Margaret
Anne

CHILD *of the* WEST WIND

———

"Whoever belongs to God hears what God Says.
The reason you do not hear is that you do not belong to God."
John 8:47

"And the light shineth in the darkness; and the darkness comprehended it not."
John 1:5

Margaret Anne

A NOVEL

Ronan James Cassidy

XULON PRESS

Xulon Press
2301 Lucien Way #415
Maitland, FL 32751
407.339.4217
www.xulonpress.com

Unless otherwise indicated, Scripture quotations taken from the
Holy Bible, New International Version (NIV). Copyright © 1973, 1978,
1984, 2011 by Biblica, Inc.™. Used by permission. All rights reserved.

Paperback ISBN-13: 978-1-6628-4923-7
eBook ISBN-13: 978-1-6628-4924-4

To: My Brother

"There was always only one who shared in the mysteries of coming to know the world around us. None but you have seen the past of this journey made to appear as some conflict driven by the cosmos innate to the whims of chaos and strife, but in truth, abounding with the plenty of the glory of our Divine Creator. We have together found many of those treasures laid out along the path of life and known the sorrows of the broken state of this place of the forever clashing forces of the darkness and light. But there was always one who held his shining light up high for me in the face of doubt and fear, anger and remorse; there was always one in wait for that next beautiful song to play its sweet melody. Just a few steps further now; and forever shall the days of innocence, discovery and love continue to shine in your heart. For the one thing holding you back or weighing you down, there exists now and forever more a million shining stars out upon the firmament and an angel of the west wind to carry you back home."

PROLOGUE

"There are certain truths manifested in earthly love that are etched into the fabric of our lives, our souls, our spirit. They are indelible pieces of art that tell the very story of who we are. A story made permanent and sung throughout the heavens. These truths are indisputable and beautiful and protected in their innocence and sincerity by the glory of God. This world shall never have them but know they do mark the time we all have shared and are a source of eternal light. We carry the truth of God's love with us always."

TABLE OF CONTENTS

Part I

The Promised Child

Chapter One

LYING-IN

∽⳺∾

THE GENTLE BUT knavish winter winds had been rolling in through the barren woodlands and fallow fields of the Carolina uplands from the west for the better part of a month. The air was cold and warned of a lingering season of darkness that would offer cover to those who wished to conceal any given sign of the light that would interrupt that cold, harsh season of the continuing march towards human suffering. Though it was known by many that the great nation founded under God was headed towards a bloody war of its manifest brotherhood, one such sign of the light still shining out beyond the depths of the approaching storm as nightfall drew near was offered up to the people as a sign that neither the deceit of the devil nor the sins of the past were set to stand eternally in the aftermath of that great conflagration of the age.

So that such an innocent and divine presence was set to survive even the night whilst the slaves to malice and the governors to none but abject cruelty roamed the American expanse unchecked, she was concealed deep in the woods and away from the tamed lands of agrarian commerce and the vital thoroughfares of American industry. She too was fighting her way through the darkness from the very flash-point of her conception, though thankfully at that moment of her distressed and near to hopeless deliverance into the confines of the flesh she was not yet made unaware of the reasons why she had accepted such a grievous task. One without an agenda born of pure love certainly would not have passed into this world under the disastrous circumstances of such an ordeal. Within the vastness of the heavens, she was the child of the west wind and given over to the troubled land by the grace of God; an angel of unmatched light and dutiful pledge to the Divine Master of all things. In that troubled season upon the expanse of the plantations of the Carolina midlands, she was breech and fighting through the tangled darkness of her mother's womb to tame the wickedness and the cold that lie beyond the warmth and safety of those once nurturing and now suffocating recesses.

If bound by the confines and limitations of the known world at that time she had been stranded between the realms of the heavens and the earth for far too long, there would have been no story yet to tell. The stern and rather pragmatic country doctor lowered his head as her fight gave way to that discomforting stillness that belonged only to the soil and what might grow from that posturing patch of unkempt lawn in the potter's yard out back that was never spoken of with an audible tone. Yet, as the doctor closed his eyes in a final sign that he would prepare to receive the lifeless little girl into the bonds of that disfavored and now hopeless calm and the tender mercies of the stillborn reticence of death before life could be known in any measure, the heavens blinked and she kicked a leg free into the chill of that February air to spite the very first man that would sell her far too short throughout the course of her unforgettable life.

Even in that turbulent year of 1859, the olive-brown skinned mother of the feisty child was a woman of some renown throughout the Carolina countryside and even down country in the port city of Charleston. She was such in spite of her skin tone that was about the most beautiful, useful and exotic that a woman of those times could possess given the hot and sunny nature of the climate throughout most of the year. Like her baby girl, who was fighting to extricate herself from a suffocating set of circumstances that a common subsequent child was not traditionally endowed to overcome, the woman was spent. Her life at that crucial moment in time was nothing more than a promise to bring forth that which she had nurtured in isolation through three seasons of that ominous annum. Her face was horribly pallid and hollow and the intense pain of the affair had given way to that discomforting serenity so often witnessed by those who spy the faces of the lingering dead before they journey to whence the angelic little girl was fighting to depart.

Thus, when the good doctor harshly took hold of the child by the feet to set her free before the need for oxygen overtook her capacity to kick on in the face of insurmountable odds, the washed out and subdued maiden of the Calhoun household was little more than an afterthought to all three persons who had gathered around her for the clandestine affair. Such was just fine by the baby's mother. She had but one duty to fulfill upon the hour of that fateful reckoning and the sudden shifting of the pressure below sang to her with the sweet murmur of a joyful hope; a joyful hope she had given up for dead in not but the blinking of an instant upon her prior thoughts of such dour constitution.

The time was not but an uncertain moment longer following the mother's holy respite from the bodily agony and mental duress caused by the nearly indescribable miracle and anguish of her labor that the child made her affecting and well-endowed voice known to the world about her. The baby's stunted cry rang out beyond the decrepit walls of the derelict, accursed and hidden structure. Her angry yet angelic peals carried out and into the twisting silence of those haunted woods that surrounded and lurched over the slightly rotting and unadorned bastard midwives cabin, which also served in the capacity of the place of execution of other and far more abhorrent abominations of the time. The shrill and ear-piercing wind of the trembling baby girl rang out through the depths of the darkness settled in over the spectral recesses out beyond the cabin and announced to the heavy spirits lingering there that the one promised by God above and divinely equipped to pave the way forward for the making of one people where once there were two had finally arrived.

On that cold hibernal night of February 24th, 1859 the nation was indeed on the brink of war. The room of her birth was dark except for the light of a few candles burning near to the very trauma of her first event. By the moment of her birth, the good doctor on site to deliver her into the world might as well have been fumbling around in the dark. The blood and fluid that had run free over the extended period of the child's disturbing conveyance had so confounded the areas near to the birthing canal that one woman standing directly over the doctor's shoulders could not make out the shape of the baby girl even as the industrious physician viciously pulled her free from the womb.

The wooden planks of pine on the floor and lining the walls of the midwives cottage hidden deep within those woods of the Carolina midlands held firm to the spirits of five generations of oppressed but loving souls that lingered along the shifting winds of the forgotten past of the countryside in wait for just such a moment. The darker spirits of those same times gone by had been relegated to the deep, undiscovered hollows of the nightshade further beyond and troubled only the shadowy highwaymen of the day. They haunted only those men passing through those parts that were of their ilk; the ones who preferred to make their passage under the cover of darkness while pledging their sanctity and their souls to none but that of a foreboding and evil talisman, which could not be shown to any by the light of day.

Those old pine boards of the cottage however, they remained tender and receptive to the heartache of those once hopeful but now lost souls who held no disregard for the worn out, bent and decaying state of the old planks. Therefore, those spirits of the ancients that had waited for the arrival of this very moment for scores heard the shrill cry of the little girl ring out into the night and startle the creatures well attuned to hunting quietly upon the midnight hour. The tremoring vibrations which gently shook the small, plain and unkempt shanty in response to the child's dreadful exclamation were the manifestations of their joy. The cold wind coming in from the west had gone still but was only to be waylaid for a short while out of solemn deference to the arrival of the newborn child that was spirit kin to its source.

Now, it was the nature of the little girl's father to strictly adhere to the well-established customs of the day which had driven the need for a woman of such renown, and already a mother of two of the most beautiful specimens in all of the Carolinas, to have marched forth from the public eye back in August of 1858 only to reach the end of that exile at this little known but highly condemned outpost in the upland wilderness. The child's father was the man upon the public throne of one of the most preeminent families in South Carolina and that family's corresponding estate; an estate which embodied the productive progress of the Southern states of the rising American empire in every way. For indeed, the estate in question and its functioning enterprises did encapsulate both the good and the bad of the era and also reflected upon each member of that reverently esteemed clan of which its constituent parts were taken under the public's consideration together as a whole, as they must within the scope of the pageantry of such formal and gallant times.

Be that as it may, only the more dignified attributes of that long-established tribe of such regal English bloodlines were spoken of openly. The child's father, Mr. Edward Christopher Calhoun, had been sworn in as the patriarch of the Calhoun family upon the passing of his father Mortimer George. Although Edward's mother still possessed considerable sway in the daily affairs of the family and held proper title to many of the various plots of lands owned, the formal recognition of that passing of the torch from father to son as it were occurred just as the cold of that winter season had begun to take hold and but a few days prior to the setting about of the Christmas decorum of the holiday fortnight, which would close out that fateful and productive year of 1858. Therefore, to be fair and not cast judgement upon the direct progenitors of the child, such stands to be noted that only the more modest of means, those merciful and buoyantly heartened denizens of that time and place whom had just learned of such an abject scandal; those kind hearted souls exposed to the truth of the events transpiring on that late-February night would certainly have been given every pretext to see the unbound promise in the birth of such a little girl who had been anointed with three Christian names and a pet name before her given name had been uttered a single time.

To the doctor and the two midwives stationed in the cabin, which was outfitted with only the transient and threadbare furnishings required to complete the clandestine task of that originally intended morning, yet was at the moment of her birth a procedure that had dragged on into the small hours of the following evening, the secret child was known simply as the Hastings miracle. To the now eerily silent little girl's spent and fading mother: who was at that time just as capable of seeing the dim pulsing light of the gateway to the realms beyond her given flesh as she was the wavering shadows cast off by the mellow, flickering yellow flames of the nearly spent candle nubs burning somewhere near to her bare feet; whilst those dark and hazy projections of human form shifted and progressed against the unadorned pine walls of the cabin and appeared to her as little more than shadow creatures that were engaged in the tender mercies of her daughter's care; her newborn baby girl and her third child was immediately known as Margaret Anne Basseterre.

To the wicked goblin crouched below the window outside awaiting any given word concerning the results of that unending episode of maternal labor while wrapped up in a wool, standard-issue army blanket of the day and cursing the devil's chill, which was abundantly given over to that night, she was known simply as the bastard Calhoun child. Lastly, to the maiden dressed only in her white, winter bedclothes, an adolescent as it were at that season of her life that danced smartly on the blossoming tenets of womanhood, and who carefully watched the always lurking Stanton Oglethorpe crouching in the darkness from the cover of nothing more than a sharp turn of the rough, woodland road that seemed to disappear into the canopy, the newly born child was known simply and affectionately as 'baby sis.'

The mother of the child would have died right there and then following the almost inexplicable and most improbable delivery of her child had the matter been conducted under normal circumstances governed only by the traditional medical limitations of the day. However, standing in direct opposition to what would have been such a miserable loss for so many that had experienced the beauty, radiant wonder, uncompromising sense of duty, and indomitable fealty to God Almighty of the Haitian noblewoman was the good doctor. In accordance with his unshakable will and steadfast determination alone, he had somehow managed to pull the baby free and do so before the disaster of their shared and uncommon predicament nearly put an end to both mother and daughter alike. Furthermore, the good doctor pulled the child free from the suffocating hold of the mother's birth canal at exactly the moment somewhere far beyond those abandoned and enchanted woodlands a clock struck twelve to chime in the first moments of February 24th, 1859.

Doctor Emmett Bailey, who was of Virginia post matriculation from his traditional doctoral studies and upon completing a rigorous and newly developed regimen of advanced courses focusing on the biological sciences, was simply the best of his medical breed at that specific time and was also perhaps even the prized blue hen of his practicing generation in all of the lands south of the Mason-Dixon Line. For the grievances of both the potential danger to his reputation and the surety that comes with the execution of potentially risky affairs by the very best, Doctor Bailey was paid a king's ransom for the deed of delivering the child in the form of gold coin and the promise of a secluded country estate south of Sumter, South Carolina.

The good doctor was remunerated directly and in secret by Mr. Edward Christopher Calhoun. Such an arrangement was fashioned for the sole reason that the newly born child's mother meant that much to the most prosperous merchant and landowner in all of the Sandlapper State. As his darkest secret, the child was to be both Mr. Calhoun's latent Achilles heel if discovered and his most cherished tangible yet eternal prize otherwise. For it was the memory of the afternoon that the gallant Mr. Calhoun at last so genteelly coaxed the child's mother, that headstrong, worldly and wholly uncompromising beauty of the mystical crossroads of the Caribbean, down the path of forbidden lust and sinful fornication upon the solitary hour she was to display such a weakness in this life, which Mr. Edward Calhoun truly prized above all else.

Following her initial belting of the winds, which duly proclaimed the child's displeasure with her prolonged confinement and the acrobatic gyrations that had been required of her to enter into the world of corporal affairs, not to mention the barbarous conditions that surrounded her in the form of her blood-stained and heinously neglected quarter of entry, the child had remained silent for far too long for the faltering mother's comfort. Miss Jeanne Jolie Basseterre-Osment had already given birth to two baby girls in her life and neither had raged as hard against the constructs of the earthborn elements nor as docilely faded into such an ominous silence; a silence that was fearfully taunted by the mounting cold and lashing winds out beyond the slightly broken window pane to her left, which was no more than an arm's length from the edge of the bed where she lay. There were crucial questions that needed to be answered by those present before the fearful and wholly consumed mother could possibly know the path she would choose to travel upon the hour.

Though she was near bloodless and had labored and suffered with such vehemence for so long, the fact that she still possessed some choice in the matter of her life or her death at the intersection of the end of the twelfth hour of the prior evening and the top of the first hour of the new day may have been considered the third miracle of that trying evening. For such was certain that the mother of the new-born little girl; a little girl who was so forcefully pried into this world by her feet just moments ago under the ominous cover of that cold and bewitching darkness and amidst the thickets of the primordial upland forest that had survived the onslaught of the colonial pioneers shaping the earth to the matters of their agrarian cause for nearly two centuries, the mother was now driven by forces older than the Carolina Colony itself and forces that perhaps predated the colonial birthrights of those European inhabitants of her Haitian homeland. There were just two things that both the spirit and the flesh of the mother's still wildly burning heart were longing to know as she lie there existing some-where within the shadowlands; that place which shrouds the world of the living from the lingering and still earthbound spirits of the dead and stands as gateway to the kingdoms of heavenly light beyond.

Like her baby girl who had just fought her way through the bounds of the well accepted impossibilities of the physical world as it was perceived in her time, the mother of the child was given over to such an unbreakable resolve and held in such high esteem by the prin-cipalities of both the realms of the light and the demesnes of mortality that no force of nature or the devil alike would strip her of that will to choose the path she would walk following the hours of her torment. She simply would not yield. She would not yield to the glory of the heavens nor pledge her featly to the future endeavors of the flesh. She obstinately refused the offerings of both realms until the rejoinders to the two enquiries tearing at the wildly palpitating rhythms and unholy turnings of her courageous yet gentle heart had been given.

As such, Miss Jeanne summoned the last of her waking strength and waved over one of the hurried midwives with her long, slender and nearly impotent right hand. The gesture was so physically bereft that it possessed a command akin to that of the armies of the angels when witnessed by those who understand the potent nature of such a willing display of frailty. She beckoned feebly with her hand while the doctor frantically worked to staunch the bleeding and repair what he could of the devastation below, though he was notably hampered by the condition of a persisting veil of darkness that the flickering light of the nearly spent candles refused to penetrate. The midwife she was attempting to summon had tended to the cleaning and swaddling of the suckling babe and had carefully witnessed the glimmer of the candlelight strike the astonishing baby girl's eyes and her heavenly countenance. The midwife was therefore equipped to answer both of the mother's pressing queries.

Though she caught hold of the mother's fading signal to come forth, the young maiden dressed in dull, dark, and heavy vestments, which perfectly concealed the stains of blood littering her light blue gown beneath and repelled the harsh cold of that windy winter night, did not want to be the one to look the long-suffering woman in those haunting amber eyes just before the moment of her reckoning. Therefore, Miss Sarah Maples turned away from Miss Jeanne suddenly and without warning when she had reached the foot of the bed. Instead of standing her ground and responding to Miss Jeanne's plea, she doubled back a few steps to approach her contemporary, Miss Reedy Cline, who was then tending to little Margaret Anne.

Having seen the signal given by the baby's mother and knowing what was to come, Miss Sarah thought it best to bestow upon her accomplice the honor of delivering such eternal enlightenment to the child's mother. Miss Sarah attempted to accomplish this feat by doing little more than placing her soft and timid hand upon Miss Reedy's shoulder. Miss Reedy had the babe wrapped, cleaned and settled. As a new mother herself, Miss Reedy was preparing to make her motherly wares available to nurse the child should the immediate need arise when Miss Sarah's always shy yet needy hand graced her shoulder. The appendage did so with just enough potency to reveal to the rather candid midwife what her next duty might be.

Without offering up the courtesy of turning around to face her fainthearted counterpart, Miss Reedy rebuked Miss Sarah somewhat hotly, "There is no time for any of your coyness now, Miss Sarah. The woman needs more water and another wet cloth or she shall not see the sunrise." Miss Sarah trembled a bit in response whilst staring into the back of Miss Reedy's only slightly turned head and replied pleadingly, "I know as much, Ma'am. Yet, I simply can't be the one to tell her about her child. I can't now, Miss Reedy! You just know that I can't!"

"Hush yusself, child," replied Miss Reedy in a much lower but still assertive voice that was just above that of forced whisper. "What did you think it was that we came out here to this accursed place to do, Miss Sarah? You and I knows how sensitive a matter this is and we done known it since we took Mr. Stanton's coin!"

Miss Reedy then turned to face her petitioner and commanded her thusly, "Now go on and tell the woman what she wants to know before she passes without the satisfaction of finding out the truth about her own baby girl. Best I can tell, this here little girl is a miracle and come upon the land to say something that matters! I wouldn't go being the one to dishonor her mother in her moment of torment and suffering."

Knowing that Miss Reedy was right and possessing nothing close to the will required to disobey one so scornful as Miss Reedy, Miss Sarah bowed her head in a dejected fashion and retreated slowly away from the taller, marginally older woman. Miss Reedy had already turned away from her and was once again studying the now perfectly contented little girl by the weak and shifting light of the nearest candle. Miss Sarah then proceeded to gather up what was needed to tend to the baby's mother before slowly and cautiously making her way past the doctor and over to Miss Jeanne's side.

Miss Sarah sat upon the old wooden stool that had last been used to get some answers from a curious Yankee gentleman passing through Sumter some months back. That Yankee man had been rumored to be stirring up trouble at night amongst the field hands. The stains and the scent of that Yankee man's fear upon the moment of that rather unconventional interrogation were still to be reckoned with on the flat base of the stool under normal conditions but certainly not presently. Miss Sarah shuffled the fouled stool back a few inches towards the wall upon sitting down. She did so to remove at least something of the pretense of intimacy implied by her initial distance from the baby's mother upon first taking to the seat. Miss Jeanne opened her eyes upon hearing the sound of the grating of the stool's legs against the old pine floor boards of the cabin.

Miss Jeanne took careful notice of the decrepit ceiling of the cabin, which came to a point some ten feet above where the ceiling angled in from the tops of the outer walls of the old rectangular woodland outpost. Miss Sarah dropped the end of a rag into the pitcher of water that was situated on the floor near to her feet and then wrung the cloth damp upon the floor boards. She could not see that Miss Jeanne's eyes were slightly opened. Therefore, when Miss Jeanne quickly and forcefully grabbed hold of Miss Sarah's wrist just as the midwife attempted to place the damp cloth on Miss Jeanne's forehead, Miss Sarah nearly dropped dead on the spot while yelling out, "Ma'am! Place no curse upon me, Ma'am! I'm just here to cool your head and get you some water before you dry out!"

The mercurial flash of Miss Jeanne's ire quickly gave way to her spent bodily condition and she released her grasp on the young midwife's arm. She did not wish to lose consciousness before she had spoken her bit to the young woman and the aftereffects of her forceful grasp had nearly rendered her senseless. As Miss Sarah straightened back up and away from the wall after being startled so, Miss Jeanne dropped her arms limply back to her side and fixed her stare, which was beset by the torments of the age, upon the frightened woman. Miss Jeanne allowed the young and still restive midwife to finish straightening up her wares before she spoke in a weak, sorrowful and cracking voice. "Why is my little girl who has been armed by the angels above so still and so quiet? Tell me woman of the night watch, will she yet live to see the first of the very light which sent her?"

While still shuddering from her fright and speaking through a mildly debilitating tremor caused by that same fear, and because she was compelled by the stunning hold of the mother's death ridden eyes; a hold that was far more potent than the shadowy, lingering specters and the darkness inhabiting that corner of the scant, rectangular room which constituted the entirety of the inside of the cabin, Miss Sarah replied, "Yessum, Ma'am. She…she seems to have taken all they had to give her and…and she…she is about as peaceful as she can be. Praise… praise God for it too. No little baby I ever seen got through something like that. You should have some water now, Ma'am, I'm begging you. Nothin's supposed to come to you now, Ma'am."

Miss Jeanne's eyes welled up with tears of joy. The gathering brine that was set to burst forth from the unmistakably captivating lower bounds of those radiant orbs, which had broken the heart of even the most hardened Caribbean vagabond or maritime scourge, softened up her piercing stare; a piercing stare that had split the intimacy of the darkness holding itself firm to that otherwise unknown corner of the upland wilderness in such a way that her eyes had appeared to be illuminated by the will of the heavens above. The mother of the child wanted to ask her second question at that very moment. Nevertheless, the grace of the gift of the young and seemingly careless midwife's words had overwhelmed her and for opposing reasons.

As it concerned her overwhelming joy upon hearing of her baby girl's perfected condition following such a horrific ordeal, Miss Jeanne took such glorious peace and comfort from the knowing that her child in wait had arrived in good order. The child to come that used to ring the wind chimes using only the tempests coming in from the west while she herself had passed the measure of her idle days in the way on a lonely porch just up the Savannah River over in Georgia, was indeed quite fine upon the moment. Miss Sarah was not lying to appease her and Miss Jeanne could see it in the trembling young woman's eyes. The child was simply taking her rest after the first of what would be little Margaret Anne's many trials in this life. Her mother was quite relieved by the certainty behind such delightful and improbable news.

When Miss Jeanne's eyes had closed and the tears once welling up within had all tickled their way down her elegant cheeks and into the twisted melding of the rough cotton blankets and warm, damp linens of the bed upon which she lay, she beheld a pen that wrote in blood. Such was a wicked pen that carried her indelible mark from Les Cayes, Haiti to Sumter and then on to Uriah, South Carolina. Now carried off from the splendors of her initial joy, Miss Jeanne remained lost in the guilt riddled hold of the depths of that immediate and searing vision for a short while. As such, she kept her tearing visage turned away from the youthful maiden now slowly and carefully raising a glass of water to her own vey parched and cracked lips. When that frightful portent at last passed in the manner of branding its eternal mark of shame upon her mind's eye, Miss Jeanne readied to ask the next question of her still alarmed and slightly trembling caregiver.

Be that as it may regarding her present intentions, Miss Jeanne's words of inquiry and the corresponding answer to her final question would be forced to wait. Miss Sarah's startling ruckus and her poorly chosen words in response to Miss Jeanne had set the wheels of something premeditated, well-devised and altogether sinister into motion. Before Miss Jeanne could turn her head back to Miss Sarah to take in the water she so desperately needed to ease the instruments of her dreadfully parched and therefore locked up throat to ask her final question, Miss Reedy had taken hold of the glass while issuing a stern warning to Miss Sarah. The elder midwife spoke with a dagger tipped tongue, though her chosen words were far more cordial than the nature of her tone would have implied. "Miss Sarah, its best you be gettin' on over to see to the child. Doc Bailey will be finishing up soon and I'll be needin' to tend to Miss Jeanne here. I'll be darned if it turned out that you didn't have the uncanny ability to jump up a mule that's been bone dry for a score."

Upon seeing the wanting look settling upon Miss Jeanne's once again hollow countenance coupled with her soft, pleading eyes and the washed-out mother's desperate reaching of her chin and lips towards the now contested glass and its rather murky yet still life-giving contents, Miss Sarah began to become possessed by a petulant cursing of guilt that had instantly taken hold of her sentiments. As such, Miss Sarah rebuffed Miss Reedy and interjected about as forcefully as the timid farm girl knew how. "Heaven have mercy, Miss Reedy! Can't you see the poor, suffering woman needs some water? I shall most certainly yield to you once she has had her fill but not an instant sooner."

Miss Reedy was having none of her accomplice's insolence. The proper moment allocated to the giving of the watchword had now changed due to Miss Sarah's incompetence but the watchword had been given all the same. Miss Reedy forcefully yanked the glass of water from Miss Sarah's hand and pulled her up from the wooden stool at the same time she began to admonish her younger accessory. Miss Reedy scolded Miss Sarah quite harshly this time. "Woman, you had better get to your senses like the tip of a whip to an ass before you feel my hands upon you! Have you not heard a damn word I have said to you? I will give the water to Miss Jeanne here once you get stuck to the doing of your own task!"

Miss Sarah had neither a commensurate power within nor a working relationship with an authority on high that would have been sufficient to deal with the harshness of Miss Reedy Cline right then. Miss Sarah yielded the cup to her counterpart and quickly finished standing to walk across the room and tend to Margaret Anne. Doctor

Bailey, who had been otherwise wholly indisposed and crossed-up within myriad shades of bewilderment over the inexplicable circumstances of the child's birth and his frustration with the limitations of his working conditions while attempting the daunting task of repairing the nether regions of the spent and now thirsting mother, was at last shocked into speaking out regarding the abhorrent behavior of the two spatting midwives.

The good doctor raised his head from beneath the primitively tented area at the foot of the bed as the last of Miss Jeanne's stiches was tied off into place. As he tended to the matters of decency regarding his patient he called out to the two women still clustered in the corner of the room near the head of the bed. "Stop it now, the both of you! Miss Jeanne will need her medication and plenty of water right away. I'll need the services of the other to get my instruments in order while I take my leave for a few minutes. How is the baby girl?"

Doctor Bailey stood up from his chair at the foot of the bed while Miss Sarah lowered her head and squeezed her way along the outer wall of the cabin past the still determined looking Miss Reedy. For her part, Miss Reedy took a seat in the soiled stool which Miss Sarah had occupied by Miss Jeanne's now slightly tremoring head and answered Doctor Bailey. She spoke loudly, as if she intended for her words to travel out beyond the confines of the threadbare cabin hidden deep within the woods. "The baby girl is quite fine, Doctor Bailey. Praise be to God and your good works. She is calm and all swaddled up like a package waiting to be delivered on Christmas Day."

The doctor walked slowly up the side of the bed opposite Miss Reedy while Miss Reedy at last gave the long-suffering mother a sip of water. By that point, the rather accomplished caregiver had mixed in some quinine from her pouch for Miss Jeanne's mounting fever. The good doctor took hold of Miss Jeanne's right hand and replied, "That is very good to hear, Mistress Reedy. The delivery has been long and trying. To bear witness to such encouraging words as it concerns the condition of the newborn child can only be ascribed to the will of our Good Lord above. There was a moment upon which I was certain we had lost little Miss Margaret Anne before we had been granted the tender graces of her likeness."

Miss Reedy studied the eyes of Doctor Bailey very carefully as he examined Miss Jeanne for a read out on her condition. She watched him so carefully through the murky darkness that one would have presumed she expected him to react in a known way to some given sign. True enough to form where it concerned Miss Reedy's apparent premonitions regarding Doctor Bailey's reaction to something that was or would be amiss, not but a few seconds passed after the good doctor had straightened his frame up upon feeling the heat emanating from Miss Jeanne's forehead before his eyes did grow quite wide with surprise. On top of that startled look of discomfort, which allowed the whites of Doc Bailey's eyes to glare disquietedly in stark opposition to the darkness that concealed the fineness and detail of his other rather charming facial features, the pipe which he had prepared with such a perfected care well in advance, yet exactly for this moment of presumed post-partum relief, fell from his hand and knocked thrice as it connected with and then settled upon the worn pine boards of the cabin floor. If the light had allowed for such discernment in reading the grueling tells of the suddenly horrified man's abjectly shaded countenance, one would have presumed the dark angel itself had seized upon the good doctor for the most grievous crimes of his past, which no man is without.

Miss Sarah had slid the far window to the cabin open without a hitch and that slippery wretch, Stanton Oglethorpe had slithered in from the cold without making a sound. The tall, thin man dressed from head to toe in a hue no different than the faint and flickering shadow he was now casting against the far wall of the cabin was the known errand boy of ill repute of Mrs. Meara Calhoun, the wicked mother of Mr. Edward Christopher Calhoun. His presence anywhere was enough to raise the hackles on a long dead hound but his presence at that place and at that hour was a poor enough omen that even the visiting doctor knew that the dark heart of evil was now directly stirring about. Miss Jeanne could not see Stanton Oglethorpe at the far end of the room. She was once again only half conscious. She had however, sensed the imminent danger to her child as the cross of gold resting upon the slick perspiration of her exposed breastbone had delivered the urgent message sent from the spirts of her ancient kin all the same.

Miss Sarah raised the wrapped baby girl from the plain old table with the upturned edges serving as a bassinette and prepared to hand the child to Mr. Oglethorpe. That was all the young maiden knew of the proceedings set to take place that night following the birth of the child. Stanton Oglethorpe however, was clearly tuned into to a differing agenda and hastily waved off Miss Sarah's offering of the neatly pre-packaged newborn babe. There was something else that was occupying the villain's mind at that moment. Not much time passed before Mr. Oglethorpe's wires got crossed up once again. Such was a common mishap displayed by the shrewd but simple minded ogre. Something that Stanton had learned about the child when he had accepted his profane assignment from Mistress Meara caused him to double back to Miss Sarah before commencing with his then primary objective. However, such was an objective that was primary only in that the task was required to be completed before he absconded off into the night with the forbidden child.

The sudden remembering of what Mistress Meara had told him about the child caused Stanton Oglethorpe to turn back and take a deep and discerning look at the child's exposed face and peer directly into her large, saucer-like blue eyes. Due to the fact that the lack of light and the still present, though only lightly concerning, incidence of Doc Bailey standing across the width of the small unadorned room from him were in direct opposition to Stanton's ability to properly satisfy his yearning curiosity to know the true nature of the appearance of little Miss Margaret Anne, the tall, lean brigand looked upon the face of the wrapped child only twice. However, such was for certain that he could have stared into the eyes of that angelic countenance for hours.

Upon completing that final look see, Mr. Oglethorpe chuckled with delight and announced to the full cadre of present company, "My, oh my, have you ever seen such a thing as that in all of God's creation? Such a creature as that one is could change the very nature of how people feel about certain things round here! Damnation to all if I wouldn't be tarred and feathered simply for believing what my eyes now just done seen!"

At that moment, the sole remaining candle that was burning in the room; a candle which had been hard pressed by the breath of the ancient and wicked spirits shifting about the cabin to burn at little more than that of a tiny droplet of flame amidst the wet, pooling wax of its shrunken nub, rose to the stance of a full arcing flame. The light given off by this rising flare set upon a small stand at the end of the bed gave a shadowy form to the tall highwayman standing in black before the open window. Perhaps heartened by his ability to at last assess the frailty of Mr. Oglethorpe's long, lurching frame, or perhaps simply because Doctor Bailey was a true gentlemen of his day in every sense of the word and had no intention of letting such a low-bred villain steal off into the night with a freshly given miracle of God, Doctor Bailey admonished Mr. Oglethorpe harshly. "You'll be tarred and feathered as it is, my man for simply setting foot in this cabin. I suggest you be leaving with exactly what it is that you came in with and nothing more. Furthermore, you skulking husk of grass, I suggest you do so before my hand is no longer empty and so hard pressed for the instrument of its satisfaction!"

Miss Reedy turned her eyes away from the intruder and began to care for Miss Jeanne in earnest. Miss Sarah was not telling a fib just a short while earlier when she let it slip that no harm was to come to the mother of the child. That unintended revelation was truth, even if Miss Jeanne had not made known her cunning perception of exactly what such words spoken to her truly meant. As such, Miss Jeanne eagerly accepted the care offered by Miss Reedy in the hopes that she would see the sunrise for the sake of all three of her little girls.

The words that Mr. Oglethorpe spoke about her child broke Miss Jeanne's heart. They broke her heart because she knew then, and perhaps she had always known, the truth about what little Miss Margaret Anne was sent to exemplify to the people of this land. Furthermore, by means of the blessings of the golden cross pulsating upon her sweat sodden chest, the exhausted woman was compelled to fight on and once again open her eyes into the splendor of the ensuing morning light for the safety and sanctity of her now threatened child. The parched mother drank heartily from the glass of water and also managed to quickly still the waxing fears of the moment rising within her. She indeed did achieve such a dutiful calm and regal poise before she separated her lips from the cold and dusty jar despite belonging to the world of the quick while also bearing witness to the swirling phantasms of the dead.

As Miss Jeanne was reengaging with that newly given and sacred promise of her recovery whilst her spent body and internally desiccated yet outwardly brackish flesh lacked the means for the formation of such hope, Stanton Oglethorpe responded to Doctor Bailey's opening words of admonishment. "Well, I must say, that wasn't such a friendly way to greet an invited guest of the two ladies up and about, and a stranger lost out upon the trail of sorrows out back to boot. Was it now, Doc?"

Stanton paused for a moment and rubbed his unevenly bristled chin for effect. He went through the overindulgent motions of the act as if he were giving consideration to something profound, though he was not. The brigand then slowly lowered his hand toward the side of his long and angular thigh and continued on with his charade. He relished having the drop on a man more than most of the sparsely offered benefactions of his meagre life. Getting the drop on a woman was a close second. "And to say such unwelcoming things at just the instant I was going to offer you the services of that fine steed tied to the post out front." Stanton shook his head confidently as if his false words and summarily wayward judgement of the facts and circumstances of the current situation were indeed Gospel true. To be plain about it, his caustic words were the very ones the devil might speak if he were standing in Stanton's shoes at that very moment.

Stanton continued on with his false deliberations while Doc Bailey remained silent and began to lock up with a terrible fright on the other side of the room. The only movement Doc made was the shifting of his eyes in an effort to better see across the dimly lit room and make a more intelligent assessment of the depravity of the situation. Just as Doc's eyes spied a slight gleam of light refracting off of the metal of Stanton's weapon, which was loosely holstered at the villain's side, the dull card dressed out in black continued on with his nearly scripted and sanctimonious twaddle. "It don't take a learned man to know that the stagecoach won't be out here again 'til sunup, Doc. That cursed little girl done kept us all well past our hopeful hour. I'll tell you what though: just to save us all a bunch of time and trouble, as it has already been a long and trying day, why don't you just go on into to your bag of tricks over there and take your best shot. If I'm still standing here after the fact, I'll go ahead and take mine. It'll all be nice and chivalrous for the benefit of the ladies present. Far better than me stepping on over there and gutting you like a pig anyhow. What says you to such a gentlemanly offer, Doc?"

Beyond being a gentleman who would never back away from such a vile man in the presence of a woman and child in need, Doc Bailey could take a bird in the eye at the distance of a furlong if furnished with a right and proper instrument for the task. His eyes were also growing well attuned to the dark. His hands, which had been flushed with the heat of childbirth and mending the rushing and then incessant discharge associated with such for so long, were thriving as the cold air began to further settle into the room following the constant commotion and angst of the earlier hours. Doc Bailey was also a keen man when it came to the ways of the world and he felt that he effusively understood the depths of Miss Reedy's treachery. He also knew that gentle Miss Sarah was little more than the harsh, cold and calculating older nurse's lapdog. Yet, as he stepped almost absentmindedly towards his old leather medical bag at the foot of the blood-soaked bed, a bag full of medical instruments that also concealed an iron capable of putting an end to something as tall and frail as Stanton Oglethorpe from a distance of fifty paces, or perhaps many more, let alone six, the good doctor missed a step while offering up his conciliation to the shrewd highwayman's terms of engagement.

Not but the passing of a brief moment later, while Doc Bailey rummaged through his old, black leather medical bag with a clear mind, a sharp eye, and a steady hand, the man dressed in black and standing across the room from the good doctor urged him onward. That dark man spoke as if his wits were exceedingly dull, or perchance more likely, well-attuned to some unrealized advantage which he possessed. "That's good, Doc. That's very good. Best option we have available to us in settling things up good and proper with the woman folk present, I say. Everything is just like you went ahead and declared to all present. There simply isn' no other cure for such an egregious trespass as my own."

Doc Bailey took hold of the well-oiled and evenly tested pistol just as the last of Stanton's words had traveled across the short distance of the room. He then squeezed the handle tightly in response to the stirring of the winds outside, which were beginning to lash out at the thinly paned windows and the sparsely planked and perhaps makeshift wooden door of the cabin. Doc Bailey had never intentionally harmed a man in his life, but at that moment he wanted nothing more than to pierce Stanton Oglethorpe's yellow and muck ridden teeth with the full force of his weapon's discharge. For some strange reason, those demented and rotten tines of his suddenly cocksure antagonist seemed to resonate in the dim, shimmering rays of the candle as the physician drew near to the middle of the room.

Stanton Oglethorpe could sense Doc Bailey's suddenly burning rage. Such was the rage of a man suddenly released from the throes of hopelessness and Stanton knew the sentiment well. Such was a rage that came so naturally to one so verily tormented prior taking hold of the cold iron of a pistol, which offered up the capacity to quickly and readily convey that heretofore mocked fury of the vengefully seeded wrath simmering within the very pith of the wronged. Stanton even obliged the good doctor with a wide and taunting smile that held back nothing of the decaying nature of his desiccate and foul-smelling dental abominations. When he saw that wicked, taunting smile mocking him in the night, Doc Bailey lost hold of the apprehension he once so sacredly held and which guided him to never take the life of another man if there was any way, perhaps even by the grace of God alone, to avoid such a calamity.

Doc Bailey could see the whites of Stanton's eyes well enough in stark opposition to the darkness to be certain that what he was sizing up was accurate. Given the near madness caused by fear lurking behind his burning ire, the good doctor braced his hands for the kick-back and he squeezed the trigger of his gun forcefully well before he had straightened up from reaching into his bag. The sudden timing of the sound surprised both Stanton and his two female accomplices as they were all three waiting for the proper pageantry of a more dignified shot. One which would be taken only once the doctor was fully upright and eye to eye with the trespasser.

However, of the three conspirators present, only the one who was now holding little Margaret Anne closely to her chest to shield the innocent little child's senses from the evils of such violence and the fury of the exploding powder was surprised by the impotent click of the well-tuned and amply oiled pistol. Conversely, the other midwife was expecting nothing different. She simply continued to hold a wet cloth to Miss Jeanne's head with one hand and thumb through her dress pocket with the other to be certain the count on the metal objects she kept safe there was accurate. Miss Reedy's reckoning was a bit quick and her fingers felt along the lining of her pocket as if they were restless or perhaps even mildly agitated. The scheming midwife remained confident the numbers were right all the same.

Stanton flinched reflexively upon hearing the hammer of Doc's gun drop so suddenly and well before his antagonist had properly squared himself up to take a gentlemanly shot. Once he recognized the muted click of the hammer striking upon and empty chamber, a sound which confirmed the reliability of Miss Reedy's treacherous handiwork, Stanton laughed like a maniacal wild man to further taunt his now once again helpless aggressor. In the aftermath of his self-serving moment of gratuitous pleasure, Stanton cackled a bit more and waved his hand sideways to direct the betrayed doctor. "Why don't you go ahead and move on out away from the bed now, Doc. Thataways I can take my shot."

Stanton waved his shooting hand a bit more robustly in the direction of the door and further taunted the suddenly maligned doctor. "We don't want anything bad happening to our new momma of that delicate little creature, do we now, Doc? You done knows who I mean, the momma of the child fit to be born in this cursed and bloodstained shanty out in the woods. My, oh my, we gots us an itchy trigger hand, don't we, Doc!" Stanton Oglethorpe chortled on further as Doc Bailey stood up straight and stepped away from the end of the bed. The habitually meek physician made his move slowly and timidly as he summed up the dire consequences of his fate upon the knowing that he had been had.

The gentlemanly doctor also thought it wise to stand a safe distance away from Miss Jeanne, who was now beginning to shift suddenly with fright while she fought to break free from the frustrating confinement of her listless body. The long suffering mother was fully aware of the events transpiring right before her eyes even if she could do little to stop them. The nearly spent woman began to shake horribly there in the bed while mentally calling to the heavens for strength beneath the soft gasping tremors of her unsettled and rhythmically spasmodic breaths; breaths that seemed desperately wanting for the primal sustenance of that now uncommonly bitter February air. Doc Bailey sorrowfully lamented his having to retreat from his tormented patient. The poor woman could do little to remedy the quite distasteful and unfortunate events of the moment that were centered on the removing of her child from her would be loving care. A sad feeling of ensuing loss slowly but uncontrollably gripped the good doctor's tender and compassionate heart. He knew well both the joys and the sorrows that accompanied the maternal spirit upon passing through the pangs of child birth. He felt deeply for the helpless woman in that moment of her certain loss.

The change in position of merely a few evenly spaced yet quite diffident steps placed the good and dignified doctor directly in front of the thin wooden door boards that were now being beaten mercilessly by the violent, lashing winds outside. Those frightful swirling tempests were lustfully searching beneath the canopy of the wilderness for the one promised them, and this particular torrent, which had cut its way directly through that blackest of February nights, seemed to know it had found its mark. The incessant rattling of that unnerving force of nature seemed to sharply magnify some mounting angst rising within Mr. Oglethorpe. Because he was servant to a witch, Stanton paid particular heed to the unease of the spirits about and more so in such a wholly condemned and certainly haunted place as this. As such, when Doc Bailey was standing directly in front of the rattling and yielding door, Stanton stopped his cackling, drew his pistol from a side holster beneath his musty, black trench coat, and called out to Doc as if he were a bit apprehensive. "That there is far enough, Doc. Fair is fair now, isn't it?"

The truth of the matter was that Mr. Oglethorpe certainly wanted nothing bad to befall Miss Jeanne for the sake of sparing the whole of the Carolina countryside the wrath of Mr. Edward Christopher Calhoun if he were finally pushed beyond that line of demarcation that separates repressed anger from the expression of wanton rage. His principal to the current engagement and a maven of the dark arts in her own right was quite clear on that point. Stanton reckoned that mandate made perfect sense. To any man with half an itching in his head, it was no secret that the publicly prim and proper Mr. Calhoun was beyond sweet on the woman.

Nevertheless, Stanton was an able bodied country boy if nothing else of gainful use to any God-fearing Carolinian. He was a good enough shot from that proximity that it would have been clear to those who knew him that the woman was never in any danger and that Stanton's true intent behind urging Doc Bailey to move away from the bed and towards the exit was to trim down on his workload once he had put a smoking hole in the center of the defenseless man's chest. None could argue against the fact that dragging Doc's corpse out into the woods for the glory of the crows and the buzzards would be that much easier from whence the legendary medical practitioner now stood a bit slouched over and fully dispirited.

Stanton had been partaking from a flask while he remained hunkered down in the cold outside and beneath the back window of the cabin. Unfortunately for Doc Bailey, Stanton's sight was still clear and his hand was still steady and true enough for the impending task. The highwayman sized up the center of the obscure object standing across the room from him with the sight of his pistol and declared for the sake of a decency that in truth he lacked, "Anything needing to be said, now would be the time for it, Doc. You's tied up in my gunsights any ways you wants go ahead and look at it. I done have to say though: I never would have taken you for a man who couldn't figure out how to load his own pistol properly." Stanton couldn't resist chuckling like a choking horse at his own ruse but halted those shenanigans promptly when a sizable branch crashed down hard on the far side of the sharply angled roof of the decrepit cabin.

Miss Sarah jumped a fright with the baby in her arms but held her tight. Doc straightened up briskly due to the sonorous and unexpected crackling and rattling of the branch slowly separating from the trunk of the tree. He then tremored some following the thunderous thud delivered by the cataclysm of the heavy limb landing flush upon the roof above. Stanton nearly flinched outright in addition to posturing up some but got back down to the business of delivering his self-aggrandizing bunkum. "But heck, rules done be rules don't they and it's my shot. You know, life is kinda funny that way, Doc. Seems like the devil is always gettin' paid his pound of flesh. He done gonna get what's his even when our intentions is in the right place and all."

Sensing some form of strength rising in the once tremoring but still visibly prostate mother of the newborn child lying directly in front of her, and furthermore, fearfully despising even the thought of what were to happen to her in the event something were to go awry before the payload of the dimwit's pistol did its savage best to put the good doctor down, Miss Reedy admonished Stanton harshly from the corner of the room. "Shut your pie hole and do what you's gonna do, Stanton! Stop pretending you got the better of an honest man when his bullets be sittin' right over here in my pocket."

Stanton kept his hand steady and his pistol true to the target as he called back to Miss Reedy in an aggressively agitated tone. "Well I'll be hooked and hanged, Miss Reedy Cline! Why don't you just go ahead and throw that coin I paid you out onto the floor with Doc's bullets. I reckon neither of you two will ever have a use for any of that metal now!"

"Stop it, you two!" interjected Miss Sarah. "I don't know nothin' about nothin' but this here little angel will be gettin' on over to her proper home across the river in Georgia!"

Miss Reedy spit fire from her eyes as she stared Stanton down. She pulled her long, spiteful hand from her dress pocket and dropped the projectiles now riddled with her guilt disdainfully onto the floor. She was not about to part ways with the coin. Besides the rattling wind, there was no other sound present in the room but for the sound of the metal bullets rolling sidelong beneath the bed until they settled into their respective nooks or cracks that ran along the old worn-out slats of the decking. One of those discarded rounds remained within arm's length of the edge of the bed.

Knowing the timid nature of Miss Sarah and by contrast the vile and callous makeup of Miss Reedy in addition to understanding the futility of trying to procure one of the loosed objects now resting somewhere beneath the far side of the bed, Doctor Bailey sensed no advantage to the brief outburst. Consequently, he thought it best to spend the last of his time upon this earth in prayer and the remembering of his loved ones. He lowered his chin to face the floorboards and awaited the instant the highwayman would have his go of it. Whilst he listened to the last of the women's voices trail off into the sheers of the still harsh and wanting winds riddling the windows and the thinly planked walls of the cabin, Doctor Emmett Bailey closed his eyes to the world at large.

When the last of the dim and wavering light of the final burning candle giving shrouded shape to the various creatures inhabiting the small, plain room in the middle of the woods had been replaced with the lovely vision of his beautiful wife, Eustice Hammonds Bailey and their twin little girls, Lily Grace and Emmaline Prudence Bailey, aged seven years, Doctor Bailey offered up his final prayer for relief in the

name of their sanctity and the blessings of love that might accrue
to them through a life well lived and devoted to God in his absence.
Doctor Bailey then squeezed his eyes tightly closed as the vibrant
flashing of those delicate visions from his past melded with the stirring abstractions of his final wish. That final wish of the good and
dutiful man was that the love rushing forth from the flooded vortex
of his maddeningly palpitating heart might somehow break free of
the rattling madness infecting these death-riddled walls and the cold,
macabre woods out beyond and softly dress over them all. When there
was naught before his eyes but the darkness, the good doctor offered
up all that he was and all that he ever hoped to be while set upon this
earth up to God above. He then awaited the fury of the report that
would set his body down to dwell in the dirt amidst the lore of the age.

Upon hearing the click of the cocking hammer of Stanton's murderous weapon of favor, Doc Bailey's heart somehow stopped itself
cold for the briefest of moments. The once bursting organ did indeed
stop dead and it went still not from fright but out of scorn for Mr.
Oglethorpe. The good doctor so wished to usurp the governing of the
matter of the timing of his demise from the hand of one so wicked
and so low as the course highwayman in the only way possible upon
the flashpoint of that thundering instant when time stood still. As
such, Doctor Bailey began his free fall onto the worn, planked pine of
the old cabin floor just a split second before the shot rang out into the
deadly freeze of the black and empty night air out beyond tremoring
walls of the old flogging cabin.

From the piercing sound of the shredding of one of the thin door
boards to the dull thud of the projectile's contact with the upper
realms of a human chest cavity, and then finally, the ungodly thump
and accompanying sharp rattling of the ground slats caused by Doctor
Bailey falling forward to meet his certain end, everything was as Miss
Reedy had hoped upon hope it would be when Stanton Oglethorpe
had finally decided to defecate rather than get off the pot as he was

often wont to do. The rogue had a yellow reputation for running to the cover of Miss Meara after shooting his mouth off wantonly or simply tucking tail and running when things got too hot up in the kitchen. While Miss Reedy doubted that option existed for the cowardly scourge of Sumter in such a circumstance as this; what with Miss Meara herself being the one that put Stanton to task here on this awful winter night, the settling of the matter was deeply comforting to the cantankerous midwife all the same.

That feeling of comfort did not hold long for the coarse and merciless woman. Even before Stanton Oglethorpe cried out loudly and disdainfully through a triangular gap in the corner of the back window's glass for Mother Mary; a cry that carried into the deepest recesses of that bewitched coppice of barren tree and thorny thicket alike, Miss Reedy suddenly came to the realization that something was horribly amiss. For one thing, the temperature outside and therefore inside the cabin was dropping precipitously to the point that no working thermometer of the day would have given a reading. Be that as it may, the foreign gales sent forth from the western mountains of the Continental Divide, a place known then only through the lore of the explorers of the day, were not responsible for the stark and evocative look of shock that seized upon the plain and hardened face of Miss Reedy Cline. That sharp, sudden burst of profane and gelid air could only take some of the credit for the morbid shade of blue that was instantaneously set upon her deathly parted lips.

Nay, it was the impulsive realization that those things exploding or falling forward into the force of the discharge of Stanton's weapon upon the moment of truth did not make a lick of sense which colored the stunned face of the midwife pale and then caerulean. Those shocking incongruities to the unassailable tenets of her expectation instantaneously ruptured her once certain beliefs as to what had transpired and furthermore, those beliefs which had been momentarily emblazoned upon her anxious mind as fact now seemed to have been projected there by some magician of the wandering carnival order. The aftermath of the assault was all wrong. The plain truth of that visible reality instantaneously transformed and then fomented her properly stunned and immediate awareness of the actuality of the cataclysm and therefore, rightly horrified the crude but sensible enough mountain girl. She had raised three simple minded men on her own and kept her daddy breathing, though she could never break him from the shine, when her momma lost hope and headed on over the gap with a preacher man to find God in the unspoiled lands off to the west. Miss Reedy Cline was a girl come down from the mountain of indeterminate lineage yet a distinctively backwoods tradition. She was no stranger to the destructive effects of a weapon fired at close range.

Not a full second passed before that gut hollowing awareness of those incongruities standing in direct opposition to the basic and inviolable laws of nature was met by that shrill, almost womanly cry from Stanton Oglethorpe. A shrill cry that was given just before that vagabond burst shoulders first through the thin glass of the back window of the cabin. Shortly after the crashing reverberations of the unexpected self-defenestration were made manifest throughout the cabin, Miss Sarah also released a blood curdling scream and rushed to take cover with the baby in the bloodstained depths of the feather bed next to Miss Jeanne. Subsequent to that brief and unconsecrated wave of utter commotion, Miss Reedy picked up on the sound of Stanton landing upon the hard, freezing ground outside. That clumsy, sidelong and shoulders first thud was accompanied by the ruckus of the last of the shattering of the glass of the back window, which Mr. Oglethorpe had used to make his frenzied and unexpected exit without having the decency to lift the lower pane. Miss Reedy quickly came to her senses and wasn't far behind in joining Stanton in a clump on the ground outside.

Doc's chin had been split open when he hit the floor like a giant felled magnolia, though his stiffened, dead weight fall was somehow due to nothing more than his own anticipation of the inevitable. In truth and inexplicably enough, beyond the clean split of that deep laceration the good doctor was left without a scratch from a bullet of any type. Doc choked in a gasp of air after he awoke from hitting the floor with such force. He then quickly rolled to his left in an attempt to take cover part ways under and part ways behind the bed at its bottom corner. Miss Sarah began wailing uncontrollably while Miss Jeanne stared up at the ruts worn into the crossbeams that ran below the hollow steeple of the ceiling of the cabin. The three remained assessing the aftermath of the brigand's ill fortune and the delivery of their own unanticipated grace for a short while and in their own differing ways.

For a short time afterwards, nothing was heard about the cabin but the rushed, heavy breaths of the two survivors feeling the need to take refuge from some unknown entity or invisible will, which waited for them somewhere out in the night. As those warm, searching exhalations were transformed into what would have been visibly expanding and then steadily drifting vapors by the harsh, wanting cold had there been but a scant source of light, all else remained quiet and still until the deathly chill delivered a sharp prodding to the wavering senses of each adherent to the scene. Couched into their respective positions both within the cabin and without, the five at least reasonably rational adults struggled mightily for a brief while to reconcile and then fully grasp what on God's green earth had just taken place.

During that peaceful interlude that lingered just momentarily, the mother of the miraculously delivered child was still quite feeble but came to understand that she was now being guided back to the unbreakable vows of her motherhood. She also understood that she was being returned to the confines of the temporal realms by the angels commissioned to protect their own. She continued to gaze wistfully upward until she rightly discerned that the smoothened ruts worn into the crossbeams above her bed marked the spots where the ropes of the days gone by had dangled and tightened under the desperately flailing weight of the innocents hoping to break free from the bonds of wicked men. While she continued to stare upward, Miss Jeanne was at peace with the fact that those once tortured and now dearly departed souls had flaunted their indifference to the bounds of both heaven and earth to ensure the proliferation of her poor baby girl; a now settled but innately uncompromising child, who had already endured such a horrifying rite of passage into the ephemeral realms of the flesh.

Indeed, Miss Jeanne knew that there were spirits of all kinds haunting the old cabin and even the woods outside. She knew the intricate details of many of those spirits because she had been wandering the shadowlands beyond the confines of her exquisite and often lusted for corporal wares for quite some time prior to Stanton Oglethorpe's unwelcome arrival. The beautiful mother of the spirited child was now catching hold of some form of useful bodily vigor and her mind was calibrating to properly understand the events of the hour and what they would mean to the days ahead which would now be allotted to her baby girl. Though she respected the fortitude of many of the spirits gathered both within and out beyond as the sounds of the tightening ropes of yesteryear haunted her scanning mind, it was the armed hand those spirits or angels had guided when all appeared lost that Miss Jeanne wished to identify.

When the once again fully cognizant woman was near to making the determination which she sought regarding the identity of their still undetermined savior, Doc called up to the women from the floor at the foot of the bed, "Miss Jeanne, Miss Sarah, are you and little Miss Margaret Anne alright?"

Miss Jeanne was not yet strong enough to speak forcefully but she nodded noticeably enough in reply to the doctor's query. Miss Sarah felt the confirming motions of her unlikely bedfellow in the shifting downiness of the pillow they now shared while the traumatized nurse was casting aside the last of her trailing tears with the dainty bent knuckle of her right forefinger. The baby remained silent. The little girl was safely and lovingly tucked in between the two women below the comforter while tightly swaddled from chin to toe. The remarkably peaceful child remained seemingly oblivious to the significance of their once and perhaps still pending peril. Sensing the unmistakable nod that was Miss Jeanne's response to Doc's checkup, the nurse began to feel for confirming signs of life upon the soft, warm visage of the little child. Shortly thereafter, Miss Sarah dutifully called back to the man awaiting her answer while nestled down upon the cold wood of the cabin floor at the corner of the bed, "Yes Sir, Doctor Bailey, we's all fine up here. Are you all right? What in the name of heaven above happened?"

Doc Bailey felt carefully along the firm bone and serviceable muscle of his chest as he lay sidelong on the floor. He was certain that he had missed the presence of a fatal wound when he examined his condition earlier due to the flood of adrenaline rushing through his still wildly pulsating arteries and veins. When the good doctor was somewhat confident he was not in fact mortally wounded, he spoke quite pointedly up to Miss Sarah in reply. He gently probed at the split skin nearly exposing the lower corner of his mandible while he spoke. "I am quite fine down here, Mistress. The villain's pistol must have backfired. Stay where you are and let me go on over and check outside the window."

Miss Sarah grew frightful in response to Doc Bailey's reply and pleaded determinedly with him, "Don't go near the window, Doc. Don't you do it! Your bullets is on the floor over in the corner. I heard Miss Reedy drop them when that beast set her off real good. I heard her drop them with God as my witness, even if you didn't. Get your bullets first, Doc! Please get them. Stanton's the type that's quite likely to try and ambush you!"

Precisely as Doc Bailey was about to rise from the floor and respond to Miss Sarah, Miss Jeanne called out to them both quite surprisingly, as if she had been granted the use of her parched out voice by way of divine providence. "Nothing misfired! Someone else is out there in the night. You keep my baby at my back now, Miss Sarah! My heart is not yet entirely settled on the matter."

On the barren ground outside of the back window of the cabin, Stanton Oglethorpe had managed to roll himself away from the shattered glass of the outwardly broken pane. The sizeable shards had copiously gathered in the dirt and in some cases had managed to become shallowly impaled in the firming ground below the unadorned window sill with its chipped and fading white paint of a bygone era. Once the highwayman had cleared his body from the area below the window, he settled under some nearby brush and rested there to catch his breath and assess his bullet wound, which was hot and pulsating at the crook of his shoulder. The spot beneath the bare but copiously branched and probing shrub was the nearest place Stanton could find that offered at least some sort of cover in the event the mysterious avenger somewhere out beyond the front door of the cabin sought to finish the job he started. The barren nook also helped concealed his location from the vantage point of the blown out back window of that hideous cabin.

Stanton reckoned on that attribute of his makeshift adytum being at least somewhat gainful. In truth, Stanton would have been quite hard to spot just about anywhere out in that blanketing darkness supposing Doc Bailey somehow got his hands on a bullet and was in turn silly enough to poke his head out the window and finally test Stanton's skills with the pistol. As such, Mr. Oglethorpe remained clutching at his own trusty revolver, which was set firmly in his right hand under the care of a determined hold that would only be relinquished upon the event of his death.

Stanton's mind was racing as he looked around apace to assess the situation despite the fact he could see very little while beset by the pitch of that moonless night. He doubted that Doc Bailey would be as brave as all of that and have a go at setting his sights on him directly. After all, the medicine man had just been inconceivably absolved by some unknown phantom of the woods that had stopped Stanton's murderous hand cold; and did so without the benefit of ever spotting its target. Irrespective of what was likely to be considered the irrelevant nature of his chosen cover at that fiercely tenuous moment in his life, the still panting highwayman took some comfort from his presumed concealment beneath the overlapping brush of the thicket all the same.

Once he was settled in a bit more, Stanton's thoughts quickly darted away from Doc Bailey and back to the still unseen specter that shot him flush in the shoulder straight through the wind riddled cabin door. Forsooth, that mysterious watchman of such deadly talents had to be stalking the brush along the road somewhere and was the more immediate threat to Stanton's hopes of making a clean break from those God-forsaken woods with his hide still serviceably intact. Due to that presumed fact, Stanton listened carefully for even the slightest scratching of dead leaves shifting upon the freezing ground or the minutest crackling of broken branches being disturbed out along the sides of the road. All the tormented man for hire could hear was the steady rifling of his exploding breath through his dismal and decaying teeth until he felt a sudden tug at his elbow.

That petulant tug was accompanied by the crisp, toothy whisper of a woman, "Psst, psst! Stanton! Psst!" The desperate highwayman declined to look away from the road due to his fear of the shadowy marksman. His lips remained silent and the position of his gaze remained fixed until his wounded shoulder received a hearty and attention grabbing smack from an open palm. At that point, Stanton Oglethorpe warmed his britches up real good. He figured the demon that had set its sights on him earlier had at last made his position. In accordance with Stanton's line of thinking, only a demon seeking his just due would have smacked at a suffering man's open bullet wound in such a menacing way. After he turned his head and quickly ascertained the identity of his far less lethal assailant, Stanton nearly bit through his tongue. He struggled mightily against the searing pain of his agitated wound to remain pledged to that life giving vow of silence; a vow which he believed would carry him through the onset of such a dubious state of peril.

Miss Reedy had remained doggedly at the vagabond's heels the entire time he rolled and crawled away from the back of the cabin. Unfortunately, as the fates would have it, the cruel midwife had sustained a frightful laceration to the side of her abdomen when she landed forcefully upon a lean and upright shard of glass wedged into the dirt below the window. Once Stanton had raised his hand to Miss Reedy in a rather threatening way to keep her quiet, the two took a brief pause to gather their bearings and further assess the situation. The unlikely pair of would be kidnappers then crawled a good twenty yards through the thicket alongside the road until they once again took stationary refuge.

In the place where they had halted their grueling belly crawl, they found a spot to lay low against a pair of fallen pine trees stacked one on top of the other. Given that the narrow carriage road they tracked from its side also angled out and away from the back of the old flogging cabin, the two were then aptly shielded by the presence of about a half-dozen sturdy oak trees that lined the road. The ancient and formidable trees, which were far too cumbersome to remove back when the road was first cleared for use, would have obstructed just about any shot taken at the two villains from the back window of the shanty or any position nearby.

When the once again gasping refugees had settled their backs against the fallen Carolina pines laying just a short ways off to the side of the road, Miss Reedy slowly but purposefully pulled the shard of glass from her side without making a sound. Not knowing what she had just endured, Stanton whispered harshly back to his supremely rugged but unwelcome sidekick, "Stop nippin' at my heels, woman! I've been shot through the shoulder and I done got but one horse to get on back! You is on your own now as we ain't got no baby to deliver to Miss Meara!"

Stanton paused for the exhaling of a bated breath and whispered more fire at the anguished midwife. "You might as well go ahead and try to take the horse out front and make for the southern edge of the Blue Ridge. I'd do it now afore they find them bullets you dropped on the floor in your haste to make a witch's point!"

Miss Reedy bit down hard on her bottom lip to conceal the existence of her injury. Stanton Oglethorpe turned his head from the gathering steam of the miserable woman and poked at the area along his upper chest and shoulder where the bullet had entered. When his finger had lightly spied the entry wound, Stanton winced in pain and whispered woefully, "The devil's curse upon me for engagin' in rightful commerce with a scornful woman!"

With those words spoken, Stanton endured a harsh slap upon the side of his face that was intended only to ground his fanciful renderings of their harsh reality. When she had the fullness of Stanton's attention, Miss Reedy whispered back to her accomplice derisively as her head tremored and contorted from side to side, "You muggins! You think I'm capable of nursing a child 'cus I don't gots one waiting back at home? What? You think Miss Meara gonna pat you on your greasy head and say, "good boy," when you go slithering on up to her empty handed? You a heck of a lot dumber than you already look, Stanton Oglethorpe! No sir, we's in this fine mess together, you and me. Ain't but one somehow gettin' along without the other as things now stand."

Following the harsh outbursts delivered by both the man and the woman while they continued to conceal their lingering proximity to the cabin in that unwelcoming spot just off of the side of the road, such was clear they were in a fine mess even if left to their own devices from here on out. The weather alone was cold enough to kill on that accursed evening. Upon developing a better understanding of the longer-term depths of his predicament and being broadsided by the knowledge that should have already been plain as day to him, that Miss Reedy had a baby to fend for back home and was therefore not likely to go her own way, caused Stanton to panic to the point of snapping. He grew agitated and woefully unpredictable as his hopes for living long enough to see the morn grew dim.

Visions of Miss Meara's beady eyes flashed throughout his oversized yet underdeveloped noggin as he raised his revolver to pistol whip the harsh and hasty midwife. He had no further use for her and could conceive of no other way to stop her from crying out into the night if he fled. Just as he was about to strike the unsuspecting and thankfully preoccupied woman, the crisp, wet smacking of the hind flesh of a horse was heard from a distance of about forty yards on up the road. The sound was unmistakable.

The unseen horse neighed roughly into the thin and now soul-crushing winter air, which had settled into the depths of those long abandoned and seldom disturbed woodlands. No man or woman with a Carolinian's blood would survive the night exposed to such an ungodly expression of the elements. Even Stanton Oglethorpe could properly reckon at least that much while he listened to the horse loose itself from the dogwood tree he had retied it to hours ago. Upon hearing his wildly galloping pony break off sharply to the east, Stanton hissed back at Miss Reedy, "What witchery are you up to, woman? We'll die of the exposure out here in this God-forsaken thicket!"

To which Miss Reedy Cline replied while holding back from expressing the manifest symptoms of her extreme abdominal discomfort, "You ain't the brightest fella I ever come across, Stanton Oglethorpe. Ain't it crossed your dim mind yet that the same fella that just put a hole in your chest without an eye on you just scattered your mangy bucktoothed steed into the wind?"

Stanton waved his pistol at Miss Reedy but held his hand before striking her. He then replied to address the depths of her disdain for him with the yammer of a spoiled child. "Maybe so, Miss Reedy, but

I done knows where the fella is now, don't I. I also knows there's a horse out front that's a fair ways off from that fella. Lastly, Miss Reedy Cline, I dun knows you won't be coming with me. You smart enough to figure on that?"

Miss Reedy had raised her hand in effort to stop the worst of the pistol whipping. Still and all, her frail, frozen appendage dressed over in the sickly blue hues of exposure and with its nails caked in the mud of her desperate struggle to seek sanctuary alongside the vile Mr. Oglethorpe in the thicket, did little to deflect the heavy iron of the butt of the gun from fatally striking her tall, pedestrian brow. In fact, the vain effort to defend her person only goaded Mr. Oglethorpe into repeating the process a few times more than were needed to send the fiery woman prostrate and senseless into the dirt and winter detritus of the dormant bramble. The inauspicious spot where the would-be abductors of the secret child took their cover.

Stanton had felt the force of the fourth strike delivered with the butt of his gun jar something loose upon the once sound footings of Miss Reedy's skull. The unnerving feeling was the same as if he had cracked an egg on the edge of his cast-iron camping skillet. At that moment, he set the bloodied gun down upon a patch of frozen earth for a brief moment and emptied the final drops of his spent flask into his parched and rimy throat. Stanton's hand trembled violently as he worked the silver flask to his lips. The intense shaking was due more to the depravity of the recently completed acts of that same unholy appendage than it was the bitter cold or even his fear of that still unseen assailant lurking somewhere out there in the darkness.

When the last of the white lightning made by the Taylor boys up in the mountains had burned the cold from his throat, Stanton took a moment to read the inscription on the flask. He did so more by memory than by sight, and the proper verbiage of the inscription was indeed slightly different than the words he silently remembered. In his mind, the flask read: "*Baby Stan done growed up.*" Suddenly disgusted by the stark meaning of the words carved into the flask he had kept at his side but seldom used since his thirteenth year, Stanton threw the silver tin deep into the woods with his good arm.

The empty canister rattled along the branches of a few shrubs and settled beneath some dead leaves gathered upon the ground beneath the canopy of that forbidden arboreal labyrinth. The unmistakable flask would one day be uncovered by an unsuspecting passer-by in similar fashion to the way all formerly hidden truths are made manifest in accordance with God's perfected timing. The unexpectedly discovered flask of Stanton Oglethorpe would become part of the fabled lore of those trying years and that fateful night upon which the promised child was given unto them all. When the flask had settled for a while, Stanton thought for a brief moment and then gathered his wares. Shortly thereafter, he launched his bid to make an end around of the cabin and procure the fine white steed tied to the old wooden post out front.

Back inside the cabin, Doc Bailey was furiously searching the opposite corner of the room from whence he had taken his cover for the three bullets Miss Reedy had scattered somewhere beneath the bed and near to the old wooden stool. The cantankerous midwife had dropped the quite lethal projectiles in that place in an effort to force Stanton to act earlier by offering up some remote sign of hope to the then luckless and deceived doctor. Doc's callous free palms remained flat and empty for quite some time and his trembling fingers began to freeze as they desperately felt their way along the smooth, tread-worn planks of the floor beneath the bed. After a minute or so of fruitless and frantic searching, Miss Jeanne implored him to stop. "Those won't be needed on this night, Doctor Bailey. We all must bunk up and conserve what we can of the heat. The cold will not relent until morning when the stagecoach arrives to take her away to safety."

Doc Bailey's stretched and pleading index finger bumped into a sidelong bullet just as he was about to end his search and seek the sorely needed warmth of the bed shared by the two women and the newborn child. His teeth were chattering and his limbs were trembling as the cold continued to set into the now still and quiet room. With its broken windows, porous front door and unsealed walls, the room offered little in the way of shelter from such a deathly chill even before the back window of the cabin had been blown out upon the calamitous withdrawal of the would be abductors. Having found at least one useful bullet for the emptied chamber of his pistol, the nearly numb and wholly stiffened practitioner was more than happy to oblige his presently convalescent charge.

After fighting through the tremoring of his uncooperative hands, Doc Baily at last worked the solitary round into the chamber of his pistol and retreated to the warmth and comfort of the bed beneath the down comforter and next to Miss Sarah. Once he was bedded down, the righteously enervated doctor set the pistol down upon the floor nearly at the ready. At the very same moment the muffled sound of Doc's pistol coming to rest upon the floorboards was giving comfort to one of the two women nestled deep into the confines of the gruesomely stained and ragged but luxuriously warm bed, Stanton Oglethorpe put his boot to the horse out front and urged the prized steed forward in the wrong direction for home out on the carriage road and heading west. Stanton believed that his only hope at that moment was to put as much distance as he was able between him and that awful cabin of known misery and death, which remained so haunted by the merciless acts of torture and other forms of abiding misery committed there for far longer than he cared to recount.

When the heavy, rhythmic reverberations of the pristinely shod hooves of the galloping horse striking the cold, firm ground of the road outside were out of earshot, Doc Bailey asked of the women, "Do we need fear the one who stopped the fiendish man with that unlikely shot fired into the door boards?"

Miss Jeanne thought deeply for a short while and then turned her eyes to the right to face Miss Sarah. Ignoring the good doctor's concerns for the moment, she asked of the now settled midwife, who was nestling the child just below the covering edge of the blanket, "How is my baby girl, Miss Sarah?"

Miss Sarah took a quick second to lower the blanket that was wrapped around Margaret Anne below the turn of the baby's chin and replied, "She is quite simply the most beautiful thing I have ever seen, Ma'am. Her eyes are large and searching like the heavens themselves and her lips are round and sweet like the cherries of springtime." Miss Sarah paused for a brief moment to get her words right and then added an addendum to her initial observations. The post scribed words were intended to warn the still very thoughtful and almost seemingly detached or perhaps simply reticent mother of the child. They were intended to do so in the kindest way that a simple girl raised on a small farm out at the main crossroads of the plantation uplands of South Carolina, such as Miss Sarah Maples was, could muster. "She is blessed with your enchanting features, Miss Jeanne. There is no doubt about that. Still and all, she most certainly does not share your complexion or that of her father, the African man good and true, Mr. Jonas Hastings."

At that moment, Doctor Bailey's eyes grew wide like a pair of tea time saucers, though none took notice of the glowing whites of his shocked orbital wares amidst the thick and peculiarly shaded darkness of the room. He had been listening to the brief discourse shared between the two women regarding the miracle child. More than that, the good doctor had been listening with extreme interest and perhaps even a schoolboy nosiness that was well-fired by a wild hair. He was however, a rather demure man who was also extremely well-mannered and had been properly schooled in the primly religious homeland of his youth up North. As such, he peered skyward into the steeple of the ceiling to deflect his unbound curiosity regarding the sweetly spoken yet supremely scandalous revelations of Miss Sarah. Nevertheless, his full attention was duly given over to the anticipated reaction from Miss Jeanne. Doctor Bailey had not seen the miraculous child since she had been relieved of the blood and other unsightly side effects of her violent fight to exit the womb in the wrong manner and breathe in the cold air of that inexplicable February night; a night which had already probed the known bounds of both terror and wonder but had apparently held safe a few surprises yet still.

Doc remained still as a corpse while a wanting to know, which was so severe he could only compare the feeling to something akin to that of exploding static bursting along the fine blonde hairs of his pale winter skin, had his mind racing in a way he had not experienced since the days of his early adolescence; those boyishly lustful days when the finely adorned ladies of the Saratoga countryside would assemble for summer church. Such was certain that the prudish medical practitioner of such a national renown craved to consume every last morsel of the abject details of such a rapidly budding exposé. He knew that this was a story capable of setting fire to the whole of the Carolinas at a time when the igniting of such a conflagration required only that of the faintest spark.

The still good but now nearly frenetic doctor's time spent in wait was not long. After a few fleeting moments of a somewhat ominous but peaceful calm shared between the four unlikely bedfellows stranded out in the woods on that coldest of nights that any South Carolina man or woman alike would ever come to know, Miss Jeanne split the silence with her strengthening voice by replying to the unintentionally insensitive midwife. "Ah, my dear Miss Sarah, let us not forget your little part in all of this. Though I absolve you of those recent sins born of both your ignorance and your worldly needs, there is the eternal perdition of your silence and the due care which accompanies the knowing of the truth about the child. Both shall remain tied to your sacred oath to her as the price to be tendered for the abetting in such an unsanctified act."

Miss Sarah began to stutter in reply and bring the child forth from the depths of the comforter so that her mother might lay her eyes upon little Miss Margaret Anne. Be that as it may, Miss Jeanne promptly cut short the foolish sputtering of Miss Sarah's youthfully ignorant tongue while she prepared to at last take hold of her baby girl. "Hush, my foolhardy child, for our heavenly Father has already shown me that my child is as white as the driven snow that shall fall in this very place upon the hour of her deliverance. Her complexion is exactly the same as her father's. Our God has also made known to me that you shall help raise up my little maiden of the angelic realms."

Miss Jeanne took hold of the precious child and pressed the babe's slightly chilled nose to her own until she felt with her own flesh the pure softness and delicate grace of her perfectly appeased baby girl with the searching eyes. She was instantly overwhelmed by the emotion of love after the trying ordeal of her birth and the terrorizing moments that followed upon which she nearly lost that precious bundle to the wicked spirits lurking out in the night. After rubbing the child's baby soft cheeks and chin for a long while, she held the wrapped bundle away from her eyes to get a better look at little Margaret Anne and spoke further for the benefit of Miss Sarah, "One day you shall be called to bear witness on behalf of the child of Edward Christopher Calhoun. That promise to speak the truth of her sacred identity shall hold but once. However, it shall remain the measure of your debt to her for as long as you still walk upon this earth. The gift of this child has not been made mine on this night, but yours, gentle Miss Sarah Maples of Solomon's Town to the west of Sumter. It is you that shall nourish her through her infancy. It is you that shall see her on her way to the fields beyond Augusta on this very morning."

Doc Bailey could not resist the forceful pining of his inanely yearning mind for a second longer. He rolled his eyes harshly to the left to venture a shaded look at the raised and fully exposed countenance of the almost ominously peaceful child. He could not make out the tone of the baby's skin as the room was now wholly immersed in the depths of the darkness that comes just before even the slightest brume of the dawn. Doc Bailey knew full well that Mr. Calhoun adored the unwed mother of the child. Why such was true was plain enough for any man to see and that verity would have held firm to its moorings even if the morning light had cast its gentle shine upon the worn out woman upon the very instant. Yet, beyond that fact, Doc knew as much about Edward's presumed desires in an almost incriminating manner given the untold value of his remuneration for services rendered. Although, while he lay there in that mussed up bed with two strange women and a swaddled babe to keep from freezing to death and perhaps even being shot at again, the good doctor now questioned the equitable nature of his contract with Mr. Calhoun given all that had transpired on that evening for the ages.

In fact, if Doc Bailey had been properly squared with his conscious and not somewhat blinded by greed and the social prestige that came hand in hand with performing a sensitive service for one as renowned as Mr. Edward Calhoun of Sumter, South Carolina at the time he agreed to deliver the child into that eternally forsaken cabin in that hopeless span of upland wilderness, he would have understood long ago at least that one spectacular nuance regarding the true nature of little Margaret Anne Hastings. Regardless, by the time the stunning words were spoken aloud, Doc Bailey had no reason to doubt what Miss Jeanne had so abruptly revealed to Miss Sarah under the presumption of secrecy where such delicately shared confidences were concerned. Those assumed promises of their continuing silence would most certainly be adhered to by the three who had been so rudely cast into such a scandalous position beneath the covers. Since he was also wholly given over to the enduring virtues of those same shared confidences, the good doctor dared not even think about silently whispering the name Margaret Anne Calhoun into the deepest recesses of his own sensibilities.

Based on what he had heard the women discussing just a moment ago and realizing that he was not to bear witness to the corporeal proof of the child's paternal lineage for at least a few more hours, Doc Bailey turned his back to Miss Sarah, as only a gentleman in such an uncompromising and wholly disreputable position would do. He prepared to rest his heavy eyes for a few prized hours. The ordeal of the birth of Margaret Anne and all that followed had carried on for forty-eight hours when the rather spoiled doctor had planned to be away from the lush creature comforts of the auxiliary quarters of the Calhoun plantation, some twelve miles to the southeast of the cabin and a few miles up the road from Sumter, for just half of a day. That estimate was in the event that there were complications with the delivery. When he was properly settled on his side to rest and thinking of the more pleasant things that awaited him back at his winter home up in Virginia, Doc Bailey called out into the darkness quite effusively, though his proximity to the women he was addressing should have dictated otherwise.

The good and rather puritan doctor could feel the shapely and warm, womanly comportment of his nearest bedside neighbor quite readily. Perhaps it was the sinful sensation caused by such intimate, albeit forced and rather incidental, contact with a blossoming woman of at least notable allure that caused Doc Bailey to speak so forcefully and so pragmatically; a tone which was delivered in stark opposition to the spirit of the cozy confines of the bed which the four now shared. "I am going to rest for a few hours before first light, my dearest ladies. Please, do wake me if that delightful little cherub or her mother requires anything at all. I shall presume Miss Jeanne's infallible instincts regarding our shadowy and unseen protector leave us with little to fear but for the torments of the deathly cold."

Miss Sarah remained too frightened by the nature of her discomforting predicament regarding her small part in the failed abduction of the child to say a word but Miss Jeanne answered back to the doctor for the benefit of them both. "Rest well, good doctor. Both your miraculous work in delivering the child in spite of her ostensibly insurmountable predicament and the other misfortunes of our circumstances on this evening have been trying affairs. The Lord above speaks of little to fear presently regarding the man who came for my baby earlier, yet there is something or perhaps someone out there. Miss Sarah will keep her guard up as little Maggie and I also rest for a short while. Thank you for everything you have done for us, most gracious Sir. We are forever beholden to a debt of gratitude accruing to your honor."

Not but the steady tick of a serviceable clock after Miss Jeanne finished with her thankful goodnight to her doctor, who was already drifting eagerly toward the initial premonitions of his dreams, the door to the old rectangular cabin began to creak steadily and evenly. The unnerving sound resonated within as if someone were slowly and cautiously entering the loathsome cottage. Doc Bailey heard the startling and then terrifying noise against the lesser remnants of the once battering winds. Those formerly strident drafts and shears were then present only in the manner of intermittently whistling gusts brushing their way past the lightly rattling walls of the cabin. He reached down quietly for his pistol, which rested cold and still upon the worn floor boards and he did so instead of returning the favor of an honorable rejoinder to the gracious goodnight offered over to him by Miss Jeanne on behalf of the three ladies.

Miss Jeanne also heard the creaking noise of the front door, yet harbored no trepidation towards the visiting spirit at last coming in from the cold and making its presence known to those it had saved from the misguided depravity of Stanton Oglethorpe. When Miss Jeanne heard the hammer of Doc Bailey's gun cock in the darkness with that tattletale click never to be mistaken for any other sound upon this earth, aside from perhaps that of the hitching hiss of a venomous snake before it strikes, she yelled out with as much force as her spent body was able to muster for such an essential endeavor, "No, Doctor! Stay your hand!"

Her warning was but a split second too late. She failed to hold back the report of the volatile discharge of the now quite useful instrument the good doctor clutched in his frightened and therefore quite touchy trigger hand. But alas, it is not but a split second that so often marks the bounds between fulfillment and disaster and so narrowly and precisely sets the line of demarcation between the living and the dead. The shot rang out harshly into the ears of the two women beginning to stir yet still partially burrowed into the blankets of the bed. Miss Jeanne and Miss Sarah had by that time grown accustomed to the supernal teasing of the lightly rattling floor boards, the intermittent spells of silence and those now hushed and familiar sounds of the rhythmically whistling winds skirting the tenuous old pine walls of the cabin. The shot was quickly followed by the shrill cry of some innocent creature that had been violently forced into the side wall of the cottage by the force of the projectile striking it at such close range. Following a brief and reconciling silence that seemed to span the entirety of the righteously shocked assailant's lifetime, what was heard next was the sound of that same gentle creature dropping into a heap of dead weight upon the floor.

Miss Jeanne screamed, handed Margaret Anne to Miss Sarah and attempted to carry herself across the room to inspect the devastation delivered upon the one she loved so dearly. She fell to the floor upon taking her second step as her lifeless legs quickly gave way. Miss Sarah began to once again weep uncontrollably while she fretfully rocked the baby safely in her arms from the depths of the comforter. The sorrow and the tragedy of that night had at last become far too much to bear for the mundane sensibilities of the young maiden; a young maiden who was so rudely tempted against the shell of her former innocence by the sweet pecuniary fruits of the inglorious grifter with the rotten teeth and a penchant for only depravity.

When the morning light at last pierced the barren canopy of that forest so deadened or perhaps only stilled by that quite uncommon and all-consuming winter freeze, the first stagecoach arrived out at the cabin. True to Miss Jeanne's word, the outer rails of the slowly turning wheels of the carriage pressed their mark into a thin layer of dusting snow that drifted fancifully along the frozen ground according to the whims of the playful and swirling morning breeze. Given all that had transpired, Miss Jeanne was adamant that the carriage would carry her baby girl and Miss Sarah safely over to her appointed home in the fertile fields beyond Augusta straight away. Though Miss Jeanne had originally intended to secretly care for her baby out there in the woods for a few days before accompanying the little one over to Augusta and beyond for a month or so before returning home to her daughters out at the farm, neither Miss Basseterre nor her newly born child of such unbound promise remained safe in that old cabin for long.

Beyond her belief that remaining stationed out at the cabin was a perilous endeavor, the spent and concerned mother of the promised child no longer felt that accompanying little Margaret Anne on such a demanding journey, which involved crossing the state line into Georgia at a time of acutely sensitive awareness to the problem of runaway slaves, was an innocuous affair given appearances following the birth of her light-skinned child. Worse than even that not at all insignificant dilemma, were her fears concerning the nature and the depths of the treachery that had occurred only hours ago. Miss Jeanne had never suspected that Miss Meara would so boldly challenge the wishes of her son, yet with such insolence now being the plainly manifest truth of Mistress Calhoun's will where that ill and potent will regarded the existence of Edward's illegitimate child, there was no telling who might be aligned with that old witch and her failed plantation boss man of a lackey. The vile woman's ties were old as the Anglican ascendency over these lands of the West, they ran deeper than Miss Basseterre would ever care to imagine here in Carolina, and in many instances, those bonds of fealty were pledged in blood throughout the passing of the generations.

On the brighter side of things for all still situated within the desolate confines of the February Cabin, Miss Jeanne never doubted that Edward would fight with all of his being to preserve the child. That is unless his claim to the auspicious wealth of the Calhoun estate were to be challenged as a direct result of the existence of his scandalous love child. Miss Jeanne worried some over Edward's commitment to the baby girl if such an occurrence were to transpire, but never in the depths of her heart and such a terrible incident as that was never a given portent emanating from the ancient golden cross resting upon her breastbone. Moreover, as Edward was the only son of the late Mortimer Calhoun, such a thing as his disenfranchisement from the Calhoun legacy was near to an impossibility without the implementation of untold treason and perfidy, which was beyond even the dour capacity of Miss Meara as it concerned dealing with her only son.

As much as it pained her heart to understand the consequences of such a reality, Miss Jeanne knew full well that her embarking upon such a journey to Georgia was neither safe for the child nor was it a journey she would be in any position to endure for some days or perhaps even some weeks to come given her present physical condition. Yet, endure the drained woman knew she now must for the sake of that gifted child. A child who was a treasure in her own right and one whose true identity must remain hidden from the denizens of Miss Basseterre's Carolina for many years to come, if not for all eternity. Furthermore, Miss Jeanne understood full well that she needed to continue on for the sake of her sweet baby girls back in Uriah if they were to endure the times to come that were the given sign of the arrival of the promised child. Sweet Miss Maime Alouette Osment, aged eleven years but soon to be twelve upon the arrival of the April blossoms, and Miss Shy Jolie Osment, aged ten years, had both been anxiously awaiting her return back at home for so long now.

With no one amongst the group of survivors of that fateful evening in any position to argue in opposition to even a solitary provision of her forcefully delivered points, Miss Jeanne's unwavering command to send the child and Miss Sarah on ahead to the fields of Georgia was so ordained. When Miss Basseterre handed her divinely spirited child, a child who had already been condemned by the unholy and banished from her rightful place amongst the landed aristocracy of South Carolina before she had taken her first breath in the world of men, into Miss Sarah's capable and welcoming arms, the inconsolable mother wept without the stabilizing graces of her traditional refinement and pleaded with the young nurse, "You make certain my baby girl grows big and strong in the months ahead. You watch over her until I can be by to see her. She is the child of the west wind. She is the deliverer of the innocent and the beholder of the purifying tempests of the light."

Miss Jeanne paused to wipe a few of the tears lingering beneath her right eye away from her high and distinguished cheek bone that was so stunningly accentuated by the expressions of her emotional distress and her tawny winter skin in the soft, lowly angled light of that February morning. She then spoke forcibly against the emptying draw of her sorrow and her exhaustion. "She is the one that shall look to banish the evils set upon this land or raze and scatter the works of the wicked out over the dust of the earth in trying." Following those words of forceful declaration regarding the nature of her departing child, Miss Jeanne bit softly at her lower lip to keep at least something of the outward show of her emotions tempered within, lowered her gleaming eyes of amber and blue to the dusting of snow lightly dressing over the packed, frozen dirt of the carriage road upon which she stood and added solemnly, "Yet perhaps in a way that none of us will ever come to fully understand."

Miss Sarah was still visibly shaken by all that had transpired and all that was now set to occur. Nevertheless, she nodded dutifully in response to Miss Jeanne. The remnants of her own tears upon preparing to leave with the child in the presence of the baby's saddened and depleted yet still radiant mother gave a sorrowful shine to her sea blue eyes while they were directly exposed to that same ambient light of the slowly rising late-February sun, which was piercing through the barren branches of the trees back to the east. Miss Sarah then turned with the child, took a few steps forward and stepped onto the awaiting coach with the promised child held safely and securely in her steadfast arms.

The soft, thin flakes of snow continued to fall outside the carriage as the sun angled its radiant light through the tall pines and bald deciduous trees of the forest. The time would not be long before that bittersweet and wholly majestic moment of their human sacrifice duly marked by the sound of the trotting hooves of the horses and the hard wooden wheels of the stagecoach crushing the pebbles, sticks and frozen clumps of dirt scattered upon the narrow and seldom traveled road were but a distant memory; a wistful and distant memory from a day gone by which once shone brightly with the promise of a stunning baby girl who had beaten back certain death and then vanished into the woods from whence she came. More so, that same baby girl was the one promised to those long-suffering under the bonds of servitude and those indirectly forced to comply with the ascribed social order of the day. That baby girl was the one who should rightfully have commanded the vast and clashing principalities of the long-settled expanse of her birthplace, yet the magnitude and splendor of her true gifts were destined to lie very still until the preordained moment of her own reckoning.

A few hours later, the old cabin was once again empty and Doc Bailey held firm to a wounded girl on the cusp of advancing into the earliest shadings of such a promising coming out into the waiting arms of her opulent caste of Southern society. The girl was tightly wrapped in torn linens at the right arm and shoulder and her body was wrapped up in both the mired cotton blanket from the birthing bed and the sorrowful doctor's arms. The day was already far warmer than that merciless chill that held so steadfast to the prior night. Miss Jeanne was sleeping on the other bench of the rather elegant stage-coach, which had just emerged from the bald canopy of the woodland road. There were not so many miles left in their journey overland to the Osment farmstead and then perhaps back to the Calhoun's Butterworth Plantation. Such a condition to the terms of their travel was a good thing. Both the wounded girl and the mother of that phantom child who had been taken back up into the westerlies were in need of proper rest and due care.

The girl wrapped up in Doctor Bailey's unwavering arms had fired the blind shot into the night that had stopped Stanton Oglethorpe dead to rights from taking Doc's life and dashing off into the haunted hollows of the night with the promised child. She had used a cov-eted Calhoun hunting rifle to accomplish the impossible feat. Sadly, she was also the recipient of Doc Bailey's own ill-fated shot that had shattered her shoulder and left the matter of her arm ever being useful once again or even kept as an ornamental appendage in doubt. The young girl's name was Elizabeth Ann Calhoun. She was the fourth and favored child of Edward Christopher Calhoun and nearly the bane of the existence of her dearly departed mother and dedicated socialite, Mrs. Libby Adams Hopkins Calhoun.

She was a beautiful child of a very curious and timid nature who carried her wares and her emotion in an always pleasant and unas-suming manner. That is to say, except when in the direct presence of her mother or until she became pressed into standing firm for her beliefs. She loved Miss Jeanne dearly from the days that elegant Haitian woman spent managing the affairs of the Calhoun household following her marriage to Mr. Osment. Therefore, Elizabeth Ann also dearly loved the one she had secretly and in the small hours of the morning learned was her 'baby sis.' There was nothing Elizabeth Ann would not do for the sake of one of her own. Little Margaret Anne could not have chosen a better sentry to guide her through so many of the difficulties she would come to face later in her life.

The three passengers on the horse drawn carriage slept for a good while until the coachman instructed his sturdy steeds to turn left up the still righteously worn for travel but visually unkempt drive to the Osment farmstead. The man of the house had been dead for some years after his heart had given way unexpectedly when he refused to yield his heavenly ordained duties out in the field to an ungodly wave of summer heat, which permitted the denizens of Hades to dance openly upon the loamy clay of the Carolina soil for a week straight back in July of 1855. Nothing was going to stop that man from transforming his still unbridled and petulant field into the cotton yielding pride of the Carolinas but for that most vital organ, which had been blessed with the gift of love in multiples of four for each corporal defect that had gone on undetected for far too long. The Wilson's, who managed the farm down the drive and were a God-loving sort of folk, had appointed their man, Shem Davis, to care for the longer portion of the drive that ran beyond the entrance to the Wilson farm while Miss Jeanne and her usual attendant, Jonas Hastings were away on some business dealings down in the Caribbean for one of Mr. Calhoun's countless merchant enterprises. Old Shem had done his right best to keep things in order under the watchful eye of Miss Stapleton, who was caring for the girls in Miss Jeanne's prolonged absence, but he had been sent on to Columbia to procure supplies for the spring planting season a few weeks back.

Sensing the change in direction of the coach and hearing the driver holler out to steady his charges for the trot down the level but in certain stretches, winding drive, Doc Bailey awoke. He turned his head and stared longingly into the barren field of cotton that was marked by a solitary oak tree, which appeared as if it might survive the entirety of the millennium. Not long passed from the moment Doc first set his eyes upon the flats of the field surrounded by a span of traditional woodlands typical to the Carolina midlands when a young girl's voice rang out from directly in front of the carriage into the thin, stilled air of the cold yet settled winter morning. The girl had been out with the hounds up to the place where the drive began to turn gently toward the south but she was still some ways off from the approaching carriage.

"Momma! Momma! Momma! Momma, we didn't expect you back until planting time in the spring! My sweet, momma! I can't believe my eyes! Momma, you're home at last after all this time!" the girl cried out as she set her sights upon the fancy carriage that undoubtedly was presumed to be arriving from the Calhoun's place.

Doc Bailey watched the excited girl begin to run on towards the oncoming stagecoach. Her gait was long and elegant like a gazelle and her smile was wide as the Savannah River at the main crossing over to Augusta. Her eyes were beaming with a light of pure joy. Hers was a glorious look and one which Doc Bailey would struggle to put into proper words even many years later upon the latent transcribing of the journals he would use to record the events of those days of such wonder, trial and hope. While the bemused doctor watched the heartened little girl run on towards them with thoughts of his own precious girls running through his head and a warm smile set upon his heart, a worn out and far too soft but steadfastly determined voice from the back of the stagecoach called out only loud enough for Doc Bailey to hear. Elizabeth Ann remained fast asleep due to the somnolent effects of her medication and Miss Jeanne's feebly delivered words possessed no hope of carrying beyond the perfectly polished, black wooden walls of the steadily moving carriage.

"Oh, my sweet baby, your momma hears you! Yes, yes, yes, momma is home for you! My God has turned my sin into the blessing of an angel but momma is home for you at last, my baby girl!" Miss Jeanne's throaty, muffled and hopelessly feeble exclamations then trailed off into a quiet and reflective whisper. More than she could possibly bear was once again weighing heavily upon her mind and her swollen heart.

"My heart is about to split my dearest. My heart is about to split my dearest sunshine, Shy Jolie."

Doc Bailey waved as the swiftly moving girl approached the evenly moving carriage. The girl took notice of Doc Bailey but remained clearly looking in earnest for someone else. The still smiling but now slightly uncertain looking girl looked to be about ten or eleven, just as the wounded girl still wrapped in his arms now was. Both were such beautiful and promising young things to behold. Doc's mind began to wander reminiscently as he continued watching the girl run on to them with no sign of tiring. He then thought about the scandalous secrets he would be forced to keep from this moment until his dying days from ones such as the little girl fast approaching.

Furthermore, the good doctor thought about the whereabouts of Stanton Oglethorpe and wondered if that villain had survived the deep freeze of the prior evening. He thought about the horrified look set upon the late Miss Reedy Cline's pasty, death-riddled face as she lie upon the frozen ground just a ways on up the road outside of the back of the cabin. The poor woman was dusted over in snow and so stiffened by the cold and the onset of rigor mortis in the limpid morning light sifting and streaking through the lifeless branches of the trees. He thought about the beautiful and mystifying face of the baby he had delivered into the exact opening of the new day. Lastly, he thought about how that wrapped up little child so resembled the girl that was near to taking hold of the now slowing carriage absent the stark contrast of the color of her skin.

As Doc readied to speak to the glowing girl still desperately searching for a given sign of her momma as she slowed her pace to meet the stagecoach, he knew that the events which had transpired in the smallest hours of the prior evening were in many ways going to shape the events of this fertile yet divided land for a long time to come. He hoped with all of his heart that gentle Miss Sarah and the little child were having an uneventful journey overland to the river and then beyond. Moreover, he once again hoped with all that he was and all that he stood to be in this life that God would grant him the capacity to save the arm of the gentle child wrapped up in his tired and slightly tremoring limbs.

He hoped for as much even if Edward Calhoun came out here to Uriah to strike him down for his unintended transgression immediately after the fact. If Doctor Emmett Bailey had come to learn anything that night, the lesson that would never leave his thoughts was that there were just some things worth dying for in this uncertain life. Those things were worth dying for because the living that transpired after not doing them was not a life worth living at all and most of all, because such eternal sacrifice, if called upon, stood alone above all gifts that might be given over for the enduring benefit of the ones he loved.

Doc Bailey then lowered his eyes from the clear blue skies of the Southern countryside, which was so haunted by both beauty and the trials of the soul. He watched little Shy Jolie Osment step onto the stagecoach and take hold of her mother while tears poured forth from that little girl's eyes. Doc Bailey then stared into the darkened locks of the mussed up yet shimmering hair of the sweet little girl sleeping in his arms. He tremored slightly whilst he considered how his impotence while standing before Stanton Oglethorpe after discharging his empty pistol had caused him to fire his weapon blindly into Elizabeth Ann a while later after the dust of that initial altercation had settled. He then pondered the dilemma now facing Miss Jeanne and her older girls as this newborn child grew into her own over on the plains of Georgia.

To conclude that moment of his passing fancy, his thoughts circled back to Edward Calhoun and his ilk and the danger that the very existence of little Margaret Anne posed to such powerful people. For that reason alone, Doc Bailey understood that he was now irrevocably tied to the fate of that long-promised child. He somehow knew right then and there that all those who had survived the night after sleeping in that bleak and haunted cabin in the woods would bear a meaningful responsibility for the protection and the care of the child along with Margaret Anne's true father.

The child had for but a moment flaunted her disdain for the wickedness of their ways in the blood stained cabin that night. She had then rested serenely with nary a worry or a cry of concern over those forces so determinedly aligned against her; spiteful forces of the accursed realms that in the year 1859 were already growing far stronger than the common man would dare conceive possible. The stagecoach began moving again toward the Osment farmhouse with its newest passenger tenderly caring for her still weakened mother. Doc began to reason that his imagination, fervently stoked by the trials of his trauma that night, was starting to get the better of him. He departed from his further considerations of little Margaret Anne knowing simply that someday he would be the one responsible for the telling of the full truth of her sure to be passionate and transformational tale. Doc then checked the temperature of his well-bundled patient and in so doing finally came to remember an even more important lesson that he would forever keep safe and which he learned upon the hour of Margaret Anne's birth. That lesson was that anything was indeed possible in this world through faith and under God.

Doctor Emmett William Bailey then smiled gainfully into the sunshine piercing the still cool February air and watched the world go by without a care to speak of as the stagecoach approached its intended destination, the quaint and comforting front porch of the Osment farmstead. The driver tightened up on the reins of his team and his eager steeds blew out heartily into the crisp, refreshing country air. The late-afternoon light remained intently angled into Doc's blue-green eyes that seemed to favor the shadings of his chosen attire on a given day. As Doc gazed out into the fallow winter field, a field which Clarke Osment had in some ways bent to his will before passing and in other ways had simply left that beautifully wild and downward sloping tract of land passing the Good Lord's gifted time in wait to once again push up the high grasses and wildflowers of its leisure, the now humbled medical practitioner of such renown found it strange that he could not bother to recollect the full measure of even a passing concern while gripped within the depths of such a heavenly ordained moment of serenity.

Looking back on those days from the lofty vantage point of time gone by, Doc found it quite strange that he possessed such a restful mind and peaceful heart as the coach came to a comforting halt between the sturdy farmhouse and the field. He found it quite strange to experience such a sublime twinkling of grace right then given all that was to be done to care for the infirmed on board. Furthermore, he found it quite strange to experience the gift of God's peace upon the very instant that many of his once sacred beliefs had been turned completely on their head. Lastly, he found it rather peculiar to experience such restful ecstasy in the very moment of the knowing that the intended direction of his own life was to be set upon a far different road than any coursing he had the capacity to even imagine formerly; formerly, in the sweet hypnotic depths of those curiously assigned pleasantries that marked the days before the one promised had been made manifest before his once inconstant and now awakened eyes by the will of the divine.

Chapter Two

THE WEEPING TIME

ᴄ❧ᴏ

IN TRUTH, THERE are no coincidences in this life. Always and everywhere we are exactly where God intends for us to be. The only question that remains on the matter is whether or not we choose to open our woefully blinded hearts to God's truth and the deeds He desires of us while the myriad moments of our lives play out before our eyes. To the ones present in Savannah, Georgia on the days of Wednesday and Thursday, March 2nd and 3rd in the tumultuous year of 1859, such a divine verity would not have been made plain to many of those who directly attended to the affairs of one Edward Christopher Calhoun during that span. In fact, such a profound truth born of the presence of some cosmic fate or manifest destiny aligned with only impossible chance on those most dismal and pluvious of dates would have remained hidden from all but a few.

Though the weather attributed to those dour turns was fit to have ascribed to it no other proper legal designation than that of an "Act of God," such blindness to the divine entity behind the outcome of Mr. Calhoun's affairs existed simply due to the willful oversight or misguided omission of some requisite facts necessary to cure such a deficiency. However, those items of tangible and direct evidence and perhaps visual confirmation of some miraculous occurrence, which are always so desperately needed to render proof of an event or confirm the mystical intentions behind a given set of circumstances where it concerns the faithless, were not present on those days. Only a select few among the fickle, those who knew the entirety of the story, had their faith in God above affirmed at a time proximate to the conclusion of those dour matters.

The number of those who have laid eyes upon that now ancient journal resting somewhere beneath the earth in one of the Calhoun crypts in or around Sumter, South Carolina is scant. However, to those fortunate few readers of Doc Bailey's unpublished memoirs and the other private publications of the archive, which served as the basis for the posthumous and wildly chaotic life story of Miss Margaret Anne Basseterre just prior to the turning of that fabled nineteenth century and of course her growing legend that continued to take shape well-beyond that time, such an inviolable truth concerning the depths of God's power and purview over His endless domain was made abundantly clear to those with eyes that truly see on those mournful days. That same revelation may also be made by the his readers of the modern era as they wander through the good doctor's carefully chosen and parsed out words and digest his colorful, heartfelt and sorrowful rendering of the three days he spent in Savannah, Georgia with the aforementioned Mr. Edward Calhoun; a titan of his day who controlled the most egregious of the concentrated mercantile and agrarian fiefdoms of South Carolina.

Edward and his entourage had arrived in Savannah on the evening of Tuesday, March 1st. The weary delegation had the delectable morsels of their evening meal sent promptly to their rooms as Edward and his various constituents of far differing natures were exhausted from the long journey down to the low country and then onward in a southwesterly direction along the coast. Therefore, it was not until the morning of Wednesday, March 2nd that the elite socialite was announced to the locals of the prospering port city over a hotel sponsored breakfast that was a rather impromptu yet grandiose affair. Even the 34th mayor of Savannah, the honorable Thomas Turner himself, was dragged out of bed for the occasion by his amiable enough wife of some thirty years. Still and all, she was both a socially and politically calculating woman in near deadly senses of the ascribed words.

Doctor Bailey was present at the head table of the breakfast gathering, which filled out a dozen tables in the grand dining room of the Wharf Side Hotel. The still enervated doctor was in attendance in accordance with his newly appointed role as Elizabeth Ann Calhoun's personal physician for the year 1859 and perhaps beyond, circumstances pending of course. His prize and now only patient remained prudently upstairs in her room recovering to the best of her ability from what was publicly described a ghastly hunting wound, the results of which had severely damaged and thus far fully impaired the use of her right arm.

Truth be told, the good doctor was beyond exhausted. His time spent in the abandoned cabin delivering Miss Margaret Anne and then delicately and very scrupulously caring for her half-sister, Elizabeth Ann in addition to nursing Miss Jeanne back to some form of useful and stable vibrancy had the poor man whipped like a mule. The rushed two day journey down state and then along the splendid coast of the Atlantic on the heels of such draining work did little to improve his physically and mentally impotent condition. With such being the case, Doc did very little speaking and diverted what little energy he possessed into making certain he had a good meal down his throat and warmly coating his unsettled belly before the now buzzing party moved on for the day.

When the large group had begun to disperse, Mayor Turner slipped into an open seat positioned in between Mr. Calhoun and Doc Bailey. The seat had been occupied by Mr. Calhoun's long-winded publicist of a sort and legal attaché, Mr. Duncan Mc Bride, also officially of Sumter. Yet at that point in his life, Mr. Mc Bride was a man who had become far more accustomed to the bustling scenes of his second residence, which was exquisitely positioned within the Market Square of Charleston. Mr. Mc Bride had rushed down his food in order to chat with the Lieutenant Governor of the state of Georgia, and of course, more so due to the nature of her perfectly positioned stance directly in between the two men rather than his desire to converse with the somewhat gossipy and oftentimes overbearing woman, Mrs. Millie Turner.

Mayor Turner was a short, round man with a voice intricately made for the political podium. He spoke so clearly and so handsomely that the occurrence was quite rare in which his listener was not instantly enamored with the man. Furthermore, such enchantment was always conjured in spite of the mayor's otherwise pedestrian and frumpy nature in addition to his nearly unpresentable deportment and sloppily arranged attire. The mayor's voice also carried in a room so clearly that his harmonious tone was oftentimes a fatal flaw, both politically speaking and socially, at least according to his dearest Millie. Mayor Turner was even considered a bit of a loose talker about town due to the fact that his acoustically blessed and often times belting voice was regularly, though of course "incidentally," overheard by those around him and because he was a very blunt man. He rarely chose to skirt the touchy issues of the day; the issues where the wagon wheel tended to firmly and irrevocably collide with the road as the now popular colloquialism may have been transcribed to suit the times.

Being seated directly next to the jocular man who refused to entertain even the slightest bit of nonsense if not spoken in jest, Doc Bailey could hear Mayor Turner speak as if that man's voice were rightly inside of his own head. The buzz of the many surrounding conversations taking place between the various people standing nearby did nothing to dilute Mr. Turner's perfectly directed effect or the charm of his thoughtful Southern drawl. "Good morning, Mr. Calhoun. Though it would appear you have brought the rain into town with you, it is indeed such an unexpected pleasure to have you in our fair city and the great state of Georgia too!"

Edward had been finishing up the last of what may have been the finest scrambled eggs the worldly connoisseur of breakfast offerings had ever sampled. After a very polite and almost dainty wipe of his mouth, Edward responded to Mayor Turner in a very enthusiastic manner. His business in Savannah had the potential to dust up some political strife if things went poorly. Therefore, Edward counted the mayor as one among friends on that grey and clouded morning spent nearby the angry, chopping waters of the bustling waterfront. "And a very gracious good morning to you as well, Mayor Turner. To what do I owe the honor of a visit from the finest government servant in all of Dixie?" Edward then offered up his hand to the visiting mayor and furthered his cordial greeting by saying, "How kind of you to come greet us at such an early hour with such short notice given of our arrival and with so much ado taking shape in your fair city today!"

Edward paused for a brief moment to properly read the mayor's only somewhat surprised facial contortions and then continued on with the pleasantries of his proper greeting. "I offer up the graces of my sincerest apologies to you, good Sir, for neglecting to send someone on ahead with our plans to visit. To defend our gentility, I will only say that we received word of the unlikely outcry at such a late hour and with so little time to spare." Edward then paused briefly to rub thoughtfully at his chin for dramatic effect and added, "In point of fact, as preposterous as such a thing may sound to you or I, we received word so late that someone in the wrong frame of mind might be persuaded to believe Mr. Butler's dutiful trustees sought to exempt the charitable sponsors of our estate from the corollary of the unfortunate event altogether; for some unknown reason or another."

Mayor Turner shifted his eyes slightly as he carefully digested Mr. Calhoun's curious combination of proper window dressing and outright poppycock. To Edward's credit however, the shrewd businessman's loosely veiled taunt of the local gentry was as to the point as ever. Mr. Turner stiffened and pulled his chair a bit closer to the table to tighten up his eye contact with Mr. Calhoun but his rotund belly kept his perfectly round and moderately balding head a fair measure from the table's edge. "Why Mr. Calhoun, for one who has so suddenly come into some of the finest yielding assets in all of Georgia, you speak as if there are those among us who do not welcome the hasty incursion of a bright-eyed, lustful and industrious sandlapper."

Edward laughed delightedly at Mayor Turner's reply. The mayor certainly was a hard-nosed man beneath that jovial and slovenly looking exterior. Still and all, he was also the type who could kick horse shit in your eye and leave you smiling with that virtuous, honeyed voice of his. In a world of fallen and egregiously sycophantic politicians, the citizenry of Savannah were quite fortunate to have such a stand-up gentleman as Mr. Thomas Turner looking out for their best interests and their general well-being. Once Edward had caught hold of the vim and vigor of his slightly contemptuous wild hair to open, he settled back down and countered with a bit of humor. "What is one to do, my good Sir? The man is a profligate speculator who knows so little of the virtues of moderation and restraint. I am altogether quite certain he would be dancing through the halls of Butterworth Plantation in naught but his nightshirt upon this very instant if he possessed even the slightest learning around probability and chance."

Mayor Turner laughed melodiously in response to Mr. Calhoun's rather humorous offering of peace and rejoined, "Aye, we lost a shrewd yet imperious mind for business when the Major died. Unfortunately, that same man possessed little time or care for the bringing along of his progeny while amassing his fortune. I suppose in the future the local gentry will just have to be more discerning around who they invite to the table for a friendly game of cards. Shame on them I say, although I had heard the hand was quite well played, Mr. Calhoun; for a Carolina gentleman, that is."

With the initial tensions of the morning detente having quickly been brushed off to the side, at least for the present moment, both men laughed heartily at the pleasant and amusing exchange. They did so while scanning the clearing room from the vantage point of the most dignified and auspicious seats in the elegant and spacious banquet hall, from the designated head of the rounded table of honor. Mayor Turner sensed that Edward was quite content to let a sleeping dog lie so he pushed on diligently to the matters at hand still capable of being cured before more feathers of the local nobility were unnecessarily ruffled as the potentially contemptuous day progressed along into the fray, or perhaps better said, the controlled chaos of the upcoming auction.

Both pride and necessity would be feverishly driving the desirous wants of his fellow denizens of Savannah once the small stage dealers and big-ring auctioneers began to accept their bids on this rare and notable occasion. For his part, the mayor was primarily seeking to keep the peace by graciously advising his dignified visitor of the potential for the miscommunication of intent and therefore, the unpleasant follow-on effects of such. The mayor understood well the passionately driven and outright contentious set of circumstances surrounding Edward's scantly welcomed presence at the impromptu two-day market fair. He spoke somewhat directly to his contemporary of a sort. "Though it appears we will be brothers in arms for the same most righteous and dutiful cause soon enough, Mr. Calhoun I have to say that I thought you had abandoned the chattel market when you did not show for the arrival of the Wayfarer out on Jekyll Island a few months back. A shipment like that has become rare since the Federal ban was levied."

Edward finished the last of his eggs and gave some thought to a subject that had tormented his rather shrewd yet easy going and every now and again slightly maniacal mind. When he had cleared his throat and set his thoughts and cares to approaching Mr. Turner with caution going forward, Edward answered the mayor evenly. "Yes, Mr. Mayor, I have no stomach for the evils and dark disciplines of the flesh trade. I do however have a keen interest in seeing to it that those who have worked our land for generations now are kept in accordance with at least the common decency that ought to be afforded the very least of God's creatures, let alone those given over to such a deplorable station in life for the betterment of only our own."

Doc Bailey nearly spit the food he was chewing right on out of his mouth and across the table upon hearing that rather rich and duplicitous remark spoken by his recently ordained benefactor of a sort. The extremely troubling experiences of his recent past were most assuredly being taken under careful consideration in Doc Bailey's suddenly piqued and rapidly ruminating mind. The mayor took the time to watchfully consider Mr. Calhoun's dangerously complex reply, which was thus given on the eve of war and therefore properly weighed against all of the potentially treacherous political entanglements that might accompany such a trying and defining moment in the country's comparably brief yet already rather prosperous history.

Mr. Turner then backed his chair slightly away from the table to relieve his compressed belly and replied, "Do understand that I do not intend to mince words here, Edward. With the trade being cut off for all intents and purposes, at least ostensibly, by the vipers up in Washington and their wandering brigades of reinforced agents that exist as a standing army in all but name, there is far more demand for competent labor in the fields than there are able bodies available to do the work. Certainly my God-fearing and agrarian brothers in arms of Georgia can ill-afford to lose Butler's lot to the already well-established grandeur of the Carolinas."

The mayor continued on with his lightly veiled directive. For his turn, Edward listened politely and intently to his "impromptu" visitor, though he had no intention of letting the mayor influence his planned business practices over the coming two days of the historic sale. "I'm not telling you anything new, Edward but do consider that those coming up at auction are considered to be the rightful property of the esteemed citizenry of Georgia by many gathered here for the event. Beyond that, most of the gentlemen about town feel you have already taken more than your fair share of what Mr. Butler has squandered from that legendary estate."

Edward laughed inwardly while at the same time pinning a look of surprise to his face for the benefit of the carefully inspecting Mr. Turner. Edward then replied rather diplomatically. "Like all of the other good and free gentlemen gathered here today, Mr. Turner, I look to accomplish no more than fulfilling my duty to both God and family. Are such virtues not what our ancestors fought so diligently to achieve nearly a century ago now?"

Mayor Turner had heard enough. He wasn't getting anywhere with the incorrigible Carolinian. He stood up and bid good day to both Edward and Doctor Bailey, whose attention had been fully drawn toward the curious and devolving conversation between the two esteemed gentlemen of the day. After Mayor Turner had stepped forward to engage his lovely wife, Millie, Mr. Mc Bride and the Lieutenant Governor, Edward turned his head to the right and addressed Doc Bailey. "How is my dearest little Miss Elizabeth Ann, Doctor? It was so good of you to accompany her on the journey here. I know this time is critical to the healing of her poor wounded wing but I could not stand to have her out of my sight for even a minute after what has befallen her."

Doc Bailey had been flipped straight from the skillet into the stovepipe fire but he cared little about his own circumstances at that point during the timeline of such consequential events. He answered Edward back forthrightly. "There are complications with the wound as you are aware, Mr. Calhoun. That being said, I am confident that with healing prayer, sound medical judgement, proper nutrition and the delicate love of those around her, the splendid little girl will be made whole again."

Edward smiled falsely to reassure Doctor Bailey that he was a reasonable man because his thoughts were confused and bitter whilst he thought about his wounded baby girl trying to recover in her room upstairs. That smile was however, easily recognized by Doctor Bailey for the thinly veiled dissemblance that it was. The sharp and revealing catch set upon Mr. Calhoun's precisely pointed eyes and the rather sour and sudden trailing off of the forced grin at the corners of Edward's indulgent and expressive mouth left little to the imagination as to the true state of the aristocrat's mind for one as shrewd as the doctor was. Nearly a week had passed since the incident, yet Edward was still burning hot with a confounding emotional muddle of both anger and anguish as it regarded what had happened to his little Lizzy.

Doc Bailey was already well beyond the point of caring how Edward felt about the accident for several reasons, most of which possessed both relevance and undeniable virtue. Beyond even those patent situational truths surrounding the maiming of Elizabeth Ann, which had said verities been made known they would have properly governed the allocation of fault for her condition in the eyes of a rational being, Doc Bailey knew the promised child given up to the world had come to be only through the inconceivable acts of a set of divine miracles. Therefore, the good Doctor's eyes were already well-attuned to a higher power working behind the scenes and the conversation the exhausted caregiver had just borne witness to only served to further strengthen the measure of his immutable indifference regarding Edward's anger towards him.

Said plainly and in summary, to Doc's credit in properly reading the man seated to his left, the present circumstances of his response pending of course, the shrewd physician knew he had little reason to fear the ill-positioned Mr. Calhoun. Beyond that, he was not inclined to fear for his own safety as a general rule while he was still one of three heavenly appointed guardians of the miraculous child. The swaddled babe was out there somewhere in the countryside with the delicate Miss Sarah, a good and dutiful but temporarily blinded woman who in the end pledged her very life to see the child on through to safety to clear the matter of her own guilt.

Truth be told, Mr. Calhoun was indeed terrified of revisiting the circumstances that culminated in the tragic set of events on the morning of February 24th. A good portion of his rage as it concerned the horrific crime committed against his favored child was in actuality cast out upon the entrenched customs and beliefs of the world at large and not entirely fixated upon Elizabeth Ann's new but seemingly tireless personal physician. Doc Bailey understood quite well the depths of Edward's unconscionable moral dilemma when it came to condemning any but Edward Calhoun in the flesh for the resultant tragedy. Doc also recognized that he was simply the one Edward chose to keep close at hand for the purpose of slowly and delicately untangling and managing the manifest outward reactions to his confusion, sadness and ire concerning Elizabeth Ann. In addition to the heavy burden of those aforementioned considerations, Doc knew full pit that Edward kept him close at hand to one day make known those same feelings which Mr. Calhoun may have harbored for his secret daughter born of the one true love of his life; a secret daughter the elite plantation proprietor, mercantilist and American aristocrat had yet to lay his eyes upon, though such a moment, if it ever arrived, would be an astonishing enigma unto itself.

Upon Edward's smile fading into that of an uncomfortably couched and unbecomingly angular look of concern, he replied stalwartly against the grain of his outward contrivances to Doc Bailey. "Your confidence in my blessed daughter's recovery is most reassuring, good Doctor. I know you are doing all that you able for the dear girl. Perhaps it is a good thing that your fates have become so forcibly intertwined. You are like two stranded travelers in need of the means of the other hoping to make safe passage out on the oftentimes perilous and lonely road to Augusta."

Now, Doc Bailey was exhausted to the point of contrariwise feeling quite fresh, and feeling so in a careless and perhaps even dangerous sort of way given the identity and the true upbringing of the man with whom he was dealing. Yet the true condition of Doc's state of mind was made plain enough by his response to Mr. Calhoun all the same. To add a bit of portrayed kerosene to the depiction of the already rapidly spreading conflagration of Doc's infernal and emotional mood, it should also be made known that Doc knew full well his host was already quite peeved by the mayor's delicately delivered yet plain enough rebuke of that one's intended wants and carefully planned doings set to transpire over the next few days.

"Let me be clear enough with you, Mr. Calhoun; I remain loyal to your daughter now because she saved my life at the very moment I had consigned as much over to God on high. I also remain loyal to her for the sake of the little one she kept from being taken off into the woods, never to be heard from again. Lastly, I remain loyal to her because my own weakness to devolve into a consciousness of fear or madness kept me from obeying Miss Jeanne's steady command to stay my hand. Do not flatter yourself, Sir by assuming that your opulence, patronage or perhaps even your thirst for revenge keeps me at the girl's side. Her lovely smile alone would impart a similar effect upon my heart far better than such puffery coming from one who sends his women in the way into the haunted darkness and the deadly freeze of those long since forgotten February woodlands."

The gallant and highborn Edward Christopher Calhoun had never been spoken to in such a way in all his life. As such, Mr. Calhoun was quite surprised to find the good doctor's novel and rather chilling spasm of backbone to be oddly refreshing to his somewhat coddled ego. Mr. Calhoun was not however, under any subset of prevailing condition or traditional custom alike, ready to address the issue of little Miss Margaret Anne in such a forthright and revealing manner; not even to one such as his rather impertinent guest who knew the facts of the matter cold. As such, Doc Bailey would receive a pardon for the moment where it concerned his assault upon Edward's honor. Beyond the stay of execution promptly offered to the good doctor and rendered in response to such an unspeakable verbal transgression upon his gentility, which was perhaps solely the result of the visiting Yankee of a sort's clever gamesmanship, Edward also believed in the depths of his heart the truth of that which Doc Bailey had just made plain enough to his slightly cosseted yet keen enough senses. Therefore, Mr. Calhoun walked the situation back a bit to learn what he could about Doc Bailey's frame of mind; and without admitting to anything damning, the nature of his newly born baby girl.

Mr. Calhoun replied to his guest's rather harsh censure in an elegant or perhaps stately tone, which also possessed an air of diplomacy and nary the discernable measure of even a menacing chord. "Among other things, I sense that you disapprove of the business which we are here today and tomorrow to conduct, Doctor Bailey. However, I can assure you that my intentions are genuine enough. I am also quite capable of assuring you that my business dealings here in Savannah are precisely in accordance with the wishes of Miss Jeanne, duly given from the warmth and comforts of her recovery bed back on the farm in Uriah; a fine estate which I so graciously gifted her upon the moment of her union to her deceased husband back in forty-five."

Doc Bailey immediately puffed up his chest to interject and put down such impossible nonsense but Edward was having no part of being scolded or admonished for a third time that day. Mr. Calhoun raised his hand sternly to still Doctor Bailey's cocked and boiling clapper and added, "I would watch your tone and furthermore choose your words wisely from here on in, Doctor Bailey. Being called a liar at my own table I daresay is not something I would treat lightly following your earlier indignities so kindly and robustly offered up in the common way."

Doc Bailey exhaled vigorously and agitatedly until he had fully repurposed or perhaps redirected his stewing ire and settled back into the depths of his cushioned dining chair in a bit of a defeated manner. He wasn't backing down from his position as it regarded Mr. Calhoun's lack of common decency or proper care regarding both mother and the given miracle that was her third child per se. However, Doc saw no advantage in forcing the issue out into the light of day right there and then while enough of a crowd was still lingering nearby in the dining room and speaking in the uplifting vernacular of the morning pleasantries.

No, to make his dissatisfaction with Mr. Calhoun's shielding tactics known, Doc Bailey shifted the topic of conversation pointedly back to the matter that concerned him more than even the unfathomable legal standing of human chattel. "Such was a harsh supposition concerning my presumed follow-on to your reply, Mr. Calhoun and not one that is kin to my own delicate graces once I have made my mind known. No, good Sir, I was merely curious to know if you had received word of the little one's arrival at her intended destination. How and for whom you conduct the legal affairs of your business is of no concern to me. Judgement and divine mercy are virtues that belong to the Good Lord alone."

Edward shifted uneasily in his chair. He was disappointed in himself that he had not considered how poorly his hand would play out once the element of fear had been driven from his antagonist. "Given the rather drastic change in plans accompanying your misadventures in the dead of the night, I suspect that word should have arrived by messenger back at the plantation not long after we departed for Savannah. What pray tell has you so concerned about the whereabouts or safety of Miss Jeanne's daughter, Doctor Bailey? I can assure you that her new home is a splendid place where she will be kept quite safely and raised in a rightful and dignified manner. None here or back home are indeed perfect, are we now, Doctor? We simply do the best that we are able with the circumstances given over to our care."

Doc was a bit put off by and more so seemed to have instantaneously tired of Mr. Calhoun's ruse. Thus he turned his head from Edward's burning irises as it was clear the man believed his own twaddle. Instead, he chose to watch another master of false pretense, the mayor's wife, work her finely-tuned brand of political skullduggery upon the Lieutenant Governor. The mayor and Mr. Mc Bride had taken their own conversation off to the side, presumably to have at the efficiencies that would otherwise not have been afforded them in the direct presence of Mrs. Millie Turner. The rain visible though the large street fronting windows of the hotel just off in the distance had begun coming down in droves. Doc took the oncoming deluge as a sign from above that the preliminary theatrics of the auction had begun up at the racing grounds; the large, open air venue which had been selected to accommodate the unprecedented demand for the Butler chattel, who were known far and wide to be among the best and most talented unpaid servants and field hands in all of Georgia.

Doc didn't know it at the time, but the Christian souls to be offered for sale in odd and broken lots determined solely by the fleeting and fanciful whims of the buyer's discretion were also generational families with strong ties to their kin and loving bonds honored over time and devoutly cherished amongst their people. As he was still somewhat unexposed to the diurnal and familial customs of those bonded over to sow and reap the harvests of the fields and therefore spared that trying detail of the horrors set to commence uptown at the flats, Doc stuck to his knitting and delivered the message to Mr. Calhoun that needed to be properly and clearly delivered.

"Well now, Mr. Calhoun, perhaps if you had seen what I had seen and lived through what we all lived through on that horrifying night of not quite a week prior, you would understand my unwavering concern for the safety of the angelic little girl. I presume that even in these parts, with the strange customs you all share in regard to certain affiliations of humanity being so prominent, laying your eyes upon a snow white baby whom most assuredly had been so improbably and perhaps even impossibly delivered from the womb of a beautiful African woman is not a common event. To further my own curiosities, I am told that Mr. Hastings is also of a decidedly African descent."

Doc paused for a brief second to keep his nerve from fraying upon staring into the scornful eyes of Mr. Calhoun for perhaps a bit too long and then delivered the last of his somewhat civil evisceration of the near to cornered and therefore quite dangerous patrician of his day. "Beyond even those visible peculiarities that may prove troublesome to the dear child's professed lineage, there can be no assurances given to any of us that the one who stalked us that night does not remain at-large and in search of the little girl he intended to take for his own; even if that foul brigand still carries the bullet your daughter leveled into his front side sight unseen."

Doctor Bailey had played his hand marvelously and Edward knew it well. Edward shifted just slightly in his chair and spoke affirmatively to clear up what little he could without stirring the pot any further. His intention was also to end the discussion promptly at that point in time. "In due turn I shall presently assure you, Doctor Bailey that the one who came upon you all that night will no longer be of any trouble to anyone, let alone the newly born child. I have it straight from an impeccable source that the foul man was taken up while he fled from a field near the crossing into Augusta some four days ago. He then possessed a second and far less agreeable bullet, which had reshaped the carriage of his skull in some demented way or another."

Doc Bailey was a bit taken aback yet also pleased by such welcoming news. Edward stared past the last of the lingering few that remained present in the large dining hall from the serving of the morning meal and out the rain soaked front windows of the hotel. He had calmed to a disposition far closer to that of his native temperament and he spoke to address the doctor's concerns in an almost reflective tone. "As it concerns Mr. Hastings, he is a gallant man and unassailable friend to Miss Jeanne yet his true identity seems to drift with the wind. I was lead to believe he was a free man by legal decree, and perhaps he is. There are some among my breed that are not at all past employing nefarious means to add to their stock of affordable labor in such times."

Edward remained silent for but a brief spell and then spoke in the same tone as before while he addressed the far more spurious claims of Elizabeth Ann's personal physician. "Where the skin tone of Miss Jeanne's child is concerned, I can only presume that she is blessed or perhaps cursed with a pigmentary defect of some form or another. Such an occurrence is not unheard of in these realms and there are some that duly obsess over similar oddities. Now, I do apologize that I must break away from the exquisite charm of your hospitality presently, Doctor Bailey. I simply must be making my way on up to the auction to save a soul of some sort…on Miss Jeanne's behalf of course. Clearly, and in accordance with the sting of your own spoken words, my good man I am far too low of a creature to exhibit such grace of my own accord."

Edward put his hands flat to the table to gain some leverage and rise but paused his measured and considerate motions before he had fully lifted his backside from the cushion of his chair. He then unexpectedly queried his guest in the manner of one delivering nary that of a spoken afterthought, "Yet before I depart, I must ask of you: what else were you angling to tell me about the little child, Doctor Bailey?"

Doc Bailey focused his eyes directly on Mr. Calhoun as Edward finished standing up from his chair in a purposeful and dignified manner. There was so much that the good doctor wished to say, but Edward's decision to retreat and live to fight on another day from the higher ground left Doc with only one option. "With the immanency of your departure being the case, I will tell you this before bidding you a good day, Mr. Calhoun: The girl is sponsored from on high. She will find a way to render you a fool or far worse if you betray her. No child without some divine purpose to achieve could have survived what that baby did in entering this world. She was settled in for only death in that womb but something drew her forth. We will talk more on the matter when the time is right. Of that I can assure you, Mr. Calhoun. As accomplished as you are, you will one day beg to know what it was I saw upon the night of her birth. She holds the keys to both heaven and hell and I pray the world of men does not abuse her."

Doctor Bailey then stood up from his seated position and offered his hand in return to his presently and impatiently waiting host. For his part, Edward replied while shaking Doc's hand firmly and staring into his eyes menacingly, "I beg of you to tread carefully, Doctor Bailey. The things you speak of are far bigger than you could ever imagine. Things happen a bit differently down here. The matter of ancestry is a sacred talisman that at times must be managed with care. I am certain things up in New York are far different in many ways. It would be best that you go on ahead and figure out in which ways that is before you speak of the child any further. She is no longer your concern. Focus your diligent care upon my dear Elizabeth Ann and all will be well."

Edward then disengaged with Doc Bailey's hand and paused to straighten up his jacket and put on his hat. When he was presentable for the graces of a lady Edward added, "Now, if you don't mind there is a family being offered that is of a primary and proximate concern for some reason or another to Miss Jeanne. I'll be seeing to it that they remain together and are properly divined to run the affairs of the plantation home of my oldest daughter, Mary Grice. Mary's husband isn't much for managing anything. Although, I do swear the man would have licked a penned in and agitated fighting bull for her hand if such had been her want in exchange for the desired promise."

When he had finished speaking, Edward walked past Doc Bailey and prepared to tip his cap to Mayor Turner, Mrs. Millie Turner, the Lieutenant Governor and Mr. Mc Bride. Upon the settling of the very

stride that placed Edward nearly out of earshot, Doc Bailey called back
to him, "Fair enough, Mr. Calhoun. Yet please do understand I have
done little more than that of a favor by you here this morning."

Edward nodded sternly in Doc Bailey's direction and continued
on to greet the awaiting quartet without saying a word in reply. The
matter of Doc Bailey would have to be dealt with at a later time and
within the precincts of a far more suitable venue. Thankfully, at least
the good and sorely tried doctor did not possess the knowledge he
did in regard to the rather tenuous whereabouts of the duly ordained
child. Edward was now certain that had Doc Bailey been made aware
of such foreboding particulars in addition to what the man had already
surmised, putting a tidy end to their publicly visible though audibly
discreet discourse would have been unmanageable.

The scene out at the most anticipated chattel auction to occur in quite
some time was dismal by all accounts. No one present that possessed
a human feeling of any resolve would have objected to such a description of both the inhospitable climate and the sorrowful mood that
weighed upon the day. The event, which would later be termed "The
Weeping Time" by those folks living in bondage and who later commu-
nicated the misery experienced during that horrific two day exchange
of soulfully shattered human flesh out along the back channels, left
even the most hardened and unscrupulous procurement agent of the
day praying for God's mercy when he had finished with such conscripted acts of inhumane profanity.

Four hundred and fifty men, women and children were offered
up to the highest bidder on those two fateful days in early March of
1859; days which were further marred by a torrential and unrelenting
downpour as the denizens of the heavens rained down their sorrows
upon all whom had gathered for the event held out at the Ten Broeck
Race Course. There was naught but the lingering effects of misery
and despair to be witnessed upon the racked and forlorn faces of the

many generational families torn asunder by the woeful indifference of the competing bidders. Those same and willing participants kept their purse strings tight on the eve of war, yet lusted after fresh help to progress the fortunes of their thriving or emergent farms and plantations.

After a wet but short and otherwise uneventful buggy ride uptown, Edward gathered with his small entourage of bondsmen and his most trusted clerk at the heart of the ovular, mile-long racecourse. Shortly after their arrival, Edward dispatched Eli Schmidt, his toughest and most notorious bargainer to the far end of the northern half of the field. That was the place where the larger lots of enslaved humanity were being offered to the agents of the notables and dignitaries. Eli had already made the rounds first thing in the morning and had properly sized up his desired lots to work the rich cotton fields of the Calhoun plantation lands back home in South Carolina. Therefore, Mr. Schmidt was already drenched from head to toe when Edward gave the thin and wormy looking man the nod to go forth as his agent and conduct their intended business of the day.

Though it did nothing to further preclude his already drenched and rather sodden attire from taking on more water from the skies above and the flooded grounds beneath his boots, Eli kept his umbrella open as the heavy, pelting rain made it difficult to see what was happening beyond the distance of a few feet otherwise. Though Edward spoke of other purposes or perhaps even differing desires to Doc Bailey just a short while ago, the clever negotiator and loyal agent of the Calhoun estate was sent out to procure no less than forty of the finest men and ten of the most mentally agile women without the added nuisance of any children. Needless to say, Eli was facing a nearly insurmountable task given the almost unfathomable contingent of competing bidders that had somehow not backed away from participating in the event in the face of such a diluvian onslaught.

After Eli and his team had been dispatched, Edward was left standing alone in the rain with Mr. Walter Sommers, his aforementioned clerk, who remained waiting in the covered buggy. Mr. Sommers was a timid man who had no nose for the actual execution of business in the real time, and certainly possessed no stomach for the awful things set to transpire on that dark and most pluvious of days. Edward spoke at nearly a yell to be certain that his rather demure voice was audible over the sloshing, slapping and crashing of the heavy rain. "Come with me, Walter. We have an obligation to fulfill on behalf of a woman with whom we have something of a debt outstanding." Walter nodded unassumingly in reply from the at least relatively dry vantage point of the buggy and prepared to do battle with the elements.

Walter hated the rain as much as he did the sunshine but being soaked to the bone seemed to add some depth and some teeth to his otherwise consistently glum mood. "Yes, Sir, Mr. Calhoun, I shall be right down to join you. Shall I bring the auction ledger? It has been quite some time since we have had a use for it. I do worry so about the legibility of its print if exposed to such weather as this." Edward laughed as Mr. Sommers disembarked from the buggy and retorted, "No, my good man, there is no need to mark the ledger until we have finished with our business. Money is no object as it concerns this matter." Walter nodded in reply as his feet sloshed down into the waterlogged turf of the inner oval. He did not reach back for the water resistant satchel which contained the ledger once his conservative and wholly unsuitable business shoes were quickly swallowed whole by the muddy swamp below.

Edward laughed as Walter stood there perfectly in place to keep his chilly, wet clothes from shifting uncomfortably along his rather sensitive ledger keeper's skin. The bookish man appeared as if he were some petrified statue; a statue which had been sculpted while the artist's prototype in the flesh had been left wanting and in desperate need of the washroom to dispatch with the unholy remnants of a disagreeable meal. "Don't stand there looking so sour, my good man. We are here on an errand of mercy. Your sacrifice will be remembered eternally by those we endeavor to serve on this day."

Walter did not say a word. He simply nodded stiffly in reply to Edward's rather comical and unknowingly ironic words of encouragement. The rain was cold and insufferable and took quite readily to Mr. Sommers' thick, winter ensemble and top hat, which was far too cheap to endure the effects of the unyielding elements. Seeing no hope for his rather timid and now quite uncomfortable compatriot, Edward turned in the mire and walked on to the opposite end of the oval to whence Mr. Schmidt had departed just a moment ago. He waved his arms every now and again without looking back into the teeth of the slightly slanting rain to be sure Walter was continuing on apace behind him.

When the two men had survived the deluge and the unconscionable puddles that had amassed on the inner portion of track to reach their intended destination, Edward laughed again and added, "There, there, my friend, that wasn't as bad as all of that; now was it?" Walter looked around and then peered into the sizeable tent raised over the outcry stand and the auction blocks; a far dryer area which the two men were unable to squeeze into given the size of the crowd that had amassed in wait to bid. Mr. Sommers then replied rather snidely to Edward in comparison to his almost intolerably dry and obedient nature by saying, "Our little jaunt would have been remembered as a far better experience had we made the cut to enter into the tented area, Sir."

Edward was now embracing the savage feeling of welcoming such a continuous and hostile offering of the elements. The brisk walk had shaken the cold from his dampened bones and he was suddenly discovering that the opportunity to perform a favor for the waylaid but steadily recovering Miss Basseterre was such nourishing sustenance for his far too sinful soul. "Your words are complete and utter nonsense, Mr. Sommers. Where else but stuck in this rainstorm for the ages would you feel so free and so alive?" Mr. Sommers wiped and then adjusted his rounded spectacles with his soaked kerchief to be certain that his known patron was indeed the gentleman speaking to him. When he was at least partially assured by a brief flashing of clarified sight amidst the steamy vapors and running droplets adhering to his spectacles, Mr. Sommers retorted rather coyly, "If I must say, Sir, the buggy ride was quite the invigorating experience, all things being measured properly and evenly that is."

Edward laughed again and gave a forceful pat to the slick shoulder of Walter's soggy jacket and rejoined, "Well then, Mr. Sommers to that sour sentiment I can only say, each man shall adhere to his own desires. Now let us focus on the matter at hand lest we endure such pleasures without the benefit of procuring our desired quarry."

Walter made no motion nor offered up any response. His indifference to Edward's unexpectedly spirited and even somewhat impish mood was just as well. The first souls to be sold as part of the historic and quite inglorious event, which would later be recorded as the largest slave auction in the history of the state of Georgia, were seen marching out across the podium blocks in chains. Many were without proper clothes and some were immediately prodded by canes and other protruding and horribly invasive extensions of the human arm. Edward, who stood comfortably tall for the era at and around six feet and two inches, or conceivably three or four inches in the right shoes, began craning his neck in search of the wise looking old man with the unmistakable white beard. The man with the perfect family of servants to keep Mary Grice's soon to be completed estate home and her yielding acreage in perfected order. Miss Jeanne had described the wise and well-seasoned man to Edward on the morning of February 28th at an hour just before his party had departed Uriah for Savannah. Doc Bailey and Elizabeth Ann had been sent on in advance from Sumter and were to join their small caravan a ways on down the road to the coast.

Although Edward and Mr. Sommers had managed to squeeze their rain withered bodies under the outer confines of the tent at around one in the afternoon, a time when coincidentally the supply of available merchandise had dwindled noticeably enough for many to presume that the best of that side lot had been claimed, there was still no sign of the wise old man with the white beard. In fact, When Eli Schmidt arrived some three hours later to inform Mr. Calhoun that the desired lots had been purchased from the stage at the opposite end of the oval; there had still been no sign of the man Mr. Calhoun was so anxiously looking to find.

The rain however, had not conceded in the slightest. In fact, as the dinner hour approached and the auction was coming to a close for the day, the rain had almost inconceivably managed to intensify without even the slightest augury being offered that the man Edward was so desperately searching for would appear. When all was shut down for the evening and the few who were still to be seen bravely scurrying about in the deluge were those tidying up the auction areas for the following day, Mr. Schmidt spoke into the commotion of the continuing rain in search of Edward's intentions. "Sir, may I suggest we move the fifty strong onto the cargo wagons and at a minimum make our way across the river to Carolina?" The Calhoun family's procurement agent had no knowledge of Edward's secondary mission.

As expected, Eli's purchases at the market fair earlier that afternoon had been a hotly contested affair. There were even rumors already making the rounds about town of shady backdoor dealings and other more nefarious proceedings taking place, which of course were the solitary pretexts ascribed to Mr. Calhoun's attendant achieving such rapid and unparalleled success. There was a fair amount of truth to several of the allegations levied and bandied about within Savannah's inner circles regarding Edward's man, although none of Edward's competitors were innocent of behaving in an equivalently dubious manner. Such behavior was just how the game was played in times of want.

At the end of the sordid affair and much to the chagrin of his many local adversaries, nothing more than Edward's unsurpassed pecuniary resources ultimately won the day. Nevertheless, the agents of the Butler trustees greatly exaggerated the offer spread required to induce them into selling to the cunning Mr. Schmidt and away from the local boys for the sake of covering their own posteriors. In any event, the time to linger on in town and perhaps even the state of Georgia was not long for Mr. Edward Calhoun and his adherents. The whiskey would soon be flowing warm into the gullets of the aggrieved and without any observable measure of constraint.

There were some men of nearly equivalent consequence to Mr. Calhoun who were ponied up to the bar back in the square, breathing fire and not in the least bit afraid of making their feelings known to Edward about his man's underhanded tactics. Those men were emboldened while taking their rest upon their home turf and of course at a time of the day when they were whiskey strong in their prejudiced and perhaps scantly reasoned beliefs. Furthermore, the grievances of all of those other once hopeful farmers and agents who had been turned back from the race course for home empty handed would be heard in the hours when the time came to shed the memories of this foul-weathered affair through the generous offerings of bourbon, port wine and the famed Caribbean rum that poured into the Port of Savannah. Those hours of the approaching evening would be dubious ones for Edward and the Calhoun party if they remained stationed nearby and on Georgia soil.

While Edward understood the nuances of local immodesty and the lowly proclivities of those he viewed to be failed men quite well, he was not leaving town without the ones promised to Miss Jeanne Jolie Basseterre. After all, retrieving the family Miss Basseterre sought safe sanctuary for was the least he could do after subjecting the woman and their forbidden child to the Articles drafted in Les Cayes some seven months ago. Far beyond that ill-advised compromise designed to protect his good name and to a lesser extent, her own, certainly the night of Miss Margaret Anne's birth and certain other and as of yet wholly undisclosed occurrences, there were other trespasses attributable to the severity of Edward's unspoken debt to Miss Jeanne. However, Edward had not yet begun to process the weight of those latter costs in either the measure of gold coin or the deadening weight of the eternal chain which was slowly being set upon his mortal soul. Though Mr. Schmidt understood none of Edward's considerations regarding Miss Jeanne and her undeclared child, Edward made his will to remain in Savannah plain enough for a man as clever as Eli to understand.

"Mr. Schmidt, while I congratulate you on your commensurate success this afternoon, you must understand that a man is no better than his offered pledge to perform for the sake of those in receipt of such a cherished promise." Eli snapped his head back from looking off towards the loading areas so fast that a sharp and disquieting crack of the man's neck was heard amidst the resounding pitter patter of the heavy drops of rain battering the tent above. So went the instant that Eli Schmidt finally understood that there was a woman out there somewhere to consider. Be that as it may, Eli had no love for taking on the not insignificant chance that he might find those same forcefully relived vertebrae dangling from the end of a rope before the dawn if he stuck around town.

His plea to Mr. Calhoun was just, well thought through and clearly delivered. "I understand what you speak of Mr. Calhoun as it concerns your honor. However, you must realize that procuring fifty slaves that have known no other home but the Georgia coast in a setting as charged as this place cannot be done without either going bankrupt or employing a bit of spirited ingenuity; if you catch my meaning there, Sir."

Edward quickly snapped out of his state of tunnel-minded disappointment with the progression of his portion of the day's affairs and replied like the shrewd operator and truly elegant businessman he was. "Yes, of course, Mr. Schmidt, you should gather up the newcomers and begin moving them on over the river right away. I will have Mr. Snider return to the hotel and prepare the rest of our contingent to depart this evening. That includes Doctor Bailey and Elizabeth Ann. Mr. Sommers and I are going to speak with the auctioneer here for a short while. We will stay the night and tend to tomorrow's activities."

Eli Schmidt nodded pointedly but discreetly in reply. Edward then said, "Please instruct Messrs. George and Trumbull to remain behind as our attachés for the remainder of the auction. I do solemnly swear that there shall be bodies to move upon the morrow." Edward then slowly wiped away some water that had gathered near his chin after draining down his steely visage from his dark, wavy hair and added, "I presume those gentlemen have drawn the short straw upon receiving such an assignment, but their devotion shall be duly rewarded."

Mr. Schmidt was not taking the bait to linger on in town, even if the undertone of such a foolish and passing fancy were present only in his own imagination and not cropped somewhere within the cadence or ancillary connotation behind Edward's spoken words. He answered Edward concisely and clearly. "Yes, of course, Sir, all will be as you desire. I bid a safe journey to you and Mr. Sommers and I wish you luck in procuring that which you seek. There are none but scoundrels out here manning the pits." Eli then paused to think for a second before he turned away from Edward and Mr. Sommers. After that brief respite to give further consideration to any loose ends that may have remained, the wily flesh trader spoke rather sincerely for one so callous and cold in the dispatching of his habitual deeds upon which he plied his hellborn trade. "Do be careful, Mr. Calhoun. Those we procured from the Island were stout and well regarded. If the price paid is made known, we are certain to have hell to pay with the stalwarts taking up their positions at the taverns back in the square."

Though Mr. Schmidt was in part lauding his own accomplishments on the day, his warning to his employer was not without considerable merit or completely bereft of actual human feeling. Edward said nothing further but nodded sharply to confirm his grasp upon Mr. Schmidt's carefully chosen words. Eli nodded in reply, turned and began his long trek back to the opposite end of the oval to begin the process of transporting the men and women purchased that afternoon back to South Carolina. The driving rain battered Mr. Schmidt's exposed head and face mercilessly the entire time he mired his way through the mud holes, shallow puddles and ankle-high pools of water still gathering upon the once greening grass of the inner oval.

Once the rest of their party had dispersed to dredge the buggy from the mud strewn swamp now claiming its virtues over the center of the inner oval, Edward and Mr. Sommers slowly yet directly approached the auctioneer who had solicited the bids for that specific venue. Strangely enough, the talented salesman was a man of color and seemed to be lingering about the staging area as if he had something further and of import to say to someone. Now Edward was clearly a man of torn ideals as it regarded his darker complexioned kinsmen. If nothing else, certainly his prior dealings with Miss Jeanne and her family spoke of that repressed internal conflict, which Mr. Calhoun managed entirely from within as the ears of his society had no patience for such progressive ideals that stood as a direct threat to the very underpinnings of their economic prosperity.

As far as Edward was concerned publicly, the law and established custom were to serve as his guideposts where it regarded the status and proper consideration of both slaves and free men alike. Beyond that, Edward saw no reason to argue with the laws of God above as it concerned the nature of his fellow man. Therefore Edward continued purposefully on towards the meandering auctioneer and offered his hand in greeting as he would to any free man engaging in the affairs of commerce and equitable trade. "Good evening to you, my good man!"

Edward called out as he approached. "It would appear that you have your hands full as it concerns this rabid crowd of dignitaries and their attendants so desperately seeking the divine graces of serviceable labor. Not even Noah's flood would keep them away!"

Mr. Claude Lemarque knew exactly who the man seeking him out was before he was ever given the benefit of his name. Furthermore, Mr. Lemarque was a man who seldom allowed those engaged within the proper refinements of his present company to remain neutral in their spoken opinions regarding most things. The current state of what Mr. Lemarque viewed as the failed yet customary societal paradigm of the time regarding skin color, legal status and human bondage was certainly not one of those things. The fact that Mr. Calhoun had not yet questioned Mr. Lemarque's station in life given the deeply brown hue of his skin was exactly such an occasion whereby Mr. Lemarque felt shorted of the opportunity to make manifest his somewhat strange and rather passionate opinions on the paradoxical anomaly of his current occupation. "Are you not intrigued by the sight of a brown man selling off the bonded flesh of his own kind, Mr. Calhoun?" was Mr. Lemarque's rather contentious reply.

While Edward remained rather surprised by the fact that the auctioneer knew him by name, he was not rattled by his rather stark opening remark in any way. He had come across a few cantankerous freed men with similarly twisting tongues who would have served as a direct proxy for Mr. Lemarque when measured according to disposition. Likeness however, was another matter altogether. Edward had encountered most of those types of men back in Haiti and therefore slightly misread the wildly intelligent and rather brazen auctioneer. Regardless, Edward elected to steer clear of trouble if such a thing could be managed as he required the assistance of the man. "Quite honestly, you have rendered me with little option but to wonder how it is that you have come across my appellation, good Sir. Furthermore,

I am certainly not one to judge the nature of a man's talents before having been given the common decency of his own name."

Mr. Lemarque knew much more as it concerned Mr. Edward Calhoun than he yet cared to reveal. As such, when given the opportunity he endeavored to cede his prickly moral high ground and engage the esteemed Carolinian from a far more gentlemanly footing. "I was told by a dear friend of a friend to keep watch for you today, Sir. I was rather disappointed when I could not spot you but of course the heathens always send the biggest and crudest of their brutes to the front to poke at my poorly situated brethren."

Edward scratched thoughtfully at his rather damp chin upon hearing such news. His curiosity had been elevated a few orders of magnitude. There could be no doubt that the rarely inquisitive mind of Mr. Sommers had also been drawn into a careful state of attention. "Such welcome news is simply splendid, my good man. I am indeed Mr. Edward Calhoun lest we allow our expectations to get crossed on the matter of identity before we speak further."

Mr. Lemarque smiled wide at Edward and retorted, "Confirmation is always and everywhere a wise practice, Mr. Calhoun. I am Mr. Claude Lemarque. I am an indentured Haitian man on loan to the trustees of the auction. My higher purpose here is to help put a comforting and more humane face on the misery we are all here to entertain. My presence as broker seems to give a strange comfort to some of the guiltier flesh traders and plantation masters. It would appear to those men in search of absolution of some impure or bedeviled sort, that my status somehow confirms that the condition of slavery is one that goes beyond skin color and rests closer to the inability of these poor urchins for sale to behave as anything other than savages without the guidance of their heavenly ordained lords of the manor."

Edward gave back a thoughtful look in response to Mr. Lemarque's rather forthright declarations and countered quite openly. "You are clearly a bright man, Mr. Lemarque. Yet you are also one who has lived the life of a freed man for perhaps far too long to understand the darker thoughts and wants of those who truly impose their will upon the hearts and minds of the good people of this land. Beyond that, I can assure you that though there a few who do commit such merciless acts, the colored man who turns on his own kind is far crueler than even the worst of the white slave drivers because he bears false witness to the nature of this grand deception. Hence, the reason I am so pleasantly surprised by your overall comportment and evenly keeled morals. Most in that camp are bootlickers who would sell their own mothers up into the tobacco fields for an official designation and some poor white man's clothes."

Though Edward had spared Mr. Lemarque the indignity of directly including him among the cohort of the stereotypical black man who might engage in this type of work, the comment certainly did its level best to bring the auctioneer down a few notches from the rather carefree heights of his presumed advantage. "This here is certainly not my usual routine, Mr. Calhoun. I am a carpenter by trade and ran aground letting my mouth jump on out ahead of my wits in a billiards hall down in New Orleans. Regrets aside, as these will not be my final hours serving these crude men, the unfortunate nature of my current circumstances seems to have aligned perfectly with the wishes of the Almighty on these few days. Regrettably, the anguish and heartbreak of my experiences here as I complete a favor for my queen are not something that I shall soon forget."

"I see," responded Edward with a slight look of further bewilderment as he gave consideration to how best to proceed. He then rejoined with, "Then I shall presume you already know the old bearded man and his family that I am looking for this evening? Five altogether, I believe they are." "Yes Sir, Mr. Calhoun, the man you seek and his family are five. There is old Solomon, his two sons and their two boys, both nearly ready for the fields. Physical specimens like none other the two sons of Solomon are as well. I suspect they are known far and wide around these parts. The tobacco toothed field martinets are going to be elbows first fighting over those two gentlemen when they arrive upon the podium."

Mr. Lemarque watched the look on Edward's face turn from cheerfully cunning to quite worrisome in a fresh lick. He remained silent for a moment and allowed the prideful man's spirits to drown into the heavy, saturated fabric of his boggy, dripping winter suit. Mr. Lemarque then allowed a thoughtful glimmer to come upon his carefully discerning and attentive eyes while he spoke of better tidings. "However, my fretful looking accomplice to the will of the Haitian queen, there are two more that have joined old Solomon's contingent as of late last night. Those less favorable additions should 'balance the load' as the seamen used to cry out amidst the choppy waters of the Atlantic when we were too many to a side or too many altogether below decks for the ship to weather a storm."

Mr. Lemarque then paused his words amidst the stillness of a thoughtful yet quite glib and nearly sidelong pose of his captivating visage before suddenly shifting those wares to a look of more scrupulous introspection and adding, "To this very day I do wonder yet still what it must feel like to be thrown into the middle of an endless and unknown ocean upon the black watch of midnight, but alas, I was never brave enough to volunteer for such an exercise during my own turn in crossing the great sea while chained to the post. In any event, I believe those two special ladies now to be joining old Solomon and his family upon the podium are the ones truly behind the beautiful madam's heartfelt request, though I am quite certain she would free them all if she could. Miss Leslie and her child have been taken under old Solomon's wing as the potential for ill tidings to befall them both upon being released at sale alone are far too horrible to even consider. Truth be told Mr. Calhoun, such is why I am here at this podium today and indeed still standing before you now."

Edward pulled his waterlogged hat from his head and drove some of the water off by slapping it forcefully against his thigh. The wet smacks caused by the act did little to suggest any progress had been made in drying out the fine appurtenance. A woman and a child were of no use to him and never mentioned by Miss Jeanne. Yet upon further consideration, Edward understood why she had remained mum concerning a detail of such weight. Mary Grice would want nothing to do with a Negro baby being raised in her house. Furthermore, Miss Jeanne knew the stubborn woman quite well and since the latter days of her privileged upbringing.

While he remained a bit directionless regarding the sudden change in circumstances, Edward raised his wet and shiny blue eyes to Mr. Lemarque and spoke a bit hesitantly. He was in a bit of a quandary, though this particular dilemma was no different than the always present complications which surrounded the entirety of his dealings with the womenfolk in his life. "Yes, of course, Mr. Lemarque, seven it shall be then. I presume that you are to assure I will become the successful bidder when they are brought forward tomorrow?"

Mr. Lemarque shook his head dutifully and replied rather stoically. "I wish it were that easy, Mr. Calhoun. The trustees are watching every move I make but there will be no argument from the supervising participant when I bring the highly regarded family out last. Unfortunately that is about the best I can do for all involved; that and keeping the seven together until the closing lot is offered at this insidious marketplace. Though such a gesture is imperfect where it concerns your resources and your ability to win the bid, the just measures will give you all the opportunity you need to wear down your rival bidders at the coin purse and the ledger alike throughout the day. Let those who are eager to oppose you win until that final lot is brought forth. Save your dry powder for the perfection of your promise to the elegant lady, if there exists such a thing as dry powder in this confounding weather. You will become undeniable in the moment the last poor souls are up for bid. Surely everyone here will be out to send you home empty handed tomorrow as some small consolation to their pride after your man's escapades at today's fair."

Edward shook his head reflexively and altogether unknowingly. He then peered out of the tent into the darkening sky. There was no way this infernal rain would ever stop before the market fair closed for good tomorrow. He dreaded working all day like a merchant's broker in the same downpour while facing up to those who despised his worldly blessings. Worse than that, he was already beginning to burn a bit hot just thinking about purposefully losing to those cads only to ultimately conjure forth the intolerable ire of his eldest daughter. Edward then turned his eyes back to Mr. Lemarque and replied rather graciously, "What you propose can be no small thing for you to execute on behalf of the elegant lady. I for one will not be the man among us to dishonor his end of the bargain. You are a good man, Mr. Claude Lemarque. I am certain that the Lord favors you in His own way."

"Oh, I am quite certain that He does, Mr. Calhoun," replied the now confident broker. "The Lord calls each of us to serve Him according to His own plan and in His own perfected way. I am honored to at last be called to serve in accordance with His divine grace as you also must be." Claude then lowered his eyes from Edward's boyish looking blues and spoke slightly out of line and even away from proper protocol. "I do hate to mix politics with business and the Lord's work, but I must know, Mr. Calhoun: given your feelings for Miss Jeanne, how do you reckon on the matter of slavery and your colored brethren?"

Edward did not appreciate the rather sensitive question at the very moment the two men were about to exchange pleasantries and part ways for the evening. A proper night's rest was now imperative given all that was to be done. Beyond that, there was sure to be trouble lying in wait back in town and the time to linger was quickly coming to an end. Edward had however, developed a deep appreciation for Mr. Lemarque. He viewed him as a man who did not deserve any less than the truth after that which they had spoken of and that which they had conspired to achieve together upon the morrow and for the benefit of Miss Jeanne. In the end, Mr. Calhoun could empathize with Claude's yearning to know how a man of his stature felt about the rather inhumane societal customs that so clearly had served to relegate the two men to worlds apart before even the slightest measure of their earthborn worth had been measured or called into service. Therefore, with all present and future circumstances being properly taken into consideration, Edward spoke candidly but also concisely in response to Mr. Lemarque's somewhat discomforting question. In truth, Edward was not entirely put off by having to humor the opinionated gentleman thusly.

"The scourge of slavery is the burning question of our day is it not, Mr. Lemarque. Owning slaves is now such an ingrained and customary practice down here that it shall drive our country into a war amongst brothers soon enough. Therefore, I shall give over to you the dignity of having my spoken opinion on the matter." Claude began to speak to intervene. He had suddenly realized that he put his own interests ahead of the needs of his call to serve and the sanctity of his noble commission.

Edward however, raised his hand flatly and firmly to silence the dark-skinned and now somewhat remorseful one-off slave auctioneer and interjected with his own thoughts on the unfortunate practice of thrall. "I will not speak long on the issue as the evening beckons, but if you must know, I do not favor the arrangement as it presently stands or at all, Mr. Lemarque. I see no differences of the mind or heart that exist between those who nurture forth the seasonal seeds of our prosperity and those such as me; those who benefit from the preponderance of the yield of that same harvest. Yet I do not set the rules of engagement and must put forth the best of my efforts to producing for my own as we all must. There is a breed far more sinister than I responsible for your plight, my good man; a wicked and ancient breed that is not to be crossed. Those of its kind are perpetually looking to usurp far more than men such as you or I would ever imagine. Heaven forbid that one of those darkened, lustful and eternally barren souls corrupts even the bloodlines of my direct progeny."

Mr. Lemarque was a bit taken aback by both Mr. Calhoun's candor and his stated opinion. Wise Claude could have spoken on the matter for hours, but he knew Edward had been forthright enough in his response to honor him as the free and well-educated man that he was. Mr. Lemarque also knew that the time to depart was indeed at hand as there were now clandestinely skulking emissaries of the trustees about. They had approached silently amidst the belting rain from the opposite end of the oval.

Therefore, the Haitian gentleman did not press Edward for more detail or question his sincerity. He simply asked one last question of Mr. Calhoun with Mr. Sommers still attentive and present. The question was one that would forever cement the bond of understanding between the two men. "That is quite fine of you to say as much, Mr. Calhoun. I do not wish to trouble you any further on the biases of your acquired morality. I am certain those beliefs are quite seasoned by now. However, if you don't mind saying so in just a few words, would you tell me how you came to plainly see something so obvious yet so seldom recognized by those of your society? Most men of your elevated status, though there are few, see the world quite differently."

Edward also spied the darkly dressed men looking to promote rumor amongst his antagonists. They were lurking out along the holding pens and the nervously twitching Mr. Sommers, who had been placed in a far too uncomfortable position already, took note of the skulking consorts of the aggrieved as well. While Edward would not linger much longer and provide those mouthy beasts with any more fuel to feed the fire that was surely already raging back in town regarding the exploits of his man Eli Schmidt, he felt compelled to say a brief word further on the matter. The topic was one that troubled his once soft and caring and now rather staid and oft times callous heart. Though he would certainly not speak openly of Miss Jeanne, there was another that had blessed the more tender constructs of his youthful spirit when he was just a child. "I will tell you what you wish to know, my very wise and very dear friend, Mr. Lemarque. We are now business partners are we not?"

Claude smiled and nodded in the affirmative with both eyes reverently closed. Edward turned to his bookish compatriot who was then shivering from the wet and the cold but still all ears. He kindly instructed him as such: "Walter, why don't you begin the journey back to our carriage and make certain that Mr. Satterfield has everything in order for our departure back to the hotel." Mr. Sommers was disappointed by the designation but also eager to get moving and get his blood flowing again. "Yes, Sir, I will do that right away, Mr. Calhoun."

Edward smiled at Mr. Sommers and replied, "Excellent, my good man. I shan't be but a stone's throw behind you. Thank you for your service today, Walter. I know this affair is well beyond the norms of your typical creature comforts." To which Walter replied, "Of course, Sir. Think nothing at all of the effort or of my presumed partialities. I wasn't born behind a bookshelf or with an abacus in my hand you know." Following those words Edward laughed cheerfully without losing his train of thought. Walter managed to crack half of a tooth chattering smile before making his way out of the tent, across the flooded dirt of the track and onto the rain soaked mire, which was once the freshly cut and seasonally renewing grass of the inner oval.

When Mr. Sommers was a dozen paces afield, Edward turned back to Mr. Lemarque and offered up that which he intended to offer up to the auctioneer, nothing more and nothing less. "When I was child there was a woman who watched over me. She was a splendid woman and a woman of fine color all the same. Miss Kinsey was her name and she taught me the true wonders of love and due care. My mother, Miss Meara Calhoun, was a wicked woman even back then. Although perhaps not expressly given over to the devil just yet, her heart had already learned to crave his bitter fruits above all else."

Edward paused to further recall those days for a brief spell and then continued on in quite the deliberate manner. "After a time, Miss Meara expressly forbade me from seeing Miss Kinsey. She lashed the poor woman mercilessly whenever she caught us frolicking about and talking of God and all the beautiful things He had put forth on the earth. As I grew older, I should have known better than to expose the poor woman. She would have nothing to do with denying me when-ever I happened by her place of work on a joyful sunny day." Edward paused again, only this time to gather his emotions. He was suddenly a man afflicted while he spoke of Miss Kinsey. Claude noticed a slight tremor in the man's neck and along his hands and asked, "Are you quite alright, Sir? Do you still speak with the delightful sounding woman to this day? Even as gentlemen, we cannot utterly ignore the throbbing aches of our heart strings."

Edward closed his eyes and flashed back some decades to just such a warm and sunny spring in the Carolinas that was full of untold hope and promise. He had taken his first game bird with the musket and rushed out along the back paths to Miss Kinsey's cabin to do nothing more than wink her way and show her the fruits of his exploits. Some two weeks earlier, the brilliant woman had helped him write a poem for the girl of his heated, pre-adolescent fancy. That was last time he had snuck out of the manor and down the servants road to see her.

As he was coming up from the marsh where the grown men took their game and foul, Edward did indeed take the shortcut that passed by the back of Miss Kinsey's cabin. Elsa Kinsey often kept the servants cottages clean during the day and watched the little children because she had passed beyond her productive years in the field. As he stood beneath the rain soaked tent, Edward then remembered the ominous silence of the children that were missing on that day when he arrived at her cabin. He then recalled the sorrowful look in her eyes as she took to the first of her lashes. The hideous sound of the first stroke drove the doves frantically fluttering upward from their perches in the magnolia trees standing watch over her cabin. Though she had waved to him to go on and get scarce long before the last of it, Edward watched the final sorrowful look the joyful hearted woman's eyes would hold upon this earth from his perch behind a juniper bush. The poem he had written had been returned to its true author and was lying upon the ground just outside the fence posts Miss Kinsey had been fastened to like some stray dog.

"Are you indeed alright, Mr. Calhoun?" asked Claude from just a few paces away as the rain continued thumping upon the roof of the tent to furiously beat the band. Edward quickly shook his head free of the mesmerizing trance and answered a bit hypnotically, "Why yes, Mr. Lemarque, I am quite fine. There was a memory from long ago playing out in my head and I could not halt its haunting message before I spoke further of her."

Edward then came fully into his wits, shifted the full measure of his focus to Mr. Lemarque's eyes and added, "What I had intended to tell you was that woman taught me all I ever came to know regarding love, the eternal promises out beyond the firmament and the maddeningly complex heart of a woman. More than that, Mr. Lemarque I was so very blessed to have learned from one such as her; one who was beyond compare in her capacity to offer such unconditional love and one who understood the world where the soul at times comes out to play or grieve or sow the seeds of that most necessary virtue, hope. No one else in my life has ever come close to matching her selfless perfections. So yes, Miss Elsa Kinsey taught me that the color of a man's skin has no bearing on the acuity of his mind or the intentions of the love rooted within his heart."

A rather shocked Claude Lemarque was nearly floored but also quite moved by Edward's reply. For the first time in his life, outside of the time his mother washed his mouth out with lye soap, the witty, now indentured man was left rendered without the capacity for speech. Edward sensed Mr. Lemarque's shock but he felt much better for having removed such a cross to bear from his chest for the first time in his life. Edward nodded sharply at the stunned auctioneer and then turned to follow after Mr. Sommers at a brisk clip.

While Edward stepped through the still gathering puddles, the air suddenly felt wet and cold whereas before he noticed nothing but the rain falling from the sky. The field smelled of torment and perhaps even death due to the fact that the cold humidity of the early evening air held such odors tight to its source. When Edward was about halfway across the mud of the track he shouted back to the still motionless Mr. Lemarque, "Good evening to you, Mr. Lemarque! Though the spot where you bed down may chain your body to the walls of this awful place, may your mind dream of the clear blue waters of Haiti and the mountain highlands just up the way from the coast. We must have our rest. For tomorrow feels as if it will be a day of considerable consequence. Consequence that we shall only ever partially understand, my friend, and never enough between the two of us to see the whole of it."

Mr. Lemarque waved toward Edward and called back mostly for the good of those secret ears listening close by, "Goodnight, Mr. Calhoun, perhaps tomorrow you will have much better luck at this end of the oval than you did today!" Edward had already disappeared out of sight and the skies had continued to darken rapidly. No reply was heard against the pounding of the rain upon the roof of the squared, canvas military tent.

The buggy came to rest in nearly the same spot as the day before. Likewise, the inclement weather and the boggy conditions of the second day out upon the open field of the inner oval were no different than the first. The sky rained down without relent and cast its curse upon those gathered to fiendishly covet and buy up what remained of the dwindling inventory at the rather notorious and similarly fabled chattel auction. The prior evening had been an eventful occasion. At least during the few hours Edward had spent at the saloon back in town once Doc and Elizabeth Ann had departed with the plurality of the remaining Calhoun contingent.

Without going so far as getting himself killed, Edward had done his level best to stir up trouble and whip his competing bidders into a frenzy that would have them arriving hot and bothered to the auction upon the break of day. Those he had set off were indeed prepared to bid early and often on all that Mr. Edward Calhoun of South Carolina would set his eye upon. Willie George and Haddon Trumbull took the worst of it on Edward's behalf but any chance to brawl or raise hell in general was nothing short of a blessing to those two gentlemen. They were deadly serious scrappers who were likely to come out ahead as long the numbers against weren't more than five to one. By the time Edward approached Mr. Lemarque's auction stand with Walter Sommers and the battered duo of Messrs. George and Trumbull in tow at precisely ten minutes before the first lot was to be offered, the stage had been properly set.

By three o'clock that afternoon Edward had come up empty handed as was his wish, but he had driven a handful of his most likely rivals for the final lot from the confines of the tent as big spending but monetarily exhausted "winners" on the day. The locals watching on in awe couldn't get enough of seeing the now legendary negoti- ator and conquering invader from yesterday's exploits, Mr. Edward Calhoun from across the river in Carolina, getting outbid time and time again. In accordance with his plan, Edward offered up a stalking bid for nearly every single lot. Often times, his losing efforts to bid turned out to be long and gut wrenching outcries, which were hotly contested and went back and forth for quite some time thanks in part to Mr. Lemarque's crafty ingenuity upon the auction stand. In each case, nearly every notable of Savannah cheered on their local champions of the Georgia cause with extreme prejudice.

The spectacle of it all left the faithful crowd spellbound and lurching up upon the tips of their boots to see more of the frenzied action so perfectly goaded onward by Mr. Lemarque's feisty Haitian cantor. When the second to last offering was set out upon the podium, Mr. Lemarque winked in the general direction of Mr. Calhoun. This was the lot so desperately coveted by Mr. Emil Lauderback of Sea Island, perhaps the single greatest threat to Edward where it concerned his intended procurement of old Solomon and his kin. The packaged offering was a fine gathering of up and coming male field hands from various families who had at least thirty years of drawing blooming cotton from the ripened stalks upon which to look forward.

In the end, Edward had raised Mr. Lauderback's initial bid to four times that of the normally scrupulous man's intended amount but dared not lay a bid any higher because he could not risk half his resources at that penultimate moment of the event. Edward knew Mr. Lauderback was the designated closer of the Savannah faithful. To Emil's detriment he also knew that the opulent man was in desperate need of additional labor out on his magnificent seaside plantation. Though Edward would remain left to fret over Mr. Lauderback's capacity to outdo him in the final round by only pushing him up as high as he did, such was how the astute bargainer saw fit to play things out unto the last. While Mr. Lauderback was pleased with his late day acquisition, his smug smile given in the direction of Mr. Calhoun suggested that the pig nosed and cloying man of a short but not insignificant stature was also the one preordained by his peers to make certain that Mr. Calhoun did not return to Carolina with even a solitary additional item of Georgia property in tow.

As another affront to Edward's upcoming fortunes to procure the final lot of the fair, the esteemed gentleman from the Georgia plantation islands was in the unconscionable position of being accompanied by his wife, Estelle. Mrs. Lauderback was a forceful woman who had taken an interest in Emil's business affairs after losing her only son some five years ago when he ventured off to the Oregon Territory to find his true calling and in so doing help close out the war with the Cayuse. Edward was only venturing a guess while watching Emil grin so snidely, but he presumed old Emil wasn't going to take kindly to losing out at the last while in the presence of such a domineering member of the female persuasion, or at least that's what the story on Mrs. Lauderback was around town.

Edward however, was not altogether sure of the actual existence of any provable feminine traits upon the woman as he glanced at her stern and tightly compacted face. Her broad haunches and shoulders remained steady and immovable as the woman continued to contort and pinch the features of her rough and overly powdered visage. Edward nudged Walter Sommers and commented sarcastically in an effort to try and assuage the slight pangs of his youthfully tingling nerves. "If you were more inclined to the effects of the spirits you might have experienced the delight of such a wonder as all of that, Walter."

Mr. Sommers nodded thoughtfully for a moment but eventually caught on to Mr. Calhoun's unexpectedly playful humor as the moment of truth fast approached. The atmosphere under the tent was electric even with the rain above cascading down just as it was for the entirety of the day. Walter was a bit nervous in his own right as he stood unceremoniously at the center of the attentions of the joyfully clapping and jeering crowd. To relieve some of his own stress that had come with being thrust into the limelight as it were, Walter nudged Edward's shoulder as he stood there wide eyed and overcome by the myriad impulses quickly transforming the overcrowded space beneath the bivouac into some form of surreal, wildly charged and oscillating pantheon of life.

When he felt Edward's elbow against his own and he was certain his benefactor was there beside him, Walter shouted to lift his naturally timid voice above that of the nearly rabid but assuredly fomenting crowd, "To undertake the act of attempting to well please something so steadfast as all of that might very well be my last adventure, Sir." Edward laughed delightedly as Walter's commentary was far looser than he would have expected from the prim and proper ledger man while under the glare of the white hot spotlight as it were. "I suspect you might be correct in that assertion, Mr. Sommers. I think it would be best if you stick close to my side while we work through this. The venue is alive this afternoon and nourished by lightning that feeds on these strange and savage emotions of such an uncommon variety!" Walter nodded wide-eyed and vacantly in reply while he remained in the midst of his stirring yet enigmatic spell.

The two men returned to business after their brief interval of lightly-humored relief. They turned their heads like they were on swivels for a few borrowed moments to size up the constituents of the buzzing crowd one last time. Not much time passed before Mr. Lemarque led old Solomon and his kin out on to the wooden blocks of the temporary lower display platform. The crowd gasped mildly at the sight of Solomon's two sons. What was heretofore known to most in attendance only through the spoken legends of the exploits of those two men out on Butler Island was now made readily apparent and in fact defied the long held belief that all things are far grander when laid out upon the abstract canvass of the mind. Needless to say, the presence of the two foreboding men did not disappoint the ogling and craning spectators in the least. The field men were so impressive that Emil Lauderback began to shift uneasily upon witnessing such specimens who placed such an exacting doubt upon the truth of his own masculinity and furthermore his expected propensity to carry the day.

Edward was fortunate enough to catch sight of the discomfort dressing over Mr. Lauderback's rather piggish looking visage. The reflexive and quite accidental tell conveyed all that Edward needed to know in regard to Mr. Lauderback's capacity to match the full weight and measure of that which was held tight by the straining Calhoun purse strings. Edward was astute enough to know that avoiding credit was preferred by the trustees running the sale as he had played a direct role in facilitating the need for such an unholy carnival at the outset. Furthermore, Edward did not want his bid subject to and therefore potentially compromised by the perhaps whimsical interpretations of credibility that might be offered by a local banker with such deep ties to Savannah. Edward slapped the side of Walter's once again wet upper arm playfully as he felt supremely confident that he had his man fully weighed, measured and found wanting as the old adage went.

All appeared to be coming up roses for the shrewd businessman on that rainy day until the last two items of live chattel were made visible upon the stand. The first of the two, although only to be seen concurrently with the other, was a tall, slender woman of color. While the strong yet lean woman was quite easy upon the eyes, she appeared somewhat worse for the wear when compared with her perfectly groomed contemporaries set up alongside her on the platform of aligned wooden blocks, and for that matter, all of the previously offered participants in the auction; an auction which was now officially a Georgia spectacle that was so very near to being etched into the history books of the period and which had already witnessed some four hundred and forty-three owned human beings legally change hands in accordance with the governing law of the time and place. The second of the two was the babe nestled into the woman's long and elegant yet wiry arms. The child was near to being completely wrapped into the depths of a beaded, rainbow colored Cherokee blanket that appeared to have been made with intricate care but quite some time ago.

Though nothing of the little baby had yet been made visible upon the instant of her unveiling to the silently mesmerized and gawking crowd, Estelle Lauderback was overcome with an unexpected and almost instantly intractable motherly yearning. The ascribable feeling was a delicate but furiously intentioned and unwavering emotion that wanted for the woman to attach her soul to some strange form of ensuing chance seemingly offered to her presently by the heavens above. A subsequent chance of sorts that somehow possessed the singular ability to offer her the occasion by which to once again share those long dormant maternal affections; surprisingly tender affections that did not align in any way with her physical appearance but which had been duly repressed for those five long, lonely and bitter years now. Those were deep and tender affections that needed to be made manifest and affections which her never found or buried solitary son could no longer afford to lovingly accept or return in kind.

Walter was the one who saw the wanting look first flash across Mrs. Lauderback's now open and wholly overcome countenance. Mr. Sommers understood the look well because he had been the beneficiary of a deeply loving mother. In fact, he could properly discern the meaning of such a look with greater ease than he could parse out an excise tax from a traditional bill of lading. Walter nudged Mr. Calhoun firmly while endeavoring to keep his eyes intently focused on the wife of their anticipated antagonist in the upcoming and supremely important bid progression.

Edward was a bit surprised to receive such a firm prompting from the usually timid man who found his ease by panning through the lines and numbers of the ledger books. He had been watching the seven poor souls up on stage closely as if he wished to understand how they endured the white hot shine of such a spectacle and even the life of servitude that awaited them beyond. At the exact moment Walter had so forcefully sought after his attention, Edward had become captivated by the woman so fearfully standing up on the podium and more so her mysteriously hidden little papoose.

Edward answered back to Mr. Sommers' urging but he had yet to redirect his eyes from the curious objects of his attention. "What has you troubled, Walter? I do believe we are in fine shape here and can have the matter settled rather quickly." Mr. Sommers still did not take his eyes off of the bewitched woman about four persons down the row from them. He tugged at Edward's sleeve doggedly as he looked upon the given spectacle of the woman's also transfixed eyes. In response to that second rather insolent and aggressive prompting, Edward turned his head sharply to the left. Right then, in naught but the twinkling of his eye, Edward bluntly and rudely beheld the almost incredulously insurmountable obstacle now mount to the heavens before them. He lightly brushed Mr. Sommers back to have a better look into the starlit eyes of the awestruck woman. What Edward saw upon further inspection of Mrs. Lauderback did nothing to alleviate the sudden onset of his terror.

Edward's throat dropped into the pit of his stomach at the very moment Mr. Lemarque stepped up to the podium in between old Solomon's grandsons, Amos and Jericho Martingale Butler. The speed with which Mr. Calhoun's confidence had been dropkicked out of his proudly puffed out lungs left him wanting a bit for air. Walter sensed that which was transpiring within his once staunchly confident employer and stepped in front of Edward to properly address the rapidly deflating man. Edward looked down from Mr. Lemarque, who was positioned just off to his left, and spoke halfheartedly and in a moderately agitated manner to the man now standing directly in front of him with those well-intentioned eyes that appeared to be sharp as a hawk's, "What is it, Walter? Is there some urgent difficulty that you feel uniquely situated to address? We will deal with the woman, but I wouldn't get too cozy with the contents of that old purse if I were you."

Walter looked down at his soaked boots that had also taken on a good caking of mud. Edward's irritation was plain enough and the accountant was quickly beginning to second guess his spirited need to say what had to be said. Nevertheless, after a brief pause and at the urging of the spirit of his dearly departed mother, for the first time in his life, Walter Sommers made his feelings known. "Sir, I just wanted to say that some peace will be granted to your soul if you make certain that the woman and the child are safely removed from this place. I am not so certain the beastly woman won't eat the child once the delirium of her fancy fades and I dare not think about what vile thoughts run through the mind of that altogether swinish man."

Walter understood the dilemma that was likely to transpire in terms of Edward's loyalties to his oldest daughter and the mysterious foreign woman who once graced the halls of the manor. Edward nodded affirmatively in reply to Mr. Sommers but more in the manner of one who was in truth disregarding his far shorter attendant. Yet in this instance, Walter Sommers would not be dissuaded. He embraced Mr. Calhoun steadfastly by the shoulders, looked slightly upward into the taller man's precisely focused eyes and said, "Please, Sir. I promise you that if one day you deem it true that I have done but one useful thing for you in this life, do know that these words of suggestion, if followed, will be that one thing."

Edward at last took his eyes off of the beautiful blanket which shrouded the mysterious child and set his gaze upon Mr. Sommers' look of pleading grace. Seeing that the man was serious beyond the typical affirmations of the mind that come from the proof of tying out some numbers on a journal entry sheet and instead spoke from a place far closer to the heart, Mr. Calhoun patted Walter on the tops of his damp shoulders with both hands and replied, "Consider your words as heeded, my good man. Now please, prepare to triangulate the bids as we move along."

Walter smiled and removed a small hand held notebook from the inside pocket of his coat. He then waved the miraculously dry scratch pad before Edward's eyes and answered, "Of course, Sir, I'll nudge you when to top and by how much." Edward smiled and spoke thoughtfully to the now rather eager looking gentlemen, "That's more like it, Mr. Sommers; for as I presently understand the situation, the settling of things shall be unto God's will."

Some ten minutes into the bidding, a process that was masterfully handled by Mr. Lemarque, Mr. Lauderback and Mr. Calhoun had seemingly shaken loose of the last of the other stalking bids. The two stubborn men were also at or near the limits of their resources. Even if the bidding had halted right then, the astronomical sums offered, amounts that had the supremely engaged onlookers gasping in unison while overcome with disbelief, would have set the record for the price to be paid to own another human being in all of the Americas. Just a short while later, Edward had reached his spending limit and suddenly became overwhelmed by a feeling of disbelief that he may yet come up empty. His bid was still the topping bid. However, as Edward watched Estelle Lauderback domineer the plump little man who undoubtedly preferred the muddy, penned up conditions of the day's venue, he felt certain that his best and final offer would fall short.

Sure enough, Emil Lauderback topped Mr. Calhoun's bid, but of course only after allowing the suspense beneath the tent to mount right up until the auctioneer's final call. Mr. Lemarque's employers and the gentry of Savannah Town would have their moment in the sun. They would have it even if the skies above continued to open up and wash every last remnant of that sorrowful time of bitter weeping out to sea before they had returned to the comforts of their second homes along the village square. Mr. Lemarque paused for what felt like an eternity before sadly and unsurely slamming his gavel down against the podium to proclaim Mr. Lauderback's offer as the winning bid.

Edward hung his head in disbelief and Walter Sommers absent-mindedly dropped his feverishly scratched in notebook down into the mud and mire sloshing beneath their booted feet. Within minutes the crowd had dispersed amidst the hooting and hollering of the heavier drinking city boys, those who were likely to walk down into town direct and continue on with the festivities. Edward and Walter remained standing in place, silently watching on as Emil and Estelle

Lauderback settled up with the designated banker and legal representative of the trustees, respectively.

Just as Edward and Walter turned dejectedly to make their way back to the buggy parked in the center of the oval, a Mr. Skip Aitcheson, Esquire called out to Mr. Calhoun from behind the podium, "Mr. Calhoun, would you mind sparing us just a minute of your time? There is a slight problem with the settlement that has come to our attention. Since you are the final stalking bid, I thought you might be interested in assisting us with remedying the matter." Edward turned sharply upon hearing Mr. Aitcheson beckon him. The move was so forceful and rapid that Edward nearly lost one of his boots when the fine leather riding wader, which he thought would perform better in in weather conditions nearly identical to or perhaps even worse than the prior day, became deeply lodged in a heavier, wanting concoction of the mire. Once Edward had nearly pulled his leg free from the rather persistent encumbrance, he called back to Mr. Aitcheson while staring down at his captured boot and trying to free it from the last of that awful brew of slop and filth.

"Well then, good Sir, if you will hold for but a patiently inclined moment, I am well known as one to be devoted in my service to a gentlemen and his finer half so gripped by the throes of distress." When Edward had pulled his wader completely free he slapped Mr. Sommers excitedly on the side of the shoulder to bring his man to terms with the rather fortunate change in circumstances. Only after Walter had offered up a proud and knowing smile that signaled his true pride in Mr. Calhoun did Edward begin to negotiate his way through the remainder of the boot cupping swill of the ground beneath the tent and return to the auction podium. Mr. Lemarque was present but standing off a measurable distance from those gathered to finalize the transaction. He remained towards the back of the settlement area and he was wearing his wrist chains.

Edward and Walter smugly approached Mr. Aitcheson, his accounting associate, Mr. Francis Noble, and a pair of rather thuggish looking boys from the itinerant farms out on the coastal inland beyond Savannah proper. The brutes were large, no nonsense boys that appeared as if they had been out on the town all night and drinking their way through the aftermath of the ruckus all day. Edward was giddy as an adolescent schoolboy and simply could not wait hear how Mr. Aitcheson's plea for appropriate remedy would be framed.

After the six men had dispensed with their formal greetings and Edward had forced Mr. Aitcheson and Mr. Noble to eat a healthy serving of crow while furtively winking in the direction of Mr. Lemarque, the seven men and one woman assembled to sort things out by getting straight down to brass tacks. Mr. Aitcheson began on behalf of Mr. Lauderback. "There appears to be some problem with the child, Mr. Calhoun. Our most gracious dame, whom we do thank for her unique and unparalleled devotion to the success of the day's market fair, seems to believe that the child in question is a white baby brought in by bounty pressers out roaming the countryside."

Edward laughed at Mr. Aitcheson due to his disbelief concerning such an outlandish claim, which would be measured in extremis as beyond that of scandalous if both of Mrs. Lauderback's accusations were true and widely understood. Edward spoke firmly in reply to Mr. Aitcheson to forcefully establish his position of strength concerning the matter. "Such a claim is simply preposterous, my good man. The child's mother was standing before the whole world to see. The woman is an angel no doubt but certainly a woman of color as assuredly as the sun will one day split the clouds of even this godforsaken tragedy." Mr. Aitcheson coughed nervously and quickly countered with, "Yes, if that woman is indeed the child's mother the matter would not take much time or effort to settle. There are however, some questions surrounding that assumed verity, Mr. Calhoun."

Edward laughed again and this time put his heartfelt mirth on display for the entire audience to gag on for quite a time. Mr. Lemarque did all he could to restrain his own joyful spirits from bursting forth onto the scene at great peril to his well-being. Emil Lauderback nearly vomited on his own mud caked boots as he was forced to shove down Mr. Calhoun's gloating due to his wife's emotional disequilibrium as it were. Edward approached closer to the gentlemen responsible for the settlement of the exchange for effect and spoke rather sternly to those suddenly glum looking men, "I will say this softly for the sake of your reputations alone, lady and good gentlemen gathered: What you are positioning as the truth here this evening is simply not possible. The woman came from the Butler Island Plantation as did the child or you would not be offering either of them for sale here today. Please, do certify the truth of my presumption before we speak a word further on the issue before us."

Mr. Aitcheson and Mr. Noble stared at one another as if the matter of who was to speak was in doubt. Mr. and Mrs. Lauderback stared at the two gentlemen whilst they postured silently with one another. The couple appeared as if they were just as curious to know what the two men might say in reply as Mr. Calhoun was. A brief spell of confusion was set upon the uncertain members of the group. Such was a befuddling confusion that threatened to burst forth in the manner of abject infamy if the fire burning beneath the surface of each adherent individually was not quenched immediately. As such, Mr. Noble stepped forward and began to speak dourly in reply to Mr. Calhoun.

"The woman, Miss Leslie Butler for clarity, went missing from the Butler Island Plantation some three weeks prior to market. She was indeed full-term at the time. She was also returned by a bounty hunter just prior to the event with the child she walked out onto the platform with and one of the younger boys included in the lot. Miss Leslie and eleven of the others had broken free and ventured into South Carolina before those three, which had been two, were returned in time for the fair. The problem before us now is that the child is of a creamy white complexion, Mr. Calhoun. She is not colored so differently than you…" Mr. Noble then paused for some strange form of effect and rejoined with, "…or I, or any white gentlemen living through the last of the season of winter and into the birthing pangs of spring."

Mr. Noble carefully studied the thoughtful eyes of Mr. Calhoun for a brief turn and then continued on with his explanation of the current set of facts and circumstances behind their dilemma. "As a gentleman of commerce you must understand there can no longer be any assurances, or perhaps an established chain of custody is the proper designation as we speak on this matter in a legal sense; whichever designation you prefer, Mr. Calhoun, there can presently no longer be any assurances given that this Miss Leslie is holding the proper child in her arms."

Edward stabbed the toe of his riding boot into the mud. He at last understood the dilemma. Old Emil was in a fine mess and had clearly dipped that snout of his into the feed bin a bit prematurely. The situational circumstance explained at least something of the colored woman's almost inhuman fear of another catching a glimpse of the child wrapped up in that old but beautiful and sacred Cherokee blanket. However, far worse than Emil Lauderback's bind, and a matter that was entirely more of a direct concern to Edward, was the bind certain to be facing Mr. Lemarque if this situation went live and beyond the bounds of this delicate negotiation; a delicate negotiation which was dancing on the razor's edge and so very near to spinning entirely out of control.

For those reasons aforementioned and in stark contradiction to his traditional instinct to strike fast and strike to kill when his business opponent had been rendered impotent, Edward backed away from his guns. He did so for the sake of Mr. Lemarque and because he became overwhelmed by the low feelings of hypocrisy mounting within where it concerned his consideration of Mr. Lauderback's quandary. In fact,

Edward spoke in reply to Mr. Noble in a far more congenial and cooperative manner. "I understand Mr. Noble. Shall we speak off to the side for a moment? I believe that we can remedy this situation in favor of all parties present with only a smattering of cooperative thought."

Mr. Noble nodded stoically and stepped off a few paces to the side of the gathered delegates with Mr. Calhoun. When the two men were speaking in confidences due to their mutual understanding of the complexities of the situation and their distance from the clever, pointed ears of those present, Edward asked, "What is your proposal, my most gracious host? You presently find me attentive to your whims and most willing to accommodate an impartial resolution." Mr. Noble nodded and spoke of a fair proposal that would provide at least something of an equitable measure of relief to all parties involved.

One catch was that Mr. Noble spoke as if he held something at hand which he could use to play against Mr. Calhoun if needed. What such a thing might be Edward could not yet begin to fathom. Be that as it may, as word of Miss Jeanne had reached Mr. Lemarque there was at least verifiable reason to proceed with caution in the face of the man's likely bluff. Accordingly, the initial scheme of settlement was not entirely to Edward's liking. "Yes, Mr. Calhoun, my proposal to you is that you purchase three of the seven offered. The three that have crossed into South Carolina without being declared fugitives of another legally divined land prior to the auction. Since you are sovereign to the state and a man of proper influence therein, you are best suited to remedy any potential conflict that may arise from the true nature and standing of the child and her accomplices."

Edward scratched pensively at his chin for a moment. Although as previously stated, Mr. Calhoun was not entirely enamored with the offer for a number of obvious reasons, he saw the merit to such a proposition. There was a certain ease by which Mr. Noble's solution could extract them all from such a convoluted and altogether gripping bind. That simple fact was in and of itself and by a wide margin, far more valuable than all of the other considerations Mr. Calhoun faced in total. Where the shrewd man of the trustees acquired the wisdom needed to refine such a proposal that relieved the undeclared and scurrilous issues facing them all, Edward would be left only to wonder. He did realize however, that he was safer to presume that the man's masterful negotiation of such a confounding shit storm, for lack of a more dignified portrayal of the fine mess within which they were all currently mired, did not occur by chance.

And so went the story of how Edward Christopher Calhoun purchased the most expensive child in American history. All rights and due provisions associated with the acquisition of the child and her keeper's papers were included in the transaction. Additionally, and in exchange for a small processing fee, Edward also acquired the runaway eleven-year-old boy who was provably reared at the Butler Island Plantation but had crossed over into South Carolina and was properly called by the name of Amos Martingale of Butler Island. Though on paper he had paid an astounding $3,500 in gold coin to essentially procure the runaway woman for the sake of her mysterious little baby wrapped in the blanket of a papoose, all liability of the selling party named in the transaction was given over to the four winds of the earth and to the incessant rains of the hour.

After parting with the entirety of the contents of his fine leather purse and signing all of the necessary provisions and paperwork, Edward Calhoun escorted the frightened woman and her deceptively white looking newborn off of the auction stage while Mr. Sommers tended to the care of little Amos. The time to explain his seemingly careless or even absent-minded deeds of the hour would not come until a few days later, following their arrival back in Sumter. Such was the place where Edward would be forced to explain the delicate predicament of the woman and the two children to his oldest daughter and her other siblings.

Later that night after the skies had parted, some rather temperate air making its way off of the warm waters of the Gulf Coast had moved overland from the southwest and settled upon the City of Savannah. For some, the warmer air was not dissimilar to a comforting blanket, which served to ward off the fresh and foul memories of the unending torrents of cold rain and foul smut of the last few days. While Edward noodled over a permanent home for three bonded slaves purchased at auction for an unspeakable sum, Mr. Satterfield put the whip to the team and the buggy made its way north from Savannah to cross over the river and into South Carolina at Augusta in the hopes that the bridge there had remained solvent in the face of such a diluvian onslaught. Such turned out to be true regarding the viability of the ramshackle old bridge. Yet perhaps only due to the fact that for some strange reason the rain, which had indeed poured down for two straight days without relent in Savannah, never made its presence felt more than ten miles inland and ten miles to the north or to the south of the Ten Broeck Race Course. In any event, the road home would be without impediment and it was a beautiful night for buggy ride with the stars above twinkling in a clear and perfected unison.

Upon crossing the river the next day, the six weary riders began their journey along the Carolina crossroads overland to Uriah and then on home to Sumter. Edward's bodyguards of a sort had been granted their leave to spend some time in Charleston sowing their wild oats as it were after their yeomanly antics back in Savannah. What the small party found along the road just a furlong or so out beyond the bridge and a short ways up from the sand creek flats of the Savannah Run was nearly beyond comprehension. The discovery was so disturbing that immediately upon reaching the far side of the river, the eyes of the woman and the boy who had been purchased down at the auction began to grow wide and shift with unease from side to side. Mr. Sommers took particular notice of the obscene amount of buzzards circling overhead in three or four very distinct clusters.

A short while thereafter, Mr. Satterfield locked his eyes upon the horseless, stripped-down carriage positioned just off to the south side of the old post road upon which they travelled. To his eyes, there seemed to be something resembling a sack of old laundry perched atop the elevated driver's pew. Though his mother had likely given her own spirit over to the blacker bents of witchery some years ago, Edward's own intuitive spirit remained strong and full of uncorrupted goodness. Thus, he quickly sensed within that the dark arts had been at play some time ago along this stretch of uninhabited carriage way; the place which perfectly resembled the embodiment of the spoken lore of those haunted old crossroads into Georgia.

The buggy and its driver proceeded with caution until the slowly moving outfit reached the empty carriage and Mr. Satterfield yelled up to the team, "Whoa now, Big Luke! Whoa now, Saul! Edward glanced up at the driver's pew and almost inexplicably found reason to believe that it was perhaps a man that rested in a slumped over fashion atop the bench. He quickly stood up from his seated position next to Mr. Satterfield and stepped onto the bridge of the abandoned carriage. After pausing a moment to summon his courage once he had identified the legs of the carriage driver, Edward poked at the mass of humanity tilted across the coachman's seat. Feeling that the upper torso of the man was dense and solid as would be presumed only with a cadaver left to rot for some number of days, Edward's arms instinctively recoiled back to his side.

Mr. Calhoun then took a deep breath and rested for a moment while he prepared to adjust the body as such that he might make out the gentleman's face, though he loathed even the thought of the necessity of the act. His first two tugs at the stiffened corpse did little to improve Edward's desired angle of visibility. As such, he placed his left boot onto the muted driver's step and elevated his stance a few feet until he turned to violently retch and then vomit off to the south side of the abandoned coach. The dead man's softer appendages and his eyes had been violently picked away and eaten by the crows. What remained of the poor chap's facial flesh was of a ghastly and pallid hue. The innards of the man's skull were visible through the scavenged at openings of his nose and mouth and he appeared as some appalling ghoul rejected from the nether realms and not fit for even the gatherings of the All Hallows Eve affairs of the fall season.

While Edward was in the throes of purging the contents of his belly from the top of the abandoned carriage for the third time, he took note of not only the ominous presence of the woodlands to the south but the speed at which his newly acquired boy was sprinting in the direction of the tree line leading into those woods. He made effort to call after the boy but another serving of gastric fluid and bile choked off what would have been his curious and hopeful call. Though Edward was quite hamstrung and preoccupied by the deep and thorough cleansing of his insides, he wondered why the woman was not also calling after the boy as he ran. Then, without a proper reason or visible explanation for his actions, the boy stopped in the middle of the field and shook his head while his mother looked out to him. Edward dismounted the carriage with an agile jump after stepping down from the coachman's pew, made his way through the initial brush at the side of the road and stepped into the high grass after the boy as neither the wide-eyed and open mouthed Mr. Sommers nor the similarly stunned Mr. Satterfield seemed inclined to assist him with rectifying the untenable situation.

In the end, the indifference of Mr. Calhoun's preoccupied adherents was no matter. The boy quickly came up to Edward's side after the flummoxed grandee had taken only four or five strides into the bending straw. He asked of the child, "Why are you running son? I promise you will not do any better than what I have in wait for you back in Sumter." Amos shook his head and answered, "No reason, Massa just thinkin' the grips was comin' in but they's not." Amos then looked up at the top of the carriage and into the empty eye sockets of the perished driver and asked, "Where he done been shot, Massa?"

Edward looked curiously at the boy and replied, "Glad you are well, my boy. How did you know that the man up there had been shot?" Amos began to tremble and shake and said, "Only way I knows of to stop a man in an army coat, ways on up there like he be." Edward nodded slowly and thoughtfully to the presently frightened looking little boy and replied purposefully, "I see, my boy. Get on back to your momma while I talk to the men here." Amos nodded and got scarce in a hurry.

Edward called over to Mr. Satterfield in saying, "Mr. Satterfield, come help me in getting this poor soul down from that buzzard's perch." Mr. Satterfield nodded and promptly came over from his seat in the buggy. As the two men were lifting the corpse from the pew of the stranded stagecoach, Edward looked down and noticed something quite worrying. The Calhoun mark had been branded into the seat of the bench. The carriage in question was a Calhoun carriage that had been waylaid or perhaps far worse. Edward quickly began to descend into a state of panic. He let the dead man fall back to his initial position, stepped back down from the carriage and walked out into the high grass until he fell to his knees and began to weep nearly uncontrollably. None followed after him for quite some time. Mr. Satterfield and Mr. Sommers took the dead man down from the top of the carriage a short while later. The past few days had been a time of sorrowful weeping for nearly all.

Chapter Three

THE CROSSROADS

❧

O N THE MORNING of Saturday, February 26th, 1859 at around first light, the carriage carrying Miss Sarah and little Miss Margaret Anne was approaching the notoriously fickle crossing at the mighty Savannah River. There was a noticeable west wind guiding the thin, brisk air upon the primary shimmering of the dawn but the weather was far more accommodating than it had been on the night of the birth of the promised child. The tasteful yet elegantly adorned four-horse drawn brougham crafted outside of London, which bore the Calhoun brand upon the coachman's seat, was not quite a mile out from the river when the driver, a retired cavalry man who had spent nearly a decade chasing several Native American tribes westward onto the lands beyond the Mississippi on behalf of the Federal Government, caught sight of a cadre of wandering slaves. Those slaves had no business being out in those parts and they quickly ducked into the high brush off to the side of the road in an effort to surreptitiously, yet belatedly, conceal their whereabouts from the oncoming carriage.

Captain Pierce, as the skilled rifleman of yesteryear was still called, hollered down to the leader of his team from the pilot's perch in response to the irregular activity, "Whoa, now, Ginny! Whoa, now!" The stagecoach came to a gliding halt shortly thereafter and its passengers were promptly serenaded by the shifting sounds of the steadying hooves of the team and the slowing wheels of the heavy carriage crushing the cold dirt and myriad pebbles covering the old post road. Not understanding why they had come to a stop so close to the river and therefore the great state of Georgia, the still somewhat anxious Miss Sarah was immediately dashed into a panic due to her thinking that the bridge might have been washed away by another flood, as it was wont to do every fifteen years or so in reality but five according legend. She clung tightly to the baby girl still curiously wrapped up in the brightly colored Cherokee throw, which the child had adorned since the morning of her traumatic birth only a few days ago, and yelled up to inquire of the coachman, "Why is we stoppin', Cap'n Pierce? We's almost all the way to Georgia now!"

Captain Pierce was an upstanding gentleman and one who steadfastly honored the discharge of his services to those who legally petitioned him according to contract for the full-measure of his readily capable arsenal of deadly talents to the bitter end. However, the Captain was no righteous crusader for any moral cause that blurred the lines of proper legal standing. He had spilled far too much blood in accordance with the laws of American sovereignty and furthermore, the country's drive to attain its manifest destiny to think too long or too carefully on the mainsprings behind any legal proclamation at this juncture in his life. At the end of the day, the Captain was under contract to protect his cartage at all cost. Once given properly over to that steadfast line of thinking, he quickly surmised that he had little to fear from the ragtag band of travelling servants, whether they had illegally loosed themselves from some nearby protectorate or another or not.

Those ducking into the brush as the stage approached were running scared and a threat to none but themselves by partaking in such a perilous exercise. Perhaps their actions were better thought of as a near hopeless endeavor which was taught to be despised and rectified with prejudice above nearly all other known transgressions of the day in those parts. Given present circumstances, such quickly became very clear to the honorable guardian of the promised one that he would not be the one to return those poor bonded souls to the horrors from whence they came. Additionally, he had no qualms about justifying his position upon the dawn of this particular day if he were ever to be questioned on the nature of this specific example of his indifference to such wanton malice.

However, there were ancillary considerations to be taken into account. Judging by the group's unusual proximity to the road and the speed at which they made themselves scarce, Captain Pierce surmised that the constituents of that particular crew were not only on the run but being forced upon their current course by some capable pursuer; someone who knew the terrain and who wasn't likely to be all that far behind them. After some additional thought and by the by, the astute and battle hardened frontier serviceman figured on the best course of action being to simply continue on towards the river and make the crossing into Georgia. He reasoned that some folks might be gathered at the crossing; honest and God-fearing folk who would be inclined to bear credible enough and perhaps even intimidating witness against the unseen brigands driving the would be captives toward the swift currents of the river which made their way on down toward Savannah. As was plain enough to decipher from his aforementioned considerations, the Captain despised the thought of being called to task by an angry bounty man having lost out on his intended quarry.

Given that he had decided upon their intended course of remediation, Captain Pierce answered down firmly but with an accompanying air of soothing reassurance to Miss Sarah, "Just thought I saw somethin' Ma'am is all. Probably nothin' but best we get on with it." Captain Pierce then called out to his prized steed and the team lead, "Yah, Ginny! Onward ho, my trusty gal!"

The forceful command given by Captain Pierce and the slowly accelerating turn of the once halted carriage wheels brought a great comfort to Miss Sarah. She tickled the baby's chin and said to her, "We almost on over to Georgia now, my little sweetie. Mean old Mr. Oglethorpe wouldn't dare set foot on that Georgia clay lest he be run on back across the river with his hide in tatters. You rest for a while. Everything is gonna be just fine, little Miss."

The baby seemed to smile and almost accidentally wink back at Miss Sara. Though most assuredly the phenomenon was simply a catching of the precious child's right eye as she reflexively blinked in response to the direct rays of twinkling sunlight that were making their way over the lower ledge of the open carriage window. Miss Sarah smiled delightedly in response to the adorable child's seemingly knowing reaction to the returning airs of comfort now dressing over her guardian's once palpitating heart. Just as the light was taking hold of the plain yet pretty midwife's stunning blue eyes, the sharp and unmistakable crack of a Pattern 1853 Enfield rang out from a downward sloping ridge some three or four furlongs across the open field to the north.

Captain Pierce was blown sideways onto the neighboring top seat of the carriage as the bullet struck his neck squarely between his jaw and his shoulder. He wasn't knocked all the way over, mind you but he fell sidelong at the hips the rest of the way onto the smoothly worn wooden seat when he violently took hold of his neck with both hands. Miss Sarah covered her mouth to keep from screaming and took to the floor of the carriage with the baby. The fleeing clan of bonded servants squeezed their bodies lower to the ground amidst the high grass and the brush lining the south side of the road. The four slavers that had been fast approaching directly upon the heels of the refugees took to a knee along the tree line to the south that opened up into the level and open field their quarry was attempting to cross. Those men then proceeded to wave and point with their arms until the position of the shooter some ways off in the distance had been identified.

Captain Pierce straightened his body up on the top seat of the wagon, which had once again come to a halt due to the scare put into the horses in addition to the loosening of the slack set upon the reins. The grizzled veteran of the western frontiers attempted to urge his team forward with the reins as his devastated throat would produce nothing but the frightful sound of a bubbling gurgle. The initial trauma of the projectile striking his throat felt closer to that of being bucked by the hind quarters of an unbroken stallion than it did a piercing nub of svelte iron. Captain Pierce had seen the wound first hand a few times out on the frontier where the scenic Ohio fed into the muddy waters of the Mississippi during the rainy season. The Captain knew he was not long for this world. His efforts in attempting to get the carriage moving along again were for the sake of the woman and the child alone. No matter the heroic yet fatal premise of his intent, when the Captain was sitting fully upright again a second shot rang out and sent him steadily to rest amid the shifting confines of that eternal good night.

Regardless of the clear intentions of that subsequent and terminal shot, the seemingly pronounced and aggressive disposition of the second echoing crack of the Enfield rifle-musket put a spur to the backsides of those already being hunted from the other direction. The abrupt explosion sent the small band of runaway slaves scurrying low and westward towards the river on their hands and knees as if there were no tomorrow. They whispered lowly but actively to one another through the covering barriers of the high grass, brush and weeds as they progressed onward in an unseen but synchronized fashion. No longer capable of containing the outward manifestations of her sheer terror, Miss Sarah screamed bloody murder from the carriage floor. Miss Margaret Anne did not utter a sound as she rested upon the stagecoach bottom with her delicate ear set against the tremoring and then hammering beats of the chest of her mentally shattered caretaker.

No, the light-eyed baby girl simply shifted her large, saucer-like eyes so that those enchanting orbs of such auspicious wonder tracked the planed rays of sunlight still beaming into the upper half of the carriage through the open windows above while the cold, steady air that scented ever so faintly of sedentary dust and old, crafted wood brought a touch of color to her exposed cheeks. The slavers set about to make a fortune from their cunningly quarried and nearly cornered prey offered up a few fairly blind, yet correct in their general direction, shots of resistance. They intended to slow whatever might be up there on the ridge in the event that some unseen force was steadfastly set upon hindering their plans to take in a king's ransom at the Butler auction downstream in Savannah in four days' time.

Up on the ridge in question, Stanton Oglethorpe was lamenting the poor condition of his arm, which was sorely in need of care and throbbing mightily from the kickback given off by his military-grade sniper's rifle. He was also cursing the stars for his continuing poor luck in regard to procuring the baby girl. The shots fired in his direction made it quite clear that he had some form of armed and unseen company at the opposite end of the expansive open field, a grove which the carriage road split near to evenly. Stanton knew he had killed the stagecoach driver dead but he had no stomach for running out into the open and across the flats to the road to procure the child with guns positioned across the way.

Although Stanton remained alone while fixed in his still undisclosed location, Miss Sarah had ascribed all six shots which were fired to Stanton's rifle. That faulty assumption caused her to panic and mistakenly believe that the next shot taken would indeed pierce the side walls of the stagecoach where she hid. In that moment, fearing what remained unknown far more than what was known, Miss Sarah grabbed hold of the bundled baby, kicked open the door to the stagecoach with her sturdy boot and went running into the brush which lined the side of the road to the south and presented away from the ridge off in the distance.

Stanton watched as the frightened nurse ran into the wild and unkempt chaparral beside the carriage road and exclaimed, "Tarnation, woman! Can't you make no sense of the fact that there's banditos lurking about!" Stanton couldn't see anyone down in the flats and figured the ones who had fired back at him were still out beyond the tree line to the south of the road due to the fact that the shots fired at him seemed to fall short of his position. Thusly, Mr. Oglethorpe quickly realized he had but one chance to get his hands on the troublesome baby girl and that his time to move was now. Stanton cursed Miss Sarah again and then made his way down the back side of the fifteen-foot high ridge to untie and mount his horse.

The four slavers or bounty hunters still taking cover in the woods were carefully noting and then pointing out any discernable shifts in the high grass and the overgrown brush of the roadside grove. They were attempting to track the refugees while those terrified souls continued on with their slithering progression toward the banks of the river. The bounty men were preparing to move in and round up their prey once they had a line on the man who had shot so cleverly to take out the stage driver from such a long ways off in the distance. That man's business with the stagecoach or its operator specifically was no concern of theirs, yet they certainly didn't want to wind up in his gunsights due to some miscalculation of intent.

When Miss Sarah darted into the field, the slaver situated on the right flank of the tight but evenly spaced out quartet offered up a few covering shots for the sake of the pretty damsel in distress. The clearly frightened woman seemed to be carrying a bundle of some sort while she ran haphazardly around the back of and then away from the fancy wagon. The well intentioned intervention on Miss Sarah's behalf only served to horrify the woman further and cause her to fall sidelong into the all-consuming overgrowth of the grove while managing to buffer the landing of the promised child's concurrent fall. One of the brigands was watching intently as his young and still overly capricious sidekick foolishly endeavored to save the day.

That rough and by then altogether soulless man laughed robustly from the depths of his rounded belly and commented, "Well I'll be damned, Jackson Strait. What'd you go ahead and shoot the pretty lady for?" The other two scourges of the Underground Railroad joined their man Shug Laing in a hearty laugh although the situation was turning into a complete clusterfuck at the quick time. Jackson, who was baby bottom fresh to the trade, retorted, "I ain't done no such thing as all of that, Mr. Shug! That man on the ridge could skin the back of a beaver with that rifle he got if he were out a mile!"

Shug laughed again and then suddenly came under the guise of a far more serious disposition. "Well, we're about to find that out rights about now, aren't we Mr. Strait? I done told ya' this was'n no business for the faint of heart when you signed on back in Ridgeland. Sometimes upholdin' the law ain't as easy as takin' up an unarmed slave boy by the collar. Now if we let those runaways make for the ridge down to the sand creek flats there's no tellin' where they might scatter off to. Why don't you go on out and retrieve the lady while Walt and Eustis cutoff that run on down to the creek. I'll keep my long rifle on that sharpshooter so you needn't worry a hair on that pretty little head of yours."

Walt and Brother Eustis Hennessey laughed and then turned to head west by skirting the tree line as it ran on towards the creek and the river just beyond. Shug grabbed his long rifle from its resting position up against the nearest tree and began to prime, powder and load the muzzle of that finely crafted instrument of death. Jackson watched on as Shug continued loading his rifle and then shifted his eyes to monitor his swiftly moving compatriots jump stepping westward toward the river along the rocky, uneven terrain near the tree line.

Jackson Strait then looked out onto a particular spot in the field, some four hundred yards ahead, where he had seen the woman drop into the brush. Somewhere between the ground upon which he now stood and the fallen woman of the field lay twelve other fleeing souls crawling along the ground in the hopes that they might still live. Jackson Strait knew right there and then that he had signed on for the wrong kind of work. Worse than that, he knew right there and then that he had signed on with the wrong kind of men; men who would put their own desires well before the needs of a proper Southern woman in distress. They were also men who were perhaps capable of far worse if the circumstances of the moment were to necessitate the use of wicked and even unspeakable deeds in exchange for hard currency or coin alike.

As the young, bright-eyed and newly minted bounty hunter considered his predicament further, he took some strange form of comfort in knowing that Shug Laing was a shrewd enough man to read him right. Old Shug knew exactly what the new blood was thinking at that point in the escapade. That harsh man who hid behind a hypocrite's call for justice just because some scornful rich men had codified moral indignity in an old dusty ledger somewhere, he had read Jackson Strait dead to rights. He knew full well that Jackson would have turned away when they approached the moment of the horrifying subjugation of those poor souls they had started pursuing so deviously and without honor out of Savannah a few days back and who were looking for nothing more than to remain together as a family. Shug Laing knew that upon looking into the eyes of the condemned young Jackson was set to head on back to the farm. Furthermore, the merciless bounty man knew that if there wasn't the safety of a lady to consider, Jackson Strait would have vanished into the wind upon the instant.

As such, Jackson Strait made the sign of the cross upon his head, chest and shoulders as he stepped out into the open grove from the cover of the tree line. Though he wondered if he was in fact beyond the deadly range of that already twice proven assassin, he took some solace in knowing that Shug would do his level best to cover him since he would not run away with the safety of a lady still to consider. Shug raised his rifle and centered the sight upon the midpoint of the top of the ridge that had to be nearly a mile off in the distance. After Shug had cocked the rifle's hammer, Jackson stooped low and began his progression further into the open expanse of the field, which was dressed in the tall but dormant high grass of the late winter season. Mr. Strait stepped ever so carefully forward while Shug spit out some tobacco juice without shifting his eyes in the slightest from his tightly dialed-in focal point up on the ridge across the flats.

Not realizing which direction she was facing as she emerged from her spell, Miss Sarah felt her way through a particularly dense patch of the copse while remaining on her knees with the baby tucked under her right arm. She continued on in that way until she found herself eyeball to eyeball with a dark-skinned man who was lying in wait for the right moment to continue on towards the river's edge. The man had large, serious eyes that shone white but were shaded in red and custard yellow due to the numerous straining blood vessels that had been forced to the surface of his sclera and a slight liver ailment brought about from malnutrition. Upon the stark and frightful meeting of their eyes, which seemed to enjoin their souls amidst the flashpoint of malice that lingered low and heavy in the air just above the shifting stalks of grass, the man desperately signaled to Miss Sarah with his hand to get lower. Miss Sarah obliged the man graciously as she feared him not and rested the bundled baby next to her cheek when she too was flat to the ground and facing the clear blue skies above.

Miss Sarah thought carefully about the man's awful predicament and how unlikely it was that she had come across a refugee in the brush after fleeing the stagecoach, even after receiving Captain Pierce's ominous warning before he was shot dead. Miss Sarah then looked adoringly at the one charged to her care and swiftly remembered that nothing was impossible with that little one. For lack of anything better to say to the still silent and now slightly trembling man from another world; a world which she knew nearly nothing about, she asked, "You's runnin' isn' ya'?"

The man did little but to lower his head in a timid sign of his reply. Soon thereafter, he looked around at his surroundings as if he were about to make a clean break from this suddenly sedated yet assuredly cracked woman and her eerily silent child; a baby who would perhaps give away their position with the uniquely disquieted cry of the new-born at any moment. Miss Sarah sensed the man's trepidation and interjected upon his thoughts of fear and taking flight. "No, don't you worry none about me or this precious little angel here. We's runnin' now too. The man who shot my driver wants the baby girl, but she's a colored girl like y'all. I swear on my honor she is! But she got a bigger secret than even that, this special little angel. A bigger secret than you or I would ever imagine!"

Black Jim as he was called back on the Butler Island Plantation was once a man of the house. He was one of the brightest minds in all of Coastal Georgia before he disappeared and made a break for the free states upon learning of the upcoming auction of his kin and kind alike. He escaped with his extended family and the widowed mother of three boys who were hanged or permanently chained until dead for running away some years ago yet one at a time and directly before her very eyes. Those boys were all like their father and just didn't have the patience or resolve required to remain living as a slave once they knew better. Miss Leslie, as that woman was called, had learned much about life on the outside from each one of her sons. Those boys were bright and they learned certain and differing aspects of life beyond the barracks and fields of the plantation before they ran away and then during the brief span they were trying to get up North. They passed much of this knowledge on to their mother in differing ways before they were so brutally returned to the manor to be set out before the others and made an example of as to what happens to those who get the itch to go on with runnin'.

Miss Leslie would have proven exceedingly useful in crossing into the North if old Shug Laing and his crew hadn't smelled discord and therefore opportunity well in advance of the Butler Island bankruptcy auction. The fact that they had all managed to cross into South Carolina and venture on for a bit before being scented by old

Shug's frightfully intuitive snoot was a testament to what Miss Leslie had learned from her three boys who were so committed to the cause of liberty. As the circumstances of their arrival upon this nearly indefensible position were presently neither here nor there, the fugitive presently considered the woman before him of her own accord. The best that Black Jim could tell, this woman was as bat-shit crazy as any white woman he had ever known. The child however, was another matter entirely.

Jim attempted to plead with Miss Sarah as calmly as he was able to given present circumstances." He asked of her, "Why are you trying to tell me that your baby is black, Ma'am? Do you think there is anything I can do for her out here with rabid dogs already at our heels? Now your own man on the hunt for y'all is up there killing folks in cold blood from the cover of the ridge. I can assure you, we folks here, we're in a mighty bad fix as things sit without a crying baby to fret over."

Miss Sarah shook her head in disbelief. She felt certain she had come across this very bright colored man hiding in an open field for God's own reasons alone. She did understand however, that he and the others, wherever they might be, were perhaps in an equivalently desperate bind. Miss Sarah lost her composure for a moment and stood up in the midst of the brush to figure out where she was in regard to the river. She did not see nor could she yet hear Stanton Oglethorpe approaching on his galloping steed, as her pursuer was still some four hundred yards or more off in the distance.

Miss Leslie was well concealed in the brush and high grass very close by and had heard everything that was said between Jim and the blue-eyed refugee woman, the woman who had fled the stagecoach with a baby in her arms. When Miss Sarah had reached her full height and then spun around frantically to face the road, Jackson Strait yelled out from a distance of about a hundred paces, "Ma'am, get down! Get down! He's riding this way!"

Stanton's third shot of the day had drifted down due his inability to precisely time the stride of his rapidly galloping mount. The bullet struck Miss Sara squarely in the thigh and sent her careening back into a dense and thorny patch of brush. Miss Leslie lurched up just a hair and dove forward to press as cover for little Margaret Anne just prior to Miss Sarah falling into the thicket. Miss Sarah was lying flat on her back after being shot but she could see Miss Leslie shielding the baby. The wounded nurse did not yet feel any pain. She pleaded with Miss Leslie from a bearing of relative calm due to her temporary state of shock, "Ma'am, please take the child out of here. She is a colored baby, I promise. I can't move my leg. I can't do no more for her. Please, Ma'am! She's a miracle child and about as sweet as she can be!"

Miss Leslie looked the child over carefully. Upon the instant their tender eyes met, the connection between the two was nearly as tight and inexplicable as the heavenly ordained bonds of any natural mother and daughter might strive to be upon that hallowed first glance. Mister Jim looked into Miss Leslie's awestruck eyes and reprimanded her sternly from his position lying flat in the high grass off to her right, "Do not get any ideas in that maternally starved head of yours, Missus. We are certain to have quite enough trouble on our hands as it is. What do you think is going to happen if we are not only caught, but caught with a white woman's baby in our midst? We are all gonna burn real slow, that's what!"

Once Miss Leslie had wrapped her arms around the child, any decision that involved leaving the babe exposed out in the field with her wounded nurse and transitory guardian went rather impulsively out the proverbial window. Miss Leslie looked over to Black Jim and replied sternly to the leader of their hapless group at the very moment of the onset of their tribulations by saying, "What we gonna do, Jim? Be leavin' one a our own to da rifleman or be feedin' her to da demons at our heels? Her only chance be wid me. None but us here knows dat I lost my baby just afore we was gettin on off a da Island. I'll be stayin' here wid her while y'all do like we planned. We will at least be slowin' dem boys down some by givin' 'em somethin' for all dat trouble they done been goin' through. Asides, a momma an' her baby gonna be looked at different than da rest a you all when we brought in."

Time was getting short but Mr. Jim gave careful consideration to what Miss Leslie had said. He was a man of God and dreaded leaving the poor woman who had already lost so much behind. However, with the child in tow they were hemmed in from both sides. They wouldn't make the hidden cave up on the eastern side of the northern banks of the river as they had planned. Jim was further troubled by the fact that they only knew about the hideaway that ran deep into the earth because of Miss Leslie's second son. While both Stanton and Jackson approached from opposing directions, Black Jim looked Miss Leslie squarely and right serious in the eye and replied, "You know we can't make it where we need to go if you insist on keeping watch over the child with the rider coming for her. What will we do without you, my lady?"

Miss Leslie smiled back at her lifelong friend and answered him soothingly, "You isn' gonna make it but for me runnin' off back to da east wid da child in my arms anyhow. But don't you worry, sweet Jim. I is exactly where God intends for me to be. Dis be my calling now an' nothin's gonna happen to dis baby while she be restin' in my arms. Maybe she be da one, Jim. Just maybe she bein' da one..."

Jim closed his eyes and fought back the tears of this instantaneous and presumably impossible reckoning. Tears which confirmed that the good and long-suffering woman's judgement was still sound, at least where it concerned what appeared to be her divinely sanctioned station as the mysterious child's impromptu guardian of the hour, if not right on through to the settlement of some long anticipated yet perhaps presently chimerical prophesy. The prophesy which Miss Leslie spoke of had endured the passing of many generations since the words were first spoken of the one who would belong to two worlds and therefore might serve to split the darkness from the light; and in so doing open the eyes and soften the hearts of their oppressors to the truth of their God-given humanity. As such, the uncommonly wise man nodded quickly, squeezed the woman of his secret adoration's hand silently and slithered his way up through the grass to prompt his companions on toward their intended destination.

Whatever that Anglo looking child indeed was, the diversion to be offered by Miss Leslie had swiftly become a necessary grace of God if any of them were to persevere beyond the throes of their dire predicament. After Jim had disappeared into the tall chaff leading toward the high banks overlooking the river, Miss Sarah asked quietly, as if she hadn't heard a word spoken between the two, "Is your man going to bring back the rest to stand up for the baby girl?"

Miss Leslie shook her head slowly and ominously in reply. She then closed her eyes and began to hum a melody to little Miss Margaret Anne whilst she prepared to rise above the vanishing line of the high grass; that sacred, bending straw which kept the exact location of their whereabouts concealed from the assassins and bounty men who were surrounding them and rapidly converging upon a solitary terminus. That shared endpoint of the exasperated end runs of those who stalked them all was the spot where Miss Sarah had fallen and those callous hunters of their human prey were closing in without relent and without remorse.

While watching Miss Leslie quietly sing to the child in preparation for some oncoming cataclysm that was set to eternally settle their temporary impasse reached out upon those crossroads to nowhere, Miss Sarah began to feel a throbbing pain shoot though her upper thigh. She was quickly shaken into realizing that she needed to care for the wound or at least staunch the bleeding. As such, she twisted herself onto her side and looked down at the blood richly staining her plain, light-blue nursing dress, her dark winter coat and the flattened winter grass beneath her leg. The nurse feigned further inspection of the wound as the dull smell of cooling blood mingled with the earthy scents of the twisted grass and the chilled soil. In truth, she dared not probe the wound any more precisely than that of an initial look see. Miss Sarah shifted her eyes away from the aftermath of the trauma and asked something of Miss Leslie while attempting to mask her mounting discomfort, "Who will be leading you on down to the river with the child then, Ma'am? Surely, your kin haven't left you to fend for yourself with that barbarian out there!"

Miss Leslie continued to turn her worn but comely visage from side to side and hum to the baby girl wrapped up in her loving arms. Her eyes remained closed when she reached the final note of the sweet melody. When her parched and swollen lips had gone silent, she stood quite abruptly and began to run with the child in her arms back to the east and away from the river. Slow to react, but seeing what had transpired before her very eyes Miss Sarah yelled, "No, please come back! He will kill you both! I swear upon all I hold dear that he will kill you both!"

When Stanton Oglethorpe saw the slave mistress rise above the shifting stalks of the long grass and the brush with the baby in her arms he had to wipe his eyes twice while his horse galloped along beneath him. He needed to be certain that what he was seeing just off in the distance on the other side of the carriage road was indeed real. Upon taking a quick moment to adjust his understanding of the situation and the about face in circumstances made manifest before his very eyes, Stanton reasoned that runaway slaves looking to make their way across the river and into Georgia amidst the shallow and narrower runs of the sand creek flats made perfect sense. Likewise, the presence of bounty men not far behind those fleeing slaves also provided a reasonable explanation for the shots fired earlier in his general direction.

He had yet to notice Jackson Strait crouch his way on out of the woods and begin to traverse the southern parcel of the open grove because he was loathe to take his eyes off of the spot where Miss Sarah had fallen. He did not want to lose his mark as he approached closer to the carriage road on horseback. With such being the case, Stanton lifted his primed and loaded secondary rifle to his shoulder and quickly set Miss Leslie into the undulating sight of that fine instrument of death. This go around, Stanton Oglethorpe prepared to time his shot in accordance with the forceful yet presently reckonable and consistent stride of his swiftly moving steed.

Miss Leslie paid no mind to the rider or the gentleman approaching from the woods. She simply ran as fast as she could muster with her eyes searching downward to be certain she didn't trip over any unexpected debris that may have settled beneath the scorched and hollow straw of the field. Shug watched on from his ready stance out along the tree line and coldly and deliberately calculated where he was to deliver the payload of his readied musket. He reckoned that the boy recently hired on in Ridgeland and presently working the contract under some fanciful name of his boyhood deliriums was too far gone. That boy hailing from somewheres over near Aiken and now slowly and steadily making his way across the grove was forever lost to him the moment he stepped on out into the open for the sake of a lady he had never laid eyes upon before this morning.

The woman the young man pursued out by the carriage was far more than a damsel in distress to Shug Laing's young apprentice. She served as some form of totem or marker sent from on high to initiate his deliverance from that cruel work; work which "Mr. Strait" had neither the heart nor the stomach to properly execute. In young Jackson's mind, all he need do to break free from these low men was somehow reach her across the expanse of that open field without taking a bullet between the eyes. While such a fact was disappointing to nasty old Shug Laing, as the boy truly was a talent with any form of firearm placed into the open palm of his well-made hand, he suspected the boy was here to serve a purpose and that said purpose was better likely than not to accrue to Mr. Laing's favor if he remained patient with the stalwart and overeager young buck.

Miss Leslie had made perhaps fifty yards along the reasonably square line of her easterly escape route, which ran parallel to and just south of the carriage road, before the shot rang out into the sound of her rushed and desperate breaths. Breaths that were sealed and muffled within the confines of her frenzied head as it bobbed in response to each desperate stride she took away from her people scurrying on toward the river beneath the cover of the brush. Within the confines of a half-step she began to glide to a stop and squeezed her eyes closed. She then readied to experience a feeling she had never known throughout the course of her life, though she had known the torments of many forms of assault both crude and clever alike. She called out to God in earnest. Yet before her plea had split the stillness and the temporary silence of the crisp February air, her antagonist was blown off of his horse. His forehead had been whipped back only momentarily but harshly in the opposite direction of his swiftly coursing steed by the force of a rapidly travelling and precisely aimed ball of musket shot.

Seeing that he had violently loosed the deadly rifleman from his horse while leaving little to the imagination as it concerned that man's rather grim and physically horrifying fate, given that the rider was traveling at perhaps twenty miles to the hour at the moment of his sudden fall, Jackson Strait dropped his musket into the grass and launched into a dead on sprint to the spot where Miss Sarah had disappeared beneath the chaff. Miss Leslie had come to a stop in the field and opened her eyes. She instantly sensed that her immediate troubles and those of the child now given over to her care had temporarily receded for at least the passing of the moment. She continued to breathe heavily while smiling into the wide eyes of the promised child and bending slightly forward to regather her wind while giving copious thanks to the Good Lord above. "Praise be to Jesus, sweet child," she called out as she straightened her formerly bent posture.

Miss Leslie continued to pay no mind to those around her while she stared into the depths of the enchanting eyes of the little girl amidst the faint and dissipating mists of her stunted but settling exhalations. That is until the crack of another rifle shot seemed to split the drifting haze of one of her panted breaths as the taut air of her lungs struck the dry chill of the morning February air. She looked back over her shoulder while turning her frame slightly to her left only to see a young man fall into the overgrowth very near to the spot where Miss Sarah was likely to remain lying. Upon twisting further to her left and facing the tree line to the south in an effort to track the sound of the most recent rifle discharge to its source, Miss Leslie noticed a small but rapidly dispersing cloud of smoke. The heavy, lingering vapors were swirling gently and billowing out from a spot beside the tall and stout Carolina pine from whence Shug Laing had taken the murderous shot which felled his boy.

To her utter dismay, there was something more frightening that caught Miss Leslie's sharp and ready eye as she spun fully around to face the woods in an effort to locate the shooter who felled the young man sprinting so spiritedly to the aid of the woman who had delivered the child unto her care. Two armed men were moving at an alarming rate of speed along the eastern bank of the river and appeared well positioned to cutoff her folk from accessing the only passable slope down to the sand creek flats. Fearing for their lives, Miss Leslie yelled out to her still hidden compatriots much to the chagrin of the once silent babe still nestled in her arms, "Make haste for dat ridge Jim and Amos! They's moving up dem banks a da river right quick!"

There was much ado following Miss Leslie's hastily delivered warning, which did not fail to reach the ears of all close enough to lay eyes upon the frightened woman standing solitary in the roadside field with the presently screaming baby in her arms. Mr. Laing promptly delivered a warning shot from the midst of his approach that produced an unnerving whirring sound as it travelled past Miss Leslie's ear just before she dropped back into the high grass for cover. Upon hearing Miss Leslie's warning and the subsequent rifle shot which confirmed that her words were Gospel true, the eleven remaining fugitives darted out from the confines of their concealment. They then scurried across the road just in front of the agitated horses still awaiting their next command while hitched to the elegantly crafted black carriage.

When Jim and his brethren had safely made the other side of the seemingly accursed thoroughfare, they ran like there was no tomorrow in the direction of the ridge from whence Stanton Oglethorpe had felled Captain Pierce just a short while ago. For his part, the decorated frontiersman remained expired and near bloodless atop the carriage, his wide, haunting eyes disquietingly gripped by the eternal stare of the dead. Shug Laing, who wasn't much for running at this juncture of his life, stepped further out into the open grove. He remained heading in the general direction of Miss Leslie and the screaming child while utilizing a high step accompanied by at least something of an urgent tempo that was applied to the otherwise ambulatory gait of an aging and ornery gentleman quite set in his ways.

Realizing that the motley band of runaways that constituted the entirety of their would be bounty to be paid by the trustees of the Butler Island estate were making for the high ground at an alarming rate of speed, the Hennessey boys made use of their perfectly calibrated rifles and took down two of the fugitives who were caught out at the back of the pack. After firing first and considering the collateral costs of their folly only afterward due to the fact that their blood was wont to run hot with both anger and the excitement of the hunt, Walt and Brother Eustis Hennessey peeled away from the banks of the river, ran down the carriage road for a short ways and then darted into the northern half of the field after the nine still spry and swiftly moving fugitives. When both the hunters and the hunted were but a short ways out from the base of the sharply sloping ridge that Stanton Oglethorpe had occupied prior to taking a musket ball to the forehead, the fugitives shocked the good 'ol Hennessey boys and broke hard to the left and back toward the river.

Brother Eustice took another specimen of their intended prey down with an adept shot to the back of that raggedly clothed man's shoulder while stopping to fire from nearly that of a dead sprint. Not long after that rather tragic development, the eight remaining fugitives disappeared from sight somewhere near the bank of the river at a point adjacent to the ridge; the ridge the Hennessey brothers thought for certain was the intended destination of the nearly cornered band of ragtag truants. Walt and Brother Eustice were perhaps seventy yards in arrears when the last of their quarry almost magically dropped out of sight along the river's edge.

At the very moment Walt and Brother Eustis were approaching the scene of the vanishing and expecting to bear witness to the would be captives standing at the ready to tempt fate by throwing their worn out bodies into the swiftly moving currents of the southwardly running river, Shug Laing had reached the faintly shivering Miss Leslie and little Miss Margaret Anne. The two were lying otherwise near to motionless upon a flattened parcel of the high, bent grass where the slave mistress had dropped low for cover with the swaddled babe wrapped securely in her arms. Miss Leslie was a good ways off to the east from the carriage and concurrently perhaps half a furlong from the spot where Miss Sarah and the young man shot through the back lay without the slightest sign being given as to their current condition. All was again silent in the open field absent the faint discord of the dry grass shifting and giving way beneath Mr. Laing's booted feet as he deliberately approached, the ominously echoing and intermittent calls of the crows perched atop the tall, leafless trees lining the woodlands from whence that dark-hearted and murderous man had arrived, and the low hum of the woman's sweet yet sorrowful voice; a voice which was directed into the child's ear and seemed to have accomplished its intended effect of once again returning the little one to her natural state of a curious and wondrous calm.

Once he stood directly over Miss Leslie and the child, Shug Laing spoke harshly and pointedly to the pair lying seemingly indifferent to his presence from the depths of his brusque sounding throat. While he opened his spiteful discourse he purposefully removed his pistol from its holster and for good measure marked the head of the woman while kicking stiffly at her flimsy shoes with a measured quotient of disdain. "Up with you now, woman! I ain't got no patience for deserters and as things is presently situated your antics may stand to cost me a small fortune. Mind you, there's a lot a things I don't fancy in this here world of ours, but losin' out on money good sits right on up there at the top of the list."

Miss Leslie halted her soothing humming and replied to the harsh man while looking into the eyes of the promised child, "Ain't dat da way a you all, Massa, but dis here little angel be fixin' to shine da light upon all dat darkness dat gots its hold over you. She gonna deliver those a her own once given over to a life in da fields from your two men for a start. If dat means you gots to put me down like da animal you done thinks dat I am, den you go on ahead an' get on wid it. You go on ahead an' bring dis here child on down to Savannah where dey gonna sell my people off like stock widout me an' see just how far you gonna get. Jus' maybe you gots a heart so black you be up to killin' a baby girl easy as your own boy runnin' out in da open to protect a lady, but dis one here, she ain't worried none 'bout ya."

Mr. Laing grew precipitously irate in response to the suddenly alluring woman's insolence but the old slave wrangler was never one to manifest the symptoms of his anger haphazardly. Therefore, he issued a command as some form of a courtesy extended to the bizarrely contented woman before making the full measure of his displeasure felt. "Well now, Ma'am, you know how all of that talk gonna go for you. As such, I reckon it'd be best if you set the baby off to the side afore I work that nasty tongue of yours right on out of that foul mouth."

Miss Leslie looked up at Mr. Laing as if she were trying to decipher what it was exactly that made the godless man looming over her tick. Where was all that hate born she wondered before answering Mr. Laing as plainly as she was able. "I ain't lettin' go a dis here chil' 'cuz I done told her I wouldn't. So you jus' gonna have to do what it is dat you gots to do while I tend to her." Miss Leslie then shifted the baby to her right arm and proceeded to stand up slowly. When she was upright, she presented the fullness of her worn but capable and noticeably effeminate corporal frame to the man with the poisoned heart and the dark, beady eyes standing before her.

Mr. Laing raised his pistol slowly and steadily to the spot at the very center of the righteously pretty looking woman's forehead and replied rather dryly, "I ain't got time to pickle your tongue none, woman, but I do aim to clear some space out in that fresh thinking attic of yours."

Miss Leslie tightened her grip upon the child, sharpened her eyes until they peered into the depths of the wicked man's soul and spoke as if her very spirit had become consumed within by an unquenchable fire, "You ain't gonna do nothin' a da sort. Your men gonna come up empty up yonder an' across dat field by da banks a dat river. You'll be needin' whatever you can fetch for me an' dis here child back down in Savannah just to be getting' on home wid food in your belly. It'd be best if'n you get on point an' accompany us on down to da river barge at da flats afore da ones behind dat rider be makin' their way on down da road in search of dis here promised child. I done seen da witch dat be wantin' her in da depths of da child's eyes an' she'll cook your flesh right slow afore she be eatin' it."

Mr. Laing cocked his fist back as if he meant to pistol whip the woman while she stood prostrate before him with a baby in her arms but Miss Leslie's eyes grew wide and burned with the rage of her possession as she spoke further. "An' don't you go thinkin' for a lick I don' know what you'd be at right dis very moment if you hadn't had your manhood melted down for messin' wid a serpent's daughter all dem years ago. Oh, I know you, you devil. I been at your back since you hung me dead from da limb of dat tree!"

Mr. Laing was aghast. Not a soul south of the Kantuck knew about what his father the preacher had done to him for messin' with his sister back up in the mountains. He looked away from the woman out of shame caused by the white hot and probing light of her truth and into the eyes of the baby girl. There he saw all of the evil he spawned henceforth from the moment the preacher had taken everything from him when he was far too young to know that what the older girl was fooling with wasn't any good. Set within the large, abounding blue and yellow eyes of the child old Shug Laing saw the depths of hell calling to him and all he knew to do was feed the fire; feed the lusting for despair fueled by the wants of those forever chained within that endless conflagration burning in the nadirs of the child's tightened, black pupils. As such, he squeezed the trigger of the pistol frantically. Still and all and very much to his dismay, the second hand weapon he had procured down in Silver Bluff while they were closing in on the fleeing slaves exploded in his hand. The ruptured pistol then fell into the depths of the grass with the pulpy and mutilated preponderance of his thumb and trigger finger.

At the very moment the pistol misfired, Walt and Brother Eustice Hennessey were exchanging the country boy wares of their rather eclectic, yet somehow still uniform, shit eating grins which were pasted across their wanton faces. They had just uncovered the entrance to the once hidden cave where the remaining fugitives had in all likelihood taken their refuge. The heads of the two men snapped back in the direction of the pistol shot while they were peering into and poking around the edges of the rather tight entrance to the underground cavern with their rifles, which were once again primed and set at the ready to fire. Shortly after being startled by the slightly awkward sound of a sidearm being fired, the two man children of a rather rigid and hard-drinking sort giggled almost absentmindedly to one another whilst they wondered over just whom that nasty old cur, Mr. Shug Laing had seen fit to shoot dead at close range.

For his part, old Shug was never granted the chance to properly holler in response to the damage done to his woefully dominant right hand by the explosion of the misfire. The sight of the pulpy nubs of his finger and thumb reminded him of a trauma far too delicate to recall just prior to the instant he colored up white as a sheet and dropped into the bed of grass held flat beneath his boots. In fact, he was so starkly rattled by the sight of his mutilated flesh that the last thing the cruel pattyroller could recall beholding where it concerned that awful mishap were the starkly portrayed images of perdition lurking in the depths of the child's rabidly burning eyes.

While the two brothers remained chuckling in such a self-satisfied manner over Shug's certain dispensation of that patented and nearly inhuman vengeance of his, they managed to stoop back over and peer into the darkened fissure situated at the base of an old oak. The tree appeared near ready to drop into the swiftly running currents of the river after a century of standing sentinel over that oft flooded and severely eroded ground at the river's edge. The newly revealed crevice was a curious discovery for the quite brutal yet adolescent-minded Hennessey boys. The root strewn opening was nearly impossible to sight absent the prior receipt of some notable marking or a determined reason to scour the proximate confines beneath the eroded base of the old oak. Beyond the narrow barriers, roots and other sundry detritus of a purely geological nature concealing the hidden threshold of a sort, the strange and subtle gap at the base of the sharp incline of the upper bank of the river opened up into an ancient cavern in the earth. A prehistoric cave as it were, which was likely to be completely inundated solely in the event the river rose as the result of some catastrophic deluge of epochal or perhaps even diluvian proportions.

Though he could see nothing of what was occurring inside, Brother Eustice fired a shot into the cave with his pistol to gauge what he could of the cavern's unknown depth and veracity. Walt chuckled again in response to the cockeyed indifference of the act and called over to his brother, "There's times I was a wishin' these here critters were brought up with a little more fight in 'em. The varmints is always cowering in some dark corner somewheres and they ain't never ready for what's comin' to 'em for what they done. What says you to such a thing as that Brother Eustice?"

Brother Eustice was busy thinking in response to the sounds he thought he heard inside of the cave once his pistol was fired and such a thing as that man thinking at all was no small matter to behold. Walt, sensing that his brother was perhaps making his way along in formulating a plan to retrieve the refugees then asked, "You gonna ask 'em to come out real nice like or you reckon we gots to go on in there after 'em? You think a hole like that opens up somewheres on over in China on the other side?" Walt laughed like an amused schoolboy once again at what he believed to be his rather witty conjecture and concluded with, "Maybe we can go grab ourselves a few Chinamen whilst we's in there as well, Brother Eustice. I hears dem boys done worked wonders wid da laying of the rails."

Brother Eustice said nothing in reply and poked his head into the open fissure until he was nearly resting flat upon his belly. In fact, he never spoke again for the brief remainder of his life. The large boulder dropped onto his head by the third generation strongman who had descended from deep within the obscure rainforests at the heart of the Congo River Basin quickly rendered Brother Eustice's cranium akin to that of an egg which had been dropped smartly upon the pantry floor. What remained of Walt's rather ordinary corporal frame was tied to the leaning oak that had so opportunely revealed the hidden secrets of the ancient gathering place last used by the Native American tribes once indigenous to the area and wont to navigate the mighty

Savannah River during the dry seasons. The macabre state of those savaged remains was enough to turn even the crows and buzzards away. As for the small band of fugitives, they made their way north along the banks of the river in the hopes of reaching the mountains of the Blue Ridge, though both their plans and their directional capacity to complete such a harrowing journey remained tenuous at best.

Upon hearing the childish cries of Walt Hennessey as he discovered the fate of his brother and then proceeded to meet a fate far worse of his own account, Miss Leslie began to march out of that grove to the south of the idled carriage and back toward the road with the child in held firmly in her arms. She was hoping to catch on with a makeshift barge or ferry that was perhaps lingering along the wet gravel bars of the sand flats. Her memories of the brief moments of her swiftly fleeting yet purposeful possession were murky at best and her haste was a good thing too. The scurvy, blanketed dregs hired on to float the only flat-raft in the area on down to Silver Bluff had heard the same ungodly commotion coming from the far banks of the river and a short ways up to the north.

At that point, the two degenerate bargemen had finally given up hope that their promised fare would indeed be paid amidst so much commotion taking place upon the tabled plains of the Carolina side of the river. Beyond those rapidly developing logistical challenges facing the stranded woman and her abruptly inherited child, Miss Leslie had a stop to make, though she knew not what she could possibly do for the woman and the young man waiting on nothing but death amidst the cover of the bent and dormant high grass of winter. Be that as it may, leaving another human being to die alone and without a proper melody to coax them along into the light simply wasn't in the motherly woman's nature.

Travelling with the seven men now to be marked as nothing more than fugitive chattel of the deadliest sort was a young boy just beyond his eleventh year by the name of Amos Martingale Butler. Black Jim and Miss Leslie had never intended to bring Amos along, as the likelihood of mischance on their adventure was better for than against, yet Amos had slipped into the midst of the escaping conspirators at a time far too delicate to the full measure of their inconspicuous cover to send him back into the care of wise old Solomon's family prior to escaping. Black Jim had rationalized earlier on in the progression of their clandestine journey that Amos was likely to be spared had they been caught due to his age and therefore his adaptability and the possibility which existed for the presumption of his innocence. Staring up at the remains of Walt Hennessey mounted to the tree as a warning to all that none should follow behind them; Jim understood full well that such a presumption no longer held even the least bit of speculative truth. He also knew that the boy thought of Miss Leslie as a mother. Likewise, Jim knew that Amos loved her as such, and that the two of them together along with the child stood a fair chance to once again be indoctrinated into the society of slavery.

As such, wise Jim put his hand on the boy's shoulder while they stood looking up at the grisly aftermath of Walt Hennessey and said, "Brave Amos, you have been like a stalwart son to me since we broke free from the plantation. The feeling of a free man you now possess in your heart is going to be with you always. One day, you will know just what to do when the white folk open their eyes to their wicked ways and at long last set our people free."

Amos had never seen anything like the skinned remains of Walt Hennessey. They were set about to look as if they had been posted up on the tree by a long since evacuated yet now apparently renegade band of Cherokee Indians come back down from the mountain. Amos nodded dutifully in response to Jim but never took his eyes off of the mutilated corpse of Walt Hennessey, which was rather cleverly tacked and tied to the dutiful oak. Jim added, "That being said my boy, I need you to understand that we are in big trouble now. I need you to run along and see to Miss Leslie and that new baby of hers or else she won't make it back to Butler Island." The boy nodded again but still dared not remove his eyes from the bloody corpse. Jim asked, "Do you understand what I am saying to you now, my boy?"

After a brief pause Amos peeled his eyes from the corpse pinned to the tree, turned to face Jim and replied, "Yes, Sir, I understand. They gonna hang all of us that's here now if not worse. I'll be gettin' on down to Miss Leslie, but tell me dis here thing first, do she be needin' me or is it really da other way around?"

Though the moment was thick with grief beyond what Jim had known during his prior life serving the household denizens of the Butler Island Plantation, he replied to the boy on time. "In truth, it's a bit of both, my beautiful boy. That little one the Missus holds is an enigma running on like a storm that's set upon cleansing the very soil of the earth. You all will look like a proper family together and Miss Leslie and the child need you for that."

Jim paused briefly and then spoke sternly concerning the opposing side of the coin related to Amos's query. "On the other side of it, you'll be in need of them if you are to get out from under these evil works now before your eyes. Do you hear what I am telling you, my boy?"

Amos nodded vigilantly and Jim quickly bent down, took the boy in his arms and spoke further, "Alright then. You get on down to the river and see to it that those two special ladies are taken proper care of. You have all of my love, my beautiful beloved boy. Don't you ever forget what it felt like to walk like a free man in this life." Jim then patted the boy firmly on the back and commanded him forthright, "Now, get on out of here before something horrible befalls those ladies given over to your care."

Amos turned and ran but stopped before he cleared the final ridge up to the grove and called out, "Where's y'all gonna go now, Mr. Jim? I can find you there one day once I escort the ladies back down the river and all." After waiting only briefly and coming not to expect an answer from the choked up man, Amos turned to crest the slope of the river bank and make haste back towards the carriage in order to get on down to the flats. Almost inexplicably, the boy stopped and yelled down, "None of this here is ever gonna be what I'm all about, Mr. Jim! That's only for what God see fit to put in my heart!"

Jim smiled knowingly at the boy and called back, "We are heading on up to the mountains of the Blue Ridge! Maybe you will know us well there in this life or in the next, my eternally cherished boy! You take good care of those ladies now and you go on back there and you be your own man! Be the man the Good Lord above instructs you to be!" Amos nodded assiduously in reply and then wasted no time in making his meager wares scarce. Duty had called him hence and he was a God-fearing and honorable boy.

Jim turned away from his dutiful charge with a longing look set upon his face and with the warmth of the boy's smile forever set upon his heart. He then stepped past the old leaning oak, which was not likely to linger on past the downpours of the spring rainy season, and joined the others who had gathered up the guns and the munitions of the dead men. Once Jim had joined his brothers in arms, they were ready to begin the long and uncertain march following the river to the north until they reached the foothills of those ancient and mystical mountains of legend called after by the name of the Blue Ridge. Whatever became of them in the end, Jim was right with his heart where it concerned the boy. He likewise knew that he had lived more within these given moments as a free man than he had for the preceding entirety of his life.

Miss Leslie nearly stumbled upon Miss Sarah and Jackson Strait while searching for them. The wounded and unceremoniously retired bounty man and his damsel in distress of a shared condition had remained lodged within the depths of the overgrowth not so far to the south of the carriage. The nurse per the true hopes and desires of her heart if not any sort of formal training had managed to tighten a tourniquet around the ghastly hole in her leg and was tenderly caring for the gunshot wound of the young man who had perhaps given his life to restore her to her finer graces. Miss Leslie could plainly see that the young man was not well. His lips were dried out and his face pallid to the point it appeared as if the otherwise capable looking lad hadn't been given over to the warmth or light of the sun in the passing decade. Though she could surmise that Mr. Strait wasn't yet dead, she knew he wasn't long for the affairs of this world either.

The runaway slave mistress touched Miss Sarah gently on the shoulder as that one refused to look away from the dying man given over to her care and said, "Ma'am, we gots to be makin' our way on down to da river if there gonna be any hope for dis here little one. I knows there ain't much to be done wid da little time we now gots, but is there somethin' I can be doin' for you all?"

Miss Sarah angled her head to the side and shifted her eyes slightly upward so that she might bear witness to that precious child one last time. Her radiantly colored yet sorrowfully held blue eyes were gleaming in the sun while she responded, "There's nothing to be done here, Ma'am. Take the child and go before the others so certain to come for her arrive. This was always the only way and you have said yes at such a cost. What more would I or those angels above watching over her ask of you?"

Miss Leslie nodded in response to Miss Sarah's reply and rubbed the suffering young woman's shoulder tenderly to console her. Miss Leslie then spoke to the child's deliverer once again with the long, caring stare of her knowing eyes steadfastly fixed upon the sorrowful nurse who appeared to be gleaming in the low angled light of the still-rising winter sun. "Ain't but one way out for her now an' dat way bein' straight into da fox's lair. But I be guessin' there a reason for dat too."

Miss Sarah turned her back to Jackson and answered her angel standing in the morning light mournfully, "It won't be long before the reason is made plain enough to your very eyes, Missus. The child is the storm beset upon the darkness and we all is just doin' what we can to keep her on course." Miss Leslie smiled sidelong as she tickled the babe's chin and retorted, "I imagine you's right 'bout all dat, Ma'am. There ain't nothin' but a good storm dat can open da eyes a dem be walking the dark road now."

Miss Leslie wrapped the baby back up in the blanket in such a way that one looking upon the promised child could see nothing of her person but for the whites of her eyes and added, "Folks be by soon enough, Ma'am. There be a Carolina doctor we be a hearin' many stories 'bout down on da Island a ways on down da road in New Ellerton. You be keepin' dem eyes on da carriage. None to be passin' by will do it afore havin' a look see at such a well-made contraption, an' wid a dead man sittin' atop to boot. But I doubts dem folks be lingerin' long once dey be havin' a good and proper reckonin' a your poor man."

Miss Sarah nodded in reply while she stroked Jackson's handsome chin with her lean and capable fingers. The bullet had missed his heart, yet by not by much. He had said such sweet things about her eyes before he went under. She figured it would be a shame if such a finely put together and kind-hearted man perished on her account, even if he had come to this forsaken place to chase a slave bounty. Miss Leslie pulled her motherly hand from the young woman's shoulder and turned to make her way back through the overgrowth and out on to the road. When the worn down yet lovely all the same woman with the child in her arms took her first step onto the dirt and gravel of the lightly used carriage way which ran some ways off to the south of Augusta proper, Miss Sarah called back to her, "God be with you and the promised one, Ma'am. God be with us all!"

Miss Leslie tightened her grip upon the child so that she might quicken her step toward the river now that she was firmly upon the level terrain of the road and called back, "God be wid y'all too, Ma'am! You'll be knowin' da face of da child when you done sees her again. How lucky she be to be findin' a mother who done just lost her very own."

A short while later, Miss Leslie and the child had made their way down to the flats without encountering much trouble. A makeshift raft sat nearly dislodged from the rocks and mud of the shallowest depths of the river where it had been purposefully run aground. The ferrymen had been awaiting Mr. Laing and the others that were expected to make to the journey downstream. The foul looking men that ran the by appointment only commuter barge down to Silver Bluff, and even all the way down to Savannah for the right commission, looked at the solitary woman with her child quite suspiciously while they prepared to launch the craft into the steadily running currents of the deeper waters. Miss Leslie called out to them, "Hold now, please, my good Massa's, we's here for da trip down da river! Sorry we's bein' late for da push off!"

The two men wrapped up in wool blankets, who shared but one useful tooth between them, looked at one another in response to Miss Leslie's plea whilst a number of dark and confounding thoughts ran through their shifty but otherwise rather pedestrian minds. Miss Leslie paid the men's initial silence no mind and continued to hop step the shallow rivulets that ran through the gravelly bars of the flats in order to board the craft, which much to her dismay from that of a closer proximity to her scanning eyes appeared to be nothing more than a haphazard arrangement of some long split-logs tied tightly together with plenty of hemp rope. When the deftly approaching woman was but a few dozen paces out, the man stationed at the back of the craft, who now controlled the jury-rigged raft's solitary attachment to the land and was therefore keeping the vessel out of the forceful central current of the river, answered Miss Leslie back squarely. He was however, quite curious as to the true nature of her predicament, "No, Ma'am. We's here to transport some slaves such as yusself back for a good turn out on the whippin' post. Surely, you want no part of that and I ain't in no position right here to come on over an' get ya!"

At the same time Miss Leslie was pleading for a ride down the river, Amos was running south towards the flats along the Carolina banks of the Savannah. Upon passing under the rickety bridge of the old post road, he quickly spotted Miss Leslie standing before the rivermen with the baby tightly wrapped up in her arms. He called out to her, "Momma! Momma! Wait on up for me! I can't wait with the carriage no more! Someone is comin' fast over the crossroads and they's just a few miles out!"

Miss Leslie knew the sound of the boy's voice nearly as well as she knew the pulse of her own rhythmic call. The boy didn't know any of it back then, but he was Black Jim's son and Miss Leslie had practically reared him by her leave when the boy's mother died out in the fields of exhaustion some eight years ago. That tragedy occurred not long after the master of hands took an unrequited shine to the comely young woman. Miss Leslie turned quickly to spot the approaching boy, though she was loathe to take her watchful eyes off of the degenerate yet cunning ferrymen. To her horror, she marked both Amos and Mr. Shug Laing converging upon the still rather improvised pathway which wound its way down to the sand creek and then out to the flats.

Miss Leslie yelled up to the boy, "Amos, get on out of there, he at your back!" Amos turned sharply to his left to have a look but was instantly swept up into the arms of the swiftly moving bounty hunter. Shug Laing spoke not a word but squeezed the boy tightly into his arms while never breaking stride as he worked his way down the path and out to the tentatively waiting raft. Miss Leslie screamed out in horror this time. "You leave him be, you devil! He just a boy! He ain't done a thing to ya!"

Little Amos was slippery as a greased pig while locked up in the confines of Mr. Laing's arms but he could make no headway to break free of the elder man's hold upon him. Miss Leslie stomped her foot upon the rocky ground, and yelled out, "Massa, don't you dare! Dat lil boy done gots da shine a God upon his eyes!" The babe remained quite calm while wrapped in the arms of the frantic woman until Miss Leslie finally lost hold of her senses and began to senselessly rush the oncoming rogue while the limbs of the little boy squirted forth in every direction from the unmerciful grip of the hard-living man's competent clutches.

Shug reprimanded the oncoming woman sternly from the depths of his throaty and guttural voice, "Stand back, woman, or none of us is gonna see Savannah with our hides fit for sittin' upon. The boy don't lie. There are hardened men masquerading as marshals up upon the carriage road at this very moment!"

Miss Leslie paid no mind to the words of the filthy heathen and slapped wildly at his sides only because the wildly squirming boy was shielding the man's softer targets. Shug Laing shook his head but otherwise ignored the useless blows of the maddened woman as he approached the ferrymen without slowing his stride, lest the writhing boy break free of his stern hold. The rivermen curiously watched the gruff and rather serous looking bounty scalper set the boy down upon the raft after striding insolently past the flailing free arm of the irate slave woman with child. Once things had settled out some, the man about to launch the raft into the currents of the river spoke up on behalf of both of the rivermen. "We don't want no trouble with the lawmen, Sir. The fare down to Silver Bluff is gonna have to be double what your man offered yesterday."

Though the appendage was wrapped in the lower corner of Miss Sarah's light-blue dress, Shug Laing shook his mutilated trigger hand before the man renegotiating the fare required for passage and retorted in anger, "Why you double-crossing swindler! Just 'cuz I sure enough can't shoot ya don't mean I can't throw ya in the river and watch you float on down to Savannah!"

The man positioned at the other end of the raft cocked his pistol beneath the cover of the blanket he had wrapped over him loud enough for Shug to hear and interjected with, "I don't think so, my friend. Now you heard Mr. Nagy plainly enough. The fare is double. You can choose to pay my friend over there or you can step on off the ferry and wait to see if the lawmen will offer y'all a ride on down to Silver Bluff. It don't make but a lick a difference to me. I'll be a tendin' to my vittles down in the Bluff followin' either happenstance."

Miss Leslie heard the demands of the foul riverman to her left, the one with the pistol about ready to put a hole into Mr. Laing. Accordingly, she stopped punching at the backside of the bounty hunter's worn but well-made leather jacket and rightly stepped out from behind the maimed brute. For his part, Shug Laing slipped his good hand slowly into his jacket pocket, pulled out two silver coins of considerable size and placed them into the open palm of the rudder man at the back of the makeshift pile of knotted pine logs.

When Mr. Nagy had closed his hand around the fare, his companion smiled and carefully let the hammer of his pistol fall back into its prone position tucked up into the barrel of the weapon. Mr. Laing nodded at the man positioned at the front of the boat and said to that man, "Paid as agreed upon. Now if'n you don't mind, good Sir, may we please be getting' on down the river?"

Mr. Paul, as the man at the front of the boat was called by most, nodded curtly in reply to Mr. Laing and spoke to his companion at the back of the boat. "Let's go on get afloat, Mr. Nagy. Lest we get tarred up in somethin' that ain't no darn business of our'n." In turn, Mr. Nagy nodded to affirm his friend's request and edged the raft slowly into the shallows of that particular side current of the sand creek with his guide pole crafted of a fine Carolina hickory.

Upon the moment the current took a slow and steady hold of the raft, Mr. Laing turned to Miss Leslie and asked, "Will such suffice for you, Ma'am?" Miss Leslie nodded and drew the child close to her chest while a wholly perplexed look remained painted across her wise countenance that was now further worn by grief and toil. Upon accepting the gesture of her response, Mr. Laing turned to Amos, who dared not shake a bone on his thin and rigid frame, and inquired of the boy, "And as for you, young man, will our current arrangement suffice?"

Amos nodded in reply to Mr. Laing only because Miss Leslie had just prior and replied to the man who had hunted him relentlessly across the midlands of Carolina with an air of eager and subservient satisfaction, "Yessir! I ain't never knowed nothin' 'bout no Silver Bluff, but it sounds like good a place as any if you ain't aimin' to tie me up to a post."

Mr. Laing smiled for the first time since the day the preacher rendered him impotent and spoke to the boy kindly in reply, "No, young man, I aim to put you up on the back of a horse so that you might help escort the fine lady given over to your care down to Savannah."

Knowing what he did as it concerned the man who had pressed him near to half-way across the state, the sound of such a an otherwise outlandish proposition sounded horrifying to the boy. As such, he stuttered back, "No, no…no, Sir…I reckon…I reckon I be fit for the branch of a tree like any other."

Mr. Paul let out a howl due to the fact that the terrified boy's answer pleased his sour heart to no end. Mr. Laing quickly stepped over to the man at the front of the raft, though that one's pistol remained positioned near to the ready, and cussed him out righteously. "Your sides done be splittin' with the laugh of one soon to be a burnin' in the fires of hell, my friend. When your rotten gums is sharp enough to eat like a man, only right about then will I solicit your opinion."

Mr. Laing then turned his back to the man he had derided, though the premise behind such a move was ill-conceived, put his good hand on the boy's shoulder and spoke to reassure Amos by saying, "None of that talk, my boy. You is set to ride on in to Savannah like some grandee of the days of old. Though dem others there will not treat you as such, I want you to remember that feeling when these fine ladies is in your care in the days to come." The boy nodded with a look of wonder set upon his eyes. Moreover, Amos had taken enough comfort from the gruff man's words to then cautiously cast an outwardly visible smile upon his appealing facial graces in return for such unexpected and amiably offered kindness.

Miss Leslie was certain old Shug Laing had lost a bit too much blood for his wits to properly function. Still and all, she seized upon the moment of the big ogre's peculiar warmth and approached the boy, put the baby gently in his arms and said, "Meet your sister, dear Amos. Her name bein' Miss Margaret Anne accordin' to none but dat angel a da field who mussa told me so. She's 'bout da sweetest chil' I done ever laid my eyes on."

Though he was quite nervous to do so, Amos took hold of the baby and held her at rest along the protruding bones of his narrow chest. Miss Leslie smiled and said, "She be takin' to you quite naturally, my child. You two is gonna be da best a friends for a long time comin'."

Amos smiled in return to Miss Leslie. As his confidence in his hold over the contented child blossomed he dared to brush aside the edge of the Indian throw she was wrapped in and glance upon her face. The look of shock immediately settling out upon the young boy's face said more than any words would have ever dared try. Miss Leslie quickly took notice of the startled posturing of Amos's eyes and squeezed his hand to silence him lest the day grow any more traumatic for all involved. Amos complied with the silently given command of his mistress but the wide and quite visible whites of his eyes did not return to a normal size for a fair bit of time. Shug Laing did not miss the boy's look of surprise but he said nothing while he continued to move slowly away from the man with the gun set to lodge a bullet into the small of his back. The remainder of their journey down the river went without incident and the men approaching over the crossroads from the east never caught sight of the swiftly floating raft.

Some two days later, the boy's pony came to a stop at a patch of grass situated next to a bubbling brook meandering its way through the woodlands just outside of Coosawhatchie. There should be no surprise that the particular cropping of field grass was of interest to the tiring steed as the full stalks bending in unison toward the life-giving waters of the eddying stream were showing out particularly green for that final day of February. The sun was getting ready to set and the three weary travelers and the babe in the woman's arms had reached the point of being about a day's ride outside of Savannah with the intention of being set to enter the city under the cover of darkness on the ensuing eve.

Shug Laing made note of the boy's hungry and distracted steed and announced his determinations to the group. "We'll bed down here for the night and work our way past Honey Hill and on down to Hardeeville in the morning. From there we can position our outfit to cross into Savannah tomorrow night." Miss Leslie was tired and had no objections to Mr. Laing's suggestion. The clearly changed man had brought them this far without further ado following their trials out on the crossroads. He seemed confident in his ability to deliver the makeshift family of misplaced chattel into the heart of the lion's den before the Butler Island auction went live in but a few days' time.

A while later, after camp had been made and the ample yet spartan evening meal was little more than a memory and a warm feeling in the pits of their swollen bellies, the bedded down travelers prepared to take their rest for the evening. Mr. Laing had not said much to Amos or Miss Leslie during their journey south toward the sea. However, he had taken more than a passive interest in the well-being of the child from time to time, even if he had yet to lay his eyes on the baby's flesh. As there wouldn't be a better opportunity to know the current station of the man's mind before they were returned to the Butler Island Plantation to meet their uncertain fate, Miss Leslie asked, "Massa Laing, what gots you up to bein' so good to us? You really be needin' to get on into town an' be havin' dat bearish paw a your'n tended to afore it go sour."

Shug Laing was watching the stars gather up in the darkening sky while lying flat upon his back when he heard Miss Leslie's question come over from the other side of now quenched campfire. For some strange reason he was stuck on the notion that in a better world he wouldn't have to return the woman, the boy and the babe to the lamentable conditions of their captivity. He even dared to reason further that the four of them might somehow be a family of a broken sort and raise some cattle up in the midlands, though the feasibility of such a presumption was beyond preposterous for far too many reasons to count. When he heard the woman's sweet and melodious voice dance sweetly upon his alert ears from the depths of the settling dusk he quickly remembered the hate lurking out there in the night no further away than the road down to Savannah; blind hate such as his own, which had been harnessed by a darker order and was always in wait to promptly devour such hapless hopes and dreams. That the man had such wishes in the first place was a minor miracle unto its own accord. While still half entranced by the heavy currents of such lively yet nonsensical emotion tugging at his wistful heart strings, the one currently in possession of the corporal features of the man once known as the meanest, nastiest slave tracker in all of the lower Carolinas answered Miss Leslie quite frankly.

"Well now, Ma'am, I don't know how to say it right proper. But for the first time since the preacher man hid the face of God from mine eyes, I seen Him up above after I done near blown my hand clean off; back when I forgot even the very least of my mercies out there upon the crossroads. In no more time than it would take me to lay my hand upon a woman's cheek, He showed me the suffering and the discord sewn by my darkened ways going all the ways back to the time that branding iron soldered my knackers, just as you somehow knowed from looking through the eyes of the child. I could feel all that pain I was responsible for and I just couldn't be that way no more no matter how bad I still wanted that moment from the past to be undone." Shug then stared at the blood soaked rag dressing his raised right hand. He could see little as the moon was new but added, "Don't look like my old work habits gonna last long anyhow. My left hand might as well be my left foot far as shootin' somethin' goes."

Miss Leslie was stunned by Mr. Laing's plain and revealing words but her heart was touched all the same. She had experienced the healing revelations of the Lord upon the death of each of her three sons and she knew that divine power could turn out even a man rotten as Shug Laing faster than a cockroach breaking from the light of day. She spoke thoughtfully in reply to Mr. Laing because she knew his heart was raw and exposed. Having all that blackness ripped away from the entangled sinews wrapped around the very essence of his heart in an instant by a flash of pure white light sent from the heavens above wasn't much different than the harsh yanking away of the wraps after a turn out at the post. "I done knows what it be to be feelin' much less den human, Mr. Laing. Most folks, dey gonna do as dey told they is. You gets told for long enough you is somethin' less than a woman you begin to believe it, though it ain't never gonna feel dat way in da heart God gave you. I knows how it be feelin' to want to be made whole as somethin' born a da flesh and da bone, but there be so much more beyond what we given to see an' touch."

Mr. Laing connected the line of twinkling stars along Orion's belt in his mind and spoke whimsically in reply, "I lived my whole life knowin' I wasn't fit for no good woman. I'm not capable of being no good to a properly needy woman, and after not knowin' any better than to keep from bein' tidied up by none but my hard drinking sister, I ain't wantin' a thing to do with a lustful woman. I reckon I can only tell of what you might already suspect. I can tell you that such a life does indeed make a man's eyes turn mean. Still and all, had I seen what was deep in that little child's eyes far sooner, what could have been, Ma'am. Oh, what could have been had I seen things right all those years ago. If you don't wants to go back, I got ways to get both you and the boy up to the free states. You might find your way along up there, though I'm told there's just a different set of chains waitin' on those who cross over."

The boy was fast asleep and dreaming of riding right on into the front gate of the Butler Island Plantation set upon his trusty albeit quirky and oftentimes meddlesome steed. As freedom of spirit is the natural state of the heart as ordained by God, it overcomes the fears of the past quite readily, especially in the young. Miss Leslie pondered the hopes that accompany such a promise as offered by Mr. Laing but quickly cast them aside as the baby beside her began to innocently stir. She answered him forthrightly. "I sure 'nuff do be appreciatin' your offer, Massa. Lord knows I do. But I reckon God be knowin' there ain't nowheres to hide a child such as dis one but in da very place they'd least be expectin' us to bring her. Though I swear she done look as white as dat harvest cotton, she be meant to gets her papers just like da ones she came to set free."

Mr. Laing closed his eyes. He was drifting off to sleep dressed over in the peaceful comforts of a good deed for the first time in decades. Before he gave way he answered back, "Strange as it may sound, Missus, such a thing as that makes perfect sense to me. She'd be a living example of just what's gone wrong for all these years now. Maybe after I get y'all back inside and outta harm's way, I'll make my way back on up to the mountains and see if I can't do somethin' for your boys. It's been far too long since I had words with the preacher or Miss Daisy Laing anyhow. If nothin' else, the air up that way is good for gatherin' one's thoughts. Assumin' I can keep my good hand from the shine that is. Night to ya now, Ma'am. You rest well. Things gonna be far different for you all by this time tomorrow."

Miss Leslie tightened the blanket around the promised child as the last warmth of the sun had dissipated and the nightly cold of winter was upon the camp. Once she had the child situated she answered back, "Goodnight, Massa Laing. If you could be a help to dem poor boys all alone up there, I'm sure dat gonna be a welcome gesture in da eyes a da Lord. You can rightly see now whereas you was blind afore, so don't be goin' hard on yusself for what bein' in da past. You know, dat boy gonna remember you makin' him feel like he be a true man in da eyes a God for all his days. He be da one dat gonna be watchin' after dis here little angel. He gonna be free one day 'cuz he be knowin' how now. You done dat, Massa Laing. No matter what a man might say 'bout what you done in da past, you gone an' done dat for him."

Mr. Laing shifted onto his back once again and the family for an evening drifted off to sleep beneath the comforts of the stars and the gently shifting branches of the low country pines. Before the man was lost to the depths of his delirium he called back, "Thank you for that, most gracious lady."

Miss Leslie smiled warmly in return. Although she was well past the need for such uncommonly given platitudes, such amiable tidings delivered upon the final hour of that purposeful evening set the tender and well-tried woman's heart aglow. It was a fine thing to be called precisely as she was seen in the eyes of the Lord by one set out among the living and furthermore, by a man raised to see her as something far inferior to that of a proper lady capable of displaying such truly elegant human graces.

Back in Uriah at that very moment Miss Jeanne awoke with a start. Her child had called to her. Though she had dispatched her people on time and Edward was likely to be approaching Savannah, there was something to be done at home before the child returned. As she lay awake in bed, she was unable for the life of her to come to grips with what such a thing might indeed be. Once the dust had settled some from her waking dream and the walls of the room surrounding her were made manifest in the form of only shadows lurking in the depths, a dark secret buried deep within her soul teased mercilessly at the confines of her troubled mind.

She closed her eyes to dispatch with the tremoring memory from her past but saw only the face of the child's father upon the very moment the half-truth of their covenant had been sealed. Only then did she understand what the child demanded of her to prepare the place for her arrival. She began to tremor and quake. She would do anything for the dear girl. She would do anything but that. With the onset of war growing ever more likely by the hour, she knew not what would return to their homeland of those things once exiled far to the North. Yet, she suddenly reckoned that with the arrival of her daughter, it was a war that was certain to come. If for no other reason than to deliver God's judgement in the face of such an affront to his pact with the nation given under His aegis and His demesne.

Part II

A Time of War

Chapter Four

SETTLING-IN

❧

IN THE HOUR before the dawn on April 12ᵗʰ, 1861 all was quiet in the manor house overlooking the grounds of the estate of Mary Grice Decker and her family. The Decker clan possessed a lovely and pleasantly undulating tract of rich and fertile land, which was once an included yet slightly divided parcel of the copiously yielding acreage of Butterworth Plantation proper. The cock had yet to crow and the darkness which had settled down low over the land seemed to rest heavy and impenetrable. On that particular morning, the nighttide appeared as if it would refuse the sun's delicate entreaty to slowly lift its veil. The soft glimmers of first light eternally waiting to gradually illuminate the morning sky and paint the quaint and quiet country-side in the opaque shadows of the various trees and structures that stood sentinel over the vast acreage of presently primed, tilled and quite arable yet still seasonably vacant land offered no sign that the day would soon commence.

Miss Leslie was in the kitchen of the manor setting out the abundant provisions of that beautiful country panty for the first meal of the day. Her customary diligence in executing the required preparatory work would allow Miss Jezebel and Miss Betsy to arrive ready to work their magic with the early spring rations and directly begin to craft the morning repast. Miss Leslie loved her Friday mornings because she was given the weekend to tend to the children once the afternoon meal was complete. Though Amos was growing up quite well, albeit as a late-blooming physical specimen at thirteen years of age, and would be busy out and about assisting with the chores of the day, little Miss Margaret Anne would be all hers until it was time to bed down on Sunday evening.

Miss Leslie most certainly did not hear the thunderclap of the munitions spent as part and parcel of the South Carolina militia's initial assault on the Federal garrison stationed at the still unfinished fort sitting out in the Charleston Harbor. Such a feat would have been quite impossible given that Fort Sumter was more than a hundred miles off in the distance as the crow flies. Nevertheless, at precisely 4:30 AM on Friday, April 12th, 1861 Miss Leslie was promptly given over to a moment of great spiritual unease. Her consternation was triggered by what seemed to her to be the very underpinnings of the earth shifting suddenly and violently beneath her feet before returning to their original footings.

The abruptly troubled woman walked over to the kitchen window which overlooked the fine garden of the Missus, but little was revealed to her seeking eyes amidst the lingering darkness of the pre-dawn hour. Though she had always known that the time of the settling-in was likely to be brief given the resplendent yet tempestuous spirit of the promised child, and while the presently mawkish woman knew not what had set the wheels of some great reckoning of the age into motion upon that very instant, she suddenly found herself lamenting the passing of two of the finest years of her life. Mr. Calhoun and even Miss Mary Grice, though only upon the flashpoint of at last laying her eyes upon the wondrous child, had been so very good to them since they had arrived in Sumter following the horrors of their travails out on the crossroads and during the Weeping Time.

Mr. and Mrs. Jackson Satterfield, who lived just down the road and towards town, had seen to the daily rearing of the child. Given the present state of the child's outwardly proffered qualities, such an arrangement progressed along far better for the sake of appearances and therefore allowed the child to experience a more inclusive upbringing than if she had been cordoned off from the public eye or socially identified as the "mulatto" or "albino" child of Miss Leslie. Although Miss Jeanne had initially hoped that her daughter would someday be stationed far closer to her while under the care of Mr. Hastings and his eldest daughter out on the Baker Farm just outside of Uriah, Miss Basseterre was well-pleased with the supervisory efforts of Miss Sarah and Mr. Satterfield in addition to Miss Leslie.

Over time, Miss Jeanne became quite contented in knowing that the child would be reared anonymously under their care and also receive the auspicious advantages which accompanied the lovely couple's gracious standing as good and proper members of Sumter society. In fact, from the first day the once recuperating pair was brought to town from Augusta by Mr. Edward Calhoun in an effort to procure Mr. Satterfield's carpentry skills upon the recommendation of Edward's personal coachman, also Mr. Satterfield, the young couple had quickly risen to the status of cherished commoners. That the child was to blossom practically under the very nose of the witch who had sought to offer her up to the devil in sacrifice to that fallen beast was a mystery that the faithful woman simply tendered over to the perfected care of God's omnipotent wisdom.

Word of the official outbreak of war between the eleven seceding states of the South and what remained of The United States of America did not reach Butterworth Plantation until the hours of the evening meal. Many involved with the higher order affairs of the plantation and the Calhoun outfit in general had already come to expect the announcement at any moment. Nevertheless, the exhausted rider delivering the news from the telegram switchboard down at the post office did not disappoint with the dramatic and patriotic offering of his colorful description of the Union Army garrison's surrender down at Fort Sumter. For obvious reasons, the news of the conflict was shared discreetly in places such as Butterworth Hall; places where the slaves present far outnumbered the distinguished gentry and other members of the citizenry about.

Upon the hour the news of the war had officially arrived out at the plantation, Miss Leslie was doing battle with little Miss Margaret Anne over the proper ration of sweet peas required as part of the child's daily nutritional regimen. In the midst of that amusing row, Amos burst into their quarters as if Master Calhoun himself had taken ill or had already been shot out on the battlefield. Amos held his tongue long enough only to marginally calm the hurried breaths of his excitement and his physical exertion upon arriving and then blurted out, "There's a war on, Ma'am! There's a war on little sis! A real honest to goodness war! The 'Lapper Militia took the Yankee fort down at Charleston this very morn afore the dawn!"

Miss Leslie heard the boy's exclamation clear enough, though she was facing in the other direction while failing miserably to feed the obstinate child. Apparently, Miss Margaret Anne also heard brother Amos's exclamation, as she proceeded to throw a fist full of unwanted peas in the direction of the loud and obnoxious intruder. Amos chuckled at the spirited child even while fully gripped in the throes of near hysteria over the buzz created by the news of war. Miss Leslie shook her head disapprovingly in response to both of her children.

She replied to the boy instead of scolding the stubborn child. She did so because she knew Amos was standing there behind her frozen in place out of respect for his momma, yet about to darn near crawl out of his skin and furthermore, because there was no way that baby was gonna eat those dang sweet peas or listen to a blessed thing she said. "My boy, what you think you be knowin' 'bout Yankees an' da fort down at Cha'ston? Who been fillin' yo' head full of nonsense? Slippery ol' Jethro or coy little Marcus? Dem's da only two I done knows dat be allowed up 'round here at da supper hour."

Now it was a fact that Miss Leslie believed the boy. However, the preponderance of doubt cast over her response to Amos's exclamation was simply her way of getting the boy to speak according to the facts, or perhaps at least according to what Amos then understood those facts to be. Amos took a deep breath and thought back to what Jethro and Marcus had both told him on the way down to the servants' quarters from the garden. After taking a brief pause to triple confirm the accuracy of his opening statement, he replied with a readily noticeable undercurrent of excitement still oscillating at the heart of his cracking, adolescent voice. "Ma'am, you knows I don't reckon a thing 'bout no Yankees but for their blue coats with the shiny gold buttons. What I do know from the folks you mentioned is that said Yankees isn' at the fort no more and that such an affront is plenty enough cause for a war."

Amos's received intelligence was indeed prescient albeit not entirely accurate as far as what was articulated and relayed by word of mouth at the time that information was actually conveyed. Much of what Jethro and Marcus spoke of was a combination of reading the tea leaves and backchannel hearsay. Nevertheless, the telegram delivering the news of Garrison Commander Robert Anderson's surrender of Fort Sumter that afternoon had reached the Town of Sumter post office about an hour earlier. The root of Amos's sources were those that traveled to the plantation by horse from back in town and those that made haste to deliver an outcry into the town square and beyond to rally the perspective enlistees. In any event, Miss Leslie's point behind cooling the boy's excitement was to prepare him for how he needed to behave in the face of what was to come.

She replied in a calm and motherly tone so as not to startle the emergent young man, "My dear, sweet Amos, your grammar be comin' along so nicely. Dat new teacher dey done brought about for da Missus here has you talkin' like a fine young man. But you need to be keepin' watch over dat excitement a your'n when you be mouthin' off 'bout a thing like a war. Things is gonna' change 'round here an' you needs to be knowin' exactly how dat is so you doesn' get yusself skinned." Miss

Leslie then paused to turn her eyes back toward the mischievous child and spoke further, "Jus' like da li'l Missus here 'bout to."

Amos lowered his head to hide his grin out of respect for his surrogate mother but then laughed nearly uncontrollably when little Miss Margaret Anne threw another helping of peas directly into the lightly defeated yet still determined looking lineaments of Miss Leslie. Miss Leslie shook her head reproachfully, stood up from the table and then began to laugh with Amos until she came over and wrapped the boy tightly in her arms and said rather solemnly, "This time been a comin' for a while but it wasn' 'til your sister arrived dat I knew it would be right soon. Things is gonna change right quick once dem boys be havin' at each other for a time. Though it be necessary in some ways an' things gonna be far betta somewheres over on da other side, big change ain't never easy for no one. Dat's why sometimes dem ways a da devil hold for so long. You need to be keepin' your head an' your excitement down low and get to doin' what you be told. You be hearin' what it be dat I am sayin' to you, young man? There's no tellin' what any of 'em 'round here might do once dem gates a hell gets flung wide open."

Amos squeezed Miss Leslie tight in response to her words and her smothering hold. Based on the feelings of both fear and wonder he felt churning side by side in the depths of his belly at that time, he knew his momma was on point. He replied softly to her, "You think we gonna see the other side of such a mess, momma? You think little Miss is too?" Miss Leslie squeezed the boy ever tighter in return and answered him hopefully, "I pray dat you two do gets to see what's on da other side of all this mess, sweet child. I be prayin' for nothin' else each an' every night. I done gots to believe da Lord do hear me. I done gots to believe He do."

Amos smiled knowingly while looking upward and into his mother's pretty brown eyes. He then stepped away from her loosening arms and walked nonchalantly over to his sister and began eating her peas off of her plate until the little girl joined him in the act. The charming boy smiled and giggled at her mussed up face while she ate. He said to his mother amidst the lapses in his mirth, "I suppose I can treat this war just like I do the fact I got me a white sister, momma." Miss Leslie smiled warmly as she walked over to join the two with their impromptu family feast and rejoined Amos with, "Dat should be jus' 'bout right, my boy. No one gonna say you been missin' your lessons wid da school mistress an' master."

Not long after that rather telling exchange the three were smiling and laughing together as the promised child worked her way through what remained of the offering served up as her evening meal. That night while the child slept and Miss Leslie and Amos lie awake in bed conjuring up pictures of what the war might bring to their once relatively peaceful little corner of the world, Amos asked of his mother, "Do you think there will be Yankees in this place, Ma'am? Do you think they gonna set us all free and let us ride horses like Mr. Laing do?"

Miss Leslie whispered something under her breath to the Lord above and then replied to the curious minded boy, "We can only be hopin' it don' come to no Yankees runnin' 'bout in dis here place, my boy. But if'n it be da Lord's will an' dat's what it do take to return what been taken from us, then I hope dem Yankees be lettin' you ride a horse right soon after dat fact."

Amos smiled and said, "That'd be somethin' momma. I hope Mr. Laing made out okay after all he done for us. Ain't no other way we woulda been lucky 'nuff to come upon Mr. Calhoun and pretty Miss Sarah. Goodnight, sweet momma!"

To which Miss Leslie replied, "Goodnight, sweet Amos. I done hope Massa Laing made out okay too, though my boys would hate me for sayin' such a thing. But maybe dey be seein' it a bit different now from up above. Dat's my other true hope, sweet boy. Now you go on and get some sleep. Things is likely to get lively tomorrow."

"Yes, momma," returned the boy promptly, though he lay awake for quite some time reliving his ride down to the Lowcountry aboard his trusty yet absent minded steed, Spice.

By late May of 1862, the outcome of the war was still in God's hands alone. The stories coming back from the front of the casualties of the war were horrific, but a long-awaited and critical victory for the Confederate ranks was finally delivered at the battle of Winchester, Virginia on May 25th following a string of dispiriting defeats for the South out on the Western front. Stonewall Jackson's decisive rout of General Banks sent the outmanned Union troops then traversing the Shenandoah Valley fleeing under constant pressure until they had crossed the Potomac River and back into Maryland. The triumph had restored some semblance of that vibrant sense of hope which had the denizens of both Sumter town and Butterworth Hall buzzing upon the onset of the war a little over a year ago.

Miss Margaret Anne was but a season into her fourth year yet the promised child had gained the lay of the land and was seen as the little darling of both the Decker family proper and the various cohorts of laboring slaves and servants alike who worked the fields, grounds and dwellings of the estate. Mr. and Mrs. Satterfield had been blessed with a baby girl of their own back in the opening days of the new year and little Miss had quickly taken quite the shine to that one. Nevertheless it was always Miss Margaret Anne who was the luminary of the show in those final years that the innocence of custom served as the watchwords for the Calhoun family and their benevolently treated servants. Just about everyone who knew the darling child believed that little Miss Margaret Anne was beloved by all and for some reason or another had even managed to captivate the heart of the esteemed patriarch of the Calhoun family, Mr. Edward Christopher Calhoun himself. The look that came upon that man's gentle yet always discerning visage was a sight to behold when the delightfully impish Satterfield child was proximate to the graces of his presence.

The mid-summer banquet of that year, which would serve as something of a flashpoint in time demarcating the end of the old ways and the beginning of the throes of the deliberate and then sudden grind into the new, was exceptionally well-attended. The Calhouns had invited the Satterfield clan, Miss Leslie, Amos and few of the other servants of the manor in addition to Miss Jeanne and her two daughters, Maime Alouette and Shy Jolie. Doctor Emmett Bailey and his family also made the extended list of invitees. By the late-spring of 1862, the formerly declared natives of Virginia had been sanctioned as permanent residents of Sumter when Doctor Bailey begrudgingly accepted an offer of employment that he could ill-afford to refuse and thereby consigned his steadfast wife and their two well-mannered ten-year old daughters to the ranks of the local citizenry. In exchange for a formidable accoutrement of amenities and professional perquisites, the good and dutiful doctor had agreed to take the time-honored and hoary yet near to unavailing reins from the tired and aging Doctor Horace Cullen as town physician.

Given that such a diversely ordained set of loosely connected attendees had gathered from nearly every walk of life, absent that of a Union sympathizer, the colorfully arrayed crowd may have appeared to the few who knew that such a thing made circumstantial if not logistical or practical sense, that the little child had somehow managed to bring together all who had taken part in the drama of her earliest days. Of course absent were the deceased Stanton Oglethorpe and Miss Reedy Cline in addition to Mr. Claude Lemarque. The maligned Haitian tradesman remained in the service of the embattled trustees of the Butler Island Plantation, though much of the liquidation of the estate had been completed long before the war broke out in earnest.

In a world already corrupted beyond repair and furthermore maligned by the wanting will of evil men and their mephistophelian overlords, perhaps the celebratory occasion given over to the softer and more genteel qualities of those star-crossed and captive for varying reasons breeds of humanity brought together in the absence of expectation, even if only for the day, was the shining apex upon which the flash of the child's enchanting smile revealed to them all what she might have been within the confines of another time and another place altogether. But alas, the time to reach such a blessed equilibrium of delicately shared union that flourished upon naught but the bonds of their humanity through only the spiritually potent yet materially bereft talisman teeming with little more than the light and love of the angelic realms had long since passed.

Her true mark was the thing which stood to defile and stain that which sprung forth from the renewal of the once scorched fields soon to be fertile with the flesh and blood of the dead; those corporal offerings which were to be valiantly or forcibly spent as naught but sacrament to their rage in response to what the devil had condoned on one side and what the devil still lusted for on the other. She would strike at the primal chord of those dark principalities that were slowly, tirelessly and mercilessly working to enslave them all. She would ensure that the primal forces of darkness did not fully inherit the void certain to linger hollow in the aftermath of that fateful reckoning of their day.

The outdoor table at the gala was long and narrow in the way of a standard, modern-day picnic bench. Such was true but for the fact that the boards stretched on for some thirty yards across the pristine front lawn of the manor in order to accommodate such an outsized gathering at nearly the peak of the seasonal summer swelter. Though the odds were stacked firmly against such an outcome, an arrangement somehow came to pass, perhaps at the old woman's insistence given sharply into the ear of her eldest granddaughter, that little Miss Margaret Anne Satterfield and Mrs. Meara Calhoun were seated directly across from one another at the center of the outdoor table, which was impeccably festooned by Mrs. Mary Grice Decker and her young children for the occasion. Of course, Miss Jeanne nearly dropped into the grass upon making a leisurely inspection of the impeccably stenciled calligraphy marking the tags used to identify the designated occupants to be seated before each elegantly arranged place setting. She understood perfectly that the seating arrangement was no accident, as few things were in this life. Yet, she remained unsure as to whether the child would be seated across from her iniquitous grand-mother by divine grace, black chicanery or the will of both in sensing that the time had come to show something of their respective hands and engage the other upon the chosen field of battle.

Under either or both conditions, the delectable midday meal went along without a snare until the table was cleared by the servants to prepare for the dessert. At that moment, Miss Meara disengaged from her conversation with Mayor Tab Odom concerning the progress of the war and for no particular reason took a sudden interest in the child seated directly across from her. Miss Sarah was having a time of get-ting the child to finish with her sweet peas while Miss Meara watched on assiduously. Something in the subtle nuances of the child's refusal awakened a long since dormant memory of one of her own children refusing her the courtesy of something far more important than the rudimentary provisions of properly dispatching with the midday or evening meal in the presence of company.

Now carefully watching the child continue to refuse her mother, Miss Meara spoke to Miss Sarah Satterfield in an almost vacant tone, which by design demonstrably conveyed the serious nature of her con-currently running thoughts. "I do apologize for taking notice of your predicament with your dear, sweet child, Madam. Yet, I suddenly felt rude, and to be honest, rather incomplete in knowing we had not yet made one another's acquaintance."

Miss Sarah shifted her eyes to her left while stopping short of delivering the payload of peas resting quite deliciously on the end of a spoon. Such was probably for the best as little Miss was about ready to combat the continuing onslaught by using drastic measures which were not limited to the about worn out repertoire of her verbal entreaties. Miss Sarah knew full well who the woman was that had addressed her. She took a stabilizing breath and turned to straighten her position at the table while returning the admonished utensil to her plate. When she was eye to eye with the woman sitting almost directly across from her, she answered Miss Meara while caking on the charm and intonation of her recently acquired status as a proper Southern lady. "Why Miss Calhoun, make no effort a'tall to petition one such as I in the name of the proper graces. I am Mrs. Sarah Satterfield. Though I am a bit new to the wonders of Sumter and the elegance of Butterworth Hall, I have known the legacy of your grace and your radiance from the very moment Jackson and I made this majestic demesne our new home."

Miss Meara looked the plain yet pretty enough maiden over for a quick second and then returned her steadfast and piercing eyes to the uncommon yet remarkable and almost supernaturally appealing features of the headstrong child. She didn't offer much by way of flattery given over to the seemingly anxious woman, instead choosing to focus on what it was she was quite curious to know. "Why thank you, my child. You do look lovely today. Your little girl appears to have quite the disdain for Mammy's sweet peas. If one could only know the mind of those so young, uncorrupted and full of vibrancy. Where is the place you and Mr. Satterfield once called home before joining the family here in Sumter?"

The experience was rather unpleasant, yet Miss Sarah felt compelled to look into the elder woman's eyes while the heiress of the Calhoun dynasty examined the child so meticulously and answered, "Jackson and I made our way on over from Augusta, Ma'am." She was understandably reluctant to offer up any detail not necessitated by Miss Meara's request.

Miss Meara turned her eyes back to the clearly rigid or perhaps anxious woman and rejoined with, "Wonderful, my dear. How is it that you came to know Sumter as a place suitable to the needs of your beautiful family?"

Miss Sarah nudged Jackson, who was at the time holding little Adelaide. Her husband was also happily engaged in a conversation with a woman seated next to him. One that had begun as little more than the exchanging of pleasantries yet soon blossomed into an exquisite compendium on some of the finest literature of the period. Upon receiving the prompting from his dutiful wife, Mr. Satterfield asked permission to be excused from the dialogue of his enchanting acquaintance for a moment, turned to Miss Sarah and asked, "What is it dear? Is little Miss making a show of begrudging her sweet peas once again?"

Miss Sarah smiled vacantly at her husband and said, "Why no...I mean, yes of course she is, but that is not the reason I so rudely summoned you in the midst of your conversation. Miss Meara, herewith, she was inquiring as to our move out to Sumter from Augusta and I thought you might be the one to better explain our good fortune back in those days."

Jackson Satterfield looked over at Miss Meara and quickly spoke to properly indulge the pride of the matriarch of the host family. She was known to be tricky to handle, and if handed enough rope by which to hang one that displeased her, prone to do so in a very public manner. "Why, Madam, your beauty exceeds even your legacy here upon the magnificence of Butterworth Hall on this finest of summer days! I am Mr. Jackson Satterfield and humbly at your service. The distracted little girl in my arms is Miss Adelaide."

Miss Meara blinked and shunted her guise to her left as if she were a bit irritated by Miss Sarah passing the baton as it were to her well-made and rather handsome gentleman of a husband. When she he had put aside her distaste for the interruption of her interrogation, Miss Meara replied to the smiling gentleman in wait of her response and spoke as if she were above the eager young man. "I am truly pleased to meet you, Mr. Satterfield. I did not intend to break up your conversation nor do I intend to keep you from returning to such elegant banter for very long. I was curious to know both how and when you came upon Sumter as the place to raise those beautiful little girls of yours. Though they appear so different, they each possess such a distinctive and pleasant beauty."

Jackson sensed the danger lurking in the shrewd and notoriously wicked woman's query. He looked at his wife who kindly enough shifted her attentions to tinkering around with little Miss's grubbed up face, in effect leaving the poor man to his own devices. "Well, Madam now that you ask the question you should know that your son Edward requisitioned us from Augusta not long after Miss Margaret Anne came into our lives." Miss Meara found the man's choice of words beyond interesting and wasted no time in summoning her son from his seated position a few spots further down the outer row of the outdoor table. "Edward, my dear son, please do come and join us for a moment. Mr. Satterfield has just informed me of your prior relationship while he and his lovely wife remained sovereign to the state of Georgia."

The second Edward heard his name called by the very dark and difficult woman who had in fact reared him; he knew trouble was not to be lagging far behind. He had never told his mother he was involved with the little girl seated across from her and certainly dared never tell her he paid a king's ransom for a white looking child without proper papers wrapped up in the arms of a slave woman. Edward graciously excused himself from present company while he pondered what he might respectfully tell the old woman without ruining the celebratory undercurrents of the day's affairs. As he stepped up and put his left hand softly and reluctantly upon his mother's shoulder, Edward called out across the table, "Good day to you, Mr. and Mrs. Satterfield! Good day to you, mother!"

Edward continued on with his hastily prepared shtick before any of those he had addressed so ceremoniously were given an opportunity to get a word in edgewise. "Why yes, I am surprised you remain unaware but Jackson's father is my coachman. When we needed assistance finishing the beautiful home of Mary Grice now adorning the lovely meadow before your eyes I went directly over to Augusta and solicited Mr. Satterfield's talents upon the recommendation of his father, Donovan. By the grace of God, the lovely family has remained with us ever since." Edward then feigned a chuckle and added, "You really ought to get out more, mother. That was some three years ago now and upon the birth of that beautiful child seated across from you."

Miss Meara cringed slightly upon the mention of God and furthermore responded coldly to her son. "I have my routines, Edward. You should know that well by now. I am quite certain Mr. Satterfield would prefer the ambiance of other settings to those which I choose to haunt. Such trivial nonsense aside, tell me why the child looks so familiar to me Edward?" Miss Meara had swiftly shattered the protocol which governed the exhibition of proper manners in the presence of invited guests. Such was entirely expected by Edward; therefore he simply gazed upon the child until the wide, rounded orbs of yellow, blue and green with the slightest dash of brown locked onto his own. At that moment he grew a bit weak at the knees as he finally bore witness to exactly who the child portended to favor upon aging some years. Miss Meara did not miss her son's lapse in physical fortitude. She asked of him again, at the very moment he was attempting to recover from the resulting symptoms of his immensely profound discovery, "Tell me, Edward, of whom does the child remind you?"

The child continued to stare into Mr. Calhoun's eyes to the point that her sudden infatuation with the man she had never known began to make the others nearby and taking notice slightly uncomfortable. Edward dared not look to his left and reflect upon the heavenly countenance of the one great love of his life as a point of reference. She was seated all the way down at the end of the table with Doc Bailey's family and her two daughters. In the end, he did not even need to do as much. When the girl turned her head slightly sidelong to continue her observations of him he saw what Miss Meara had seen. He saw that the child possessed or at least mimicked what he believed to be something of his own childhood peculiarities.

As Edward remained silent and frozen in place, Miss Meara began to cackle self-assuredly, as if her cauldron down in the basement back home were boiling over with its toxic brew of lethal, black stew. She then openly taunted her only son, "Do tell me again, my dear boy. How is it that you came across the parents of this electric spirit of the world's beyond? Did you really think you would succeed in hiding such a thing right beneath my very nose? Do you remember who it was that delivered word to you of the child's arrival to the farm outside of Augusta?"

Edward could say nothing in reply while Miss Meara stood up from the table and shook her boy by the shoulders and admonished his imprudence further. "Do not play me for a simple woman. There is nothing of this world around us that remains unknown to me, my dear child. Some things just take longer than others to be made manifest. Open your eyes, my dear boy before it is far too late!" With that, Miss Meara began to walk across the lawn and back toward the house while she laughed to none but her busied thoughts.

At that very moment, Miss Leslie passed by to gather up some of the plates from those who had finished with the main course of the meal. Miss Margaret Anne spotted Miss Leslie and yelled out, "Mammy!" She then proceeded to hop down from the bench, circle half of the table and wrap her arms around Miss Leslie's legs. Those gathered in attendance remained speechless upon witnessing the spectacle of the white child and the colored woman. For her part, Miss Meara stopped, turned back toward towards her still stupefied son and lamented aloud, though none present could hear her voice, "Such is just perfect, Edward. Isn't it all just perfect! You have some hard learning to do, my boy; some very hard learning to do indeed!" Miss Meara then cackled one last time and made her way up the stairs, onto the front porch and into the manor home of her granddaughter.

Miss Jeanne watched the old woman carefully and bowed her head to pray while her baby girl took joy from none but the servant woman. Miss Leslie laughed awkwardly and called over to Miss Sarah for nothing more than the sake of appearances, "I be sorry now, Ma'am. Da little ones don' tend to be knowin' any better 'til their schoolin' start."

Miss Sarah's face became glossed over in the look of an open yet vacantly contrived smile, which embodied the emotions of fear and bewilderment swirling about in her head and tremoring along the softer climes of her insides. She answered back with a slightly shuddering and hollow cadence, "We's all family now, Miss Leslie. You have known that since we first came to town. You better believe that we's all family now."

Miss Leslie nodded in reply, looked down at little Margaret Anne and pleaded with the little child, "Run on back to your momma now, little Miss. You's gots some work to do on dem there sweet peas yet still."

Miss Margaret Anne failed to understand the need to maintain appearances and by all accounts and for better or for worse would retain that trait for the entirety of her life. However, she quickly took notice of the untold number of eyes gawking at her and Miss Leslie while they stood out in the open upon the lawn behind the long, outdoor dining table. As such, the child endeavored only to hide her head behind the blushing servant woman's legs and lock her arms ever tighter around the bends of her knees. The child remained positioned that way with all in attendance watching on until Miss Leslie picked her up in her arms and walked her slowly back over to the other side of the table and the proper motherly attentions of Miss Sarah. None of the onlookers dared utter a sound while the scene slowly and painfully reached its conclusion.

Though she was seated at the far end of the table with her daughters, Maime and Shy, Miss Jeanne had no trouble seeing either the little girl clinging to her former nurse maid or the frightened maid struggling to cope with the intense unease generated by being the spectacle of the moment. Doc Bailey and his daughters were seated with their backs to the two that had become the center of attention. Since he could see little of what had caused such a protracted silence amongst those gathered for the afternoon meal, Doc Bailey watched Miss Jeanne's eyes very carefully. Though she had remained stoic throughout the majority of the spectacle, he noticed a tear drop fall from the corner of the beautiful woman's eye and run down her cheek until it landed upon the hollow of her clavicle when Miss Leslie handed the reluctant but evenly mannered child back to Miss Sarah. That she was overwrought by emotion was of little surprise to the good doctor, who had reckoned long ago exactly who the enchanted little child was. For he was one of three still amongst the living present when the child was first called by the name formerly given over to her in that frozen old cabin so tormented by the shifting and disquieted spirits of yesteryear.

When Miss Jeanne realized that a tear had fallen loose from her eye and run down the length of her cheek she pulled her napkin up from her lap and excused her person from present company. She feigned a casual smile as she departed and then made her way into the parlor of the beautiful countryside manor. Edward had remained inanimate as far as outwardly appearances went, yet he did take notice of the woman walking into the house by way of nearly the exact approach Miss Meara had utilized just a short while ago. When the child was again seated at the table and the broken conversations amongst those gathered began to slowly and cautiously resume, Edward took his leave in a gentlemanly manner from those within earshot of an evenly keeled spoken word and followed Miss Jeanne into the house.

When Mr. Calhoun had keenly extended his coursings beyond the threshold of the front door, the Haitian mistress was nowhere to be found. She had boldly stepped into the parlor of the spacious and elegant home. The open and expansive sitting room situated at the back corner of the house also happened to be the very place to which Edward's mother had retreated upon publicly admonishing her son. The shrewd woman had sought a place to gather and reticently sift through her bubbling ruminations concerning the sudden reshaping of the grand chess board and Miss Jeanne knew it well.

Miss Meara Calhoun now understood why the soulless lords of her witchery had coveted the girl far beyond that of her own wants. Those hateful, sinister and lustful wants to snuff out the crimson stain of the half-breed's foul bloodline from the Calhoun lineage and place the line of Miss Jeanne's fabled golden cross under her thumb in so doing paled in comparison to the harshly conveyed desires of her hell-born masters, men and demons alike who most assuredly feared something moving beyond the firmament to behave in such an unnaturally precipitous way. Yet upon having seen the child in the flesh, the wicked woman presently and principally needed to understand what it was that the child possessed deep within, regardless of its undeclared lineage. She had not seen eyes so readily capable of staring beyond the veil of darkness and deceit which had been steadily and meticulously draped over the land as if such an unbridled obscurity were no more than some passing inconvenience of the times. For that same darkness had rendered many a seasoned and God-fearing man blind to His eternal light before driving them into the confines of that deranged and primal madness which spawns hideous intent.

Miss Meara was looking out the back window with the long stare of the conspicuously distrait that took in only blurred visions of the expanse of the planted field before her eyes. She was instead focused inwardly on those images conjured up in her twisted mind of the foul images of death and destruction that were wont to occupy the entirety of her thoughts as the war progressed onward toward its still uncertain outcome. After her husband had died some years back, she no longer faced the restraint of having to pretend she hadn't offered her soul up to the dark one long ago in an effort to win that burdensome man's hand and take on the coveted Calhoun name. Furthermore, the Pinckney clan had severed her connections to the Trust which held the ancient wealth of the once united family. Given that nothing beyond the presently quite unlikely marriage of Edward's only son Aubrey, who remained among the missing following the Confederate defeat at Shiloh, to one of the Pinckney daughters would reestablish those ancient bonds under the terms of her censure and in her day, she no longer saw any reason to put on airs or aggressively hide her skullduggery. She had failed thus far in driving her son Edward to pledge his fealty to that same awful patron of malice and despair but few of her waking thoughts remained idle or away from that consuming desire spawned by the hot whip of her now merciless and eternally tireless champion of the realms of heat and fire.

Miss Jeanne stepped quietly into the room so as not to startle the preoccupied elder woman, who was still quite handsome to look upon for those who were blinded to the murkiness of her soul. Irrespective of her subtle approach, Miss Meara sensed that the Haitian mistress had arrived all the same. Miss Jeanne had not spoken to Edward's mother directly since she first arrived in South Carolina back in 1843. As such and given the woman's taciturn posture, she spoke softly to the back of the stilled woman, though Miss Jeanne's heart was rife with the toxic brew of the swirling emotions of both fear and anger. "Good afternoon, Miss Meara. I am sorry to trouble you. However, your gentler graces would be most appreciated if you might spare kindness enough to endure a moment spent obliging my concerns."

Miss Meara cackled spitefully in response to Miss Jeanne's entreaty and then replied harshly to the dispirited woman standing solemnly at her back, "Ah, Yes and right on cue! If it isn't the Haitian whore come in search of my blessings of consent for her wicked and devious ways."

Miss Jeanne stepped closer to the hostile woman and abruptly silenced her before she could wriggle her parsed tongue to spit deceit any further, "No, ma'am. Your blessing is of no concern to me. I know full well where you pledge your loyalties upon the witching hours. I have come to beseech you to leave the child and Edward be. Though I may yet prove to be, they are not of the dark concoctions of your foul master and stand to remain innocent of all that we are."

Miss Meara thought for a moment before replying to Miss Jeanne's rather crass entreaty and then rebuked the beautiful woman standing behind her. "You have little right to ask a thing of me, woman of the night! What words are spoken from the watchful eye of that fine specimen of a husband of yours? You know the one, the one who died of a ruptured heart clearing the field for you and those little urchins of yours. Don't think for an instant that I don't know what you and Edward have been up to all these years."

Miss Jeanne pressed the golden cross to her chest just as she did on the night she had at last given all of herself over to Edward. If she was uncertain before as to whether or not she had rashly walked dead on into the witch's lair, she presently knew that she had. "What would you have of me to keep the touch of your evil hands from the child and her father? I have already surrendered all that I am able by decree within The Articles that define my pledge of silence to both Edward and your family."

Miss Meara turned to face the woman and then approached her slowly and thoughtfully. When she was directly in front of Miss Jeanne she spoke coldly and callously of her black desires. "You are a beauty to behold, woman. The ancient cross you bear is nearly part of the family now due to your treachery. If you hadn't possessed such a powerful and eternally valuable aegis I wonder how long ago you would have been lost to the sea. Your dead husband was all man by my own considerations but don't fool yourself into thinking I would have permitted Edward's coy little experiment with your Mr. Clarke Osment and his Negro farmstead if the treasure tied to the pendant wrapped around your neck was not real."

"I see," responded Miss Jeanne while giving further thought to Miss Meara's hateful remarks. Miss Meara looked away from the cross as it made her eyes throb nearly as evenly as the sunlight of a cloudless day. She spoke harshly again before Miss Jeanne could counter her earlier provisions and revelations. "Never mind all of that now, you foul seductress. There is a war on and the outcome is uncertain. Therefore, I must remain loyal to Edward, though he refuses me and the ones wishing to possess him. The child is another matter altogether that will soon be beyond my control. However, now that Edward believes he knows who the little girl is he will protect her at all cost. Since I have just revealed to you that I am loyal to Edward while such uncertain conditions persist and that Edward will pledge his life to shield the sanctity of the child if needed, there is nothing presently that should worry that pretty and so very lustful little heart of yours."

Miss Meara stepped away from Miss Jeanne and began to stroke the ornate wall clock adorning the impeccably furnished room and spoke further. "Time is such a tricky phenomenon is it not, my dear woman? When you desire it most it flies swiftly and direct like the crow. Yet when you desire what is beyond the given ticks of a beautiful old clock such as this, the hands remain steadfast and motionless; as if they desire that you dance with the disquiet of your torment until the mind flees elsewhere and takes refuge within the dimensions of the soul."

Miss Meara stepped slowly away from the wall clock and rather deliberately paced her way back into the prior stance she held standing before Miss Jeanne and added, "Yes, my dear. Based on what my eyes have seen, I do believe that I have been granted the authority to agree never to directly harm the child well beyond the days of this little war of ours. Yet you must do something for me in return."

Miss Jeanne closed her eyes so as to dilute the truth of whom she was agreeing to bargain with and asked, "What might such a thing be, Ma'am? What is one so compromised as I am possibly able to offer you in return for such a blessing? I am not permitted to pass the golden cross to one who is not of my own flesh and blood per the sacred oath of my ancestors."

Miss Meara gripped her cold, lifeless hands around Miss Jeanne's own, looked up into her eyes and prompted her firmly, "See me now, woman. Know what lies beneath the one you bargain with before I make my offer." Miss Jeanne opened her eyes and stared into the strikingly blue yet horribly possessed orbs of the elder woman before her. As her hands were tied by Miss Meara's own, she could not clasp the golden cross to take her refuge. She trembled upon witnessing the untold depths of the cold, black void that lie deep at the heart of the frightful woman's slightly dilating pupils. She spoke not a word but held her gaze firm.

Seeing that she had Miss Jeanne's full attention and that the beautiful Haitian queen had been given the facts required for her proper consent, Miss Meara whispered with a vile hiss, "That is good, my dear. All you must do is keep your secret safe and I will be of no trouble to the little urchin. Though I see the danger in such a thing, there are those I am beholden to who also lust after her essence. They will wait for one such as her to ripen and approach with care when I tell them what I have seen here today." Miss Jeanne nodded reluctantly in reply to the horrible woman and recited her pledge of acceptance. "I will never tell a soul of the existence of a child born of your son Edward and me."

Miss Meara's eyes opened wide with shock and she hissed back abruptly at the woman, "Make no effort to deceive me, whore! There is no bargain until you pledge the sanctity of the secret!" Miss Jeanne's mouth opened wide in response to the woman's harshly delivered accusations and she exclaimed, "What secret is there then that lies far enough away from the eyes of the devil's witch?"

Miss Meara shook her head and then steadied her forked tongue before she spoke further for clarity. "Speak the truth of it, whore! Speak the truth of it or fret for the child each and every moment of your life during the times beyond the very instant the fighting stops! You can't hide one so bright from me and you know that to be true."

Miss Jeanne grew agitated and began to plead with the woman, "Tell me what it is that you seek to know and what I must never speak of!" Miss Meara narrowed her eyes and studied the woman carefully. Sensing that the elegant Haitian woman would not reveal the source of that darkness presently within her pith of her own accord, the old witch began to forcefully induce the response she was seeking. "Tell me the truth about the..."

Upon that very instant Edward stepped into the room and called out frantically, "My dearest ladies, what have we here? The guests are beside themselves without the presence of your company!"

Miss Jeanne flinched with a start upon hearing Edward's rather stark and unexpected introduction, which he delivered hastily while he entered the room with the purposeful intent of cutting short the conversation taking place between Miss Jeanne and Miss Meara. When he was much closer to his clearly agitated mother, Edward added, "I wasn't under the impression you two were so friendly with one another," purely for effect. Miss Meara had no axe she was able to grind openly in the presence of her son. As such, she simply let the extent of her displeasure with being so rudely interrupted be made known while managing to simultaneously slight her present company, "My goodness, Edward! If you were not in fact my own son I would be left to presume you were raised with the savages of the field!"

Now knowing before that moment that their child was in fact present in Sumter and at times living on the very estate of Mary Grice,

Edward refused to let such an ill-mannered and downright reproach-able remark slide, "Mother! How dare you make such an insinuation that reflects so poorly upon those given over to producing all that you now take for granted!"

Miss Meara offered up a snide and rather deleterious screech in response to her son and quickly knocked him off of his high horse. "My suggestion to you, my son is that you go right on ahead and loose every last one of them as your God commands. I would go on and do it now before the Yankees do it for you and allow them all to fit your neck with a handsome noose." Edward gasped in response to his mother yet he remained at a loss for words while the vile old woman made a show of taking her leave. Miss Jeanne, who was quite happy to have the disruption serve as an adequate deflection from her prior conversation with Miss Meara, remained quiet and presented stoically as if nothing said was of any concern to her.

When Miss Meara was out of the room and well on her way to the front door, Edward spoke to Miss Jeanne in an excited manner using the airs of a pronounced whisper, "The initial fabrication of the child's arrival to the farm outside of Augusta was all well and good enough given the circumstances. But Jeanne, how is that you never came to tell me the child was here before this very day!"

Jeanne lowered her head in a show of her shame. She thought back to all of the times she had considered telling Edward that the child was living directly under his nose but for one reason or another, including her own dilemmas caused by the existence of the charming baby girl, she did not summon the courage to do as much. She answered Edward with the very first of the reasons that caused her to hold her tongue not long after she knew Miss Leslie, Amos and the promised child had arrived with Edward to Butterworth Hall from that horrible auction down in Savannah.

"I am so sorry for letting the secret be held from you for so long, Edward. When she first arrived and I had come to see her, I didn't have the heart to tell you that you had purchased your own daughter at a slave auction. Please, do understand there was no other way to keep her safe once I knew she had been taken down river by the bounty man. Afterward, the days began to pass and Miss Meara didn't seem to know any better so I kept things as they were; always with the intention of telling you upon the morrow. Always afraid your mother might one day read the truth of her present station in the beating of your heart or in the glint upon your eye if you knew the precious little girl was kept safe so close to that sorceress and so close to the focal point of your daily affairs. I was only thinking of her safety, Edward."

Having just endured the distinct pleasure of an encounter with his wicked mother, Edward was quite certain Miss Jeanne was correct in her assertion about his mother reading him properly under the premise that he had known the child was here. Such a fact however, did little to fill the void of his disappointment with how things had transpired regarding his unexpected discovery of the true identity of the child or the fact that he not only owned but purchased his daughter outright on paper and in exacting accordance with the law. The correspondence of her feigned delivery into the care of those he had solicited for the sacred task had done wonders for his broken heart when he thought she had been lost to them forever. Yet now he felt betrayed and undeserving of any measure of the child's future love.

Lost in the cross currents of his disappointment with both his own actions and the presumably protective measures taken by the beautiful woman standing before him, a woman that he was always and for evermore powerless to deny, Edward lowered his head in a show of both disapprobation and shame. He shed a tender tear for the little girl and for the state of affairs of the very world he appeared to have wrapped around his finger and subservient to his every command not more than an hour ago. Edward then lifted his head suddenly and proclaimed, "We must never let mother know the true identity of the child!"

Miss Jeanne shook her head in the manner of one overcome by sadness and answered her forbidden lover directly, "She knows, Edward. I watched her decipher the true nature of the child while we were seated at the table. The public spectacle she made of you and the questions she was seeking answers to were no accident. That is why I followed her into the house."

Edward's eyes grew wide with incredulity and he asked, "Do you know the essence of her intentions as it regards our forbidden child?" Miss Jeanne stared deep and long into Edward's moist and shiny blue eyes. She too was at a crossroads where it concerned her faith and her standing as the mother of a little girl she had already betrayed more than once. The confounding premise of her need to protect the child at all cost did nothing to assuage her guilt. She answered the heartfelt plea of the man that was her solitary forbidden desire in this life and the man who had swept the young woman she once was off of her feet and taken her so far away from the beauty of the coastal mountains and the madness of her Haitian homeland. "As far as her spoken word is concerned, she intends to remain loyal to you for as long as the war persists. What occurs beyond the day the fighting stops is a question to be given over to those who would be in a position to affirm the moment of her reckoning in the wake of such a calamity."

"I understand," replied Edward thoughtfully. "She is both mad and condemned to the realms of the demons that possess her mind. She will honor that pledge if it was given to you, as it was offered for a reason dear to her wants. Yet we must prepare to make due provision for the days waiting beyond the settling of this great reconciliation of a sort. As she slips further into the darkness of her insanity her thirst to desecrate all that is good grows to be nearly unmanageable. Unfortunately, my father was neither discerning nor diligent in dealing with the affairs of his estate once he took ill. He rendered me near to impotent where it regards culling her madness while she still lives and breathes."

By the look set upon her troubled yet still warm and timelessly elegant visage such was easy to surmise that the honorable woman had become preoccupied by another thought long before Edward had finished with his statement. Her response left little doubt as to the verity of that perceived occurrence of her distracted state. "I cannot be certain how she views her subsequent offer, but she also pledged an oath to hold the child harmless beyond the end of the fighting, Edward. However, she asked something of me in return and I received no occasion by which to satisfactorily reciprocate in accordance with her desires. You stepped into the room with such an uncommon potency that our dialogue was immediately halted."

Though upon that instant while standing before Edward, Miss Jeanne would have answered the same question asked of her by Miss Meara truthfully and without the slightest air of hesitancy, Edward had become preoccupied by his effort to calculate his leverage in dealing with his mother as it concerned little Miss Margaret Anne. He spoke in reply to Miss Jeanne as such, appropriately distracted and unaware of the consequences that may hinge upon her bearing forth the secrets of her soul right then. "No matter if she has pledged a vow to the sanctity of the angelic child or not, she stands to lose all that she has attempted to take for her own if she betrays me in these months and perhaps years of conflict."

Miss Jeanne nodded as both the necessity and concurrently the will to speak form the depths of her guilt ridden conscious quickly passed upon once again currying to the consequences of the flesh presented before her eyes. Such was if her need to announce a sudden confession while in search of absolution had been carried away on the wings of a dove hastily scattered by the hunting hounds lunging into the brush. "She spoke of as much, Edward. As long as you remain here or stand to be forced into a position to deliberate concerning the fortunes of the estate upon the settling out of the war, she will not move against her colored grandchild; no matter how hot the burn of such an abomination remains to the darkened purity of her beliefs."

Edward turned his focus back to the eyes of the woman appealing to his better senses and responded somewhat hopefully, "But of course she will not, my dear. She cannot yet bargain with one who remains without a name or a face if the war is lost and she will never chance pledging her fealty to something, nay anything, that cannot provide her with some semblance of certainty on the other side of chaos. Furthermore, none are likely to willingly inherit the grisly mischance of that vagabond, Mr. Oglethorpe now that the uncertain hours proximate to her birth have passed. Mother surprised us all on that night. However, my sacred pledge to preserve the child at any cost was made known to those few who need to properly understand such loyalties when I received false word of her safe passage into Georgia. The sorrow I was forced to endure when I thought she had died out on those crossroads was far too much to bear."

"I am not disagreeing with you in the least, Edward, yet there is perchance one other truth that stands to set the child free from your mother's grasp. Something that would free you from the burden of trying to defend the tender needs of the very one you can never acknowledge as your own."

Edward shifted his attentions fully over to the delicate yet almost kaleidoscopic and tormented expressions of the woman's alluring mien and professed his steadfast will as it concerned their child. "Such talk is nothing more than whimsical fantasy, my dear Miss Basseterre. From what I have seen of her she is as much of the world of your people as my own. She is also kin to both slave and nobleman alike. None have stood to deny her. Who but I will abide by her if the Yankees come through Sumter and the world around us burns beneath the mounting hatred of their boot heels? Speak no more of who or what may be conjured to stand in my place, dearest Jeanne. Whatever the words that now sit restively at the tip of your tongue, cast them aside as meaningless and graciously accept the honor of my solemn vow to eternally stand before my mother as it regards the child. She is in fact precious and dear to me; as is her mother."

Miss Jeanne summoned the last of her courage and her fading will to for once allow the truth to stand above her doubts and fears. She looked deeply into Edward's eyes and beseeched him to do no more than hear her words. She entreated him to listen intently before the moment given over to her to make right that which she had forced him to endure at the conditional mercy of an evil far darker than even Miss Meara vanished forever more. When Edward was silent and calm she spoke. "There is something you must know, Edward. Something you must know as it regards the now broken woman standing before you. The child is equivalently of the light and the darkness. Though I consider "my people" no different than your own, there is another reason why her capacity for both goodness and destruction are without bound."

Edward edged his body upward as if he intended to apologize for his earlier and accidental slight, but the elegant woman of uncommon repose put her well-formed and lissome finger to his lips to silence him. Such was the first time their skin had touched since they returned from the signing of their ill-fated pact down in Haiti in August of 1858. She kept her finger to his lips while she spoke softly to him. For she knew if his chivalrous tongue pierced the sanctity of the moment she would never speak the words to him in this lifetime; the words tearing her heart in two and slowly consuming her soul by the day. "There is a reason she was purchased by her own father to shine a light on that man's sin, Edward. Just as there is a reason she has disavowed the conscription of my motherhood from the moment of her birth because she knows the nature of both my sin and my treachery."

"Yes, she goes freely between both the provinces of the landed nobility of this hypocritical place and the shanties of the slaves who toil of the earth but such is not near to approaching the limit of her capacity to be of two worlds. You must only say the words I spoke to you when we were overcome by the want and the passion of our forbidden lust in an otiose effort to fill a void in our hearts; a void intended to be occupied or made whole inimitably by God above. Speak those words that conjured you into that unspeakable sin and the truth will be made known to you."

Edward remembered the words of that eternal promise driven by his insatiable desire: 'I am yours no matter what the morning brings or the enormity of the curse that may be cast upon us.' Yet for some unknown reason he dared not speak those words now.

He had suddenly grown ill at the paunch in considering the meaning of the words proffered from the presently enchanted woman's tongue. Those words remained so close to poisoning his ear and infecting his heart, though he knew not why. Furthermore, in his mind there was nothing which could be said that would change his stance as it concerned his will to keep the little girl from harm. In truth, he could have done more for her if she was another's child and away from the chains placed upon him by his society at such a delicate juncture in the affairs of men. Yet in looking upon the mother of the child, who was that one great and always forbidden adoration of his life, such a price was far too dear for him to either tender or endure. If she had fallen prey to the devil in attempting to absolve her guilt in the aftermath of their conjoining, he would still refuse to forsake the child in any way from this moment forth.

Edward pulled her finger slowly and gently from his lips and he asked of her, "Do you remember when you agreed to accompany me here from the docks at Jacmel?" "I do, Edward. I shall never forget the day. I hope you know at least as much," the reverent woman standing upon the precipice of the age replied solemnly. "What did you think of me then, dear Jeanne? Was I more to you on that day than the renown of my name or the command of my influence?"

"We were so young and full of light back in those days, Edward. You were so handsome in an unassuming way for man of such stature.

The others were so boastful and filled with the very pride which consumed them. I saw a man who stood above the wickedness that broke my father's heart and it was as if I would have followed you anywhere no matter the difficulty of the entanglements of the past standing between us."

Edward smiled whimsically and replied, "Do you still see something of that man standing before you now?" Miss Jeanne lowered her head and spoke to ease his mounting angst. "I do, Edward though there is much that weighs upon those fine and rather debonair shoulders of yours. That is why I must allow you to understand the true nature of the child."

As had always seemed to be the case over the passing of the years of their star-crossed union, the two would be lovers were once again set upon differing paths that were unlikely to be reconciled while standing in the beautiful sunlight shining in to the ample windows of the parlor. "I had seen far too much of the presumptive ways of my father back in those days. The visions I had for us made no sense for a woman of such presumed virtue and I am eternally wretched for such poorly configured wants. The lives we live here for the public consumption and the deeds of so many that thrive in the darkness are of such differing peculiarities. Will you forgive me my transgressions, dearest woman?"

Miss Jeanne looked back into the reflective and penitent man's eyes. She had never seen him look so raw and exposed in her presence and at the very moment he would have been wise to remain far away from the postures of one prepared to bear their soul before another. She pitied the man for his poor timing and his broken understanding of the matters of a woman's heart and the depths to which even an expectant mother will go to protect her own flesh and blood. Though the gallant man was perhaps missing the mark presently to the point of indeed squaring off in the contrary direction, such was how it had always gone between the two. Still and all, she believed she was beholden to the man for far more than the graces of accepting his apology. For no matter what might be said of his shortcomings in regard to what he was far too blinded to see of her in the days of her youth and what he failed to grasp as it concerned the complexities of the world around them, the man did love her dearly. There were even times that he had proved out to love her almost as much as he adored the fabled House of Calhoun.

"Edward, you owe me nothing. I surely did once love the man who swept me off of those Haitian docks at Jacmel but he was a man of another time and another place altogether. The man who belongs here was already given over to the commitments of this existence. That man was good to me, my adoring husband and my beautiful girls beyond the bounds of expectation. That man deserved better than what I came to offer him." Miss Jeanne then closed her eyes and waited for the response from the man standing before her. The response which she believed was destined to seal or lay bare the truth at the heart of the fate of Margaret Anne and her progeny before both God and man.

Edward lowered his head as he understood at least something of the meaning behind Miss Jeanne's carefully chosen words. "I see, my dear Miss Basseterre. I thought for a time I could have both, as little was ever denied me, but such thought was nothing more than a fool's errand when it came to the heart of one so noble as you are. Forgive me at least for that. Whatever it was that finally compelled our union and thus the moment upon which the child was conceived, please do not tarnish or take that from me. The existence of that moment alone shall be enough to endow me with what is required to see not only the child, but all of us on through to the other side of whatever evil portent or scourge of malice is yet to be endured. Do you understand what I am now saying to you, my dear woman?"

So it was that Miss Jeanne did comprehend what it was that Edward meant even if his presumptions as to why such a wish might prove advantageous could not possibly be on the mark. No matter, she would honor the man's desires as she was in truth beholden to him for a great deal more than that small sliver of decency and her debt superseded even Edward's insensitive insistence upon the secrecy of The Articles and the provisions termed out therein.

Now set upon the words she would convey, Miss Jeanne looked over Edward's shoulder and stared into the planed and dusty light coming in through the window of the adjoining room. She spoke in a haunting and reflective tone that mirrored the twisted fixing of their destinies just words away from being but a foregone conclusion. She remained baffled by the resiliency of the devil's subterfuge that seemed in that defining moment to show no proper course for untangling its venomous web. "There have only been three men that have known me in that way, Edward. The second was a brutish man who threatened all that I held dear for the favor of his company. I was weak and foolish so I obliged out of fear for his wrath. I was never the same woman upon giving into that fear but I believe my weakness in the moment may have opened up the door for the darkness that looms over us now. The child is dear but susceptible to the same soulless principalities of only cruel intent that her mother once was. Such is the only way she can possess and command such an inordinate amount of the light…"

At that moment Mary Grice came running into the room with Elizabeth Ann. Mary Grice's younger sister's arm was not quite what it was before the birth of the promised child but Doc Bailey had done wonders to bring it back to a rather useful semblance of working form. The limb was plenty strong enough to wrap her arms tightly around her father whilst Miss Jeanne smiled joyfully. "Father! Father!" Elizabeth Ann pleaded while she held the man tightly and looked up into his eyes. "You simply must come and see little Miss! She is leading the hounds around the yard as if they know her voice and understand every word she says! I have yet to witness such a thing quite like it in all my days!"

Miss Jeanne smiled at the spirited young woman who plainly adored her father and interjected upon the vibrant request. "Little

Miss, you say? Well I for one must go out and view the spectacle of such a wonder with my own eyes!"

Edward looked down at his daughter with a warm and welcoming grin. The vibrant and charming young woman was simply not going to take no for an answer. He looked back up at Miss Jeanne and apologized to her with his eyes, while she shook her head in a care-free manner and mouthed, "All is fine." Upon receiving Miss Jeanne's blessing, Edward exclaimed to his starry-eyed daughter, "Well then, let us be off before the show comes to an end!"

Mary Grice was far more grounded and less susceptible to impressions of show than was her little sister, yet even she was impressed. "I must say, you will not be disappointed father; you either Miss Jeanne. I do believe that even grandma Meara would be impressed." Edward shook his head while taking Elizabeth Ann by the hand and spoke in jest, "Let's not go running after Miss Meara just this moment. I will tell her all about the event."

The girls both laughed, knowing precisely what their father meant while Mary Grice locked her arm into her father's unattended limb to further nudge him along. Miss Jeanne smiled at the three of them looking so happy together. She was both excited and saddened by the moment conceded to her to watch her precious child shine while the truth of her motherhood remained hidden beneath a continuing veil of obscurity.

Elizabeth Ann let go of her father's hand and took Miss Jeanne by the arm to bring some sunshine into her heart. She knew the truth of the matter and had for quite some time before the child was born. She also loved Miss Jeanne dearly. "You simply will not believe what the child can do, Mammy Jeanne. She truly is a wonder!" Miss Jeanne welcomed Elizabeth Ann's embrace and stepped forward as Mary Grice took a playful hold of her other arm. "I am quite certain that she is, my dear. I am so happy that the two of you thought to seek us out. How are things progressing along with your schooling now, young lady?"

Elizabeth Ann smiled and said, "On account of all you once taught me I haven't missed an A yet, not even in arithmetic." To which Mary Grice quipped, "That, Ma'am is a minor miracle unto itself." Miss Jeanne smiled wide at not only the young woman's accomplishments but her excitement regarding her learning. "I had a very astute and capable teacher of my own back on the island in preacher Calvin. I think the man knew enough to fill the entirety of the volumes of the library back in Sumter. When I was a young girl such was a rare moment that I didn't find the man reading or studying something of the sciences. If I had minded my assignments half as well as you do, dearest, there's no telling what I might have come to know. Now, my mother was a seamstress but she knew every tongue I tried to teach you by rote and many more."

Miss Elizabeth Ann smiled with wonder and asked, "Are you going to stay over in Sumter tonight, Miss Jeanne? I would love to hear more stories from the island! Your old cottage remains vacant as it has since you moved out to the farm over in Uriah. You know father would never allow another to step into your shoes. Besides, Mammy Jeanne it has been ages since I've spent time with Maime or Shy."

When the four of them stepped out onto the front porch in nearly a perfected line suitable for an evening dance, it reminded Miss Jeanne of the happier times they all spent together before the girls' mother and her beloved Mr. Clark Osment passed on within the same year. After Clarke was gone her visits became more sporadic as many concerned with the progression of the Calhoun dynasty kept a watchful on both her and Edward while they remained unwed. As it regarded Elizabeth Ann's question of the moment, her heart told her that tonight would be a fine time to reunite the girls while Edward was certain to be headed off to town to get the latest news on the war and turn some cards.

"That sounds like a delightful idea, Miss Elizabeth Ann. The girls will be thrilled. They are not much for traveling as it is and would most

certainly welcome an extra night in the company of such fine and genteel women. The farm just isn't the same for them with Clarke gone.
It's hard to believe he died nearly seven years ago now. I don't know
if you've seen the girls yet, but at fifteen Maime is nearly a woman of
her own accord and of course Miss Shy will never be far behind her."

"Simply splendid!" interjected Mary Grice. I will send Eastman
over to Butterworth Hall proper to prepare the cottage for your arrival."
Miss Jeanne wasn't certain what had taken hold of Mary Grice's sensibilities, as she had never been one to be quite so welcoming or even
treat her as the free woman such as she was in times past. Perhaps
she was something of a changed woman with her husband Tanner
gone off to the war for more than a year now. Whatever the reason,
the change in the innately rather uptight woman was quite noticeable
and quite refreshing.

Once the plans for the evening had been set, Edward called out
while the foursome made their way down the stairs of the front porch
arm in arm, "This is such wonderful news! I will cancel my appointments in town straight away!" To which Miss Jeanne replied cattily,
"There is no need for all of that Edward. I don't reckon you were made
to endure an evening with seven or more ladies gripped by the occasion of a long-overdue reunion." Edward laughed and retorted, "Fair
enough, my dear lady but do not let my absence give reason for you all
to pick at my many shortcomings." The women all laughed and Miss
Jeanne jested in return, "Whatever do you mean, dear Edward? We
have all always known of your uncanny nature to so precisely decipher
a woman's mind."

The foursome continued laughing in unison while they stepped
onto the front lawn. Not long after that they bore witness to the promised child schooling the pups as if she had known them all from the
trying moment of her birth. The sight truly was something to behold
and the large crowd still seated at the extended yard table did not
utter a word due to their sheer amazement over the child's miraculous

capacity with animals at such a young age. Edward knew not what to make of such a talent. None but Elizabeth Ann was even capable with the horses and his own dogs were known for running roughshod all about the grounds of Butterworth Hall. In any event, the child's capacity with the normally awkward and unruly beasts so often difficult to set to task was beyond the description of uncommon.

From a second story window, Miss Meara watched on shrewdly and cunningly while remarking to none but her deviant sensibilities, "Perhaps she is indeed the promised one of lore. You should have accepted my bargain with your words, dark woman."

Irrespective of her vilely murmured words of the prior instant, having seen the heartfelt smile set upon Edward's face while he watched on from the side lawn, the shrewd sorceress knew that the woman set firmly in the sights of her oftentimes lethal spite had remained in-line. There was little left for her to do in regard to the blossoming child until the war had reached its anticipated conclusion and those set to govern this land in the aftermath of the bloody conflict were made known. There was however, the interesting case of the refugee slave later discovered to have been listed by the name Black Jim Martingale of Butler Island. He was a man who had recently been apprehended by a few scavenging men loyal to Miss Meara somewhere up along the Blue Ridge while playing the role of a Yankee scout. Perhaps, she conjectured in silence, it was time to pay that man a visit out in Collier upon the morrow.

Chapter Five

SUMMONED

⚬❦⚬

SOME TWO AND a half years following the mid-summer celebration at the annexed grounds which comprised Mary Grice's
plantation estate, at noon on Wednesday, December 21, 1864 to be
more precise as it regards that always properly marked but fickly perceived dominion of time, those who were responsible for the care of
Miss Margaret Ann were summoned to an informal assembly by Mr.
Edward Christopher Calhoun. While the rather surreptitious and
initially nondescript event was loosely branded as a holiday planning affair for the benefit of those not requisitioned to attend, hence
the reason for diligent secrecy and proper watch, Mr. Calhoun's true
motive for the conclave was to discuss the safeguards to be placed
around his illegitimate daughter in his absence. Edward would be
departing Butterworth Hall to join General Wade Hampton's cavalry on the following day. The regiment of the newly commissioned
Confederate Captain and belated entrant to the war was assigned the
hopeless task of endeavoring to defend South Carolina from Sherman's
Army of some 60,000 strong. The Union ranks were camped outside
of Savannah upon completing their brutal and destructive three hundred mile scorched earth march to the sea from Atlanta when the invi-
tations to the attendees set to comprise the newly formed fellowship
went out on 14th December.

The location of the somewhat clandestine meeting was some
seven miles outside of Sumter proper, north by northeast, at the fairly
novel and rather quaint Leonard Brown Plantation. The three-story

clapboard house of the Oswego estate, which served as the main facility and homestead for the plantation of some twenty slaves, had been completed in 1856 thanks to the diligent labor and agile mind of Mr. Ancrum Murphy. Though Mr. Murphy had been granted his freedom for his fine work on the home he remained domiciled on the premises and served as caretaker of the modest grounds surrounding the handsome yet rather unassuming dwelling.

Mr. Murphy was offered a suitable percentage of the yield to manage the labor but kindly refused the generous offer. He was a well-principled sort who could no more claim dominion over his brothers and sisters still given over to bondage than he could deny the fundamental God-given rights of any living among the various cohorts of his fellow man. Furthermore, Ancrum believed that life, liberty to pursue the wishes of his Lord and Savior, and the striving for a better future for those who would carry his name into a finer day were the unassailable provisions of simply being born unto this earth. As such and due to the fact that Master Brown had marched on down to Charleston to join the Confederate ranks in September of that year when Atlanta fell to Sherman, the one who greeted the separately arriving guests would in fact be the architect, fabricator and caretaker of the very home in which they would find themselves comfortably gathered.

Mary Grice was horrified by her slight where it concerned a properly delivered invitation to the event. She had pryingly discovered the existence of the planned gathering from her contrariwise invited sister, Elizabeth Ann. Though many would have scorned the means by which Mary Grice discovered the coming eventuality of the secret assembly, the eldest of the Calhoun children believed it was her duty to stay apprised of even such innocuously labeled events. Therefore, with her husband off to war, Mary Grice conveniently made a point out of staying over at Butterworth Hall on the evening prior to the gathering with the oldest of her two children, an unfortunately neglected yet rightly spoiled and haughty little girl near to the same age as Miss Margaret Ann by the name of Constance Emmaline Decker. With the stagecoach picking up Elizabeth Ann set to arrive at 8 AM on the ensuing morning of her stay, Mary Grice was up with the sun at around 6:30 AM and working with the ladies of the kitchen to prepare something special for the morning meal for both Connie and Elizabeth Ann. As such menial work in the service of others was generally far beneath her presumed station in life, there could be no arguing that Mary Grice was determined to know who would be accompanying her second to youngest sister on the trip from Butterworth Hall to the undisclosed site of the event.

To her surprise, only Edward's coachman and concurrently Jackson's Satterfield's father, Mr. Donovan Satterfield and Doc Bailey were aboard the finely polished coach which had departed from just down the road at the carriage house of Butterworth Hall Plantation. Mary Grice had hoped to scold her father in an indirect or offhand sort of way for his oversight of the necessity to have one such as her present for any holiday planning event, even if the result of the affair was to surprise those of his immediate family not in attendance. However, Mr. Edward Calhoun was nowhere to be found as the carriage approached the front circle of Butterworth Hall after entering the front drive from the auxiliary road. Mary Grice's disappointment was palpable though she kept the focus of her front porch discussion with her sister to that of the irrelevant and recondite or that of the mundane. Discussing such routine affairs where her standing as the oldest sister added to the self-assessed perception of her own worth or those things which her sister did not understand somehow made her feel superior to the darling daughter and apple of Edward Christopher Calhoun's eye. Though she was often times speaking of things that sounded rather frivolous or even absurd to her teenaged sister, Mary Grice was nothing else if not a sedulous woman. Therefore, the motives behind several of the more eccentric topics of their morning discourse were also designed to secretly nudge Elizabeth Ann into accidentally revealing something more of the clandestine gathering.

"Do you prefer the Christmas Star or the Christmas angel, dearest sister?" asked Mary Grice before coloring up her question a bit for show. "Though the traditions behind both are supremely important to the story of baby Jesus, I find that I take heart from the presence of the westward leaning star lighting up the night sky for all to see."

Elizabeth Ann saw that the stagecoach approached but she surmised that it would be a few minutes yet still before the driver would beckon her to embark. She indulged her sister though she knew precisely what she was up to. Touching upon such a sore subject for her older sister to address was simply the result of her innocent mind plainly revealing its responsive ruminations to a given question. "I do so love both of them, Mary Grice. I hope that Jackson and the rest of our boys so torn up by this war see the star as they drift off to sleep wondering if their tomorrow will be their last. Furthermore, I hope they hear the good news of baby Jesus from the angels if they no longer wake to see the morn such as we do. I do pray for our men, Mary Grice. I know not how they continue to endure in the depths of winter with the Yankees pressing down upon them so, and without relent. I have heard they lack food and proper clothes. As such, I worry that our boys will starve or freeze or both if they are not first brought before God by a Yankee rifle."

Elizabeth Ann caught on to her lack of care concerning her older sister's obsessive worry over her husband and clumsily managed to only add more fuel to the fire while trying to right her wrong by asking, "Have you heard from Tanner of late, Mary Grice?"

Mary Grice said not a word in reply until she stood from her rocker on the porch and approached her daughter Connie. "Dearest, the carriage arriving for your aunt will be stationed in the circle shortly. Will you kindly run inside and retrieve the biscuits in the kitchen I made for the gathering? They are on the silver tray." Connie went cross-eyed as if she were slighting her mother and complained in a manner unbecoming of a young lady, "Mother, Miss Sally can do it when she comes to escort Aunt Elizabeth to the carriage." Mary Grice grew cross and admonished her daughter, which in and of itself was a rare event, "Young lady! You go on and get scarce and we will discuss your manners on the way home!"

Connie shook her head, stood up and stomped her foot on the floor. She then shunned her mother by turning her head swiftly away from her while she stepped snottily toward the front door of the house. The obstinate young child then opened the door and shouted, "Miss Sally! Get that tray from the pantry!" Upon hearing the child mock both her and the dignified graces of the assiduously proper Miss Sally, Mary Grice turned away from Elizabeth Ann, grabbed hold of her child rudely and sharply escorted Connie the rest of the way into the front hall of the house. She then promptly shut the door behind them.

Elizabeth Ann laughed contritely upon hearing Mary Grice tear into the child through the glass of the ornate front door. Little Connie was growing more rotten by the day in the absence of her father. As her pleasant titter faded into the chill of the morning air of an overcast December sky, Elizabeth Ann watched Mr. Satterfield patiently lead the carriage team up the grand drive of Butterworth Hall and past the drive's bald yet still beautiful rows of overarching magnolias. She hoped the carriage would outpace her sister's return but knowing Mary Grice as she did, she was not hopeful about the prospects of such pleasant conjecture. She did however feel quite badly for so insensitively reminding her sister of Tanner's plight and leaving poor Connie to promptly know the aftereffects of such inopportune candor, though she believed the child probably deserved a similar excoriation under any circumstance.

When she returned to the front porch, Mary Grice was carrying the tray of buttermilk biscuits. Miss Sally had opened the door for her and stood patiently in wait. Mary Grice was suitably embarrassed by her daughter's behavior and at the same time once again agitated by her exclusion from the upcoming assemblage. She spoke sternly into the winter chill. "Elizabeth Ann, you should know better than to mention the girl's father in front of her. There has been no word from him out on the Western Front for months if you must know. As her behavior would indicate, the little child is clearly beside herself and quite frankly so am I."

Elizabeth Ann abhorred being placed at the center of controversy. Therefore, she simply apologized in persuasively remorseful fashion. "Please, do accept my sincerest apologies on behalf of the both of you, Mary Grice. I lost my head for moment. I had no idea that you had not received word from Tanner for such a span. I do hope and pray that he will return to you all soon enough. He is a good man and a gracious father to his daughters."

Mary Grice reached forward with the tray of biscuits she held in both hands with the intention of giving it over to Elizabeth Ann and retorted rudely to her sister for good measure, "The child also knows that father will be leaving tomorrow morning for Charleston to pledge his services to General Hampton. Do not be so callous as it concerns her feelings!"

Elizabeth Ann accepted the tray from her sister and replied, "I am truly sorry, dearest sister. There is so much to consider as the world readies to burn beneath our feet. Shall I tell father that you are awaiting him when he returns from planning your holiday surprise?" Mary Grice shook her head and answered, "No, with all that remains to be done I have no time to await you all like some hand maiden." Elizabeth Ann frowned and rejoined her sister mournfully. "Do not let your anger with me affect your feelings for father. He will be beside his mercies if you are not present before he departs." Mary Grice closed her eyes and offered over her reply quite spitefully, "Father could have had me to your gathering if he was that concerned over my whereabouts before he departed."

Doc Bailey yelled up the elegant steps of the grand front porch to the two ladies while he made his way over from the carriage now stopped and ready to accept additional passengers, "Good morning, beautiful ladies! I hope your day has begun on a bright note and you have managed to retain something of your holiday spirit in the face of such adversity."

Upon further consideration, Mary Grice was in fact a bit surprised to see Doc Bailey as there was no end to the manifest maladies of the malnourished back in town. Beyond the question of the always unbearable demand for his immediate attentions, the good doctor certainly did not fit the profile of one given over to the more effeminate qualities required to prepare for a secretive and festive holiday event. In point of fact, given the suddenly odd circumstances surrounding the doctor's presence, Mary Grice's attentions had been immediately diverted from the trifling manifestations of her displeasure with the oversight of her inclusion in the clandestine gathering to Doc Bailey's unexpected arrival. The tried woman called down to the carriage riders as if the effort to do so was far beneath her. "Why as I live and breathe, if it isn't Doctor Emmett Bailey in the flesh; and a good morning to you as well. I had presumed the days of you accompanying Elizabeth Ann around town like a maidservant had long since passed."

Doc Bailey paused and looked up as he approached the base of the steps to the beautiful and magnificent grand veranda of Butterworth Hall. He intended to size up Miss Decker before he approached upward to escort Miss Elizabeth Ann to the carriage. Doc's thoughts were quick as greased lightning in attempting to get at the immediacy of the grievance behind Mary Grice's sour salutation. However, his propensity to proceed upward with one so deviant and childish in wait, especially when she was turned out without proper supervision while in the throes of one of her moods, was a few unsettled moments in the making.

Doc remained silent until he took a bow before Miss Decker at the top of the stairs and rejoined her while simultaneously offering his guide hand to Elizabeth Ann. "Mrs. Decker, you look as lovely as always. A radiant vision amidst our otherwise parched and starved land yearning to break free of the torments of war. As it concerns my chaperoning of your sister, nothing could be farther the truth. Such is now and such shall always be that her prospering heart is the radiant light that illuminates my path."

Elizabeth Ann blushed mightily at the doctor's deflecting flattery. Though she was fast approaching the years suitable to be married off and in spite of her innocent beauty, her natural modesty and the war had left her bereft of the conditions required to know the differences between the gentlemanly subtleties and more evocative innuendoes layered deep within the kind and becoming words fit for public consumption of a man of any sort. Her sister Mary Grice was rather the opposite. She was rumored to know the absolute devilry of a few men beyond that of her own husband, but none would dare speak of such things openly, or perhaps even in private.

Mary Grice poked at the good doctor further in an effort to further her own agenda. "What will the abounding masses of our wartime infirmed stand to do during the hours of your inconceivable indisposition, Doctor Bailey?" Doctor Bailey knew the sort of woman Mary Grice once was when left unattended with those predisposed to the poorer graces of the small hours. The Doctor's strange ability to at times seemingly operate beyond the command of her father had filled the once lustful young woman with intrigue enough to coax those demons out upon the flashing of an ill-advised parcel of time. As incredulous as such a thing might sound given that the woman of such esteem was married and into the years of her child rearing, the rebuttal was never forgotten.

Doctor Bailey said nothing as he whisked Elizabeth Ann down the steps while taking note of the miraculous improvement in her arm of late. The long and slender appendage suddenly looked as if those years of anguishing limitation and rehabilitation, which had done wonders of their accord, had never happened at all. When the two were at the bottom of the steps and safely away Doc Bailed turned back to Mary Grice and answered her rather cattily, "Miss Greta and Miss Sula will be at the office all day tending to the suffering in my absence. I do recommend that you join them in their most gracious efforts on behalf of all who face a need if you are indeed worried they will be overwhelmed."

Mary Grice looked carefully down at Doc Bailey and nodded coarsely, as if to convey that such an inconvenience deserved no more than a tremoring of her thought let alone something of her precious time and vitality. The Doctor's response was quite ingenious as it concerned putting an end to the prying and patronizing ways of Mary Grice at that moment, yet as far as the long game would go he had made a grievous error. Mary Grace bided her time patiently in wait to respond as Doctor Bailey and Elizabeth Ann boarded the carriage. When the doctor and her sister were set and ready to depart and precisely before Mr. Satterfield issued his command to commence, while likewise flapping at the reins to urge onward the very last of his horses still boarding at the plantation and not in engaged in the services of war, Mary Grice called down in earnest while striking the pose of one delivering a suddenly remembered afterthought, "What then of Amos, Doctor Bailey? I was told he was to take his leave again today to assist you back in town."

Doctor Bailey looked sharply over to Elizabeth Ann while they sat facing one another in the carriage. Elizabeth Ann quickly took notice of the present dilemma and sweetly called back up to her sister. She spoke as if there were not a trifle of worry to be cast about where it regarded Mary Grice's ancillary concern. "Amos is to be watching over little Miss today, sister. I'm certain he merely acted a bit rashly by accepting Doctor Bailey's earlier invitation. Miss Leslie is the official administrator for the planning committee and you know that Miss Sarah has been over in Columbia making something of use with the old threads since the trains stopped running from Atlanta."

"Yes indeed," added Doc Bailey while displaying the requisite touch of a forgetful mien. "The boy doth speak the truth though. The two will be at my office in the afternoon with Miss Greta and Miss Sula passing out some little Christmas treats confectioned by Miss Eustice and our girls!"

"Simply wonderful," returned Mary Grice snidely as she cunningly devised a plan for the after-hours that would catch them both in their shameful lie. "Perhaps Connie and I shall indeed join them in the afternoon to assist with such a show of goodwill toward our fellow man in these trying times!"

Doc Bailey shook his head with concern and Elizabeth Ann subtly raised her open palm to let the presently frazzled man know that she would be the one to end the discussion. "Such a deed of kindness would be a truly amazing gesture of you both, Mary Grice. The thought of the act alone warms my heart to no end! There are so many among us in need!"

Mr. Satterfield, picking up on the need to put an expedited end to that long and uncomfortable goodbye, gave his call to the leads of his team. "Get on now, Big Luke, up with it, Saul!" Though they were perhaps a bit long in the tooth presently for such a vocation, the trusty steeds were all that were available to pull the carriage during such an enduring turn of miserable war. No matter, the dutiful old beasts relished in the honorable nature of their given task and wasted not a moment in proudly taking to their march.

Mary Grice crooked spitefully away from the slowly turning wheels of the carriage as they began to gather momentum against the sound of clacking hooves working their way down the cobblestone portion of the upper drive. She took two quick and determined steps forward and called back over her shoulder to her sister upon preparing to enter the house as Miss Sally alertly opened the door for her, "Sister, in your haste you forgot the biscuits!" To which Miss Elizabeth Ann called back while nudging her pretty, ornamented head out the window, "Take them into town with you, dearest sister. There is such need!"

Mary Grice stepped back out on to the porch, grabbed the overlooked sterling silver serving tray topped with still-warm country biscuits and pushed it harshly at Miss Sally by way of silently lashing out at the unsuspecting woman for no particular reason. That is to say no particular reason apart from the fact she was present and beneath her. The angry woman then calmed a bit upon taking a deep and hearty breath and commanded the still bonded maidservant. "Have Mackey deliver these to the doctor's office in town." "Yes, ma'am," was poor Miss Sally's only answer back as she shifted quickly to steady the glimmering tray while Mary Grice turned from her and stormed up the stairs and into the sweetly remembered haunts of her childhood bed chamber. Only after Mary Grice slammed the door to her room with due measure of audible authority did Miss Sally scurry back to the pantry to care for the forgotten morsels.

A good while later, the invitees to Edward's secret conclave were gathered and nervously sipping tea in the living room of the Leonard Brown Plantation. The time of day was precisely noon, yet there was no sign of Edward. Miss Leslie, little Miss and Amos were sitting on three stools assembled in the corner of the room near the old careworn piano. Doc Bailey, Mr. Satterfield and Mr. Sommers remained engaged in conversation while standing before the wide, doorless entranceway to the room, which opened into the quaint front foyer. Miss Sarah, Miss Elizabeth Ann and Miss Jeanne were sporadically conversant from their seated postures on the plush yet antiquated sofa.

The three uneasy women were far too on edge to allow the forced smiles accompanying their offered pleasantries to hold for more than brief fits and starts offered in conjunction with their conversant gesturing concerning the holiday season and the effects of the war on those they knew and held dear. Miss Jeanne and Miss Sarah had shared a ride over from Columbia, where both women had dreadfully made note of the threadbare defenses that lay in wait to stop the march of Sherman's brutal and insuperable army; an army already widely known to deliver naught but death and destruction in its wake. The fear in the eyes of the two women as they watched their doomed brothers and sisters of the cause vainly throw up nothing more than the veil of proper defense works around the perimeter of the city was palpable.

At around fifteen minutes past the hour, Ancrum Murphy stepped by Doc and Mr. Satterfield and took a position standing in the center of the room near the round, wooden tea table. When all eyes were upon him, Mr. Murphy spoke clearly to the congregation. His voice carried smoothly and effortlessly throughout the quaint and comfortable room. To those listening to the pure, unwavering and harmonic voice of the steadfast man it seemed as if his words were to be treated as nothing more than matters of present fact. "Good day once again, ladies and gentlemen gathered at the request of Mr. Edward Calhoun. The pleasure of welcoming you to the Leonard Brown Plantation is my own. For those with whom I have not yet had the opportunity to make a proper introduction, I am Ancrum Murphy, plantation groundskeeper. For those that know me well, Mr. Murphy then smiled at Miss Jeanne; you must understand that every provision of our humble homestead remains at your command for as long as you see fit. For the benefit of all present, you should be aware that Mr. Calhoun will not be arriving until sometime around the top of the one o'clock hour. I am aware Master Amos and little Miss Satterfield will need to depart for town. I shall begin the journey with them upon the instant."

Miss Leslie had been made aware of the need for Amos and little Miss to make appearances at Doc Bailey's office back in town by

Elizabeth Ann. As such, she kissed her children heartily and directed them towards Mr. Murphy as he continued to stand stoically at the center of the room not but three or four paces away from the happy family born of such tragic necessity. Miss Sarah stood up from her seated position upon the sofa to hug little Miss. She was heartbroken by the news of her surrogate daughter's departure. She had seen little of the charming light of her heart while she and her daughter by way of natural childbirth, Miss Adelaide Satterfield had been stationed in Columbia with the emergency outfit of seamstresses trying to keep the soldiers furnished in at least something resembling proper military attire. Miss Jeanne watched the women kiss and embrace her daughter while her heart grew heavy and her shimmering light eyes, which contrasted so exotically against her olive winter skin, grew sullen. Not knowing how Miss Margaret Anne might react, she dared not complicate matters by approaching the little angel at such a difficult juncture for all present in the room.

While little Miss dispensed with her heartfelt goodbyes, Doctor Bailey asked of Mr. Murphy, "If you will be so kind as to regard the necessity of my pardon in asking you such, Mr. Murphy, do you perhaps know if Mr. Calhoun is late by design?"

Ancrum turned to face Doc Bailey and he spoke evenly and openly in reply. "I know only that I was instructed to tell you all to converse freely amongst one another as it concerns the little girl. I believe Mr. Calhoun wanted you each to share what you know of the child so that all gathered would come to understand the very full picture of her life. There is to be nothing known by one that remains hidden from any present. You are to proceed with your discourse in the true spirit of family union. However, Mr. Calhoun asks that you guard the arcanum you take away from this place as dearly and as capably as you have the smaller, fragmented secrets of the child's past."

The look of silenced astonishment that dressed over the countenance of each and every person in the room outside of Mr. Murphy and little Miss herself, due only to the five-year old child's lack of under-standing or perhaps her otherwise standard and angelic indifference to most concerns of the corporeal realms, was a sight to behold. For they all held puzzle pieces of varying shapes and sizes that were part and parcel of a larger secret, which in its entirety told the true story of the early years of Miss Margaret Anne Satterfield. Each broken and fatefully confided secret of their own was shocking beyond reproach in its own right, yet to witness the colorful canvas of her life take form, and to in turn be entrusted with the safekeeping of said knowledge by a man so revered and so respected in the ways of the world as Mr. Calhoun then was, was something honorable that each and every one of them would never forget for all of their days.

"I see, Mr. Murphy," replied Doc Bailey after taking a moment to gather his thoughts upon absorbing and then swiftly contemplating the gravity of the ensuing moment. "I will take your statement to mean that Mr. Calhoun had planned for an hour to be spent in the absence of his presence." Mr. Murphy stepped toward the good doctor and replied to the man as evenly keeled as he had spoken the words of his prior announcement. "Such a thing as that I cannot say, doctor. For I am not one given over to speaking of the corners of another's mind not made plainly known to me. What I can say for your benefit and with a fine degree of certainty is that Mr. Calhoun will not appear in this chamber before the one o'clock hour, whether he is on the premises now or still finishing with his appointed rounds." "Very good, Ancrum," answered Doc Bailey evenly. "Thank you for both the gift of your dis-cernment and the gift of your hospitality. We are indebted to you for both blessings." Ancrum Murphy nodded kindly yet rigidly to Doc in accepting that man's gratitude.

Before he departed the room, Mr. Murphy asked of the partici-pants gathered whether or not they wished to remove the presence and authority of their person from the assembly of the fellowship before the conversation began. Hearing none that wished to do so yet witnessing many who visibly appeared as if they did, Ancrum Murphy bowed and put the matter properly to rest. Ancrum then turned, took his proper leave of the ladies, bowed before Doc Bailey, Mr. Satterfield and Mr. Sommers and escorted Amos and little Miss out of the back of the house, where there was indeed a previously prepared carriage awaiting their arrival. As originally planned and accounted for by Mr. Calhoun the prior afternoon, the empty coach had been sent up to the Brown Plantation for any who wished to depart before the whole truth of Miss Margaret Anne was made known to them all.

Edward did not suspect Mary Grice would cause little Miss and Amos to be absent. However, he did believe that Miss Jeanne would leave the entirety of the scandalous discussion to the others and assist Mr. Murphy with the care of the children for the majority of the free flowing discussion that took place prior to his arrival. He never fully understood why he initially believed she would linger upon the outskirts of the exchange but such was not the case regarding the woman that would forever haunt his dreams; at least not in the absence of the children.

Upon an initial reckoning of the most pertinent facts and circumstances surrounding this rather sensitive sharing of information regarding the promised child, the group decided Mr. Satterfield, Jackson's father that is, would open and that Miss Jeanne would end the testimonials. The reasoning behind such a decision as recommended by Doctor Bailey was that those to speak first presumably possessed the least amount of undisclosed knowledge regarding little Miss. Furthermore, those who would close out the discussion, while knowing more, could avoid the repetition of restating any plainly implied or previously revealed facts and thus reduce their burden to an equivalent amount of time as those who spoke first. Such was the theory anyhow, as one might have it from the lips of the good doctor himself.

When the dialogue actually began to commence in earnest, Mr. Satterfield and Mr. Sommers spoke together of the same events that occurred down at the Savannah auction in complimentary and nearly alternating fashion. Mr. Satterfield's revelation, given in conjunction with what Mr. Sommers had to add for the sake of clarity, of what Mr. Calhoun effectively paid to acquire the child at Miss Jeanne's request and what they saw out upon the crossroads on the way home did indeed draw a few discernable gasps from the assembled audience. Gasps quite similar to the ones released by both men a short while thereafter upon learning from Miss Sarah and Miss Leslie, respectively, that the adorable child once standing before them in that very room was the illegitimate daughter of Mr. Calhoun and for a brief period a hunted fugitive from the clutches of Miss Meara before nearly being absconded by the frightful Mrs. Lauderback.

That Edward most certainly did not know as much about the origins of the child he purchased while he attended to the matters of the Butler Island liquidation auction down in Savannah was made abundantly clear to all present. Miss Jeanne even stepped in prior to her formal declaration to corroborate that fact, which seemed to shed such light upon Edward's behavior and the true nature of his character. Be that as it may and however a given participant felt about the actions of Mr. Calhoun upon their learning the truth of the child's origins, none were left to doubt the divine miracle of little Miss's birth and eventual settling-in amongst them all here in Sumter.

As the details of little Miss Margaret Anne's life were made manifest during that telling hour, all present in the room began to grasp the entire picture of the child's brief yet barbarously disrupted existence. Each of them was forced to come to terms with something of the blossoming little girl's life which was supremely uncomfortable to their reckoning of the world they thought they once knew swirling so conveniently or perhaps even violently about them. For Elizabeth Ann, such was the knowing that her own grandmother was the one responsible for the horrible man she shot blindly through the door of the February Cabin. The young woman was drawn to tears and nearly unable to remain in the room without the presence of Miss Jeanne's tender caress as Miss Sarah spoke of the plot to kidnap the newborn baby she had foolishly and devilishly participated in with the late Miss Reedy Cline and Stanton Oglethorpe.

As Miss Jeanne had pardoned the would be midwife for those despicable intentions long ago, for Miss Sarah, her demons gnawed at the knowing of what it was like for Miss Leslie to stand for sale with a white looking baby in her arms at the very auction she had just fled for nothing more than the sake of a child she had never laid her eyes upon prior. Miss Sarah also understood intuitively that Miss Leslie had nobly accepted her ward instead of running north into the mountains with her fellow captives upon escaping the sights of the very rifles once carried by her husband Jackson and the dubious bounty man; the one who had torn her dress at her request to staunch the copious bleeding of his maimed hand. Furthermore, Miss Sarah came to discover the very depths of the true blessing it was that Jackson had been shot in the back by that same bounty man after killing Mr. Oglethorpe, as it was that deed alone which had liberated her husband to be born anew. Concerning the proliferation of Miss Margaret Anne directly, being so close to death's ostensibly cold and eternal promise was the defining moment which later directed Jackson Strait to accept responsibility for the protection of the perchance illegally obtained child upon Mr. Calhoun's request.

Beyond even those aforementioned life altering realizations, Miss Sarah had always known that Jackson being shot in the back had kept the otherwise robust man held back from the Confederate ranks and at home long enough to know the catching smile of his blood child, Adelaide. The injury kept him home with her, little Miss and their beautiful baby girl until the coming days of their desperation caused the senior military men directing the war efforts for the Southern cause to remove such suddenly puerile restrictions; restrictions once set in accordance with their former conveniences and quite illogical preference for something of a more humane and noble face to be placed on the unmerciful suffering and quite ugly innards of war as experienced by the human senses in real time. Amidst the reality of the brutal conflict, which would come to be known as the opening stanza of modern warfare, it did not take such cunning men long to understand that a man with one good lung could stop a bullet just the same as a man with two.

As for her own reckoning of the events associated with being summoned to the Leonard Brown Plantation on the last day of winter in 1864, Miss Leslie was shocked by little where it concerned the patchwork quilt being woven by those present to represent the true life story of little Miss Margaret Anne Satterfield. She had witnessed and experienced the vile deeds of the white plantation men and knew of their secret progeny. She had borne witness to or been told the legends of unthinkable family feuds resulting from similar affairs in the past. Though the unfortunate coincidence of a landed white man purchasing his very own child at auction was indeed a first for the well-traveled slave woman, she had no trouble fathoming such an awful thing taking place in a society so twisted up by some deeply entrenched breed of evil; a diseased breed which was rotting out their flesh and the vibrant looking complexion of their land once promised up to God slowly and from within, and best that she could tell, them Yankees throwing around hopeful words like emancipation while burnin' up and butcherin' everything in their path weren't free none from that same diseased breed either. In Miss Leslie's eyes, the world was on fire and the devil had set the blaze from both sides, but there was hope yet still set deep within the eyes of the promised child.

No, having given birth to three healthy and sizeable baby boys and having miscarried her fourth child not long before being hung out on those troubled crossroads, Miss Leslie's amazement stemmed from hearing of the miraculous birth of the child; a miraculous birth which tied right into that mysterious look of awe and wonder set deep within the powerful child's eternal stare. She saw what was deep within that enchanted baby girl upon the very moment Miss Sarah had handed her the child in the high, dormant grass of that winter field at a spot just south of the overland carriage road and not far off from the river. She saw the eyes of her own unborn child who had recently perished just before she would have been born out on Butler Island deep within those swirling galaxies of amber, blue, green and dusty grey. Miss Leslie swore back at that moment just the same as she would swear to now if asked: the spirit of her little one, who never once breathed in the air of the outside world, had gifted her essence to the propagation of that swaddled babe for the age with some big job to do waiting for her out there somewhere.

Though such a spiritual presumption was a difficult leap of faith for some, when Doc Bailey had finished telling the impossible tale of the birth of the little girl to those gathered, they all verily believed that she was indeed a promised child of the old wives' tales and the oral legends of their ancestors. The primal source of such lingering lore of the centuries gone by was different for each constituent of the budding fellowship of the child, yet they all had heard varying forms of the stories of those born with the blessing of the light from beyond the firmament. They had all listened carefully as children when their grandparents spoke of those born to fracture some ancient and phantom malice of the age. Perhaps that common authenticity of their varied upbringings along with their ability to sense the love of the divine in a world cloaked in the nightfall of the damned was why they found themselves gathered that first afternoon of winter to bear witness to and furthermore pledge to protect the precious yet scandalously illegitimate child.

Once Doc Bailey had gone so far as to reiterate his belief that the little girl was nothing short of a heavenly ordained miracle, there remained little of her mercurial yet still ephemeral story to be told.

That which did remain to be said regarded the revelation of her origins prior to the night of her birth at the February Cabin; an accursed old haunt heretofore spoken of at measurable length which remained standing yet still lost in time and still lost somewhere out in the enchanted woods to the north of the road out to Uriah. Only at that juncture and as was appropriate, did Miss Jeanne begin to speak timidly of her part in all of this from the purview of her seat next to Elizabeth Ann at the end of the dated and exceedingly comfortable grey davenport of the blithely classical yet certainly country time living room of the Brown's modest plantation home.

Miss Basseterre spoke of the very first day she met Edward while overseeing the portage transfers out upon the cargo docks at Jacmel, Haiti. She admitted to being in many ways taken by the rather handsome in an unimposing way and gallant yet strangely humble American who had come to port in the hopes of expanding his successful mercantile merchandising and maritime freight businesses. The two had dined that evening back in 1843 on the occasion of her 17th birthday as Edward had travelled unaccompanied to Haiti and she was living alone. Miss Jeanne's father had placed her officially in charge of the family ventures, which included a considerable sugar plantation in the hills and a small shipping operation amongst other sundry endeavors. The preacher or Irish minister as she liked to call him, Calvin Eoin Basseterre had taken his leave from the island for a few years to visit with his mother's family on the West Coast of Ireland before she passed on. Her father had never recovered from the death of her mother and furthermore, he had lost his way in seeing the island in that same enchanted light of his younger days amidst the failed politics and poorly considered concessions to the French colonialists in the aftermath of the revolution.

Miss Jeanne spoke of the connection she and Edward had made while at dinner that evening and then while continuing to explore the island together for the remainder of that beautiful week in early-May.

When Edward returned in July of that same year he made her an offer she would never dare refuse, though her more than commonplace feelings for a married man troubled her so once she had transferred the care of the Basseterre family properties over to one of her cousins. Beyond how she came to arrive in Sumter, she plainly narrated her way through her arrival to South Carolina and the disquieting months of that first winter spent organizing the affairs of Edward's thriving merchant business while managing the household at Butterworth Hall in conjunction with Edward's wife, Miss Libby, Elizabeth Ann's late mother.

Toward the end of that fanciful walk down memory lane, which was quite necessary given that her conjoining with Mr. Calhoun had occurred out of wedlock, she relived the years of her marriage to Clarke in 1845, their move to Uriah, the birth of their lovely daughter Maime in 1847 and then the arrival of the spitfire of Uriah, Miss Shy Jolie on this very day back in 1848. The gallant woman came near to tears upon reliving the trying death of her husband out in their field in the summer of 1855. Still and all, she fought her way through to the finish of that sad tale and the tale of her estranged relationship with Edward following the death of Miss Libby a month later. When the stage had at last been properly set, she meandered her way through the years following those tumultuous affairs right on up to the moment of that fateful afternoon spent with Edward in late May of 1858 that resulted in the birth of Margaret Anne.

As she was committed to her vows given to both Edward for his sake and Edward's mother for the sake of the safety of her daughter, she spoke of that afternoon in the only way she was permitted according to the bond of her word. She spoke of that tender love that had always existed for Edward and spoke of her moment of weakness in vague terms primarily for the benefit of the virgin ears of Elizabeth Ann. Lastly, she spoke of the existence of The Articles which bound her to secrecy amongst other things and her fear over how those provisions

listed within might one day impact the descendants of both Margaret
Anne and her sisters back home in Uriah, though Miss Basseterre provided little if any detail behind that disquieting assertion.

At that time and right on cue, Edward stepped quietly into the
room so as not to be an immediate disruption to any in the midst of
speaking. Upon passing under the large open entranceway that joined
the living room to the front foyer, he surveyed the faces of those assembled that were from that day forth to pledge themselves as undisclosed guardians of Margaret Anne Means; her legally given name
according to the aforementioned Articles, though the child was never
able to settle under that intended moniker for even that of a flash
out upon the heavens as her named father was called by Mr. Jonas
Hastings on the morning she was born. Upon first glance, Edward
was quite pleased by what he bore witness to in the room and he
firmly believed that the blindly enjoined entendre had suitably served
its intended purpose.

Behind Edward, stood the final two members of the heavenly
ordained group set to protect the sacred child while the war came to
a close. The two men standing in wait to be introduced to those already
assembled along with Mr. Calhoun formed a rather unlikely ternary.
The first man standing behind Edward and to his right remained hopelessly locked onto the living image of Miss Jeanne Jolie Basseterre. That
kind-hearted yet somewhat shifty looking gentleman with the groping
eyes was Mr. Claude Lemarque.

To Mr. Lemarque's left stood a rough looking rogue with but
three fingers on his right hand. He wore a dark winter riding coat
and was known to none present but for Miss Leslie, whose countenance warmed considerably upon seeing the man step up to the wide
entranceway to the living room behind Edward. He looked woefully
out of place standing indoors and the man's face appeared older but
far softer and much kinder than Miss Leslie remembered it to be. As
he was the only man ever to stand for her in any way outside of Black

Jim back on the Island, she found that the novelty of the outrider's ragged yet confident glow tugged quite amply upon her heartstrings. Her cheeks quickly warmed accordingly.

When Edward finally spoke, the room was deathly silent with the undercurrent of a static charge waiting to explode due to the anticipation of nothing more than Master Calhoun's eloquently delivered word. The man of the moment began by introducing Mr. Lemarque, who was also only a known quantity in the flesh to Miss Leslie, and in name alone familiar to Miss Jeanne. Mr. Sommers needed no introduction to any present upon the passing of the prior hour, though the reclusive man had never been formally introduced to Miss Leslie. In any event, Edward called his ledger keeper out before all present to be certain the sheepish man hadn't managed to simply fade into the woodwork as he was wont to do in Edward's absence. Like the other man who had accompanied Edward belatedly to the conclave, the introduction of Mr. Laing, as previously touched upon, was an enigma to all already present in the room but for the slave woman he had returned to Savannah under cover of darkness and Miss Sarah. Miss Leslie knew why the towering outrider was standing in the room, but Miss Sarah most certainly did not. After some brief pleasantries were exchanged between those already present and the new arrivals, Edward promised to allow the two gentlemen to mingle amongst the adherents of the fellowship shortly thereafter. The room then grew deathly silent and once again settled in wait.

Edward began at the very heart of what had driven him to bring these fine folks together on that 21st day of December in 1864. "I have come to learn a few things of significance upon living this blessed life of mine. Though the thought is paramount, I will not speak of the faith that binds me to our heavenly creator. I intend to leave such a matter as one divinely set to the affinities of each of your hearts exceptionally until the time comes to share my beliefs with you all. Rather, what I will tell you now is that there is something which has been made apparent to the very depths of my heart and to the furthest reaches of my soul. That revelation I now share with you all gathered here today is that there is no evil darker than a lie bound in many ways by the truth. The unassailable truth of that conviction became plain enough to me upon the knowing I had purchased the tag set upon my very own child."

Edward paused for a moment to regather his gentlemanly fortitude while the faces of many seated or standing before him dressed long and uncomfortably stricken by the expressions of reticence or sadness. "As such, my hope is that today we few gathered here as one will embark upon a journey to remove the stain of the cowardly lie I have allowed to taint the very essence of such a precious gift as the little girl. Who among us but her revels in the blessings of the nobleman and the servant of the field alike? Who else may dance smartly and fly so free in times of both sunshine and rain; and who else can as sweetly induce the featly of the creatures of the earth, both those tamed by man and those still wild with the essence of the land? You see, while I have endeavored to plant the black seed of a lie into the very pith of her legacy she remains free from the taint of my transgression. Yet perhaps, only free of that lie as to who and what she is will she be set free to act in accordance with her divine provisions and in turn be understood by all as the spirit of the west wind which she truly is."

Miss Jeanne was rather impulsively overcome by her emotion upon hearing the crux of Edward's initial message to the fledgling convocation. She stood up from the sofa abruptly and immediately began to plead with the man to reconsider his proposed haste in dealing with the truth of her little girl. "Edward, I do grasp what you are saying and I understand the desperation driving your desire to seek both truth and light for the child. I know those feelings are tremoring in the depths of your gentle heart after what you have done. Be that as it may, you must consider the dangers the child faces from the one who still possesses ways to subvert the dominion of your authority back at

Butterworth Hall. With Miss Sarah here before us, surely you understand that the man hired by Miss Meara and who shot Captain Pierce
in cold blood possessed nothing but lethal intent. I truly believe that
woman prays from her knees now to the darkest of the demons set in
opposition to the light."

Edward bowed his head in response to Miss Jeanne's startling
entreaty and gave solemn reply to the woman now nearly maddened
with worry over the fate of the little child. "The war is nearly lost,
my dearest. Though the gift is long overdue and little more than a
token gesture upon the hour of our doom, I do plan to offer those so
wrongfully set in chains by my family under the bloody letter of the
law the option of their freedom this very Christmas morning to come.
Mister Sommers has been instructed to make the announcement in
my absence. I will not presume to do the same for my own daughter
by upholding the validity of the very contract of her purchase." Edward
paused to settle his wits for a moment and then added, "Shall I proclaim from the rooftops that more was paid for the child than any
slave in the country's history? Does such a feat absolve me of my sin?
Could any father live with such a public denial of one of his own flesh
and blood?"

Miss Jeanne grew frantic as she began to fully grasp the depths of
Edward's remorse. She knew the old woman had seen what awaited
them all on the other side of the war, whether by way of evil premonition or through the keen workings of her wicked mind in conjunction with the foul connections of her political apparatchiks; those who
offered up betrayal as easily as a morning greeting when it came to
either coin or their own self-preservation. "Edward, the vile woman
will stop at nothing to have the child or worse if her identity is made
known as an affront to The Articles; and I do mean nothing, Edward!"

Miss Elizabeth Ann stood up from the sofa and wrapped her arms
around the trembling woman. She then pleaded with the solemnly and
stoically resolved Mr. Calhoun, "Father, I do worry so for little Miss. Is

it not better that we set things right only in passing through the wake of the great cataclysm that appears set to come? You will not be here to guide us or to hold Miss Meara at bay come morning. Now that I know what she has done, such is easy to see that Grandma does grow darker by the day while the Yankees draw near. I could not bear the pain to come if any harm were to befall the precious little girl due to your absence!"

Following the heartened pleas of both Miss Jeanne and Elizabeth Ann, Doctor Bailey quickly stepped in to voice his support for the concerned if not outright frightened women in earnest. "Edward, Miss Jeanne and your daughter are correct in their assertions. The little girl is free the moment you let the world know exactly who and what she is, assuming the laws of man could ever bind such a miraculous creature to begin with. Yet, is it not better to keep her hidden and away and safe from both your mother's ungodly wrath and the shifting whims of the foul miscreants soon to be ravaging the land in the aftermath of what is now nearly a certainty to come? We shall all be subject to none by God's divine mercy when the Union men commence their march through Sumter upon losing so many of their brothers in arms."

After taking in what Doctor Bailey, his daughter and most thoroughly, Miss Jeanne had offered up for his consideration, Edward turned his soft and nearly broken blue eyes on each person sitting in the room for a probing turn that felt like an eternity to each one of them. Those ceaselessly searching orbs, which seemed to pierce the soul of those Edward surveyed, were stayed when they reached the bowed and penitent head of Miss Leslie. The woman was examining the poor case of her timeworn shoes and recollecting the color, form and tractability of the earth upon which she stood trembling in those same boots when each of her three boys were tormented for their need to take flight in the face of the absolute devilry of their enslavement. She was thinking what a wonder it was that the soles of those shoes had now managed to carry her to the very threshold of her own freedom amidst the tears she once again softly and warmly felt her eyes crying for her lost children.

She could feel Mr. Calhoun's eyes upon her. She remembered the fear that once struck her heart when white men of similar stature had done the same in the days gone by. She marveled at how much of that once prevalent evil God had already torn asunder as the celebration of the Christmas miracle readily approached along with the bitter Yankee battalions and the eyes of those foreign men from the North certain to be burning brightly with naught but vengeance. She then thanked God for Mr. Edward Calhoun and his family. She was awed by how her saying yes to the Lord above from the depths of her terror and blindly accepting responsibility for the child's fate had already blessed her so. On that day near to six years ago, she had been hunted like some rabid dog while she crawled along on her barren belly through that dry, scratching winter grass, always afraid the devil and his men for hire would see her no matter how low to the ground she stayed. The dull taste and the earthy smell of that grass and the dirt beneath were now and forever to remain the smell of her fear, just as the rich scent of warm leather and worn out flesh baking in the summer sun were the fragrances eternally tied to that of her mortal sorrow.

But those days were gone now, along with her three boys. God had already pulled the pilings of that foul church of slavery from the moorings of the earth and all those Yankee boys needed do presently was push a bit on the outer wall. She was here in Sumter now with Amos and little Miss and the others around her who had come to love her because she said yes to God and delivered the promised one back into the very den of vipers in Savannah from whence she had barely escaped. In truth, she had indeed barely escaped with her life that day whilst she came to be crouched on all fours in a southward leaning grove lining those scantly traveled and for many years now, auxiliary crossroads into Georgia very near to the river, a river which possessed such life-giving waters running faithfully down from the ancient mountains and into the sea for all time.

Up until being summoned to that place, Miss Leslie had always believed that she brought the child to the auction because it was the promised one's only hope of escaping and continuing on with a momma that was ready to feed her. She now knew that she had carried Margaret Anne back to Savannah so that her daddy could pay the freight for his own sin and properly deliver the child unto the place she was always meant to be as born anew and do so without a soul beyond her true momma knowing otherwise. Miss Leslie understood that only God could make such things happen and furthermore, she understood that the outrider standing in the room with her would have killed her dead without the Good Lord or one of His angels sending down a miracle on behalf of her account. Only when she was ready to speak, did Miss Leslie dutifully lift her tear-stained eyes to the man who patiently and kindly awaited her while the others watched on anxiously.

Miss Leslie lifted her chin slowly until her moist eyes were fixated upon Edward's own wet and grief laden orbs. She spoke with the temperate cadence of remorse. "I knows you been a waitin' on me Mr. Calhoun, but I had to gets me some things right afore I be speakin' 'bout little Miss. I's ready now if 'n it was indeed me you was waitin' on."

Edward never took his eyes off of Miss Leslie while he spoke warmly in reply, "Yes, Ma'am. You were indeed the one I was waiting on but take your time if you need. Nothing that rests quietly and virtuously in your heart need be hurried on our account. You are the one having acted through faith and kindness alone set among us. There is a reason you are here that is above each and every concern of the others; mine included."

Miss Leslie turned her head slowly to look upon every soul gathered in that homey country living room. Her tears of both joy and sorrow began to flow again but they did not tie up her tongue any. "I be thankin' ya' deeply for da kind consideration, Mr. Calhoun. As one who done seen what come from da half-truths you done told us 'bout, dere isn' no part a me dat wants nothin' to do wid no more lies buried deep inside a da truth. Y'all sees da world as it be comin' into your eyes. What you den go on an' reckon a da place go on in your heads an' be based on what it be dem noodles been filled wid. Only after all a 'dat an' a bit less, do y'all reckon on how da world be comin' into your heart. I done been forced to see da world through my heart for all my life. So there be no chance a hidin' what da devil doin' to us all from one like me or any a us dat been in dem places where our eyes gets to bein' pried open so wide by da whip dat our hearts don't be missin' none a his tricks."

Edward turned his eyes to Miss Jeanne as she stood listening to the woman who had been told she was nothing but a slave her whole life. He could not read where she was coming out so he responded to Miss Leslie while also endeavoring to win the favor of child's mother. "I agree with you, Miss Leslie. None of us can afford to face the tribulations of the days ahead with any of the lies of the old ways still scarring our hearts like the fateful burning letter of scarlet which perpetually castigated Miss Hester Prynne. We must reveal to the world who and what the child is and do our best to protect her under God's patronage. Only then will she be set free to do what it is God intended for her to do while she is among us."

Miss Jeanne began to tremble again because her pact with the witch was now holding strong upon her heart, almost as if some fantastical spell had been cast over her. Be such a belief truth or coincidence, Edward's mother devoted little energy to anything else but enforcing from afar that half consented to pact of Miss Jeanne's while she lurched to a fro around her foul smelling pot of rotting animal flesh deep beneath the family sanctuary back in Sumter. Miss Basseterre continued to tremble noticeably before all until she took hold of the golden cross around her neck and called out frightfully, "Edward, you have no right to effectively doom the darling child to clear your own conscience on the eve before you venture off to war!"

With all eyes suddenly upon her, Miss Jeanne stood up from the sofa and continued on with a touch more elegance and calm interwoven into both her tone and her cadence. "I speak truthfully in saying that I once held such contempt for you when we signed those Articles of Les Cayes with what seemed to be our own blood. Yet, I did not know the true will or nature of your mother back in those days. I always believed the reason you pushed for the agreement was due to nothing more than your own commercial concerns, which you held so dear and rightfully, though not righteously, sought to protect. Only now do I understand your more noble reasons behind never wishing to stand for the child. Presently however, I also see clearly that in your current condition you will never understand why I cower from making such revelations all the same."

Miss Leslie was the one who instinctively picked up on something stirring beneath the surface of Miss Jeanne's nearly frantic plea to both Edward and all present. As such, she began to lament the sour taste of knowing that the truth of the child was not to be cleared to come forth on this day. Two choices stood before her as she readied to make her mind known: push to override the nearly insurmountable sanction of the child's natural mother by way of calling for a group vote or; concede the battle for the truth today in the hopes she would come to know the woman's mind and furthermore, in the hopes that Edward would return alive to Sumter following the war and that upon his arrival this wrong would then be set right. Miss Leslie understood that the witch had rendered Mr. Calhoun limp as a eunuch through the words of Miss Jeanne. Therefore, she spoke to make something of a peace amongst those gathered. She believed that all present but for her and Edward were likely to be leaning in favor of keeping the true identity of the child concealed until a more opportune moment arrived. A time following the war when it was safer to make the revelation a matter of the public record, which would be properly presented according to the prevailing wishes and whims of the social collective swirling so uncertainly around them all at the present juncture.

"Now Miss Jeanne, I ain't one to be sayin' da child should be put afore da mouth's a no hungry wolves or even any of dem wolves in sheep's clothin' be posturin' 'bout town for what dey gonna offer up to dem Yanks when they's comin' through here like they done Georgia. You knows 'dat I love da child if'n she was my own, her an' Amos both. My believin' in her safety after da truth a her be made known be comin' through my faith in God alone. Since we all be needin' to work dis out together for dat promised child, maybe it be best dat we agree to let Mr. Calhoun make dat truth known once da war get settled out. If'n, an' God forbid it, Mr. Calhoun be known to have staked out his life for da Carolina cause, I'll take dat to be da same as God's will to be leavin' da matter in da hands of da child's mother while dis world go on get reborn form da ashes a all dis here killin' an' sufferin'."

Miss Jeanne nodded appreciatively in response to Miss Leslie's colorful and heartfelt concession. Afterward, she looked carefully into the eyes of all present and gathered in the room. She then spoke cautiously because she was aware she was standing on a pile of tinder with the flint capable of scratching up the only spark necessary to ignite a conflagration within the room and beneath her feet no further away than Miss Leslie's chair. "I thank you for your earnest consideration of the matter, Miss Leslie. It saddens me so to know you are far more aware of the mind of the precious little girl than her mother, who stands humble and heartbroken before you all begging of you to think only of her safety in the absence of gallant Edward. I have made my sacrifice to forego the feel of the child's skin against my own for the sanctity of her life. I offer up the continuation of that sacrifice to you all now in the hopes that we dare not render the child to a fate far worse than that of not knowing the full warmth and love of her true mother. Certainly, I cannot presume that such a plea will fall upon deaf ears."

Edward nodded and angled his long frame fully upright in the gallant manner, as if he were to speak in response to the wise and heart rending words of both Miss Leslie and Miss Jeanne. Be that as it may, Miss Leslie spoke somewhat surprisingly, as she was in fact out of turn according to the rubrics of proper Southern etiquette. "Now, Miss Jeanne, don't you go takin' dem words da wrong way, but I aim to say but one more thing to all dats in here since my heart won't be havin' a lick a peace otherwise. That is if'n Mr. Calhoun done give his say so."

Edward's eyes quickly met Miss Leslie's and he nodded dutifully while interposing with, "Of course, Miss Leslie. Please, do speak your piece."

Miss Leslie nodded in return and stated, "I done want y'all to know I isn' condonin' what we here is 'bout to do. I believe Master Edward is right, there isn' no darker evil out there than dat a dressin' a lie up like it be da truth. What it be dat I's tellin' y'all is I been livin' wid such a thing all my life but the lie a it be concernin' da truth a me bein' a woman afore dem eyes a God right up 'til it done gets down to da color of my skin. What I'm tellin' all you all here is I's not condonin' what we is doin', I jus' ain't got no authority to be puttin' my faith in God as it do regard dat precious girl into da hearts of y'all in dat same way it be sittin' in my own. What I do knows is dat da easy road always gonna be lined wid da devil's will."

Miss Jeanne raised her chin slowly and looked over into the awaiting eyes of Miss Leslie and responded in the only way possible at that moment. "All a fallen woman can say to such truths is that if her own faith were indeed strong enough the child would have never come to be at all. Therefore, if my weakness must be the sin to see her through to the other side of this awful war, I am willing to accept such a righteous form of condemnation from all gathered in the knowing that my current will is born of little more than my loving intent. However, I will not commit to such an act without Edward's blessing."

Edward looked over to Miss Jeanne and he sensed the very same emotion that was overcoming him while he spoke with her during the midsummer picnic at Mary Grice's estate. He sensed that there was but one hope to set things right but that in so doing, and for some odd and arcanely intangible reason, his heart might not survive the moment of passing through such a crucible. The weight of what lurked within the shadows of Miss Jeanne's troubled soul was simply a burden he could not bear before joining the ranks of the beaten men that remained fighting in a war that was lost some time ago. He lowered his eyes to the floor in knowing that he had somehow flinched in the face of his mother's witchery, yet he did not know how he had been outflanked by the black-eyed mistress who so often wandered the midnight woodlands.

The feeling of being outmaneuvered in a world that up until that moment seemed to bend to both his dutiful will and his fancy alike was entirely foreign to him. He spoke to them all in a defeated tone. "I shall return from the war and in doing so I will make things right by that precious child of God. Let us keep her safe as she is now known until that day arrives. Perhaps God will still hear the prayers of his fearful children who possess only the blessings of love and goodwill resting deep within their hearts."

Miss Leslie felt the finality of the moment come to pass and knew they had done wrong but she had no way of changing the outcome. Such had been the case with most things in her troubled life as a slave, absent the glorious time she said yes to God and yes to the promised child. Mr. Satterfield was conversely set at ease by the decision. He was worried sick over his son, as Jackson had not been heard from since his outfit was surrounded and then came under attack as part of the brutal Yankee siege at Vicksburg. He did not wish for Miss Sarah to be overcome by the situation surrounding the child; a dire situation which was sure to follow if the whole truth of the matter was to be made known at home in Sumter and perhaps throughout the entirety of the Carolinas.

Likewise, Miss Sarah, who unlike her father-in-law lacked some of the star-crossed history surrounding the origin of the tryst occurring between Edward and Miss Jeanne, was comforted by the pledge to keep the child's identity hidden and have her remain in the care of Miss Leslie while she and Adelaide were away in Columbia. Elizabeth Ann remained uncertain as to what was best for her little sister. Her instincts told her that the child had been unintentionally wronged there on that cold and overcast winter afternoon, but knowing even something of what stood in wait to oppose the truth; she was not of the mind to dissent to the will of the child's true mother and therefore the will of her father.

Doctor Bailey had been impressed by Edward's gallant will to make the truth of the child known. He had always found fault with the man for the very reason of his past refusal to do so alone. Therefore, according to his thinking, the reasons behind Miss Jeanne's objection must have been consequential enough to keep the man from bearing his soul to them all before he was just as likely to die as not in marching out to haplessly defend South Carolina from the onslaught of the soon to be arriving columns of the Union Army gathered under Sherman. Be that as it may, Doc Bailey had experienced first-hand perhaps three of the many miracles that surrounded the little girl. Part of him felt she deserved to once again fight the odds of all that stood in her path as nothing short of the full truth of the one God saw fit to deliver into that haunted February Cabin from the very throes of death. To make his decision sit easier, the good doctor offered to serve as Edward's proxy in the event he was killed defending the state and Miss Jeanne saw fit to undo the every last one of the current provisions set out to guide Margaret Anne's anonymous and inconspicuous life.

There was however, one who remained fully in agreement with Miss Leslie and the need to allow the child and those around her to know the truth of Margaret Anne's life before the lines of demarcation, those of both a political and a social context, were wholly redrawn in the aftermath of the war. To the surprise of some hearing this tale both presently and in times long since passed, that man was not Mr. Lemarque but Mr. Shug Laing. Though the reformed man was a sizeable and still foreboding presence, all the more so in a relative context when contrasted against the rather genteel nature and appearances of the ladies and gentlemen included amongst present company, Mr. Laing stepped into the room rather meekly and hat in hand to briefly speak his mind.

He was then the child's hired protector, as per the terms of his agreement with Mr. Calhoun and his pledge to his Lord and Savior on high upon the instant of his salvation. Certainly the proposition of revealing the true nature of the child to the swiftly shifting and highly charged scrutiny of the public eye in such times of uncertainty and chaos would serve to put Mr. Laing under further duress while within the confines of the fulfillment of his service to the promised one. Be that as it may, the notable burden of Margaret Anne's exposed truth to his sworn duty mattered little to one such as Mr. Shug Laing. He was now a man who had seen the light and a man who knew a thing or two about the dark and vile nature of half-truths.

Mr. Laing nodded reverently to the only woman he knew in the room and the woman he admired more than any man set upon green's earth for her courage and her faith in standing to deliver a white baby into the hands of the unkind hoards frothing at the mouth to possess yet more flesh by way of whip, unbroken chain and lawfully written bond. "Afternoon, Ma'am, its sure is good to see you well again. How is the boy who come running back down to the river after you?"

Miss Leslie smiled at Mr. Laing while taking note of his right hand, which held his weathered hat and which possessed only three discernable fingers and a shortened nub for a thumb. She had never seen the raw extent of the damage caused to that hand when his gun backfired in the field. The quiet bounty man had had kept the appendage wrapped haphazardly right up until the moment he delivered the three of them into the hands of the cloaked man. The faceless yet foul smelling urchin who had slipped the escaped mother and her two children into the auction pen and adjusted the ledgers accordingly after verifying their prior whereabouts with none but that same Mr. Laing.

Miss Leslie spoke sweetly and soothingly in reply to the changed and fully redeemed man. "Oh my, Mr. Laing, it sure be good 'nuff to see you too after all you done for me, da boy an' li'l Miss. Amos, he be well. He been waitin' to ride hisself a horse again ever since we done crossed over to Savannah from Silver Bluff all 'dem years ago now. Maybe you could take him out ridin' some time while you be watchin' over li'l Miss mischievous."

Mr. Laing smiled with his eyes alone, like any hardened frontier man might, and answered Miss Leslie in kind, "I'd like that, Ma'am. Fine boy that Amos and a natural rider too. I look forward to keeping time with you all."

Miss Leslie smiled a bit bashfully and rejoined the suddenly handsome cowboy, who once stood as the scourge to the more liberated of both mind and body alike of her bonded kinfolk. "We done look forward to havin' you 'round, Mr. Laing. We couldn't be askin' for none better to watch over us in times such as dese here be."

Mr. Laing nodded dutifully in reply to Miss Leslie and then turned to address the remainder of his waiting audience. He spoke in a dignified manner, which was clear and easy to grasp. "I just want to say one thing to you good folks. I aim to take up my duties concerning the child with the help of Mr. Lemarque here one way or another. What you decide on how to proceed don't make but a bit of difference to me. But do know this: I lost more than I aim to discuss with you all here because there was always one little lie at the end of every truth my daddy ever told me; my sister too. But we was alone up in them mountains and the moonshine let the devil taint even the word of God in the eyes of the preacher man that was my daddy. I don't have no easy answers for you all now but for some reason I felt the need to speak up for this brave woman here. She took that child sight unseen from Miss Sarah while runnin' for her very life from the barrel of my own rifle. Then she went ahead and presented her body to the devil one last time to get your little Miss where she needed to be. That is all I gots to say." With that Mr. Laing stepped back and duly retreated into the foyer to his former position at Mr. Sommers's side.

Once Mr. Laing had finished speaking, Mr. Calhoun stepped back into the center of the room while acknowledging Mr. Laing's thoughtful notice of a sort. "Thank you for that, Mr. Laing. With Mr. Laing's prescient advice being administered for the benefit of the group are there any who now stand against protecting Miss Margaret Anne as she is now known until I return from the front?"

Miss Sarah and Miss Elizabeth Ann shifted a bit uneasily but seeing that Miss Jeanne's classically beautiful countenance appeared firm as ever in holding to her former resolve they said not a word. Doctor Bailey was the closest of any to throwing caution to the four winds and entreating the group for the removal of the veil of secrecy which surrounded the child, but he remembered how wise and pre-scient the girl's mother was on the night of her birth. As he stared at Elizabeth Ann's miraculously healed arm, he starkly recalled the cost of not heeding Miss Jeanne's warning in time. He would not make the same mistake twice and therefore, he also remained silent.

After a solid minute of silence had passed, Edward spoke again to confirm the group's intentions and furthermore confirm the honorable bond of their vow of secrecy until the proper day came for the truth to be known. When all had agreed by nodding their head and saying aye, Edward adjourned the formalities concerning little Miss Margaret Anne. He then called out to Miss McKinley in the kitchen to bring out the refreshments so that the far more festive holiday planning could begin. The much needed and well-deserved merriments continued on for a few hours out at the Leonard Brown Plantation and then carried on late into the evening back at Butterworth Hall in the form of a farewell celebration for Edward.

Maime and Shy came up to the manor from the servants quarters where they were staying with their mother and where Miss Jeanne first lived when she arrived in South Carolina with Edward back in 1843. The night was also the occasion of Miss Shy Jolie's 16th birthday and both she and Edward were serenaded well beyond the midnight hour. Even Mary Grice and Connie were in attendance that evening when Edward gave notice that all of the slaves of the plantation were free to stay or go at their leisure as of sunup. He did not wish to leave them at the mercy of the highwaymen rounding up the uncertain and unorganized refugees roaming the countryside. Many of those lost souls had been freed or in some cases revolted in the face of dwindling opposition to hold them captive while believing they were set free according to edict due to President Lincoln's Emancipation Proclamation issued more than two years ago and taking effect on the first day of 1863.

On the later side of the evening, Miss Leslie had remained in a festive mood. Thus, Mr. Laing had happily agreed to accompany Amos and little Miss back to their quarters situated on the Decker Estate just to the north of Butterworth Hall. Miss Margaret Anne was near to turning six years old by that time, though her diction, comprehension and arithmetic were several years ahead of schedule. The three played gin and poker for a while until little Miss had gathered up all of the chips and points in each contest and Mr. Laing began to drift off to sleep while he sat in his chair before the round wooden table in the main room.

When Amos was off tending to the fire, Miss Margaret Anne quietly approached the sleeping man and looked carefully into his eyes though they were closed. She noted that his face was marked and tired but possessed that knowing glow of the soul, which carried him forth on this unexpected and perhaps final journey of his. His lips were parched and sat cold and motionless while his cheeks and nose were sharp and stalwart though ragged with the tattletale signs of age and hard living. The maturing man appeared as if he had pressed the once handsome definition of his lineaments to spite the very west wind that had so spiritedly conveyed her into the abject confines of the February Cabin for the entirety of his life.

The little girl then carefully studied his deformed hand and thought to make it better in a way that was a bit abstract yet would have floored the man had he awoke to such a marvelous change in the usefulness of the limb. Yet in reading the man's thoughts, Margaret Anne came to realize that Mr. Laing did not wish for that hand to be able to do the terrible things it once did so callously and without remorse. She understood that the deformation was received as some sort of blessing by the sleeping man because the injury kept his eyes always watching for God, even upon reaching for his morning tin of coffee.

Beyond that, the promised child sensed that the man was broken in some way she did not fully stand as mature enough to reconcile with her thoughts. To her innocent and majestic mind she could only translate the feeling conveyed as the man's inability to properly convey his love, or so he thought. She sensed that as a result of this strange and uncommon deformation of some semblance or another his heart was horribly bound up in a similar way. Therefore, she simply pressed the palm of her hand to the man's chest until she could feel that erratic organ beating haphazardly beneath his canvas winter undercoat. She kept her hand placed there until Mr. Laing awoke with a sudden start just as Amos was approaching.

Mr. Laing's eyes popped open as if he had been shocked back from the dead. They were wide and brown with strings of green that ran like vines climbing the bark of a stout and aging tree. He inhaled quickly as if his wind had been pressed out of his lungs while he slept. Amos watched on silently from over Shug's shoulder as Miss Margaret

Anne stood there with her hand upon his coat. When Mr. Laing had evened out his breathing with a slow and steady exhalation he looked down into the eyes of the wondrous child and asked something of her as if she were his barely known mother, "What is it? What do you notice there?"

Margaret Anne looked up into the man's shifting and refocusing eyes while she lowered her hand and said, "Something was stuck but I think it is gone now. Are you quite okay, Mr. Laing?" Mr. Laing felt rather different but he couldn't properly reckon in what way. He rejoined the little girl after a brief pause by saying, "I do indeed feel quite fine, little Miss. A little shut eye always does wonders for an old man like me. I suppose the elders are having quite the time back at the Calhoun house. I should be gettin' you two rascals on off to bed!"

Miss Margaret Anne giggled and said, "You're silly, Mr. Laing. I think that's why Mammy likes you." Amos rolled his eyes in disgust before making his presence known to Mr. Laing with a loving tap on the shoulder and then marching on across the cabin to his bunk.

Mr. Laing smiled at Miss Margaret Anne and retorted, "Not many women around these parts done take to a man for being silly, but I reckon your mammy's glad God got to me when He did for your sake alone. Now, let's get you settled in for bed afore you swindle me out of the last of my money playing cards."

Miss Margaret Anne giggled again and said, "Your heart can see again, Mr. Laing. You tell me what you see in Mammy's eyes when the sun is up come morning." "Well that'll be enough of that talk, little Miss. You get on into bed and I'll do the waitin' up for the night owls," replied old Shug rather precipitously while blushing to beat the Dutch.

"Okay, Mr. Laing. Goodnight to you then. We forgot my story, but tomorrow is just as good a day for that as any," answered little Miss while intending to cede to her overseer's wishes.

Old Shug Laing laughed at the adorable little child and answered her kindly. "I dare say, little Miss, you are quite the persuasive pint-sized lady. Get on into bed and I will tell you a story that will be yours for all time." Miss Margaret Anne smiled, winked artfully at Mr. Laing and ran over to her bed very excited to hear any story by such an adventurous and well-travelled man.

A short while after Mr. Laing had begun his tale, Miss Leslie returned home to the cabin from the last of the festivities winding down at Butterworth Hall. The fire was burning out as Mr. Laing had intended and in the low light of the abode she could see very little. As she felt her way around the front room she heard the voice of the old rogue whispering softly to the little child, "And the woman took hold of the baby wrapped in the Cherokee blanket; the baby she had never laid eyes upon afore, and made her way through the high grass as the vile, old murderous man approached. Then, she suddenly stood up with the child in her arms and began to run with all of her will summoned in the other direction for the sake of her friends…'"

Miss Leslie smiled into the low light of the dying fire as she eased her hand onto Mr. Laing's shoulder and whispered, "Dat's a good story for her to be knowin', Mr. Laing, but little Miss need to be getting' on to sleep."

Mr. Laing looked back over his shoulder and saw little but the shimmering whites of the tired, yet so pretty in their pureness, eyes of Miss Leslie. He answered back to her and little Miss simultaneously, "Alright then. You heard your mammy, little Miss. We shall continue on with the rest of the story tomorrow night."

Miss Margaret Anne pulled the blanket over her head and giggled again before calling back with a muffled voice, "Very well, Mr. Laing. It's a good thing that you are listening to Mammy. She always knows what's best."

"That she does, my dear child. You rest well and we will see you in the morning," replied old Shug the softy.

"Goodnight, my little angel," whispered Miss Leslie from over Mr. Laing's shoulder. "Goodnight, Mammy," replied the child from beneath the depths of her blanket.

Mr. Laing and Miss Leslie then walked back up to the front of the cabin to discuss the sleeping arrangements for the evening. "You go on and be takin' my bed, Mr. Laing. Ain't enough hours left in da evenin' for me to take my rest afore I needs to be getting' on up to Miss Mary Grice's kitchen. I shoulda knowed better den to be drinkin' dat wine but after today I was feelin' da need to partake of at least somethin'."

"And rightfully so, Ma'am," interjected Mr. Laing. "I think they all is making a horrible mistake but all we can do is our very best to make sure our intuition don't get proven out right in this case. I'll be having nothing of keeping a tired woman from her own bed. I'll go on ahead and pitch my camping roll over by the fire."

"It be okay, Mr. Laing, we knows we ain't doin' no harm nowheres bein' as we is. Take da inside half and I'll be up an' off in da mornin' afore you even knows I's was ever there. You done had a terribly long journey today. We done gonna get da place all set up for you afore tomorrow night. Master Calhoun never said you was comin' to keep an eye on us. We's so glad to have ya, though. Amos be talkin' 'bout you from time to time."

Mr. Laing shifted a bit uneasily but also strangely hopefully all the same. Though he was effectively a eunuch and wasn't much use to a lady at this hour of the evening, he hadn't lay next to a woman, let alone a colored woman, since he had haplessly spent some nights at a brothel outside of Savannah many years ago. Back then he was just hoping to know at least something of the feel of an at least partially effeminate creature. Beyond that, he was used to sleeping on rough ground and in open spaces. Thus, such a proposed accommodation stood contra wise to his standard modus operandi. Yet, he was for some unknown reason drawn to the unexpected proposal all the same.

"Why thank you, Ma'am. I am sorry to be such an inconvenience to you until we get things settled."

Mr. Laing winked coyly at Miss Leslie, though it was difficult to make out such a gesture in the dim and still waning firelight of the cabin. He then spoke to add to his prior thought for good measure, "But you amongst all know you ain't got nothin' to worry about as it concerns this old fella. I sure could use a proper night's rest."

By the time Miss Leslie had changed into her night clothes and laid out her outfit for the early morning kitchen detail, true to his word, Mr. Laing was fast asleep. She managed to find an almost comfortable bit of space upon the slender bed, yet there was little doubt that the unwittingly sprawled out man was used to sleeping in the woods in much the same manner that a bear might, precisely as he had on the nights they travelled southward together to the auction down in Savannah. The inconvenience was a small matter to the hardened woman of far more trying circumstances. She came to her rest swiftly while discovering that she actually appreciated the presence of the coarse man in the cabin since she never knew what to expect might come their way where it concerned little Miss. Not but an hour later, everything the former slave mistress thought she knew about the man, and everything which had in fact once flashed brightly before her eyes in the manner of a vision of his horrific neutering whilst she was riding upon the lightning of the moment that was standing prostrate before him in that accursed field, had changed. Her strange and wanting consent was the first she had given over to a man since the father of her boys had been beaten to death out in the field for taking ill.

In the silent minutes before she knew to take her leave to begin her chores of the day, the woman was inexplicably both grateful for the cover of darkness that hid her shame and thankful for the man currently by her side and the miracle that had somehow overcome him. Her world had changed suddenly and her champion of the times to come was a rough man touched by the hand of God to abandon his wicked ways. Such was a strange and powerful thought for the righteous woman who had never experienced the feeling of a free and virtuous man. Though she still bore some of the shame for her ease in acquiescing to the gentle yet lumbering guardian of the promised child, the purity and sanctity of the moment of her want enjoined by the freedom of her assent was one that was such a long time in coming to the otherwise abused maidservant. When she had slipped away from his kind yet brutish arm to dress for the morning, she felt as if she had never known the banal terms of her slavery, even after she tied on her smock in the darkened kitchen of Miss Mary Grice Decker.

At the same time Miss Leslie was coming to terms with the freedoms of her given affections, Master Edward Calhoun was kissing the foreheads of his daughters Elizabeth Ann and Blair Raimi while they slept off the innocent effects of their late running revelry and dancing, which held the darling girls up well past the customary appointments of their proper bedtimes. The melancholy father looked quite gallant and rather well-suited to the fit out of his officer's regalia, which had been carefully prepared by Miss Sarah back in Columbia. As Miss Leslie continued to work in the kitchen while reflecting upon the recent interlude that seemed to have somehow touched her soul just hours ago, Edward began his slow and thoughtful march down to the stables to deprive Mr. Satterfield of Big Luke. He hated to take something so dear from the always dutiful coachman with his son seemingly lost somewhere out west of the Mississippi River, assuming Jackson was indeed lucky enough to make it that far when Vicksburg had fallen, yet none of the horses present at the stables excepting Big Luke were fit for such service.

Not long before he reached Mr. Satterfield while the somber enough looking older gentleman was shoveling hay into the stalls of the three remaining carriage horses, though such a designation was a bit of a euphemism for the kind yet timeworn beasts better suited to the leisurely strolls of the women and children, a dour thought flashed across Edward's mind. Concurrently, the same thought crossed the mind of Miss Leslie a mile or two up the road as she toiled to set about the provisions for the morning meal to be served at the Decker mansion. Though Mr. Calhoun did not fear for his return to Butterworth Hall, he suddenly understood that the man who would return from the war would be a far different specimen than the one who departed on this cold and damp December morning in the year 1864.

Furthermore, the two wistful thinkers came to possess an understanding that welled up from the depths of their hearts and was spoken from the essence of the spectral realms that held sway in the hours surrounding the reticence of the dawn. Such was an understanding that the true gift of the promised child had been eternally compromised by the forsaking of her identity in the dark days that were to follow and certain to favor the black, cunning and wholly unseen posturing of the strengthening witch lurking below the town of Sumter in the Calhoun catacombs. Though both Edward and Miss Leslie would shake free of that awful premonition in the days to come due to their unassailable hope for a brighter tomorrow amidst the always uncertain and oft times calamitous affairs of a fallen postbellum society that awaited them somewhere out on that discreetly emerging horizon of the half-light, the witch would haunt their souls for a lingering span with the failings of their denial of God's given gift.

Edward put his hand on Mr. Satterfield's shoulder while the elder man continued to preoccupy his saddened mind by steadfastly engaging in his morning chores. Edward spoke solemnly to his longtime adherent. "I'm sorry to take the old boy from you at such a sorrowful time, Donovan. I know he's part and parcel to your family right now. I promise to send word of Jackson's status out west upon reaching the ranks over in Columbia. I will pass along your love to Miss Sarah and that beautiful granddaughter of yours as promptly as I am able once I arrive in town."

Mr. Satterfield at last put down his pitchfork by leaning it against the wall of the stable and turned to heartily embrace Mr. Calhoun while tears ran down his face. He spoke somewhat brokenly into Edward's ear while his chin rested upon his captain's shoulder. "Whatever becomes of my boy, I know he will do it gallantly all thanks to that little girl who is due to one day cause quite the stir."

Edward gripped his hands firmly upon Mr. Satterfield's shoulders and set his man back some so that he could properly look into the depths of Donovan's forlorn eyes of emerald green. He spoke firmly and in the dignified manner of a Confederate officer. "Do not give up hope just yet, Donovan. Many yet still are left to scavenge the woodlands in wait for that final moment of surrender. Many are taken prisoner and will be freed when the fighting comes to a halt. Hold out hope for your boy, my noble charioteer. He may surprise you with the gift of his return one fine morning."

Mr. Satterfield stared back into Edward's eyes with a vacant glare set upon his otherwise disquieted mien. After biting his lower lip to steady the onslaught of his emotion he answered his captain. "Nay, Master Edward. The boy was always wild-eyed and loyal as was his mother. Just as he walked out into that pretty grove resting on the southern side of the crossroads for Miss Sarah, Jackson wouldn't leave a single one of his own behind only to face captivity or time spent wandering the wilderness. You bring word of his end, however you must find it. I, in turn, will give all that I have to keep that child of the light safe. She saved the soul of my boy by causing him to be delivered from the hands of wicked men and into the arms of Miss Sarah. There will come a day when each of us that knew her understands that in truth, she saved us all from the miserable depths of the great reckoning soon to come."

Edward nodded, patted Mr. Satterfield heartily on the shoulder in a show of mutual affirmation and mounted Big Luke. He slapped at the golden stallion's side with his fine, leather riding boot while directing the massive steed towards the road by pulling on the reins. When the horse had reached a steady trot and was heading down the storied plantation drive of Butterworth Hall, Edward called back, "If I should fall, please press Miss Jeanne to do the right thing by the precious child."

Mr. Satterfield nodded and called out down the road in reply while the cool of the morning dew added a milky and swarming potency to the mist of his breath upon striking the gelid air of first light, "Aye, my captain! You give those Yanks hell for my boy and for the others back in town that will never return! The world as we once knew it is fading before our eyes!"

To which Edward cried out, "Devilry always hath a price so dear, my good man! Yet, the good Lord above forgives if we only ask and brings a new day to those meant for the other side all the same! Hug my baby girls and keep them far from those scourges of Sherman if they arrive before me!"

"Aye, Sir! Such shall be as you have asked!" Mr. Satterfield hollered down the road at the magnificent looking duo trotting so gallantly away from him. The old man then dropped to his knees upon a haystack resting next to the grand stable door, which had been swung open in anticipation of both Edward and the rising of the sun. He dropped to his knees upon a firmly bound haystack and wept for hours over the loss of his boy and all the things he never told him while he was present.

Chapter Six

THE SEASON OF THE WITCH

༄

M ISS MEARA CALHOUN returned to her cavern beneath the heart of Sumter from Martinsville, Virginia on Friday, February 24th, 1865. Columbia and Charleston had fallen into the hands of Sherman's men a week prior, yet the rail lines running through Sumter, throughout the central regions of the state, and parts of the Lowcountry were still running or at least functional in the rare instances there were available stocks of produce, livestock or other commercially viable commodities to transport. Edward remained out riding with the skirmishers protecting those rail lines and the soldiers retreating from those fallen cities as Sherman's two armies marched rapidly through the state in an effort to join forces with the Union brigades fighting up in Virginia to close out the war. He had yet to return to Butterworth Hall since the moment of his departure on the morning of 22nd December, the very day Sherman had marched his troops into Savannah, to serve with the South Carolina defense forces as a cavalry captain under Confederate General Wade Hampton.

Accompanying Miss Meara on her trip to the scenic mountains of Southern Virginia was Allan Worthington, a venerated South Carolina attorney whose firm kept essential records on some of the most prominent sandlappers and their viable interests dating back to the close of the American Revolution. The two were gathered there in the mountains outside of Martinsville to secretly meet with the man who stood to become regional director of their little corner of the world when the postwar reconstruction efforts began in earnest. As it turned out, when they arrived at the appointed meeting house, the man they had been directed to beseech on behalf of the more "moderate-leaning" members of the American citizenry merely "caught out" behind Confederate lines upon secession was a man that was familiar to them both from his days as a Union Army officer stationed in various towns throughout South Carolina prior to the onset of the war.

That Miss Meara had ways of knowing who the man was that stood to become provisional director of Sumter and the city's surrounding counties following the war was not a surprise. That she had secured a meeting with such a man before the war had officially ended, though in truth it had already been lost, also made a fair bit of sense to those who understood the need for local political posturing by those Yankee gentlemen to be placed in charge of Confederate protectorates given what was known of Lincoln's proposed ideals for the process of the reuniting of the war-torn nation. What was a surprise to any and all who learned of her journey much later on was the fact that a man as thusly renowned as Mr. Worthington was had been willing to expose his neck to both parties still engaged in the conflict long enough to journey through North Carolina and into Southern Virginia as the result of either a preciously called in favor to Miss Meara or as payment in kind for something of extreme value rendered by same. Perhaps his presence out on the road on such a devious errand was the prelude to something far more sinister that saw prominent allies from across the country gathering to address what might transpire in the aftermath of such a bloody and resource depleting conflict.

In any event, had the reason behind the journey been made known to Edward or any other patron of Sumter of significance, such an endeavor would have ended poorly for both participants while good men, spent beyond any measure of human understanding from four long years of misery and death, were still spilling their blood for the Confederate cause. That reality was certainly not to be lost upon such shrewd operators as Miss Meara Calhoun and Mr. Allan Worthington,

Esq. Clearly, the juice was to be worth far more than the squeeze for both of the long-standing denizens of Sumter, whose history together dated back to the years following the close of The War of 1812.

More concerning than even the act of their prescient treachery in seeking safe harbor with the presumed enemy prior to the end of the fighting, was the fact that their venture must have proven to be a success. Upon their return, Mr. Worthington accompanied Miss Meara into the crypt to execute some contract documents, which had been prepared well in advance of their departure. By way of their premediated perfidy so common to the ruthless that bask in the idolatry and the authority of deceitfully obtained or forcefully compelled abundance, such was clear that the devious tandem of lewd confidants, only by way of mutual benefit of course, yet in all unholy senses of the expression as they shared such dark religion, had moved to preempt the loss of the war and consolidate their power base in the face of the inevitable Yankee occupation. The dour repercussions that accompanied such a sudden shift in the way of things to come remained unbeknownst to the loosely federated fellowship of little Miss Margaret Anne Satterfield during that desolate fortnight which spanned the weeks beyond the event of her sixth birthday.

The two conspirators embarked upon the rather harrowing journey only after Miss Meara had finally allowed Edward to ride off and play soldier upon the closing stages of the bloody and bitterly contested conflict. Of course after having been cleared for service, there was little the noble gentleman could do to halt the progress of the dark mistress who once bore the name Meara Clay yet had always remained zealously loyal to the exiled Morgenthau clan of Edward's maternal grandmother, who were never to be spoken of due to the heinous nature of their religion and sacrament back in their native provinces of Germany. Such fealty to that dark order of yesteryear was of primary concern to the Pinckney trustees upon attempting to drive Miss Meara's clan from their blood connection to the auspicious generosities of the Trust.

The presence of little Miss, had her paternal lineage been made known, certainly would not have aided in the restoration of those currently broken or perhaps only legally cordoned off ties.

By the time Edward had reached his final day of military service on Easter Sunday of 1865, the very same day Lee Surrendered to Grant at Appomattox Courthouse in Western Virginia, Miss Meara had finished with the devious consolidation of her legal claims to the various land titles within the Calhoun estate. Edward's final day as a fully commissioned Confederate Captain would not however, go without incident. At that time, Captain Calhoun and his men were an integral part of Lee Fowler Pressley's informal congregation of Confederate militiamen. They found themselves engaged in battle out at Dingle's Mill just south of Sumter upon the three o'clock hour and remained tormented by the lingering darkness of an ominously approaching dawn. Edward had escaped suffering any serious casualties during his prior months of service and the same held true for Big Luke, though some of their rather valiant yet otherwise meaningless escapes had been notable. Edward and his trusty steed were stationed just three miles south of Sumter proper and he had planned to return home later that day until the fighting broke out.

Near the end of the battle, as both sides were scattering due to a lack of impetus, direction or leadership, Edward made an ill-advised decision to follow along on the heels of a fourteen-year-old farm boy from up around Florence who was energetically chasing some disconnected Yankee infantrymen into the swamplands near the rather ambiguous banks of the Wateree River. The boy was a wildcard for certain and had ridden down from the north of the state to join his long-suffering Confederate brethren as they dug their heels in just south of Sumter at the mill. While there was little peril in chasing some lost Yankees who had dropped their rifles in favor of hastening their escape into the marshes, the thought of returning home and the tantalizing proximity of the end of the war caused Edward to lower the guard of his restraint ever so slightly. As such, he missed spotting the rifleman who had taken an interest in trying to cover the backsides of his precariously exposed brothers from the mountains of New York upon endeavoring to join the rambunctious farm boy in the hunt.

The shot was never heard amidst the scattered rounds still being fired from one side of the breastworks at the center of the battle site onto the other. The well-aimed ball caught Edward's knee cap clean with a glancing blow and then explosively pierced the lung of Big Luke with the accompanying sound of a morbid thud when rupturing that vacuous chamber. Big Luke held firm upon being struck instead of falling, which was likely the only thing that saved the already damaged leg from being crushed beneath the girth of one the largest animals in service throughout the Carolinas. Though he was galloping out at a good clip after the Yankee miscreants split out from the Union flank and a few strides ahead of Edward, Virgil O'Keefe heard the bullet strike Big Luke's side. The sound reverberated across the short span of open field between the raging boy and his Captain like a vacuous boom of the rolling thunder of a swiftly moving storm set upon the high skies and foretelling of the displeasure of the heavens above.

Virgil O'Keefe lamented for the flashing of an instant what was to be the passing into history of his fleeting and unfulfilled destiny to attain battlefield glory by skinning the hides of a few Yanks. Yanks so lost and confused they were willfully running into a bog along the Wateree as if there might be something of their salvation to be found in such a place. Virgil could picture them standing there stuck in the mire as he emptied the full bevy of his country boy arsenal into their chests while his brassy minded mare, Val reluctantly slowed at Virgil's command and gave up the chase. Before Virgil turned the mare to retrieve his Captain, one of the frightened Yanks turned and looked at him from the distance of no more than forty yards before stepping into the bog. Virgil raised his rifle as the shot was no more challenging than taking a duck sitting on the still water of the family pond from the vantage point of his porch back home. The man's eyes widened with terror while Virgil slowly and methodically tickled the trigger of his supremely accurate weapon.

Virgil was suddenly overcome by a vision of the man's little children running through an open field filled with snow that looked like cotton and the Yankee officers rounding him up later to settle out his conscription fees. His finger began to twitch as if some darker thought, which simultaneously possessed his mind, felt the moment of murder dissipate. Virgil threw his weapon from his hands down onto the ground and yelled, "Thataways, you Yankee fool!" while pointing off to the south to a spot sure to be blocked from any sort of Confederate advance. "Don't y'all do no scoutin' no more while you be burning to the ground every darned thing that be crossin' your path!"

The man received his prodding unconditionally and waved at Virgil before running off in the direction Virgil had so graciously pointed out for his benefit. Virgil hollered out in reply, "Don't you go wavin' at me you filthy Yank! I will pick up my rifle and shoot 'ya dead on my own ya yella' belly!" Virgil then laughed and dismounted from his horse while the man made haste for the higher ground of the river bank to the south.

Edward had remained seated upon Big Luke trying to comfort the old boy while the steed began to falter. Virgil approached and took a look at both the side of the horse and Edward's knee while Edward continued to comfort Big Luke by whispering gently to the animal. Upon making his initial assessment, Virgil O'Keefe spit out some of his tobacco juice into the greening grass of the spring season beneath his feet and reported back quite agitatedly, "Aw' hell, Cap'm Calhoun! We's gonna have to put the old boy down. Damnable Yankees! Not a one of 'em can shoot straight is the problem!"

Virgil then removed his hat and lowered his head to impart a blessing upon Big Luke while his soothing left hand stroked the animal's right flank. When He had finished, Virgil looked up at Captain

Calhoun and said, "Let's get you on down from there, Cap'm afore one of them imbeciles shoots you down. They might have a chance of hittin' sumthin' now that they guns is pointed in the other direction while they disperse."

Edward patted Big Luke once more and dismounted quite awkwardly in favoring his right knee while Virgil assisted him with the effort. When the two men were seated on the ground and much more challenging targets for any sharp shooters still lingering about the field Virgil said, "Don' be lookin' like that knee a your'n is ruined, Cap'm. But you gon' be on dem sticks for a good lick."

Edward shook his head spasmodically in an effort to gather his bearings and replied almost absentmindedly, "Never mind me, son. You think the horse is lost? I hoped to return the steed to his keeper as he lost his boy already somewhere out near the Mississippi." Virgil spit into the grass again and give a long hard look at Big Luke from his seated position in the grass. "I reckon' he can't breathe so good, Cap'm. It's a real shame. I ain't seen one bigger'an 'em and only a few older. Ya' still gots your pistola on hand, Cap'm?"

Edward's knee had locked up with pieces of the shattered bone catching like a broomstick in a bicycle wheel. Virgil was primarily right about the knee but Doc Bailey would once again have his work cut out for him in mending the partly crushed joint. He looked up at Big Luke and thought it a shame the only thing he would get to killing during his short time serving with the Confederate ranks was his own horse. Then he pictured Mr. Satterfield's face when he had departed Butterworth Hall for the war and realized he was not capable of taking the animal from the devastated man. "We don't have but four miles in front of us to get on home, son. Are you certain the horse can't make the trip?"

Virgil scratched at his chin while the thoughts of a simple country boy ran through his mind. He had never had the pleasure of talking to a true grandee man before and he remained a bit baffled by the continuing discussion over something that was set in stone and plain as day. Virgil looked over and across the field. There were a few Yankees still gathered and providing cover for the retreating infantrymen. One of the men gathered was the one who shot Edward and Big Luke concurrently. That man had watched Virgil pardon his conscripted mate from up in the Adirondack Mountains of New York State and he was wondering what was keeping the two men from putting the suffering animal out of its misery.

Virgil spoke solemnly to Edward while he kept his eyes on the man who had taken notice of them from across the field amidst the chaos. "Ain't gonna be doin' the old boy no good, Cap'm. He be dead by this time tomorrow, if not sooner, best I can figure. It'd be best if 'ya go on and put him down 'afore more of the Union men take notice." Edward shook his head and asked of Virgil, "Do you think you could do it on my behalf, son? I don't have the heart to tell my man I was the one to put his prized stallion down."

Virgil looked down at the ground in a disappointed manner. What he was first coming to learn of the Aristocracy was not something that suited his fancy. "I ain't one to be shootin' no livin' and breathin' man's horse, Cap'm. I just tryin' to get 'ya to do what's best for the big fella. We can leave him here and see what he does, but you need to be movin' on out. I can pull 'ya on up if you be willin' to put yur neck out there in sayin' goodbye. My horse Val be waitin' and we ain't doin' no favors to none by lingerin' in this here spot, Cap'm." Edward began to tear up. He pulled his pistol and properly showed the handle to Virgil O'Keefe.

Virgil refused the offer by waving his hands in denial. Virgil then turned his head to the Yankee still stationed some fifty yards or so across the flats watching them carefully and tipped his chin in the direction of Big Luke who looked as if he were getting set to scatter amidst the chaos and his agony. The bullet struck the large, playful and loving animal's head in such a way that his pain was violently yet instantaneously no more before the massive beast fell insensibly to the earth with a resounding thud. Edward began to cry in earnest when he heard the awful commotion of the bitter end of his only friend in this horrible war.

Virgil O'Keefe tipped his hat to the Yankee gentleman and thought silently, "I only been signed up for a few days but war gots to be the darndest thing I ever did knows to be set upon God's green earth. Ain't a thing 'bout it that is what it seems but for all the dyin'. God, please do bless 'dat horse. He ain't had nothin' comin' to 'em."

Virgil and Edward rode into town on the back of Val a few hours later with a host of the other men who had scattered for home when the fighting stopped down at the mill. The Yankees had decided to hold their position as the daylight of what turned out to be a fine April morning had begun to break in earnest. The rail lines had been taken offline under cover of darkness and General Potter saw no need to press on into town on the heels of the tattered infantrymen doing little more than drifting off for home and numbering no more than a few hundred on the morning of Easter Sunday. Doctor Bailey had stepped out of his office on Calhoun Street when his assistants were drawn to the window by the frightful sight of the first of the ragged Confederate soldiers marching by the front window of the single-story brick edifice. Though there were not inordinate numbers of the rank and file who were seeking to return home by way of the heart of the town, the boys were rough looking and certainly not expected even though the artillery being fired during the early morning hours of the battle was easily heard by all. Doc had been up since the first of the munitions was fired and as always, had been doing his level best to help heal, nourish or simply soothe the cadre of the hungry orphans scattered about town.

Doctor Bailey quickly spotted Edward and Virgil riding behind the slow-moving band of tattered soldiers. He ran up next to the gallantly pacing stallion and immediately took notice of the blood which had seeped through the torn grey shirt cloth requisitioned to perform as the dressing wrapped around Mr. Calhoun's wounded right knee. Seeing that the injury was not insignificant, Doc called up to Edward while Mr. Calhoun leaned into Virgil's back to keep from falling into the road. The wounded man had grown weak of both body and spirit and he failed to hear Doc Bailey calling up to him while he watched his wretched brethren in arms continue on with that final march in the face such uncertainty and the sour taste of both death and defeat infecting even their thoughts of shortly returning to their loved ones and the farms they called home.

Doc walked in stride with Val and studied Edward's leg wound a bit more intensely before beckoning to the boy directing the lively and headstrong steed through town. "What happened to Captain Calhoun's leg, soldier?" Virgil O'Keefe looked down at the good doctor who had such concern glinting from the depths of his tried and tired eyes and replied, "Rifle shot glanced off his kneecap before goin' on in to his mount. Big fella stood strong though and kept from fallin' and finishin' that leg off for good. He gon' live but if you's the doc some proper care wouldn' be a hurtin' the Cap'm a bit."

Doc Bailey nodded hastily as he continued to step lively in an effort to keep up with the horse. "Yes, young man, I am the doctor here in Sumter and my office is just a few doors back down the road. Bring him around and I'll go have my assistants prepare a place for Captain Calhoun." "Yes, 'um, Sir, doctor, Sir. Ol' Val here's gonna bring 'em right on up to your door," replied Virgil as he steadied his mount. Doc nodded and ran the short distance down the street to the office to alert Miss Kitty and Miss Grace, who had replaced Miss Greta and Miss Sula after those bright and beautiful souls had left town when their husbands were freed from a neighboring plantation.

When Edward awoke in the back room of Doc Bailey's office a few hours later, the quarter was empty except for Miss Kitty. The recently minted widow, whose husband had died prior to the burning of Columbia back in February, had also been left childless when her two boys were killed side by side at the second Battle of Bull Run. She sat in a chair in the corner of the unadorned room with vanilla cream walls reading a journal highlighting the exploits and explorations of Merriweather Lewis and William Clark back in 1805. Edward did not recognize the threadbare woman right off as the once full bodied and vibrant woman he had last seen just before her boys died back in the summer of 1862. As such, he simply addressed the woman as Ma'am. "Ma'am, if you will accept my begging of your pardon, do you mind telling me where I am presently situated?"

Miss Kitty finished up the paragraph she had been reading and set the periodical down on the stand next to her chair. She stood up, straightened her careworn spring dress and replied to the awakening man as she stepped over to the table upon which he was resting, "Why, Mr. Calhoun, I do hope the journal I was reading before my eyes or the lingering fog of your delirium have kept you from your proper manners as a Southern gentleman. For I do certainly yet still answer to the name Miss Kitty Manning Jones, though all who shared the name of our blood kin seem to have paid the dearest cost for our cause."

Edward began to sit up but the pressure set upon his broken up knee was far too excruciating to finish with the exercise while a lady was present. He grimaced and exhaled steadily to compose his wares before addressing the woman now standing over him. "My deepest apologies are offered unto you, Miss Kitty. Yes, the magazine was shielding the depths of those majestic eyes of yours. I cannot bear even the thought of the oversight. How are you presently, my dear and gracious lady? I have never recovered form the story about your gallant boys up in Virginia. They are to be made heroes of for all eternity."

Miss Kitty took Edward by the hand and replied with exuding warmth to the man who was then drowning in his shame, "Ah, my gallant Edward. You always were the dreamer amongst our lot when we were coming up. Unfortunately the losing side will have but a few heroes when the history books are written and only then to bolster the legend of the very same men burning us out of our farms, plantations and towns. The affront of what we have done to the helpless Africans will not age well in a land founded upon liberty. Be that as it may, I know my boys and my Archibald did what they felt was right by their people and their way of life. The devil set in somewhere amongst us and we reap the harvest of that vile pact sown so long ago amidst these sorrowful days. I do believe the Yankees will ride into town upon the dawn tomorrow. They are not so vile or so vain as to shake their fists at our God on the very day Jesus defeated the scourge of this death that is all around us."

Edward laid his head back to rest on the pillow set upon the table where he lay and spoke wistfully of the happier days of their youth. "My dearest Carrie Alice Manning, you were always the prettiest girl in the school house. I lamented the day Archibald swept you off of your feet for longer that I care to admit. You still look every bit the vision of those carefree days gone by now."

Miss Kitty smiled musingly for but a fleeting moment in reply to what she viewed as Edward's listless fawning. The woman was no longer capable of taking joy into her heart. As such, her scant and nearly hollow countenance hastily hardened again before she spoke in reply to Edward's senseless flattery. "By the glint of the hope still hiding in the depths of your eyes I can see that you have not received word from home since you set off to join the cause back in December. If you knew what I know or had seen the things that I have seen, even such a lightly twinkling glimmer of hope would be speckled in black and wholly consumed by the reality of our despair."

Edward closed his eyes to shield his soul from the truth of the emaciated woman's face. The veracity of her soulfully spoken word was written upon the give in her grey flesh and the pronounced visibility of her skull where once shone the pretty little tattletale traits of the most beautiful young woman north of Lake Marion. Such was now made manifest that the life they had once known was quite clearly a bill of lading consigned over by and then shipped back to the devil so that the accursed angel could later bask in the very wickedness, want and despair rotting out the essence of the once blooming pith of the woman looking down upon him. The curse upon them all that was always coming as the freight to be paid for each chained man sent out into the fields to do their bidding had arrived. One look at the morbid, empty flesh of that woman's face spoke of as much.

Thusly, Edward did not ask Miss Kitty about the recent events taking place around town. No, Edward spoke of the end that came to her husband as what stood before him seemed suited to take sustenance from only misery and he did not wish to beguile her by way of offering hope that would only drive her to rain sorrow down upon his already tensioned heart strings. "I was not far from Archibald when he made his stand in Columbia. He was already a broken man and mad with the devil's blasphemy when they began to set fire to the town. There was something about the rising flames that drew him in as a group of us stopped to watch before riding off into the cover of the pinelands to the north. It was as if the man saw some saving grace in sending his body forth to be consumed by the conflagration bursting forth from the windows and the doors of the first of the buildings to be set alight. He spoke not a word when he put his heel to the side of his mare and began riding straight back into town as if he would not stop until he was burning alive in the center of the statehouse."

Edward then opened his eyes and carefully studied the twitching orbs of the woman who most certainly was driven just as mad as her suicidal husband by the death of their two boys. She waited for him to say the words but Edward would not begrudge one so overcome by evil in much the same way his mother was. She waited for him to speak, squeezing his hand and wanting nothing more than for Edward to tell her of the screams he let out as his flesh curled and bubbled from the heat but he would not oblige her. Finally she begged of him, "Did he ride the horse into the heart of that inferno, Edward? Did he give his body over to the fire? Did he scream for all to hear when he committed to the very desecration of his own sinful flesh?"

Edward shook his head mournfully as he knew the woman was of the coven now or at least so spiritually deprived she had found her way upon those same morose beliefs. He could have told her what she wanted to hear to set things somewhat at ease by pacifying the blackened wants of her heart. He could have done as much just as he had done so many times in his adolescent existence with his baleful mother when she openly revealed the cold nature of her heart. Yet he refused the craven woman that nostrum and instead held to the flickering light of his hopes for a better tomorrow that might yet rise with the promised one from the ashes of this bitter war; those hopes he held so dear in the face of such destruction and death, and he told her the truth. "No Miss Kitty, the sharp-shooters keeping watch over the torch bearers from the rooftops above shot the maddened man for sport before he ever made the stairs to the statehouse. Still and all, if you must know, I do presume Archibald intended to ride the horse into the fires of hell with him. Both the man and the boy who went before him into this life, they always despised being alone."

Miss Kitty turned her eyes sharply away from the man who had so rudely disavowed her but quickly returned them in a shrewd and cunning form set to knife their way into the depths of the wounded man's soul. She would indeed entertain his undead aspirations for the things not yet possessed by her dark master set upon perishing all things still beholden to God above. "You have been away for far too long Master Calhoun. The world you once knew here is gone or given over to the wants of your unfaithful mother. All that you held dear is no longer serviceable to your God above us. Therefore you shall walk alone or you shall walk in the mists of this eternal darkness."

Edward became hastily fearful to the point that bringing his frame upright was little more than afterthought, even with the pain in his knee driving him near to madness. When he was eye to eye with the grey-orbed mistress whose opal pupils seemed to consume those once vibrant windows to her soul he asked of her, "How can the presence of such wanton and unbound wickedness be true, Madam? For, I have only been away for but a season and some weeks."

Miss Kitty squeezed the frightened man's hand ever tighter in her wiry hand and her eyes began to smile that wicked, sinful smile he was so accustomed to seeing glimmer in the eyes of his mother. She tasted his fear and it was good. She then began to feed on the man's dread as if she were possessed by some entity directly connected to the nether regions below. She sensed the absoluteness of her advantage and spoke to the man as one who deserved to be pitied for what he would come to understand in the days that followed. "Ah, yes, my dearest Edward; you have been away for but a season in the midst of four long years of the devil's war. However, none have made you aware that the time passed here in your absence has been the season of the witch. Go and see my dear boy if you must. Only darkness settles over the land and few remain free of the deadly noose of the harridan's rope."

Edward began to tremble as his mind was set loose to imagine in such vivid color the myriad horrors that may have transpired while he was away. He pulled his hand hastily from the woman's grasp and feigned a stoic look of indifference to the impact of her spell. "Clearly, Madam, the death of your boys has spoiled your heart. What you see with those now enchanted eyes are merely the things my foul mistress wishes for you to see. I intend to see what has been kept sacred by God above upon returning home, though I do believe the expanse of my demesne shall be a far different proposition than what it once was. Such is intended to be a good thing after the many years of our sin and folly alike."

Miss Kitty laughed luridly and then swiftly softened the garish expressions of her depraved wants for the sake of appearances. She knew that the truth of what awaited Master Edward Calhoun would do far more to break his spirit than her baiting and presumptuous words ever could. "My dearest Edward, I do not intend to be present when the dreamer in you dies in the days ahead. That blessing is tabled for your mother and those she serves alone. Moreover, and for little more than the sake of the handsome boy who once possessed such beauty and the grand and wonderful hopes of a joy filled imagination, I do wish you the best as you return to the infernal comforts of the home fires now burning."

With that said, Miss Kitty departed the back room in search of Doc Bailey as it was her sworn duty to do so upon Master Calhoun's awakening. For his part, Edward grew mad with anticipation as he sat in wait for word from his friend, the good doctor of Sumter town. Doctor Bailey entered the room not quickly but purposefully and then approached Edward carefully with the thoughtful guise of a concerned father. "Edward! It is so very good to see you!" exclaimed Doctor Bailey as he stood in place next to the table of his convalescent patient.

Edward shook his head to clear the waft of dankly fragranced air that remained lingering from Miss Kitty's presence and which continued to corrupt his thoughts. He was pleased the deranged woman had not returned with his friend and laced his tone with the undercurrents of that very relief when responding to such an energetic greeting. "The pleasure of reuniting with you is mine, Doctor Bailey! You truly are a sight for sore eyes! Perhaps you should think about retaining the services of one still given over to the glory of our Almighty Father," replied Edward in a level tone which reflected the gradual lifting of Miss Kitty's dour spell. Doctor Bailey nodded and replied, "There are no others beyond Miss Kitty or Miss Grace available for duty and suited to the despair of my trade, which is tied to the misery of the passing of these recent months spent in your absence. I should have watched over you myself but the children are so malnourished. We lose one of the poor abandoned souls near to daily."

"Nothing to worry over, my good man," retorted Edward almost happily. "You must have your hands full and I am certainly a man comfortable enough in his own skin to look past the devilry of a woman so woefully cursed by such terrible loss."

Doctor Bailey nodded with a look of consternation crossing over his well-defined and rather Irish leaning facial features. He spoke with his head down to begin but then eased back into his usual form of warm and expressive gesturing. "Indeed, and there is much to discuss, Edward. First, let us have a proper look at that knee of yours. I do believe it will heal based on what I first saw upon your arrival but you will be limited in your movements and your capacity to rely on the appendage for a month or two. I will have Miss Grace prepare a reasonably useful set of walking sticks that should suffice in allowing you to get around some in the meantime. The good news in that you appear well otherwise." Doc Bailey then winked at Edward while his patient responded, "Thank you, doctor. Thank you for your blessed works and thank you for being a man of noble character. I worried so very little about my people back at home knowing you were around and caring for their needs in addition to the needs of your family."

Doctor Bailey angled his head a bit sidelong to study Edward's rather neutral yet subtly postured mien. His shunted look of mild relief alone suggested to the doctor that Mr. Calhoun would have much to digest in the days to come. However, Doc's immediate concern had to do with the young man watching the affairs of the day transpiring out on the main road through town from the relative comforts of a wooden chair in the front lobby of Doctor Bailey's office. "Edward, Mr. O'Keefe tells me that you managed to get shot upon chasing after the rather wild and unsanctioned escapades of a newly enlisted farm boy. The boy admitted to me that he was but fourteen only after our conversation had continued on for a bit."

Doctor Bailey then turned away from Edward to procure a new bandage for his wounded knee. He was a firm proponent of proper hygiene being critical to the healing process. While he reached onto the wooden shelf for the last of the cloth which would suffice for such a need, Emmett Bailey added, "Wonderful boy, yet he possesses the vernacular suited only for a seaman."

Edward thought back to what had drawn him to the young man while watching him run that detached column of lost Yanks straight into one of the most notorious bogs down along the Wateree. While he remained a bit detached from Doctor's Bailey's preparations to treat his wound as he focused wistfully inward, Edward replied a bit nostalgically, as if the event had taken place years ago. That his perception of the span of time allocated to the memory of the boy had been stretched, as if the boy was certain to fill those present gaps in the years to come, was another sign to the oftentimes intuitive man that his encounter with Mr. O'Keefe down at the mill was not by chance. "Yes, Emmett, something did draw me to that wild injun of a young man. He turned upon his horse and put the screws to six seasoned Union soldiers as if he understood their predicament before they themselves did. There existed a certain brilliance to the madness set upon his eyes that I cannot properly explain but to say that the scene appeared to me as if the boy saw things occurring before they actually took place out there. I was immediately drawn to the young man and not knowing the limitless bounds of his proficiency with a rifle and a horse sought to give him aide in the event the table set to his advantage was suddenly flipped away from his favor."

Doctor Bailey returned to Edward's side as Captain Calhoun sat flat-legged upon the table. He sought to distract his patient from the agony of removing his current wrappings by steadfastly remaining engaged in the conversation. "Though some lye soap for his tongue is a proper compliment to his rather 'loose' diction, I will say the young man is both fearless and charismatic. Perhaps there is a reason he is here now and furthermore, a reason you failed to keep your hide out of the line of fire during such a senseless fray."

Edward bit sharply down on his right index finger to hide the unpleasant grimacing caused by his pain while Doc worked on his knee. When the wounded man had composed his outwardly given response to the less than tender maneuvering of his injury he answered, "I do believe you have hit the mark with such a presumption, Doctor. There is indeed a reason I followed him out there and indeed a reason he was the one to escort me home. I do presume that in due time we will come to understand how it is that our fates have become intertwined beneath this shroud of presented coincidence."

Doctor Bailey had made his assessment of the condition of Edward's knee. Captain Calhoun had been quite fortunate that the patella bone had not ruptured or even splintered beyond the depths of what appeared to be a few shallow fractures that would one day heal. The doctor then prepared to dress the wound and replied rather thoughtfully to Edward's prior assertion, "What I am able tell you about the boy is that he lost his folks when Sherman's columns marched right on into North Carolina. I will also tell you that the boy is afraid to speak nothing of his mind. If he is as talented as you say with his rifle and that beautiful stallion the two of you rode on into town, there presently exists the certainty of his capacities being put to good use."

Edward nodded in reply and then shifted his line of thinking back to what may have befallen those awaiting him at home while he was away. His tensions mounted in accordance with his spoken thoughts. "Doc, Miss Kitty was rather taken by the vile spirits looking to exploit, or dare I say feed upon, the somber news of her husband Archibald's demise. Beyond that, she caused me more than a tremor and a twitch when she spoke of what I may find upon returning to the home fires of Butterworth Hall. Are you aware of what she may have been alluding to, my dear friend and caretaker? Certainly nothing has befallen little Miss Margaret Anne or another of my dearly beloved children without word being sent!"

Doctor Bailey tied down the dressing covering Edward's right knee and stepped up and to his left to address the man from a closer and more personal proximity to his suddenly troubled guise. He then gave a searching look into Edward's eyes to take note of how fragile the gentleman might be in his current state. Though nothing as dire as what Edward had proposed with an almost rhetorical and certainly dour connotation had in fact taken place, there was much to discuss and the time to begin that dialogue was of the essence. "I dare say, Edward, nothing as final as death has gripped any of your beloved, my good man. I know you refuse to speak of Aubrey until he returns from the battlefields of Virginia, but we have received no word of his condition in the preceding months. However, the season of your absence has most certainly been used to set the stage of the postbellum world here in Carolina away from the advantages of your favor."

Edward spoke hastily in reply to Doctor Bailey as he could no longer repress his desire to know what had occurred while he was off fighting the last remnants of an already decided war. Hearing the name of his own boy did not help with the easing of his mounting anxieties. "Precisely what has mother been up to whilst I was away for the entirety of the winter and the opening fortnight of the spring?"

Doc tensed his lips for a moment and ruminated under a bit of duress on exactly where to begin. The first of the news to strike his thoughts occurred for no particular reason excepting the fact Mary Grice was likely to involve the most intense of his lamentations. "We received word of Tanner's death up in Virginia near the end of January, Edward."

Edward's eyes grew wide with shock and he asked, "How have Mary Grice and my precious granddaughters handled news, Emmett? The poor girls aren't but seven and five. That earnest man would have stopped a battalion of Yankees of his own accord for little more than the flash of the refined smile of my first born child. He was a good man and a loving father. That is such sorrowful news. May the brave Mr. Decker rest in peace, Doctor Bailey."

"Your granddaughters were quite saddened by the news and they remained distant while processing their grief. As for Mary Grice, she refused to come out of her childhood room at Butterworth Hall until your mother returned from her journey abroad in late-February. After that moment…" Doc paused to steady his gaze and then continued, "This is difficult for me to say, Edward, but she was a changed woman and presently she remains fully allied with your mother."

Edward shook his head and lamented that he was not there to soothe the angst of his prickly yet well-intentioned first child and her daughters. "I cannot say that I am surprised but we will turn her graces back over to the light once I have returned home to care for them all." Doctor Bailey shook his head and added, "There is more Edward. Mary Grice is no longer domiciled at Decker Hall. She has taken up an abode to the west of town where it is rumored she negotiates on behalf of your mother with the Yankee gentleman presumed to become administrator over the Sumter region."

Edward gasped as if someone or something had punched his gut with a considerable amount of force set behind the blow. "I cannot believe such a thing, Emmett! Who is caring for her children? Her husband has not been known to be dead for but a few months!"

Doctor Bailey shook his head and continued on with what he believed needed to be said. "There is more Edward. There are rumors Mr. Lemarque now calls the same place home." Edward began to lose the footings of his temporal and spatial equilibrium and the room began to spin far too fast to place any of its objects, including Doctor Bailey into focus. The good doctor saw the man falter upon receiving the news and placed his left hand upon his shoulder. The gesture did little good and before long Edward had lost his hold upon the world of the quick while also losing his hold upon the morning meal he had shared with Mr. O'Keefe while the two rode upon the back of Val in the wake of the steady death march of the tattered Confederate soldiers limping and grinding their way towards town.

A few hours later, the carriage driven by Mr. Satterfield and drawn by the two remaining horses stabled out at the Calhoun's livery began its journey down the long and awe inspiring plantation drive culminating at the beautifully columned, grand antebellum veranda of Butterworth Hall. Edward awoke when the carriage throttled and caromed some when the front wheels caught for an instant and then forcibly worked their way over a sizeable fallen limb. Such a disturbance was once an uncommon occurrence while navigating the splendid approach yet now something Mr. Satterfield had grown accustomed to in the absence of the long since scattered groundskeepers. Shocked forth from his swoon and harshly vaulted into the startled wares of his proper sensibilities, the wounded Captain of only the winter season of that final year of the war perceived his person as exposed and primitively feared for his safety before taking stock of his surroundings. Upon waking, he had temporarily lost track of the prior affairs of the day in his mind. Edward asked almost hurriedly, "Have the Union men marched into Sumter?"

Though the grounds had been left unattended for some weeks, when all but five of the remaining servants ran off to join the nearby communes of the freed slaves, Virgil O'Keefe was quite overcome by what remained of Butterworth Hall's once former grandeur. The fields had not been turned for the spring planting and the slave quarters off in the distance beyond the nearest boundaries of what now appeared to be meadows on each side of the roadway remained eerily vacant. Still and all, the magnolias lining the road were a sight to behold as was the magnificent mansion directly ahead with its legendary columns and wide, floor-to-ceiling windows that adorned both floors of the sizeable and stately estate home. Doc Bailey had prepared to answer Edward's question to calm the startled man but he was promptly broken off before he was ever to begin by the spirited young lad to his left; the upstart soldier boy who had so garishly stretched his neck out of the window of the carriage to have a better look at the spectacle of the unkempt grounds. "'Dem Yanks ain't likely to show their faces up in town 'til the morrow, Cap'm. Is you the king a dese here Carolinas or sumthin'? I ain't never beheld such a sight as all a 'dis here is!"

Doc Bailey smiled at the wild-eyed boy so full of life and wonder. He complimented Mr. O'Keefe's observations while Edward turned his head to the window to ascertain his whereabouts. "The boy is likely to be correct in his assertion regarding the Union men, Edward; it being Easter Sunday and all. Are you quite alright?"

Edward shifted his eyes to take in the current condition of Butterworth Hall. Though the place certainly did not present as it might have in Easters past, he counted his blessings presently upon having witnessed the destruction of other similar plantations, those much closer to the wake of Sherman's columns marching at the quick time through South Carolina back in March to join what remained of the fray up in Virginia. Upon having some time to take in scenery, Edward was actually quite pleased by what he saw. The land had so quickly adapted back to its natural state and the old homestead built by Mortimer's grandfather, Charles Edward was still a sight to behold. While he began to wonder what now awaited him within those vaunted walls of a colonial origin, Edward replied, "Yes, Doctor Bailey. I am quite fine. I see we have a new guest to Butterworth Hall as well."

Edward then winked smartly at Doc while gesturing with his smiling guise toward Virgil. The good doctor chuckled out a reply while Virgil O'Keefe continued to crane his neck out of the carriage window. The bold and unabashedly unaware farm boy remained completely oblivious to the state of his 'unrefined' behavior while continuing to take in the splendor of the estate. "Yes, Edward, indeed we do. I was quite certain you would not have had it any other way."

While all that he had borne witness to thus far was enough to convince Virgil O'Keefe that everything laid out before his dumbstruck country boy eyes was little more than a mirage, when Elizabeth Ann came running out of the house concurrently with the approach of the carriage to the front circle, the young man nearly lost hold of his wits altogether and exclaimed, "I think I done died and gone straight to heaven, Cap'm! If I thought me a one of 'em could a hit the side of a barn from fifty paces out I'd swear one a dem Yanks must a got me while was pinin' over Big Luke out in the flats by the marsh." Virgil then shook his head robustly in the manner of one pinching flesh to be certain they are awake and asked, "This here is bein' the place y'all calls home, Cap'm?"

Edward and Doctor Bailey smiled at one another in response to the boys antics. Doctor Bailey had to choke down an outright laugh while he nodded at the approaching girl's father in a signal of acquiescence to the one now appropriately suited to both answer and reign in the young hellion. "Well, my lad, this is indeed the place I have lived for the entirety of my life. I must warn you however, the women are far more challenging to deal with than the men." Virgil scratched his chin while keeping his eyes locked on the approaching young woman as if he might go blind if he lost sight of her and called back into the carriage, "Well it ain't no mystery as to why, Cap'm. We needs to be gettin' on to boarding the place up 'afore those Yankee dogs come snoopin' 'round wif gifts a the Lord above like her on the farmstead!"

Doctor Bailey coughed up a laugh that was anything but subtle while Edward's face grew a bit red in the knowing he was to have his hands full with this young country buck. No one had ever addressed one of the most opulent and stately plantations in all of the Carolinas as merely something of a farmstead, which Edward found hard to fathom even if the old estate was presently but a shell of its former grandeur. Yet, the girl's father had bigger fish to fry as it were in the immediacy of the moment. "Yes, young man, but allow me to be quite clear by saying that is my daughter of whom you speak."

Virgil objected in reply to the Captain's loosely veiled insinuation rather quickly. "Aw, shucks, Cap'm! I ain't mean nothin' by it. 'Dem Yanks absconded with my own sis' after killin' my folks is all I be sayin'.

As far as I done cared, they could a had all 'dem Yankees left over at the stockade up in Florence and done left my folks and my sis alone. I shot me a few a 'dem Yanks though, 'afore they gots to havin' their sights set on Val. You can't trust but a one of 'dem dogs exceptin' maybe the one gone and done me the favor of puttin' your horse at peace."

Edward was wistfully watching his beautiful daughter approach as the boy spoke and he lowered his head when Virgil had said his piece. He couldn't even imagine what the boy's parents had endured when the boy's sister was abducted or otherwise. He spoke solemnly in reply to Virgil as Mr. Satterfield called the last of his aging steeds fit for duty to a halt. "I am truly sorry for all that you have lost, son. My boy, Aubrey never made it out of Fort Wagner when the Union stormed their defenses back in July of sixty-three. I was told for a time that the few who remained of his company had been transported back up to Virginia by sea and were once again fighting somewhere up there. I have recently learned that was a lie spawned by an old enemy of mine back in Georgia."

Edward began to tear up while Doc and Virgil sat silently and solemnly in wait to hear what the man still wished to say regarding his only son. Edward firmed up his guise and drew his shoulders swiftly inward in an effort to clear the visible traces of his emotion. He then continued. "In any event, I had never spoken of the incident or at least the possibility of his death in the hopes that he might one day return to me if his name was never mentioned along with the perished. Perhaps I owe him a far more appropriate eulogy than that of my silence which stands guardian over those places within that cannot yet form the proper words. One day soon, I will offer up my testimonial to my boy for the benefit of the ears of all. In the meantime, as a show of my gratitude for what you have done for me out at Dingle's Mill, you are welcome to Aubrey's room, young man but please; do give proper deference as it regards the ladies of the house."

Young Virgil O'Keefe had tilted his head back into the carriage when it came to a halt to listen to his Captain but he never took his eyes off of the young mistress. "Yes Sir, Cap'm, Sir! I was only speakin' of the defendin' any lady in need wit' dat of my own life! I is truly sorry 'bout your boy. I don' know how to thank 'ya for such an honor as 'dem quarters. But you needn't worry for any of the pretty little ladies out at dis here farmstead! No Yankee gonna lay eyes on a one a 'dem with Virgil O'Keefe scoutin' about!"

Edward nodded begrudgingly to the young man, though Virgil was still looking directly at Elizabeth Ann as he did so. The young man's eyes then proceeded to track his daughter quite precisely while she crossed in front of the steadied carriage to open the door on her father's side and greet him. Once the fine wooden door had been sprung open, she noticed the tearing of Edward's pant leg and the bloody bandage right away. "Papa! Papa! Welcome home, dear Papa! What have those terrible Union men done to you while you were away?"

Edward smiled at his purely and puritan pretty young woman of a daughter, who appeared to have blossomed so in his absence. After taking in her radiance for a long moment, he answered her greeting warmly as if the young lady had whisked away every last one of his burgeoning fears in an instant, "My dearest, Elizabeth Ann! Let me have a good look at you! You so look the part of a grown woman now. Have you all been well in my absence?"

Elizabeth Ann's face became a bit flushed upon thinking of the current condition of things at the manor but she decided there would be time for discussing such unfortunate actualities later. "Yes, father we are all quite well for the most part and very well upon considering the state of affairs in the world around us." Elizabeth Ann then looked over to Doctor Bailey and asked, "What of poor father's leg, Doctor Bailey? Will he yet live?" Doctor Bailey smiled at his forever favorite patient and replied soothingly, "Why of course, my dear girl. If I was able to have that arm of yours fit for proper use again, I do believe I will have your father back to his full complement of activities before June arrives."

Virgil O'Keefe became a bit slack jawed upon seeing the woman up close and upon hearing the sweet, melodious sound of her voice. If asked, Doc Bailey would have noted that the boy had lost hold of his slobber as it concerned the corners of his mouth. Elizabeth Ann artfully took notice of Mr. O'Keefe before answering Doctor Bailey. "That is wonderful news, Doctor Bailey! We do hear of and see such awful infirmities set upon the men who have been fortunate enough to stagger home from the war." Elizabeth Ann then smiled wide enough at her father to melt the poor, drooling man's heart and added, "Oh, my manners! Who is our distinguished guest for the evening father?"

Not used to having another speak on his behalf, Virgil interrupted Mr. Calhoun quite neatly and fumbled awfully through his introduction to one so well brought up as Elizabeth Ann was to boot, "Howdy, Ma'am! I bein' Virgil O'Keefe if the fancy suits ya. Rode with the Cap'm here down at Dingle's Mill and woulda shot me up a half-dozen a'dem Yanks if the Cap'm here had stayed put where'n he was at." Virgil then laughed nervously of his own accord with his hat pressed to his chest and colored his greeting with, "I's always at the service of a pretty lady like yusself, Ma'am!" Now, Miss Elizabeth Ann Calhoun had never seen, nor heard for that matter, one quite like this young man. She evenly raised her delicate fingers to her open mouth in a show of perplexed wonder.

Doctor Bailey slapped the young man firmly on the back to take something of the wind out of his wildly blowing sails and attempt to slowly coax the rather eager gentleman into displaying mannerisms at least lightly resembling proper etiquette while in the presence of a young lady, "Alright now, son. Let's move on out of the carriage so we can get Captain Calhoun into the house and appropriately positioned to greet his family."

"Yessum, Doc," answered Virgil while he placed his hat back onto his head. His heart skipped a beat as he moved closer to the young woman standing in front of the open door on Edward's side of the coach. Doctor Bailey quickly slapped the oblivious Mr. O'Keefe on the shoulder and continued to guide him along as to the proper course of affairs when a lady is present. "Other side, young man, lest you run right on through the lady in wait for her father."

Virgil was a bit stunned to think the contraption had more than one way in or out, yet he heeded Doc's request; though he did so rather begrudgingly. Edward laughed at the young man in a wholly bemused manner while Miss Elizabeth Ann backed away from the carriage door slightly in the event this Mr. O'Keefe wasn't quite clear on his instructions. Edward then interjected jovially to spare the boy any further unease, "Don't worry, Mr. O'Keefe. You shall get familiar with the lay of the land soon enough. However, and as I have already advised you heretofore, you may find the ladies of the manor far more difficult to enmesh than a few lost Union boys caught out in the heat of battle." Doctor Bailey shared amply in Edward's mirth while Virgil grimaced at his own folly. Mr. O'Keefe then briskly straightened up his appearances on the other side of the carriage. He may not have been able to place all of their uppity words, but the young man knew when he was being played the fool.

A short while later, Edward found himself limping up the stairs to the beautiful storybook front porch of the mansion while Doc and Virgil propped him up from beneath his arms. When the three men had nearly reached the final stair, Elizabeth Ann walked across the porch to open up the heavy and ornate mahogany front door. With the door opened wide enough to nearly accommodate the three side by side gentleman in the exact manner by which they approached, and in the manner of something resembling a loosely given warning to her father, Elizabeth Ann announced, "Grandmother will be very glad to see you home and generally well. She has taken up permanent residence in the attic and inquires of your whereabouts almost daily."

Edward frowned as he cleared the threshold and subsequently feigned his happiness over such a joyous circumstance, although in truth he expected nothing different from his mother with the Union soldiers stationed so close to town for such a notable stretch now. Thusly, Edward did manage to contrive a loosely credible smile in the direction of his daughter in reply. Just as proper etiquette would dictate. Elizabeth Ann began to look around the house in a premeditative fashion and to think through other ways in which she might be of use to the gentlemen situating her father when Edward replied rather cheerily to the news, "Simply wonderful, my dear. Perhaps she will join what remains of our assemblage later for the evening meal to celebrate Easter."

Elizabeth Ann twisted coyly away from her father and indulged the charade as such: "Of course, I don't venture up to her quarters, father. However, I will most certainly see if Amos is feeling up to the task once we have you situated and comfortable." Edward nodded and rolled his eyes at Elizabeth Ann in the manner of a shared jest and said, "Do not trouble the good lad over such an errand. I will send Emmett up after our cherished matriarch once he is no longer fit to be tied over lugging me all about town."

Edward laughed but the good doctor did not join him in unison and simply stated, "I owe Amos a fair sum for all of his wonderful work back at the office. I do believe the young man aims to be a doctor, or perhaps even a barrister one day given the way he marks his hours. I'll tack a bit more on to his kingly sum for such dutiful work should he accept my revised proposal." At that, both men shared a laugh while Virgil O'Keefe scratched his head with confusion until the beautiful young lady of his fancy returned from a quick trip to the adjoining sitting room. At that point, the young man's eyes grew wide with

THE SEASON OF THE WITCH ❧

uncontrollable delight and he forgot all about the strange circumstances surrounding Mistress Calhoun.

Easter dinner that evening was a joyful affair if proper weight and measure were given to the ancillary circumstances of the hour surrounding the unlikely gathering of tradesmen, nobility, former slaves, and rather rough looking outsiders happily welcomed into the bunch on the very eve of the formal Yankee march into Sumter. With the full complement of the family gathered for the celebration of the resurrection of the Risen Lord, absent Miss Meara of course, and also in celebration of Edward's welcome return to both home and hearth at Butterworth Hall, nothing of what remained of the finest of the threadbare provisions or the culinary talents of each member of the eclectic congregation was overlooked upon the commencement of such a joyous occasion. Prior to Mistress Tabatha bringing forth the cleverly engineered bread pudding for dessert, given the dearth of necessary ingredients available for what turned out to be quite the delectable concoction, Edward addressed his new family by chiming dutifully upon his dinner glass. "I have a few matters of extreme importance to discuss with you all before our not so gentlemanly Yankee callers arrive upon the morrow. The very first of which is that I cannot tell you how proud I am of everyone gathered here in attendance this evening. You have all done so well in the face of such extreme adversity in my absence."

Following his congratulatory benediction, each member of Edward's audience assembled in the grand dining room of Butterworth Hall glanced appreciatively around the room and nodded to one another in acknowledgement of the fine work and dutiful sacrifice of their compatriots during the trying winter season of 1865. When enough time had passed to allow for the building comradery to peak, Edward worked his way onto the ill tidings. The news they all stood to gain from by hearing, in that such palpable portent would aid them in beginning to prepare for what tomorrow was set to bring forth to their severely altered and beset by hardship though not yet utterly scattered existence. "The second item I would like to address with you is this: based on what I have experienced during my service to the Confederate cause in other areas of the state given over to the smaller cohorts of persisting Union occupation, there exists a more likely chance for than against that Butterworth Hall will serve as the center of command in this region for our uninvited guests. As such…"

Edward should have known by the look of astonishment melting down the faces of his adherents that something sinister beyond the sour news of his announcement was afoot. However, he was far too focused upon carefully choosing his words to notice that Miss Meara had ever so slyly and sveltely slipped into the room and currently stood directly behind him. Not long after hearing the first few syllables uttered from his mother's mouth, which was the only apparatus Edward had known to be capable of producing such an interposing and juxtaposed cadence of wickedness intertwined with self-satisfied joy, Edward instantly realized that Miss Meara was indeed standing over his left shoulder as she was wont to do during the business convocations and ceremonial dinners of his younger days.

"Why are you filling the minds of your people with such fear and anguish, my dear Edward? As well as you know me, you should have surmised that I would never stand for such a thing as Yankee officers desecrating the hallowed halls of Butterworth Manor with their hideous slander and brutish ways. As always, your dear mother has taken care of everything for the lot of you lost souls. None of you present above that of the less than distinguished graces of chattel need worry a bit about what is to come if you simply remain loyal to my, admittedly at times, somewhat eccentric whims." When Miss Meara had finished addressing the assembly, she walked over to Doctor Bailey and put her cold and sterile yet shapely and outwardly stately hands upon his shoulders. The Doctor flinched instinctively upon sensing the cold soul of the woman through those eerily docile and bloodless appendages.

Edward did not turn and face his mother but instead carefully studied the face of each man, woman and child situated at the table. When he confirmed their continuing disdain for the woman now putting the good doctor into such a state of unease, he responded to his mother's antagonistic disruption of their heretofore enjoyable evening; "Hello, mother. I am glad to hear you sounding so well. Yet I must ask, who or what have you sold into Yankee hands for the favor of your advantage as it concerns Butterworth Hall? Surely you do not possess arts dark enough to requisition one who is yet to be named with naught but the queer potency of your cabalistic allure."

Miss Meara shook her head disparagingly at her corporally wounded and otherwise ill-prepared son and admonished him in return, "There, there, Edward. You know far better than to think I would exchange anything of value to you if it were not in return for something or someone you held ever dearer. I simply exchanged what remained of our title to land over in Uriah for the aegis of the gentleman who is to be the Union administrator over Sumter and the surrounding climes. Forsooth, I just knew you would find such an arrangement to be a far superior option to submitting your precious daughters, I do know how you love them so, to the whims of murderous Yankee gentleman and outright vagabonds."

With that Miss Meara fixed her eyes sharply upon Virgil O'Keefe, as the rather uppity faced young man was seated directly across from where she stood behind Doctor Bailey at the table, and added for good measure, "Though it would appear we do yet welcome vagabonds to Butterworth Hall in such dark times as these."

Virgil shifted as if he were to stand in objection to such a soul rending stink eye and personal affront but Edward hastened to the boy to remain seated with his level hand motioning toward the table. While Mr. O'Keefe did oblige his Captain, the farm boy's mouth was slipperier than a greased pig in knee high mire. "Listen here now, Ma'am. I ain't no vagabond and we fightin' men don' take kindly to no one negotiatin' with no Yanks while we is out there dyin' in the field a battle!" "Well, well, well…exactly what do we have here, Edward? A boy of lowly, sustenance farm stock with an attitude in need of some adjusting such would appear."

Miss Meara then turned her eyes from Edward and fixed them sharply back on the boy until he began to shrink back in his chair from the silent onslaught of such an unholy glare, which gnawed at his rapidly beating heart and somehow pressed sharply upon his windpipe. She then shifted her guise to that of one lost in thought or extremely puzzled by a recent development as she rejoined the suddenly startled young man. "Has no one been kind enough to tell you the war has ended as of today, my dirty child?"

Virgil made a quick move to rise from the table if for no other reason than to escape the tension of the piercing clutches those black, beady nighttime eyes of the harridan. However, Edward leveled the enthusiastic young buck back into his seat with his hand once again and kindly refuted the vile woman. "Why must you speak out of both sides of your mouth mother? Is such to avoid ever telling the truth? What makes you think the war has come to an end? Our valiant boys continue to defend what they are able."

Miss Meara might as well have pulled out her pointy hat and her broom at this point in the one-sided entendre. For her laugh in response to Edward's hopeful rhetoric left no doubt as to the true nature of her religion. Some were forced to cover their ears as the shrill noise evoked the pretense of hot, bubbling blood thumping through their eardrums. When she had dispensed with the theater of her ungodly and mocking joy, Miss Meara responded to her son, "My poor, poor, boy, Edward. He is always so far behind the workings of his cunning mother. If you have not heard, Lee has surrendered to Grant at the Court House up in Appomattox, Virginia on this very day." With such joyous news crushing the final hopes of so many in the room, Miss Meara heartily reignited her awful, self-aggrandizing cackle once again.

Edward lowered his head in defeat but called back to her sternly, "Stop it, Mother! Though I understand what you are doing, Elizabeth Ann and Blair Raimi do not need to see you like this!" Miss Meara shook her head in taunting her boy and replied cattily, "What, are you not equivalently offended to see me behave in such a way in front of your black child, Edward? Perhaps her unholy breeding is better suited to my affinity for the arcane."

"Mother! You stop that right this instant! The child does not know any better!" replied Edward as harshly as he could muster without screaming or throwing his plate directly into her exposed throat. Miss Meara giggled again and taunted her boy further, "My goodness, Edward, how can the child not know she is colored? By June you will no longer be able to see her at night but for the whites of her eyes! Just like the rest of those sneaky devils running off into the darkness while our boys are off dying on the front!"

Edward attempted to stand in defiance to his mother's spiteful scorn and the irreparable damage such hateful words would inflict upon all three of his daughters present. Yet his leg gave way in a lame and wretchedly painful manner, causing the broken man to fall back into his chair awkwardly. He began to weep with his head bowed near to the table while he begged of her to stop but the rotten woman would never answer to such a shriveling plea on the very eve of her long awaited subjugation of Butterworth Hall, which stood to put her firmly in control of the Calhoun family dynasty. Those gathered sat open mouthed or closed their eyes upon witnessing both the impotence and the public shame and suffering of their benefactor and patriarch. The humiliation and sorrow of the man they adored and the vile, hideous joy of the woman they had come to despise whilst sleepwalking through the stygian haze of that soul rending season of the witch were equivalently hard to bear.

None of the men in the room were in a position to stop the woman from unleashing the full complement of her unbound madness. The prospects of what lie in wait at the hands of the occupying Yankee mercenaries put the gentlemen at great risk and they would certainly never lay their hands upon the slight yet comely woman, no matter what venom she spit forth from her beguiled tongue. In the interest of protecting little Miss however, Miss Leslie did stand and face up to the woman. As she approached, Miss Meara taunted her likewise. "Do not come in front of me to pass judgement on my words, slave woman! You have lied to the child about the true nature of her origins for the entirety of her life! Have you told her what she fetched at auction yet? She's so confused now; she doesn't know whether she's supposed to befriend the proper citizenry of the estate or the lowly chattel. She has you and that scourge of a widow drooling in the corner of the room, Miss Sarah, to thank for that!"

Miss Leslie lowered her eyes from the witch as she could sense rather acutely that those eyes had powers beyond warping the waking thoughts of those who looked into them. She replied rather sheepishly to the ill and diminutive creature with such a fiery tongue. "If'n you don' mind me sayin' so, Ma'am, li'l Miss don' be knowin' any better 'cuz 'dats da way God intended for her to be. She gots herself a white momma, a black momma an' one 'dats somewheres in 'tween. She don' even be knowin' dat skin color mean somethin' an' I don' reckon proper 'dat God gonna look kindly upon you takin' dat from her."

Miss Meara's eyes grew wide and her face went stark and hollow before she lashed out at Miss Leslie in reply, "Oh, you insolent woman! I aim to take far more than that from the child! I aim to take far more than that from you all come morning when the blue jackets arrive. You have no idea the ways in which I will make each and every one of you suffer until I have taken exactly that which I seek!"

Miss Meara then paused to calm both her mercurial tone and her vile mannerisms. She had not intended to break Edward so thoroughly until he was rendered essentially powerless in the face of the Union occupation. In the event she had provoked any of them emotionally beyond the extent of rational counter measures, the witch added quite smugly, "Furthermore, if anything should happen to me they'll burn you all out and lay your bones upon the road for the scurvy dogs staved by war and famine to gnash up in their teeth. Now you colored folk get on out to the cabins for the remainder of the evening and you be on off of my property by sunrise. That includes the bastard child. Send her back to Uriah to her whore of a mother. I believe someone special aims to be tending to the Haitian princess there."

Miss Meara then turned her back to Miss Leslie and the rest of the stunned folks gathered for that once warm and welcoming Easter meal. Before she had departed the room, Miss Leslie stepped to her rather swiftly and put her hand on the haughtily departing woman's shoulder. The witch spun around quickly and put the palm of her right hand on the sullen woman's forehead while clutching her index finger and thumb firmly to her temples, though it pained her so to touch Miss Leslie's exposed brown skin. Miss Leslie turned her head away from the deathly grip of the witch, but Miss Meara held firm with her hand until Miss Leslie began to go mad with unceasing and rapidly progressing tremors of doubt and fear.

When Miss Leslie's knees grew weak from the onset of her madness, Miss Meara pushed her adversary's head back frightfully by rapidly straightening out her right arm. Though the force of the thrust from such a slight woman as Miss Meara was should have sent Miss Leslie back only a half-step and no more, she was cast halfway across the room. The suddenly possessed and much maligned woman back-pedaled awkwardly until she fell at the feet of the back of the chair of Miss Margaret Anne, who was facing away from the entrance way to the dining room and towards the far wall. The child had been listening intently with her eyes closed.

As Edward had been rendered incapacitated of both body and now mind, Mr. Laing sprung up from his seat next to Amos and made for the entrance way to fetch Miss Meara before she made the stairs upon her exit. Miss Margaret Anne grabbed hold of the gruff man's hand as he slowed his progress toward the grand archway leading out of the dining room to be certain Miss Leslie was not hurt. The gesture caused Mr. Laing to halt completely as he did not wish to inadvertently pull the child off of, or far worse, over the backside of her chair. Margaret Anne did however, take full advantage of the handsome ogre's three remaining fingers and use them to hop down from her chair and speak with her mammy. By that time, Miss Leslie remained coiled up on the floor in the fetal position. Her mind was still racing with waves of eternal guilt over the death of her three sons that would not stop tormenting her heart, which had mended over the years in such a brittle fashion. The child put her hand gently upon Miss Leslie's forehead and the horrible thoughts came to a halt straightaway.

Miss Leslie looked up at Margaret Anne with a slightly startled and wholly confused bearing and asked, "What been a happenin' to me, li'l Miss? How did you make it stop?" Margaret Anne smiled at her mammy and answered her plainly, "I took the bad things away. I can always take the bad things away, Mammy. Didn't Mr. Laing tell you that?"

Miss Leslie began to sit up with the help of that same Mr. Laing. Suddenly, the true nature of the child was beginning to make sense to her. The little girl was an angelic expression of the light, precisely like those her grand mammy used to tell her of when they couldn't sleep late at night while tucked up tight together in the corner of the overburdened cabin out on Butler Island. She was like the spirit wind that eased the tormented souls of those tender, frightened creatures crossing that great unknown leviathan into the west while chained to the darkened underbelly of some blood and feces stained vessel or another. Before Miss Leslie could respond to little Miss, the child asked of her, "What did you wish to say to say to Grandma Meara, Mammy? I will ask her in your place."

Miss Leslie smiled at the beautiful little child and replied as warmly as only a loving mother would have been able to reciprocate upon enduring such a doleful spell. "I was just gonna ask her not to be sendin' you off to Uriah 'til mammy Sarah get better from da knowin' dat yur daddy died off in da war; 'til she be well enough to be makin' da trip wif ya."

Miss Margaret Anne smiled at Miss Leslie and replied, "I shall ask her for you, Mammy. I shall ask her right now. I fear for what is to become of little Adelaide if we are sent away." Miss Leslie shook her head slowly as one still gathering her wits about her and said, "No, my child. She don't wanna be bother 'wif dat now. Best you be stayin' right here aside me."

Miss Margaret Anne laughed and said, "That's silly, Mammy. We shall never know the answer if we do not ask." Miss Leslie nodded uncertainly in reply as she rose to her feet and then proceeded to answer the promised child. "I be askin' dat a her in da mornin' lil' Miss."

Irrespective of her mammy's request to stay put, by the time the still slightly confused Miss Leslie had finished straightening up her dress, the child was already standing out in the dimly lit front hall not but a step or two beyond the archway to the dining room. Margaret Anne was calling up the stairs after Miss Meara, who was not all that far along in her progress to ascend to her lair beyond the upper floor of the manor. "Grammy, Meara! Grammy, Meara! Miss Leslie wants to know if I can stay here until Mommy Sarah is better again. Would that be okay?"

Miss Meara stopped suddenly, turned and stormed down the stairs until she was standing in front of and in fact looming over the promised child. She looked down at the enchanting little sprite and asked of her out of a mouth smartly angled with disbelief, "What did you just call me, child?"

Miss Margaret Anne looked up at Miss Meara and responded plainly, "Grammy, Meara. That's what I called you, Grammy Meara." The woman nodded slyly and returned shrewdly, "I see. And who exactly put you up to calling me Grammy Meara?"

Margaret Anne thought for a moment and replied as candidly as a six-year-old might, though her diction and cogitation were closer to that of a rather adept eleven-year-old. "No one put me up to anything, Grammy Meara. That is simply your name. You are Edward's mother and Edward is my father of a sort. Even though I imagine the papers he has on me are going to turn up worthless right soon if they are not already."

Miss Meara began to grow cross and asked a question a bit forwardly of the uncommonly astute child, "How would you know such a thing as that, child? No one has spoken of such things openly that still lives."

Miss Margaret Anne smiled all the same and answered the woman no differently than she had before. "I know all of the secrets that run true within the darkness in your heart, Grammy Meara. I knew them before you were born. The man who told you of my papers under duress is kin to my mammy and father to my brother, Amos."

Miss Meara became impulsively irate in response to the child's portentous warning of a sort, which was clearly delivered from the realms beyond their present earthly station. As such, the witch hastily bent down and slapped the child quite firmly upon the cheek. The sound of the little girl's youthful, smacking flesh was both painfully lush and unconscionable. For good measure, Miss Meara followed the blow by admonishing the child quite harshly. "You watch your tongue, you heathen Negro child! I'll cut it right out of your mouth and feed it to the snakes! Why have you let them all lie to you for all this time if you knew the truth? Why do you not despise them all for their deceit?"

Margaret Anne felt at her reddened cheek almost absentmind-edly and answered the sorceress evenly, "Because all that was hidden remained as such due to you, Grammy Meara. Those who love me feared you might come to harm me before I could remove that black-ness from your heart and this very land which you have cursed through the bloodletting and the chains of your time."

Miss Meara was aghast and now clearly engaged well beyond her element in dealing with whatever had possessed the child. She shot back rudely, "Who taught you to speak of such things, child? Do you think that I fear you as one who might dare put a stop to my reign over this place? Try me child! I beg of you!"

With that, Mr. Laing stepped into the hallway with the grand staircase and was poised to interject on behalf of the little girl when Miss Margaret Anne replied; once again in a deadly calm yet strangely cheerful voice. "To try you is one of the very things I am here to do, Grammy Meara. Come closer to me and I will show you."

In many ways, Miss Meara should have known better than to appease the phantom fairy of the west wind, but the vile witch had never come across one such as the promised child. Moreover, the wicked and prideful woman was clearly not going to cower before anything while being carefully watched by the very people she wished to torment for all eternity, and most certainly not a sweet and inno-cent-looking six-year old child. Therefore, Miss Meara smiled rogu-ishly and obliged the child by crouching down to her eye level. Miss Margaret Anne smiled warmly into the eyes of the heathen witch and said, "You will be quite better after we are one, Grammy Meara. I promise you as much."

Before the vile woman knew what the child meant, her small hand was upon her heart and in the far corners of her body there was suddenly warmth where before there had existed nothing but the infinite cold; an emptiness unable to be appeased for long by any and all manner of cruelty delivered as tribute to her malicious masters. The demon that controlled the witch on behalf of a far darker and more powerful prefect instantly felt the seismic dislocation caused by the child's hand upon the woman's chest. The succubus enigmatically tied to Miss Meara sent tremors along the arms and legs of the woman to flee, whether by walking, flailing or even crawling away from the light of the child's touch, yet those warnings were for naught. Miss Meara remained frozen in place and rendered utterly prostrate before the mercies and whims of some phantasmal entity bent on bringing into the light that enduring sickness within her; a sickness which had festered in the dark corners of their world for far too long.

In an instant, Miss Meara was once again half human and her blood began to run warm as it did in the days of her childhood. Had the child a dozen ticks of the clock longer to work her light into the wicked woman, the world would have worked itself out to be a far different place in the days, months and years to come. However, the evil seed had been firmly planted in the soul of Mary Grice Decker when Tanner had been forever taken from her, in that her husband had been pronounced dead during those dark months that passed while Edward was away. Although she and Mr. Lemarque were late in arriving upon the premises, she bound through the front door to the manor when some unholy connection to her grandmother had beckoned her forth.

Upon entering, Mary Grice ran into the front hall of the stately plantation mansion and quickly took notice of what little Miss was doing to her grandmother. She then stepped forward and took the child harshly by the arm until Margaret Anne's hand was pointed toward the vaulted ceiling above. The violent dislocation of the promised child's electric connection to her evil host caused the chandelier overhead to shatter into grains of dust that landed softly upon the floor and the hair and wardrobes of those engaged beneath the beautiful and ornate creation of a now forgotten century. The mesmerizing spectacle of it all was a sight to behold.

Miss Meara lurched back away from the child and came to a quiz-zically driven rest upon the bottom stair. Mary Grice was forced to immediately release the child's arm as the sensation upon gripping that galvanized appendage was akin to standing in close proximity to a lightning strike. The ostensibly possessed child had promptly blacked out and fell limply to the floor upon becoming disengaged from the family matriarch and gatekeeper standing sentinel before the still unknown or perhaps merely unseen focal point of her unresolved des-tiny. Mr. Laing would have inherited the upper hand in sorting things out upon the reckoning if Mr. Lemarque had not accompanied Mary Grice over from Decker Hall and been neatly brandishing a compact firearm set at the ready. He waved the pistol at Mr. Laing and backed the large man under the archway and alongside the standing atten-dants who had abandoned their seats at the table upon taking notice of little Miss Margaret Anne's escapades with Miss Meara.

Mr. Laing was not surprised by his one-time friend's betrayal. Near everyone in town knew Claude had fallen in with Mary Grice. She was now a woman who had quickly learned to leverage the full potential of her commanding if not exquisite beauty subsequent to the passing of her husband, and in ways that would have driven to madness those only familiar with the essential understandings of the passions of the flesh. Mr. Laing addressed the presently revealed Judas among the fellowship of those properly summoned to address the unique circumstances of little Miss back in December. "Though you done lost your mind to the forbidden patch where the useful wits of a man can disappear and never be heard from again in this lifetime, Claude, show enough decency to allow me to tend to the very child you once swore to protect with your life."

Claude laughed thoughtfully in response to Mr. Laing and called out over his right shoulder, "What you be sayin' to such a noble request as all of that, Miss Mary?" Mary Grice was looking into her grand-mother's bedazzled eyes and answered her man cogently, "Yes, Mr.

Lemarque, do have that beast remove the accursed child from this place. Then help me get grandmother out to Decker Hall until it is safe for her to return here in the morning."

Claude nodded and instructed Mr. Laing by brandishing his silver pistol in the direction of the child while poking a bit of fun at his former associate's country grammar, "Ya done heard the lady, Shug. Best we get to the deescalatin' a dis here 'little misunderstandin' betwixt family and friends." Mr. Lemarque then looked Mr. Laing squarely in the eyes and conveyed a message that resonated closer to his true feelings on the matter. "The war has them all confused and none of us knows what's in it for tomorrow."

Shug would have spit on Mr. Lemarque's fine yet careworn leather boots if the act wasn't bordering on obscene in the presence of such noble young ladies. As such, he simply nodded silently at Claude before stepping forward and gracefully sweeping the girl up off of the floor and into his arms. Once the promised child was secured within the hold of those lumbering limbs, Mr. Laing carried little Miss Margaret Anne devotedly over to Miss Leslie, where Doctor Bailey quickly joined them to make a proper inspection of the senseless creature.

When Miss Margaret Anne was well attended to, Shug Laing called back to Mr. Lemarque, "Thank you, Mr. Lemarque. Such would probably be best if you would oblige your mistress and get Miss Meara on up to the Decker quarters of the plantation. Edward and Miss Meara have had a heck of a trying evening. I'll see to it that everything is in proper order when the Yankee boys come a calling in the mornin'."

Claude nodded to Shug in a hasty and distracted manner and asked, "The little one, is she going to be alright?" To which Mr. Laing snapped back harshly, "That's for God to know, you serpent of the grass. Now get your folk on outta here afore I needs to eat me a bullet on the way over to chokin' the very life outta you with my eight good fingers."

While Mary Grice was slowly escorting her grandmother to the front door, the uncertainty of the moment overwhelmed the eleven-year-old little girl who had no functioning memory of her true mother, Miss Blair Raimi Calhoun. Accordingly, the frightened girl went running up to her oldest sister and grandmother to assess the situation. She was not yet infected by the witchery of those two, yet Mary Grice had taken responsibility for a good deal of the raising of the child after their mother had passed not but a year after Miss Blair was born back in fifty-four. Such was especially true during the years following the birth of little Miss, those impressionable earliest years of Blair's cognizant childhood when Elizabeth Ann was off to having her lame arm tended to around the clock by Doctor Bailey.

Outside of Elizabeth Ann and at certain times the girl's predominantly busied and habitually traveling father, the youngest proper Calhoun child was far closer to Mary Grice and Miss Meara than any of the others gathered for the impromptu celebration of both Easter and Edward's return home from the war. Things may have turned out differently if Miss Jeanne had been present. Be that as it may, with her father in the altogether shattered mental state that he was, the scared little girl believed there was little else to do but run out of the dining room and right up alongside her stalwart and rather formidable oldest sister; the woman of that dismal hour who seemed to hold some form of strange dominion over the ruinous situation and the future reconciling of those events. Blair Raimi lightly grabbed hold of Mary Grice's elegant, dark-green evening gown before asking, "Is grandmother going to be quite alright, sister?"

Mary Grice patted her little sister on the head while she prepared to usher Miss Meara Calhoun out of the manor by way of the grand entranceway to Butterworth Hall and replied, "She will be fine, my dearest Blair Raimi. Father has made a fine mess of the family legacy and the little slave girl gave grandmother a terrible fright is all.

Accompany us up to Decker Hall and grandmother and I will explain everything to you properly in the morning."

Blair Raimi let go of Mary Grice's dress and looked up at her reasonably tall and rangy oldest sister while she crossed beyond the threshold of the front door with her grandmother. She then asked her oldest sister a string of frantic questions, "Are there to be real live Yankee soldiers at Butterworth Hall in the morning, Mary Grice? Are they not frightful and barbaric heathens as they all say back in town? Are you not afraid of what they might do upon their arrival? Will father be better come morning before they arrive? Why has no one told me little Miss was a slave girl and yet sister to us all? I had always believed she was a Satterfield proper. What does such a scandalous affair make of father's reputation as true Southern gentleman?"

Though the questions asked by her little sister were of a serious nature and all the more so given the harsh words that had been spoken by many present and furthermore, what had just transpired to close out that dark and deceitful manifestation of the season of the witch, Mary Grice could do little but smile warmly at the inquisitive little whipper snapper. In a rather shaded and devious manner, Mary Grice then proceeded to answered only the questions that would strengthen the young girl's resolve to walk away from those inside the manor, including the always charismatic and lovable Elizabeth Ann, "My dearest little sister, Blair Raimi. You have nothing to fear from the Union Army officers arriving tomorrow. Grandmother has already provisioned ahead to make arrangements with their commanding officer to limit their presence here."

When Blair Raimi breathed a noticeable sigh of relief in response to such welcome news, Mary Grice continued on with her shameful politicking and rather unabashedly spoken lies. "While it would appear father has lost his mind for a spell, as he did back when mother died, he will be left to make his own accord of peace with the gentlemen representing the Union during the occupation. Those inside our home are his family now and there is nothing you can do to change that unfortunate reality. He has always favored the slave child over us all. Father even went as far as sending Aubrey off to the war to be killed down at Fort Wagner so that he could leave everything to her behind our backs!"

Blair Raimi stood in the threshold of the doorway for a moment and glanced back into the old manor home, which held the preponderance of the once wonderful memories of her childhood. She stared briefly into the eyes of those standing in wait. She watched carefully as Miss Leslie, Doctor Bailey and Amos tended to little Miss. She then glanced over to the right of those crouched down to the floor and looked curiously upon her seemingly senseless father, who did little but appear to stare at the ornate china cabinet on the far side of the dining room. When she was satisfied that what remained of the man who once stood larger than life and at the very center of her known universe was not coming over to plead his case, she turned coldly away from those she once loved. Miss Blair Raimi Calhoun then stepped out into the lively air of early-April on that enchanted and starlit Easter evening; an evening which would forever change her life.

Those she left behind would do little to restore the broken fairytale of her life. Her grandma Meara was not one to be left without means and Mary Grice would fight for their legacy and the legacy of their deceased mother even if their father no longer would. The myriad notions and beliefs which were left to be misunderstood or wholly looked over in the aftermath of the cataclysm would remain that way until the day of their proper reckoning.

Blair Raimi joined Mary Grice and her grandmother on the front porch while Mr. Lemarque closed up shop as it were behind her. The shrewd Haitian man never once took his eyes off of old Shug Laing, who stepped slowly forward in following them out at a reasonable distance until they had boarded the carriage and Mary Grice's coachman, Mr. Churchill, had called his threadbare stable ponies to task for the short ride up to Decker Hall. Back in the house, Mr. Satterfield did his level best to implore Mr. Edward Calhoun to break free from his overbearing miasma and do something in the name of his youngest proper child.

The spent and quite broken elder coachman found even the thought of the task of heartening Edward to be nearly as futile as speaking to the late Jackson Satterfield's similarly shattered widow earlier in the evening while he worked to corral little Adelaide. The poor woman had turned hollow inside in the days since she had learned of Jackson's death and had later become inconsolable upon watching Columbia burn to the ground before her soot filled and watering eyes. While Mr. Satterfield pulled at Edward's firm yet cadaverously unresponsive shoulder, he made careful note that their season of death and untold loss was also in some ways the season of rebirth for so many that had known nothing but a life in captivity. The blackened sorcery of Miss Meara Calhoun and the war had duly marked that season upon which the antebellum glory of the Calhoun dynasty had been torn asunder as the price to be paid for their enduring cruelty to their fellow man. In many ways, the strife caused by the promised child had brought about this night of their own intimate reckoning with the sins of the past; a night which if they had been honest with themselves was a night they or their forebears had known to be coming from the very first of the days slaves were brought up this way from the chattel markets down in Charleston.

While Mr. Satterfield continued to futilely shake the unresponsive limb of his gracious benefactor, he caught sight of little Adelaide hovering over her beloved big sister of at least the shared and tender heart if not by blood or legal entreaty. He then realized that whatever unholy monstrosity arose from the dead in this place upon the sorting out of the war, at least while the estate remained under the thumb of the witch of Sumter, would certainly be a cold and nasty bane upon all attempting to walk in the light and do right by those dreadful sins of the past. Still and all, Mr. Donovan Satterfield also realized that resting within the hearts of those two little girls was the seed of God's eternal hope. Such was a tender and blessed seed that in God's time would blossom and indeed wash away the evils that had beset both their own generation and that of their forebears upon settling this great land under the equitable laws ordained by the divine master of all things. Lastly, Mr. Satterfield realized that in due time Edward would rise again and that the true work of the promised child, which would set the wheels in motion for that joyous season of their own liberation from the heavy yolk of those wicked men and demons alike still bearing down on them all, was still to come.

Miss Margaret Anne came to from the spirit worlds when the carriage carrying her antagonist had separated her from the connection she had tunneled into the vile essence of the witch; that heinous harridan who had pledged her soul long ago to realms, which upon bearing witness to the misery and despair existing within, nearly broke the essence of the little child's spirit of the light. Upon looking into the swirling cosmos of amber, blue, green and grey that were the child's once again opened eyes, Doctor Bailey found the little girl's present lack of focus to be rather unsettling. She was always one to hold things so easily within those beautiful orbs. He asked of her, "little Miss, are you able to hear me properly?"

The child stood up without uttering a word while Doc motioned to the others to give her some space. When those once surrounding her had backed away, she stepped slowly yet purposefully over to her father. The promised child then stood next to him and she put her hand on his forehead until the once bemused and stupefied looking man turned his head to the left and looked warmly upon the darling little sprite. He smiled down upon her as if he had been made privy to some great and wonderful mystery of life, and perhaps he had. Strangely, the child did not smile in return as she was without fail wont to do when looking upon any of God's wonderfully made creations. Instead, she bowed her head before her father and said, "There is time yet still before things are settled. Use it wisely. I must return to my mother for a spell."

Edward nodded thoughtfully to acknowledge the curious words of the little girl. Margaret Anne then firmly grabbed hold of Edward's wounded knee until she fell back to the floor senseless. Those gathered for the evening were left to wonder what had transpired between Edward and the child of the light but Miss Leslie had at least some semblance of an idea. That is to say she knew at least something because her grandmother had told her the tale of one no different than her darling little Miss. She stepped over to Mr. Laing and beckoned for her man to retrieve the child amidst Mr. Calhoun's feeble attempts to stabilize his daughter while the others, including Doctor Bailey, remained spellbound and perfectly still.

When Mr. Laing had secured the child, Miss Leslie spoke plainly and evenly to the small and dispirited congregation. She delivered no pretense of false hope. "Those a us dat wanna come along, we best be makin' our way on over to Uriah in the mornin' afore dem Union men arrive an' Miss Meara return. Best I can reckon, 'dat be Master Edward, Elizabeth Ann an' my folk but y'all's all welcome. My kin folk settlin' out dat way ain't got no axe to grind. Dey smart enough to be knowin' da devil's work when dey sees da thing an' dat there devil gonna be right here reapin' what he done sowed for da time bein.'"

Part III
Fables of the Reconstruction

Chapter Seven

EXILE

∽✎✐∼

TUESDAY, APRIL 11ᵀᴴ, 1865 was a fine spring morning in Uriah, South Carolina. The sun was shining brightly off to the east and the air was thin and invigorating when taken in upon those first sacred breaths of the new day. The greens of the fauna of the field were so crisp and so clear upon the focus of the naked eye and so teeming with vibrancy against the backdrop of the cloudless blue sky one might have believed they could reach out and touch the pulsating song of new life being given off by His Majesty's natural order. There simply were no words to be offered which could have painted an equivalent scene of that which was sensed by the skin and tremoring within the lively havens of the human spirit when staring out into the lush lucidity of that cool morning air and taking in the richness and splendor of even the slightest nuance or offered deliberation where it concerned God's creation. Mr. Edward Calhoun and Miss Jeanne Jolie Basseterre were casually sitting in two of the three beautiful pine rocking chairs delivered as a gift to Miss Jeanne and the Osment girls by the Wilson family. The rather unexpected but quite treasured gifts were given when the now childless couple had abandoned their neighboring farm just down the drive in late March, not but a few weeks before the war was officially lost but certainly not before the deleterious effects of the lingering hostilities had driven the very last of their hopes and dreams from their soft and simple hearts.

Helen and Clay Wilson had lost their three boys, Grayson, Landon and Elijah, when they all perished on the same day fighting over on the western front somewhere near the Cumberland River in Tennessee when Fort Donelson fell to the Union brigades. With their small contingent of slaves all run off down the road when even the rangers had been called into service to defend pockets of South Carolina from Sherman's twin columns set to march on through the state from their camps pitched near the Georgia coast, the aging couple offered up the property to the late Shem Davis's oldest son, Barbury and his extended family in exchange for a small stipend to be paid them from the annual profits of the harvest until they met their end. Barbury was thrilled with the offer, which was quite generous when translated into the appropriate financial terms of the day.

Mr. Davis honored the agreement and then some until Mrs. Wilson died quite naturally as a librarian down in Charleston in 1885. Before passing on, Helen had made an annual pilgrimage up to Uriah to visit both Barbury and his rapidly expanding family and the old homestead with its peculiar haunts where her boys had become men. She made the sacred journey for the last score of her life. Each spring when she arrived and without fail, Mrs. Wilson fell to her knees in tears upon reaching the base of the drive and ran that old familiar Uriah clay through her aging fingers. The sight of the ritual was quite contagious and it choked Miss Jeanne up something fierce upon witnessing the poor old woman pining for the days of her vanquished happiness, which seemed to be resting peacefully somewhere within that soft, settled dirt of the drive. Perhaps that was the last place Helen Wilson had seen her three boys standing together, smiling and alive before they marched off to Columbia to join the South Carolina militia in the spring of 1861.

Though none of the others quartered at the Osment farmstead for at least the prior evening were close to waking up at that hour when the sun had just crested the horizon, the truth of the matter was that at least a few more chairs were going to be needed for the homey country veranda in the days and months to come. Miss Jeanne and the girls had done what they could to get some cotton planted that year. Yet, without any help in the large, verdant field undulating downward and off to the south before her and Edward's eyes, the ladies of the farmstead had spent far more time grooming the large, seasonal gardens surrounding the house. Their rather astute expectation given the dearth of available labor was that the continuing need for necessary produce provision would far surpass the benefits of harvesting surplus cotton stocks, which would have proven quite difficult to get to market under the existing war time conditions.

Upon seeing all that had been accomplished by the three industrious young women from the vantage point of his rather serene rocker and after having made an erstwhile inspection of the premises from various angles of the finely constructed front porch, Edward verbally applauded their efforts. "I have to give credit where credit is due Miss Jeanne, you ladies have done a wonderful job out here since you came to visit us back in Sumter over the holidays."

Miss Jeanne smiled reminiscently while looking over the field under the glorious purview of the first shimmering rays of daylight weaving their way through the still budding trees of the surrounding woodlands. She then replied rather appreciatively to her somewhat unexpected guest, "Why thank you, Edward. We do what we are able with what God above is so gracious to provide during such times of hunger and malady alike. Maime and Shy are quite tireless in their efforts both here and back in town where they care for the suffering who are without. They truly are women of their own accord now. The truth is that we do indeed learn of what God has created within us during times such as these that so tirelessly try our souls."

Edward smiled broadly for the first time since his mother had so rudely broken in on their Easter celebration before he spoke in reply. "Their father would be proud of all you have done out here since his passing. Clarke was a good man, even if he had managed to take the enchanting woman of my fancy for his own. Upon seeing the girls and all they have done in this beautiful place, I do believe God was once again correct in His infallible discernment on that rather tricky matter."

Miss Jeanne laughed pleasantly at Edward's admission, which was some twenty years overdue yet still better than never having arrived at all. She had taken a strange comfort from Edward, Elizabeth Ann, Virgil, Mr. Laing, Miss Leslie, Amos and most certainly little Miss's arrival out to the farmstead. To the now wistful woman, the occurrence of their unannounced visit gave the impression of something so natural that the days prior to their having been warmly welcomed into their humble home were absent something necessary or even innate to the functioning essence of the place with Clarke no longer present. Perhaps that feeling of comfort was likewise derived from their all being together in the manner of an extended family yet tucked away from the expectations and the cross-currents of a society that saw only the radiant gifts of what Miss Basseterre had inherited of her mother's skin tone upon taking notice of her and furthermore, perceived those blessings to be something of a beautiful curse in such an outwardly steadfast and traditional culture; a peculiar and decidedly particular culture that had once come to thrive upon an appalling and bestial practice that was plainly an affront to the wishes of the Almighty.

In places such a Sumter, where the carriage class was known to put on airs, there always existed that ascribed unease which emanated from those of the Anglican female caste who used such visible traits as a way to control or demean her classically handsome yet unbridled beauty, which graced both her heart and her striking outward appearances. Beyond even those aforementioned considerations, perhaps the comforting warmth explicit to the Edward's presence stemmed from the significant distance they presently presided away from the black cloud of the witch's spell. Such was a dour enchantment that had chained their love, or perhaps ill-timed adoration, to the earth with shackles of iron from the very moment she first set foot upon the abounding plantation back in Sumter with only expectant wonder and awe emanating from her shinning, Irish eyes.

Some combination of both advantages which their current setting possessed over the pageantry and the accompanying dark secrets of Sumter seemed to ease the hearts and minds of the both of the somewhat estranged paramours on that splendid spring morning upon which they were gathered together as one. Additionally, the peaceful ambiance brought about by the added blessings of her humble home's perceived drawbacks as naught but a common farmstead amongst many gracing that beautiful countryside when compared to one of the most glorious plantation estates in all of the Carolinas converged with the aforesaid to contrive the conditions present; conditions which rendered the graceful woman unafraid of either their sinful past or the once impenetrable ramparts that had accompanied Edward's inclusion amongst those of the very apex of the Southern gentry. Of course, the outcome of the war and Edward's reasons for being there upon the daybreak were also secondary factors regarding the situational ease of Miss Basseterre's disposition while taking in the morning ambiance with said company.

Regardless of the trivial pontifications one might ascribe to the comfort the lady of the house now felt with the man who had both warmed and troubled her heart from the moment she first laid eyes upon him down in Haiti, the entirety of the confusion, the gravity, and the guilt that had existed between them, and which had served to forever taint her relationship with both Edward and little Miss back at the stately plantation, seemed to Miss Jeanne to have melted away with the rising of the sun on that lovely April morning of 1865. And just perhaps, those once formidable trepidations had suddenly drifted away into the open meadow of the field stretching out before their eyes and scattered into the woodlands beyond like whispered rumors; like softly spoken hearsay of the past woefully concocted yet dissipating into the mist well beyond the ears of those desiring to know such devilish morsels concerning the folly of their fellow man.

She spoke in a reflective tone that embodied the serene yet thoughtful look set upon her comely visage. "I told you one day you would thank me for accepting Clarke's proposal, Master Calhoun. I was unsure of the decision of my own accord for a short while. That is until through your gracious gift of this beautiful and once wild plot, my determined man was able to turn this feisty land into our home and the home of my baby girls. I do so wish he was gifted more time to be out there turning that field he loved nearly as much as he loved the three of us. He took such pride in being a free man of color out there upon his own demesne."

Miss Jeanne paused for a moment to laugh silently at the passing stations of her fondest memories of her former husband and then added, "At least Clarke came to feel that way after the Lord above and that unforgiving dirt began to bless his back breaking efforts to have the lower meadow cleared when the upper tillage did faithfully yield the first of his bumper crops."

Edward laughed whimsically and retorted, "He was a good man and an earnest man, my dearest Jeanne. You chose wisely with Mr. Osment. I must say I was certain you would rebuff even the very last of your countless and diligent pursuers until the moment I witnessed the word yes seep into the lightly shifting breeze from your tender lips on your wedding day. Though I feigned not to be as such on account of my dutiful Libby Hopkins, I was a broken man on that day, Miss Basseterre. Perhaps I would not have been so hard pressed if my dearly departed had ever behaved as more than Miss Meara's bootlicker. Yet, I do digress. At least there were the few times she believed it appropriate to procreate. I shall always have the memory of those rare interludes."

Jeanne tittered freely again such that the lightness of her spirit was easily taken in by her companion of the first light. She laughed lightly yet joyfully as she did back in the olden days when they would share their deepest secrets with one another. The Caribbean mistress was indeed aware however, that she had in fact broken Mr. Edward Calhoun's tender heart on the day of her marriage to Mr. Clarke Joseph Osment back in 1845. She was back then, and remained so to this day, certain that the outcome of her marriage was best for them all, Edward included. The culmination and release of the poor man's self-inflicted frustrations some thirteen years later was a matter upon which her womanly pith remained decidedly mixed, whereby her feelings on the tryst still touched both ends of the emotive spectrum.

Irrespective of the lingering impropriety overshadowing the catalysts which drove that fateful span of their conjoining to such an extended and long overdue climax; sinful sensations of the flesh, which she had imagined so vividly not long after the very first evening they had dined together back in Haiti, she blushed slightly with a feeling of ecstasy and not shame in the present moment. In truth, her cheeks warmed due to the fact Edward would be so very pleased to know he had touched off that uncontrollable sensation within that was somehow made manifest in the mind yet governed by such innate and wild yet strangely sensitive passions deep beneath the beaded sweat of her exposed nut-brown skin on that sultry May afternoon.

She replied to the gentleman's light sarcasm with the full measure of her intent to bestow upon him something sacred in return for having had to break his heart in the years since passed. "The hours I gave myself over to you were precisely how the young island girl you swept off of her feet had always dreamed they would be, Mr. Edward Calhoun. I wanted you to know that and to have that with you no matter what may come of us in the days ahead."

Edward was rocking back on the ends of the rails of his chair and staring up at the porch roof deep in thought when the dam burst in his head upon the hearing of the words he had always wished to hear. The words he wished to hear more than any others that could have been delivered so sweetly into his tenderly awaiting ears. The overpowering reaction to Miss Jeanne's unexpected admission drove the poor man over the ends of the rails of his rocker and onto his back with a resounding thud when the posterior of the chair firmly struck the pine decking of the veranda. Edward knocked his head some upon the fall, yet the Haitian mistress could not help but appease her inner mirth by laughing at the clumsy, love-struck stripling he still remained. Her heart began to swell for the man all over again, just as it did when she was only seventeen and possessed no given notion that the American gentleman was married with two young daughters and a baby boy.

Edward attempted to spring forth from the awkward mishap of his ham-fisted fall but only managed to twist the chair over and on top of his body. Miss Jeanne continued laughing like a giddy child while she stood up, walked over to Edward and pulled the chair free from his discombobulated limbs. Edward had done little but smile shamelessly and remain prostrate on his back upon the porch while she had liberated him from the clutches of the finely-crafted rocker. When the chair was off to the side, the still wonderfully laughing woman reached out her hands to pull her mischievous bungler off of the deck. Edward took hold of those stately appendages and pulled such that the still giggling mistress was caught off balance and left with no option but to fall on top of the wounded gentleman. Once she had landed as lithely as any woman gripped by similar straits might have managed, Miss Jeanne beamed brightly into the waggish man's eyes with that delighted smile of the willing. He in turn kissed her sweet and perfectly sculpted lips as if they were the final sampling of the rarest honey collected up along the eastern peaks of the Blue Ridge.

She returned the favor and offered the soft warmth and succulent prowess of those mindful lips eagerly to the suddenly hopeful man. For the first time in the twenty-two years they had at various points in their star-crossed union both wanted so badly for the exact passions now popping like charged static both within and without that of their intertwined bodies and pulsing readily along the softer and at times unbearably sensitive formations of skin and raw nerve alike, there existed no cause for remorse as their lips continued to explore, discover and ignite but for the potential exposure of their present lack of common decency. That concern was far secondary to the knowing of what it felt like to take in the living flesh of the other freely and without the burden of guilt.

Had another thirty seconds passed there would have been no turning back; nothing of the sort. Thankfully, Miss Leslie hollered in an outward direction from behind the door to the porch about as loud as she could muster without causing those still sleeping denizens of the overcrowded house to believe she was being inconceivably massacred by little more than the child under her care or the low, twinkling shine of the morning light. She had been sleeping in the front room and was startled into waking by those formidable eyes in the back of her head when she heard the commotion of Edward falling backward in his rocking chair onto the sturdy pine boards of the front deck. The richly intuitive woman had then looked out the window and witnessed what followed, though she was shortly thereafter forced to cover her eyes for the sanctity of her shame.

Miss Leslie interrupted the two provocative early birds by showily reprimanding her mischievously angelic ward. "Now, li'l Miss, what do I be tellin' ya 'bout wanderin' on out a dis house afore no one is awake! You best be gettin' on back up to your room wid Miss Elizabeth Ann an' Miss Shy afore I works dat li'l hide a your'n right on outta line wid dat sneaky little mind you gots!" In response to such formidable provision, the rather astute six-year-old turned sharply before reaching the front door and scurried back on up the stairs without saying a word in reply.

When Miss Leslie heard the wooden rocking chair get put upright out on the porch followed by some innocent giggling in unison, she shot out of the front door like a cannonball and announced her presence to the would be lovers like the crowing cock of the yard. "Well a good, God-blessed mornin' a y'all! And I was thinkin' I'd be da very first out here to look upon dis new day."

Miss Jeanne attempted to cut in for the sake of normalizing the burning blush of her folly but Miss Leslie would have none of it. "Good morn…" "My, oh my! A fine spring day da likes a dis one an' even an ol' handmaiden da likes a me might gets to thinkin' 'bout love! Do be pardonin' my forward approach now, Master Calhoun. But umm, umm, umm, dis here be da weather a da Good Lord Hisself! It do indeed!"

Miss Leslie began to laugh knowing that the ruse was up while Edward remained unwilling to yield to the animated woman. "Why, good morning to you, Miss Leslie. If it wasn't for the burden of our ungainly need of accommodation on such short notice, I might be led to believe the birds were a chirping and the bees were a buzzing somewhere near to the confines of your nest last evening."

Miss Leslie put her thumb and forefinger to her chin in earnest and proceeded to soundly beat the rather cavalier gentleman at his own game. "Dearest, Mr. Calhoun, if I didn't knows me a thing or two 'bout 'dat wounded knee a yours, I'd swear 'dat you done be wearin' da hair of a brothel man. Must be da wind or somethin' a da like I presume, yet I wouldn't go hangin' me a bedsheet out to dry in dis here air dat be stiller den a hussy preachin' in da pulpit."

Miss Leslie laughed indulgently in response to her own wit and Miss Jeanne cracked a knowing smile, though the guilty woman was quite close to giving up the ghost and laughing outright. For his part, Edward likewise struggled to keep a straight face, giddy as he was over what had just occurred. Ever the consummate gamesman however, the stubborn man was not yet ready to give in to Miss Leslie. "Well now, Miss Leslie, not knowing what a brothel man might do for the sake of appearances, I am at a loss to respond to your clever insinuation. Perhaps I should sequester Mr. Laing as an exhibit of said likeness?"

Miss Leslie lowered her eyes playfully in the direction of Edward and followed with, "Fair 'nuff, Master Calhoun, but your hen da one out here cacklin' like she just laid down a fresh dozen an' we sure 'nuff could use dem provisions wif all dem moufs we gots to feed. Asides, Mr. Laing be more like da werewolf. He only be up to howlin' when da moon be full."

The three laughed together for a good long while as it felt joyous to be human again, away from the torments of the war and beyond what seemed like that rank and heavy passing of the season of the witch. After a while talking through the hopes and plans for the days ahead, Miss Leslie asked Mr. Calhoun how it was that his knee became so spry that he was up to foolin' around on his backside with a woman atop that leg. Mr. Calhoun answered solemnly after a discomforting pause. "Miss Margaret Anne put her hand upon my knee and I have felt nothing but weightless warmth in the joint ever since I lay down to sleep last night. Moreover, little Miss said I should seek Mr. Laing's pertinent advice regarding the phenomenon. Is there something I should know about prior to putting forth a query before old Shug that is seemingly quite innocuous?"

Miss Leslie looked curiously at Miss Jeanne and shook her head slowly while replying to Edward, "Oh' Lawdy. I done told dat ol' brute never to speak a da thing 'cus I ain't want Miss Meara knowin' of it an' I be guessin' he heard me if li'l Miss be da one done told ya."

Miss Jeanne remained rather smitten and therefore quite distracted by the effervescence of the moment latterly passed like the sweet sunrise song of the meadowlark yet she grew quite curious upon hearing of the manifest works of her baby girl. "What happened with Mr. Laing, Miss Leslie?" she asked with a slightly vacant tone, which epitomized the divergent and racing distractions vying for the attentions of her mind on that fine morning out in the country.

Miss Leslie lowered her head and spoke hesitantly yet in turn. "I don' wanna go talkin' out a school none but Mr. Laing done had it bad in da ways a his'n manly affections. But den lil' Miss put her hand upon da man's heart like she done Miss Meara an' I's could tell ya dat da man done been paid back in full for all a 'dem years he missed." Miss Leslie stopped there for decency's sake and for the application of proper discretion where it concerned speaking of her lover and perhaps her husband to be of a sort.

Edward wanted no part of that discussion. He felt distractedly at his practically healed knee while Miss Jeanne asked a follow-on question of Miss Leslie as delicately as she was able, "Do you mean the girl freed the man's mind of some horrible reconciliation of the past or was it perhaps something else that had the otherwise rather robust man all bound up, Miss Leslie?"

Miss Leslie looked around to be sure no one had approached while her guard was down due to her funning around with the two lovebirds. She lowered her head again and spoke quietly. "Well, Ma'am when I done come about takin' da child on behalf a Miss Sarah in dat winter field to da south a dem haunted crossroads into Georgia, God showed me da moment a Mr. Laing's curse an' it wasn' no triflin' thing. Nothin' even Doc Bailey could be settin' right if'n you catch my meanin'."

Miss Jeanne turned to Edward sharply and asked, "And what of you Edward? What of your leg?" Edward stood up for the purpose of making a demonstration and replied, "The bullet that put an end to Big Luke back at Dingle's Mill glanced sharply off of my kneecap. Two nights back the appendage was lame as the leg of a horse that had stepped into a post hole sight unseen. Today..." Edward paused, grinned slyly for effect and then cattily expounded upon his revelation. "Well, my dear, surely you among all stand to properly ascertain the difference the child has made."

Edward's expression then gradually sagged into something of a blank and unresponsive stare while he added, "There was more though, my dear. The dark and faithless thoughts of Miss Meara, or perhaps another of the damned more potent than she now is, had begun to pierce my mind and fracture my thoughts for a time following my mother's arrival to Easter dinner. Little Miss made it stop until I was overcome by a blanketing feeling of eternal warmth and the cognitive expressions of some radiant light. My wits were not far from cracking or dissolving into the abyss of some consuming desolation when the dear child made it stop with little more than the touch of her tender hand."

Miss Leslie had desired to further Edward's thoughts based upon her personal experience with the child's healing light. Margaret Anne had also mended her frightfully broken and bewitched thoughts on that now infamous Sunday, April 9th, 1865. However, Miss Shy Jolie, who was a stunning yet rather impulsive sixteen-year-old lady and much the mistress of her own accord by that time, came running out of the house and onto the porch with the promised child hot on her heels. She stopped suddenly in front of her mother's rocker, stomped her foot on the porch in anger and announced, "Mother, this little imp of the woods is up to thinking that you are her momma and that therefore we's up to bein' sisters! I know she ain't but six be she sounds a heck of a lot smarter than that ten-year-old Davis boy from up the drive!"

Miss Jeanne remained sitting calmly in her chair with her hands folded across her lap. She was quite thankful that the sudden intrusion hadn't occurred moments earlier. After allowing her hot blooded daughter to cool down some, she asked of her with a smooth and steady calm laced into her tone and projecting outwardly from her almost rigid but certainly evenly kept demeanor, "Has she now. And what else did little Miss have to say for herself?"

Shy rushed out an exhalation and pressed her foot firmly to the porch boards but she did not stomp that long and slender appendage as she had earlier. "Well, she said that Miss Meara is her Grammy and that woman got the devil put into her in a bad way." Miss Shy paused for a moment to cool her burning lips and added, "My apologies, Mister Calhoun. The child has the wind set to her tongue today."

Miss Jeanne repressed a laugh in sensing the benefit to keeping a straight face in the presence of her wildly beautiful, fitfully tempestuous and clearly agitated daughter. Edward smiled and replied to allow Miss Jeanne some additional time to gather her wits about her regarding the more sensitive matters contained within the unexpected and painfully forthright disclosure. "That is quite alright, Miss Shy. Little Miss Margaret Anne is absolutely correct. If she were speaking falsely we wouldn't be so harshly imposing upon you all here today absent proper notice. Thank you for your gracious hospitality. We were situated with no other option on account of my mother's darker tendencies as it were. It truly is a joy to lay my eyes upon one so lovely as you have become."

Shy Jolie replied quickly on account of the fact she did not want Mr. Calhoun to think she felt put out by having to share her room with Elizabeth Ann and little Miss. "We are so happy you all could be here, Mr. Calhoun. Think nothing of it. We are hoping you will be so kind as to stay for a while. We sure enough could use the help around here." Edward smiled delightedly and replied, "We will look to more permanent arrangements for some but you just may get your wish regarding the others, pretty lady."

Miss Jeanne decided to interject at that point. "You need to mind your grammar, young lady. Your grandfather would turn a fright in his grave if he heard you speaking as you were earlier." "Yes, Ma'am," replied Miss Shy while lowering her head to display the proper shade of shame. "Now I know you believe what little Miss has told you or certainly you wouldn't have displayed such hostility in addressing your dear, sweet mother. Does the fact trouble you, my darling child?"

Miss Shy lowered her head further and her voice cowered considerably as she spoke in response to her suddenly and once again dignified mother. "No, Ma'am, the truth is never going to trouble me.

However, it would have been far more considerate of you to tell Maime and me that you and Mister Calhoun had been married in secret. We sure enough always reckoned that you two was sweet on one another once daddy and Miss Libby died so near to the same time."

Upon hearing that, Miss Leslie turned harshly toward the door and scooped up little Miss while abruptly announcing her rather impromptu intentions. "The little Miss an' I best be getting' on in to look after dat breakfast. There aims to be a lot a dem mouths to feed on dis here fine morning. We to be workin' wid da provisions we brought over from Sumter."

Miss Jeanne nodded quite eloquently and replied, "Why thank you, Miss Leslie. That would be so very kind of you." "Think nothin' of it, Ma'am," was the departing woman's rather curt reply as she swiftly whisked the little girl inside the house while the unsuspecting child remained wrapped up in the comforts of her mammy's arms.

When only Edward and Shy remained with her on the front porch, Miss Jeanne spoke evenly yet with a sympathetic bent intended to comfort the confused young woman. "You spoke of Mr. Calhoun's mother a while ago. Margaret Anne was right about the woman. She is very powerful and her heart has become infected by that power and her greed among other things. The situation that exists between Edward and me is muddled beyond the visible complications plain enough to your tender eyes, young lady. Furthermore, things are the way that they are between the two of us primarily because of Edward's mother now that your father and Miss Libby are gone from us. We had not planned to tell anyone of the child to keep little Miss safe. That is why the truth was kept from you and your sister; to protect little Miss and to protect the both of you. Be that as it may, the truth always has a funny way of making itself known. Margaret Anne had no will to allow such a veil of secrecy and deceit to prevail for long. Your sister is an amazing child, my dearest Shy Jolie. Just as you and Maime both are."

Shy stepped forward to the stairs of the porch and looked out over the field she so fondly remembered her father planting, ploughing and harvesting when she was just a young girl no older than little Miss. Her mind was filled with the reckoning of a dozen things so innate to her very essence that had suddenly changed. The world around her had rather abruptly become a different place, yet somehow she realized that all of those memories of her father which she held dear remained both as true and eternal as they ever were. Still and all, there lingered a slight twinge of anger sitting restless in the depths of her heart and she became determined not to leave the veranda before the fullness of the truth had been made manifest to her so that she might properly settle out her shifting emotions. "Did you and Mr. Calhoun wed while you were down in Haiti before you were removed from the public eye? I thought you might die upon your return home that morning. Had you just given birth to my sister?"

Miss Jeanne nodded subtly to Edward in such a way that the gentleman knew the time had arrived for him to take his leave. The still beaming aristocrat kindly obliged in a dignified manner and winked at the beautiful mistress of his dreams while he passed by appearing as if everything in his life had suddenly been set right by little more than the caress of her willing lips. Miss Jeanne was left to ponder for an instant what might have been had she kissed the man the very moment his wife had passed on but such thoughts born of her fancy that involved the reordering the past were spurious affairs incapable of coming to any good. They were all here together now on behalf of the promised child and such was the gift they had been given to make the most of God's eternal promise to them all. As to what would be properly accepted of such a gracious bounty was a worry for another time.

When Edward was inside the farmhouse and well on his way to helping out in the kitchen, Miss Jeanne turned her thoughts outward to appropriately address her daughter's concerns. "Yes, my dear Shy Jolie, your little sister had been born the night before and Doctor

Bailey believes her survival of the ordeal was nothing short of a miracle. She was breech in a horrible way and the delivery took a lot out of me. I am so sorry I did not tell you the moment you ran up the drive to greet me. The situation was so perilous for both you and Maime and also the little child."

Shy continued staring out into the field where the dreams of her loving father lingered thick and pungent and then dusty in the planed rays of sunlight leveling out across the acreage of the expanse from east to west. When she had taken enough time in digesting what her mother had told her she asked, "Have you always loved Mr. Edward and not father? Will little Miss be the apple of your eye now because of who her father is?"

Miss Jeanne stood up from her chair and wrapped her arms around her daughter. She turned Shy's chin towards her searching eyes and spoke mournfully due to the pain she had caused her dear second child. "Miss Shy Jolie Osment, I loved and do love your father dearly. He was the only man never afraid to approach me and ask of the true feelings of my heart. None of those other men, including Mr. Edward knew how easy it would have been to light up the warmth of my affections. Beyond that, Mr. Clarke Osment was just about the most handsome man to set foot in the Carolinas and his daughters take after him in that regard."

Miss Jeanne paused for a moment to further reflect upon her beloved husband and smile soothingly down upon her daughter. She then turned her eyes to look out upon the unturned field and continued on with her message from the place where she had broken her thoughts off prior. "When your father died my heart was broken in a way that is still yet to mend. Just as you do right now, I still see him out in that field breaking his back tirelessly for the three women he loved. I miss him and I miss what we all had together when he was with us. There is nothing I would place before having all of what we shared together back if only I could obtain such a mystical wish. Yet, you must understand that there is also nothing that will ever taint the endearing nature of those moments kept safe right here in my heart."

Shy smiled warmly while looking up into her mother's eyes, as if the stunning young lady then understood the proper ordering of those mysterious confluences of the elegant mistress's life beyond her time spent in this place with her beloved family. Miss Jeanne took such comfort from the look so delicately tendered by her daughter alone, yet she spoke of more upon kissing the warmth of Miss Shy's forehead. "Edward was a seed planted in my heart when I was a young woman not much older that you are now and set about with wanderlust to see the world beyond my precious island kingdom, which was at the time being subjugated from within. He will never possess that corner of my heart eternally set aside for that dashing man who gifted me you and your precious sister. There will come a time when you shall understand such things, my dear, but let it not be upon this day. Though such is not the only reason I will never marry Mr. Calhoun, the eternal stations of my heart are pledged faithfully to your father."

Shy gave further thought to her mother's words. In some ways the young lady did understand how differing men could belong to differing colors of her love, though not in the way a more seasoned woman might. She smiled in thinking of her daddy raising her up to the sky in that beautiful field laid out before her eyes. She then turned to give her mother a proper hug and said, "There is a purpose to everything, my sweet momma. The child is a blessing unto us, even if she is illegitimate. God our Father and His decision to deliver little Miss into to our care certainly stands above the notions of any flawed constituency or belief held by them uppity folks that are always proclaimin' this or that. How long have those same ones who make such rules been shackling the colored folks up to the post at night and whipping them when they tire out amidst the unrelenting heat of the field on that day? God most certainly made no such law tied to all of that misery." Miss Shy's memories of those terrible things she had seen and heard in her younger days then began to fade and she proclaimed in earnest, "I love you, momma!"

Miss Jeanne hugged her darling yet impetuously opinionated girl tighter and said, "Don't you go thinking I haven't sinned now, my sweet child. I have. My only wish is that one day you will come to understand that such sin was never intended in the way you once thought. I owe the crimson flag of my impurity to my lack of faith alone. Yet in some ways, my hopes that some good might come as the result of my own weakness were all hopes tied to you and Maime."

Shy backed away from her mother but held her shoulders with her hands while she spoke to reassure her. "No word of judgment will ever pass over these lips, sweet momma. I know you are right with God where it concerns little Miss."

Miss Jeanne quailed slightly but refused to let such a seed of doubt creep into her thoughts during such an intimate and truthful moment. She steadied her sidelong leaning eyes and spoke softly yet resolutely to affirm the attestations of her daughter and calm that shrewish feeling of unease. "I know one day I will be right with God for all of the things I have done to spare my three girls any suffering. I see that truth now in your pretty smile, sweet girl. Is there anything further I might clarify for your benefit before we return to the others, my dearest Shy Jolie? I do not want to see my baby girl hurting any due to the improper things I have done."

Shy looked probingly into her mother's eyes and asked, "Will you tell Maime? She is not likely to look past such a thing as easily as I have. You know she spends every free minute she has over with the Episcopal congregation back in town."

Miss Jeanne nodded and replied, "As it was with you, I will leave the matter up to the child. No one here will speak of her lineage openly. Furthermore, if Maime asks I will tell her the truth, as should you. We shall not allow any more lies to fester out on your honorable father's demesne. The four of us are now one, precisely as things were always intended to be from the moment little Miss was born. The child chose to return to her father and then return to me for a reason. I believe she is somehow tied to the wishes of the angelic realms."

Miss Shy nodded and smiled warmly in reply and took her mother playfully by the hand. "Let us go help Miss Leslie and little Miss with the morning meal. The gift of a little sister and having so many good folks about the place is truly wonderful. Perhaps Doctor Bailey and his family will be by to pay a visit from the Claibrooke farm. I do love that man dearly after all he did for both you and Elizabeth Ann."

Miss Jeanne smiled at her daughter and answered her in the freshly expectant tone of one having passed through the worst of the repercussions of a woefully dreaded secret made manifest, "Perhaps the Baileys will be by later today, my beloved. I suspect it will take them a bit of time to adapt to their new surroundings if they choose not to return to Sumter."

With those words spoken, the two wistfully delighted women returned to the house and began working with little Miss, Miss Leslie and Mr. Calhoun to do the best they were able to get the Sumter contingent and Miss Maime properly fed. All went relatively smoothly until young Mr. Virgil O'Keefe made his way his way down to the kitchen from the guest room upstairs he was sharing with Mr. Laing. Miss Elizabeth Ann followed not far behind the eager and orphaned farm boy, who upon meeting Miss Jeanne's family with Elizabeth Ann randomly at his side thought for certain he had done died and gone to heaven.

The summer, which was not far off as the Carolina seasons went, was fixin' to be a hot one for the young man so akin to operating while displaying all the obvious tells of a full-blown nuclear meltdown taking place inside of his mind and who was likewise, quite new to handling the scattershot wares and emotional urgings of his blossoming progression into manhood. The world beyond was indeed on fire, but here in this sacred place born of Edward's chivalrous generosity and Clarke

Osment's sheer will to provide for his beautiful ladies, the heavens seemed to touch the earth in a beautifully simple and uninterrupted fashion. Edward, Elizabeth Ann and Virgil shared the farmhouse with Miss Jeanne and the Osment girls. Doctor Bailey and his family moved on into town when the diligent physician set up shop in the village square of Uriah with Miss Sarah present but unawares of her surroundings and little Adelaide and Mr. Satterfield also hired on as dutiful helpers. Miss Leslie, Mr. Laing, Amos and little Miss built a little cabin at the edge of the woods on the far side of the pond down the slope to the west of the main farmhouse, and of course there was the constant influx of countless and quite varied Davis children running about the place.

Mr. Laing and Virgil had the fields yielding quite nicely in those three harvest seasons of Edward's exile in Uriah. Much of their profit or excess production had been requisitioned by their Union Army overseers trying to restore order to the Carolinas, yet there was always just a bit more than enough to go around and keep some coin available in the event unforeseen expenses did arise. The Confederate notes once circulating in abundance were all but worthless in those days but the gold and silver coin of the times that was held dear during the war did the job just fine. As for Virgil, the young man never missed church once in those simple and contented years when none of the notable constituencies vying for power in the Carolina Midlands following the war were pushing the envelope all too forcefully in an effort to exert their will before a more permanent state of government was installed.

The primary reason behind Virgil's perfect attendance at the Sunday sermon was the fact he was escorted right into his pew by the three prettiest and also eligible young ladies in the county in Miss Maime, Miss Shy and Miss Elizabeth Ann and of course, there was little Miss Margaret Anne to boot. Though the young man was indeed tightening his bonds with God in those years to the point that he regularly attended church with Maime on Tuesday nights in addition to the family's Sunday pilgrimage into town, the zenith of his three years spent as Captain Calhoun's adjutant in exile was his late afternoon kiss of Miss Elizabeth Ann Calhoun. The event Mr. O'Keefe would never come to forget occurred in late August of 1868, and took place beneath the once pesky and now monolithic old oak that Clarke Osment had left standing on the eastern side of the upper field.

The crop had been put in late that year due to the unseasonably cold spring. As such, by that final day of August the two might be lovers, still far closer to the inseparable and similarly antagonizing bonds of siblings or the comforts and deep empathies of true friend-ship at that time in their lives, found themselves wading through a waist high sea of white, ripened cotton as the radiating orange sun settled down below the tree line to the west. They approached the old rope swing dangling from the low, stalwart eastern facing branch of the oak filled with laughter and tired from the demanding chores of another day of righteous toil out on the farmstead. The air was heavy and warm, and thick with the sweet scent of the late summer wild-flowers lining the edges of the field but quite pleasant and perhaps even comforting to those who had endured the peak heat of the searing summer sun on that day.

Virgil had scaled the trunk of the broad shade tree to hang the swing back during that first summer of his stay in Uriah to impress Miss Elizabeth Ann and Miss Shy Jolie while the initial cotton crop of the postbellum era began to blossom out in the fields of the Osment farmstead. Elizabeth Ann had fallen in love with the spot and the slow, ranging motions of the swing Clarke had lovingly crafted from a loose section of Eastern Pine that had fallen over well before its time out by the pond. In truth, Miss Calhoun's affinity for the swing took root the very moment Virgil had swung the rope over the branch and, in doing so, nearly broke his neck in front of the very women he had set out to impress with his farm boy talents and emergent physical prowess each day from sunup until lights out.

Elizabeth Ann was in a playful mood as she cleared the last of the cotton stalks near the base of the tree and took hold of the rope swing. The young lady was enchanted in the ways of one given over to mischievous frolic; although she believed the time to talk seriously with the young man she had trained in the proper ways of a Southern gentleman for a spell beyond three years now was upon her. Virgil steadied the swing and was set to give the contraption a gentle push as he always had when they came out this way to trade gossip and ponder the meaning of life's great mysteries as the day began to cool upon the setting of the blazing summer sun. When his hand was properly placed on the small of Elizabeth Ann's back, the young lady instructed the willing young man, "Not yet, Virgil. I have something important to tell you."

Virgil smiled warmly and replied in earnest as he admired his companion's summer work gown, which was certainly never intended to endure such taxing agrarian labor. "Swinging carefree in the breeze has never stopped you from speaking your mind prior to the present moment, Miss Calhoun." Virgil still spoke with his back country tongue while working the fields with Mr. Laing or any of the Davis boys doing their part to prepare the harvest. Still and all, both Mistress Stevens back at the schoolhouse and Elizabeth Ann had worked wonders on the boy's diction and grammar, which he ventured to employ when given over to a setting properly suited to his fancy talk.

Elizabeth Ann stood up from the swing and turned to face Mr. O'Keefe suddenly while squeezing the ropes of the swing together in her right hand. "What I should have said to you, Virgil is that there is something I must do before I tell you of father's plans for the coming season."

Virgil shifted both excitedly and a bit nervously while he considered both tenets of the statement so hopefully offered over for consideration by the dangerously purposeful young lady. He answered her calmly and thoughtfully, though he was explosively being set into gear with anticipation as he sensed something was different by the look in the pretty lady's shimmering sky toned eyes. "What is it that you must do before you make your thoughts so plainly known, beautiful lady?" he asked expectantly of her.

Elizabeth Ann looked deep into the star-struck young man's eyes until the blazing tell of her intentions settled glistening on the outer edges of her shining blue and grey irises. When Virgil correctly sensed the moment he had waited more than three years to experience was imminent, he softened his lips and leaned forward while his imagination exploded with a thousand differing thoughts, which all flashed into one and served to put the moment forever on an untouchable and indelible pedestal. The savage yet tender flaring of his senses upon the instant her warm, soft lips met his own was unlike anything the young man had ever experienced. The kiss was deep and full and held for seven glorious seconds before the pretty girl pulled ever so slowly away and opened her eyes to examine how she may have changed the still gruff yet alluringly handsome young country boy.

Standing in the twilight of the afternoon, Virgil revealed what lie at the depths of his soul to the young woman with little more than the transfixed look set upon his twinkling grey eyes caught in the very last of the direct, planed beams of the settling golden sunlight. Elizabeth Ann took a soft and comforting hold of Mr. O'Keefe's rough hands, so scarred by the labors of the field, such that the beaming young man would know she was pleased by what she had felt. Looking down at his worn, leather boots, which so perfectly mirrored the unwavering constituency of the man standing in them, the young woman asked, "Was that all you had hoped it would be, Virgil? I did not want to disappoint you upon the intersection of a shifting fantasy and naught but the soft warmth of the reality of my tremoring lips."

In truth, Virgil had been overwhelmed by the event and in the fashion of a true gentleman granted the beautiful graces of a woman he had sought above all else for so long, he wished to do little more than run off across the field and have a whiskey drink with Mr. Laing to celebrate. Be that as it may, the other half of the man's wildly pulsating heart wanted to fall down on his knee right there and beg for the gallant young woman's hand until she acquiesced. As the stunned farm boy had taken too long to respond, Elizabeth Ann grew frightful and asked, "Are you quite alright, Virgil? Have I done something wrong?"

Virgil shook his head spasmodically to get his thoughts square and replied excitedly, "My heavens no! Have you any idea how long I have waited for that moment? The reality of your tender gift has far surpassed even my wildest expectations."

Since it was obvious from the enthusiasm he was then exuding that the boy was not fibbing, Elizabeth Ann smiled coyly and replied rather demurely, "I thought you may have felt that way and I am glad you waited for me. I too needed to know what existed there in the depths of that mysterious act; the thought of which alone has made my heart flutter so this past season of the summer sun. Though the feeling you have set upon my heart complicates things in some ways, what rests there now is true and honorable and belongs to you no matter what becomes of us in the days and years ahead."

Virgil hitched his head ever so slightly sidelong and asked, "What do you mean by speaking such vague thoughts, pretty lady? This beautiful place before our eyes will be the same tomorrow when we kiss beneath the old oak tree as it is today. I belong to you now and that will never change. Everything is exactly as you know it to be out here. There is nothing present in this life of ours set upon this perfect place that is drawn about to confuse or trouble that pretty little heart of yours."

Elizabeth Ann lowered her head and spoke softly into the scattered patches of grass beneath their feet that took in only the scant light that the strapping shade tree would allow. "Virgil, you should know that father aims to take residence in Charleston for a time when the harvest is in. He wishes to reestablish his merchant business with

Miss Jeanne now that the majority Republican government has been established at the state house over in Columbia and our Carolina has been readmitted to the Union. He believes the authority of Miss Meara's provisional men will be dampened now that the military government of the Reconstruction is being phased out."

"That is wonderful news, Elizabeth Ann! We shall be married in the spring when the Captain returns from his business ventures down at the port." Elizabeth Ann looked up at Virgil O'Keefe and pondered the direct nature of the young hellion who feared nothing and no one. She had done wonders for his speech over the years, but the young man remained little more than a raging bull in a Market Street house of china, which in truth was a large part of what had ultimately drawn her to the Florence farm boy during their time spent in exile from Sumter.

She spoke in reply to dampen or perchance ease the excitable young man's enthusiasm. "Father wishes for me to join him and remain behind for a time to pursue my studies in literature. He believes we will all return to proper society one day. I for one cannot understand the mind of the man. I have never seen him happier than during these past three years away from all of the madness back home and focused on little more than the woman who has haunted his waking dreams since he first came to know her down in Haiti. My mother was a competent woman but I always believed that the marriage was an arrangement of Miss Meara set to keep my father and his children in line with the proper expectations of grandmother's society."

Virgil remained somewhat confused by Elizabeth Ann's rendering of her father's intentions and her own desires. No matter, the young buck was never one to back away from a challenge, especially not when he had been fighting for this moment for so long now. He constricted his sights on the pretty lady's eyes and stated plainly, "Then we shall be married come the holidays when you both return from the city for a spell. Surely the Captain will not remain away from Miss Jeanne longer than such a span as that."

Elizabeth Ann took hold the gallant young whippersnapper's hands and spoke somewhat expectantly, though her internal consternation was readily audible. "There is more to being married than simply kissing beneath the tree, Virgil. There is a courtship and we must make plans for our future together. Though I have no doubts whatsoever that Miss Jeanne will keep you on as long as you wish, there are no provisions by which we should raise a family in this beautiful station of our wonderland away from the harsher realities of life. Have you considered any of the necessities more akin to a proper couple in thinking of asking for my hand?" Elizabeth Ann then peeled her eyes away from the suddenly flummoxed pioneer of a sort and added for context, "Life is not as simple as what we have come to know here, my dearest Virgil. I had hoped you may have come to understand as much."

Virgil raised his eyes to the spot where he had hung the rope over the branch. If he could accomplish that feat without breaking his back at the behest of the young lady, he could reckon his way around this obstacle set in his path and make her see the necessity behind honoring their love under any circumstance. "I shall accompany you both to Charleston then. I am just a simple man of the backcountry but the city shall not be the end of me. Besides, Edward is not safe in such a busied place without me watching his backside and he knows as much to be the God's honest truth."

Sadly, the more the young man spoke the more the lady's mind, which was still somewhat preconditioned by the whims of her gilded upbringing, took the reins from her heart. The situation was such that Mr. O'Keefe was suddenly standing in quicksand. The more he fought against the gripping pull of his suddenly dire fate as it concerned Elizabeth Ann, the deeper he sank into the seemingly smarmy earth swaying and faltering beneath his feet. Elizabeth Ann replied evenly as the moment continued to slip away. "Grandmother has offered a truce to my father in exchange for his return to Sumter. He will not accept the terms of course, yet he knows he need not fear for his safety any longer. Whatever little Miss did to the woman by putting her hand upon her, Blair Raimi reports that she remains only half as vile as the frightful demon we left behind at home at the end of the war."

"Stay here with me then," pleaded the young man near frantically as he felt his hold upon her wavering heart loosening further with each word she spoke and each instant that passed away from the brilliant flash of their tender kiss.

Elizabeth Ann looked intently into Virgil's desperately pleading steel-grey eyes once again and offered the young man an almost unforeseen gesture of conciliation. As if the heavens had opened a door to the future before her eyes, she suddenly realized her expectations were unreasonable and that she had known all along that the young man was a simple and direct farm boy; nothing more and nothing less. Furthermore, she understood clearly that the truth of his abiding nature was precisely what had endeared Virgil O'Keefe to her from the onset. There was however, something else lurking in the shadows behind her father's wish for her to accompany him to Charleston that further complicated the tempestuous ebbs and flows of her emotion. A young man who Elizabeth Ann had always been naturally fond of back in Sumter had taken up residence in the heart of the city as a physician.

That same young man with such currently abounding potential regarding his esteemed vocation had invited Edward and Elizabeth Ann to reside in his lavishly grand Victorian brownstone home, which was vacated by a hideous slaver who was suddenly without a viable source of income following the emancipation and the forfeiture of the Confederate war effort. In the letter addressed to Edward, a letter that followed a prior correspondence with Elizabeth Ann, Doctor Roger Jemison Dawson made manifest his intent to court Elizabeth Ann during that time they were to reside with him in town. The proposal delighted Edward. His lovely yet diffident daughter's prospects for a suitable marriage were nonexistent here in Uriah and she was fast approaching the fading bloom of her twentieth year. Whether such beliefs in the dour nature of Elizabeth Ann's hopes for an impassioned and blissful yet still befitting marriage were true or not, such was how the eyes of the noble aristocrat still very much alive within the chivalrous man looking thoughtfully out upon the changing landscape of their world saw things as it concerned his pious and rather demure daughter when the dispatch arrived.

Regardless of her father's confused or perhaps shaded beliefs, Elizabeth Ann had learned quite enough of the tribulations that always seemed to accompany those who failed to follow the impulses of the heart. As such, her feelings turned on a dime and she replied warmly to Virgil while nearly laughing at her own impracticality of but a minute to the erstwhile, "Very well then, Mr. Virgil Denton O'Keefe. If you are to ask me properly, I will agree to your courtship into the Easter season."

Having thought the battle already lost, Virgil nearly fell over upon hearing such agreeable terms. Only his uncommon dexterity saved him from the disgrace of such a clumsy blunder at the most inopportune of moments. When he was properly situated once again, he answered the beautiful lady back. "You will not regret a minute of your decision, my pretty Elizabeth Ann. With your father soon to be gone, I reckon I best be moving on down the road for a spell..."

Right then and upon the very moment the young man was to solidify their open and ambiguous yet devoted pledge to some incipient form of joyous union, a twig crackled and then snapped in the underbrush garnishing the nearby tree line to the east. Virgil turned to his left and hollered recklessly, "Who's out there?" The firm warning was answered by the unmistakable giggling of two children. Virgil looked back to Elizabeth Ann and smiled cleverly upon making the general identity of the harmless assailants, though the stunned woman had covered her gaping mouth with her hand upon realizing they had been discovered.

Now, Virgil O'Keefe was only playing for effect but he couldn't resist the opportunity to brandish his fine silver pistol in front of his newly proclaimed consort in an effort to put a scare into the still thinly veiled brigands off in the bush. Looking back on things later in his life, the decision would remain one that haunted the fits of his darker thoughts for the entirety of his days set upon this earth. "I gots my pistola at the ready, your villainous fiends," Virgil called over in the general direction of the pair of soon to be appropriately identified miscreants. The two children chuckled louder and cringed in the way of one certain they would soon be discovered while Virgil stepped away from Elizabeth Ann and over towards the edge of the woods. Virgil smiled glowingly at Elizabeth Ann while he prepared to push aside the branches of a nearby bush and thereby uncover the intruding rascals.

While the twigs began to rustle as Virgil pulled them aside and the two accomplices began to giggle louder, a rifle shot echoed out like a cannon blast from the woods to the south of the field. The children, who belonged to one of Barbury Davis's direct descendants or another, were startled something fierce in thinking Virgil had fired his pistol. The shocked accomplices to the crime of only mild voyeurism screamed in horror and took flight back toward the Osment farmstead, which was the closest bastion of safety. If the rifle had not been fired, the children certainly would have harmlessly scattered back into the woods and toward their home.

Elizabeth Ann cowered closely alongside the bark of the girthy oak tree and shouted, "Virgil O'Keefe! You'll give those poor devils a heart attack!" Virgil looked over to his right, towards the southern woods, which separated the lower forty from the upper field and called out, "Who goes there?"

The vile sounding laugh that emerged from the depths of those woods was certainly only half-human, though such a distinction may have been gracious. Upon hearing such an unsettling response, Virgil ran over to Elizabeth Ann and quickly tucked her behind the oak tree such that she was not exposed to anything out beyond the tree line of the southern woods. Elizabeth Ann had covered her ears in the event Virgil was not finished with his shenanigans and did not hear the low yet hideous laugh emerge from the wooded stretch at the end of the field. She still believed Virgil had shot off his pistol to scare the eavesdropping children and as such asked, "What are you doing, Mr. O'Keefe? Have you gone quite mad that you would handle a lady in such a way?"

Virgil put his finger to his lips to try and quiet Miss Elizabeth Ann and whispered, "Someone took them a rifle shot in this here direction from the divinin' woods down by the end of the upper field. Did you hear the villain laugh in the way of Miss Meara?" Elizabeth Ann put her hands firmly upon her hips in a show of disgust and spoke sternly to the seemingly beguiled young man. "I don't condone what you did Virgil, but the lying about a thing is not something I will look past lightly. Now you put that silver pistol of yours away and let's get on up to the house and calm those poor children before the gossip runs hot as the midday air! I must have lost my mind in thinking you had grown some!"

Virgil shook his head and replied again in a whisper, "No, don't you move from this spot. Whatever is out there just might set its sights upon you. He could be one of Miss Meara's men or worse."

Elizabeth Ann shook her head furiously and derided the young man rather scornfully, "In all my days, Virgil O'Keefe! I have never seen such behavior from a gentleman in all my days! I should have known better!" With that Elizabeth Ann stormed off toward the house while Virgil set to trim his sights on whatever was moving steadily to the west and off of the property by way of the cover of the trees. Seeing that Elizabeth Ann was now exposed out of the corner of his eye, Virgil fired a shot in the general direction of the last twig he heard rustle near to the spot where he believed he had seen the shadowy assailant swiftly withdrawing.

Elizabeth Ann turned around furiously and shouted back to Virgil, "I hope you realize what you have done, Mr. Virgil O'Keefe! You had better get the last of those laughs out now because I will not tolerate you belittling me!"

Virgil paid the pretty and rather agitated young lady no mind. He had by then spotted the darkly dressed man scampering off beyond the property line but there was no way he could hit a mark that far off in the distance with the weapon currently resting in his calm and deadly precise hand. Only after realizing it made little sense to have another go at the unknown rifleman with only a pistol at his disposal did Virgil shift his thoughts to effecting damage control with the angry young lady and the certain to be loose lipped Davis boys. He tucked his pistol into his working britches and went running up the slope of the field after the surprisingly swift young woman before she had any more time to look things over in the wrong light.

Virgil did not catch up to Elizabeth Ann before they had made the front garden that ran the length of the house just beyond the front porch. To his dismay, Henry and Thaddeus Davis were pointing out toward the old oak and speaking frantically to Miss Jeanne and Mr. Calhoun when he had finally made the swiftly moving target of the young lady's side. While the frazzled young man relished the opportunity to set things right with Elizabeth Ann by having the boys now stationed up on the porch bear witness to the fact he didn't fire off his pistol by their ears, of course and conversely, the eventuality of such an exculpatory admission would depend upon on how much the little heathens had actually seen and heard while hiding down there in the brush. Beyond the uncertainties associated with the clearing of his good name of the sin of such childish sport and alerting Elizabeth Ann to the tangible dangers then present when he actually did discharge his weapon, there were other dilemmas mounting away from the favor of the young man as Henry and Thaddeus continued to bear their souls before the Captain up on the porch; additional snags or difficulties as it were, which were perhaps far more severe than calming the young lady down by absolving him of such boorish behavior. In any eventuality, Virgil O'Keefe understood intuitively that the chips had been forced down upon the table and the cards were near to being turned.

Elizabeth Ann refused to speak to the eager young man pulling frantically at her elbow as they approached the stairs to the porch. For his part, Virgil dared not grab hold of her hand or forcefully impede her progress with the young lady's father carefully eyeing them both while he listened to the two Davis boys plead their case before God and Miss Jeanne alike. To Virgil's dismay, when he and Elizabeth Ann were near to stepping upon the first of the stairs leading up to the deck, Miss Jeanne scurried the children and then walked quickly into the house with a muted look of indifference set upon her face. Such ominous portent and hastily executed actions certainly did not lead Virgil to believe that the testimony of the two boys had been only that of innocuous.

Though Elizabeth Ann was still incensed over Virgil's exhibition of such dangerous tomfoolery with a loaded pistol, upon looking into the eyes of her waiting father she quickly realized that there would be another matter to address. Virgil called up to the porch in the direction of Mr. Calhoun cheerily and rather innocently. He spoke as if nothing of a material nature had taken place upon the interlude of their typical exchange of the morning pleasantries, "Howdy, Cap'm. I trust you had a good day with Mr. Sommers back in town. Where has that old boy been hiding since we left Sumter?"

Mr. Calhoun was not angered by the young man's planned engagements with his daughter but worried by them all the same. He understood the complications young and perhaps even impassioned love could pose to a woman's overall sensibilities and her proper understanding of how the world works. As far as Virgil putting the fear of

God into the Davis boys went, Edward had accurately calculated that the matter would be one to sort out with Elizabeth Ann, who was unlikely to approve of such childish antics. Where Captain Calhoun was losing some of his respect for the audacious young man was in the fact he had gone behind his back in seeking to court or perhaps wed his daughter, depending on which Davis child one chose to believe at the time.

As such, Edward narrowed his charming guise and replied in earnest to the young buck's cheerful and woefully benign greeting. "Come on up here, son. Mister Sommers is quite fine but I would relish in the opportunity to speak directly with you presently." Though his heart had dropped like a hot stone into the empty pit of his right before supper stomach, Virgil nodded distinctively in the affirmative and replied in the military way, "Yes Sir! Cap'm Sir!"

While Virgil made his way up the porch stairs with Elizabeth Ann lagging uncomfortably behind, Edward answered the young man's rather ancillary question for the sake of knotting up a potential loose end. "Mr. Sommers has been quartered in Charleston on my behalf since we departed Sumter for Uriah. I needed some boots on the ground and some ears to the tracks down at the port for various reasons. He visits with good news and therefore our little incident, which we shall address upon the instant, presents itself as quite timely."

Virgil realized the boys had spilled it all as he stepped evenly upon the pine porch boards at the top of the stairs with his heavy, worn-out working boots. Nevertheless, Virgil attempted to cut the more serious issues off at the pass by focusing on the more mundane matter at hand. "I swear I never fired my pistol, Sir! I was just brandishing the weapon around some to put a trifling scare into them nosey boys when a rifle shot gots fired from the woods to the south!"

Edward now had his opening upon Virgil's hotly declared reference to the nosey boys. The very delineation left little doubt concerning the sensitivity of what the prying eyes and ears of 'them boys' had discovered down by the old oak. Nevertheless, the shrewd businessman and passive negotiator waited for a bit to address just exactly what Henry and Thaddeus Davis had been eavesdropping upon to cool down the fiery young buck just a hair. "Elizabeth Ann, I'd appreciate you coming on up here as well, my dear." Captain Calhoun's daughter lowered her head and replied rather timidly, "Yes, father."

The sullen young woman walked up the remaining stairs to the porch deep in thought so that she might prepare her mind to defend the wishes of her heart. Virgil's antics with his pistol hadn't strengthened her resolve to stick that pretty neck of hers out any on behalf of the out of order farm boy. Still and all, she felt that she would vigorously defend Mr. O'Keefe's actions in their entirety when push came down to shove with her father; and if she knew one thing at that moment with any semblance of certainty, it was that her father would eventually push the tumultuous situation beyond its boiling point. Her father's ideas around the betrothal of one of his daughters were no different now than they were before the war despite all that had changed and all that had been rendered to ash around them. Unfortunately for the young lovers, Elizabeth Ann was not as strong willed as her older sisters Mary Grice and Susannah Jane were when it came to their insistence upon marrying Tanner Decker or not marrying Tines Murdoch III, respectively, nor did her father currently possess the resources to put another common man such as Tanner right in the ways of a proper Southern gentleman upon marrying into the family.

When she was beside Virgil standing on the porch, Elizabeth Ann began with the same unsuccessful tact as her would be courtier. "Virgil says he didn't fire the weapon, papa. I for one believe that if he did indeed do so that the act was not intentional."

Edward studied his daughter carefully, more so to gauge the tendencies of her heart than to discover if she was speaking the truth. He then spoke to her in a calm but certainly formal manner. "Though I would not condone such irresponsible behavior, whether or not Mr. O'Keefe fired his weapon in the presence of unsuspecting children is not my primary concern. What is my primary concern is the chastity and proper behavior of my daughter. The boys said they found you two kissing beneath the oak of the field. What do you have to say for yourselves as it concerns their dour accusations?"

The potent memory of that fire burning in his heart when her sweet and tender lips overcame his own caused Virgil to laugh a bit nervously. Such was the only expression of a feeling so overwhelming that he was raised to know. He then answered the Captain plainly and in a forthright manner. "I plead guilty to the act, Mr. Calhoun as I ain't one to call no man, or boy in this instance, a liar. However, you should know Miss Elizabeth Ann ain't never knowed it was coming to her."

Edward had to smile upon facing such youthful and inexperienced chivalry. For as displeased as he was with these rather unexpected turns of events, though they should not have been surprising to any man with eyes that see and wits currying to the more gracious favors of common sense during that summer of 1868, the boy was charismatic and Mr. Calhoun appreciated the fact that young Virgil was standing up for his daughter's honor under fire. He queried his daughter in response to Virgil's gallant denial on her behalf. "What say you, Elizabeth Ann? Were the lips of the young man yet faster and more cunning than an unseen serpent of the grass?"

Elizabeth Ann blushed heartily, lowered her head in shame and replied penitently, "No father. The thought and the act were both of my own accord. Virgil is a gentleman in that regard and would never have tricked me thusly."

"I see," replied Edward rather scrupulously. He rubbed his chin with his thumb and forefinger while considering the possibility of the young lovers for a moment but then dispatched with the silly idea upon heeding to the necessities of tradition and his nearly impoverished state. The shrewd man knew how to devilishly break the angelic spell his pure and lovely daughter had cast over the exceedingly honest and likewise hardnosed young man. Though he despised being quite so underhanded, he really saw no alternative solution to quickly dissolving their rather determined affections for one another at that point.

Beyond the kiss, the Davis boys, having been scared senseless into his unwitting arms, had told the Confederate Captain of both the softly bandied about proposal and the planned courtship. Edward folded his hands under his chin and stared the both of them directly in the eyes before plunging the dagger devotedly into their backs and then driving the wedge between them. "Now, do understand that I am not privy to your correspondences, my dear Elizabeth Ann. However, based on what the seemingly affable young man requests of me, I have to believe he has received at least something of an affirmative word from your delicate hand. As such, I must ask of you; what would Doctor Roger Jemison Dawson have said if it were he behind the bush in place of the Davis rapscallions?"

There was little doubt, if any, at this point that Captain Calhoun had brought in the heavy cannon to divide and then dishearten his young and sorely unprepared opponents and moreover, to mercilessly bend them to his will in precisely the same fashion he might have shamelessly neutered any adversary to his business dealings prior to the war. As to why the disavowed member of the elite planter class clung so dearly to the traditions and desires of his past where it concerned the future of his daughters was something of a mystery. Particularly in light of the fact that his heart had finally settled warm and true in the arms of Miss Jeanne over these past three annum of his exile, and done so with little more than a rudimentary material stipend, which had been provided only by the exacting yet satisfying necessities of their physical labor. Whatever the unwavering actuality behind his present motives, precisely as Edward suspected would be the truth of it, Mr. O'Keefe took the bait concerning his ruinous revelations around Dr. Dawson first.

The teenaged farm hand turned to Elizabeth Ann with a look set upon his deflated mien that spoke of a mortal wound to the heart. His lips quavered and his cheeks twitched spasmodically at the slight hollows above his prominent jaw. He chose his words judiciously out of respect for the young woman's father alone. However, sudden jealousy so viciously set to such depths within him was a hideous handmaiden, one which laid such a deadly clutch upon Virgil's raw and exposed emotion that the young man was left nearly helpless in trying to manage such a dark and consuming force of nature rising within him. "Does your father speak the truth, Elizabeth Ann? Did you simply wish to make me want for you all the more while you were away and spending time with another who seeks the very thing I have requested of you?"

Elizabeth Ann was guilty as surveyed as it were in that she had not rebuked outright Dr. Dawson's inscribed entreaty so cleverly set within his letter received by her back in May. At that point in time, she was aware that she had feelings for Virgil stirring deep within her heart but she did not wish to offend her one-time confidant from back in Sumter; a man who knew so little of how drastically her life had changed in these last seven years since the onset of the war back in sixty-one. Where her sin or folly took hold was in the fact that much of her decision not to address Dr. Dawson's softly laid proposal rested squarely in the veracity of her inability to accept the fact that her desired husband might endeavor to be little more than a common subsistence farmer in a town such as Uriah, which was destined to be heavily influenced if not controlled outright by the majority of its inhabitants that belonged to the class of freed slaves.

The reason she had lured Virgil out beneath the old oak tree to kiss him was to discover if the bonds of her heart would thus override her fears of such a common existence; fears that were nearly innate to her being in that they had been brought about by her privileged upbringing. The good news on that late-August afternoon was that her heart had won the day once Virgil's firm lips had pressed so dutifully against her own. That was until she came to presume that Virgil had scattered the young Davis boys from the bush with a twelve year old's prank. Now, with her father standing so firmly and openly against the young man for the reproachable sin of not seeking his approval, the confluence of rushing emotion and the battle raging in her head and in her heart left the young woman at a loss for proper words to respond to Virgil's sorrowful entreaty. Thusly, her cheeks shone red against the shimmering blues of her twisting eyes due to the embarrassment of her unintended yet so bluntly revealed deceit.

After settling out some, Elizabeth Ann came to the singular determination that she would not lie to the fallen gentleman serving out his exile in Uriah or the misguided and overzealous young farm boy. She spoke in reply to the darkening young man with a courageous voice given the depths of her unease and the almost maniacal tremoring of her moral compass, which was caused by such a forceful assault upon the dearest of her sacred values. "Virgil, Roger Dawson did write to me back in May as father has so eloquently stated. I have not looked upon the letter in quite some time, yet written within was certainly some form of a request to properly court me during the time father was set to take up residence with Dr. Dawson in Charleston. I did not say yes to my long-time friend, but alas, I did not properly rebuke him either."

With that being said, Elizabeth Ann hung her head and looked upon her worn out working boots, which would have been a ghastly and furthermore unfathomable sight back at Butterworth Hall. She found it strange that she had taken such pride in those boots with each culling of the garden and reaping of the field up until this very moment. She wondered why this peculiar desire for all of the fine things she never once wanted for as part of her former life was suddenly mounting within her shifting mind. She then began to speculate as to what spell had been cast from the depths of the earth below Sumter town; what enchantment of Miss Meara was drawing both her and her father away from the very demesne of their paradise found and so deceitfully luring them toward some abiding antebellum stanchion now glorifying their return to something of a mirage or perhaps a foreboding and grossly demented likeness to the abundant ways of old.

Although the odds appeared to be stacked against the young buck at that moment given everything which had conspired so suddenly and so perfectly against him, as if by the will of the devil itself, Virgil would have won the day had he only stayed true to his heart. Still and all, this new and ungainly contraption which was Virgil's jealous mind was a dark place that ran black with spite and was fed copiously by the murder of his family and the rape and dismemberment of his sister; those tragic events that left him orphaned at age fourteen and seeking blood retribution and the forced comforts of his fellow man only offered up in the temporary camps of the warring soldier. The young man's sudden spite for both his beloved Cap'm, who had clearly turned on him and did not find him worthy of his daughter, whether his own accidental skirting of proper protocol was reason enough for such an attitude or not, and his climaxing love and sudden and simultaneously accompanying disdain for the deceitful young woman were so powerful that Virgil O' Keefe was set to take flight in the face of a fight for the first time in his life.

The young man knew but one way to end the hideous cross-current of these feelings, and that was to separate his mind from the torments of his soul. He learned the trick after his family was violated and murdered. He spoke harshly and in his provincial tongue to the both of them before leaving the main farmhouse for good, though the dutiful young man, of course, saw to it that the harvest of that season was brought in for the benefit of his family.

Virgil set his eyes upon Captain Calhoun first. "Well 'den, Cap'm, if'n the man dat done kept a bullet outta your'n hull ain't good enough for the likes a your'n daughter, shame upon you den. My folks was always sayin' dat your kind and dem men dat be pushin' those wicked Yankee boys was one in the same."

Virgil O'Keefe then turned to Elizabeth Ann. Though her eyes pleaded mercifully with him not to travel down the road lined with the black thoughts of his current mind and the road that he appeared so set to traverse, nothing but Virgil asking for God's grace would have turned back the young man's spite. For his was an incendiary spite, so suddenly and unexpectedly released from some dark inner sanctum of his guarded soul, and the violent release of that awful stew of hot piss and sour vinegar was some four years in the making from the day those Yankee boys took everything from him.

Needless to say, Virgil did not solicit such divine grace in responding to the pretty and already quite broken young lady. "Dancin' wif' two gents is always better den dancin' with the one if you can spell your mind a da deceit I'd be supposin', purdy lady. But I ain't no man to pretend that I's somethin' I ain't. Yessum, I talk like a country boy and I act like a country boy dat ain't gots no folks exceptin' y'all. I ain't never gonna aim to make mine more den a country boy can pull outta dat there field or another one jus' like it. But jus' know the heart of dis here Carolina farm boy with none left behind dat still be wearin' the same name was to have been yours if'n ya had wanted it, Ma'am."

With that, Virgil O'Keefe tipped his worn out old field hat to Edward Calhoun and turned the other way from Elizabeth Ann in stepping down from the porch. After he had said his piece, he could not bear to look into her eyes even one final time. The act alone nearly sent the broken hearted young lady to her knees. The young man then marched off to the west to take up Amos's bed at the Laing's cabin since his brother of a sort was off in Columbia with the Republicans trying to promote the rights of the former slaves in the new govern-ment. Virgil had always figured Amos's efforts wouldn't come to much with all the hatred burning like brush fires across the countryside and within the cities and towns of the postbellum state, but he sure did applaud the brilliant young man for trying. Amos Martingale Laing was about the smartest young man Virgil ever did know and he was hell bent on setting things right after all those years of lies, chains and the cracking of those horse whips upon human flesh.

Edward was also a bit broken by the boy's words. In his mind, the young man was set to simply live his life out happily on this farm in his proper place. That such a life was a thing not suitable for his daughter was not in accordance with any fault of his own, or so he believed. However, the reality of those young and primal forces of innocent love and their accompanying light clashing out in the open before his very eyes evinced a near overwhelming feeling in him of compassion for the doting young man who did indeed look up to him like a father. Things did not get any better for the still half-shaded mind of Mr. Edward Calhoun from there. Elizabeth Ann shed a tear while her guilt over what she had done to the now scorned and sorrowful Mr. O'Keefe kept her from running after him; running after him and whisking off with the brash and warm-lipped farm boy and forever disappearing into that last light of the low settling aura of the gloaming and the silhouettes of the summer trees off in the distance.

Instead of following after Virgil, the incensed young woman set her eyes scornfully upon her father and made her feelings plainly known. "You had no right to misconstrue such a thing as Roger Dawson's correspondence, father! Virgil didn't seek your blessing because he knew nothing of my feelings before I kissed him heartily by that rope swing. He only asked to court me then because I told him I was to be leaving with you for Charleston when the harvest was in for the season. I am beginning to think that Blair Raimi was quite astute in leaving us behind for grandmother! Perhaps Susannah Jane was the smartest of us all to get on with the leaving of this twisted place behind for good before the war was known to be lost!"

Elizabeth Ann paused to steady her wind. She knew she had wounded her father badly, if not near to mortally. Yet, her hatred for what he had done was burning hotter than the flames which had consumed Atlanta back in the winter of 1864. As such, she behaved in much the same manner as her father before her and went for his exposed throat upon the very moment of his faltering. "Why is it that you cannot do the honorable thing and take Miss Jeanne's hand? Is it that she is also unworthy of the name of the disgraced son of Meara Calhoun? Is the price of such infamy of marrying a colored woman dearer than even that which you paid to procure your own child by same? You will turn on even me one day, father if my station in life becomes but a burden to your wants!"

With those harsh delivered to her still somewhat unwitting or perhaps gobsmacked father, who somehow continued to believe that the young woman was simply confused and overwhelmed by a transitory rush of late summer affection, Elizabeth Ann stormed into the house. To his credit, Edward had at least rather precipitously come to once again understand that the rules of engagement as it concerned the affairs of a young woman's heart were far more challenging beasts than even negotiating with the vile serpents of the business and political realms. As such, Edward meekly attempted to plead his case while his daughter stormed by like an afternoon cloudburst of late July. "Perhaps I am confused, my dear. Why would Roger Dawson ask for my permission to court you if you had not led him to believe such a thing were at least agreeable?"

Elizabeth Ann stopped hotly at the threshold of the door, turned to her father as if she were caught up in a tropical cyclone and rebuked him thusly, "Because, Mr. Dawson is the very same as you and the remainder of your ilk, father! Unless slapped in the face directly, that sort of man will not stop until he has what he wants! Thank you for turning me over to such a fiend as one who would solicit my own father for the benefit of my affections without my proper consent! Have you learned nothing during the entire while we have remained so happy here?"

Edward stuttered a bit, precisely as he did while only a boy in front of his mother when he was caught making time with Miss Elsa, the lovely elder colored woman Miss Meara eventually had beaten to death. He did so in an effort to speak but he had no words to express his confounded thoughts driven so swiftly towards remorse and depravity. Elizabeth Ann had no time for such feeble impotence. She put her back harshly to her flummoxed father and finished storming into the house and up to her room, leaving the fumbling man to stew in the juices of his deceit disguised as some twisted form of paternal shepherding. She soon reached the room she had shared with only Margaret Anne for the past year due to the fact Shy had moved on over to Augusta to continue her studies under the aegis of an older industry man, though many believed the true reason behind the move was to keep the stunning woman from setting the entire town ablaze with her painfully candid tongue.

Upon entering, Elizabeth Ann saw that the promised child was studiously reading at the desk set in between the two slender beds lining the walls of the modest quarters. Elizabeth Ann paid no mind to the child's previously serene environment and slammed the door closed aggressively before falling headlong and distraught onto her bed. Furthermore, she did as much with all of the groans of anguish and misery that precisely mirrored her deep-set anger and her heartache. In response to her sister's dramatic rendition of the pangs of death, Margaret Anne placed her book calmly down on the desk like a good and proper student having reached the end of the period and asked, "What is the matter, sister? What is it that has you so troubled on this perfect day that the Lord has so graciously made?"

Elizabeth Ann was sobbing into the near suffocating depths of her pillow and did not reply to her little sister of a shared father. Margaret Ann stood up from the reading desk and promptly sat down on the bed next to Elizabeth Ann. She then stroked Elizabeth Ann's radiant, dark-brown hair lovingly and stared blankly into the nearest wall for a time while her older sister continued to cry it out. The nine-year-old child then spoke vacantly as if she were focusing on something else while her words were delivered. "Father has driven Virgil away, has he not?"

Elizabeth Ann was surprised by her little sister's unprovoked knowledge and pulled her face free of the smothering warmth of her pillow to give the growing child a curious look see. "Yes, father has driven Virgil away, little Miss. How did you know?"

Margaret Anne Basseterre put her finger to Elizabeth Ann Calhoun's cheek and wiped away a stray tear that had begun to run sidelong towards her sister's prim and slender nose. "Do you plan to run off with Virgil, sister?" the little girl asked quite innocently as if the occurrence of such an event were naught but a slight consideration.

Elizabeth Ann sat up and wiped her face free of the last of the loose tears trending down her cheeks and replied, "No, of course not, little Miss. What good would come of such a turbulent escapade without father's support? Virgil is still in many ways just an oversized boy much younger than I and no more prepared to raise a proper family without father's benefaction than any of the Davis children he consorts with daily out in the field."

"The prospects of the man who seeks your hand down in Charleston are far better I presume?" asked a suddenly perplexed Margaret Anne of her older sister.

Elizabeth Ann didn't pause to bother with the little girl's impossible knowing of another man as she was neck deep in the thinking through of the persisting quandaries of her present dilemma. "Well he is a physician of some renown down at the port. The need for his services seems to be without end as more infirmed souls and folks left pitifully wretched flock to the cities in search of charity in the aftermath of the war. He has always been fond of me…and perhaps a few of the other girls from school. The betrothal would be an honor and a boon for father's uncertain standing with the old guard if he remains in town to revive his business prospects." Elizabeth Ann then shook her head in disbelief and concluded her brief discourse with a pronounced air of the same, "But for heaven's sake, why am I saying such things to a nine-year-old child?"

Margaret Anne delivered another frightfully puzzled look in the direction of her sister and spoke with that almost eerie calm so distinctive to her insouciant disposition, "Virgil is a good man. Perhaps you should talk to him. I do know that he loves you dearly. He inquires as to the nature of your feelings often and he will not fare well if he believes you and father have betrayed him for being no more than what he always has been."

Elizabeth Ann smiled wistfully and complimented her rather astute and exceptionally intuitive bunk mate, "You are such a bright girl, little Miss. I do wish there was something I could do to change father's mind but he is woefully set in returning to his life of yesteryear, though the ways of the past are today little more than an illusion of his nostalgic mind. I do worry so over what will become of Virgil if he truly believes father has found him wanting. He does look up to father so and seeks direction from him almost in the way of a little lost puppy dog."

Margaret Anne shook her head at her sister and retorted flatly, "I think it is you who are set in the old ways, sister. Father has little to do with your desire to be true to your feelings. In time, you will know the longings of today to be quite real and you will experience a desperate need to reconcile the veracity of your spurned love to the very beating of your heart. There will come a day when one of those primitive urges will not function properly without the other."

Elizabeth Ann exhaled in a frustrated manner and exclaimed, "You are far too young to properly understand such delicate intricacies, little Miss. Perhaps you should return to your reading and the simple affairs of a child."

"I will soon enough do as you say, sister. Yet Virgil is somehow tied to my destiny just as he is yours. If you and father have both broken his heart, I fear the undercurrents of his undoing will have dark repercussions for us all," replied the promised child with that same emotionless calm.

"Listen to you pontificate, little Miss," interjected Elizabeth Ann. "You speak as if you are a woman of some thirty years and a common practitioner of marriage counsel. Do not worry over Virgil. He is like a wild stallion and will find another love when I am gone and long since forgotten. Moreover, he is but a boy of seventeen with a heart as tempestuous and unbound as the winter sky."

Margaret Anne said nothing in reply and quietly returned to her reading table. Once there, she found the spot upon the page she had been so peacefully perusing when her sister barged into the room and she was forced to place her book down flat upon the table. After she had read in silence for but a moment, she turned and spoke thoughtfully to her sister. "All dark things stem from the denial of the heart, my dear sister. Over time, your compromise will make the place of your deceit raw and then turn cold when you seek to shield those tender throbs stemming from that eternal truth of your love for the young man both within and without. Let us hope such is true and that you merely remain uncertain as to your feelings for sweet Virgil, lest you play the devil's hand of vying for comfort over love."

Elizabeth Ann giggled brilliantly at the preposterous nature of such a thought in that the idea had stemmed from the mental wares of a nine-year-old child and asked of her sister, "What may I ask are you reading over there, dear child? The prose has you near to speaking in tongues!" "Oh, I requisitioned one of Miss Jeanne's romance novels from the shelf in the family's room. The grade level material they provide at school is both dry and trite," was little Miss's straightforward reply.

Elizabeth Ann laughed heartily while being rightly shocked by the prodigious child and replied, "Well your preferred material is precisely on point as it concerns your older sister. Perhaps it will serve you well when a man comes a calling for your own precious hand." To which Margaret Ann responded, "I know as much, sister. That is why I am reading the novel, so that I will understand the mind of Virgil O'Keefe when you are gone from us here in Uriah and set to return to society in Charleston." Elizabeth Ann shook her head in disbelief and moved to close the oddly prescient conversation. "I suppose such a thing can't hurt, my dear child. No one in this household seems to know a whit about love to begin with."

Margaret Anne then looked over to her sister from the pages of her book and announced, "Here is another appropriate thought for you, my dear sister of the light. 'Do know well that the truth of the world is never as it is given over to appear before our eyes that are so easily deceived. Never deny your heart for the sake of only the false promises of those who spin lies and condition the minds of the ones they seek to control.'"

At that moment, Miss Leslie called up the stairs to little Miss so that she might come down for their evening stroll with her baby girl. "Good evenin', Li'l Miss! We's a be waitin' on da porch for ya when you is ready!"

Little Miss set her book to rest face down on the desk and addressed her sister one final time as she began to make her way out of the room. "I'm off to walk with Mammy and Sweet pea. I hope you feel better before long, sister."

"Tell them I say hello, little Miss. It's fixin' to be a beautiful evening," Elizabeth Ann called back. "I will, sister" replied Margaret Ann as she finished dashing out of the room and down the stairs into the waiting arms of her mammy.

When her sister was out of the room, Elizabeth Ann picked up the book little Miss had been reading. She began to skim the open pages more by the light of the candle than the light coming in through the window as darkness fell over the land. None of the words that little Miss had recited to her were written anywhere within the text of the open pages. Elizabeth Ann shook her head with amazement and said to none but her firmly yet slowly catching thoughts, which were working their way around her head like the gears of an ancient clock, "Certainly the child does not come up with such things of her own accord! The pure wonder of such an impossibility!" Elizabeth Ann then lay back down on her bed. Though she tried to imagine the serenity of her dashing return to Charleston society, she was able to consider little more than the sweet, precious lips of Virgil O'Keefe and what insanely maddening sensations might lie beyond those warm and wanting gate keepers to the wildly blunt yet stalwart young man's heart.

Some five weeks later, on Friday, October 2nd, 1868 to be precise, Edward and Miss Jeanne were to be found once again sitting alone on the quaint front porch of the Osment farmstead. The hour of the occasion was a fine fall evening upon which the annual cotton harvest had been shipped off to market. The air was dry, waxed warm and scented of the drying leaves of the upcoming fall season and the pruned stalks of the field. The profits that remained that season were far more abundant than they had been under the expedients of the Union Army skimming operations or protection rackets of the prior years. The new state government in Columbia was predominantly Republican in both the nature of its stated representatives and its intended policy, but the planter class displaced by the war did not intend to let such a state of affairs stand for long once the presence of the blue bellies was little more than an unpleasant afterthought. Mr. Satterfield would be heading in from Sumter and not town in the morning with a full and proper team to draw his steadfast carriage and begin the journey of

Edward and Elizabeth Ann out of their exile in Uriah and on to their triumphant return to the reemerging elite society of Charleston town.

Though returning to Sumter was still an outright impossibility with his mother floundering somewhat under the new political regime and incapable of turning a profit on the sizeable plantation without the benefit of slave labor, with Mr. Sommers's assistance Edward had managed to dredge up something of the old leases and titles to his Caribbean merchant trade business. His primary hopes in venturing forth to the old port city were to rekindle that enterprise and see to it that his only legitimate daughter who had not turned her back on him was properly married off in the event he was unable to get back up on his own two feet by reestablishing his trading ventures. Though he and Miss Jeanne had not shared a room while he lived out at the farm for the sake of appearances in the eyes of their children, the two had not been without their intimate moments. Furthermore, they were treated as a singular head of household by all present and nearly all who they crossed paths with back in town. They were in those simple and tender years, nearly all which they had both, at various yet misaligned times in their lives, always hoped they would one day be.

Over the past few months, as the once blocked path before Edward's return to at least something of his former glory began to clear, Miss Jeanne had come to realize that Edward was not a man made to sit idly by out on the farm for much longer. Be that as it may, she fretted terribly over Edward's decision to take up residence in Charleston for a time before things with the new elected government in Carolina had a chance to settle out some or properly mellow with age as it were. While the two sat peacefully out on the porch, Virgil O'Keefe could be seen off in the distance in the dusty haze of the gloaming that followed the setting of the sun. The industrious young man was down the slope and beyond the harvested rows of cotton slowly disappearing before their attentive eyes at the southern boundary of the upper field. He was clearing the gap between the woodlands and its accompanying underbrush and the outer perimeter of the planted soil. Virgil was still very much a broken man more than a month after his unceremonious disavowal by Edward and his pretty daughter, yet he had finally stopped hopelessly searching those southern woods for the shell casing of the shot fired by the shadowy hobgoblin with the ill and foreboding laugh.

While the two watched Virgil work by his lonesome off in the distance of the fading half-light of the dusk, Miss Jeanne calmly asked of her sometime lover and ofttimes confidant, "Have you spoken with Virgil since the episode on the porch with Elizabeth Ann? I do not find him to be of his usual good-natured accord in the rare moments I have crossed his path now that he has taken up residence down at the Laing's cabin. Miss Leslie is also worried about him."

Edward turned to look at Miss Jeanne and replied somberly, "I have not spoken to Mr. O'Keefe since that day. In fact, he usually remains scarcer than even his present station from my proximity. I feel for the boy, I truly do, my dearest Jeanne. I do not know what I could have done differently to avoid such a bitter end to our time spent here together. He is such a vivacious and enjoyable young man when his head is ruminating properly."

Miss Jeanne looked at Edward as if her jaw might drop into her lap and exclaimed, "Edward Christopher Calhoun! You either have rocks in that two-bit head of yours or your desire to prosper away from me down in Charleston has driven you mad! After all we both have endured for the sanctity of these few blessed years unmolested by the expectations of the world around us, how is that you of all people dare to say such a thing about the boy with a straight face?"

Edward's face instantly flushed red with shame. He had not been rebuked so sharply and so openly by the elegant woman since he nearly had a come apart over the Trust barrister's lustful behavior down in Les Cayes back in 1858. He fumbled brutally through the testimony of his defense. "What would you have me do, my dear? Subject Elizabeth

Ann to little more than a subsistence living here in this place? She would not survive the year in the permanent care of the young man."

Miss Jeanne gasped openly and shot back, "My word, Mr. Calhoun, you certainly are a man who knows how to belittle those he intends to leave behind after three years of skimming for his needs and biding his time. I now understand why the boy is distraught. He loved you like the father he no longer has, Edward! I too once loved the man whose heart had come to be free here in this place. But this man before me now, the one who knows nothing of true dignity or heartfelt kindness when the opportunity to reestablish his broken name presents itself, is the same man I refused to give my heart over to for some twenty-two years prior to the first of these golden moments we have been so blessed to share. It now appears I would have been well served to abide by such wisdom for the remainder of my days!"

Once those words had been harshly given in reply, Miss Jeanne stormed back into the house and did not reemerge until an hour before Edward's carriage arrived the following morning. Edward had been left to ponder his callous indifference to the hearts of those so endeared to him; hearts which he planned only to prosper once he was effectively reestablished back in the port city. The war had claimed his only male heir and being forced into exile by his mother had cost him two daughters and what claim he once had to the family fortune. His fourth daughter had left for the free states up North after leaving Butterworth Hall to reside with an aunt up in Greenville following the death of her mother. She was last known to have settled somewhere near Boston. Edward's aggressive resolve to return to prominence, it now appeared, was close to costing him the great love of his life, his remaining daughter and the young man he considered to be the closest thing to a proxy for his heroically fallen son he would ever come to know.

Be that as it may, the suddenly pigheaded man was still somehow fooled into believing that returning to some semblance of his former

nobility and wealth would set all things right and was indeed a very
necessary sacrifice to be made on behalf of those given over to his
care; those who as of the present moment still failed to understand
the always threatening bondage of resource poverty. Perhaps his
drive for more was brought on by the angst set upon his mind when
thinking of the helplessness he would face when left to little more
than the common provisions of this fine land he had gifted to Miss
Jeanne more than a score ago upon her once devastating, yet as he
had come to understand over time, quite necessary betrothal. That
she had loved the man she married beyond his understanding was a
verity that Edward never considered or let taint these beautiful years
of their settling in during his banishment to Uriah. Perhaps his need
to recapture what once was had also been driven by his ego and the
feelings of his mounting inadequacy that seemed to fester on occasion
while the seasons of his exile and his relative uselessness out in the
field and around the house wore on. In those otherwise blissful years,
he worried ever more over keeping his hold on the beautiful woman at
his side each morning when they warmly greeted the new day as one.

Though Miss Jeanne was still quite angry at Edward the following
morning, she arose an hour before the carriage was due to arrive with
hopes of talking some sense into the man. After watching her husband die in the field, the woman of such innately guarded emotion
also knew never to leave a thing unsaid when the days ahead were set
to become uncertain. The air was cool and dark when she stepped out
onto the deck that Saturday morning of 3rd October 1868, but the
intuitive senses of the elegant Haitian woman alerted her to the fact
that the morning light was not far off from splintering the pitch of
the lingering darkness. Mr. Calhoun and Elizabeth Ann's travel cases
were packed and resting near the stairs to the front porch in wait for
the impending arrival their coachman.

She spoke as one set upon resolution and not the vile allowances of
continuing spite when she greeted the lonely and reticent man hoping

amidst the enduring darkness before the dawn for little more than the breaking of the light and the sweet promise of her arrival. "Good morning, Edward. I see that you are well situated and ready to be off on your next adventure." The incidence of her soothing voice was of immediate comfort to him, though he remained uncertain as to her present frame of mind. "Yes, my dear. There is a man who awaits our arrival into Charleston on Tuesday. Leaving now should afford us plenty of time to make our appointed rounds in town," was the suddenly hopeful man's not formal yet still rather factual reply.

"Where is Elizabeth Ann?" asked Miss Jeanne in the hopes there would be time enough for them to speak at length. Edward laughed off his daughter's sluggish ways in the morning and replied, "Oh, you know how the young ladies are as it regards their beauty sleep, my dear. I suspect she will not arise before first light. Nevertheless, I have personally seen to the preparation of her travel provisions." "That is good, Edward," answered Miss Jeanne in a plaintive tone. "I was hoping we would have some time to talk before she made her way outside for your journey back to the sea."

"Well now, a useful span of time we have been thusly granted, my dear. So please, do make your concerns known to me. I am quite regretful over how things ended between us yesterday." Edward remained even keeled as he was filled with equivalent amounts of childish excitement over his trip and consternation over his dour abuse of Miss Jeanne's feelings the prior evening. Virgil O'Keefe remained on the man's thoughtful mind as well. Furthermore, though he did not fear for little Miss's safety in his absence, Edward wondered how the little sprite would respond to the actuality of the deficiency of his presence in the weeks ahead. The confusion the child had already endured as to the true nature of her family and lineage was far beyond the bounds of the ordinary and perhaps now bordered on the surreal following her lawful adoption by Miss Jeanne when she had turned eight. Yet just perhaps, Edward thought within the charged recesses of his lively and ruminating mind, the child was always intended to be gifted unto something far larger than even the true ancestry of her blood father and mother.

Miss Jeanne opened the dialogue cautiously. "Edward, I have not had hopeful presentiments about your return to Charleston for some time now. Nor do I have a good feeling about you and Elizabeth Ann leaving Virgil and little Miss behind. I do believe that little Miss shall be quite fine. However, you are the one who stands to suffer most from your separation from the promised child for a time. Beyond the matter of the child, Virgil is your ward from the day he returned you home from the field of battle and he deserves far better than your crass indifference to both his professed love for your daughter and his endearment to you. Lastly, there is a man who is likely to seek you out who seems to have the capacity to offer all means of material folly at the very price of one's mortal soul. I believe he is the one who brokered the deal with your mother just before the war came to an end. The deal that was so spurious to your future hopes."

Edward turned his head from the open darkness of the field and looked over to Miss Jeanne. There was much to consider both deep within and openly without regarding her spoken words. He could see very little of the due consternation set upon the woman's furrowed brow when he asked rather curiously about her final revelation. "How is that you have come to know a man in possession of such blessings or perhaps, in truth, only that eternal curse? What would such a man seek of me, my dear? I have so little of value to offer him."

While Edward's answer spoke volumes of what he valued down into the depths of his heart at that moment in life, Miss Jeanne proceeded forward with him in the hopes of steering the good Captain Calhoun back to at least something of the benevolent mind he possessed upon the afternoon of his arrival to Uriah. He was at last free of his burdens on that day and came to her with a pureness of spirit she had not seen lingering in the depths of his eyes since he looked her over almost improperly on the docks back in Haiti. The golden cross had always spoken to her of the man's pure heart and unwavering dignity when he was able to look away from the vanity of his idolatry, which unfortunately Miss Meara had driven into his innocent thoughts from the moment of his first spoken word. As such, she aspired to at least plant a seed upon fertile soil as the sun neared rising on that fateful morning of his departure for Charleston.

Nevertheless, the span of Mr. Calhoun's benevolent reprieve had been far too short-lived out here in Uriah. There was once again a harrowing danger present for such a worldly man in possession of an innocent and unbound spirit at its pith when that gentle spirit was left unmolested for a time by the wants of the world at-large. Furthermore, Edward's mother had managed to protect something of his birthright through her efforts to draw him into to her own vile degradation of the light and her soulless worship of the darkest arts, which are of course, eternally bound to perish within the inner sanctums of the earth. In the unsettled postbellum world of the South, the bright-eyed Edward saw nothing of this shadow of iniquity creeping onward and nearly unnoticed, though steadfast in its approach, over the emergent quarters of the Carolinas during that much maligned yet euphemistically fabled period of the Reconstruction.

"Edward, do you remember when the Union Provost was gracious enough to have our picture made out by the pasture fence back in town on little Miss's eighth birthday? The day her own mother adopted her because Miss Sarah had been deemed inadequate to care for her and then taken over to the asylum in Sumter?" asked Miss Jeanne with a steady voice and guiding cadence.

Edward nodded in the affirmative while he thought back on that specific moment of the very day in question and replied candidly, "I do remember both the gentleman and the day very well, my dear. Are you suggesting that a former Provost turned carpetbagger has been inquiring of you on how to go about entering into a business venture with me?"

She replied as one lightly irritated upon being asked a question to which they did not fully know or at least wholly comprehend the answer. "I don't know what I am suggesting, Edward. He has asked about you from time to time when I have seen him passing through town. Perhaps he believes you might be able to help him protect his business interests in the state as the new government continues to gain a proper footing within the fading shadows of the Reconstruction efforts. Whatever the source and nature of the light the child touched your mother with, Miss Meara now seems incapable of or perhaps unwilling to execute upon her given promise to deliver both you and the child to those she kneels before. Whatever he wants, I am only warning you that the golden cross has burdened my heart with some shadowy omen attached to the man's soul, assuming he does indeed possess the graces of such a human essence at all."

Miss Jeanne did not know that Edward intended to meet the very same man she now spoke of in Charleston come Tuesday. Likewise, Edward did not know the man had provisioned for his safety for a span; these very times he had been left undisturbed with Miss Jeanne within the soft golden light shining down upon the requiem of his former life and the peaceful contentment of his exile. Edward looked to the heavens and the belt of Orion flashing mighty and strong upon the pre-dawn sky as he considered what he might say in reply to such a dour revelation concerning his immediate prospects.

After a short while, he proceeded to answer the vexed woman truthfully, though deceitfully, through the tact of his omission. The always clever man did not reveal his plans to at least entertain the strange Yankee gentleman's uncommon notions for a business venture in the postbellum impression of the Carolinas. "I will promise you, my dear that having survived the bitter curse of my mother, I shall never consent to an agreement with one of her ilk in this lifetime. You may rest easy now upon receiving the honor of my word faithfully given over to the one who has always held her place at the very center of my heart."

Miss Jeanne smiled some and followed Edward's eyes up into the stars. She worried that he did not understand nearly enough of the dangers he was jumping headlong into by reentering the constant fray raging between the principalities of the darkness and the forces of light. Be that as it may, she knew the man was honorable and would never renege upon a spoken vow to her and that his judgement of character was without compare. As such, she simply took hold of the golden cross and prayed into the cool, dusky air for that of his safe passage through to whatever destination the unsettled man was seeking to attain.

Miss Jeanne then answered Edward compassionately. "Thank you for delivering that promise, dearest Edward. In exchange for your faithful and sanctified vow, I will see what I am able to do on your behalf for the sake of both you and your daughter where it concerns Mr. O'Keefe. Little Miss and I can be quite the persuasive duo when set to task."

Edward smiled and turned his eyes back to his lover and friend and spoke with only that of an indulgent whisper as the plight of Mr. O'Keefe flushed the well of his rawer emotion with sorrow. "Thank you for that, my dear. Upon the fulfillment of my expectations while abroad in Charleston, I do sincerely plan to provide for that boy beyond his wildest dreams."

Miss Jeanne walked slowly and purposefully over to Edward and guided him up from his chair with her long and elegant hands. When Edward was up on his feet she pulled him by the collar and kissed his lips as if she would never see the man again. For perhaps, she would see some phantom of this being in the flesh from time to time, but the fullness of the man she had once again dared to fall in love with while he was out here in Uriah and set upon this simple and pleasant countryside was never to return. In some ways, that man had already vanished into the ether. As she knew she was set to break the tender man's heart if she bound him to stay and was likewise unable to keep him safe when she set him free to go find the truth of the darkness still waiting out there in the world at-large to swallow him whole, she simply gave thanks to the Good Lord above for this time they were so blessed to have shared with each other and their beautiful yet make-shift family born of only love and opportunity.

She paused her kiss for but a moment and then returned her lips to his in earnest and quite lustfully, as if she wished to consume his heart or at least keep something of that tender throbbing organ safe within her own. She continued on in that wanting manner until Elizabeth Ann stepped out onto the porch and blushed righteously at the raging fire set ablaze upon the primal whispers of the first light and placed directly before her waking eyes. Only then did the eternally elegant woman retreat from the tips of her toes and free his heart and soul to journey back toward the timeless ocean; that haunting sea of the shifting tides which would forever keep safe all that was both innocent and pure of their now storied and one day fabled union of these strange and shallowly considered days of the Reconstruction. The days which marked the passing of the moment of their shared and glorious exile.

When the wheels of the carriage began their slow and grinding turns prior to that more harmonious glide over the dirt drive of the Osment farmstead, Miss Jeanne called down to both Edward and Elizabeth Ann, "I am glad the child has returned with you. We have much to atone for as it regards the little sprite, Edward. We owe that to her before the world is turned on its head once again. Travel safe, dearest ones! We shall have the place ready to welcome you upon the onset of the holidays!"

Edward and Elizabeth Ann waved up to Miss Jeanne and Edward called back, "It shall be a truly wonderful Christmas this year, my dear!"

And somewhere out in the upper field of the Osment farmstead under the cover of the last of the lingering shadows of the dawn, a young man dressed in a plain yet freshly laundered white cotton shirt, his field britches and cap, and the boots his father had refurbished for him when he had reached his thirteenth year, began the slow and lonely walk back to the Laing's cabin. He never spoke a word as the carriage turned out of sight.

Chapter Eight

DEAL

～⊙⑥⌇～

E DWARD SAT DOWN with Mr. Lucian Reed Morgenthau
on Tuesday, October 6th, 1868 just as the two gentlemen had
planned via letter and telegraph wire during the spring and summer
months of that same year. Mr. Morgenthau understood quite well
that Mr. Calhoun was not to come to terms with any arrangement
he proposed on that day for a few differing reasons. To the layperson,
perhaps the most prominent of those reasons to oppose any offer
Mr. Morgenthau laid upon the table imminently was certainly to be
Edward's reluctance to do business with the very man that had aided
his mother in nearly cornering him at the end of the war. Yet, Mr.
Edward Calhoun was no stranger to the shifting loyalties of uncertain
bedfellows in the realms of the ruthless seeking to obtain the things
which they covet. Therefore, a far superior impediment to even that of
Lucian's known deceit was, but of course, to be the stunning woman
from Uriah's cautious reprisals. Reprisals which were certain to come
before Edward had departed the farm for Charleston and reprisals
which would have been no secret to or perhaps better understood as
entirely expected by the Yankee gentleman.

All the same, Mr. Morgenthau wished to plant the seed of his
deceit on that afternoon and then nourish that dark kernel over time.
By accomplishing his devious deeds in such a way, Edward would
be given a healthy bit of rope to gradually come to terms with the
disastrous situation he faced in the wake of his fairytale hiatus from
the harsh turnings of the worlds of both need and unbridled want.

Certainly, Mr. Morgenthau could not fault Mr. Calhoun for keeping time with or adhering to the wishes of a woman whose beauty was destined to be renowned throughout the span of the age, yet he did worry some that the once shrewd man had lost his fiery penchant for proper gamesmanship and the procuring of the fruits of the flesh, which included the reestablishment of his rapidly fading legacy.

Though Edward had no knowledge of such a clash, at least as it concerned Mr. Morgenthau specifically, in fact he remembered the gentleman as being quite affable on the afternoon he kindly stood for a picture with him, Miss Jeanne and little Miss to celebrate the child's adoption by her birth mother and her eighth birthday simultaneously, the former Union Provost of the Reconstruction had been waging a tangible war upon Mr. Calhoun from a time even before Fort Sumter fell to the Confederate brigades to elicit forth the dire seasons of the war. Miss Meara had failed in her task to subvert the child of the light and draw Edward into their world beyond the staunch and misery ridden pillars that marked the gateway to the realms without hope. Worse than even Miss Meara's prior failures, the miserable evil set free to control the aging bounds of the lustful and wanting woman's heart and soul had been beaten back into a state of permanent impotence by the powerful light working of the spirit warrior of a child. Thus, in suffering what he had now come to quite clearly understand as his defeats on the Easter Sunday that ended the war, Lucian had simply realigned his always abundant and well camouflaged arsenal of minions set to do his bidding as the spiritual trench lines shifted in the aftermath of the cessation of the violent bloodletting on the carnal fields of battle.

Miss Meara was now nearly useless to the former Provost as she was near to bankrupting the plantation and would soon face liquidation if something was not done about both her impuissance and her incompetence. Though the aging woman remained quite miserable in her day to day outlook on life, she no longer possessed that evil bent which had for so long enabled her to so wickedly govern the thoughts and deeds of her fellow man. What Miss Meara did still yet possess that was of value to this devil of a man, or perhaps even the devil himself, on the redrawn battlefield of the postbellum Carolinas was the key to restoring Mr. Edward Calhoun to his once former glory. That is if she could keep a hold over those once productive assets for long enough to entice Edward to cut a deal with her miserable handler.

What Mr. Morgenthau in turn possessed in regard to controlling the long ago fallen woman was a valid deed, contract good, on the mortal soul of the presently waylaid succubus to be, though Lucian was rapidly tiring of what remained of the once wicked sorceress upon the aftermath of her heart being so bluntly corrupted by the light. So things had gone, and those dire miscarriages of his past now drove Mr. Lucian Reed to begin to move his chess pieces into position for the second assault upon the presently faltering Calhoun dynasty. Upon meeting with the unlikely scenario of his further failure, he would simply allow the postbellum residuals of the once quintessential estate to splinter into the wind as the forces of the light aligned against him would have preferred occur for more than a century now.

The trick Mr. Morgenthau needed to pull off to take hold of his long sought after prize, which was the once purely innocent and quite robust soul of Mr. Edward Christopher Calhoun and all that such a powerful talisman might command while under his influence, was to over time convince the man that all of his hopes and dreams rested squarely within the power of his consent to Lucian's Faustian bargain. The process of finally taking that trick somewhere down the road with a hand not quite flushed with spades was set to begin upon the hour. Mr. Calhoun's guardian child of the light was a far differing matter altogether and a far more valuable totem entirely, though she was one that remained entirely unassailable until Edward was his and had along with her other living guardian, offered her up for the benefit of his craven wants.

The dialogue exchanged between the two men during the late afternoon entendre was quite agreeable to begin. Mr. Reed, as he was called according to preference while abiding in Charleston, quickly seized upon Edward's naturally hopeful nature, which was in full bloom upon Mr. Calhoun's return to the coastal city, in offering that man nearly his every wish. "I am quite delighted to see you in person after all of this time, Mr. Calhoun. I hope you were not surprised to learn that I was an entity not entirely foreign to you. You look well and sound surprisingly enthused by your prospects upon the expectancy of reentry into your commercial affairs," were Mr. Reed's near to opening remarks.

The restaurant the two dined at that fine, early-fall afternoon fronted the market square. Edward was caught out watching the passersby from his seat beside the window while Mr. Reed spoke, primarily to avoid looking into the man's evocative eyes, which possessed a peculiar reddish tint to them when compared to the purely opal hues of the more the traditional human pupil. Truth be told, Edward had to double check the glare and the reflections of the light within the establishment more than few times to be certain the devilish shade he so very clearly witnessed was not simply some strange but explicable optical illusion. Edward responded to his host while his eyes remained distracted by following the escapades of a mother and her two small children as they navigated the busy pedestrian thoroughfare of the square. "Presuming to succeed at anything whilst maintaining a dour outlook upon the world is proximate to being something near impossible, my friend."

Mr. Reed rubbed at his chin attentively and replied, "What a wonderful and purely arcane outlook on life you have, Mr. Calhoun. Do you not believe that the laws or habitual redundancies attributable to one's success are directly in line with the very limitations of the world before our eyes? I am beginning to ascertain that you do not fully understand the dire nature of your situation in the uncertain times upon which we now find ourselves making our way."

Mr. Calhoun turned his eyes back to Mr. Reed and replied in the same hopeful tone as before, "Those who remain confined to the obstacles of a particular situation as such a reality is presented before their eyes at a given juncture are to persist only in the service of the king, my good man. The bright-eyed boys who set out to liberate our nation would never have lifted a finger against the most devastating military of their age if they had looked upon the world with only the rational deliberations of the eyes and not the eternal flame of their unbridled spirit."

Mr. Reed shifted a bit uneasily upon confirming that this shrewd and notorious man of commerce was far more of a dreamer than he would have imagined. The devilish man was by no means delivered into an impasse however, and he quickly set about his work of demoralizing Mr. Calhoun in a rather mechanical and perhaps slightly maniacal fashion. "Ah, yes. The victory of your forefathers was one for the ages. However, many still remain who are hard-pressed to beset such rebellious things so insolent to the established religion of concentrated power standing for far too long in a world heretofore dominated by harsh and wanting men. Such is just one of the reasons we untethered Americans find ourselves in the aftermath of such a deadly conflict. While I admire your brighter outlook on the possibilities of the common man, a group to whom you now belong part and parcel given your standing as near destitute, I am left to wonder how you plan to return your adventurous merchant concerns to their antebellum glory without proper access to financing."

Edward smiled coyly at the man seated across from him and took note of the smell of dusty wood and the low-burning hearth that abounded in the old brickwork establishment. He then laughed at the man's brazen approach and said, "Miss Jeanne mentioned that you would be a, how shall we say, 'less hopeful' sort to deal with. I am in turn left only to conclude she was correct in her assertions formed while crossing your path during your days as Provost over Uriah and the surrounding prefects. I have many connections around town firmly rooted in the more opulent memories of our younger and more prosperous days, good Sir. I think you will be surprised by the willingness of many to back my proposed business ventures."

Mr. Reed nodded in silence and spoke a bit testily as he slowly drew his chin up from his chest upon his final gesticulation of affirmation. "Well then, Mr. Calhoun, I am certainly not a man to be little more than a wet blanket to one so confident in his own resources. However, I am also not a man who is used to being denied that which he seeks. Take heed of that fact while you venture forth of your own accord. Do you not even wish to hear what such a man as I might offer to a fallen icon of the planter class to tempt his hopeful spirit before we part ways?"

Edward laughed and replied lightheartedly. "I promised the woman of my dreams that I should refrain from doing business with you; at least until I have had the chance to speak with her upon my return to Uriah over the holidays."

Mr. Reed laughed in response but the sound was so rudely unnatural it aggrieved even the good folk gathered over at the next table. His eyes then tightened and grew deadly serious once again, shimmering red with the fires of Hades but in a somehow seductive manner. Once he had set his sights properly upon his mark, Mr. Reed made his proposal known regardless of Edward's feigned disinterest in same.

"It is a little known fact that many of the brightest business minds of our day take their heed from their feminine consorts. I did not project you as such a man, Mr. Calhoun but that is according to my own very rare oversight. In any event, know that the bargain I struck with your mother is foundering. As such, I am willing to offer you full recourse to Butterworth Hall and quite favorable financing in exchange for only a minority position in your upstart merchant and trade enterprises." Mr. Reed paused to carefully study Edward's eyes and then added, "Of course, only in the event you find the current state of affairs concerning business equity and finance to be wholly distasteful to your proper graces."

With his best and final offer made, Mr. Reed stood up to depart from the table. Edward took due notice of the proper 'all-in' riverboat gambler and asked, "That is quite the offer, Mr. Reed. Do you not intend to sit for supper? I am certain it will arrive upon the moment."

Mr. Reed smiled snidely at his guest and replied, "No, the establishment lacks a cut of meat rare enough for my tastes, Mr. Calhoun. Nevertheless, I knew the place to be one of your favorite haunts in town prior to the war. I must be off to see my new doctor about the prospects for a proposed venture of our own."

Edward nodded in reply and was about to wish the frightful yet charismatic man good day but suddenly felt compelled to ask, "What else would you be seeking from me outside of a minority interest in my merchant ventures, good Sir? Surely the deal would be found wanting from the vantage point of one as astute as you are, given that you would be destined to put up the lion's share of the emergent capital."

Mr. Reed smiled wryly as he went about setting his cap carefully upon the thick, black hair of his head and retorted, "You should ask around town on that question, Mr. Calhoun. There are many you may seek out that know me well. I am permitted to speak openly only of what we shall set down in writing. The more nebulous enjoinders of the contract are subject to very particular interpretation."

"I see," replied Edward directly. "Well I bid you good day then, Sir and I wish you luck with your follow-on appointment." Mr. Reed nodded in the gentlemanly fashion in reply and said dryly, "Likewise, Mr. Calhoun." He then stepped away from the table and called back to Edward from the area near the bar, which was but a few honest steps out from the front door, "He is a wonderful surgeon with his eyes set upon having the world but at the moment he remains somewhat side-tracked by a woman of uncommon purity and delight."

Edward caught on to Mr. Reed's meaning upon the instant and called back, "When does your offer expire, my good man? I am beginning to sense that you have been some time in executing upon the necessary provisions."

Mr. Reed turned sharply with an about face that was completed very precisely in the manner of a military pivot and replied dutifully to the suddenly inquisitive man. "Ah, Mr. Calhoun, you of all people should know there is no expiration set upon an offer of such blessings to the giver. Yet, as with all things worth having in this life, the sooner done the better. If you are expeditious in your affirmation, you shall be celebrating Christmas with all of your girls back at Butterworth Hall. Excepting perhaps Susannah Jane of course, though she may one day return to you in knowing that your slaves have been set free. My offer does, however, include the one who mimics her father with that outrageous Haitian lover of hers." Mr. Reed then laughed rather snidely while turning his back on Edward to exit the premises.

Edward nodded uncertainly and flushed a bit red. Many of the patrons of the very proper and long-standing establishment had turned to have a full-on stare at the man professed aloud to be having an affair with a colored woman. "Thank you for that, Mr. Reed!" Edward shouted across the room loud enough to be heard over the dubious whispers of those now tracking what was transpiring at the table of one.

When Mr. Reed was out the door, Edward's food arrived. As impossible as such a thing seemed to him at the time, he would have sworn he heard the voice of the red-eyed man whisper into the hollows of his head while he bit into his choice cut of steak, "You are most welcome, Mr. Calhoun. Our union has been such a long and trying time in coming to fruition." Accordingly, Edward set his silverware down upon the table and promptly exited the establishment as many of the patrons continued to exchange whispers with one another over the scandalous announcement of the prior moment.

Edward did indeed return to Uriah that Christmas season as he had promised Miss Jeanne. Elizabeth Ann however, did not make the journey; instead electing to remain in Charleston for the splendor and decadence of a holiday season spent amongst the city's socialites. Beyond her desire to see and be seen with her dashing husband to be amidst the nearly outlandish regalia of the Christmastide upon the Market Square, the darker truth behind the young lady's reluctance to join her father in returning to their home in exile out in the country was her fear of encountering Virgil O'Keefe. Irrespective of Elizabeth Ann's reluctance to face up to the sins of her past or the still tender yearnings of her once pious heart, the dashing young lady's courtship was proceeding quite well and she was indeed thriving as a lady about town pledged to the arm of one of the finest young physicians in all of Charleston.

During that expectant season of her life, Elizabeth Ann felt as if all of the pomp and pageantry she had trained for as a young girl growing up at Butterworth Hall had at long last begun to return the just dues she had always expected in exchange for the time and sacrifice of the normalcy of her childhood years. There was not a social circle in town to which the charming couple was not only welcomed but undeniably sought after and in unremitting fashion. For short spells, she tired of the false pretense behind so much of what she spent her time doing, yet the side of her that was her mother's daughter quickly took to her newly appointed position alongside the former icons of Charleston society that were boldly reemerging throughout the Reconstruction Era as the Union military presence receded into the annals of faded memory.

Unfortunately for Edward, Elizabeth Ann and Doctor Dawson remained his only allies of financial standing in town after nearly three months spent away from Uriah. The scant offers Mr. Calhoun received to finance his business ventures were entirely unworkable and to make matters worse, Mr. Sommers had just informed him that his financial condition was approaching precarious levels on the eve of his return to the country. Still and all, the resilient man was far from disheartened upon his return to the Osment farmstead and all the more invigorated by the prospects of returning to the place of some of his happiest years and the ones he now loved.

Virgil O'Keefe remained noticeably absent from all of the functions and gatherings that Edward attended. As such, Mr. Calhoun was left without a means by which to apologize to the young man, though it was a bit spurious of him to attempt to do so only now that Elizabeth Ann was safely away down in Charleston and perhaps only days shy of her official engagement to Dr. Dawson. Edward and Miss Jeanne were cordial and, at times, perhaps even intimate, but with Edward living in another place and dead set upon rebuilding something of his former life, the patient yet wise woman knew it was only a matter of time before the ties that still bound them were found wanting and then altogether nonexistent, though she knew Edward would choose to believe that nothing had changed between them in the slightest. By contrast, Edward did in fact view the world in a precisely mirrored fashion to the shifting whims of the wise Haitian countess. He coveted the days when he would properly define their heretofore always mutable relationship by asking for her hand as a man of gentlemanly means and, in so doing, abundantly provide for the elegant woman of such uncommon radiance and the angelic daughter they discreetly shared.

The one matter of significance that Miss Jeanne delicately pointed out on Edward's final night in Uriah upon the commencement of the holiday season was the blossoming bond that was forming between Mr. O'Keefe and their daughter of nearly ten years. Because Edward was used to dealing with many of the more nefarious types during his days as a young man expanding upon the reach of the Calhoun estate, he asked timidly of Miss Jeanne, yet only out of due precaution, "You don't suppose that the young man has taken little Miss under his wing to exact some form of vengeance upon me or Elizabeth Ann, do you? I know the idea sounds preposterous at first blush, but there are ill winds and dark shadows making their way overland while the absence of a lasting authority persists; my own absence to be included in such where it pertains specifically to the needs and desires of and likewise, the bounds to be set upon Mr. O'Keefe."

Miss Jeanne shook her head purposefully in the negative turn and then shot a reprobate glance in Edward's direction before reprimanding him thusly for his boorish considerations of such a fine young man, "Of course not, Edward. The boy is not like us. He doesn't even know how to think such things. Neither is he one to change his beliefs upon being influenced by those beyond the property line. The two of them are both simply lonely and seem to thrive upon the common bond of their unwitting innocence. Little Miss can no more carry on a conversation with a typical ten-year-old child than you are able to correctly ascertain the thoughts of a young woman."

Miss Jeanne then laughed at her own playful wit for a fair spell and proceeded to add the following to her deliberation for good measure, "And you know how lonely Virgil was set to become with both you and Elizabeth Ann gone in addition to Shy. Doctor Bailey's daughters have been sent up to board for school in Virginia upon the coming semester and the Davis boys are often up to no good back in town while Virgil picks up the slack of their indolence out here on the farm. The two are like brother and sister and the match makes sense for the time being. Besides, Edward I am not certain that little Miss was ever intended to be held long by any man of this earth."

Edward rejoined Miss Jeanne promptly in an effort to keep the poor thoughts of his prior frame of mind regarding Virgil from being misconstrued beyond the point of her initial perceptions or, furthermore, considered as prevailing. "Yes, yes, of course you are right about Virgil, my dear. How dare I expound to the detriment of his honor due to my own folly and mistreatment of the willing young man. You should also know that irrespective of what you believe to be the nature of my intent, Elizabeth Ann and the young doctor are a wonderful couple, perhaps the most glorious young pair in all of Charleston."

Miss Jeanne lowered her chin a bit and sharpened her eyes some while responding rather indifferently for effect, "That is nice, Edward. In as much as she is happy for the reasons that are true to the intentions of her heart."

Edward smiled proudly and replied warmly as if the thought alone of the debonair couple did warm his heart so. "Oh that is for certain, my dearest Jeanne. You should travel to town to visit for a spell and witness the two of them. If you do as much, I promise you will no longer doubt my wisdom on the matter."

"I doubt my presence with you in Charleston would accrue to your benefit right now, Edward," replied the unconvinced lady of the house. "However, do know that I anxiously await the hour of your return to us here in Uriah. Have you stayed clear of the man I warned you about? Speak to me true now, Mr. Edward Christopher Calhoun!"

Edward shifted his eyes to the side but answered the woman honestly. "Mr. Reed did make me a binding and quite suitable business offer that was near impossible to refuse, but I merely sent him on his way due to your redeeming counsel. The man certainly looked the part of his true nature. That is to say he appeared as one who would consort quite naturally with mother. He almost spoke as if he were older than the trees and as if he dealt in the trades of the spirit world. In any event, I found the entirety of the rendezvous to be rather unsettling as it were, my dear."

Miss Jeanne looked Edward over carefully and spoke sternly to the man who was being candid yet clearly protecting some secret of a greyer nature. "Whatever you do while you are in Charleston, Edward;

you promise me that you will not consent to anything delivered from the lips or the blood red pen of that man. He is a consort to the darker principalities and a comely liar of shifting context and twisted words. Whatever he promises you will cost you ten times that much as it concerns receiving any of God's peace into your soul."

"Fret not, my dear woman. I am far too familiar with the consequences of not heeding to the whims of your intuition or even the premonitions given by the cross of gold that speaks to you with such wisdom to do otherwise." Miss Jeanne stood up from her rocker on the porch and reminded the man of the sanctity of his promise in passing. "I am going into the house to check on little Miss, my dear. Always remember that I intend to bind you to those words eternally."

Edward smiled lightheartedly at the Haitian princess and replied acquiescingly in saying, "Of course, my dear. All that I do is for you, the child, my other daughters and all who share in the bounty of this beautiful land. The man promised me Christmas with my children at Butterworth Hall back in October and I refused his offer. I do not presume that he will ever be in a position to offer better. Please tell little Miss I will be up to say good bye shortly. She is such a wise and darling creature. I sometimes struggle to believe that she is of the flesh of one such as I am."

Miss Jeanne smiled a bit ponderously at Edward's remark. He was a good man whose only perhaps fatal flaw was his unwavering belief that material worth was in large part the true measure of a man in this life. He had certainly benefitted in many ways from his social status and the advantages of his wealth throughout his existence, yet the golden cross at times spoke to her of a price far beyond the measure of those fleeting endowments of his birthright that might one day be paid if the gift was sought by him beyond the auspices of intended grace. The feelings passed through the cross from some spirit or another of a prior age were never conclusive and she believed those premonitions were intended only to heighten her watch over the man as his position grew ever more precarious.

However, beyond those hazy notions of the heavens and the spirit realms, there existed a certain thought that crossed her mind from time to time. A thought which was purely of her own accord and based solely upon her familiarity with Edward's deeply rooted beliefs. The thought was sorrowful and made her worry so for the sanctity of the good man's soul while he ventured into such squalid waters in an effort to once again feel whole. That thought concerned the truth of the fact that the man would never in this lifetime believe that she would have been equivalently taken by him, if not more so, that day upon the docks down in Haiti if he were penniless all the same. Such an association by which one believes in the ability of wealth to alter the will of the heart was an exceptionally dangerous proposition in its own right. Beyond that, Edward never once realized how poorly that presumption regarding her character made her feel about the totality of the star-crossed intersection of their lives.

By the mid-summer season of 1871, the winds of change had fully remade the existence of many of those still living off of the rich acreage of the Osment farmstead. Margaret Anne Basseterre had blossomed quite early into the explosive beauty of her womanhood at just twelve years of age, which forced her older brother by proxy, the twenty-year old Virgil O'Keefe to spend all of his time not laboring in the field fending off her would be suitors. Some of the eager young men journeyed to Uriah from as far off as Kershaw just to have a glimpse at the proper Carolina girl of the winter season and the Haitian duchess of the summer season. Since the two had both been in a way abandoned with separate yet powerful gifts and were then so far away from whence they came into this world, and as there was always time to discuss a given matter while out picking or pruning in the fields, manicuring the gardens or stacking wood for the winter months, there was not a thing of this world that had been made manifest to either of the two separately that was not known by both severally. Margaret Anne even knew the fullness of the horrific, obscene and lurid story of how Virgil's sister, Casey Meredith O'Keefe had met her untimely end at the hands of Sherman's Union men while they marched north through Florence to clear the Confederate stockade there.

Though the two were joined in the unbreakable bonds of their companionship in the way of a brother and a sister, Margaret Anne's emergence as a woman in the corporal sense, which had coincided perfectly with the spring season of 1871, had created some awkward moments for the brazen and heretofore pure farm boy, who had remained in that untainted stead well beyond the years for such an enduring trait out amongst the simple folk of the countryside. In fact, it was in May of that year the bizarre thought crossed the young man's mind to wed the promised child once she was of a proper age. Virgil did not tell Margaret Anne of these plans, though she had already surpassed the age of consent for the times down in Carolina.

To be fair, the thought of the complications that would arise from being transformed into the properly consummated legal protector of his soulmate and sister of a kind never crossed the young man's mind back in those days. Perhaps if such unsettling consequences regarding the true nature of a proper marriage between a man and a woman had drifted into the simple confines of the young man's thoughts, Margaret Anne might have sensed where Virgil was getting crossed up in the deliberations of his future ideals. Regardless, such dreams of his waking mind were nothing more than fanciful certainties of another day while dressed in the innocence of those abundant turns of the sun back in the spring and summer seasons of 1871.

Of a more pressing concern while Shy approached her scheduled August marriage to Mr. George Ridley Brown of Augusta was the fact that Edward was being squeezed at every turn in his endeavors to get his business off of the ground. He had honored his promise to

Miss Jeanne where it concerned Mr. Reed as of that sweltering July day in question, but his finances had reached the point that drastic measures needed to be taken lest he retire out to the farm and live the remainder of his days as the ward of the woman of the house. Edward and Miss Jeanne strolled by the eastern side of the burgeoning cotton field until they reached the old oak and the swing where Virgil and Elizabeth Ann had last confided in one another; that sacred spot to all who graced the confines of the Osment farmstead where the two young might be lovers had indeed kissed for the visible pleasure of their, as of that life-altering moment, undiscovered audience. Edward set Miss Jeanne down upon the swing and set her off in motion in a playful way before he began to bear the depravities of his soul to the smiling woman as she relished the breeze generated by her free and continuous motions through the hot and sultry air of mid-summer.

"I need, to speak with you about a matter of considerable import, my dear," began the man who had that same summer reached the end of the very last of his provisions. He needed the miracle of a life-line cast into the water; water which was beginning to cover his open mouth as he gasped for that precious and rarified air of the drowning man while his limbs went limp with fatigue and could no longer lift his head above the waterline.

She replied in the manner of one set perfectly at ease whilst she caromed languidly upon the swing, which was hanging from the lowest of the eastward leaning branches of the stalwart oak. "Of course you know that I will always indulge you, my dearest Edward, but do push me yet a bit higher before we begin. I am suddenly reminded of the days of my childhood when I would swing into the calming currents of the easterlies sweeping over the high, twisting grass of the mountains overlooking the bay."

Edward stepped back in perfect time with Miss Jeanne's return from the higher altitudes beneath the overarching canopy of the old oak so that she might glide seamlessly into his arms. Because he had become fully distracted by the severity of his predicament upon receiving her long, svelte figure from above, he delivered a forceful thrust with his arms in an effort to elevate the elated Haitian queen ever higher. The ill-advised, awkward and poorly timed impulse nearly sent the beautiful and well-dressed woman in her summer whites forward without the swing. They both laughed like little children once Miss Jeanne rather adroitly, though clumsy in its gangly and sidelong appearance, rescued her wares from the perils of a frightful face-first fall into the dirt and grass of the ground below. When she had settled back into a more rhythmic and continuous motion that nearly assured her safety, Edward stated plainly, "Though I have generally spoken otherwise upon my visits into the sanctity of your patiently waiting arms, my affairs are not progressing well down in Charleston, my dear."

Miss Jeanne shifted her weight upon passing Edward's shoulder in an attempt to soar into the neighboring branches of the oak by way of the wonderful contraption and called down to him, "I have known the truth of your condition for a while now, Edward. Elizabeth Ann has written to me frequently over these last six months. She is worried about you and she believes the situation down at the port is untenable. That is why I am smiling and laughing so."

Edward took the jubilant and enigmatic woman's meaning entirely the wrong way but only ventured to ask rather quizzically, "How can it be that such an emotion runs utterly congruent with my ruin, my dear?"

Miss Jeanne propelled her legs forward through the down stoke as she passed by Edward and continued to extend the elevation of the apex point of the swiftly undulating swing. When she was set to return toward the earth after a brief pause in her motion upon reaching the height of her rise, she called down to him, "Because, Edward that means it is time for you to return home to me before you dig your way into a deeper hole with those that love you and the money men to boot. You have done all that a man is able to do given your current station. Yet, God has answered you with the perfect appropriation of other gifts; blessed gifts such as your return to the woman of your dreams and your daughter who is near to being a woman now."

As he was prone to do when focused on another matter, Edward looked directly past the truth of those bountiful blessings which Miss Jeanne had tried to make plain enough. "So you have heard that Elizabeth Ann's courtship has stalled? I begged of her to look past the oversight of a young man with the world at his feet but I think that the witnessing of such treachery with her own eyes has forever soured her on any future proposal."

Miss Jeanne brought the swing gently to a halt after few more decelerating passes and stood upon the broken clusters of grass covering the roots of the tree to take Edward by the hands. "Listen to yourself, Edward. Though you have avoided consenting to the wicked man's proposal you have played for far too long in his house and allowed him to reset the rules of the game entirely in his favor. The Edward Calhoun I once knew would no more stand to see his daughter endure a marriage of such infamy than he would send her off to work in a Market Street brothel to make the ends meet."

Edward lowered his eyes but not his chin in responding to the still graceful, yet in his mind, distastefully heartened woman. "As always, you are unerring and factual in all that you say, my dear. Yet if she disavows Dr. Dawson we will be left homeless before we have a single ship out to sea and under contract to deliver freight. That is why I have returned to you off turn and prior to the wedding. To beg of you for something of the blessings of the golden cross that has protected and so wisely guided you over the years of our differing turmoil. I am well over my head in endless liability yet the business you probably remember so fondly from our earliest days together is not so very far from its first sources of revenue."

The horrid look of fear that suddenly dressed itself over Miss Jeanne's once delighted mien was not without merit. She looked up into Edward's eyes and asked, "Speak plainly to me Edward, what do you mean by saying as much regarding your debts? You did not enter into an agreement with that rapacious man against my will, did you now?"

Edward shook his head like an admonished puppy dog and replied rather demurely. "I have not, my dear. The scoundrel will no longer honor the terms of his initial pledge as he understands that I am two years' worth of future revenues into debt. I stand to be barred from the business and far worse if I falter in my obligations. The men to whom I owe gold coin are not the more scrupulous types we were used to dealing with during our Haitian trading ventures. These men are deadly serious and precisely uncompromising in both their provision and their subsequent requirement for timely repayment."

"Are you in danger, Edward?" Miss Basseterre gasped frightfully as she grabbed hold of his slender yet prominently featured shoulders. This time Edward lowered his head while he spoke in reply. "Aye, Ma'am. I am in grave and certain danger if things progress into the harvest season in their current state."

Edward then paused to look back into her eyes, which were lilting with such radiant and uncommon color when set against her beautiful cocoa brown skin of the summer season, and furthered his plea, "But do understand that I had no choice in the matter of entering into an arrangement with such brutal men. The man you forbade me to transact with made certain every honest provision for my success was withheld from me back in town."

Miss Jeanne was familiar with the loan sharks that operated down on the docks of Haiti. At times, they were sanctioned by the more ruthless governors of the island, and at other times they plied their trade in the alleys and the shadowy back rooms of the more disreputable establishments of the port cities. She shook her head as one presently distraught and asked Edward candidly, "What is the hell born man offering you now to fend off your demise at the hands of such awful brutes? Have you come to your end, Edward?"

Edward shook his head dubiously and replied with a trembling voice to the starkly frightened woman in earnest whilst his tears streamed down his face like heavy raindrops streaking to the bottom of a windowpane. Those bulging tears ran over his pallid, haunted cheeks in such a way that left no mistaking the baleful accords, devoid of all hope, to which Edward Calhoun was now destined in some manner or another to remain beholden while he still lived and breathed, or conversely, for all eternity. He answered her plainly. "He asks that our baby girl be promised upon your consent as her legal guardian and adoptive mother to marry a man up in Vermont, or some other Yankee quarter where the wind blows cold across the barren mountains for the preponderance of the year."

Edward went silent for a moment to steady his voice. As if the forthright proposal of another betrayal of his beautiful and perfectly illegitimate daughter was not beyond reprisal, there was more. He wiped his face, which caused the dirt and dust kicked up by Miss Jeanne's energetic turn upon the swing to smear woefully across his once bright and still somewhat boyish features. When Miss Jeanne was near to interjecting quite frantically once again, he raised his finger delicately to her tremoring lips and spoke wistfully yet kept a steady command over his intonations. "There is more. In addition to the impossible betrayal of the child, he seeks some sort of contractual pledge, as collateral only of course, of the assets of the golden cross. He swears such a writ will permit him to make the bondsmen I am dreadfully in arrears to whole. Likewise, he swears that the pledging of such eternal collateral is in proper accordance with some law or edict of which I am unawares, yet one I presume to be sacred to the demonic sect or ancient coven to which he must certainly belong. The rest of his offer stands as it did before. In that regard he remains true to his word, though by no means honorable in his conduct."

Miss Jeanne shook her head and whispered in fits and starts with a twinge of insanity laced within her tone that was altogether foreign to her nature, "No, no, no, no…you understand neither the nature of our baby girl nor the provisions of the golden cross, Edward…such simply cannot be…it simply cannot be…" Upon hearing those vacant and unnerving words from her perfected lips, Mr. Edward Christopher Calhoun fell to his knees once again and wept like a child while chanting, "Then I am undone, my dear woman! Then I am undone before both you and God above!"

Miss Jeanne promptly pulled Edward up from the ground and began to speak frantically in doing little more than hurriedly thinking aloud, "The provisions of the golden cross can only be obtained for use upon some given sign from the heavens. It is written and spoken down through our generations that a blinding light will shine forth and only then shall the ancient treasure of Cesar Maduro be spared for its intended purpose. Until that moment arrives, touching that gold is akin to a curse upon my forefathers and all that such wealth touches…" Though Edward's already practical mind, which had become deadly pragmatic upon the instant out of necessity, understood little of the need to adhere to such an esoteric pledge, who was he as a now indentured man to argue with two centuries and more than a score of unblemished wealth preservation. Thankfully for his sake and his sanity alike, Miss Jeanne stopped her words abruptly as a dark yet hopeful thought exploded into the confines of her mind.

Shortly thereafter, she continued on with her self-deliberating far more evenly than before, as if she had borne witness to some viable plan that would somehow alter the sealed lot of the fated man standing before her. "If it is only collateral which the devil seeks, and make no mistake about it Edward, that man is some form of the devil incarnate, we can provide as much to keep you alive, my dearest love…"

Miss Jeanne then trailed off before she could be heard uttering, "What of the betrothal…we can consent all we want yet the child so near to being a woman of her own accord will only act of her own will on the matter of her matrimony…perhaps we can save you yet still, my dearest…perhaps we can save you yet still…"

Edward covered his saddened face with his hands now also soiled by his lamenting in the dirt and begged of her, "If returned to my prior station, which the agreement will achieve, I can undo everything until it is precisely the way it was before Miss Meara banished us all from Sumter. The way it was before this dark day. Have you ever seen me fail from the perch of my prior advantages, my dearest? The betrothal, if such an outrage ever stands, is not set to be sanctioned for three and a half years' time. That is when our darling girl reaches the age of her consent according to the provisions of Vermont law."

Miss Jeanne lowered her head and began to think more clearly while she took note of the burgeoning rows of cotton growing up in the field around them. "I am set to gift the golden cross to my darling Shy Jolie upon the evening of her marriage to Mr. Brown. God above has called for the passing on of the ancient relic on that very day. Though I do not feel entirely honorable in doing as much, we must set the collateral provisions before that time. When such a collateral contract has been arranged, we will consent to the future betrothal of little Miss, with you remaining as but a silent voice. Yet you must promise me that the man is given no legal remedy to enforce little more than the continuance of our whims upon the darling child of the light. You must promise me that, Edward!"

Edward nodded while he began to shed larger tears of shame. He then came to a sudden realization perhaps even more horrifying than dying at the cold, black, empty bottom of the Charleston Harbor with a boulder fastened to his ankles. "What becomes of me if I consent to a contract with this man, my dearest? What was the price you have feared for these three years now?"

Miss Jeanne looked into the man's eyes and replied starkly, "If you cannot find a way to beat the devil at his own game you will join your mother in the place where the fires burn hot and eternal, Edward.

But I know you will vanquish that beast to save us all who need you here in this place for a far longer turn. I know you will vanquish him because I cannot stand to lose you now and if I have been warned of such an emptiness set to possess my heart when you are gone, I have not heeded the truth of it. Before God, I will not leave you to die now cold and alone, my love. Such is not a price that I am willing to pay to this thing that haunts us without mercy or even decency. After what he has done, any contract he offers to you is null and void in the realms where those with souls step lightly upon the dust of the earth or upon the glorious ether beyond the firmament!"

Edward nodded and replied softly, "I hope that you are prescient as always in delivering such words, my dear. I have never been so afraid. The devil is indeed knocking upon my door."

With Miss Shy Jolie Basseterre set to wed Mr. George Ridley Brown at the Osment farmstead on August 23rd, 1871, Edward returned to Charleston on Wednesday, August the 9th of that same month to retrieve Elizabeth Ann and return her to Uriah in time for the wedding and furthermore, to enter into a formal accord with Mr. Lucian Reed Morgenthau. He would have returned some weeks earlier but he felt it wise to remain away from town while the notice day of his formal default loomed on the horizon. In truth, and wholly out of character, Edward did not even remember the exact terms set within some of the piggyback loans he took out at the end to keep the business from a state of legally recognized bankruptcy. Therefore, he remained loosely uncertain as to the precise moment he would become a marked man, or perhaps better said, some semblance of the walking dead.

What Mr. Calhoun was greeted by when he arrived at the spacious brickwork home of Dr. Roger Jemison Dawson on Market Street that fateful evening was nearly beyond description. At a minimum, the scene was certainly riddled by a perverse and ritualistic undercurrent that was far baser in its nature than anything he had heretofore even heard scandalous musings of during the gilded yet surreptitiously hedonistic peak of Southern planter class prominence before the war. That his beloved daughter was mixed up in the entanglement of burning flesh and other assorted sundries of a wholly deviant nature nearly drove the poor, worn down and beaten man into a state of cardiac arrest. He found the hardwood floor of the main room of the residence far less forgiving upon his knees than the soft dirt and tufts of grass at the base of the old oak standing sentinel over the Osment field.

Of course with Mr. Reed not only present but prominently featured in the midst of the scene of the dissolute melee, the timing of the encounter had certainly not been left to chance. That the man possessed near carnal authority over his daughter's inability to wear white on her wedding day, at least in accordance with proper tradition, drove Edward into a fit of helpless rage. Following an almost, but for the circumstances, maniacal outburst of awkward and comical futility, Edward's cursing and flailing about finally achieved its intended purpose of clearing the home of all those partaking in such madness with the exception of Mr. Reed, the owner of the stylish residence and Elizabeth Ann. The latter two of the remaining contingent scattered in shame to the upstairs while Mr. Calhoun and Mr. Reed talked business before Mr. Calhoun and his daughter were to depart with Mr. Satterfield for Uriah in the morning.

The deal between Edward Christopher Calhoun and Mr. Reed was formally struck the following morning, on Thursday, August 10th, 1871. Only then had Edward's boiling cauldron of emotions from the prior evening been calmed to a more manageable simmer. In accordance with the terms Edward had discussed with Miss Jeanne back in Uriah in July, Mr. Reed was promised Miss Jeanne's consent to the marriage of Margaret Anne Basseterre and Mr. Jacob Asher Bromley of Brattleboro, Vermont. The wedding date was to be set upon an appropriate hour following the child's 16th birthday. Mr. Reed also received a certificate of collateral pledged via telegraph from a vault in Jacmel, Haiti, or perhaps another depository on the Haitian island, to remove the venomous lien set against the life of Mr. Edward Christopher Calhoun. Lastly, Mr. Reed received a one-third share in the ownership of Mr. Calhoun's merchant enterprises.

In exchange for signing onto the agreement, Edward received the invaluable revocation of his termination for default upon settlement by Mr. Reed, which was set to go live sometime in September, the unencumbered title to Butterworth Hall and the requisite financing to properly launch said merchant operations in the coming months. Not that such a thing was needed to effect the agreement, but in an effort to expound upon what kind of man Mr. Reed truly was, no provision was made for the care and quarter of Miss Meara Calhoun upon her expulsion from the manor back in Sumter. She was simply no longer of any use to the vile gentleman and he treated the then impotently stationed and woefully aging woman as such. Her hold over the crumbling remnants of the once enviable and rather powerful Calhoun Empire came to an end on that searing and miserable Thursday, which embodied the typical heavy and stifling heat of August down at the port.

Sometime after the common law agreement was signed, Mr. Reed and Mr. Calhoun went over the darker and more nebulous terms of the ancillary blood contract. Elizabeth Ann could be heard crying hysterically from the upstairs apartment she shared with her father the whole time the two men were discussing the murkier nuances of what Mr. Reed viewed to be an eternal, or evergreen in the legal parlance of our own day, settlement. That is to say Mr. Reed simply needed to remain a viable entity of the flesh to collect upon his just due and he was an ancient and steadfast soul. Though the young lady did not know as much while she cried the tears of the suddenly wretched, her somber yet somewhat muffled undertones as heard from study below, were quite fitting given the circumstances of her father's longer-term arrangements with Mr. Reed, even if those tears of her shame and rebuke were wholly unrelated to what was transpiring between the two gentlemen on the ground floor of the spacious and impeccably clad Market Street residence of Dr. Dawson.

Though Edward felt partly responsible for leaving the young lady alone in Charleston while she was trying so desperately to the impress the young surgeon given over to perhaps masochism yet certainly unspeakable forms of debauchery, and doing so for little more than the proliferation of her penniless father at that point in her stalled courtship with Dr. Dawson, he spoke not a word to his daughter during the three days of their staggered return trip upland to Uriah. Such an enduring silence was fine by Elizabeth Ann. She was forever ashamed of what her father had witnessed her endure and even appear to pine for. As such, she struggled to look the vacantly guised man directly in the eye while caged within the confines of the painfully ponderous carriage, which she believed might never reach their intended destination. During the ride and in the times she found her mind wanting for a distraction, she was left to ponder how she had permitted her corporal temple to be abused in such a shameful and prurient manner. She soon came to realize that the young, expectant and pious woman who had departed Uriah nearly three years ago had died that August evening upon little more than the knowing.

By the time they were approaching the scant outposts not far beyond the county line, Elizabeth Ann began to wonder if she remained even near to resembling the same woman who had turned her back on Virgil O'Keefe those three years or a lifetime ago. She wondered as much due to the fact she was now returning to Uriah as little more than some fallen harlot of the elite order. She prayed without end that the young girl who had heeded the mystical call of her newborn sister to the February Cabin with a hunting rifle near frozen to her hand was still alive somewhere within. She hoped upon hope that the honorable Virgil O'Keefe would speak to her after all this time spent hiding the shame of her rebuke of him and then ultimately prostituting out her very honor in return for some form of financial sanctuary that was never to be properly reciprocated in kind. The dark man with the beady, reddened eyes had used her up to achieve his desired ends with her father and left her unfit to wed a man like Virgil; an honest man who remained as pure of heart as the endless blooming fields of cotton upon the harvest season.

Though there was a time during her society years in Charleston that the very essence of the world of men seemed to beckon to her every whim, Elizabeth Ann had quickly come to realize that she had turned her back on nearly everything that she once loved for little more than a fleeting glance at a lavish lifestyle that no more suited her than the witchery of her grandmother or the brutality of the slave quarters back at Butterworth Hall. As they approached the familiar farms lining the countryside but a few miles out from her only true home in this life, she began to wonder why she had given some meaningful part of her soul to the proliferation of all three of those great evils present in her life. While she ultimately fell short of answering that particular peculiarity now so clearly tied to her uncertain temperament, before she and her father arrived in Uriah, the now tainted young woman made her father swear never to speak of what he witnessed of her back in Charleston.

The always prudish gentleman was in turn elated to be held to such terms. In truth, he was rather uncertain if he could properly describe what he saw unfolding before his eyes just a few evenings back if he had been forced to do as much. Deep down in his heart, Edward Calhoun only hoped that his favored daughter, who was once little more than a sweet and innocent young woman of such uncommon delight, would recover from her sordid exposure to such a harsh, lustful and self-deprecating experience.

Beyond those uncertain hopes for the once bright and always expectant young woman who had once possessed the man of her virtuous fancy while Mr. O'Keefe stood at the ready to conquer the world for the favor of her hand, he also knew in the pith of his soul that what had happened to his daughter was simply the summation of that ruinous calamity which were the years he spent down in Charleston. For those were the years he had spent trying to reincarnate something once dead according to the bonds of equitable right in exchange for the sins of his past. Even now, the fledgling roots of his nascent kingdom were sponsored only by the forces of malice which were certain to sow only an entity of grotesque form upon such an unnatural rebirth. In looking upon his daughter while she stared listlessly out the window of the slowly moving carriage against the backdrop of the quaint and peaceful countryside, Edward Calhoun understood full well what price he had tendered to have what he wanted. Beyond that, he understood that what now spawned from the once proud and formidable Calhoun family lineage and which ultimately rose from the ashes of the war would be forever subjected to a lingering bondage equivalently dark to the savage fornication of that evening and his eternal pledge to that dark master of the realms without light or hope.

Miss Jeanne and all three of her daughters were sitting in wait on the porch for Edward and Elizabeth Ann's arrival when the carriage began its final turn down the drive to the Osment farmstead. The sun was preparing to set somewhere off in the western sky in a patchwork blaze of fiery oranges and deep, luminous pinks. Because Miss Jeanne knew much of what the two had endured during the past three years away from Uriah, she allowed the excitable bride to be to serve as the one to take care of the boisterous welcome for the four of them in wait. The proud and once again hopeful mother of three did so simply by not objecting to Miss Shy's running down the stairs to the porch and into the nervous and still shame riddled arms of Elizabeth Ann once the weary traveler had stepped out of Mr. Satterfield's still beautiful black carriage.

"Let me have a look at you, you beautiful thing!" cried Miss Shy Jolie as she stepped away from their heartfelt embrace to make a suitable inspection of the fallen queen of Charleston with her own always animated eyes. Miss Shy's true intention in doing as much was in actuality to gauge the extent of the trauma lurking within the young lady's heart. "You look as brilliant as you ever have, my dearest Elizabeth Ann! Come now; walk with me down to Miss Leslie's cabin. Miss Leslie made me promise to deliver you hence before you sat down for supper at home. Little pea is quite the diminutive lady now and Amos should be in from Columbia within the week!"

Though Elizabeth Ann felt as if she had betrayed her proper manners in scampering off with Shy so quickly, she did step over to the lower stairs of the porch to hug Miss Jeanne, little Miss and Maime in that order. When the two ladies were near to reaching the pond beyond the western side of the farmhouse, Elizabeth Ann asked of Miss Shy in a tone that attempted to mask her question in such a way that her voice sounded as if her queried interests were that of little more than a passing fancy, "Is Mr. O'Keefe now abroad, sister Shiloh? I noticed you did not mention him earlier. I haven't seen the young incendiary since he sent two of the Davis boys running for their lives before I departed for Charleston."

Shy quickly shot a look over to Elizabeth Ann that reminded her former bunkmate and lifetime confidant to dispense with the twaddle in her presence. "Sister Lizzy, why must it be so that you are the only one in all of Uriah, or Augusta for that matter, to call me as such? Mr. George Ridley Brown, who is set to be my husband in just ten days, is not even aware that Shiloh is my rightfully given name. But enough with all of that, young lady; the term of endearment remains your gift alone. Now, as to Mr. Virgil O'Keefe, he's managing the fields for my momma, Barbury Davis and Miss Penny Claibrooke. He has what one might call a little agrarian consortium going on right here in simple little Uriah. Sensing that Miss Leslie and Mr. Laing were having a hard enough go of it trying to find some time to be a proper married couple with Little pea running wild over there, the wild-eyed boy of our fancy went and built hisself a nice little cabin down by the property line with the Claibrooke's."

Miss Shy paused for a moment and looked Elizabeth Ann over quizzically before shifting both her tone and her diction for the sake of both familiarity and effect in declaring, "But that ain't really what you is askin' about now, is it, girl?"

Elizabeth Ann smiled coyly and her temperament warmed commensurately. The feeling of being around one who spoke so true and knew the girl she once was brought such joyful warmth to her to heart. As such, she replied glibly in accordance with the feigned maintenance of her easily discovered ruse while in the presence of her dear confidant. "No, sister Shiloh, I suppose that wasn't what I had desired to ask of you. Why don't you go on and be a dear by speaking to the question I was truly intending to ask."

"Umm, umm, umm, the city girl is as sassy as the reputation that precedes her. Oh, we will get to that later, my dear. That is if we gonna figure out how to contain such blasphemy in a place where most folks ain't got much more to do on a Sunday besides talk," was Miss Shy's forthright and colorfully delivered reply.

Elizabeth Ann instantly flushed ruddy at the cheeks. Flashing that blush the color of a ripened summer strawberry due to her shame caused the blueness of her eyes to show brilliantly in the trailing light of the setting sun. Though the possession of direct experience with such taboo doings did accede to her a bit of an older sister type edge where it concerned the brazen Miss Shy Jolie while they remained near to the same age, Miss Calhoun would have gladly traded in any advantage offered by such a salacious badge of honor in a heartbeat. Shy laughed in sensing that there existed at least some semblance of truth to the scuttlebutts concerning Elizabeth Ann, which seemed to begin swirling around town at the same time Bradley Jemison took up a position as one of the county sheriffs about a day ago. The timing of the local gossip was certainly not a coincidence given that Bradley was a blood cousin to Doctor Dawson and that they both grew up raising hay together back in Sumter. However, whether or not there existed any legitimacy to those rather ruinous back alley whisperings had remained unknown to Miss Shy prior to that instant.

Elizabeth Ann swatted playfully at her should be step-sister and began to walk at the ladylike configuration of the quick step in effort to change the subject without so much as addressing its existence. Shy chased right on after the roiled young woman. When she caught up to Elizabeth Ann, Miss Shy spoke to ease the still blushing young lady's consternations some after doing her sisterly duty. A duty which included ensuring that her trusted confidant would not be caught off-guard in the event the rumor mongers kicked their ponies into a sprint while Elizabeth Ann was making the rounds back in town. "Virgil isn't keeping a woman out there at his place and he's still not fit to be kissed, let alone married, if that's what you are wondering, sister Lizzie."

Elizabeth Ann halted her swift stride and turned quickly to face Miss Shy before inquiring of her with a keen sense of interest. "You don't suppose Virgil knows anything about the story behind my failed courtship; do you now, sister Shiloh?"

Miss Shy interjected quickly upon her sister's query with her typical vigor. "Honey, a story that raw gonna make its way through these here parts like greased lightning. However, if there is set to be one man in town that knows nothing of the scandalous affair come Monday morning, it'd be Mr. Virgil O'Keefe. That handsome young man doesn't fancy a thing besides his work in the fields and putting in his time watching over little Miss. Still and all, given how you left things here, it'd be best if you told him before he finds out of his own accord from other less reliable sources."

Elizabeth Ann nodded thoughtfully in reply, though she was beginning to grow curious over what the official narrative being bandied about town indeed was. Fortunately for her, Miss Shy did not mince her words while she continued on with the delivering of her prudent advice in the manner of one tied to the business end of a live wire. "And let me tell you, that's no small thing! Because sister, that story getting passed around town is sizzling with sin! The tale makes me blush just thinking of it! I'm quite certain that the truth of the matter, which is what you'd be delivering to our boy, is far more sedate."

Elizabeth Ann reddened considerably again due to the fact that Shy's teasing about the lewd affair caused brilliant flashes of the sights, sounds and seismic sensations of the flesh hogtied to that vile moment to erupt throughout her mind. Shy not did miss the meaning behind the rosy, bemused look set upon her sister's lineaments and called out, "Oh, Lawdy now! That poor boy is going to have a come apart! The rumor out here has it that the lonesome buck is near to being arrested for unruly provisions he accords to none but hisself!"

Shy laughed again at her own wit but then quickly looked at Elizabeth Ann in a far differing light. She suddenly possessed something of a strange reverence for the most pious woman she had ever known due to her known time spent on the darker side of the proper doling out of affections. Shy knew she would never journey down such a base carnal path in her own lifetime. Moreover, she found it hard to believe that the virtuous young lady she had spent so much time with had seen and perhaps experienced directly those things that most sober folks would never dare speak of to another. Miss Shy now knew for one thing that she would never leave her own man alone with sister Lizzie if even half of what she heard making the rounds back in town was in fact the truth.

Elizabeth Ann seized upon the advantage of Shy's silent time spent trying to reorder her expectations regarding the rather 'experienced' woman Miss Calhoun now was. "Virgil shall get nothing but the truth from my lips, sister Shiloh. He's a good man and he deserved far better than what I came to ultimately offer him. I'm glad to hear that he is well and perhaps also quite selfishly happy to know that he has not found another. I have thought about him and about kissing him beneath the old oak often, and from the very moment I left Uriah for Charleston."

"Well, I suspect he's been thinking about you just the same, but you know damn good and well that our boy is not one to easily look past being belittled as he was by both you and the Captain," Miss Shy shot back in the manner of one warning the broken young lady not to get her hopes set too high. Shy then paused briefly to consider the slowly shifting eyes of Elizabeth Ann and added for good measure, "What you say is all well and good, sister Lizzie. However, one of these days you and I are going to have a serious talk about what happened to you down in Charleston. The world can be a cold, cruel place and you look as if you have tendered your wares to the service something harsh and forbidden."

Elizabeth Ann's eyes grew wide with surprise upon learning that she was wearing her feelings tied to such unspeakable debauchery so blatantly. She hastily lowered her eyes to the grass near to her feet and then began moving on down the slope towards Miss Leslie's cabin once again. When she had taken a few steps deep in thought over how to reply to this brazen young woman who knew so much of her former mind, she offered up her countermeasure in a vague and monotone soliloquy.

"I only hope that Virgil will forgive me for what I have done. I certainly have no right to expect anything more than that from the principled young man who has done so well by you all while I was off chasing the fanciful dreams of the girl I was for a time always raised to be. In the end, sister Shiloh, I have paid far more dearly than even my imagination would have permitted me to fathom. The act of denying both the wishes of my heart and the intuition of my good sense for little more than the promise of wealth, society, and subsequently, lust has a price that is dear and a price that I will never be able to properly convey. Though I do not wish to speak much on what you may or may not have heard from Mr. Jemison, I will say that judging by little more than the look set upon your face earlier, the rumors and the truth of it seem to be playing into one another hand in glove. Those in possession of money and power in such places will always use up all they wish to of those lacking the same to possess even the most trivial of their wants. Such is an awful state of affairs and one that I hope you are never forced to endure, my precious sister Shiloh."

Shy picked up her gait and began to once again walk alongside Elizabeth Ann. "Never you mind all of that, sweet child. You are home now and the man that always belonged perfectly to the lovely chambers of that delicate heart of yours is still all by his lonesome, excepting little Miss. I just know he still has a place for you in that stubborn country boy head of his. You just gonna have to give it some time and go gentle on that boy. You and your daddy done him wrong, sister Lizzy, and there ain't no two differing ways to knowing that fact."

Elizabeth Ann nodded solemnly in response to Miss Shy's assertions, which did seem to brighten her spirits considerably. She then provoked her soon to be wed sister and friend. "Shall we race on down to Miss Leslie's like we used to, sister Shiloh? I do believe I can still best you, even situated within this monstrosity of a travelling gown."

Shy laughed and took advantage of her opponent's lack of readiness by running off into the high grass of the slope that gracefully worked its way down to Miss Leslie's front yard. "Elizabeth Ann took a determined late jump and called after Shy, "I should have remembered that you were always worse than even the Davis boys when it came to seizing upon an advantage!" To which her sister Shiloh responded, "Nonsense now, you just as slow in gettin' started today as you ever were!"

The two girls laughed at their own childish shenanigans while they ran dressed for supper all the way down the hill to the front door of Miss Leslie's cabin. Who the winner of the race turned out to be was of little import to either of them, yet far too close to call. Miss Leslie chuckled heartily when the puerile women arrived at her door so winded, teased them considerably for their childish ways so close to Miss Shy's big day and then hugged them both so tight the young ladies thought she would never let them go. Elizabeth Ann basked in the afterglow of the unexpected yet welcome exertion and the sadly fleeting return to the carefree and innocent ways of their youth. She would remember the moment fondly well into the closing hours of her life.

On Thursday evening, August 24th, 1871 Miss Jeanne Jolie Basseterre and her daughter, the recently declared Mrs. George Ridley Brown, were talking on the front porch of the Osment farmstead. Shy and her husband, a man with some forty-three years' worth of living under his expanding belt strap and far older than his twenty-two year bride upon the moment of their openly declared nuptials, were set to depart on the following morning for Augusta. The newlyweds would then be traveling on to Atlanta for an extended stretch as part of their honeymoon. Shy was fondling the golden cross draped around her neck and taking notice of the strange markings so delicately carved into the ancient relic in the low light of the setting late-summer sun when she asked, "Momma, why did you not pass this pendant down to Maime? She is older and far more faithful to God than I. I know sissy already knows lots about who our folks were back in Haiti, but Maime would just about melt upon hearing the fully annotated story of our ancestors and those two sacred truths of this here glorious cross."

Miss Jeanne smiled as she watched her daughter curiously inspect the legendary heirloom of the Basseterre clan that had been in the family since the second score of the 17th century. Though Shy had never legally disavowed the name of her father, nor would she have ever done such a thing publicly and for the record of things, Miss Jeanne was sad to see her radiant hotspur of a daughter lose something of the Basseterre moniker she favored and had generally kept to brandishing publicly following the Emancipation. Shy had done as much regarding the manner by which she was called for the primary reason that unlike the Osment appellation of her beloved daddy, which originated from an Anglo slaveholding family up in North Carolina, the name Basseterre had been passed down to her momma through the centuries by the little boy who once stood before a hideous cloven witch of a bygone era and had managed to keep both the cross and its timeless wealth safe from the lustful greed of a Spanish King.

The mother of the bride then smiled inwardly upon recalling the look set upon her daughter's stunning guise when Shy had learned just how true those old stories of her childhood were. Only after her slightly mawkish moment of reflection did Miss Jeanne give some thought to her daughter's question and reply openly to Miss Shy, although she had wondered over that very same peculiarity the moment the next bearer of the pendant was made manifest to her in a waking dream on a radiant yet rather cool morning back in May of that same year. "Only the future holds the answers to the reasons behind why our mysterious Creator decides such things in the manner He does, my dear child. Perhaps Maime is far too delicate of a flower to be saddled with such a burdensome responsibility. I do know in my heart that your sister wanted nothing to do with the medallion while I still lived and breathed and the time of the cross's intended passing has arrived."

Miss Shy shook her head affectionately in response to her mother while not taking her soft brown eyes off of the golden cross and answered her only partly in jest, "It's probably more likely that the Good Lord knows I'll be needin' such a blessing the way my mouth is always runnin' off on its own before I can ever get to taming it any."

Both of the ladies laughed heartily at the introduction of that patently evident and therefore entirely plausible theory. Yet before they had finished giggling over the humorous thought, Miss Shy abruptly inquired of her mother, "What about little Miss, momma? I thought for certain your cross of gold might be destined for the mysterious sprite. There were times I even got to the thinking that such was her given purpose since the world was raging all around us, both during, and for a time, following the war."

Miss Jeanne shifted uneasily in response to the complexities and the still hidden deceit lurking behind such a pertinent question. She replied rather directly, as if she wished to forcefully splinter the curious thought of her daughter altogether. "Perhaps it is best that one with the mysterious gifts and lineage the child clearly does possess is kept from the further notoriety certain to be caused by possessing such a powerful icon and all that you now know to be tied the cross's legacy. I don't know much about the dark bent driving the sickened and perhaps possessed mind of Edward's mother. However, what I do know is that some part of why she wanted for the child on the morning of her birth, the morning you came running up to Doctor Bailey and I when we returned home in the carriage, has to do with that cross now draped around your neck. Stay on your guard and see to it the ancient relic remains safely there until the time comes that you are called to pay the gift forward. Never forget to be watchful, my child."

"Perhaps what you say is all true, momma. Perhaps little Miss being blood kin to both our people and the Captain's folk means somethin' of significance beyond our understanding," responded Miss Shy a bit distractedly before slightly modifying her thought by saying, "Yet I can't help but feeling that both Maime and little Miss are still tied to the legacy of this beautiful pendant all the same. Maybe I'm just the one made by God to keep it safe while all this mess going on around us gets properly sorted."

Miss Jeanne nodded her head in response to her daughter and said, "Yes, my dear. I have felt the same thing for some time now. That is why I took special care in pointing out that the future will reveal the reasons behind both the blessed and cursed decisions of our past. When Calvin Eoin passed the cross to me, there were no others in line for the inheritance. Nevertheless, the cross was destined to leave Haiti upon little more than my wanderlust for reasons that lingered far beyond even my fleeting fancies at the time. So it is with little Miss and all that swirls about pertaining to the mystery of her origins. What is clear about both that promised child and the golden cross is that they are now here for a reason that we do not yet entirely understand."

Miss Jeanne paused and smiled wistfully into the fading light of the eventide while her daughter took time amidst the resolving silence to consider her mother's words. Miss Jeanne then spoke further on the matter in a soothing and reflective tone. "Beyond all of that, my dear, there is something else that has also become abundantly clear to my eyes over the course of this turbulent yet blessed life of mine. The folly of our ways is but something God takes into consideration when He goes about implementing His perfect and wonderful work. The three of you are all strong with the Lord in your own way. Therefore, I do believe you are all still tied to the legacy of the cross of gold through your children's children and so on down the line until the day arrives to reveal and put to God's use the abiding provisions of old Cesar Maduro's remaining treasure. As you know from the story I told you about the legacy of the relic, Cesar was a wicked man for a time too. Yet as it was with Cesar, God puts all things, both good and bad, to His intended purpose to achieve His desired ends in His perfect time."

Such a thought made perfect sense to Mrs. Brown. She nearly acquiesced to her mother's opinion accordingly while at the same time shifting her thoughts to another concern drifting through the confines of her active mind. "I understand what you are saying to me, momma. Still and all, I do remain left to wonder what is to become of little Miss. What with her being illegitimate, colored or white depending on the season of the sun, and all else that is wrapped up into the beautiful ball of wonder that she is. Do you think that you and the Captain will ever be married, momma? I know you said you would never marry another man outside of daddy, but I would feel a whole lot better about her prospects with all that is going on in these parts if you two

were to properly enjoin and get her out from under all these lies bein'
told about just exactly who and what she is."

Miss Jeanne blushed a bit, though thankfully such a telling predilection was not visible upon her August skin. "Well isn't that right
forward of you, Miss Brown! As with all things that may or may not
come to pass in the days ahead I do not have a definitive answer for
you. The will of my heart where it concerns the occurrence of marrying
another beyond your father has not changed any, though I have come
to develop a far more robust appreciation for the redeeming qualities
of a more determinate form of companionship as you all continue to
come up so wonderfully and conduct lives of your own accord away
from our beautiful little corner of the world. Be that as it may, my
dearest Shiloh, Edward is set to return to Butterworth Hall to try and
return to the seemly graces of his beloved daughters Mary Grice and
Blair Raimi once his mother is satisfactorily situated."

Shy quickly picked up the slight twinge of concern lingering deep
within her mother's otherwise reminiscent tone and offered up a rather
forward suggestion, "You could return to the plantation with Edward,
momma; you and little Miss both. I doubt Maime will ever leave this
place, even if she one day finds a man suited to her deeply spiritual
inclinations."

Miss Jeanne smiled warmly at the innocence or perhaps brash-
ness of her daughter's suggestion given the convergence of portended
impediments certain to accompany such a notion and replied a bit
pensively, "A marriage like ours remains quite the radical notion in
a place like Butterworth Hall and perhaps more so in these times
upon which we find ourselves now living. There is a hatred burning
far brighter across the land now than it ever did when those of our
shared ancestry were chained to the demesnes of others. In the eyes of
those now rightly tainted by scorn, those having lost so much during
the war and when the Yankees set our people free, who else is set to
pay for all that death, suffering and the loss of the only way of living

they had ever known still festering in their hearts? I posit that it shall be none but our long-suffering people; the ones who are so beautifully adorned yet easy to set aside and then admonish."

Miss Shy let the golden cross fall back upon the firm skin of her chest after teasing it some with her thumb and forefinger and asked, "Are you speaking about marrying the Captain with you bein' colored and all, momma?"

Miss Jeanne focused her eyes, that shone of flashing amber and a twinge of blue in the low yet still lingering light of the setting sun, tightly and lovingly upon her daughter. The beautiful bride looked so radiant and full of wonder in the aftermath of the heat of the day and set out before the stillness of the gloaming, which was offering up those lingering last traces of the haloed light. Though she was never much for the men in her daughter's life, Mr. Brown included, the girl was a spitfire and rarely left a thought rattling around in that stunningly beautiful and witty head of hers unshared or solely to her own devices.

Miss Jeanne then smiled reticently into the afterglow, wrapping its soft and ambient light around her second child like an angel of the heavens, and replied blithely though sensibly to the very direct line of questioning her daughter always employed when she wanted to get right down to the absolute truth of a given matter. "Yes, my dear, most here do see me as colored, although I am the daughter of a black-breed Irishman of a sort and arrived to the Carolinas free as any of them turning the earth ever were given the state of affairs here. Those once slaves have been emancipated by edict and by Carolina's return to the Union. Likewise, many of the tainted strain of Miss Meara Calhoun and the other brutal chattel proprietors have been rendered impotent in the aftermath of the war. However, I fear the subsequent struggle for those of color, a group to which we now belong just like any of the others and without distinction, is only now beginning."

Miss Shy kept her eyes firmly upon her radiantly illuminated mother and stated plainly, "I do sure enough believe you are right about that, momma. Ain't no way any of those old minded Confederates still stirring about are going to let their grubstaker folk see their just due without a proper fight. Just as you have said, but for the title to this here farm, we are now just the same as the ones that been set free. I've been talking to Amos some about the work he has been doing back in Columbia. You know how bright that boy is and he seems quite worried over the direction in which the proposals for the new state government are heading."

Miss Jeanne responded enthusiastically to her daughter's astute annotations. "What you speak of is the God's honest truth, my dear and a burden far more pressing than I believe Edward understands while things continue to settle out after passing through the heart of chaos and what still awaits us all somewhere on down the road. If it makes you feel any better, I do believe that Edward intends to marry me and look after little Miss. Yet, you know the two of us have been down this road of a differing sort, both for a time before I was married to your father and in the moments of our grief in the years after your father and Miss Libby passed near to one another back in fifty-five. Beyond the persistent torments of our troubled past and the limitations posed by the world at-large, Edward is presently in a bad way with the man whom he's been collaborating with to get out from under the difficulties brought about by that season of the witch that marched in the footsteps of the closing of the war. Thankfully, little Miss delivered the light of the angels into that suffocating darkness possessing Edward's intolerable mother before she had her way with the very last of us."

Miss Shy got her dander up upon hearing about Miss Meara. Beyond the legend of her ill deeds, she hadn't had much direct exposure to the repulsive woman while growing up, outside of the time Edward's mother had taken hold of her hand and looked crossly into her eyes. That solitary act alone was more than enough for one such as Miss Shy to tremor frightfully upon the knowing of what was lurking deep within the cold and empty heart of that devilish woman. "What a nasty enchantress she is, momma! Little Miss must be cooking up something good for the soul in that playful heart of hers to trim mean ol' Miss Meara's wick like she did. I can see why those devils want her. The fact that Miss Leslie has herself a Little pea by that former bounty man whose daddy branded him like a steer, done tell you all you need to be knowin' about what little Miss might do one day."

Miss Jeanne nodded reflectively and replied almost vacantly to her now spirited daughter while the calm and welcoming cool of the dusk brought about the soothing and rhythmic reprise which was that fine evening's compendium of the variously strummed love songs of the crickets hiding in the grass. "I suppose a miracle the likes of that does tell us all we need to know about what our sweet child is capable of, my dear girl; I suppose it does. Please, do not go sounding off about her workings with the light to Mr. Brown now that you two are married. Discretion is the far better medicine to be applied while engaged in the devoted care of our little Miss and in this instance, Mr. Laing also."

"You know I never would say a thing about it, momma," answered Miss Shy excitedly while coloring her reply as such: "Miss Leslie know my lips is sealed too or she wouldn't have told me but for the fact she wanted someone else to know for the sake of little Miss. You know, in the event anything happened to the both of them and some of the others that might be knowin'. I just presumed you knew what she done, momma."

Miss Jeanne did not answer her daughter as to whether or not she knew about the miracle Margaret Anne had performed for her mammy and Mr. Laing. Such silence was intended to be a lesson to her impassioned daughter on the merits of that aforementioned discretion without fibbing any. Miss Shy allowed her mother's unresponsive silence to pass and asked her the question to which she truly wished to know the answer. "Surely, you don't believe that Captain Calhoun will allow anything to stand in his way where it concerns his doin' right by you, momma," beckoned Miss Shy with a look of incredulity settling in upon her otherwise restful mien.

Though she wished to mildly reprimand her daughter for the slack grammar Miss Shy continued to employ whilst she was in a spirited frame of mind, and all the more so when she was under the recent influence of Mr. Brown, Miss Jeanne chose to instead gladly step through the open door to another topic. "I do believe Edward's decision to stay on for a time in Charleston was the end to our hopes of living out our days happily ever after out here on the farm he gifted to your father and me."

Miss Jeanne paused for a moment while deep in thought and then expounded upon her candidly given insight. "And you know something, my sweet girl; as truly beautiful as our time spent together in this beautiful and secluded refuge from the odium of the world beyond was for both Edward and me, perhaps the moments we shared these past three years shall remain all that the two of us were ever intended to peacefully lay claim to as one. The truth of the matter will always be that the man was married when I followed him like a little lost puppy dog to the Carolinas, regardless of my reasons or the wanderlust set upon my dreams by the pull of the golden cross. There is a price to be paid for being guided by such improper wants as it concerns my intercessions with Mr. Calhoun back then, no matter the potency of the rationalizations of my enchanted mind."

Miss Shy turned her willful brown eyes away from the field and back toward her mother. She asked of her bluntly, "Were you in love with Mr. Calhoun when you followed him here from Haiti, momma?"

Miss Jeanne smiled soulfully while continuing to reflect upon the days of that seventeen-year-old girl still waiting to break free somewhere deep inside of her. As such, she spoke redolently in reply to her always outspoken daughter. "I knew I loved something deep within that man the moment I set my eyes upon him, my beautiful Miss Shiloh Jolie. With such an example of what not to do where it concerns flirtatious interludes with a kept man given over to you, I do pray for the best of this life for both you and Mr. Brown in the years ahead. Love in its proper setting, the likes of which your father and I shared, is a right powerful thing blessed by God, my sweet girl. Never look past such a precious gift no matter what forbidden fruit gets dangled low and sweet before your eyes like a summer peach. Lest you be pushed into to making a deal with the devil incarnate in an effort to extricate yourself from the consuming folly and destruction of your prior want. The most precious gift of the golden cross is the necessity for unrequited forgiveness to be offered by the bearer. Never forget that truth or that the sacred bearer of the cross is now you, my dearest. Hold the thought dear when you and Mr. Brown leave this place to make your way together in the beautiful yet fallen world beyond your home."

Miss Shy replied to the wise and thoughtful words of her mother with a touch of sharp wit spoken in her country tongue to wind things down, "That untamed old rake sure enough gonna be needin' such a gift as all of that to survive this here storm if I be catchin' him up to his old tricks as a properly married man!"

Miss Jeanne laughed knowingly and said, "Don't I know that all too well, my dearest Shiloh. Perhaps you now have your answer regarding the passage of the golden cross." Both of the beautiful women laughed warmly and proceeded to sit quietly together and watch the darkness settle over Clarke Osment's beautiful, versant field; a suddenly tranquil and eternal field when shaded by the last of the dusty light of a summer day and one teeming with the endless bursting boughs of white, ripened cotton for as far as the eye could see. Miss Jeanne then smiled inwardly in honor of the past and made a mental note to walk on down to Virgil's homestead and thank him for all of the exacting toil he continued to put forth on their behalf.

As for the old estate home outside of Sumter that following spring, with her grand, white front porch columns and large, beautifully adorned windows, she was looking as good as Miss Jeanne could ever recall seeing her. Though the posted date upon the cover of the Sumter Chronicler that morning read April 22, 1872, but for the lack of activity around the house and out in the fields, Miss Jeanne would have sworn to even those dear to her that it was the spring of 1843 once again. She would have sworn that she was just arriving to assume her duties at the old estate home after her long journey to the Carolinas from the sugar plantations up in the highlands overlooking Jacmel, Haiti.

Although her 46th birthday was just a day shy of being two weeks out, the still splendid yet maturing widow smiled to the whims of none but her fancy as she ascended the steps to the storybook veranda, which in its restored state of grandeur seemed to stand as both cenotaph and sentinel to the passing of the era of the great Southern plantation. The shifting spirits of the heads she turned on that day back in forty-three were still haunting her chosen pathway to greet the renascent lord of the manor. As such, the beautiful maiden possessed not the slightest care for accidentally offering an affront to any of the presently ordained groundskeepers then lingering about the premises of this grandiose and meticulously reordered American dreamscape.

One of those heads which she had turned on that day of nearly thirty years ago was a devilishly handsome one that belonged to a young indentured brick worker, carpenter and fix-it man laboring as part of a maintenance crew from up in the Northern Carolinas by the name of Clarke Osment. The fine woman thusly enchanted by the memories of all that had come to pass so long ago wondered if she would have lit that same fire in the young man's heart on this day. She questioned as much in the knowing that the blooming and lively young man had ultimately passed on in trying to bend the resolve of that gorgeous and so very promising yet obstinate old field to his will in an effort to sustain her and furthermore, because she was presently on the verge of entering the years of the spinster. Regardless, such doubt brought about by the passage of time did little to taint the crystalline memory of the look of wonder in that beautiful man's eyes back on that fine day and never would.

Beyond those cursory reservations concerning Mr. Osment in his youthful form, which stemmed from the unnatural and bootless union of the present being melded into the past amidst the haze of some nostalgic presumption, Miss Jeanne presently felt that uncertain way about her dearly departed husband's thoughts, if he were indeed looking down upon her now, because she had so dishonored his legacy through the depths of her sin. Though in many ways, by acquiescing to the depths of that carnal immorality of 1858, she was in truth trying to forever honor the beautiful verity of what that honest and adorning man would leave behind as his lovely and eternal gifts to this world, she struggled to see the hopelessness of her predicament back then when the thoughts of those sinful deeds were presented before the glorious sunlight of that fine spring day so far beyond the aftermath of what had transpired between her and Edward. Be that as it may, there was no doubt that same fire for the woman well along into the living out of her fifth decade continued to precariously burn in the now slightly twisted and in many ways callow heart of the current patriarch of the still somewhat financially challenged and nearly idle plantation estate.

When Miss Jeanne reached the top of the steps and hopefully stepped onto the grandest front porch in all of the Carolinas, her thoughts remained of a melancholy and nostalgic temperament. There was also no doubt that a great weight had been lifted from the spirit of the land upon Edward's return and the coincident banishment of the black countess. For many reasons that spring, there was at least some semblance of hope tingling in the air at Butterworth Hall where once there was none, yet something sinister stirred out beyond the old abandoned slave cabins. The relief now granted to those once persecuted so mercilessly while they toiled without wage upon the premises was tendered only in the mirage of visible half measures offered up to those once owned outright along with the other fairytales incorporated into the fables of the Reconstruction served up for the public's consumption.

In reality and in practice, the subsequent rights and the fractioned off suffrage of the freed slaves were far from the perfect intentions of God above and fell well short of equitable treatment under the common laws of man. Although the source of the prior authority and the influence of those usurping their sustenance from the bonds of servitude had been scattered by the brutal marches of the Yankee infantrymen, those that had been freed were forced to wander the land without resource or equivalent claim to the tangible needs of their suffering families. As such, the reckoning of those sins of the past had been waylaid for a time and the darker principalities were once again gathering in the shadowy haunts beyond those standing tributes to the past now lying dormant near to the fields. The craven men responsible for the fabrication and administration of those abandoned cabins and those of the ancient bloodlines also infecting the body politic of the North were currently conjuring up new methods by which they might continue to enslave not just the race of their African brethren but the denizens of the gradually healing nation as a whole.

The war and the hell which it had wrought had passed into the settling mists of the dawn years ago now but the promise of the Reconstruction had already been falsely seeded by the corrupted arbiters of malice and the servants of greed. This was true of both the freshly anointed governors of the Yankee and Confederate dominions alike. The slaves had been set free from their physical chains, yet indeed the bonds of their continuing depravity and the hatred that governed the minds of those who had lost so much of their earthly kingdom was a prison that was in some ways worse than what those freed people had grown accustomed to over their generations spent living in bondage. And indeed, those Southern captains of the Reconstruction falsely cried foul in saying, "Look here at what you have done to the poor souls we once cared for," while at the same time setting out a nearly impossible path for those delivered from their chains to travel in reaching self-reliance or the spoken proclamations of their God given equitable standing beside their fellow man.

On the brighter side of things where it concerned the former captives, the seed of their own redemption had been firmly planted in the aftermath of that bloody conflict. While their own memorable journey through the wilderness was perhaps only just beginning, the sick and demented paradigms of the past, which had allowed for the construct of slavery in a nation under God, had slowly been scattered into the four winds; scattered like the countless grains of sand drying upon a windswept beach at low tide while the able bodied American boys and men of their day slaughtered each other mercilessly on the field of battle only to enter into a lasting bondage of debt of their own accord. Those electing to continue on with such savagery concerning their former chattel in the days ahead would be forced to do so openly, mercilessly and without the cover of those colonial religious abominations serving as the tenets of a society which subjugated the very humanity of any and all not accustomed to the brutal doctrines of modern European warfare.

And so it was that the strange, shifting political conditions of this somewhat deformed time for rebirth and for some type of healing to work its way across the land at last brought Miss Jeanne Jolie Basseterre and Mr. Edward Christopher Calhoun to the long avoided moment of their reckoning following the deal that was struck by Mr. Calhoun that prior fall. A deal that was signed in accordance with the ancient laws of the darker principalities that were both blood and spirit kin to his mother. For her part, Miss Margaret Anne had remained in Uriah for this first meeting with the conspicuous Yankee industrialist by the name of Jacob Asher Bromley.

The well-learned, Harvard man and avid Reconstructionist had come to town to assist Mr. Reed with the spreading of the glories of some form of Yankee enlightenment or another. However, such was simply propaganda that no Southerner who had experienced the heavy handed dogmas of the carpet bagging executioners of Washington's "kind and forgiving" policies designed only to reunite the nation ever came to understand in any way whatsoever. When the dissemination of that bootlicking propaganda, which served a far more sinister cause than that which was readily apparent to the naked eye in the aftermath of war, was taken as an aside, the truth became quite clear to those who knew the bookish and slippery Green Mountain man that he had designs on making the locally renowned and exotic beauty of only thirteen years his bride; when the time was suitable according to the tenets of Vermont law, of course.

Edward had arranged for the meeting between Mr. Bromley and the child's adoptive mother to take place at Butterworth Hall that spring as part of his prearranged ascension to the station of unbound and undisputed Calhoun family patriarch. In actuality, Edward did remain fully encumbered to Mr. Reed in the darkest possible senses of the word. Though at times, Edward could sense the sword of Damocles hanging over his head, Edward flourished in the role just as he always had in the days prior to the war. His merchant and railroad businesses were beginning to thrive and he had even managed to return some semblance of prior normalcy to the lives of his once disenfranchised daughters, the widow, Miss Mary Grice Calhoun-Decker and the oft times shy yet highly regarded eighteen-year old debutante, Miss Blair Raimi Calhoun.

Miss Elizabeth Ann had not returned to Butterworth Hall until late-January of that same year. When she arrived, she was still keeping time far away from the public eye following her second failed attempt to find herself happily married; this time to the man she had always truly loved. To say that the young woman was distraught or at least a long ways off of script would have been putting a bit of lipstick on the proverbial pig as it were. Given the scandalous and desultory rumors that persisted about the fallen young socialite throughout the state, her reclusive state was understandable while her father returned to prominence and the spectacle of the always critical and oft times disparaging views of his wealthy Southern peers.

Miss Jeanne had seen to it that both Miss Sarah and Doctor Emmett Bailey were brought to town to attend the introduction to Mr. Bromley, as the two remained the child's anointed guardians of the miracle of the February Cabin. She did not trouble Elizabeth Ann over the affair, though it was true that the eliciting of such an opinion as that of the young woman's in her present state would have made for a rather challenging afternoon. Miss Sarah being brought in from the asylum without the proper recourse for speech or the capacity for even a rudimentary understanding of human dialogue at this juncture in her enduring madness seemed to be little more than an accommodation to Miss Jeanne's enduring superstitious beliefs, yet there is always a purpose to all things under God. Doctor Bailey was, of course, a bit dismayed by the whole situation and found that his feelings for Edward had returned to the lows of that fateful journey to Savannah, where Edward had purchased his own child in accordance with what Doctor Bailey considered to be both a righteous meting out of justice and a standing testament to the glory of divine providence.

Doc was made aware of Edward's dire straits upon entering into the agreement with the Yankee industrialist and former Provost of Uriah to have little Miss married off by word of mouth delivered directly from the lips of a founding member of the somewhat foundering fellowship of the promised child, Mr. Sommers. According to the good and faithful doctor's way of seeing things however, the existence of such extenuating circumstances did little to absolve Mr. Calhoun of this third treacherous betrayal of the promised child. The man had been offered grace at every turn where it concerned his secret love child, the most prominent form of which was manifest through the presence of the promised child herself, yet he had sold it all and perhaps then some for little more than the promise of a dream divinely requisitioned to die when Lee's Army marched back to their homes upon that sorrowful day of Confederate surrender.

Now here the man stood before him, pawning off the very one who had put a stop to the vile persecutions and inquisitions of his mother at the precise moment Edward Calhoun both literally and figuratively lacked a proper leg to stand on. Though Edward had cried foul due to the resultant folly brought about by those of the darkness beset against him, Doctor Bailey now understood that the man's temporary kindness was but a provision of his state of despair and that in truth, Edward felt coldly justified in offering the terms of little Miss's betrothal in exchange for that satchel full of gold he had tendered to retrieve her unwittingly on behalf of her mother some thirteen years ago. The man was cold and calculating to say the least, and perhaps under the auspices of his mother's warped and smothering upbringing, which denied him nothing, also self-absorbed enough to try and play the very forces of the darkness and the light one against the other while his kingdom flourished back in the confines of the waking world governed only by the self-obligatory and fleeting needs of the tangibly driven mind and body. Doctor Bailey had been waiting patiently for Miss Jeanne's arrival to do so, and as such, when she arrived he quickly departed the room without saying a word to any present as a conscientious and passive objector to the arranged betrothal of the promised child.

Miss Jeanne had already lost much of her nerve and her appetite for appeasing those soulless men when Doctor Bailey made the full extent of his displeasure known by turning his back upon the lot of them. She smiled half-heartedly at the hollow man standing before her as the intended husband of her beautiful baby girl, and who clearly stood ready and somehow uniquely enabled to squeeze every last remaining ray of light from the divinely touched spirit of that precious child. She had never come across a man that presented more in the manner of dried and thirsting flesh, though his skin was moist and creamy white like the sweet, spring milk of the Claibrooke farm. Upon touching Mr. Bromley's hand, Miss Jeanne was alerted by the tremoring of her heart in the place where the golden cross used to rest cool and dense upon her chest to the starkness of the cold and empty black watch that had indeed hollowed out the man's once human heart and gutted his perpetually starving soul. That she had for a time held out hope that the one delivered over to be the future husband of her daughter, in accordance with Edward's deal with the serpent, would be at least human, became an idea that quite suddenly existed well beyond the capable tenets of her womanly sensibilities.

Miss Jeanne drew her hand back from the cold, smooth skin of the man in earnest and turned to face Edward. She shook her head fitfully in response to what had become of not only the man she loved, but any man who sought to allow such a travesty to be perpetrated upon one of his own. She knew full well Edward saw that demented and hollowed out entity for what it was. She stuttered some in trying to parse her words carefully so as not to put Edward in harm's way. Shortly after the onset of her predicament had commenced, Miss Jeanne's nervously shifting eyes beheld the woman divinely proffered out and set apart from the insanity of the moment she had always hoped would never arrive, though in truth, she had always known with certainty would surely come.

Miss Sarah had been left to wallow in an unseemly accumulation of her own drool upon Doc's departure. Miss Jeanne quickly stepped over to the poorly cared for and inanimate woman and wiped her chin very sweetly with the towel set upon the constant stillness of her lap. As she finished with the wiping clean of the always delicate and foamy corners of Miss Sarah's loosely bated lips, Miss Jeanne called back over her shoulder to the three gentlemen standing in wait, "I am sorry, my dear Sirs. Clearly, poor Miss Sarah is in no condition for this assembly. I must see to her return to a place of proper care right away. A situation such as this is a dishonor to one forever bound to my sweet daughter. I was heretofore hoping she would be granted some form of temporary reunion with her senses."

The two foreign, or at least Northern, gentlemen looked dubiously at one another and then over to Edward to seek his counsel on what exactly seemed to be transpiring in spite of both their wishes and their expectations. Edward shook his head, shrugged his shoulders and then lightly waved off the stern yet silent concerns of the two visiting gentlemen while asking of Miss Jeanne, "There is nothing to worry over is there, my dear? Our esteemed guests are to be off to Atlanta within the hour."

Miss Jeanne hastily finished up with her efforts to make the slack-jawed woman appear presentable and then stepped directly behind her wheelchair. "My apologies to you as well, Edward, but I can give neither you nor the gentleman in wait your anticipated answer today. Without Doctor Bailey present, there is no way for me to know the mind of the child's heavenly ordained overseer. I simply must be getting Miss Sarah on back to Sumter for her treatment straight away." Having said that for the benefit of all company present, Miss Jeanne turned Miss Sarah fully around in her wheelchair and began to motion her forward toward the door leading out to the front porch of Butterworth Hall.

Mr. Reed had a brief history with the elegant Haitian woman and he could readily sense her repulsion toward Mr. Bromley, which was not an uncommon reaction coming from those with eyes that truly see and a heart that yearns for God above. He nodded discreetly toward Edward with just a slight lowering of his chin and a purposeful closing of his eyes. The look suggested that Mr. Calhoun needed to properly address the situation with the clearly disheartened woman. In response, Edward stepped toward the front door with the intention of assisting Miss Jeanne in delivering the debilitated woman over the threshold and into the care of the lingering Doctor Bailey, and foremost, to prod the suddenly stricken mother of the promised child for something of a response that was far more serviceable to his further plans and perhaps his well-being. "Surely your resolve has not been shaken so suddenly, my dear," uttered Edward as he pulled open the front door in the direction of the main foyer. "Perhaps you could offer something of a more heartening nature to the esteemed gentlemen who have traveled so far to offer such wonderful prospects to our little Miss."

Miss Jeanne stopped cold and turned to face Edward before replying rather drily, "But of course, Edward." Miss Jeanne then turned to face the gentlemen still standing in the front hall, though it pained her mightily to do so, and addressed them in a formal or perhaps sterile manner. "To the gentlemen standing in wait, I am not denying your request for my consent concerning the betrothal of my child. I simply cannot offer you an answer today. Doctor Bailey has made his feelings known and nothing of the poor woman in this chair has given me due provision to overstep the doctor's objection."

Mr. Bromley motioned to step forward and plead his case but Mr. Reed quickly stilled his cousin with a gentle brush delivered from the back of his forearm. Mr. Reed then addressed Miss Jeanne, "Of course, my dear. Take all the time you need to feel at peace with the inevitable decision. I understand your reliance on those who stood by the child when she was abandoned to be born in the woods and then tendered for as if naught but chattel by her own father. There is plenty of time for us to receive your affirmation in the form of a properly offered consent. It is after all, little more than a formality; yet a formality of the highest order that will keep our beloved Mr. Calhoun here from being understood as a petty man and a liar."

Miss Jeanne nodded as evenly as she could posture in the direction of Mr. Reed and Mr. Bromley but uttered not a sound. When she had pushed Miss Sarah out onto the front porch she turned to Edward, who was helping at her side, and spoke to him with tears running down her cheeks, "You must find another way, Edward! The child has endured far more than she ever should have in this life already. Beyond that, she freed you from your mother. I will not subjugate her to what lies beyond the outer walls of that hollow man's dwelling. I never will. You have some time to set things right. You must keep her from the hold of that man! We all must!"

Edward stopped his progression walking towards the stairs of the porch beside Miss Jeanne. He watched Doctor Bailey gently take the mentally shattered Miss Sarah up in his arms from her wheelchair, step down from the grand veranda and make his way over to the waiting carriage piloted by Mr. Satterfield. Miss Jeanne delayed in following behind the doctor until Edward had come to his senses and began to take up Miss Sarah's chair. The Sun was still warm and pleasant and the spring flowers, which were all properly blooming in the front garden at the base of the veranda, had been meticulously attended to by Miss Blair Raimi and Miss Elizabeth Ann. Before Edward and Miss Jeanne began the short walk across the front circle over to the carriage, Edward beckoned to the clearly disenfranchised woman a final time. "You have given your word, my dear. You know better than I, as it was you who made effort to warn me off of the Yankee gentleman, these men do not take kindly to changes in circumstance once contractual consent has been granted."

Miss Jeanne turned back to Edward and replied forlornly, "I granted you my consent, Edward. I am not denying as much. What I am asking of you now, for the sake of the child, is that you release me from the bonds of that pledge. The promise was not mine alone to give. The time has come to do right by the child and abide in accordance with our faith in God. I will do whatever I am able to do for you, Edward but it cannot be that. It simply cannot be that."

Edward stiffened in an almost petulant manner as if her plea was something altogether expected of only a child playing out by the schoolhouse. "You act is if the child stands to do better in marrying some sharecropper of color from back in Uriah. No white man of the

Carolinas will endure the political suffering of the betrothal in today's world. Be sensible now, woman!"

Miss Jeanne wiped the tears streaming from her eyes in knowing that the man she once loved had been taken from her. She knew that her words would do little good in waking the man from the unbroken sleep of the devil's mirage now showing upon his glossy eyes as if his bargain belonged to the realms of pleasant and eternal summer shade, yet she spoke the words anyhow. "Just as I was in doing the same back in my day, I do believe Margaret Anne would be far happier in marrying one who took only his just due from the offerings of the land. Be that as it may, I doubt any man of this world is set to have her. Do what you must, Edward, but know that I stand by at the ready to protect the child at all cost. You must understand by now that I made the promise of her hand for the sake of another man altogether. Be well, Mr. Calhoun. I bid you good day and I wish you well in your remaining deliberations with such demons cast out upon the earth within the hour."

Edward set Miss Sarah's cumbersome wheelchair down upon the pristine cobblestones of the circular ending to the drive, turned in disgust from the one he now viewed to be a treacherous woman, and made his way back up the stairs and into the manor without speaking a word. Doctor Bailey lovingly set Miss Sarah down into her seat within the confines of the carriage and then turned to embrace the inconsolable woman of such dignity, elegance and beautiful grace. While he held her tight, the good doctor wondered precisely what had been set in motion and what twisting of the fates was set to be unveiled in its proper time.

Chapter Nine

VIRGIL O'KEEFE

❧

E LIZABETH ANN ARRIVED at the southern edge of the
property line and perhaps what she then viewed as the final outpost resting at the edge of the earth. According to the young woman's present beliefs and the nervous tremoring of her broken heart,
both righteously shaken and then tied into confounding knots by the
trauma of and associated with her prior abuse, she now stood before
the only remaining gateway to an accepted return into the gentler
graces of life out at the Osment farmstead and perhaps the realization of some passable form of happiness at all. Though she remained
a woman of her own standing at the time, given her desolate spiritual
and mental condition, Elizabeth Ann had remained under the care of
Miss Jeanne in the months that followed her father's return to Sumter
to reclaim Butterworth Hall on the final day of the summer season
of 1871. She had adored Miss Jeanne since the earliest days of her
remembered childhood and the Haitian woman's presence in her life
during those emotionally turbulent months was the shining grace of
that far too brief season of her return stay in Uriah.

For all intents and purposes, the man of the modest white farmhouse before her eyes was also now the principal operator of the
cooperative of farms that covered the rolling hills and intermittent
woodlands to the west of Uriah proper. He was also the man that
held the key to her broken heart and the key to what she believed was
her only recourse to tread upon the still hidden path to her salvation,
both out here on the farm and also within the hallowed haunts of

Butterworth Hall. What she had subjected her father to witnessing back in Charleston was a thing she intended never to speak of, but for once, beyond her conversation with Miss Shy upon her arrival out to the farm while her father still lived and breathed. On that cold December evening, Miss Elizabeth Ann Calhoun knew deep down in the places that still quivered with the ill sentiment of what she had been subjected to back in August that her father's opinion of her would only be set right if she took the hand of a man that would vouch for the reordered remnants of her chastity. There was only one man that had ever belonged to her heart and only one man that could set her father's own sin right, and he was somewhere lurking within that quaint yet comely cottage set before her eyes. A cottage that would do quite nicely in keeping her from the public eye until she was ready to move past the condign scarlet badge of that sultry summer evening back on the Market Square of Charlestown town.

The wintry air settling into the flats of the gap that marked the ancient seasons of the creek's shifting progression throughout the ages caused the elegant young woman to shiver slightly. Over her uncovered shoulder she could hear the buggy piloted by old Barbury Davis make its way back onto the upland road that traversed the boundary between the main field of the Claibrooke farm and the lower bounds of the Osment acreage. She wrapped her velvety shawl, which radiated crimson against the white and gold of her fine Charleston evening gown and the semi translucent grey skies above, around the chilled skin of her creamy white shoulders. Her slender, low-heeled shoes that stepped along the fitted shards of natural slate which comprised the front walk were crafted of a fine, white polished Italian leather, and taken together with the shimmering fabric and elegant cut of her dress set against her raven hair, ravishing blue eyes and crimson accoutrement, gave her the look of some untouchable countess of the Victorian Court.

On another day and in another lifetime she would have been the lady in wait known as Elizabeth Ann Calhoun. The very same Miss Calhoun that all who knew her back before the war would have expected to see in all of her exquisite joie de vivre on this final evening of 1871. Yet, the woman who nervously approached the handsomely crafted cedar door to the farmhouse nestled beneath the canopy arching over the harmoniously running creek off to the side of the property, she haunted the landscape before her shifting eyes as but a shell of that once and future promise to Carolina society. The skeletons now settled upon the cupboards of her closet were ruinous and hardly a secret to any with a penchant for the gossip of the day. Fortunately for her, the man inside the attractively constructed farmhouse was not one of those types. However, she had already revealed the fickle nature of her heart to him the only time in her life she was pressed on the matter of her commitment to the truth of her feelings, and some years before she had ventured into the depths of the carnal sickness shared by so many of means that are no longer bound in spirit to the light and love of their Creator.

Her right hand trembled something fierce as she knocked upon the door to finally engage her would be lover, who had always been kindred to the very pith of her heart for reasons so numerous she could no longer count them all out in one sitting. She still remembered the taste and feel of his lips on that cooling August afternoon out by the rope swing. The two had spoken a few times awkwardly in the months since her return from Charleston late that summer, but had never reconciled the severity of her slight of the young man back in those days before her world was turned on its head. This moment however, would not be the time for such words. The woman had no appetite for confounding the feelings now burning like a fired iron upon her heart. She wanted nothing more than for the man behind the door to have his just due where it concerned her once faltering heart whilst she offered him every sanctum of that former glory of her blossoming womanhood that made his eyes go crossed and set fire to his dreams on that dark day of the war's end.

Upon the third set of knocks that echoed slightly into the settled chill of the crisp air of the creekside flats, Virgil O'Keefe opened the door only to be pushed across the main room of his cabin until he fell firm to his backside upon the davenport. His lips were overwhelmed by the famished softness and warmth of her mouth. His mind lost hold of its grip upon the confines of reality. His wits exploded in flashes of throbbing light while the muscles at the back of his neck convulsed violently and then seized up due to the blood rushing hot and flush to the sensitive crux of his masculinity. Unfortunately for the young man so inexperienced in the ways of a woman, the overwhelming sensation delivered him back to the singular time and place of his life upon which he bore witness to such beastly want. Furthermore, that remembered moment of his sister's distress was a time he would have altogether rather forgotten if such a nightmare weren't etched into the soft, tender skin at the back of his eyelids when he closed them each night upon drifting off to sleep. As such, he was no more than a limp and confused puppet on a string when she guided his hand inside of the tricky wardrobe accessories tended to only by the handmaidens of the elite and the spot of an unknown likeness to his sensations of touch, which was like glory and the safety of soft warmth resting upon quicksand.

The young man had stood upon that quicksand before in dealing with the uncommon beauty. Consequently, Virgil O'Keefe retreated suddenly from that promised land upon which he had been so forcefully delivered. He needed to breathe and to assess his formidable inexperience with such endeavors and far more importantly than all of that, he needed to properly define the gap still dividing their understanding of what had been done when she left him to wilt before her father upon the porch, and done so for only the written promises of another man once familiar to her. Elizabeth Ann reacted first to the retraction of the fuel so rapidly firing her passions and tried to set back into motion that which had been so abruptly quenched like a flame doused by cold, heavy water.

When Virgil O'Keefe broke free of her reaching lips and her searching hand, the clarity and promiscuity attached to his firm rejection of her brought about the sudden and cutting retreat sponsored by the lustful young woman's shame. She rose from the sofa like the exceptional athlete she always was and rushed towards the door but Virgil caught hold of her. He asked of her forcefully while taking hold of her slender wrist, "What is happenin' with you, Elizabeth Ann? What have those city folk done with the woman who so softly and sweetly gave up those lips to me out by the old rope swing with the flutterin' heart of a little girl?"

Elizabeth Ann turned into his hold and buried her tearing eyes into his chest as she cried her words softly into the flesh of his heart pounding just beneath the cotton fabric of his checkered, winter dancing shirt. "I thought you might forgive me for all that I have done if I gave over to you all that I once was when you first took to me back on that day you arrived at the plantation with Papa. All that I have done since I left you has been wrong and hopeless and infernal. I am a ruined woman, Virgil O'Keefe! I am lost to the eyes of God and fit for only the role of mistress in the world of those I tried so hard to affect. The woman you once knew has been paraded around Charleston in scarlet for all to see."

In truth, Virgil understood little of what the suddenly distraught young woman was trying to tell him outside of the fact that the man in Charleston clearly had his way with her in some regard beyond the bounds of what she presumed to be the sanctity of her chastity. His diction slipped quite noticeably back to its country roots due to his confusion. "Nothin' dat be happenin' down in town gonna be a come a cropper out here on dis little bughill. I ain't got me a care in the world for dem affairs a dat city and their piddlin' ways, Elizabeth Ann, and dat be includin' whatever dem folks be reckonin' dey done gone an' claimed a your'n virtue. If my sis had lived to see another day beyond the hot, whiskey riddled breath a'dem accursed Yanks, I'd a put a bullet in any man that spoke poorly of her. That bein' said well enough, we do gots to settle out on what happened when you left. In my eyes, the woman dat returned to me ain't none different den da one who turned her back on dis here home of ours."

Elizabeth Ann sobbed all the more and finally said what she should have returned home to tell him after the very first of it. "I'm sorry for what I did to you, Virgil. There wasn't a day I didn't regret the way father and I treated you for little more than the promise of a prominent and filthy man. Such is the truth before all the other verities about me that are yours for the knowing if you only say the word."

Virgil rested his chin on her pretty dark hair and took a deep breath. He then answered her kindly, as he knew full well that she was hurting in a bad way. While he wished for her to know his mind, he knew by the tenets of her behavior alone that she had suffered far beyond any word that would have ever reached her tender ears from even the hottest burn set upon his lips for what she had done to him. "Listen to me, Elizabeth Ann. We gonna figure out dat past and set the road we gonna walk in the future accordingly, but it ain't gonna be on dis here day. We's both too raw for any of dat."

Virgil then removed his chin from the velvety feel of her soft, dark hair that smelled of ripened summer peaches and looked into the deepening blue abyss of her tear-stained eyes. He spoke further while attempting to align his grammar with the ways of her sweetly offered teachings of the past. "Now, why don't you see if you can set that pretty smile back upon that restless beauty of yours and let's go and have us a time tonight. We both done been through the mill these past few years and we both deserve a bit a dat ol' holiday carryin' on, no matter the circumstances been keepin' us apart."

Elizabeth Ann looked up into Virgil's eyes and smiled such that her tears nearly absolved her of every past sin still settled black and cold within the simple young man's tender heart. Virgil looked into those moist blue eyes and followed his earlier thoughts within the medium of a kind and caring tone. "About the only thing I do know right now, pretty lady, is that this world of mine is a much better place with you in it. I waited a long time for you in the knowin' you would come back to me. God done granted me that grace and I don't aim to be the one to spoil it none. I been workin' hard to make sure we gots all we need right here out upon this beautiful land. All I need now is the pretty girl that once walked these fields with me talkin' poetry and paintin' the wildflowers of late summer."

Elizabeth Ann and Virgil straightened up their appearances and, for a time, began anew in talking over all that had been happening out at the farm over a bottle of passable wine Virgil had kept tucked away upon the recommendation of one of the Davis boys for just such a moment. Elizabeth Ann had kicked the New Year's festivities off a bit early, sharing some wine with Miss Jeanne and Miss Leslie before she arrived. The slowly and awkwardly reconciling young couple discussed little Miss some but Virgil kept much of what lie at the heart of his relationship with the young woman to the confines of his own sentiment. Elizabeth Ann didn't think much about Virgil's defensive posture concerning her little sister and was in fact happy the beautiful little sprite had such an honest and stalwart protector now that her father had committed the preponderance of his energies to the restoration of Butterworth Hall to its past grandeur.

The truth be told, the two had a wonderful time as the warmth of the wine settled out their anxiety over their hopes and fears concerning the uncertain days ahead. They laughed over the always humorous goings on over at the Davis farm and they reminisced about the glorious times they shared together with Miss Shy, Maime and Amos during the years following the war. By the time they departed for town from over at the Claibrooke's farmhouse, the two were in a good place where it concerned the properly mending and recoupling hearts of estranged young lovers. They only tenderly probed around the more delicate matters that kept their worlds neatly separate while they worked to reestablish the foundations of their deep rooted and near filial fondness for one another.

All continued to go well with the two somewhat queerly reunited young lovers as the night progressed, and such a state of affairs held true to form even following their joining up with a few of Virgil's rowdier acquaintances from the other side of town. That is to say, all continued to go well right up until the flashpoint the white lighting had taken like the explosive electric currents of a midsummer storm to Elizabeth Ann's rather intolerant head. Her filters that typically governed her actions within the confines of such a socially active yet common place during such a festive time, where the more salt of the earth rungs of Carolina society had gathered to rather boisterously ring in the New Year; those filters precipitously melted away and her thoughts were aggressively assaulted by those darker whims and fears lurking just beneath the surface in the violent shallows of her broken emotions. As she became more inebriated, she grew resentful of her deep seeded love for Virgil O'Keefe as a broken and manifest response to her own acquiescence to the perversions of her former lover and his demonic handler, yet oddly and for no particular reason known to her, she began to lament her inability to satisfy the sickly, intimate bents of Doctor Roger Jemison Dawson.

While Elizabeth Ann was converging upon the darker haunts of her troubled mind whilst she approached the climax of her stupor, Virgil had for a time also been overcome by the spirits of the grain mash and had completely looked past his spurning of the young lady's rather unexpected and quite forceful affections earlier that evening. In a directly opposite manner to the dimming emotional state of his thwarted paramour, Mr. O'Keefe was feeling his oats and considered the traumas of the earlier hours to be little more than a hot flash of insanity and Elizabeth Ann's currently unexpressed, yet certainly dour, feelings as little more than the temporarily triggered sentiment of one new to the effects of the backwater 'shine. Virgil had tried the concoction a few times with a few of the boys from back in town, but had sworn off of the stuff given its tendency to do little more than rekindle those old wounds from his past and due to the impacts of the after-effects on his production back at the farm in the days that followed succumbing to those rare wild hairs of his.

Tonight however, the personal effects of the whiskey were suited just fine to the lively atmosphere of the New Year's Eve square dance. Accordingly, Virgil had made the mistake of taking his eyes off of the young, intoxicated woman, who viewed her person as little else but scorned in that bent and twisted light of the drink, to festively yet harmlessly indulge some of the more pronounced and even eccentric dancing women of Uriah. The mistake was near as fatal to the reconciling young couple's plans for the future as was the frame-up of a calamity that drawing his pistol in the vicinity of Thaddeus and Henry Davis was, back when those two miscreants were found eavesdropping on him and Elizabeth Ann from behind the bushes near to the rope swing dangling from the eastward leaning branch of the old oak. While Virgil was off making time with the local ladies at the line dance, Elizabeth Ann had cordoned off a few of the younger and unaccompanied boys from out near the county line. Worse than that, the three had disappeared into the lumber room of the meeting hall in response to some sadistic manifestation of Elizabeth Ann's twisted need to prove her worth to the hedonic gods that had commandeered the waking thoughts of her husband to be and, thusly, set ruin to her life back in Charleston.

The lively and quite strenuous dancing of the last quarter hour had Mr. O'Keefe feeling rather alive and a bit more in tune with his senses of the flesh than he was after that last violent swallow from the old tin flask of Bennett Scott, an older scamp of about thirty who wandered about the area occasionally yet spent the majority of his time completing contract work mending the rail lines throughout the state. When the soulful band got into a spirited rendition of *Carry Me Back to Old Virginny* kept at the slow time, Mr. O'Keefe at last remembered that he had come accompanied to the New Year's Eve celebration and broke away from the couples joining together in the traditional way for a reluctant bob.

Virgil asked around for Elizabeth Ann but nobody had seen her in quite some time to the best of their recollections, none of which would have sufficed as testimony in a proper court of law due to the soggy condition of the givers. Such was safe to say that the 'shine had been copiously and pervasively dispensed amongst the revelers gathered back in Uriah that evening. While Virgil wasn't yet to the point of panicking as he canvassed the various groups gathered about the town hall, he did recall that the uncharacteristically ruttish young woman had spoken of partaking in her fair share of wine before Barbury Davis had dropped her off at his homestead out by the Claibrooke property line prior to their trip into town.

It wasn't until one young lady by the name of Beatrice Stewart seemed to recall Elizabeth Ann funnin' around with Lloyd Brooks and Ephraim Moncton back by the administrative offices that Virgil took to worrying over the young lady on a couple of different fronts. When the band broke out into the playing of *Dixie* to welcome in the New Year, not a wallflower once clinging to the outer confines of the main assembly hall or its adjoining vestibules was left out of the wild and captivating menagerie of the dancing fray. Such an occurrence made Virgil's job of finding Elizabeth Ann a bit easier yet did not improve the results of his thorough and possibly even frantic search for the besotted young socialite perchance bent on exhibiting some form of chaos or self-deprecating destruction. When Virgil was about to give up hope and step outside into that gelid January air of the first hour of 1872, he recalled a favor he had accepted responsibility for years ago accruing to the benefit of Mrs. Evangeline Stokes near to the very spot upon which he now stood at the front of the building. The good deed of yesteryear involved an old storage closet that could only be approached by a short and smothering auxiliary hall, which also happened to open at the side of the building and was only accessible from the exterior of the premises.

With his heart beginning to pound almost audibly against his ribs and breastplate from the onset of some horrifying premonition; a horrifying premonition involving the young lady who had along with her father already once ripped his still beating heart directly from its moorings while that vital organ still rested within the proper confines of his stalwart chest, Virgil stepped out of the assembly hall and into the crisp evening air. His hot, whiskey riddled breath exploded like the billowing cloud of a cannon blast into the surrounding environs of the night while lit up by the light escaping from the slowly closing door to the assembly hall. Virgil made his way slowly and watchfully to the side of the building shifting hastily in his mind from thoughts that derided the madness of such horrible portent regarding the young lady to those that once again condemned the two-sided nature of anything with cold, calculating Calhoun blood running through its veins of porcelain or glass. Upon seeing that the door to the auxiliary hall was ever so slightly ajar, Virgil quickly came to terms with the worst of his fears over what had become of the young woman; the once pious and gracious young woman that had owned his heart from the very moment he first saw her cross the drive at Butterworth Hall back on Easter Sunday in 1865.

Left to only the guidance of the suddenly shaded spirits of the whiskey, the cold air of that darkening January night, and the memories of what the young woman had already done to him now duly tied into his ominous presumptions of the offing, regardless of where the two traversed together from here; Virgil made his way down the narrow, unlit hallway that scented of old, damp wood until he heard the first of those unholy sounds emerge from the lumber closet. Having no knowledge or even rightful pretense as to the resultant exposition of raw lust beyond what he had experienced earlier that afternoon, the young man could only equate the grating sounds clawing at the porcelain enamel of his simple soul to that of a stray cat in heat that would never know the gratification of its duly given satisfaction.

What had been done to his sister near to the end of the war occurred far beyond the reach of his tender ears, though not his rifle's sights when he had made the top of the bluff far too late to be of any use to the horrifically abused girl. Unlike the events transpiring behind that door, what those Yankee animals did to his sister surely only occurred upon the mortal precipice of her helpless stance against so many brutes fashioned in the ways of only death and dismemberment for four long years. He remembered that the ones he had killed also smelled of rotgut whiskey, like he now did as he warily approached through the pitch of blackness to what he remembered to be the warped wooden door of the old, musty closet. He placed his hand flat upon the door as his tender and simple heart burst once again in accordance with the maddening sounds that held not even the slightest portent of discretion.

He listened closely with his ear set upon the dry, prickly wood of the door boards until the frightful hollowing out of the voice of one of the boys confined to the closet seemed to signal some sort of an end to the savagery taking place inside. Virgil did not know it then, but the other boy had been tersely cast aside as spent some minutes ago. Following that brief moment of calm, he heard her affecting some mysterious ritual that brought her own cadence close to what the boy had hastened from the depths of his ecstasy before she crassly mocked their inadequacy and crudely dispatched the young ruffians from the dark and dusty quarter of their emblazoned sin.

The thinly planked door hit Virgil square in the nose as Ephraim Moncton burst forth from the closet while trying to reconcile the mess of his britches that were still at half-mast. Virgil retreated back a step and against the wall while drifting into a daze to avoid a second happenstance of what had just bloodied his nostrils. The move was prescient because it was not long after he fell out of the way of Mr. Moncton that Mr. Brooks came scrambling out of the closet hell bent on returning to some semblance of the light beyond that old and frightfully opaque hallway.

Virgil remembered nothing of the awkward time that rested between the smarting of his nose and his submission to naught but a vision of what he thought accompanied him within those dark, musty quarters that suddenly scented of strange and wafting yet clearly human potions. In the fantasy of his ensuing madness, he followed her ever hastier commands until his legs gave out from under him upon the seizing of his very pith and the frightful tremoring of his limbs that refused to quit even after he had fallen limp to the floor. Somehow, in the aftermath of that derisive stupor of frenetic aggression, the two returned to their apportioned buggy for the evening as if all were normal and that they together as one now possessed some forbidden knowledge far beyond the notions of all those others back inside the town hall still living within the confines of their shame.

Still and all, the effects of the alcohol faded and the sun brought with it the revealing truth of those first rays parsing through the canopy with the lustrous shine of the morning light. Though it was cold, the sky had cleared absolutely and presented itself as some crystalline form of powder blue resting over the span of the horizon when Elizabeth Ann exited the cabin and made the few miles walk home to her room up at the Osment farmstead. She slept until the supper hour that evening and never responded to those beckoning her to attend the traditional New Year's Day meal of black-eyed peas, smashed potatoes and honey baked ham.

Virgil's memory of the incident was broken yet not altogether absent. The stationary flashes he did remember were enough to induce the young man to travel out to the county line and put the fear of God into a few young men that had been rumored to be speaking nonsense about the behavior of Miss Calhoun on New Year's Eve. Be that as it may, Mr. O'Keefe never spoke a word to the young lady until little Miss's thirteenth birthday arrived some eight weeks later, on February 24, 1872. For her turn, Elizabeth Ann had eventually retreated to Butterworth Hall after making no progress with the young man during the first few weeks of January.

Her memory of the incident was naught. While such a verity heartened her efforts to draw out Mr. O'Keefe at a time when she would have otherwise run away in shame, that point in time customarily being the very day the alcohol freed her from the twin sicknesses of withdrawal and nausea, her lingering bravado brought about by her lack of functional recall was certainly no mea culpa for just about anything Elizabeth Ann endeavored to achieve against the grain of the scandalous affairs of that night. At least not during that first fortnight in January, and at least not as far as Mr. Virgil Denton O'Keefe was concerned. And perhaps such a response was justified, given what had transpired upon the ringing in of the New Year and the still misfit reconciliation of Elizabeth Ann's slights of the young man in the past.

The aforementioned late-February of 1872 gathering for the celebration of the thirteenth birthday of Miss Margaret Anne Basseterre was a family affair that was generally quite cheerful in the early going, outside of the blatant eschewal of Miss Elizabeth Ann by Mr. O'Keefe. In fact, while effortlessly observing that her big brother of a sort was to have nothing to do with her older sister and understanding intuitively, though perhaps not distinctively, that Virgil had taken a bite of the proverbial forbidden fruit of mixing alcohol with fornication back on New Year's Eve, the actuality of which was quite likely to change the nature of her own relationship with Mr. O'Keefe while she was now a woman of consenting age in South Carolina, Margaret Anne quietly slipped away from the party. On the way to taking her leave from the guests gathered together in her honor, little Miss bore down upon her wholly overcome older sister and graciously guided her by the hand down to Miss Leslie's cabin for a sororal chat.

At that point in time, Margaret Anne was no longer oblivious to the rumors concerning Elizabeth Ann once again swirling about town like the rifling tempests of the tides. When the two young ladies were settled down within the otherwise empty cabin, the then still lean yet near to robustly situated in the ways of a proper woman of the times and woodland sprite of a far more mature nature, pulled no punches in addressing the fallen former socialite. "Why have you come here, my sweet yet so sullenly appearing sister? Uriah is such a long way to travel from Sumter for little more than the formal notice given of my progression into the ranks of womanhood. You should know that Virgil would no more speak to you now than he would one of those Yankee boys that assailed his sister. While I am a firm believer in reconciliation, your ill-conceived treatment of the young man will take far longer to heal than only these dreary few months of the passing of winter have allowed. Tell me now what it is that I already know, sister."

Elizabeth Ann lowered her head from her seated position and spoke dourly yet evenly, "I am in the way, little Miss. I am in the way and though I hold no rightful expectation that Virgil would do so, I was hoping he would do the honorable thing and marry me."

Little Miss turned her head slowly in disbelief, precisely in the way that her mammy used to when she would ask such wild and inappropriate questions back when she was but a child. Margaret Anne Basseterre then replied to her sister with that same air of mounting incredulity that was conveyed so naturally by Miss Leslie's otherwise gentle yet candid mannerisms, "Have you gone and lost your mind, Elizabeth Ann? You must speak of this to no one! Virgil will never consent to a betrothal where the question of the child's father stands in doubt! Furthermore, if you press the matter for the satisfaction of your appropriate consent and presumed paternal patronage, it shall be the first of the three men present with whom you will depart the church." Little Miss did not bother to clarify that such an opinion stemmed solely from the thoughts of her brother Amos, who had spent countless hours poring over legal volumes related to the matter of paternity back in town, and was based upon a purely fictional state of affairs involving a woman of the brothels Margaret Anne had conjured up in her inventive mind.

Elizabeth Ann shook her head with her eyes to the floor in a distraught manner and replied, "I am ruined, then little Miss! I am ruined just as father is by that awful contract he entered into with such an awful man!"

Little Miss stood up from the sofa and approached her older sister, who was sitting in her mammy's reading chair. When she stood directly in front of Elizabeth Ann she spoke plainly, as she always did, "Give me your hand, my beloved and abused child."

Elizabeth Ann looked up frantically at little Miss and replied, "Are you going to send the child away to the places of the light from whence you came to us?" Little Miss kept her eyes squarely focused upon her sister's quivering countenance and said simply, "No, I am incapable of such things. The child is not here of my accord but of yours and father's."

"What do you intend to do then, my darling angel of the light?" was Elizabeth Ann's suddenly hopeful reply. Margaret Anne Basseterre sharpened her eyes and answered, "I aim to heal your heart for the sake of the child, just as I did with Grammy's and Mr. Laing's. Now give me your hand, sister, before those who govern the light now once again teeming within me deny my plea."

Elizabeth Ann tendered her svelte right hand cautiously to Margaret Anne and watched her sister's eyes ever so carefully as she did so. Margaret Anne studied her sister's palm shrewdly with the thumbs of each of her protracted yet handsome hands that reminded Elizabeth Ann of Maime's and Miss Jeanne's long and beautiful appendages. Little Miss then looked back up at her sister and said, "The child is of the seed of Mr. O'Keefe."

Elizabeth Ann became overwhelmed with emotion and cried out, "Then Virgil and I shall be married!" Margaret Anne spoke rather directly and in fact to the contrary in reply. "No, such is no longer possible based on what you and father have done to Virgil when accompanied by the bounds of your horribly knotted adultery. Nevertheless, you will care properly for the child as he stands to be Edward's heir."

Before Elizabeth Ann could object, little Miss squeezed her hand forcefully until she drove a wickedness far more forceful than she had ever experienced from the very core of her sister's soul. Unlike with Miss Meara, the demon man infecting Elizabeth Ann had been granted access to the far more remote corners of her being. When Elizabeth Ann was healed of that opal seed growing someplace within and the connection between her and the promised child was broken, little Miss was sent bounding into the wall at the far side of the room. She lost consciousness upon striking the reinforced pine boards of the partition and slid senselessly to the floor.

As had been the case with both Mr. Laing and her grandmother, Elizabeth Ann was gifted a scene from the worlds where the creatures of the light, such as little Miss was, abounded. She rose from Miss Leslie's reading chair, stepped evenly across the cabin and picked Margaret Anne gently up off the floor, though they were then near to the same physical apportionments. When Elizabeth Ann had an appropriate hold on the promised child, she worked her way out beyond the cabin door and began the arduous trek up the slope covered in deadgrass and back to Miss Jeanne's. The terrified older sister screamed as she labored forward into the cold, incessant winds of that February evening, "Help me someone! Help me! Help me Virgil O'Keefe! Little Miss is going cold!"

Virgil did not hear the cries of the young woman stumbling through the high grass of winter out in the night. Yet, there was some connection present to her harrowing distress that set off a dreadful feeling of unease within his distracted mind. He bounded out onto the front porch of the farmhouse and looked down the entire stretch of the upper field and the surrounding environs. He knew each corner of the darkened terrain before his eyes just as he knew the back of his hand. Virgil then ran down the stairs of the front porch and off in the direction of Miss Leslie's until he found Elizabeth Ann crawling through the grass and screaming hoarsely, "Help her! Help her! She is going to die because of the seed of my wretchedness!"

Virgil looked sternly at Elizabeth Ann as she cried the tears of the damned and pulled futilely at little Miss's limp arm through the dormant stalks of the long, shifting winter high grass. Virgil presumed that the vile and sinful woman had intended to break his blossoming relationship with her younger sister and was only after the fact of the foul deed met by the reproach of her own guilt. Therefore, Virgil spit with disgust into the grass as he looked over Elizabeth Ann with only scorn set upon his handsomely chiseled visage. He then scooped up Margaret Anne with one rather fluid and athletic motion and rushed the darling cherub up the slope and into the main farmhouse. He left Elizabeth Ann crying hopelessly in the high grass and said not a word about her whereabouts until Edward asked, "Has anyone seen Elizabeth Ann of late?" Mr. Calhoun's query had occurred just prior to his having been made aware of the severity of the uncertain situation with the birthday girl.

Miss Jeanne, having some intuition on the matter but certainly not knowing that Elizabeth Ann had been left lying within the bending straw in front of the Laing's cottage to die of exposure, walked over to Edward and brought him out onto the porch. When the two had reached the deck out of doors, such was likely the temperature had dipped into the low twenties at that late hour of the afternoon or perhaps early evening. Edward was looking curiously into her eyes when Miss Jeanne spoke soothingly to the still very troubled patriarch of the profitless Butterworth Hall. "Edward, I believe Elizabeth Ann is down at the Laing's cabin where she was speaking with little Miss. You should go to her and speak to her about the condition of her heart. Things have not progressed well for the poor woman since that awful day prior to your return from Charleston."

Edward grew a bit cross upon hearing mention of that day and replied coldly, "What am I to say to her as it concerns such low form, my dear? Do you think that even a man of standing can undo such things tied to the measure of one's virtue or character?"

Miss Jeanne hugged Edward and rubbed his upper back while whispering, "You must remember, Edward, Elizabeth Ann was there in town for you and so was the man with whom you struck your bargain to return to Butterworth Hall. Go down there and speak to her and let her know that you are there for her no matter what she has done. Butterworth Hall will one day crumble into the dust of the earth, but your love for your child will span the ages set about by the heavens if you honor that love appropriately."

Edward kissed the lips of the thoughtful, caring and prescient woman and then turned to descend the steps of the porch and head down to the Laing's cottage to speak with his heartbroken daughter. Before he departed in earnest he asked of Miss Jeanne, "What of little Miss, will she be quite alright then?"

Miss Jeanne nodded wistfully and replied, "Yes Edward, in time she will be back to her old self. Elizabeth Ann will not fare as well if you do not watch over her now." Edward nodded in acceptance of Miss Jeanne's proposal and ran off into the biting west wind of late February as the skies continued to hasten in response to the whims of the night watch.

By the time the frantic Mr. Calhoun had made the bottom of the slope down to Miss Leslie's place, Elizabeth Ann was laying on her back amidst that high blowing chaff of late winter. Given the overcast skies and the absolute setting of the sun upon the moment of his progression down the slope, he did not see his daughter lying prostrate out upon the gently sloping hillside before he reached the front door to the Laing's cabin. He opened the plain wooden door rather hastily and began to call for Elizabeth Ann while looking throughout the few rooms of the small, single-level cabin that suited Miss Leslie, Mr. Laing and Little pea just fine. Seeing no sign of his daughter nor hearing any response from her upon concluding a cursory check of the settlement, Edward stepped back out onto the small, ground level porch at the front of the cabin and began calling out into the teeth of the wind, which was now whistling down the hill, for any sign of his daughter. "Elizabeth Ann! Elizabeth Ann! Where are you, my dear?" He received no response from out beyond the cavernous hollows of the night well-staid before his rapidly searching eyes.

The temperature continued to drop precipitously. Near to the way that it had on the night Margaret Anne was born. Edward remembered the depths of the cold of those early morning hours well. Such was in fact the only moment he could liken to the raw provisions of the current weather. He had been sitting out on the back patio of Butterworth Hall those thirteen years ago presently and awaiting word from one of his coachmen on how the affair of the child's birth had progressed. He nearly lost the fingers on both of his hands to frostbite on that cold and eternal evening he spent in wait and also watching for any of Miss Meara's henchmen moving about the grounds.

Elizabeth Ann remained lying flat on her back in the grass. She rested motionless while watching the intermittent patches of cottony white clouds stream by overhead, though they appeared as little more than shifting obstacles mount before the glimmering light of the stars. She had reached the depths of her trance set upon her by little Miss to root out the evil sprig so treacherously laced within the inner sanctums of her soul by that coarse and brutal Mr. Reed; the man or demon that had abused her thusly on the night she traded her virtue for the unrequited favor of Dr. Dawson back in Charleston. She felt so well and warm that she never once considered the possibility of frostbite or hypothermia while she lie there praising the few stars twinkling in the heavens in between the leisurely passing stratospheric clouds; those billowy and dreamlike nebulae which appeared to shift gently above the cover of the thin lower phalanxes of vapors racing across the sky at the prodding of the west wind, which was moving swift and low across the land. She heard her father calling from differing locations in front of the Laing's cabin. Be that as it may, she presumed his voice was merely part and parcel of that wonderful dream of her reconciliation with the celestial bodies above.

Making no progress in the dark and with no reason to presume his daughter was set down into the depths of the high grass, Edward raced back to the farmstead to solicit the advice of both Mr. O'Keefe, who had so graciously brought little Miss back to the house, and then Miss Jeanne. He made good time in returning to the farmstead, though he was rather frantic and difficult to understand when he arrived. Thankfully, Miss Jeanne and Maime took charge and began to provision for the recovery effort necessary to retrieve Elizabeth Ann from the teeth of the arctic winds cutting their way across the farmstead while also assuring that little Miss would remain well in hand in their absence.

Elizabeth Ann was eventually found by Mr. Laing, who was canvassing the hillside as part of a larger search party. She had remained exposed to the cold for some twenty minutes following Edward's initial abdication of his quest to speak with his daughter and the temperature had dropped into the single digits by that time. Though the young woman's facial skin was blue and her fingers purple, her eyes remained open and staring up into the passing clouds when old Shug

Laing picked her up off of the freezing grass, brought her into the cabin and set her down by the modest hearth. Shug then wrapped the frozen young woman in nearly every blanket within the cabin he could lay his meaty and frozen paws upon. Not but thirty minutes later, Elizabeth Ann fell off to sleep by the fire and did not awaken until the midnight hour. Her father had been sitting in the room with her checking her vitals from time to time as she thawed from her exposure to the harrowing winter winds and their harshly delivered and attendant cold snap.

When she awoke, her hands were dressed in Mr. Laing's stovepipe mitts. Though the sensation coming from her thawing hands could have been likened to that of some sort of burn to the flesh of her extremities that had remained exposed, she made no motion to free her hands or back away from the vigorously burning fire. She sensed that her father was present on the sofa behind her but she did not speak a word for quite some time upon returning to her senses. She simply watched the flames of the log burn in strange and repeating patterns of yellow, orange and blue until she fully understood the precious nature of the gift bestowed upon her by little Miss Margaret Anne.

After coming to terms with the beauty of the promised child's healing light, she spoke into the warmth, silence and flickering firelight of the quaint room. Elizabeth Ann did not turn to face her father while she spoke. "I am well, father. Thank you for coming to find me. I had no notion of the danger present to my perfectly still and hidden wares. Though you may not understand such a numinous conviction, the malice the wicked man seeded within my soul has been taken away by the promised child."

Elizabeth Ann then turned her shimmering blue eyes away from the fire light and toward her father while asking, "Is she well, father? She struck the wall with such force when she parted her hands from my own. The violence of the affair was beyond unsettling and so unjust due to the beauty of both her intentions and what she did for me. I had no prior notion that my heart had been infested thusly until she lifted his curse."

Edward looked down upon the young woman dressed in a winter blanket and now sitting in front of yet facing away from the fire and towards him. He could see a measured change in the shadowy lilt of her eyes and he answered her comfortingly while the undercurrent of his tone remained appropriately pensive. "Yes, Margaret Anne is well, my dear child. She has been set to rest in her bed after responding sensibly to both Mr. Laing and Doctor Bailey. Hopefully she will be just as she was by morning; just as she was before you two so unsettlingly ventured down here alone amidst the freeze."

Elizabeth Ann wrapped the loosened blanket, which had fallen behind her back some, tightly around her shoulders after freeing her hands from the impromptu mittens, as the bulky contraptions were far too clumsy for such an exercise. She then sat upon the cloth davenport next to her father and replied to his well-intended rebuke of the prior haste exhibited by both her and her sister. "I am truly sorry we caused you to worry over us, father. I will only presume that little Miss sensed I was in a bad way upon witnessing me make no headway in my attempts to enact amends with Mr. O'Keefe. She brought us down here to free me of the will of that accursed man, though I had no notion of the truth of such a thing until I felt her pull some phantasmal succubus from my soul by the very roots. Margaret Anne is an amazing creature, papa."

Edward smiled into the gilded half-light of the fire and replied warmly, "That she is, my dear, but so are you. All that has befallen you was of my accord. The things I wanted for were ultimately intended for the benefit of you ladies and Miss Jeanne. Be such as it may, if I had only understood before we embarked for Charleston that the blessings of the Lord above had already been provided in abundance and were waxing warm and true right before my very eyes, that heathen fiend would have possessed no claim upon either of our lives. Miss Jeanne warned me of his prowess and his potency, yet I did not listen and it has cost you so dearly, my sweet child. I should have come for you far sooner and I should never have stood so firmly between you and Mr. O'Keefe. Sadly, I cannot undo my misdeeds of the past. I am only able to hope that what has been set in motion will one day put an end to that man's foul curse upon mankind. I have wagered far more on the come to the advantage of such a result than I ever care to divulge."

Edward then flashed back to that awful moment Mr. Reed had taken possession of the innocence of his little girl and he shuddered violently in response. Elizabeth Ann still possessed a faint current of the light put into her by Margaret Anne. Therefore, when she placed her hand upon his own to calm him, the charge exploded like a static burst and wiped the vile scenery from his mind. Accordingly, Edward's heart was promptly settled for a time. At that moment, Edward truly believed that somehow and in spite of every obstacle mount against her, the child of the light would indeed endeavor to accomplish precisely what she had revealed to him that prior July.

Elizabeth Ann did not fully comprehend her father's final two statements. Nor would Edward have expected her to suitably ascertain his meaning at that moment in time based upon what had been made manifest to his daughter. Those words were left to her as scrawled markers; signposts as it were, which were to be understood only after the dust stirred up by these tumultuous affairs had long since settled out and her vantage point of the road they had travelled together was that of a far loftier perch. They were the words bestowed upon her thoughts now, in the event he was not present to respond when that which remained hidden from her eyes came into the light.

All the same, seeing the restful calm sweeping across her father's heretofore anxious brow, Elizabeth Ann set aside that which did not resonate with her current awareness and instead responded to her father's heart-rending apology. "Do not think of such things, father. We are both to blame for what became of us as we approached poverty back in the city. Where it concerns what we did to Virgil, those deeds of our self-righteous desire occurred long before we allowed ourselves to be bent to the will of that awful man. Moreover, you should not fret over Virgil. He has been made whole in accordance with due providence."

Edward glanced sidelong and rather quizzically at his daughter. He knew she did not know the hand of Margaret Anne had been pledged to an unknown scion of the Yankee cause in exchange for their return as a family to Butterworth Hall and the financing of his emergent business ventures. Therefore, Edward quite dubiously presumed Elizabeth Ann was speaking of the progression of the blossoming relationship between Virgil and Margaret Anne. To hide that truth, he spoke rather cryptically of the folly in seeing the intricate bond between Virgil and little Miss as a blessing upon Mr. O'Keefe. "I wish more were to come of the fondness little Miss and Mr. O'Keefe share for one another, yet she is only now of the marrying age while he is a well-developed man of some twenty years. I highly doubt Miss Jeanne would approve of the match beyond what they now share with one another."

Elizabeth Ann chuckled warmly in response to her father's suggestion. She was still giddy with the warmth of her sister's light traversing through the inner depths of her being and therefore not prone to any discernable measure of deception. "Such a match would certainly be quite the feather in Virgil's cap, father, though I suspect little Miss is not fit for the traditional ways of the world as we now know them. I highly doubt that any man would survive what she possesses inside."

Edward smiled a bit circumspectly, his eyes gleaming warily in the light of the fire in response to Elizabeth Ann's thoughts on the matter of Virgil and little Miss. He rightly sensed that there was something more that he lacked knowledge of lurking beneath his daughter's colorful annotation. "Such might very well be true, my dear. However, if you believe the young lady's future to be thus, how is it that Mr.

O'Keefe has been properly provisioned for as it regards our abuse of his loyal feelings towards us?"

Elizabeth Ann chuckled sweetly again while considering the marriage of Virgil and little Miss. She remained half entranced by the aft light of her purification when she replied rather candidly, "Because father, with Aubrey now passed away, my male child of Virgil's siring is set to be your proper heir to the continuity of the Calhoun legacy. Little Miss spoke to me of as much."

Edward jumped from the sofa like a man having unknowingly sat upon a sharpened nail and proclaimed, "What is this heinous tomfoolery of which you speak, dear child! The man will not speak to you yet you declare that you are with his child!"

Elizabeth Ann giggled innocently again and replied warmly, "Of course, father. The only shame in the truth of it is that Virgil will never stand to know, or perhaps believe, what little Miss drove from my soul and thus never forgive me for the terrible sins of my past. I am willing to accept his indifference toward me if the cause of such has resulted in my bringing forth the legacy of you both into the world."

Edward quickly realized that his daughter was not yet well from the aftereffects of her exposure to the promised child. He had experienced as much firsthand and he knew well the irrational euphoria that accompanied the touch of her charged hand. As such, he sat back down next to her and they talked through the matter calmly and then lovingly. Though Edward knew she spoke the truth on the matter of her pregnancy after a certain portion of the deliberations had concluded, he also knew she was not ready to face the truth of what was to come as she prepared to bring an illegitimate child, which the father of said child could never know about, into the confines of Butterworth Hall or the world at large. When the smoke had cleared from the excitement of the evening, Edward would have the young woman speak to Miss Jeanne about her condition. For he had correctly presumed that he possessed no proper standing to either condemn or advise his favored child on the suitable meting out of such a firmly seeded scandal in wait. Furthermore, it was simply one of many sordid affairs that now belonged to the recent legacy of the much maligned young woman.

Some years later and a few years after the birth of Francis Virgil Calhoun in early October of 1872, on Sunday, December 27, 1874 to be red letter of the law precise, Virgil O'Keefe and Margaret Anne Basseterre got wind of Edward's promised vow to marry off his illegitimate daughter to Mr. Jacob Asher Bromley of Vermont on the occurrence of her sixteenth birthday. Miss Jeanne had tragically passed on less than a week prior in a rather mysterious and completely unexpected fashion on the night before Miss Shy Basseterre Brown's 26th birthday. Coincidentally to the events behind her mother's death or not, Miss Shy had also been to town for an extended visit over the Thanksgiving holidays of that same year due to difficulties of a domestic variety back in Augusta. What was clear concerning the events ambient to little Miss's discovery of her quite unexpected or at least heretofore unacknowledged forthcoming nuptials was that the details behind the secretive plans were bluntly delivered to both her and Virgil by Miss Shy on that final Sunday evening of 1874.

Virgil and little Miss were quite close by that time and had tempted the status of their sibling style relationship by bussing daintily in the way of would be sweethearts every now and again when they would part ways for the evening while standing waist high in the blossoming bounty of the summer cotton. Those few kisses were little more than the brushing of dried out lips charged with only the salt of a tiring day out in the field. Little Miss had remained indifferent to such harmless displays of affection that did not seem to trigger her still convalescent inner light in the hours of her fatigue. Likewise, Virgil struggled in attempting to further those trifling amorous experiments beyond that stage due to his brotherly affections for the stunning and elfishly pure young woman.

In those years following Elizabeth Ann's discreet yet permanent retreat to Butterworth Hall in the aftermath of her unwed pregnancy, Virgil had taken on plenty of help out in the fields of his little cooperative. There were scores of freed men wandering about Uriah in search of sharecropping work and Virgil O'Keefe would have hired them all on if he could have afforded to do so. Such was especially true once the new state government in Columbia had rendered it near to impossible, through the implementation of post Reconstruction Era legislation and the proliferation of segregation, for those of color without significant resources to procure an arable patch of land of their own.

Virgil treated all of his people exceptionally well. Moreover, after his disturbing lessons in both inexperience around proper intimacy with a lady and the consequences of not partaking in the manlier affairs of life following his humiliation at the hands of Elizabeth Ann, he took to drinking heavily and gambling on those rare occasions that the moon was full and the work due upon the hours of the daybreak was manageable. On those raucous evenings, Virgil put on his Sunday best and proceeded to consort with the looser sorts who came to work out on the farm for a span no longer than the passing of a season. In fact, by January of 1875, Virgil had crossed over into the other side of town by the light of the plenilune often enough that he was known by the majority of the church going folk in Uriah as something of a cocksure, though clandestine and infrequent, ladies' man with a preference for the free-spirited women of any persuasion with whom he took his whiskey.

Consequently, the still young man of twenty-three years who had devised the plan to marry Miss Margaret Anne Basseterre in an effort to circumvent the prior promises of her legal guardian, and in truth her blood mother; though they were promises only once given by the Haitian countess to in effect save the skin of her sometime paramour of the last seventeen years, was not the same man of woeful inexperience that had escorted the radiant yet dishonored society gal, Elizabeth Ann Calhoun, to the New Year's Eve ball back in Uriah in 1871. This rendition of Virgil O'Keefe was a revel hard work harder gentleman. His only cherished belief, esteemed above either of the two sides of that simple yet antithetically and authentically decorated coin, which represented the totality of his life out on the farm, was the protection of the angel who presently stood in for the sister that was so brutally taken from him near to the end of the war. As such, adapting to the particulars of marriage given the history of his relationship with Margaret Anne was to be near to impossible for one with the past traumas of Mr. O'Keefe, at least where it concerned the few women he once loved in his brief life.

Following a trying outcry amongst the promised child's surviving guardians and relatives still back on or tied to the farm, an outcry between those in favor and those set against Virgil's proposal of marriage, though the only sustained verbal objection came from the mouth of little Miss's other brother of both sentiment and situational circumstance, yet who was not a blood relation to the promised child, Mr. Amos Martingale Laing, the two were married by the lawful albeit not practicing Pastor Shug Laing of Uriah all the way out in Silver Bow, South Carolina on Sunday, January 31, 1875. The 'family' row over the contentious betrothal became so lively and drew so close to revealing some of those frightful skeletons buried deep within the closet of the by that time doggedly rebranded Calhoun family, in addition to letting the sun shine down upon other delectable sundries of dubious portent to high ranking officials back in both Sumter and Columbia, that eventually Miss Shy, and thankfully not too long thereafter, her briefly orphaned children, all found themselves exiled to or at least living in Haiti a little over a year after the whole sordid affair of little Miss's solitary legally binding marriage began to take shape.

Poor George Ridley Brown, with his not entirely immaterial gathering of worldly assets, which was all the more impressive when measured against the diminutive wealth of his colored contemporaries of the day, perhaps suffered the worst of it in the aftermath of his wife's openly speaking in regard to certain family secrets pertaining to the promised child. The hard drinking man about Augusta town turned up dead of the drink and was discovered in said condition scandalously intertwined within the long and luxurious extremities of another also senseless, though only comatose, intemperate by the name of Miss Lucinda Bowers. While being caught bang to rights in the bed of a notoriously provocative woman and dead of the drink to boot were certainly happenings that were a bit circumspect for a man so well versed in plying the routine of his self-indulgent trade, of an equivalently bizarre nature were the proclamations of many that somehow linked Miss Shy to the untimely demise of her shamelessly cavorting husband.

In any event, Miss Shy was ultimately sent forth to the shores of Haiti to begin the divinely inspired task of properly adhering to the only marginally encumbered bullion stocks of the Jeanne Basseterre Trust, which was simply a timely and lightly modified continuation of the enduring Trust of Evelyn Elaine de Carrefour and Katherine Evelyn Elaine de Jacmel, both one in the same. To Miss Shy's amazement, the Carrefour Trust had been established by Andre de Basseterre in exacting accordance with the dying wishes of Cesar Maduro de Bilbao, just as her mother had told her when she spun her lavish yarn of the history of the golden cross. In fact, every last morsel of information her mother had conveyed to her pertaining to that ancient treasure of theretofore only spoken lore had checked out exquisitely with the fiduciaries and the once legendary Caribbean goldsmiths of Haiti. Irrespective of the aforementioned and in conjunction with her mother's wishes and proper tradition, the often woefully beset and once again Miss Basseterre never spoke of the treasure to anyone, until by manner of perfected rite she dutifully passed the golden cross on to her twelve-year old son Andre in 1883 when she was released from prison. The warmly executed ceremony attended to by none but a mother and her child occurred some three years after Miss Shy had physically tendered the relic over to Andre's care upon commencing with that first of her two Haitian prison terms back in early 1880.

The night of the honeymoon of Mr. Virgil Denton O'Keefe and Miss Margaret Anne Basseterre, both of Uriah, South Carolina, was spent just across the river and a ways on up to the north from the site of their secretive wedding. The establishment of some local renown, The Sentinel Hotel of Augusta to be exact, was one that would forever live in infamy after the small hours of that first morning of February had come to pass. Following some aperitifs, the newlyweds dined and followed up their mouthwatering meal by taking in a mélange of rather prodigious cocktails with a few friends of the already moderately blackballed Miss Shy before returning to their room in a state of celebratory disarray. Virgil and little Miss both were hastily overcome by the uncertainty of what was intended to follow upon arriving within the confines of their secluded quarters.

Margaret Anne had never touched alcohol before and certainly not the anti-fragmatic the honeymooners had been sampling that evening. She was unaccustomed to operating in such a way by which her always prescient premonitions or extrasensory perceptions were rendered ineffectual. As such, she did not pick up on Virgil's drunken and obstinate need to properly consummate the marriage earlier on in the evening. In fact, when the initial mechanics of their intimacy began to progress, Margaret Anne was quite pleased by the suddenly cogent carnal and emotional sensations that seemed to be amplified by her intoxication, which in turn seemed to deaden her usual reconciliation of and control over the powerful tremoring of her inner light. She had been drained of that light for a time following the exorcism of that nascent yet frightfully potent and maliciously virulent spawn of the darkest order taking root within the pith of Elizabeth Ann. Tonight however, and some three years removed from the affairs of that trying ordeal, the promised child's inner light was once again teeming within and bristling with charged currents of pent up electricity waiting peevishly to be set upon its supernally intended coursings.

The two carried on like a normal married couple that had been thusly repressed by the piety of virtue prior to being wed until they reached the point of consummation. Only at that time and rather unfortunately for the both of them, did Margaret Anne's internal alarm bells begin to siren in the proper warnings of the disaster set to ensue. She suddenly shot back to the state of her usual coherency and declared, "Virgil, you mustn't! Though I would freely give all that I am over to you in the name of your sacrifice alone, I am not meant for such a soulful union of the flesh in my current condition. I am but the nectar glistening within the confines of a deadly snare."

Virgil was good and drunk by that point in the evening and well beyond the point of no return as went the typical brothel parlance of the day. He scratched his head doubtfully while the rest of his bodily wares remained trembling at the ready. He was not to accept such a denial on the night of his own wedding in his current state. "Oh, don't you go a worryin' none, Maggie. I ain't no ignoramus like how I used to be when I done went through it and den some with your sister."

Virgil then inched his way closer to the point of the event horizon but Margaret Anne abruptly shielded the gateway to his promised oasis and answered back sharply, "You don't understand, Virgil. Such a thing simply cannot be. I am so sorry I let things get so far along. Please, do forgive me! I possessed no tolerance for the spell of the drink!"

Virgil shook his head in a bemused manner as the visions of Elizabeth Ann's varying forms of treachery ran through his trenchant mind. He grew desultory and obstinate while answering back snidely, "You ain't gonna need to be forgiven for a thing, my darlin', 'cuz we's married now."

With that, the young man moved swiftly and aggressively to take that which he felt now belonged to him in his appallingly altered and woefully bereft state of mind. Not even a one of the ladies out watching him throw the bones had ever told him no. Certainly, it was not possible that his bride would try and entertain such an absurdity on the very night of their given nuptials. "Virgil, no! You must stop! You don't understand!" were the final words the promised child beckoned frightfully in the direction of her husband. After they were spoken, the seal separating the boundaries of their humanity had been broken and the marriage was consummated by law.

Upon the moment of the finality of his rather abrupt transgression, Virgil seized up as if he had been razed square in the head by a lightning bolt sent from the heavens above the firmament. He retreated quickly from his ill-advised position and fell back against the wall standing beyond the end of the bed. The numbing electric current travelling throughout his body and roaring like some savage mania of infinite incoherency throughout the vaulted hollows of his mind did not yield, even upon his sudden acquiescence to his bride. He grew maddened with rage as he could not stop the exploding tingles or the rifling sensations screaming throughout his body and scattering any and all reason within his thoughts. The raging feeling of utter madness and unbound overindulgence set fire to his skin and the nerves behind his eyes. The tendons and muscles within his limbs pulsated wildly, as if he had just arisen arisen from the bloodless sleep of a thousand years.

Virgil turned away from the bed and clutched at his face. The overwhelming feeling of the exquisite torture that would not end and his shame over violating the most precious gift his life had ever known overwhelmed his fraying essence. He remained beyond mortal consolation or bodily reprieve until his quivering hand took hold of the silver pistol resting on the bed stand and the business end of the barrel pushed into the soft flesh lining the underside of his mandible. Her hands had covered her eyes but she hoped he would dislodge the trigger before his thoughts grew darker and his soul was emptied of the light.

He complied commendably amidst his continuing fits of madness until the top of his skull was painted onto the ceiling above and the bullet shot from his silver pistol entered the bottom of the whiskey tumbler of the couple copulating on the floor above. Though the look set upon the dead man's face, with its hollowed-out cheeks and pallid, macabre flesh, in addition to its eyeballs melting like candlewax into the horrid forms of those drooping lower eyelids, spoke of another message altogether when the authorities had arrived, Margaret Anne smiled warmly. She smiled warmly while her delicately sculpted forefinger ever so gently grazed the hardened callouses covering the palms of his sturdy, farm boy hands in the knowing that Virgil O'Keefe had left those horrors of his past behind and stepped swiftly into the light. The young man had been fiercely loyal to a fault and remained dreadfully stricken by the horrors of his past. Though the promised child had no intention of cleansing Virgil of those phantoms of yesteryear and seeing him off to the ethereal realms, such was a far better outcome for the fastidious yet savagely wild young man than had things progressed otherwise while she ventured onward to meet with her appointed destiny.

On Monday, February 15th, 1875 Doctor Emmett Bailey and Mr. Edward Christopher Calhoun were at last permitted to enter the Augusta jail to visit the prisoner while accompanied by Mr. Darley June Haskell, Esquire. When Mrs. Margaret Anne O'Keefe entered the cold and drab visitation cell in her oversized boiler suit with the rather recognizable white and light blue stripes, she was still a sight to behold. She had grown tall in the elegant and not overbearing manner like her mother as she approached the now dubious marker of her 16th birthday. Her lush brown hair had been set into twin French braids that ran down past the backs of her shoulders. Her light eyes of shifting color, though predominantly flashing amber at the moment, set against her only lightly tanned winter skin shimmered radiantly with that inner light of hers. She approached the standing gentleman with that trademark look of bemusement set upon her spritely yet somehow also classically gracious mien, which gleamed at the cheeks and the rounded tip of her nose with the gloss of her inner shine.

Doctor Bailey understood the look Margaret Anne now possessed to be the tell of the young woman's internal compartmentalizing and realigning of her thoughts to compel spoken notions more akin to how these three men standing before her would so strangely look at the truth of the world under the guise of the inauspicious circumstances of the last few weeks. He greeted the beautiful prisoner warmly and hugged her tightly. "Good morning, my precious angel of the light! We have been worried so over your condition in such a place! Have they treated you well since the confusing turmoil of your arrest?" He was about to offer his condolences for the inhumed condition of Mr. O'Keefe but thought better of being the one to introduce such a live topic so suddenly. Doc had taken to the bright-eyed boy from the moment Virgil had first arrived at his office in Sumter while delivering his Cap'm to safety following the skirmish down at Dingle's Mill.

Margaret Anne hugged Doctor Bailey in return. In such a lonely place as this, it was quite comforting to see the last of her surviving and mentally fit guardians of this world as so ordained by the spirits of the west wind and the tormented souls of the February Cabin of her birth. She smiled wide, as if all was suddenly right with the world again, and replied, "Why yes, my most gracious Doctor Bailey. They have treated me well yet my confinement to the indoors is a burden upon my soul that is beyond the station of troubling. Still and all, the pleasure of seeing you does warm my heart so! You look exceedingly well! How are Miss Eustice, Lily Grace and darling Emmaline?"

Before Doctor Bailey could respond and in keeping with the limitations set upon his precious time, Mr. Haskell stepped over to the young lady, made his very polite and proper introductions, offered his condolences for the miserable fate of her husband, and then proceeded to question her in a rather rhetorical or perhaps simply confirming manner. "I presume you wish to stand for a plea of innocence regarding the serious charges set against you, Ma'am."

Margaret Anne looked curiously at the rather wormy appearing gentleman and answered him plainly enough yet with an unexpected design tied to her spoken thoughts. "The prosecutorial delegation advises me that the primary charge leveled against me is that of the murder of my husband. How does any good woman or even a bride of only hours accept innocence in the matter of her betrothed taking his own life, my dear Mr. Haskell? I would hold your hand and read your offered thoughts to save you some of that time you so urgently esteem, but alas poor Virgil has consumed so much of me that I would presently be found wanting in attempting to effect the exercise."

Margaret Anne then turned her eyes away from the presently grimacing barrister, smiled thoughtfully in the direction of the drab limestone of the ceiling and rejoined her prior thought by coyly offering up a mocking suggestion, "I have been pondering the matter some, Mr. Haskell. Perhaps we shall instead plead negligence in the handling of our divinely ordained blessings over the accusation of murder? Certainly the state cannot presume to punish me for driving the man mad with little more than the light of the angels designed for far darker principalities than the poor, honest, loyal and most certainly broken man my husband was."

Edward had been staring out between the bars of the only window in the room, which was primarily used for prisoner interrogation and meetings of the accused with counsel, such as today's gathering was. He was deep in thought while she gave her rather curious reply but he sensed where the young woman who possessed no capacity to lie was headed with her response. He needed the feisty young lady to trim back her wick some while addressing Mr. Haskell or much would be compromised. Margaret Anne was upset and what had become of Virgil had been anticipated by none.

As such, Edward stepped smartly away from the window and walked up in between the modestly aggressive barrister and Margaret Anne. He then spoke firmly to the thinly configured man who would be the young lady's sanctioned counsel. "There will be no need for all of that showmanship, Mr. Haskell. The young lady has been offered the provision of her release in exchange for the honoring of a promise set to come due in but a few weeks' time. There will be little record of anything let alone the entering of a plea to stand trial." Edward then smiled while he shaded his guise to favor his right side to address Margaret Anne and asked of her, "How does such a settlement sound to you, my dearest?"

Mr. Haskell turned his stark, brown eyes away from Mr. Calhoun and slowly backpedaled his deficient frame into the far corner of the room to regather his thoughts. For his part, Doctor Bailey returned to his seat at the small table in the middle of the room. He was quite satisfied with allowing the situation between Margaret Anne and her father to draw down for a while before he would intervene. There was already much to consider according to his proximate reckoning of the affair and beyond that, far more to reflect upon than he would possibly come to realize upon that sitting.

Miss Margaret Anne replied flatly to Edward's offer and gestured indifferently in the manner of one thoroughly unimpressed by the man's ostensibly remarkable solution to her present quandary. "I know what it is that you are offering me, Edward. The supposition is the same as it was before Virgil and I lost our minds trying to escape from all that you have so graciously arranged on my behalf. I also know what is at stake for you and why mother initially consented to the match, though later changed her stance. As she is now among the dearly departed, the burden of consent belongs to you." Margaret Anne paused for a brief moment, shifted her captivating lineaments into that of an outwardly pensive guise and then asked, "Did you think that I would oppose your will while you remain under such duress, Edward?"

Edward turned to face the open wall of bars that lined the inner boundary of the dank and middling-sized room that seemed to secrete the desolate emotion of the cold stone, brick and iron of which it was fabricated. He spoke away from the promised child yet he spoke with remorse riddling the cascading undercurrents of his somber tone. "I am truly sorry about what happened to Virgil, dearest child. I did love the boy like my country son. I had hoped to ask for his forgiveness one day in response to my lack of refinement in attempting to sort through the sudden clashing of our worlds."

Having said his piece regarding the dearly departed, Edward shifted his eyes back to Margaret Anne and spoke with a bit more aplomb, "However, my dear. We cannot change what has come to pass. We must now look to the promise of your bright future away from these dour walls that you find so suffocating to your tender spirit. If the knowing of such may ease your grief any, I am told Mr. Bromley is a good man and that the match is destined to be filled with love and unimaginable prosperity. His industrial ventures seem to know no bounds where it concerns their expansion and their notable margins of profit."

Doctor Bailey was about to rise from the table in objection to such blatant supposition but Margaret Anne signaled playfully with her fluid eyes for the good doctor to remain seated. Thusly, the irritated doctor did remain where he was situated and made no objection. Little Miss turned back to her lawyer, who was now pacing thoughtfully in the far corner of the cell, and asked, "How long will I be destined to remain here if I seek the path of clearing my good name, Mr. Haskell?"

Darley Haskell approached the young woman and replied to her question quite sternly. "That is difficult to say, Miss Basseterre. The time needed for a proper capital murder trial could take up to a year and the judge has already unequivocally denied our request for bail to be set in any amount. His rather harsh ruling was ascribed to the severity of the charges brought against you and the flight risk associated with your current legal status as a colored citizen of South Carolina. However, you do face a far more serious problem than even that, Mrs. O'Keefe; with my apologies now being offered for referring to you as Miss Basseterre earlier."

Miss Margaret Anne smiled whimsically at the middle-aged barrister such that the man grew uneasy given the weight of what he had just revealed to her. She then asked of him rather directly for effect, "And what exactly may said problem be, Mr. Haskell?"

Mr. Haskell slid his eyes away from the intensity of the naturally pretty prisoner's tightening glare and replied, "The current political climate does not favor you or your predicament, my lady. Those whose opinions matter around these districts somehow seem to know that you are blood sister to Miss Shy Brown and therefore also a woman of color according to your proper lineage. A few may also suspect that Edward is your father and unfortunately, Mr. Calhoun is a man of endearing infamy to some of the most powerful men on this side of the river."

Mr. Haskell then turned back to face his calmly postured client and offered up the remainder of his sobering discourse. "Many here in Georgia are now using brutal methods to establish the new boundaries of race through openly enforced segregation across the state. Those opposing you, whomever they might be, will foment the locals to despise you such that they will not relent until you are dangling from a rope in the town square for the murder of a hard working white man. In the eyes of those men looking to sharply define the living reality of the new racial order here in Georgia, nothing trumps the offering up of the spectacle of a very public hanging; a very public hanging of one such as you are for the benefit of those of color that may remain, how shall we say, a bit confused by the proper meaning of emancipation.

That is about as plain as I am able to rightly convey the situation to you, Ma'am."

"I see, Mr. Haskell. Thank you for making my untenable position so very clear to us all," replied the prisoner rather smugly when compared to her rather innocent and therefore obliviously direct habitual nature.

Margaret Anne then turned playfully toward Mr. Calhoun and asked rather whimsically of the quite concerned albeit sternly presented man, "What say you to these frightful claims made by the clever carpet bagging man you have propositioned for the favor of my defense, Edward? Am I little more than a murderous woman of color purchased unwittingly by her own namesake for more than any other slave to go before the auctioneer, just as those looking to promote their agenda are presumed likely to say? Or am I simply a misunderstood phantom of the light sent off to be born in a flogging cabin in the middle woods? No wait, perhaps I am the daughter of the woman born of the island easterlies that possessed the whims of your heart before your soul was sold away to the principalities of the darkness, and for little more in return than the proliferation of the accursed confines of that old estate back in Sumter."

Edward muttered something unintelligible in the manner of one set to interject but the young woman spoke harshly over his fumbling utterances. "No, you hold that thought safe for but the passing of a moment, Edward. For I now know who it is that I am. I am the pregnant wife of the man so ruined by your sale of your white daughter to some frothing heathen of the flesh that upon reaping the pureness of the light from within he took his pistol to his chin to put a halt to the madness splintering every last belief he once held dear."

At that, Mr. Haskell had heard quite enough and knew when it was time to take his leave. He addressed them all upon departing the holding cell. "To be quite clear, Madam you should take the offer and do so smartly. With that, you all have my dutiful and diligent opinion on the matter. I will certainly defend the young lady with the very last drop of my legal capacity and fortitude if that is what you all decide is best; against the whims of my better counsel of course. I will await word of your decision out front while you speak confidentially amongst one another." Mr. Haskell then picked his hat up off of the table and signaled for the guard to open up the barred gate to the ancient prison's interrogation room.

When Mr. Haskell was heard exiting the adjoining hallway through the bars of the makeshift cell of a sort, Edward did finally reply to his daughter's harsh suppositions concerning his prior conduct. However, both her tone and her uncharacteristically catty conduct had driven the shrewd man into a far more defensive posture. "My dear, I understand the depths of your anger centered upon my actions of the past. Surely you know that I had nothing to do with what happened to your mother. As you have so bluntly made known to all then present, she was indeed and forever will be the one great countess of my heart. Yes, the circumstances behind your upbringing have been both unfair and unsuitable at times for one so blessed by the gracious heavens above as you are. But do understand that your grandmother was a powerful woman before you placed a hold upon whatever dark spell was controlling her. She wanted you dead or consumed by her dark order on the night you were born. Doctor Bailey has certainly spoken to you in the past regarding as much."

Edward paused and paced back toward the far wall and its solitary squared window to the outside world. When Margaret Anne said nothing in reply, he continued on with the long overdue bearing of his soul directly for the benefit of the promised child. He spoke in a clear and squarely penitent tone. "Your escape from your grandmother's hired man, thanks to the sacrifice of Elizabeth Ann, was how I came to purchase you down in Savannah when you were but a few days old. I had no notion of who you were when the fates offered Mr. Sommers and I provision by which to take possession of you and return you to your divinely intended home."

Edward then turned fully away from Margaret Anne while she studied him scrupulously to understand the absolute truth of his intent. The man suddenly twisting in the wind as it were, once again looked out through the barred window of the cell. He carefully watched the rushing currents of the Savannah River making their way down to the coastal city, which was also the tributary's namesake, though the thought had just dawned upon him that perhaps those names had passed from one entity to the other in much the same manner as the steadily flowing currents of the river ran so timelessly from the mountains out to the sea.

Upon allowing a fair bit of time to pass and hearing no objections from those present at his back, Edward continued on with his statement of contrition. However, from that point onward and for no discernable reason outside of one that perhaps the promised child might pick up on, Mr. Calhoun offered up his spoken expressions of regret in only the antiseptic tone of one delivering half-measures, those formal treatises that had so often come to replace his bent toward heartfelt remorse since he had returned permanently to the old plantation estate; returned and so thoroughly cleaned house back where the home fires were now once again burning in a suitable fashion. The change in his outlook and the almost menacing subtleties shaded within his tenor while addressing the sins of his past did not go unnoticed by either member of his audience. One of his listeners understood what it was Edward Calhoun was trying to accomplish and the other did not. Such was precisely as Edward had intended.

"However, my dear child, I believe that we have all done the best that we were able to by you under the conditions given over to us at the time. I had no plans to force you to accept the esteemed Mr. Bromley's proposal and clearly your mother did not either. Yet when that day of you glorious wedding arrives, you will shortly thereafter see all of the wonderful things that have been provisioned for you and your progeny. In all honesty, my dear girl; as things now stand, Mr. Bromley's ability to advocate for your undisclosed release from this horrible stanchion to none but the depraved has turned out to be a hidden blessing."

The one who understood the true nature Edward's ever so subtly revealed ruse responded in kind. "You know, Edward, both Mr. Lemarque and Black Jim were through the farm to visit and make a few dollars back near to the end of the last harvest season. Such would appear that you left the two gentlemen in dire straits upon Miss Meara's passing. Is such a man of color provoking the intentions of your eldest daughter far too much for you to endure in the restored state of your former glory?"

Edward turned back sharply from the window and stepped in a measured manner towards his now insolent daughter. He rejoined her harshly but with his standard gentlemanly airs still intact. "Do you not recall that Mr. Lemarque had betrayed us all on the night you confronted your grandmother? The man is rather fortunate that he still breathes. As for Black Jim, I presume his service to my mother in revealing to her the true nature of your origin was compelled and not offered willingly. Because I have no obligation to the man, I freed him to take his leave. Shall I instead have them both stretch for what they did to you, my dear?"

"Of course not, you arrogant man," Margaret Anne shot back as testily as she could manage. Yes, you indeed did free them both, Edward. You freed them without a dime in their pockets to procure the slightest morsel of provision. You left them penniless after all they had done to see me back to you. Furthermore, you received me in exchange for the insignificant cost measured as little more than that of the entirety of your coin purse set aside for the procurement of chattel. You never endured anything near to the mortal dangers those two men withstood for the sake of my deliverance!"

Margaret Anne then sharpened her eyes on Mr. Calhoun and began to slowly approach him in such a way that even Doctor Bailey's nerves began to jitter as he watched her doggedly from his seated position at the table. She spoke rather darkly as the man standing before her retreated slowly back toward the solitary barred window carved within the brickwork of the far wall of the cell.

"Regardless of your harsh treatment of those men, Edward, they both seemed to be quite convinced that the debonair aristocrat who first fell in with the manifest demons of this world while his heart still beat warm and soft, like that of a man, was no longer recognizable to the eyes of either gentleman. Have you indeed fallen so far as all of that, Mr. Edward Calhoun or were those simply the words of desperate and spiteful men? I know the truth of it because that is why I am here; to guide you where you chose to go and furthermore, to remove a lasting curse from the land. Though there is so much more I could offer to you all, those who believe in the primacy of the darkness as both governor and primal arbiter in this near faithless world of men will never understand or therefore accept the possibilities of the workings of the light. You have been consorting with those who relish in the pangs of torment and suffering for far too long already, dearest Edward. Yet, I want to hear the truth of your will and the current station of your heart spoken directly into my waiting ears from those now cold and scaly lips of yours."

Edward stopped where he was and stood his ground. Quite possibly because he had but a Mississippi half-step left to retreat toward the hoary, kilned brickwork of the outer prison wall. He understood that if the world was to remain as he had once again sculpted it to his favor for those requiring the benefit of his grace, that he and the presently hot tongued woman were to remain adversaries. That discovery was a strange realization for even such a cunning and harshly calculating man when dealing with one of his own flesh and blood.

Back when he had feuded with Mary Grice, he understood the greed rooted beneath the tenets of her betrayal. He also understood that she would shift her loyalties on a dime to the one that could satisfy the material and societal privilege of her wants. The impetus behind this creature of the light, which now appeared as some darkly shaded imp of the woodlands whence she was reared, he no longer, at least visibly, comprehended in the least. He tried to lie to her without revealing even the slightest of pantomimes that would undo his credibility while Doc watched on with that meticulous eye of his. If Edward's words had been spoken to a mere mortal given over to the traditional analytical limitations of the horribly shunted human mind of our age, he would have succeeded in covering his lie.

"I am but the same man you have always known, my dear child. I have made my mistakes in the past as it regards you all. Yet I now proceed from a far superior position, though admittedly, my improving fortunes do remain of an extremely delicate standing. There is a growing hatred for the coloreds being sparked in our time and the resultant flames are presently and quite tenaciously being fanned by the darkest of men among us. In time, such burning hatred will grow so dire you will welcome the day both you and Mr. O'Keefe were spared the fallout of such a poorly thought through arrangement."

"The nation remains united but the old girl is now duly beholden to her creditors in paying for the war. Those administrating over the fallout and the enormity of the bill come due have no interest in seeing a united brotherhood of properly sovereign Americans living in a land where the color of a man's skin means little more than the chosen spelling of his given name. You, who are of two worlds even here on earth, will fare far better in the North, where there is an established faction that supports our brothers and sisters of a decidedly African descent and where the war and their resultant freedom is considered a victory. The hatred of man is set to burn far less intensely in those Yankee quarters of your new home."

Margaret Anne stepped directly in front of Mr. Calhoun. Although she did not explicitly question the verity of his assumptions buttressing both the current condition of his heart or the danger she faced if she were to depart these bloodstained walls and remain where she was known to all, she inferred through her tone her lack of commitment to the belief in either supposition. Subsequent to her rebuttal, she raised her hand to place it on Edward's chest but the man standing before her flinched in an ungainly manner and interjected sharply with a vehement yet backpedaling objection, "There is no need for any of that, my dear child! I promise you that I am quite fine!"

Edward then laughed nervously while Margaret Anne slowly retracted her hand and replied to his rather boisterous insistence with an eerie calm, "There is one choice left to be made, Edward. I can heal you now or you can send me up North to marry a man I have never set eyes upon while I am in the way with the child of the same man who delivered unto you your heir by way of Elizabeth Ann. Such is all the same to me, as I am always and forever tendered over to the care of those who sent me. But do know this Edward, if you choose to send me away the blackness settling in your heart will be a curse upon the house of Calhoun until the day one of the line within me burns it to the dust of the earth and scatters the ashes to the four winds."

Edward rather precipitously circled around the table and away from Margaret Anne while acting as if it were essential that he put his hands upon the shoulders of Doctor Bailey. Mr. Calhoun then indirectly petitioned that silent man by way of his continuing pleas delivered in earnest to Margaret Anne. Doc was in fact doing little but watching along with such focus and discernment when Edward took a forceful hold of his haunches and announced for the benefit of all, "I am sorry, my dear but it has become readily apparent to me that you are quite stricken by the loss of Mr. O'Keefe. Any sensible woman would give thanks for the opportunity to keep such a beautiful neck from being stretched upon the gallows out in the square. Tell her, Doctor Bailey! Please talk some sense into the maddened creature!"

Doctor Bailey closed his eyes and uttered not a sound in response to Edward's haphazard and aggressive plea for relief. Margaret Anne filled the gap of her guardian's silence and replied cattily to Mr. Calhoun.

"Am I stricken in such a way that I will agree to honor the legacy of the man who betrayed me thrice by in turn dishonoring the legacy of the child of an honest man who so kindly and lovingly looked after me all these years; all these years while you were off trying to reassemble a cracked egg without the use of some form of black magic until you came to realize the futility of such a thing. Your own faulty presumptions are what sound like madness to me, Edward."

Edward lowered his eyes to the floor and made his final play in a level-headed fashion. "Unfortunately the option to honor the child of Mr. O'Keefe is no longer available to you, my dear. If you remain here, the best you can hope for is that the child will be born in the very prison set to undo you for the murder of your unborn child's father. The man who owns the one that seeks your hand up North will make certain of that. His bloodlines are of the creditor class. Said otherwise, those of that dark man's dark breed are the ones party to the creditor agreement set about up in Washington in seventy-one. The courts and the magistrates are beholden to them all and also the crown by way of the incorporation of the postbellum government. You will never leave this place until you hang if you chose to fight them, my dear."

For the first time in her life, the promised child began to cry in response to any circumstance of her human condition. Such a visible spectacle was only for the darkening fate of her unborn child. The emotional pangs of nascent motherhood had brought her far closer to the essence of her humanity than she had ever been prior to that moment. While she wept, she begged sweetly of Edward Calhoun, "Promise me I shall step foot before Virgil's grave before I am delivered into the strange precincts of the northlands. I presume he has been appropriately laid to rest back with his beloved sister and parents in Florence."

As Edward postured that he was too afraid to touch the broken child, Doctor Bailey stood up from the table and hugged the precious creature dearly while whispering in her ear, "Of course you shall visit the grave of your beloved, my dear. Nothing of the heavens or the earth shall hinder me from delivering upon such a promise to you."

Edward twisted nervously over by the window. While he was not enamored with the slight detour made as a late amendment to his envisioned plans for the transfer of the promised child to the Green Mountains of Vermont, he realized that fulfilling Doctor Bailey's now spoken promise to her was a necessary caveat. Particularly in light of the additional wrinkle of the young woman's pregnancy, which would need to remain forever shaded from both Mr. Bromley and Mr. Reed. While he watched the steady current of the river run toward its mouth along the coast of the Atlantic Ocean, he added something special, unsolicited and of his own accord to Doctor Bailey's promise for sporting measure. "Of course we will make certain that you visit the grave of your beloved Virgil, my dear. Beyond that, we will see to it that the marker is adorned with the salutations of a war hero for his saving of my life back at Dingle's Mill."

On Wednesday, February 24th, 1875 the entirety of the living contingent of the promised child's over watch assembled by Edward Calhoun back before that Christmas season of 1864 attended a formal funeral service. The lovely outdoor service was held in honor of the posthumously decorated Civil War hero, Mr. Virgil Denton O'Keefe and his family out at the sustenance farm where Virgil's forever beloved kin were killed by Sherman's men marching through South Carolina. In addition to Adelaide, Mr. Satterfield even brought Miss Sarah over to Florence from the asylum outside of Sumter. Beyond those folks mentioned heretofore, of course Mrs. Shiloh Jolie Basseterre Osment-Brown, Miss Maime Alouette Basseterre Osment, Little pea and many from the Davis and Claibrooke clans were in attendance. Before the preacher gave a benediction over the newly marked and beautifully adorned gravesite, Miss Margaret Anne, who was now both famous and infamous alike throughout the rolling hills and fields of the postbellum South Carolina countryside, depending on one's lingering preferences or situational bent, laid her hands upon the head of her other living guardian, though the poor heartbroken woman remained ensnared within the enduring confines of a near vegetative state.

Legend has it that the shattered widow was restored to at least something resembling her former vibrancy just a few months later. As the result of his daughter-in-law's miraculous healing, Mr. Satterfield and his granddaughter, Adelaide, in addition to Miss Sarah and some of the others who knew well the bright and simple farm boy that they all loved so dearly, made the pilgrimage out to Florence at the end of every harvest season back at the Osment farmstead. They made the journey over to Florence and they laid some of that ripe cotton of the Carolina Midlands at the foot of Virgil's grave at the behest of the fallen soldier's bride of only a few short hours. The ceremony continued on in some form or fashion right on up to the onset of the Great Depression in the early 1930's. Some still lay a branch of cotton at the foot of the O'Keefe family tombstone right up to this very day. The identities of those furtive and faceless purveyors of the nearly forgotten tradition remained shrouded in mystery for near to another century after the official progression out to Florence had come to a rather silent and unceremonious yet strictly enforced halt due to the whims of the Depression Era patriarch of the Calhoun family. The legend and the truth behind that faithful pilgrimage never died.

Miss Margaret Anne boarded the train up to Greensboro with Edward and Doctor Bailey later that afternoon after many a tear filled goodbye shared with those who loved her. Right before she left the platform of planked wood to step up the stairs and onto car five, she reached into her bag and handed the old, dusty hat Virgil used to wear out in the field to Elizabeth Ann. Her dutiful overseer was standing beside the promised child's other sister, Miss Shy to properly see her off. Elizabeth Ann accepted the cap she remembered so vividly with a tear in her eye. The source of that tear was the feel and the smell of that old hat so delicately tied to those fondly lingering memories of her past, and of course, the tear was brought about by all that had come undone since the last time Virgil had removed that hat to push her on the rope swing and then sweetly kiss her lips. Elizabeth Ann had brought her son, Francis Virgil Adams Calhoun on the journey to see his father's gravesite without making due note of the rather substantive yet undisclosed occurrence. The young boy of just two years and some months took to the hat immediately and graciously held it for his mother while she hugged her departing sister goodbye.

The old steam train, one of the last of its kind from the Confederate era to survive the war and that far beyond, slowed its progression and gave a series of raucous blows from its horn as it approached the station marked by a small, solitary depot in the heart of Greensboro. The skies were overcast and the soft, misty and intermittent rains falling upon the smokestacks and old tobacco warehouses of the city were slow and indulgent and wistfully binding upon the soul on that otherwise raw winter afternoon. The smell of the drying tobacco wafting through the stagnant, damp air of the city alerted Miss Margaret Anne to the fact that she had indeed arrived in a differing corner of the world. Mr. Lucian Reed Morgenthau could be seen standing underneath a black umbrella smeared by running droplets of gathering rain at the furthest reaches of the ground level platform while the train braked and glided its way up to the brick, whistle-stop depot with its angular roof of heavy slate. Outside of her sale at auction during the Weeping Time down in Savannah and the ill-fated evening of her honeymoon down in Augusta not but a month ago, this was the former Mrs. Virgil Denton O'Keefe's first foray out beyond the sovereign confines of South Carolina.

She was looking nostalgically out the rain smeared window when the train rolled slowly past Mr. Morgenthau, who loomed long and lean and ominous beneath his raised black umbrella against the backdrop of both the old and the new contrivances of the cityscape. She could not recall having laid eyes on the darkly dressed figure before in this lifetime, though she had seen him some eight years ago for but a fleeting moment in time upon the event of her legal adoption by her mother. The man from the picture taken that day presented as far less foreboding, and perhaps almost charming. All the same, she knew from the instant she looked upon the man who appeared so comforted by the presence of the cool, fleshy rain that he was the one that would one day draw forth the last of the primordial light gifted upon her spirit and her soul. When that shadowy man once standing directly outside of the train car window was perhaps half a furlong behind them, Margaret Anne looked into the distracted and musing blue eyes of her Edward.

She then spoke with a deep longing for the moments now passed. The moments that had been presented to the once bright-eyed and affecting man to fill his heart with love and keep his soul from the hands of those that had overtaken his overambitious mother and left his listless father, Mortimer George Calhoun to die slowly and alone of the drink. For that stodgy old man did truly die right before Edward's eyes in the aftermath of his catastrophic marriage to that once beautiful gold digger of yesteryear and servant to the occult with such a serpentine ancestry. "Edward, I hope you will always know I would have served as your daughter whether you had known the truth of that still hidden betrayal or not. I would have done so faithfully had you only asked. I would have done so with love in my heart just as I have now agreed to serve as the cup of your earthly salvation…"

Margaret Anne then looked over to Doc and changed her tone considerably to one of a much more scathing bent to conclude her thought. "…though I know you now walk the darkened paths of this life so cleverly shifting between the needs of the transient flesh and the falsely seeded dreams of the interminable spirit."

Edward kept his eyes focused on the misty rain drifting and then angling downward in sheets of visible vapor until that rain seemed to disappear upon the slate and brick rooftops of the city out beyond the droplet dressed window of the cabin car. He did not shift his tearing eyes over toward hers when he asked reticently of her, "Then why do you offer up so much of yourself for the benefit of one such as I, who has in your eyes only betrayed you, if you had another way open to you?"

Margaret Anne searched with her large, round eyes for the man standing out on the far end platform that they had slowly passed not but a minute ago. The confines of her window did not offer her the luxury of such a sharply angled line of sight back from whence they came. She spoke softly and reverently in reply to Edward's faithful query. "I do this for you now because there was a time when you once openly stood as my father before many and because in God there is always hope in tomorrow. I do so now because you have not yet been made whole for the gold tendered to acquire my colorful flesh that shifts its likeness and therefore its attachments to the various consorts of our society with the changing of the seasons. Surely your world would have been a differing place back when you signed his eternal deed if only that wealth had not been spent on one so worthless to the bearer."

Edward remained haunted by the vision of the man standing on the platform and her response did nothing to ease his consternation over that day far off into the future that was perhaps so certain to come. Upon seeing the man standing there so still, his fear of the day, hour, minute and flashing of an instant when he would pay in full for the unholy reconstitution of his earthly empire was near to driving him mad. In his mind, that darkly adorned man waiting so patiently upon the platform was still in possession of his favored daughter in that horrific manner; that horrific and ritualistic manner that his mind refused to abide as reality or likewise allow him even a once remembered glimpse at a reincarnation of some horrific likeness of that foul sickness, which would always and forevermore be staked to the crux of his heart as quite genuine, though he would never again picture or recall anything of the sounds and the color or the scent of that phantom deformity.

Edward had heard the words of the promised child but he had not listened amidst his distracted state. Upon seeing the man outside his window in the flesh and in his mind then brandishing the silver pistol of Mr. O'Keefe, Edward's overwhelming fears drove him to focus on but one solitary and quite cruel concern. He replied vacantly to the young woman still dressed in black and hidden from the world behind her veil of mourning. She was forced to keep covered while she remained in the South and, rather conspicuously and soon to be notoriously attached to the crime of the murder of Virgil O'Keefe. The liars ancillary to the demons they had bargained with would certainly create that stir to keep her from fleeing her new home up north and returning to the land of her lovingly remembered and virtuous youth. The twisted perversions of contract with the darker order knew no bounds.

Of course, it was true that Mr. Reed had provided for the impetus behind Miss Basseterre walking out the back door of the old, bloodstained haunt as if nothing away from the ordinary were occurring. As part of the arrangement behind her escape, she was from that moment on to once again be called publicly by the name Miss Margaret Anne Basseterre. Such a name was in proper standing with the communal obliteration of any record pertaining to her presumed to be illegitimate marriage to Mr. O'Keefe. Furthermore, the documentation behind and other sundry items pertaining to the veracity of said marriage were only to be kept in the bowels of the Calhoun family crypt and duly overseen by that first keeper of Miss Margaret Anne's family history, Mr. Walter Sommers himself.

Both Miss Basseterre and Mr. Calhoun had dutifully held up their end of the bargain. Yet, in the true fashion of one acting in accordance with some demon lurking in the night, Mr. Reed had also, and just as swiftly as he had provisioned for the young woman to be pardoned by way of reckless indifference, prodded the local magistrate back in Augusta to convincingly stir up the sentiment behind those hell bent on hanging the colored woman and escaped convict. Of course, Lucian had committed to the execution of the latter only in an indirect and entirely blameless manner. As the newly reconfigured story went, Miss Basseterre had allegedly, yet somehow also certainly, most heinously and most illicitly propositioned the morally bankrupted warden of the prison in obtaining her freedom from the old haunt. The evidence however, remained decisive that the lustful woman had indeed committed the deceitful murder of a fine and prosperous white farmer making a suitable living within the confines of the presently enacted tenets of the fabled glories of the Reconstruction.

In any event, Edward's cold, distracted and vacant reply went as such, "Thank you, my dear. All that stands ready to be granted your progeny is dependent upon the success of your marriage to Mr. Bromley. Take good care of the child within and take good care to assure that the marriage has been legally consummated in the mind of Mr. Bromley. Your legacy to your children and the children of your children will be remembered long into the passing of the age."

Miss Margaret Anne stood up from her seat and grabbed Doctor Bailey's patiently waiting hand so that he might be the one to offer her up to Mr. Reed; the man with whom she would travel to New York to meet Mr. Bromley. Miss Basseterre and the two Yankee gentlemen would then continue onward to the site of her wedding and her new home in the southern mountains of Vermont. Though she knew Edward was fully compromised by his presently revived fears of the powers and principalities of obscurity and death, being offered up to the likes of those who awaited her with language suitable only to the gifting of a whore in some backroom lounge was a bridge far beyond what the promised child was willing to cross following Edward's rather empty response to her final plea.

"I will of course honor Virgil's child, Edward. My passing of what little light I possessed into the shattered mind of poor Miss Sarah, who had endured the worst of the war's dire cruelty, should allow the heathen beast to have what he wants without incident for a time. Therefore, your kingdom built on folly and the tribulations suffered as the result of your avarice shall also persevere for a time, Mr. Calhoun. I bid you good day until the occasion of my return home, which you know is certain to come. Also certain to come is the hour of your ceding to the devil the remainder of his due should I fail in protecting my charge of such angelic command."

Edward nodded graciously in reply but he could not pry his tear stained eyes away from the window for the sake of something far larger than the promised child's current feelings. He knew that Doctor Bailey mustn't see his tears. To spare him the remainder of his pain, Margaret Anne drove the last of her dagger home to rest within the warm, pulpy confines of his rapidly beating heart. "Finally Edward, if any further harm befalls Elizabeth Ann or Virgil's dear child in your haste to achieve empire, I shall see to it that you are fed to the same dogs you send me off as chattel to face as payment in kind for any forthcoming lack of faith or courage that causes you to falter in sheltering them both. The act shall be piecemeal, as if you were little more than the loose ends scattered about the morning trough."

Hearing anew that the promised child remained in some way infallibly bent to his will and that somehow there was little risk to the endeavor of the betrothal coming undone; the formerly distracted man grew somewhat heartened in making his reply. "I have never known you to speak in such a way, Miss Basseterre. Enjoy the lavish gifts of your coveted betrothal and think to thank me at least some when every opportunity of this world is afforded both you and your children in the years ahead." Edward then tightened the focus of his eyes upon something moving out beyond the raindrops running down the train car window. He suddenly wondered if the black master of his soul would appear by the door to their car. But alas, that man never arrived.

Miss Margaret Anne took the hand of her proper escort for such an affair from the moment of her birth and spoke bluntly to the now nearly vile and wholly corrupted man facing away from her and off toward whatever had suited his fancy out beyond the dreary window of the train car. "You have never heard me speak that way, Edward because you have never known the truth of what I am. Though I am made manifest through the workings of the light, I could not be present in the flesh if the forces of the darkness were not also existent within me like a flushing hand of high spades. Remember the gift I offered you back in the prison well in the time that I am gone from both you and the land of my birth. Though Miss Meara did not seek as much from me when I freely gave of my light and delivered its warmth into her blackened heart, I do believe your mother fared far better than you ever will from this moment onward, dearest Edward." Edward Calhoun made no reply and kept his eyes sharply focused on what lie out beyond the window pane.

As Miss Margaret Anne and Doctor Bailey approached the tall, darkly dressed man still standing at the very edge of the old wooden boards that comprised the station's platform, the rain came to a summary halt. The woman dressed in black and the concerned looking physician came to a standstill from their matching gaits shortly thereafter, while the shadowy man folded up his umbrella and shook it free of the precipitation gathered upon the contraption's outer skin. Miss Margaret Anne lifted her veil and turned to face the worried looking man who had miraculously delivered her into this world. She addressed Doc somewhat remorsefully in knowing she would not see or speak with him again in this world, though she did not reveal as much to the already hurting man who at least still possessed the hope of seeing her upon her return.

"Remain here, my beautiful aegis of that February Cabin. Know the man's face, yet never approach close enough to know what lies within the depths of his eyes. I shall be fine. Your beautiful girls are both grown now and making their way in the world. Go visit them with Mrs. Bailey when you are up this way again and spend some time with your grandchildren. Please keep watch over Miss Sarah from time to time before you return to your native haunts. Mr. Satterfield is not long for this world and Adelaide is not yet ready to support her mother, though Miss Sarah will be fully well in time."

Mr. Reed began to approach the two looking so warmly into one another's eyes but Miss Margaret Anne raised her hand to halt his progress. The dimly featured gentleman courteously complied. Doctor Bailey hugged his little Miss tightly and responded warmly to her suggestions. "I will see to Miss Sarah and Adelaide until Mrs. Satterfield is suited to the task of managing her own affairs. After that, I do believe the Mrs. and I shall return north, at least as far as Virginia, to be closer to our girls and their families." Doctor Bailey then lowered his eyes and asked, "Are you certain you are up to this, dear child? Surely, you owe nothing to either your father or the man who awaits you."

Miss Basseterre smiled in that innocent and spritely way that she used to when the two of them sat upon the porch of the old Osment farmstead and he would fascinate her with scientific facts that made little sense to her spirited mind so infused with the light. She then replied quite expectantly to Doc's question, though she only spoke in such a manner with the intention of lifting the poor man's broken spirits. At times, she still beheld the glory of what existed on the other side of this life. Nevertheless, the good doctor's little Miss was also quite stricken by this sorrowful, and in some senses, eternal parting of the ways.

"All things with me will be just as God has always intended for them to be, my beloved man. The one before us is an old and deeply wicked soul. There was a time not so long ago when I thought I could both save Edward and remove some great and eternal curse from the land. I will have accomplished the latter one day, yet it appears this dark man has pushed off the final settlement of the undoing of his heinous acts for quite some time to come. He outflanked me in spoiling Virgil beyond the measure of my ability to understand the depths of the sorrow resting in that poor boy's heart. Yet Virgil's legacy is all that shall remain as a sign to you all and your progeny that follow you of my promise that one day closure will be brought to this darkness that owns Edward's fall from grace."

With those words spoken, Miss Margaret Anne Basseterre wiped her eyes and stepped away from the embrace of the man that had against all odds forcefully tugged her into this world by her feet. At the very moment she had realized that she recognized the darkly shrouded man in wait from the photograph taken upon her eighth birthday, yet before she took hold of Lucian's outstretched and patiently waiting gloved hand, she called back to her protector, "I love you, Doctor Emmett Bailey! I shall never forget a single moment we have shared! There is always such fondness to be taken from our memories!"

Doctor Bailey raised his hand to the promised child in response to her final call but his throat became so stifled by his emotion that the organ was left bereft of the capacity to utter a sound. He shrugged his shoulders helplessly in the way of a little boy who was missing his assignment for school and pointed at his neck to signal the existence of his dilemma to the promised child. She smiled that angelic, knowing smile of hers while walking off towards town at the side of Mr. Reed and then blew a kiss in his direction. Doc lifted his hand and then squeezed his fingers tight to show her that he had caught the offering. He then pressed his closed fist to his heart. She laughed beautifully in that carefree and innocent way that only she could and repeated Doc's gesture when he blew a kiss to her in return from his open hand.

Doctor Bailey then turned sharply to run and board the train, as the once slumbering goliath was whistling and laboriously clambering in anticipation to depart while its engines began to roar back to life. All that the good man saw as he ran back down the platform were visions of the myriad variations of the unforgettable flashes of the smile of the little girl he once delivered from the fates haunting an old flogging cabin somewhere deep in the woods of the Carolina Midlands. He cried like a child in a separate cabin until the train pulled into Charlottesville, where he and Edward would dine with his daughter Emmaline, her husband Cortland and his baby grandchildren.

Part IV

Deliverance

Chapter Ten

RENEWAL

❦

T HE WEATHER OF those first flashes of the afternoon of
March 13th, 1875 was a temporal clime near to the prevalent
embodiment of a standard noonday hour to be expected by the local
denizens during that final fortnight of the winter season in Southern
Vermont. The temperature in the town of Brattleboro remained near
to forty degrees for the entirety of the afternoon prior to the arrival
of the first of the long, eastward leaning shadows of the evening shade.
Not much, if any, of the snow pack lining the compact cordillera of
sharply rising foothills to the west of the lovely little riverside hamlet
had begun to visibly dissolve on that cloudy, wet and raw afternoon,
though the temperature had held above the pour point for the preponderance of the passing of the daylight hours.

The resiliency of the snow was primarily due to the low, cheerless
cloud cover of an ominous and heavy, leaden-grey, which had settled
still and seemingly absent the bounds of time some ways below the
fabled crown of Wantastiquet Mountain, which loomed unseen as
both menacing and unapproachable on that day from its permanent
station directly across the river to the east in the equivalently quaint
New England province of New Hampshire. The aforementioned,
beautiful and sharply rising slopes just beyond the western limits of
town, which were still donning their winter whites, also happened to
be majestically situated along the perimeter of the level and sizeable
rear grounds of the substantial Victorian estate home belonging to
Mr. Jacob Asher Bromley. Given the awe inspiring natural splendor

of that ideally situated terrace of such regal design and aesthetically pleasing contrivances originating in places the world over, none were surprised that such a spot was chosen for the wedding of Mr. Bromley. The season of the event however, left many at a loss for proper words that might convey any sort of useful comprehension of the groom's motives behind the selection of such a luckless time of the year for an outdoor gathering.

The wedding of the Northern industrialist to the rather bright-eyed and exotic looking Southern belle of a nearly unknown origin went off without a hitch beyond the rather drab and uninspiring doling out of the elements that accompanied the otherwise grand affair. What little was known regarding the radiant young bride of just sixteen years was delivered in the form of taglines and propaganda which were quite familiar to those in attendance that supported the Yankee cause. Therefore, the proceedings of the afternoon had not carried on for long before all present knew that the long-suffering young lady was in some manner tied to and rescued from the depths of the brutal saga of the waning aristocrats of the slaveholding planter class of the Deep South. For her part, Miss Margaret Anne sustained no objections to the rather broad yet consistent classifications of her past life, or at least not an objection substantial enough to cause her to do anything other than nod in agreement in reply to those stodgy Northern women so obsessed with offering up their condolences for the poor and unenlightened state of her prior condition.

The non-denominational rites of matrimony were well attended by those of the local citizenry not afraid to brave the lingering rime, snow and ice of a late-season storm that had blanketed the Connecticut River valley not but a week prior to the beautiful ceremony. Strangely enough to many in attendance, none who knew the bride were present that afternoon by invitation. Furthermore, the absence of the bride's father to formally give away such an enchanting and delicate creature at such an extravagant affair was an outright shock to nearly all.

There was however, an older looking man of African descent working behind the bar; a man who seemed to some of the more perceptive delegates in attendance to cast a familiar eye in the direction of the well-paraded about lady of the manor from time to time. However, given the potency of the ballyhoo regarding life in the South the good folk of the Connecticut River Valley had all tirelessly ingested for the past fifteen years or more, the few who had made such an outlandish connection did so merely by way of speculative or illusory inference.

A day following the splendid reception upon which no expense or lavish indulgence was spared, at least according to the puritan standards of the town of Brattleboro and the whole of Southern Vermont, the often envied yet somewhat awkward couple made the moderate journey west through the southern peaks, valleys and winding streams of the lower partitions of the Green Mountains over to Bennington. Once there, they spent a week in the manner of those enduring a rather sterile yet functionally correct honeymoon of a sort. Truth be told, while Mrs. Bromley had struggled to the point of manifesting physical illness throughout the continuing progression of the repetitively reinforced acts of copulation, Edward Calhoun had little to fear from Mr. Bromley questioning the proper sire of little Miss's first born child while he continued to administrate over his reestablished fiefdom back in Sumter. At least not until the child reared its head into the world of the living some eight months or so on down the road.

While Mr. Bromley was appropriately vile to the beautiful young woman due to his soulless disposition and his embalmed flesh, which felt and scented of a bloodless cadaver yet somehow mimicked a living breathing entity of God's creation, the marriage was tolerable in the moments that Mr. Bromley traveled into town. More agreeable to Miss Margaret Anne's favor than even those uninterrupted hours of her reprieve, were the times Jacob traveled beyond the confines of the Hamlet of Brattleboro for work or to participate in the quite lude and wholly unspeakable fancies craved almost fortnightly by the sedentary yet always famished beast of the night church. Of course, such a distinguished man as Mr. Bromley indeed was at that time remained keen enough not to defecate where he ate and lay his head down for his proper stretches of rest. Therefore, Miss Margaret Anne's husband kindly remained away from the manor for a full day both before and after the consummation of such appalling bawdiness and salacious rite.

Though the lord of that rather particular and, at least in accordance with little Miss's very Southern and entirely divergent upbringing, peculiar Yankee manor had in some ways tired of his proper mistress mere months into the marriage and pestered her less frequently to fill that cold, interminable and morbid void within him, Mrs. Bromley wasted no time in declaring her pregnancy to all living and working within the confines of the manor. She did so in accordance with her sheer joy over the convenience of such an obdurate obstacle to the exhibition of the proper affections of the newly betrothed. While there were times she played her hand a bit high regarding her condition for the shrewd Mr. Bromley's liking, there was always a commensurate distraction to such blatantly exposed disdain available to an affluent and silently powerful man such as Jacob was. Therefore, the skulking dead man and high priest of the midnight hour did not brood long over Margaret Anne's distant lifestyle and near to deviantly prudish ways.

By the time the October harvest season of 1875 came to pass in New England, Margaret Anne Bromley's pregnancy appeared as if it already had progressed to the point of going full term. However, she should not have been set to deliver her child until sometime after the puritan rendition of the Thanksgiving holiday in late-November. Be that as it may, the exceptionally young mother to be went into the unyielding pangs of maternal labor late in the evening on 3rd November of that same year and her nearly devastating delivery did not occur until the afternoon of that following day of 4th November.

Having her child at such an inauspiciously premature point in time may have alerted Mr. Bromley to the woman's pregnant state upon the hour of their given nuptials but for her birthing of twins; one of which was a large and healthy Anglo looking baby boy. The fortuitous events that followed upon the unfortunate timing of the beginning of her labor cleared the air for a time of those concerns only privately noodled over by her kind and endearing physician and the cold, harsh man of little to no empathy or valid and not entirely concocted warmth.

As has been already stated, the first of Margaret Anne's twins to exit the womb was a warm and seemingly affectionate baby boy. Of primary interest to Mr. Bromley was the fact that the child appeared to express the genes of an entirely European air by way of those myriad traits which stood to be offered from the worldly and exquisitely diverse pool of genetic markers possessed by Miss Margaret Anne. Mr. Bromley was well aware of his spouse's confounded lineage and his solitary worry in accepting Mr. Reed's proposal to somehow dampen her clearly devastating inner light was that he would remain without an acceptable Anglo leaning heir to his Northern industrial dynasty. In accordance with those prior worries of Mr. Jacob Asher Bromley, the second child, who had been hiding at the back of the young woman's womb for eight months, at least according to little Miss's attending physician, was of another constituency altogether. Her outward appearance was a shock of a directly opposing nature than Miss Margaret Anne was to her own delivering practitioner upon the moment of her birth nearly seventeen years ago.

Now, none knew as much, since his parents had been deceased for about a month before the brazen farm boy ever even came across the Captain at the skirmish occurring down at Dingle's Mill on the final day of the war, but Virgil O'Keefe's mother was a pleasant yet rigorously made and bipolar physical specimen of German and West African descent. Given Margaret Anne's own tendencies to only favor the skin color of her mother in the summer seasons of the South, and only then upon the working of long hours out in the field, and furthermore, Mr. Bromley's always pallid or deathly ashen hue, the child appeared to be toned a bit out of the expected sorts upon her arrival. Nevertheless and of course, her mother loved her dearly and at times seemed to love her all the more for the struggles, the forced humility and the shared bond between them that accompanied that rather distinguishing trait.

Mr. Bromley was nearly a cultist adherent to the ramifications of lineage and an ardent student of the proper bloodlines of the European order that still ran somewhat purely throughout the Western Hemisphere. He had remained so from the days of his childhood, irrespective of the fact that those increasingly diluted pedigrees were becoming harder to trace or verify as time marched on in the Occident. Such would have been the enduring case with the derisive splitting away of the Calhoun branch of the regal Pinkney line, an occurrence which was the temporary result of that score of years surrounding the war when Miss Meara's deviant religion and her illicit alliances infuriated a number of the blue blood trustees. Mr. Bromley had been loosely following along while those matters played out as little more than a passive adherent to Mr. Reed, yet he did make a proper note that the curable disenfranchisement of Miss Meara's family was ultimately justified in accordance with the dreadful witch's blood connections and stained allegiance to the rather taboo Morgenthau line to which Lucian belonged. In any event, Mr. Bromley's small sliver of say in his mandated selection of Miss Margaret Anne as his bride was partially the result of her presently unheralded yet readily traceable ties to the once emergent bloodlines of Cesar Maduro and his uniquely potent cross of gold, which was forged and improperly consecrated to the faithful warriors of Jesus by some deviant turncoat among those furtive men who had spent seven years beneath the Temple of Jerusalem during the crusades.

Her paternal lineage was nearly unmatched and was accepted by all of Mr. Bromley's equivalent standing without question. Margaret Anne's paternal grandsire of the Calhoun's first American generation, Isaac Able Calhoun was a second generation descendant of and assign to the primary recipient of the Pinckney Land Trust. Furthermore, even the wicked and salty taint of his own vile Morgenthau clan of the German lowlands by way of his bride's paternal grandmother's infected line was of direct and valuable interest to the wandering and soulless provocateurs and takers of the earth. Such as Mr. Bromley now was after his unfortunate run-in with his cousin, Mr. Morgenthau.

Those of Mr. Bromley's breed, they were both men and demons alike. They were hell-bent and defiled creatures who were always attempting to strengthen, add to and isolate the traits of their vulgar line as their lineage evolved on down through the generations. They accomplished this age old desire by marrying beautiful blue or black-blooded creatures such as Margaret Anne was upon the eve of her marriage. Furthermore, those of Mr. Bromley's ilk wed those properly-endowed women nearly as a direct affront to God's perfect ordering of each of his splendidly diverse, uniquely gifted and wonderful children; those not eternally rendered to little more than the confines of the soil and death or the infinite emptiness of the conflagrate realms below.

By the summer of 1880, Miss Margaret Anne Basseterre Bromley and her three children, David Emmett Bromley, Leslie Sarah Bromley and Elizabeth 'Liza' Morgan Bromley were thriving in the beautiful countryside just outside of Brattleboro, Vermont. Miss Margaret Anne missed her home, her twin mothers back at the farm, her extended family, and she missed the days spent with Mr. Virgil O'Keefe out in their beautiful field of summer cotton. Still and all, at just twenty-one years of age, the children kept her plenty busy and always smiling, Mr. Bromley hadn't laid his clammy, deadened flesh directly upon her skin since the birth of Liza Morgan some three years ago and she had managed to procure the comforts of a confidant who was one of the many on staff at the manor. Likewise, the town and its surrounding districts quaintly nestled up against the broad, rushing river sourced from the northern mountain ranges and which split the territory of New England near to directly in half had come to suit both Margaret Anne and her young children, though the little ones knew of no other confines by which to compare their beautiful home and their beautiful little hamlet filled with honest yet sterile, God-fearing folk of a fervently religious bent.

Mr. Bromley and Mr. Reed had not seen each other during this span of some five years since the birth of Mr. Bromley's patchwork twins, as Mr. Bromley had spent the majority of his time travelling between Manchester, Burlington and Montreal up in the Canadas. For his turn, Mr. Reed had remained quite busy down in the Carolinas managing a few of his own ventures there in addition to his continual yet detached oversight of Edward's almost unimaginable success in taking direct advantage of the burgeoning pockets of the Post-Reconstruction economy of the South. However, on a pleasant summer afternoon, the two men reunited over lunch at the mouth of that same Connecticut River that ran past Brattleboro; a place where the wide and swiftly running watercourse emptied into the Long Island Sound and a place which was also the site of the southern wards of the fully incorporated seafaring town of New London. The mid-July gathering was rather harmless and actually quite dull right up until the point Mr. Reed began to push firmly in advocating for his always dark agenda.

"I thought you had turned rebel, never to return back home to us," was Mr. Bromley's rather flat attempt at some light humor while the two gentlemen were near to finishing their early afternoon meal. Mr. Reed looked up from his plate with a wicked and angular smile that stretched out devilishly across his long, handsomely narrow and strangely crimson-eyed visage in response to Mr. Bromley's half-hearted attempt at wit or perhaps just levity. "You were never suited to the more agreeable tendencies of tasteful humor, Jacob. However, do take note that I offered you an ample smile in return. I have learned a great many things while I have been living abroad and behind enemy lines as it were. A few of those pertinent nuggets of relevant information I gleaned while pressing for the proliferation of my broad array of rather dubious concerns down in Dixie may be of import to you, my friend and cousin forever pledged to the blood order of the line of Morgenthau."

Mr. Bromley daintily wiped at his chin with his cloth napkin after a bite of his warm and mealy seafood chowder. He then returned his table linen to his lap and raised his eyes to thoughtfully stare over the shoulder of Mr. Reed and out the window of the establishment situated just beyond the footpath bordering the rocky coast and facing out to the sound. He suddenly found that he had grown tired of and possessed little patience for Mr. Reed's antics.

Jacob Bromley had been married for some five years now to the most beautiful thing in all of New England by a fair margin. An exotic Southern beauty of such renown that many a Yankee boy up in Vermont would have marched on down to Dixie of their own accord to procure something as equivalently fine had there not been such a danger of being shot dead while given over to the act. That finest woman of all those he had ever come across, and there had been many, had borne him three satisfactory children of varying appearances that he knew very little about, although he understood instinctively that the first born would certainly do just fine in serving as the proper heir to his abounding fortune if such a thing now mattered at all.

While he remained given over to his now customary habits of wanton indulgence and greed, her vivacious and childlike approach to even the simplest pleasures in life had somehow stirred something warm and expectant within his once wholly deadened and empty soul. The vile man seated across from him could offer him neither the pleasant delights of his pretty caged bird back home nor the satisfaction of his insatiable carnal want to command and possess warm flesh. That man now watchfully looking him over was naught but wavering lips and the fabricated conceit of the demon of the age, who by decree owned him outright and eternally.

His wife continued to avoid the touch of his cold, dank hands that belonged to some Frankenstein's monster like the plague. Yet, he still possessed the ability to bend her to his will, even if he hadn't bothered to put her out in such a manner since the onset of her second pregnancy, perhaps some four years ago now. Though he was a wicked man of the highest order and had many a man sentenced to death for little more than the presumption of treachery, he had actually ventured forth in the years of his marriage to the nymph of some curious angelic shine to find that his only true enjoyment in life now came from the rare moments that his wife was kind to him. He cared little that in those moments she was only abiding by tradition to deliver her warm and soothing pleasantries against the backdrop of the soft, cascading morning light coming in through the large, lightly curtained windows of their spacious bedroom.

Mr. Reed could see plainly that his man was going soft and becoming the product of having far too much going his own way for far too long. While he never feared the man's outright disavowal of the hedonistic ministries of the flesh and the sacrificial rituals of the demon realms, one such as Mr. Reed despised witnessing even the slightest sense of comfort pervading throughout the thoughts or the cold and empty souls of his fallen attendants. "You may want to brace for yourself for what I am about to tell you, cousin. Though you may appear disinterested in my news, I do assure you that smug look of self-satisfaction or a longing for the sea is about to morph into the guise of one twisting beneath the gallows in short order."

Mr. Bromley lowered his eyes back to the shifting red silhouettes dancing somewhere in the depths of Mr. Reed's infinite pupils and pretended to care about what words the devil's top adjutant, or perhaps even the devil incarnate, might speak. "I apologize for the distractions set about my drifting eyes and my wandering thoughts, cousin. I have been pondering if there is not some way I might draw closer to my elegant wife in the years to come."

"Elegant is one word for the woman, cousin but deceiver and murderous whore are others that fit far better in accordance with the actions of one such as her," replied Lucian rather scornfully.

Mr. Bromley closed his eyes and lowered his head only slightly. He understood that Lucian had left him to his own devices for far longer already than he would have presumed when he first agreed to have her on his behalf and then later lavished in his good fortune upon improperly marrying Miss Basseterre. Furthermore, Jacob knew the time had come for him to dutifully do his part where it concerned whatever was behind that devil's interest in his bride. She had never belonged to him but had always belonged to the red-eyed demon capable of such horrific chaos and unspeakable destruction. As such, Jacob spoke obsequiously in reply. "You have piqued my interest as always, Lucian. Please, do tell me what the young woman has done to deceive me."

Lucian looked away from Mr. Bromley as he realized he would be allotted little satisfaction from Jacob's reaction to the divulging of his dirty little secret concerning Miss Basseterre. As such, he spoke forwardly and in a manner conducive to one conducting his affairs of business. "She married a common man prior to you back in Carolina, Jacob. She then killed that man who was like a brother to her. She did so with the hopes that she might escape both her mother's sacred promise of her betrothal to you on the anniversary of her 16th birthday and the sanctity of her properly consecrated commitment to that rather plebian man."

Jacob opened his eyes and looked at Mr. Reed until that strange red shading of his counterpart's irises was etched into the depths of his mind's eye. He then spoke flatly and candidly. "Therefore, Lucian, you never murdered the man to stop the consummation of the marriage on my behalf and then framed her for the crime to drive her away from home. You only bought the local politicians and the judiciary to stoke the rumors of her savagery after the man was dead and she was imprisoned for his murder to force her into my waiting arms. Furthermore, you now expect to evince the nonexistent emotion of my surprise by revealing that David and Leslie Sarah are not the fruit of my deadened loins to draw me forth and set me purposefully against the woman. Have I hit near to the mark with my conjecture, if not precisely splintering its eye?"

Lucian turned his eyes back toward the brown brick of the side wall of the tavern by the sea. He rarely guessed wrong when it came to leveraging the emotions of a man useful to the practice of expounding upon his evil wishes. Yet, he should have known that this already dead and now soulless creature incapable of feeling even the slightest vestiges of the warmth of human emotion, and as such had been perfectly chosen for the task at hand concerning the preparation of Miss Margaret Anne for his own consumption, would not flinch upon learning that his two oldest children were of another once bright-eyed and warm-blooded man. Lucian lowered his eyes to the last bits of the raw cut of hare resting upon his dish and simply gave the orders to which he needed Mr. Bromley to adhere. "Yes, you have hit the mark directly, Jacob. What I require of you is to enrage her by slaying the children of the Southern farm boy and at the height of her madness treat her as your proper wife. You must draw the very last kernel of her inner light away from her."

Mr. Bromley took Lucian by the hand and gripped the demon's cold and slippery appendage tightly while he spoke rather assertively to his counterpart in a low and somber tone. "The trouble with you, Lucian is that you must by your nature ultimately destroy those who you employ to enact your sinister and unholy plans. I have always known that you would one day press your knife into my own back when you had what you wanted from me, which is in this case the woman in some form of neutered state whereby she is safe for you to touch. Though I must abide in accordance with the provisions of our proper contract and agree to the terms you seek of me, do understand that I will spend the remainder of my cold and joyless days warning those still of the human condition off of your eternal bargain that does little but open the gates of hell for the blindly damned."

Lucian looked back up from his plate and pulled his hand hastily away from Mr. Bromley's deadened yet humid flesh. "Simply do what you are told, Jacob. I own you. I know that you are nearly cold to the remaining depravations that this world has to offer you. Yet do me the favor of basking in the glory of taking the light out of the young woman for her treachery served as such a cold dish to one, who in his own vile way, doth care so for the tender woodland sprite. You are the only one capable of opening the door to my future line as you have been dead for all intents and purposes these past twenty years now. As such, I will not stop you or even attempt to hold you up for a time if you spend the very last of your moments free of the fires of hell disavowing my future dealings in the realms of human commerce and procurement."

Jacob Bromley stood up from the table and looked out into the chopping waves of the visually endless sound beyond the window yet directly before his eyes. When he had thought for the moment on the meaning of such eternal beauty he answered vacantly back to his man in wait. "All shall be as you wish, my proper governor. I shall return to Brattleboro via the river and the lovely young woman shall be in the way by which you intend to possess her. I will need but a week's time. Promise me no harm shall come to my daughter. Nothing of her condition was ever pledged to my own bargain."

Lucian looked Jacob over carefully one last time from his seated position upon the worn but unforgiving wooden chair of the tavern set by the chopping waves of the water. When he was satisfied Mr. Bromley was properly set to do his will, he answered him back in a flat yet sinister tone. "Your daughter shall know me just as you have since I spared your slipping life in the only way that those of the darker realms can effect such a thing. What she chooses to do when she is a consenting adult is beyond my control. Thank you for being honorable in your dealings. I know you favor the children and even now, knowing what you know or perhaps always knew, still favor the Carolina woman. Spend what time you have left after you have honored the final terms of our agreement preparing your daughter to understand the ways in which I will bend both her perception of time and her perception of reality in the human realms to possess her. Perhaps then, she will know a different end than her father."

Jacob nodded coldly in reply. "That is good advice, Lucian. I think that those may be the only words you have ever uttered that I will in truth take solace in abiding. Have a pleasant evening. I shall see you up in Brattleboro in just over a week's time set to deliver the wholly mortal configuration of my wife."

Lucian nodded firmly to confirm and took up the last of his serving of hare. He relished the cold, bloody taste of the meat and he wondered what awaited him when he might at last approach the child of light. Jacob turned and left the tavern abruptly. He spoke not a word more. Upon exiting the old, colonial establishment, he chose to walk the wind addled coastal path back uptown toward the harbor and the docks of the boats that traversed the river northward against the rushing flush of its currents derived from the gathering brooks and streams flowing down through the peaks and valleys of the ancient and indelible Green and White Mountains of the north country. After he finished his meal, Lucian set his hellish eyes upon a lonely mistress seated at the bar who had once belonged to some rough seafaring man; a seafaring man long ago lost to the depths of the timeless sound.

Six days after his first meeting with Mr. Reed in nearly five years, on July 22nd, 1880, Jacob Bromley sent his three-year old daughter,

Liza Morgan, up to the mountain town of Montpelier to spend the remainder of the summer with the children of his only true friend of this world. He brought his four-year old twins of clearly muddled and starkly divergent constituencies into the master bedroom that evening to have an impromptu, yet of a formal accord, discussion with their mother. He stood a few paces behind them when he drew his old Union Army sword from the war and prepared to drive the tip of that blade through the heart of his son by way of his back. When the sword was fully free of its sheath, Black Jim stepped out from the lady of the manor's closet to the side of the raised bed with its overhanging floral bed dress. He held firmly in his rough, worn-out hands, which had picked more Georgia cotton than could rest in the sea, a newly manufactured double-barrel shotgun set at the ready. Miss Margaret Anne raised her hands to cover her face and specifically her shocked and accordingly gaping maw at the sight of both her husband's drawn sword and the chosen instrument of destruction in the hands of her co-conspirator.

Mr. Bromley turned to his right upon hearing the commotion of Jim's haphazard and irascible exit from the lady's cloakroom and beheld the only enduring flash of light that would leave a lasting impression upon his shadow favoring eyes. Jacob had smiled joyfully and with a sense of relief at the sight of the African man just before the violent and expanding blast of the weapon took the head clean off of the walking cadaver with its sword drawn for the conclusion of some vulgar ceremony. Unfortunately, the broad array of the timely and rather unexpected discharge of the shotgun also prematurely exited a percussion fracture in the right barrel of the weapon. Several of the errant pellets struck the head and upper body of little Miss Leslie Sarah. The frightened and then rightly stunned child was blown forward and onto the end of the bed next to which her mother was standing in a frightful state of near shock amid the dreadful calamity of the reckoning.

Upon seeing that her little girl was in a bad way, Margaret Anne yelled, "Take Davey, Mister Jim! You two make your way south with Mr. Lemarque until you get all the way down to Carolina to Miss Leslie's place. I will take Lessie Sarah into town to see the doctor and suffer whatever consequences must be endured to keep the precious creature among the living!"

David remained standing in the middle of the room trembling and too afraid to move otherwise upon having his eardrums nearly rupture from the thunderous clashing of such proximate and violent discord. He had turned away from the source of that untamed, mechanical rage only to bear witness to the headless corpse of his heretofore eternally absent and perpetually inattentive father. The strangely soothing warmth running down the inside of his leg from the back of his properly suspended leisure trousers did nothing to spur him into motion, nor did such awareness stoke the emotions of his shame. The righteously shaken boy knew only fear and the deformity of the absent face of death, which had been so harshly robbed from his father.

While Miss Margaret Anne began to frantically attend to the little girl she looked over to her boy and pleaded with him, "Davey, you go on with Mr. Jim now! We will be out to join you in time! I will see you again my beloved boy but your sister needs care. Do you understand me? Mister Jim has your travel bag ready for you. You both must go now!"

The boy turned his head back to the eyes of his mother that were so riddled with fear. He nodded to her in reply with fluttering eyelids in a frightened and wholly confounded manner as he had heard little of what she said. In accordance with the proliferation of such fear and bewilderment, his beautiful, brown leather shoes remained firmly anchored to the polished floorboards that glimmered in the light of the setting sun from in between the two plush oriental rugs adorning the room.

Jim took a careful look at the shattered right barrel of the shotgun while the smoke from its brutal and unequivocal deliverance of absolution finished clearing from the chambers. Seeing that the gap left behind when the gun had splintered remained close to the opening in the tube, the aging man and former runaway from Butler Island, Georgia held out hope that the darling little girl might survive the ruinous failure of the integrity of the weapon. Jim had been working odd jobs around the estate for years for the sole purpose of executing that savage, yet near to remarkably pure in its delivery, reprisal upon Mr. Bromley when the proper time arose. The sweet child who had caught the errant shrapnel in the head or neck reminded Mr. Jim Martingale of her namesake, the tender-eyed Miss Leslie. She reminded him of Miss Leslie in the days when little Miss's mammy was just an enchanted little slave girl back on the Island. The Miss Leslie that Jim likened to Lessie Sarah was a memory set upon Jim's mind long before the woman of his fancy had given birth to the first of her three ill-fated boys. Likewise, such was a memory that was born some years before Master Butler had taken a secret shine to the lovely girl he remembered brushing up against near to the well on the sunny, September morning he was first sent up to the manor to learn the proper ways of his white masters back in 1838.

Jim dropped the shotgun to the floor and rushed over to the spot at the end of the elegant bed where Miss Margaret Anne was frantically tending to her daughter. In the midst of his wide-eyed guilt over the accidental harming of the dear child, he was suddenly gripped by the onset of a consuming trance. Whilst he was within the confines of that waking dream, Jim was reminded that the sacred linens of that bed were far too proper and clean for a freed black man of his sticky, unwashed summer skin; skin so perfectly suited, at least by way of and according to the harsh, unending propaganda of the day directed at him and his people, to only the dark, steaming jungles of the African continent that he remembered so little of and the once prosperous cotton fields of the Georgia Coast.

As Jim stepped slowly closer to the place where the child fell amidst the inundating haze of his mounting guilt, he held out hope for the little girl being gently yet frantically prodded and tended to by her angelic mother of the spirit realms. In the midst of his continuing confusion upon that unholy reckoning, he considered that the assaulted child's distraught mother was the same woman who was once a child wrapped in a Cherokee throw that he had rebuffed to die in the arms of the white woman maddened by fear. And in truth, Margaret Anne would have died that day out on the crossroads to nowhere but for the purity and faithfulness of the slave woman he once loved without ever telling her as much. Jim continued to slowly and cautiously approach yet closer to an interval proximate enough to the end of the bed that would allow him to plainly see the full extent of his brutal recklessness. At that moment, he came to realize that the same child of the light he had once disavowed and who then came to be delivered into her rightful place upon the Calhoun estate some days later by only the grace of God and His angels among us; the man formerly known as Black Jim came to realize that the promised child set out upon those crossroads for reasons then known only to the Lord above had no rightful business being up here in the mountains of the North, or perhaps any place upon this earth so accursed by the low morals and filthy wants of corrupted men.

When he was almost near enough to bear witness to the trauma of little Lessie Sarah's ordeal, Miss Margaret Anne wrapped the child up to her chin in a folded blanket resting at the foot of the bed. Not but a second thereafter, Black Jim saw clearly the gammy side of the child's bloody head that was resting in her mother's firm and capable hands of such a contrasting skin tone. He understood immediately that she would live based on what was then revealed to him but he fretted over the unknown condition of her swollen, bloody and pulpy right eye until he witnessed the beautiful nymph of the woodlands press her fingers firmly into that place of such wretched disorder.

"I am so sorry, Miss!" he begged of the distraught mother with the pleading eyes of a guilt-ridden child. "The gun was defective upon its issue. But we can all make it on over to New York and the old lines of the Underground. They are still up and running in some form and we aim to seek every advantage that they offer for the concealment of our journey home."

Jim paused to still his rushing breath some but his eyes still flashed naught but fear. He then augmented the thoughts of his prior appeal. "She won't bleed out from the smattering of pellets, Ma'am! Mr. Lemarque is waiting out over the first of the mountains at the edge of the property line with the mules to get us on over to the west by way of the southern mountain pass."

Miss Margaret Anne shook her head steadily and solemnly as her tears streamed off of her softly squared chin and onto the hot skin of her bloodied baby girl. Jim pleaded with her again in an expeditious and rather forthright manner just as he did with Miss Leslie back when she first took Miss Margaret Anne into her motherly arms that had by that time lost their hold upon all of the beautiful fruits of her womb. "If you stay behind, they will hang you up high for all to see, and in short order, my lady! There's no telling what they might do to your colored child once they take you away. They might go on and properly reckon what the man of the house was up to before I..."

Jim's voice trailed off upon his looking over at the mangled heap of human remains slouched into the corner of the room where the late Mr. Bromley was blown by the discharge of the blast. "...Before I did that to him..."

Margaret Anne took a deep and cleansing breath upon hearing Black Jim's assessment of the child's condition and looked lovingly at the little girl who so endeared her to the memory of her beloved Virgil after he had been working his endless shifts in the summer fields of cotton back home. She then looked lovingly into Mister Jim's eyes and replied to him with a kindness that resonated above that of any fear the rapidly aspiring man of an unmatched intellect had ever known, and he had known the depths of many an enduring terror during his tumultuous life as a freed, captured and then freed again man nearly born into bondage. "She was not meant for what shall come to pass, Mister Jim; just as her dear father was not formed of the clay of this earth to endure beyond the moment of my having been offered up to the demons of these curious lands to the north for a time. God is calling her home to Him and I must remain with her to prepare her to pass on into the heavens."

Margaret Anne then lowered her eyes from the still rather frenet-ically disposed man and spoke solemnly. "The dearly beloved child's condition reveals that the time has come for me to endure the last of my trials of this peculiar reality unto which I was so unceremoniously born. Take Davey and make haste, my good and honorable man. Just as your brave deeds did accomplish all those years ago upon mine and Miss Leslie's unfathomable return to Butterworth Hall, you shall be the one to deliver my darling boy to the place where he now belongs. He was always meant to return to our shared homeland, the lands his father loved so dearly."

Upon hearing a slight clamor that arrived to her ears hastily from out in the hall, Miss Margaret Anne quickly snapped out of her wistful state and sharply lifted her enchanting and colorfully bespeckled yellow eyes to Jim's. Those abundantly oversized orbs were suddenly beset by a startling look of alarm. She spoke to Mr. Jim with a renewed sense of urgency. "You must hurry now! The aftermath of what has been justly served upon the poor, soulless man is already no secret to those working in the house below and the others lingering outside the door!"

Black Jim stared blankly into the swirling kaleidoscopes of bril-liantly flashing colors that were the beautiful young woman's radiant eyes when purely charged by her static yet bristling inner light. Shortly thereafter, he also snapped back to his heightened state of alert and begged of her, "Please now, Ma'am! Amos will never speak to me again if I leave you both here to die!"

The promised child let the fullness of the light arriving to her from some unknown source within the spirit realms radiate from her sparkling eyes for a bit longer while she replied to the frazzled man with the same tone of comforting kindness as before. "Go now, my dear man. Tell Amos that I love him and that I will return to you all in the proper time already allotted by God above. Tell my brother to be ready to take me in on that day. Take care of my sweet baby boy, Mr. Jim Martingale! He is lost and afraid right now and I love him dearly!"

Jim nodded uncertainly and then turned quickly away from the promised child. He took the perfectly stunned and righteously soiled boy up in his arms and made his haste to exit out the back of the manor home by way of the dark, low-ceilinged and secretive passages known only to the headless victim, Miss Margaret Anne and their most trusted attendant, Miss Natalie Washburn. Jim and the boy then ran in tandem across the lush, green summer grass of the level back yard under cover of the rapidly converging shade of nightfall. They ran with the spirit of the west wind until they reached the concealment of the pines at the base of the nearest ridge, about a half-mile off in the distance from the rear of the house and back to the west. They moved like two silhouettes against the shade of the mountain shielding them from the last of the dying light given off by the setting sun. When they began their ascent up the primary ridge at the back of the yard, Jim and the boy continued to progress fluidly along their intended coursings even as that subtly resolving orange orb closed out the confines of the day with streaks of purple, orange and pink lighting up the horizon in the stratospheric planes just above the most magnificent of the southern mountains of Vermont. Those majestic and ancient peaks still to be tamed to by the swiftly travelling fugitives stood somewhere off in the distance from the shrouded expanse now blending into the all-consuming shade of a summer evening directly before the frantically searching and wildly tremoring eyes of both the man and the child.

About fifteen minutes later, Miss Margaret Anne kissed her dear Lessie Sarah on the forehead and removed the edge of the flowered comforter from the instantly fatal damage to the artery running through her baby girl's neck. The poor but not long-suffering child had bled out only minutes into her ordeal after being thrown by the force of the blast onto the end of the bed. She expired far faster than the promised child could employ her light to heal at least something of the inadvertent damage caused by the shotgun's terminal fury. Margaret Anne had covered her up earlier because she did not wish for Jim to know what he had accidentally wrought and because she needed the always helpful and gracious man to keep his wits about him while he guided little David along the uncertain path of his own deliverance.

The child had passed on without speaking another word. Yet her mother had spoken into the depths of her soul and blanketed her cheeks with the love shimmering deep within her cascading and then softly rupturing tear drops while little Miss Leslie Sarah O'Keefe stepped carefully into the light and began the wait for their devotedly anticipated reunion.

When Mr. Lucian Reed Morgenthau entered the room near to an hour later, Miss Margaret Anne remained weeping like a distraught mother subjected to the most difficult of realities to assault the human condition, the loss of a child. None in attendance nearby to complete their daily duties at the Bromley estate that evening dared to broach the threshold of the master-bedroom door prior to Mr. Morgenthau's arrival. By the arrival of that late hour of Miss Margaret Anne's Yankee exile, most of the staff had heard the rumors in some form or another of the woman's miraculous capacity. Although she was none but kind to them all, albeit often times eerily distant from the relevant cours-ings of any given day outside of her affectionate interactions with the children, none of the hired help wished to face one as she was believed to be whilst she remained in such a miserable and uncertain condition. That is to say that those amongst the colored contingent of the staff with Southern roots or ardent connections to the lore of Dixie, and whom represented a fair percentage of the after-hours staff, believed she was a child of the light dating back to the very earliest days of little Miss's arrival to Vermont. Beyond their fears of such a mythical creature presented in the corporal form, none wished to be the first to bear witness to what was certain to be the gruesome remains of the strange and deviant lord of the manor or whatever was at the business end of that thunderous explosion delivered from the hull of the double-barrel.

Mr. Morgenthau closed the door slowly but firmly behind him and walked across the room to curiously inspect the headless remains of his cousin and long-time consort. Being that he was unawares of Black Jim's prior presence in the room, he stood before the weeping woman as one quite impressed by the capacity of her will to deliver retribution upon the poor bloodless sot who had sold his eternal wares and served him so honorably in exchange for little more than a twenty year continuation of his degenerate religion. "Where is the boy?" asked Mr. Morgenthau in his typical emotionless manner by way of an effort to begin the process of tidying up loose ends.

Miss Margaret Anne set her lifeless child gently to rest in the middle of the bed. She did so not to address Mr. Morgenthau but because her daughter had passed out beyond the places of the wistful lingering tied to the torments of the dead while the departed hovered near to the earthly remnants of their memories that were not permitted to pass beyond and into the light. She did not want to confound the child's journey with her own inner radiance, which did so efficiently and effectively permeate the bounds of both worlds. When she had closed the child's eyes out of respect and her enduring love for the deceased, she looked up at Mr. Morgenthau and asked scathingly,

"What leads you to believe that my boy was ever present, you demon of the accursed realms?"

Mr. Reed responded in a dry yet rather glib manner as he continued to probe the remnants of the body from a safe distance using the tip of his purely decorative walking cane. "While our headless friend here left no pumpkin, nor do the markings of his trusty steed of the sleepy hollow linger nearby, it remains clear to me that his sword was drawn to remove the entirety of the dull stain of Mr. O'Keefe from his line."

Mr. Morgenthau had finished with his crafty reply while shifting his eyes away from the sagging remains blown back into that far corner of the room. In response to her visitor's demonic glare, Miss Margaret Anne shuttered her eyes and replied with a slight edge to her otherwise even tone, "So it was you who told Jacob that the first of his line were delivered from the virile essence of a proper Southern gentleman."

Margaret Anne then opened her now dulled eyes of amber and blue and asked thoughtfully of the vile and heartless man, "How did you know the truth of my children's origin in the capacity of one set to so candidly reveal such a verity without doubt to the deposed father of his own dearly beloved, Mr. Morgenthau?"

Mr. Morgenthau laughed wickedly in reply to the sorrowful woman and stated forcefully, "Who else has stood by to betray you at every turn of his miserable existence to protect the vile legacy yet perceived grace of his birthright, my child?"

Margaret Anne lowered her eyes back to her precious daughter, who looked so similar to her father in a darker shade while she was lying lifeless upon the bed and answered Lucian in kind, "Edward bears your mark now and his chosen path is one that I am now only set to see unto its conclusion. I knew that he would betray me again because such is the fruit of his faithless nature and his fatal desire to serve his own only by shaping the ways of the world according to his will. That you both have conspired to take my angel from me has set me firmly upon the path of undoing you Mr. Morgenthau. Certainly you now know the truth eternally beset upon my will after all of this time. Certainly you have always known that you cannot be left to tend to the ill seed of what you have so delicately sown for all of these years now. You are an abomination to our Heavenly Father and I am called to return you to the realms of eternal sorrow and emptiness. Four-hundred years in some form or another is far too long for one such as you are to remain among the living."

Mr. Morgenthau nodded stoically in response to Miss Margaret Anne's claims and approached the radiantly weeping promised child. The potent expression of her earthborn sorrow only made him lust after her all the more. "If you come with me I will see to it that she is buried properly. Otherwise, the resultant effect commensurate with that which shall be assuredly perceived as your heinous deeds upon the hour is that the poor, assumed to be bastard child of some way-ward, slave-bred rebel of the land of cotton will be fed to the hogs while you hang from the sturdiest limb of the stalwart chestnut tree out front. Of course, you do understand that I will personally see to the deliverance of such a forceful serving of the king's enduring justice with my own hand, my lady. I will do so in reciprocal accordance with what you have so hastily done to my man here."

Miss Margaret Anne elegantly stood up from the bed and pulled at her dress to reveal something of that which Mr. Morgenthau had always sought after and called provocatively over to him in her demented state, "Why go anywhere, Mr. Morgenthau when you can take what you have always lusted after and therefore needed upon this very instant. Surely none at the door will stand to interrupt the wishes and desires of a nearly immortal man such as you." She was distraught and beyond tired of being twisted up in the upside-down lies of this insidious devil. She would not stand to let his curse upon her and all those that she loved survive what were certain to be the tortuous remains of the day.

Mr. Morgenthau cackled in vein to rebuff her but his very pith began to be drawn toward that which his dark essence had so sadistically sought after for so long now. That which his wanting and covetous soul, eternally pledged as the bone collector and deliverer of sorrow for the high priests of the darkness for centuries now, sought after from the moment of that photograph he obliged on the occasion of her 8th birthday back in Uriah. The crux of his eternal wickedness disregarded the perfectly calculating nature of his well-traveled and experienced human mind and he approached to within a step of her exquisite, lightly olive skin and the beautiful adorning light now beginning to once again shine in her otherwise hollow and deadened eyes.

Now, as a matter of indisputable fact, Mr. Lucian Reed Morgenthau was a man who knew to practice restraint. He hadn't survived in the Americas from the moment the first settlers had arrived without possessing healthy doses of such a trait. However, he had never suspected that Mr. Bromley would let him down. At his very essence, Mr. Reed was a frothing entity of base cravings and wants. Once he had both set his mind upon having the promised child and then had in proper turn stepped into the room alone with her, there would be no turning back if she pressed him. Such unbridled want had always been the man's fatal flaw, his Achilles' heel as it were, which his deep awareness of same had heretofore served to keep him far removed from such a precarious entanglement. He knew right then the magnitude of the trap he had unwittingly sprung.

She turned before him seductively as her stylish and graceful, yet swollen in accordance with the fashion of the era, dress dropped from her shoulders to the floor. He no longer controlled his actions and therefore began to quickly and deviantly unlace her inner garment, which had to do little at all to keep the long and lean muscles beneath the smooth, tightened skin of her midsection flat and without the slightest draw. The delay caused by the undoing of the intricate contraption almost freed him of the blackened want of his accursed soul.

Yet the sight of her bare, smooth lower back, which so perfectly angled outward and seamlessly intertwined with the gentle goosebumps electrifying the tightened peel of her upper leg forced him to take hold of her; take hold of her like a proper demon of the night and roughly tear away every last vestige of clothing and cumbersome accessory that remained upon a properly adorned lady of the nineteenth century American nobility.

When she was exposed before him she pressed the palms of her hands flat to the bed as she had been forced to do years ago now while accommodating the headless man slumped into the corner of the room just behind his fallen officer's sword. He tried to turn her around when he had freed himself to take that which the interminable darkness within, ever incapable of being satisfied, demanded, yet she held her proven ground while not obstructing him in any way. She had but one chance to unleash all that been assembled within her spirit and her soul to finish him. Furthermore, she knew he would somehow restrain her abounding light if he glared at her with the hunger-driven madness of those ruddy yet mottled and soulless eyes. That light within had been repressed for the span of some four apocalyptic years now and had been set loose from both its moorings and its source to shatter the darkness upon the instant of the senseless killing of her beloved child.

She closed her eyes and held her ground waiting for the moment he would be just as vulnerable as any man being inundated by the currents of desire and then so suddenly overcome by the deepest throes of his fulminating urges. He raged like a maniac frozen to an electric fence with a charge leveled to repel even the largest carnivorous game of the open prairies of the mountain west. In return, she summoned the epitome of her passions by reliving those brief moments spent with Virgil and succumbing in the way she wished to that night; that night when she so dreadfully fractured his already ruined mind and further shattered his broken heart with the cosmic current of her light.

The full and unattended delivery of that unexpected payload produced a raging insanity within the already broken and confused young man, which was far too powerful to bear for longer than the flashing of an instant before death or any end to such vehement and exquisite torture was preferable to the ensuing madness suddenly raging within both Virgil's body and his by then deeply twisted mind.

She then looked carefully at the still, lifeless face of her beautiful daughter. While staring at her she coupled the insatiable inferno of her unspent desire of that evening of her honest and faithful honeymoon with a burning hatred that served to compress the primordial essence of her inner light by way of some universally expressed magnetism of a polar antithesis. She sensed that he was hoping to break free before he had gone too far but she turned quickly while closing her eyes and wrapped his hindquarters in the womanly strength of her farm girl calves and picked up with the motions he had so hastily discontinued until she heard him burst like an exploding water mane in the dead of winter.

She pulled him closer as the once razor sharp tensions of his muscular body went limp and she grabbed hold of the bare flesh of his chest and squeezed and clawed at his creamy, white skin like some savage and ravenous beast of the wild with all of her might. The spent man tried to draw away but the light rushing directly into the infinite darkness within could not be tamed or deferred in the least. The pulmonary valves running into his aorta exploded in such a way that the sound was audible across the room and also quite distinct to those eavesdropping near the door while lingering out in the hall. Mr. Lucian Reed Morgenthau then tensed up rigidly for a final instant and dropped like a weighted sack of flour through the gap in her intertwined legs, which were locked at the ankles, and fell dead upon the floor.

When the demon had expired and then dropped to the floor, the woman screamed bloody murder as the last of her angelic aura, which had graced the warmth of her heart from a time prior to the moment of her birth, exploded in a blinding flash of light. The blazing gleam erupting forth and radiating through the paned glass of her bedroom windows and into the night sky could be seen by Jim and her boy as they made the crest of the first of the low mountains that lead into the southern pass. Jim shook his head sadly for a reflective moment and then quickly ushered the boy over the bald, rocky apex of the stalwart peak and back downward and into the cover of the Eastern white pines and sugar maples.

When it was finished, Miss Natalie Washburn, who had been about the closest thing Miss Margaret Anne likened to a friend during her exile in the beautiful mountain woodlands of Vermont, finally turned the perfectly polished brass knob to the master chamber amid the ensuing silence. Once the latch was freed, she slowly pushed the white, wooden door partially open and quietly slipped inside the room before once again shuttering the master chamber to the prying eyes of her contemporaries. She would never forget the scene she beheld upon the moment of her entry into the gorgeous and perfectly adorned room of such a New England or perhaps traditional Yankee flair. Miss Washburn had never seen one set amongst the dead outside of a proper funeral parlor, let alone two dead men, one of them being headless, and of course there was the poor, peacefully stilled child of just four years, who had always been her favorite. She worked quickly while glancing around the room to rectify the indecent nature of the child's stunned and motionless mother before any of the others dared to step forward and arrive upon the ghastly scene.

At the same time the local law enforcement officers were trying to piece together what had taken place without the benefit of a useful witness, as the only surviving participant of the ordeal had been rendered not only speechless but inanimate in the aftermath of the horrors of that hour, Jim, David and Mr. Lemarque had boarded their pack mules and begun the forty mile journey through the southern mountains over to Bennington. From there, the somewhat conspicuous looking ternary would proceed on to Albany, where they would prepare for the long journey back to the Deep South along the old Underground Railroad lines out of Skaneateles, which were by the summer of 1880 primarily used for more nefarious endeavors. There would come a time, the preciseness of which was unbeknownst to the two gentlemen escorting the child at that juncture of their journey, when the boy was sought after by the highest order of the authorities in Vermont and perhaps New York as well.

There was no trial for the maddened widow of Mr. Jacob Asher Bromley. Instead, Miss Margaret Anne Basseterre was promptly remanded to the care of the doctors on staff over at the Brattleboro Retreat on the morning of August 6th, 1880. While there, the shattered remnants of the once elegant and vibrant young woman remained sitting in the shadows of her red brick asylum cell in total silence and an unbroken solitude for nine long and lonely years. She never even spoke a word upon the birth of her fourth child, a demented looking baby boy with a strange twinge of crimson lurking in the depths of its pupils. The doctors were stunned that the child progressed along to a natural birth at all given the near absolute lack of proper nutrition or sleep that the insane mind and haunted soul of the woman subjected her body to endure.

Within a few years of his being born, the baby boy was promptly taken up to a convent outside of Quebec City to be reared at the request of a strange man of few words by the name of Erasmus Delmar Sinclair. Mr. Sinclair hailed from the wooded upland mountains of Central Maine. As the child was difficult to behold, seemingly brilliant beyond all compare and physically challenged to the point of expressing some lingering forms of permanent debilitation, there were no objections to the boy's relocation from any of the child's custodial wards, who took their pay directly from the revenues of the state. In fact, the child secretively tagged as the sole heir of the line of the deceased Mr. Lucian Reed Morgenthau was never heard from again stateside but grew to be of a peculiar and reclusive renown up in the busier cities and provinces that lined the full length of the Saint Lawrence Seaway. He exhibited a preference for spending much of his time alone with only his caretakers on the eastern coast of Nova Scotia in his later years.

Some nine years after her initial institutionalization, in the late summer of 1889, Edward Christopher Calhoun was celebrating his 68th birthday back in Sumter, South Carolina. The decade of the 1880's had finally been that long awaited season of rebirth back in the Carolina Midlands as the last vestiges of those hideous and corrupted Reconstruction Era policies were being phased out of existence. Furthermore, the influential positions of government had been fully handed over to the current breed representing the local gentry of the day.

  With Mr. Reed passing on and his one third ownership stake in Edward Calhoun's booming industrial and trade centric business ventures in the hands of an administrator by the name of Mr. Erasmus Sinclair of Maine; a man who served as trustee for an unidentified eight-year old boy and Canadian national, who himself was the only named heir of Mr. Lucian Reed Morgenthau, Edward thrived financially and finally returned to something of the warmer graces of his youth. The existence of the boy, who was also Edward's legal yet publicly undeclared grandchild in accordance with the provisions of the Articles of 1858, was not documented by Mr. Sommers until around the same time as that 68th birthday celebration for the rejuvenated yet still oft times concerned looking Mr. Calhoun; sometime during that latter third of another typically hot and sultry summer season in 1889. For it was then, that for the first time in more than twenty-five years, Edward Calhoun received word of the intentions of his daughter, Mrs. Susannah Jane Devening.

The racial climate throughout the state remained unfavorable and even hostile towards the freed slaves in many prefects and counties of the state. The continuation of such an unjust state of affairs was rather unfortunate given that the subjugated majority of the one million or so folks presumed to be living in the state at that time were now well into their second generation of being liberated from their status as human chattel. Under the new yet wholly biased way of things, the liberated remained bound by other political and social constructs now deigned as legal segregation or the separate but equal doctrine, which was in fact upheld by the highest courts in the land. At least as far as Edward Calhoun was concerned, the doggedly determined man was at long last on his way to delivering upon something of his aging promises made to his former mistress during the years of his exile from Sumter.

In a broader sense, those were sanctified promises made to those less fortunate members of his impromptu clan that were sharing in the quite pleasant years of his banishment out on the Osment farmstead. They were the promises made directly to Miss Jeanne for the benefit of all whom he considered given over to his care when he departed for Charleston to reclaim what remained of his fortune and reengineer his once legendary estate over a score ago back in 1868. With such thoughts streaming through his mind and such volatile happenings set as a backdrop upon the events of the day, following the week of his birthday celebration, Edward Calhoun traveled across the state to meet with Mr. Amos Martingale Laing, Esquire, a renowned attorney then approaching his forty-first year of breathing in that warm, sweet Carolina air. Edward was slated to meet with Amos to discuss the legal, political and financial prospects of setting Uriah aside as a Negro commune under the current or perhaps necessarily newly attuned laws of the state.

At that time, Maime, who was just a few years older than Amos, and her family of four had taken over the day to day responsibilities of keeping the Osment acreage producing. Mr. Laing and Miss Leslie

were well along in life and into their seventies by those days and Little
pea remained unmarried and off attending Atlanta University as part
of the college's upcoming graduating class of 34 students. In any event,
the current matriarch of the Osment farmstead sternly objected to
Amos's plan of turning Uriah into a Negro only commune or incorporated township under the guise of little more than reverse segregation.

Both Maime and her husband, Jefferson Sidney Duval, a wandering evangelical type by trade before marrying Miss Osment and
settling down out at the farm, believed the realization of Amos's near
lifelong dream would only serve to proliferate the racial differences
being promoted and legally defined throughout the state. Furthermore,
the religiously zealous couple worried that such a designation was an
affront to God's law and would perhaps bring those same racial epi-
taphs and accompanying tensions home to roost in a place such as
Uriah; a place where farmers of all creeds had coexisted together since
the day Miss Jeanne was gifted the deed to the Osment land. Though
the Wilsons had departed years ago and acquiesced their acreage adjacent to the Osment plots to the ever expanding clan of Barbury Davis,
the Claibrooks, Evanses, Dunwoodys and several other white families
of note with a rich and deeply rooted heritage in the area had remained
over the years even while other colored families were given access to
land and settled in the county following the war.

Edward had learned the hard way the near impossibility of making
something right by acquiescing to the tactics of and utilizing affiliations with those of a more malevolent bent. Nevertheless, he not
only felt obliged to promote Amos's idea of transforming Uriah into
the all-colored town of Blackville to visibly repent for his own sins
of the past, but also because the idea was not without some form
of merit given the way things had been going for the former slaves.
Furthermore, his support of Amos's endeavor, even if the young man's
ideals were slightly misconstrued, would certainly go a long way in
restoring him to the finer graces of Elizabeth Ann, Lizzie's prospering

and nearly seventeen-year old boy, Francis and his estranged daughter of some twenty-six years now, Susannah Jane Devening.

That was of course assuming that the woman about Boston town for decades now ever bothered with the future inconvenience of being updated on their lives down here in the Southern partitions of Carolina. Susannah had ultimately fled into the arms of a Yankee Colonel during the war after residing with her aunt for a time up in Greenville prior to the war due to Miss Meara's outwardly vicious treatment of their field hands. Still and all, always at the essence of Edward's estranged daughter's ire was her father's openly displayed indifference to his mother's cruelty, particularly given that Miss Susannah had always known that Edward's heart catered to even the slightest wistful whims of the uncommonly learned Haitian mistress she had always loved so dearly.

All the same, the winds of change were also blowing through the river valley that split the boundaries between New Hampshire and Vermont during that same summer of 1889. The twelve-year old daughter of both Jacob Asher Bromley and the voiceless woman of the asylum had been returned from the woods of Maine to the welcoming auspices of the fine Brattleboro estate home that had remained under the diligent care and proper oversight of her great-uncle Erasmus. At around the same time as Liza's return to the manor, a Boston socialite of some scholastic renown and forty-eight years of life experience by the name of Susannah Jane Devening had begun asking around town about the condition the murderous madwoman both of the asylum and of notorious local lore; local lore that Mr. Sinclair would have preferred aggressively came to a suitable end, or at a minimum, profited from a reworking of the tale for the benefit of the ascendant Miss Bromley.

Such a reordering of the most shocking and dubiously gossiped about happenings of the days gone by was difficult to achieve in a quaint little town where little else of such scandalous rapport occurred with the madwoman still present, irrespective of the fact that she had spoken nary an audible or at least discernable word in the past nine years. Thusly, Mrs. Devening's arrival to the Bromley estate for tea on the sunny and pleasant afternoon of August 28th, 1889 was received as a rather auspicious event in the jaundiced and bloodshot eyes of the aging Mr. Sinclair; a man who never would have fathomed the untimely and exceedingly dire earthly demise of Mr. Morgenthau, the previously reigning prelate of their ancient and iniquitous order, before visiting with the drained woman of such parched, grey flesh, distended eyes and hollow cheeks, who was somehow still something of an enchanted lightning rod direct to any man's willing heart back when he last witnessed her hauntingly bated condition in the asylum some years ago. And indeed, Mr. Sinclair did receive Mrs. Devening onto the back patio of the large, perfectly groomed summer yard with aplomb in the hopes that perhaps something might be done to rectify the regrettable circumstances surrounding Liza Morgan's estranged mother. The summer patio was the appointed place where the charming yet perfectly cold-blooded child of twelve, by way of the incessant and righteously inundated teachings of some schoolmaster of a sort to the children of the noble classes, awaited the otherwise unknown New England socialite of only a deeply sophisticated repute.

The three exchanged pleasantries out back before the tea arrived while the perfectly trained and groomed servants buzzed about the patio in an effort to keep their employer and her guests quite con-tented. Such was a wise practice where it concerned the rather fas-tidious and nearly adolescent lady of the manor. It wasn't until the altogether toothsome tea had been sipped on for quite some period of time by all present and party to the simply splendid delights of that temperate and bright afternoon of late summer that Mrs. Devening felt comfortable enough to openly initiate her intended request of either Mr. Sinclair or her undeclared niece of a sort. "I must declare the true reason behind this wonderful time which we have shared together. I was hoping that you would provision for me to visit with my half-sister.

I am fitfully worried that she will lose all hope of returning to a sound mind if she does not speak with someone of her family soon. Surely she has paid for her sins of the past with the price of her solitude for quite long enough now."

Mr. Sinclair looked thoughtfully at the pleasant looking woman of a decidedly urban sophistication and flair, which exuded from her pores and was highlighted by nearly all of her somewhat eccentric mannerisms. The aging gentleman was captivated by her dark but greying hair that flowed without end from the brim of her white, straw hat, which was of a clearly archaic and Southern bent, a few generations stale in the essence of its fabrication, and otherwise out of place on the comely head of the academic aesthete. He answered her rather starkly. "None but her doctors are allowed in to see her as she is quite mad. Additionally, she possesses a penchant for the murder of her past husbands, their associates and even her own child, the Madam here's colored half-sister, to satisfy her blood lust. She is wanted back in her homeland for much of the same sorcery and none have found her once blooming son, who apparently vanished into the ether some nine years into the offing now."

Mrs. Devening had done her homework on the Bromley affair and was certainly not a woman to back down from any challenge of her own accord. "Let us presume for a moment that the woman was not capable of wielding, let alone loading and firing the broken shotgun, dear Sir. Moreover, since she has never been granted her day in court, you are speaking in a purely speculative manner as it regards her alleged crimes."

"Fair enough," replied the rather impressed Mr. Sinclair. "All the same, I can tell you that the second man found dead in her chamber of a ruptured heart was a steadfast man of uncommon and in the minds of several, eternal resolve. Do you not fear for your own safety, my dear lady? Irrespective of who decapitated poor Mr. Bromley and ended the life of the precious though somewhat ostracized child, what manner of woman is capable of delivering her lovers into that eternal goodnight with little more than the use of her bare hands or a contraption far worse and wholly ungovernable?"

Susannah replied a bit hastily to Mr. Sinclair as she was now somewhat put off by the presumptive and chauvinistic nature of the elder gentleman. The young woman off to her side watched her in an attentive yet callous fashion while she spoke. "Only a man would speak so foolishly about the true powers of the heart possessed by that of only good a woman. In any event, am I to understand that I would be doing a considerable favor to you both by arranging for the estranged woman's treatment to resume under the care of the doctors back in Boston?"

Mr. Sinclair nodded discreetly in reply to his guest. He then turned his eyes toward and signaled with his pointing chin away from the young lady of the manor, so that the mistress might know the time had come for her to take her leave. Miss Bromley begrudgingly humored the old man. Yet, not before she let out a vile sigh of misplaced disgust directed toward Mrs. Devening. When the heiress had finished making a slight scene of dutifully parting ways with present company, Mr. Sinclair replied, "Your presumption would be quite accurate, my dear. There are none in the vicinity that are not aware of her malignant deeds and those that know the story of her past will not have her."

Mr. Sinclair then rubbed pensively at his chin with the long, prominent fingers of his right hand and added quite solemnly for effect, "I would be forever in your debt if you were a person capable of granting such wishes, my lady. She will never leave the confines of her cell for even an hour until she speaks coherently for the benefit of the doctors in charge of her care. And quite frankly, given the benefit her notoriety to their 'studies', I believe that such is the way those self-indulgent practitioners prefer for things to remain."

"Well such is not how I intend to allow things to remain for the poor woman who has been so awfully abused by the other men of your ilk that coveted after her," Mrs. Devening shot back soundly and confidently. Mr. Sinclair was intrigued by her zeal but not yet hopeful as he replied to his guest's rather blunt assertion. "How is that you intend to make the tormented soul speak to you, my dear?" Susannah raised her steel-grey eyes to the old codger of a coarse, yet strangely enough, uncommonly refined disposition and deportment and answered back, "Have your men at the asylum draw back her medication for the next two days and on the third day I will go and speak to her. I will return on that day and report back to you on what she has said."

"Have it your way, my dear, but your presumptions concerning the finest or perhaps shrewdest of our psychologists up here in God's country are going to condemn you to fall short," was Mr. Sinclair's inattentive reply as he slowly rose from his comfortable outdoor sitting chair. I must depart for another engagement across the river in New Hampshire, but Miss Washburn will show you out; once you have finished with your tea, of course. The blend is quite exquisite and worth the time taken to sit and reflect while you finish what remains in your cup. I will see you back here when you return to me in but a few days' time, my love."

Mrs. Devening rose to embrace the darkly presented gentleman with her hand in the manner of saying goodbye, but Mr. Sinclair stepped away far too spuriously to be held up by such a courteous gesture. The callously spurned woman called over to his back while Erasmus entered the house by way of the music room, "You will honor my request then, kind Sir?"

Mr. Sinclair stopped suddenly while halfway over the open threshold and replied to her rather hopefully and rhythmically when compared with his usual tone. "Why of course, my dear. I am certain the doctors will grant me at least that request. I dare say however, that had those dutiful men been of another order or commensurate affiliation closer to my own, we would never have been granted a reason by which we might be having this conversation at all. Your sister has someone watching over her and I am prepared to concede to her obstinance for the benefit my intended heiress. I wish you well in your endeavors, my dear. I will see you again in but a few days."

With those words spoken, Mr. Sinclair disappeared into the house. Having no one to respond to and likewise, needing some time to digest all that Mr. Sinclair had so watchfully divulged, Mrs. Devening stepped a bit further into the open grass of the yard to bask in the pleasantly warm afternoon sunshine of late summer in Vermont. Shortly thereafter, she began to examine the beautiful flowers at the base of the mountain, which lie at the furthest reaches of the perfectly manicured back lawn.

About thirty minutes later, Miss Natalie Washburn approached the spellbound woman at the furthest reaches of the yard while Mrs. Devening was carefully observing a set of delicate Monarch butterflies extract the sweet, tempting nectar of some long stemmed gladiolas blooming near to the short, swollen pines at the base of the mountain. Mrs. Devening watched as the beautiful creatures, incidentally to their intended purpose of feeding upon the nectar, unwittingly attracted the pollen of the flower. Mrs. Devening marveled over the exquisitely efficient reciprocation of the act, which was quite necessary to the distribution of the flower's seed and therefore compulsory to its germination and the proliferation of the species in the seasons to come. Based on what the urban socialite had learned in passing of her father's forbidden love child, Susannah Devening couldn't help but wonder if the trapped and isolated woman, whose solitary asset of endearing value to any in these foreign lands was the brutal audacity of her legacy and her corresponding silence, was in the same manner as the stationary flower working her seductive magic to evince Mrs. Devening's being to effect a similar result as that of the butterfly for the benefit and unlikely proliferation of the mysterious and cordoned off woman.

The colors of the dancing butterflies, the beautiful violet bloom of the flowers and the surrounding lush greenery of the accompanying summer scenery had Mrs. Devening simply spellbound. However, she remained locked into the depths of her recently discovered doubts concerning her mission when Miss Natalie Washburn gently and silently tapped her on the shoulder. The startled lady now made leery of the touch of an unseen stranger by her years spent within the bustling urban environs of her Boston home jumped a fright before shading her off-angle eyes in the direction of her sweetly fawning pursuer.

Miss Washburn quickly spoke to calm the visiting woman's nerves upon knowing she had inadvertently surprised her. "I am so terribly sorry, Ma'am! I did not mean to startle you. Your coachman was asking as to your whereabouts and I was hoping to have a word with you before you departed the premises."

Miss Susannah slapped her open palm down upon her rapidly beating chest and replied kindly enough after the calming buffer of a lightly held yet hastily withdrawn breath, "No, no, no, my dear. The apologies called for have accrued to only my account for the depths of my distraction. The natural order of the world out here during the late summer is simply stunning."

Miss Natalie grabbed hold of the visiting woman's hand in an effort to continue to comfort her and replied rather spiritedly to her endearing observation, "Miss Margaret Anne did love it out here so at this time of year. Perhaps she would have thrived in this mountainous land so foreign to her if only the summer ran for a good stretch longer."

The humanity that Miss Washburn applied to the tainted legacy of Miss Margaret Anne's prior life as a living, breathing woman of mortal feeling soothed the startled Bostonian more so than even the warm pleasantness the maidservant exuded from the depths of her charming and unassuming aura. "Well, my dear, one would be hard-pressed to overlook the splendors of the current season in this beautiful country. Did you know my sister well?"

Miss Washburn smiled wide and divulged a secret that had heretofore remained her own since her furtive relationship with Mrs.

Bromley began to blossom back when little Miss was a much younger woman all those years ago in 1875. "We walked the yard like this from time to time. Although she revealed little of the particulars surrounding her mysterious past, she spoke quite often of the natural warmth and light that enveloped her beautiful heart. Knowing her like I did, I for one was never set to believe she could have done any of the hideous things they said of her. She loved that poor child so very dearly."

Miss Washburn then pondered the moment of her arrival into the room that evening nine years ago now and expounded further upon her initial thoughts. "Most certainly she never would have consented to the giving of herself to that vile man found dead of a ruptured heart at the foot of her bed. Some say that man was the devil incarnate and had owned the souls of many."

Miss Susannah took hold of both of the woman's smooth but firm and wiry hands and replied, "Thank you for that, my dear Miss Washburn! I have never met the poor child. However, when the aggrandized crumbs of her sordid tale made their way down to me in Boston just a short while ago by way of a doctor I know who paid a work visit to the asylum up here, I was for some reason drawn to come up here and try to help her or comfort her if I was able. I loved her mother as if she were my own. Yet, before you approached, I was beginning to doubt the beneficial nature of what lurked behind my sudden calling to this place."

Miss Washburn beamed brightly in reply and said, "Yes, you must somehow take her away from that ghastly place. My husband's sister was there for a spell some years after her boys died at Gettysburg under conscription. She will never be the same after the horrible things done to her there."

Miss Washburn paused to think for a brief moment and then continued on with her thought while picturing Miss Margaret Anne exploring some delightful corner of the yard near to where they stood.

"Your sister was of another time and another place altogether, and perhaps another world also. None understood her but all sought to cage at least some small parcel of that angelically radiant beauty of hers. She did not speak to many people up here but I was always of the belief that she was an angel of some sort trapped amongst the rest of us mortals within the confines of the waking world."

Miss Washburn paused briefly once again, squeezed Susannah's hands in a pleading manner for effect and added, "You simply must take her out of that place! I have been so distraught over what I presume to be her deplorable condition after being confined to that madhouse for so long!"

Miss Susannah nodded in reply to Miss Washburn's heartfelt plea and answered the pleasant yet troubled woman hopefully while she strolled amiably back across the lawn and toward the house. "I do believe the time has come for her to leave that place and return home to live out her days in relative peace and quiet. I was told by a knowledgeable professor of spiritual history back in my hometown of Cambridge that the man whose life I believe she did in fact take was, as you have said, a vile demon of the highest order. Perhaps that sounds like silly superstition to many, my dearest lady, but the professor had met the man in person and he likewise, and dutifully so, believed that the deceased once owned the souls of many."

Miss Washburn bashfully looked away from the stoically classic, rangy and honorable woman's eyes. When she was focused on one of the most prominently blooming gladiolas radiating violet and white in the low angled sun of the late-afternoon hours of the end of summer in the northern climes she replied, "I should not speak of such things, but the wicked men of that family have cursed many a good man from these parts over the years. When I heard they had been plying their craft way down in Dixieland, I knew it was only a matter of time before one such as Miss Margaret Anne arrived to put an end to their insatiable and evil ways. God began the healing of the horrific sin of slavery by ending the war in favor of the Union but these darker sorts of an ancient breed stepped right in to corrupt the resulting balance of power and seize upon the country's weakness. I hear with sound ears what those gentlemen speak of from time to time. I wouldn't doubt that one such as Mr. Reed was responsible for the killing of Mr. Lincoln, even if they blamed it on a Southern gentleman."

Miss Susannah thought for a moment and replied warmly with a slightly bemused twinge to her tone. "That is a lot to take in from one with such an impeccable source. Yet, I have seen the work of those demons with my own eyes. In point of fact, their hideous nature drove me from my homeland at such a young age. I am actually looking forward to the moment of my return home with my unknown yet hopefully soon to be renewed little sister."

Miss Washburn smiled wide, patted Mrs. Devening lovingly on the hand and answered her back thusly, "I take solace only from the fact that your sister has perhaps freed many a man from some confounded and eternal damnation by putting an end to that foul beast. I am told he was the worst of the living purveyor of souls. You need to return her to her homeland. I believe that she has done all that was asked of her in this place."

On Saturday morning, the 31st of August, 1889, Mrs. Susannah Jane Devening entered the cold, haunted and blood curdling confines of the Brattleboro Retreat. She was escorted down several dark hallways locked tightly by bolted doors of ancient, black steel until she reached the dour, cushioned cell stained by the bodily excrement of the madwoman at the end of the furthest hall from the entrance to the keep. The doctors that had escorted her to Miss Bromley's cell propositioned her to remain present while the two interfaced, purely in the name of the ward's benefit, of course, but Mrs. Devening nervously declined. Once the harshly sonorous echoing of the sound of the forcefully closed steel door simmered down into the lowly reverberating quietude of the dungeon hallway in which she stood and when all was quiet within the padded confines of the barred and presently occupied chamber before her eyes, Susannah made her introduction to the back of the presumably deranged woman staring out through the bars and the thick, cable-reinforced window of her cell and into the yard.

Before she had finished with the final syllables of her name, Margaret Anne answered back to her visitor without turning from the unclear view of the dense glass mounted to the brickwork behind the black, steel bars of her cell window. "I have been waiting for you, sister. I would have summoned you sooner but there was no hope in such an exercise before my daughter had returned to assume her place within the manor. Thank you for putting a halt to the vile poison corrupting my blood and my mind. We are but little more than unwashed animals to these madmen torturing us at every turn. I refused to speak to them and never will, dear sister. Except to say to them, kindly open the door and step aside you beasts."

Susannah's jaw dropped until her mouth was agape. She could not believe this creature of such monstrous and eternal myth while locked away for nine long years, both in this awful place and now in the shifting confines of her academically trained mind, had spoken in a direct and coherent manner to her. "Tell me, my child what is it that I can do for you? If I plead your case properly to Mr. Sinclair, you should know that he wishes to see you gone from the whole of New England. He presumed that your condition remained impassable for the execution of such an endeavor."

Miss Margaret Anne turned from the window to face the sister she had never set eyes upon. A sister who herself was little more than some imagined myth of the Calhoun legacy by the time she had been sold into marriage up in this place. She approached her slowly and steadily. She replied softly to Susannah as she made her way toward the bars at the front of her cell. "What do I wish for, sister? I wish to return home to my boy and shepherd him away from what remains of that vile demon's madness back in Carolina. There is much you don't know and much that remains to be settled back home."

Miss Susannah took hold of the now wretched creature's hands as they rested upon the bars plied so stridently to the brickwork of both the ceiling and the floor and which were now positioned directly before the narrowing gap between their searching eyes. She spoke softly to the hideously abused woman. "Your wish is a good one, sweet child. For, I too must also return home to face our father. I thought I could run away and never look back but the smells of those warming fields of late summer cotton haunt me annually in the August seasons such as this one. I have been happy away from the devastation of the war and the foul treatment of our fellow man but there comes a time when all must make a certain peace with the torments of the days of their childhood innocence."

Margaret Anne smiled warmly at her sister and spoke rather cryptically in reply. "Few understood the capacity of that monster, yet strangely enough and though he fell to that demon for a time, Edward always did know the truth of what was out there hunting them all by invitation from Miss Meara."

Susannah lowered her eyes from the mussed and stained append-ages of the otherwise delicate and still mildly alluring, though wholly hollowed out, facial formation of her sister, who was the only one of them to be delivered from the womb of Edward's true love. Given the urchin of the asylum's current state, Mrs. Devening could never dream of affecting even some crumb of her once imagined jealousy for the one who was in truth what she had always wanted to be, the daughter of the elegant and mysterious Haitian mistress that haunted Butterworth Hall in the days of her childhood. She shook her head contritely to dispel the lingering fumes of that vulgar thought in addi-tion to repudiating her sister's comment by saying, "Edward is now and always was a man to care for his own needs first. Only then, was he prepared to properly see to the needs of those given over to his care. He is not a bad man at his pith. He is simply a man trained by his mother to fear the pangs of want and being without above all else."

Margaret Anne shook her head dejectedly and replied, "One day you will understand, sister, but only if you see me on to our home country, for it is there that the fullness of the truth stands to one day be made known to you. Are you indeed the one who can deliver upon such an essential wish? I have answered the call of those of the eternal realms who sent me here to you all and I have remained forsaken as I knew that I must. I gladly did as much because from the vantage point of the heavens I once beheld the world where that man remained presented in the flesh. I have waited out the old man who still mourns the loss of his devil incarnate of the age in silence until the hour my living daughter was set to return and my son of that demon's configuration began to reveal his dark promise. I waited in silence until his concerns for the reordering of the future would dampen the fires of his once all-consuming vengeance."

Mrs. Devening stood silent and in awe of the being beset before her upon her proper reckoning of the magnitude of the words spoken by the promised child; words to be tended to for all time and words which depicted entities and events so foreign to Susannah Jane's predominantly academic footings yet so keen to her always Southern heartstrings. Margaret Anne lowered her head in response to look of spectacle set upon her sister's handsome guise and spoke to the floor concerning the rapidly approaching hour of her desolation.

"Yet, now that I have unsealed my thoughts for your consideration after all this time, I cannot bear the thought of another day of this place and the vile energy it circulates like the oncoming rush of fouled wastewater gathering near to a stagnant stream. Will you take me away from here before I perish within, my dear sister Susannah? Have I presently endured enough loss and loneliness to once again bear witness to the rising of the sun? The sorrow which accompanied the breaking of my now human heart was always the burden I was never predisposed to bear, but God speaks to me now and reminds me that nothing is lost that is of His hand."

Mrs. Devening began to cry at the sight of the poor, wretched child of the light and declared, "With God as my witness, my sweet child I will deliver you home to the endless fields of cotton awaiting your return back in Carolina."

Per his own wishes of far more than an innocuous predilection, Mr. Sinclair could not provision for Margaret Anne's accompanied release given the inmate's sudden return to the finer graces of her more humane sensibilities until Monday, 9th September, 1889. On that day, Susannah Jane Devening and Miss Margaret Anne Basseterre boarded the train to Boston and a week later set sail from Hyannis Port on the Cape for Charleston. They arrived at their Market Street hotel on 17th September, where they would await the now deceased Mr. Satterfield's replacement, Mr. Cawley, to shuttle them overland to Uriah via the same refurbished carriage the newly born promised child had ridden in prior to being delivered into the arms of Miss Leslie in that field of bending winter high grass to the south of the auxiliary post road to Augusta.

Edward had kept the carriage perfectly maintained and postured at the ready for the moment of little Miss's return to Carolina. On that day in Charleston, the promised child did not recall the exquisitely detailed coach of her frightful first journey amidst the haunting portents swirling about the wanderlust of her thoughts upon the long-awaited instant of her homecoming. Though she was but a suckling babe during that first harrowing ride, she would not forget the comforts and curiosities of the elegant contraption twice.

While in Charleston, the two ladies poured over the scant offerings of mail delivered into Miss Margaret's Anne's asylum cell over the past nine years that had not been previously opened, inspected and filed or returned to sender, as was the case with any letter originating from South Carolina. The last of the unopened letters was one that had arrived from the hand of a Miss Shy Jolie Basseterre via Port-au-Price, Haiti back in October of 1884. Little Miss's maternal sister had been in jail for a time back in Haiti or remained there when she wrote the letter. The status of the author's then present liberties was not made entirely clear to the reader because Miss Shy Basseterre had addressed so little concerning her own condition upon writing to her sister by way of that correspondence secretly forwarded on to the asylum in Vermont by Elizabeth Ann under the care of a direct courier. The letter would have been a stunning surprise to nearly all amongst the living, yet was not entirely unexpected, albeit disappointing in its permanence and its certainty, according to the tenets of the promised child's once brilliant extrasensory perception. In either case, the letter was promptly burned before the eyes of Mrs. Susannah Jane Devening, the ashes of which were left to settle upon the eddying crosscurrents slapping up against the old brick of the inner break wall of the Charleston Harbor.

Back in Uriah at a time concurrent with the arrival of the ladies into Charleston, none but Elizabeth Ann was expecting the clandestine return of the two daughters of Edward Calhoun living in exile up North. Miss Calhoun had arrived at Miss Leslie's cabin without her son, Francis Virgil Calhoun, who was fast approaching the eve of his seventeenth birthday. Unlike his mother, who understood well the healing prowess of the inner light the promised child once possessed, Francis did not buy into the premise of little Miss's innocence where it concerned the death of his father; an innocence that Elizabeth Ann faithfully preached to her son, though her pleas continued to fall upon deaf ears. Francis Calhoun was a man firmly of his own mind and his mother's story about Virgil's sad demise ran contra to nearly everything which he understood to be humanly possible. Beyond that, his mother's unwavering conjecture cut against the grain of every legend that was bandied about in the presence of Francis's always pricked up ears concerning the night his father died. Moreover, those legends that spoke to the harshly blunted honeymoon of Mr. and Mrs. Virgil O'Keefe coursed fluently through the surviving lore of their people in much the same way that the thriving tributaries of the mighty Savannah ran throughout and gave life to the farms, fields and unyielding woodlands of the Carolina countryside.

Elizabeth Ann had returned to Sumter a day before the ladies arrived out at the Osment farmstead under the cover of darkness. Little Miss and Susannah Jane were dropped off by Mr. Cawley at the end of the drive per their request to the physically stout coachman and decorated war veteran. The prodigal sisters were travelling light and wished to surprise the unsuspecting denizens of the farmstead with the endowment of their arrival. Miss Margaret Anne possessed nothing outside of the few things to wear that her sister had purchased for her back in Brattleboro, Boston and Charleston and Miss Susannah Jane had brought only the essentials needed for the two of them to complete the journey to Uriah by way of rail, sea and then land. As such, Mr. Cawley graciously saw to the furtive delivery of the ladies' few bags to the nearest side of the main farmhouse once the women had wandered off down the dirt drive and into the upper field. The normally emotionally stifled coachman remained inspired by the accounts of the two weary travelers when he reached for their bags. Not but a brief spell subsequent to his taking hold of the first of the travel cases, Mr. Cawley could hear the lighthearted ladies serenading each other somewhere off in the night. They sang beautifully intoned refrains of *Dixie* against the backdrop of naught but the resounding silence and the intermittent anthems of the restlessly chirping crickets.

Susannah Jane opened in grand fashion with, "*I wish I was in the land of cotton, Old times there are not forgotten; Look away! Look away! Look away! Dixie Land.*" Miss Margaret Anne then rejoined dutifully in carrying on with the second verse, "*In Dixie Land where I was born in, Early on one frosty mornin', Look away! Look away! Look away! Dixie*

Land." Shortly thereafter the two women joined together in singing the chorus to celebrate their long-awaited return to the loamy clay of Carolina. "*O, I wish I was in Dixie! Hooray! Hooray! In Dixie Land I'll take my stand, To live and die in Dixie; Away, away, away down south in Dixie!*"

Miss Margaret Anne had been away from home for nearly fifteen long and trying years when the once again fugitive from the law in her native Carolina knocked innocently upon the door of the cabin where she had removed the demon seed of Mr. Morgenthau from her sister, Elizabeth Ann Calhoun back on the eve of her thirteenth birthday in 1872. Though the promised child had been thrilled to simply walk barefoot though the harvested fields of cotton and set her eyes upon the old farmhouse where she had done the majority of her coming up, the haunting and permanent absence of both her mother and Virgil were difficult losses to once again revisit upon the moment of her arrival. She had been whisked away to her appointed rounds up in the North so soon after the two pillars of her adolescent life had suddenly and unexpectedly passed. Though she was presently little more than the mortal shell of her former self and abhorred the enduring sorrows that accompanied even the memory of her trials up in Vermont, upon that moment, Margaret Anne wished that the mystical creature she once was had been far more prone to the pangs of her ephemeral heart, such that there may have existed a permanent marker etched upon the places within that her mother and Virgil had graciously touched with their love before they were both so harshly torn away from her during the pitiable years of her adolescence.

Though she was asked to remain home that night by Elizabeth Ann in the remote event a friend of the family passing through town required accommodations, Miss Leslie was no longer expecting company on that evening when she opened the door to greet whoever had arrived at the threshold to her cabin like some phantom in the night. Mr. Laing was fast asleep and snoring like a bear after a long day assisting with the preparing of the harvested cotton to be shipped to market. Upon the instant Miss Leslie caught sight of the promised child standing before her in only the light of the forward lantern of the cabin, the astonished aging woman folded her hands together, fell to her knees and then wept with her arms raised toward heavens. She wept near to as inconsolably as she would have if the Risen Savior had at last arrived to carry her home to the lands beyond the soil of this farm still wearing out her tired and aching bones. Such was the joyous nature of their long overdue reunion.

"My child has returned to me!" she cried up to the slightly bent silhouette standing upon the ground level porch boards just beyond the cabin door. "I knew you was fixin' to return to me afore I passed on! Sill an' all, I wouldn't a said no if'n it was Jesus come to take me home like an angel in da night!"

Mrs. O'Keefe dropped to her knees before the overwhelmed woman of her earliest memories and hugged her tightly as if there were no tomorrow. Miss Leslie cupped her hands to the promised child's sunken cheeks and asked, "What dey gone an' done to my angel a dat west wind? You gonna be okay, my baby?"

Miss Margaret Anne had eaten well from the moment of her release from the asylum, yet she was still ten pounds or a bit more underweight. Beyond the hollowed out caricatures that were her declining facial features, the rot to her teeth and her sagging left eye, which was the direct result of pressing her face into the bars of her cell window for hours on end in an attempt the feel the warmth of the blurred, streaming of the light out beyond that hideous madhouse, there was something else that was missing or that had changed about Miss Leslie's eternal gift given over to her upon those ancient cross-roads into Georgia.

Miss Margaret Anne smiled brightly, though she quickly took noticeable measure to conceal the damage to her teeth due to her shame, and answered her mammy softly and in kind. "I will be okay,

Mammy, but I had to return the light back from whence it came once that awful devil had dropped dead upon the floor. I am just like everyone else now. I see the world with my eyes just the same as you or Pappy. I reckon I might finally be up to eating me some of those famously delightful sweet peas of yours."

Before she could even smile in response to her own wit, the broken-down rendition of the promised child lowered her head mournfully and wept for all of the sorrows of the fourteen years gone by and the once again yet hastily and woefully remembered death of her mother too. Miss Leslie raised little Miss's chin up with her thumb and forefinger and admonished the child to heap praise upon her in the way any old Southern woman from out in the country would, "Nonsense now, my child! You ain't a bit like none a us here. You gone an' done exactly what dem angels a da Good Lord been askin' a you an' you be lookin' da part of an angel for it too! You be hearin' me now, my pretty baby?"

Miss Margaret Anne smiled in return for little more than the receipt of that beautiful comforting voice that had carried her beyond so many of the fears and uncertainties of her childhood. She hugged the woman again as if she would never let her go and the two of them cried it out for the quarter hour until Mr. Laing was at last stirred from his seemingly interminable slumber. Little Miss then began to lament the sins of her past while she continued to weep. "I never meant for any harm to come to Virgil, Mammy! Everything was so right upon the moment but that boy was so broken up inside by what had been done to him and the horrors of his past that some parcel of my light went away from me and seemed to shatter his mind. I could see it in his eyes; everything was too much and too fast and Virgil just couldn't anchor his wits to anything sensible beyond that silver pistol of his."

Miss Leslie drew a breath in deeply while continuing to brace Margaret Anne's shoulders. She then exhaled evenly. She knew what she wanted to say to her daughter but not in the presence of others.

Before her mammy could signal as much, the promised child frantically rejoined her prior thought, "He got the shot off in time. I know he got the shot off in time, Mammy! But why did he have to suffer so in staring direct into those vacant hollows of the insane mind, those infinite places where only broken thoughts belong, for doing little more than being such a good man to me?"

Miss Leslie waived Mr. Laing back into the cabin and Miss Susannah Jane along with him. When her husband and the estranged daughter of Edward and the late Libby Calhoun were back by the sofa of the main room making uncomfortable yet proper introductions amidst the sorrows and the joys of the moment of the promised child's return, Miss Leslie pulled her child up off the porch planks and hugged her. She then whispered into her ear, "You an' I's gonna take us a walk an' talk over all dem things your momma never gots to afore things started movin' in on us all way too fast. Dat be soundin' good to you, my baby? 'Cus you always gonna be my baby since da moment I said yes to God to take you on, you beautiful thing."

Miss Margaret Anne cried harder on the woman's shoulder for a while and then nodded to acquiesce to her mammy's earlier offer to walk off into the pleasant climes of a splendid evening in September. When they reached the rope swing of the old oak, Miss Leslie sat little Miss down and began to push her gently yet firmly enough to stir the air as she made her passes by the old woman relishing in the return of her lost child and the comforting night air. After some of that calming slow time had passed silently between them, Miss Leslie allowed the troubled creature to take in the tantalizing beauty and perfected warmth of a late-summer breeze. When the night air had settled cool and calm again, Miss Leslie began to speak. "You know how evil be presentin' itself in dis here world a ours, don't ya now, my sweet child?"

Little Miss kicked her feet forward just like her mother and sister before her always did, right as the swing once again began to return to the nadir of its course. She relished in the feeling of the soothing evening air upon her cheeks as she called back, "I know only of where it hides itself, Mammy. You know that I never understood the bad things lingering in folks' hearts or why a lie could seem to proliferate for so long."

Miss Leslie smiled as some form of life returned to her promised child and called up to her as she reached the apex of her latest pass, "Dat's'cus you always done had da light dat belong on da other side, my child. I for one can be tellin' ya first hand there ain't but three things dat allow evil to be hidin' for so long in plain sight in dis here world of ours. I'd be willin' to bet my last dollar you don' be knowin' what even a one a dem is or at least what it be feelin' like."

Little Miss laughed as she passed by the thoughtful woman and called back, "You'd a been right back when you last saw me, Mammy, but I truly am not like that anymore. I'm just the same as you or anyone else now. I just haven't had a chance to learn to think like one who believes this world is what it seems to the naked eye."

Miss Leslie shook her head in disbelief and laughed heartily at the more womanly and more human version of what remained of the woodland sprite. "Yessum, well you sure enough do be actin' just like dat girl who went an' left me a waitin' here for her. Well, I'll just go ahead an' tell on ya den. Those things be a wantin', fear and wrath. Dem's all dat evil be usin' to run dis here place."

Little Miss let her feet catch upon the spotted grass beneath the old oak as she passed by until she came to a swaying stop next to her mammy. Her face took on that haunted look of her asylum days and she spoke vacantly as if some strange notion heretofore foreign to her just infringed upon her thoughts. "There is one other thing, Mammy. There is deceit."

Miss Leslie could not see the harrowing expression set upon the promised child's tender mien in the midst of the well-settled darkness. Therefore, she spoke in the same lively and jocular manner of the moment just prior. "Well now, baby girl, I reckon you is at long last catchin' on to da way things work down here. Yes, dem lies dey do be tellin' rules over dem all. Yet even dat clever deceit ain't worth a darn to any of 'em but for da rest a what I done told ya. You can't trick no one into doin' a thing dey could care less 'bout doin' or stealin' a thing dey ain't after havin in da first place."

Little Miss lowered her head to the ground, though she could see little of its form and contour beneath her feet. She asked rather abruptly, "Am I a fallen woman now for what I let those awful men do to me, Mammy? I can't seem to wash myself free of the stain of their ugliness. Everything I did to send that vile demon back from whence he came turned out all wrong, excepting the fact that he's gone now."

Miss Leslie rushed over and wrapped the child in her loving arms once again. She spoke soothingly into her ear as the one among her three mortal mothers assigned to care for her nearly unassailable heart. "What done happened wid Virgil wasn' none your fault, dear child. Just da same be da truth if'n for a moment you done lost your wits in wantin' to know da man in dat way. All things of dese here fallen realms be backward, upside down an' downright inside out. You ain't known no better 'bout da brittle state a Virgil's mind. Heck, none a us here dat ever gots to knowin' da boy woulda guessed a thing like dat, an' there ain't nothin' getting' learned when you givin' da mule a second kick."

Miss Leslie paused a moment to further recall those days back when Virgil ran the farm and added, "Now Virgil, dat boy always done come off like a wisecracker or tough as da leather an' otherwise unawares. How was you to be knowin' dat havin' you 'round a man be like bringin' on a cannon to a rock tossin' fight. You was just built from above for da doin' a somethin' else 'cus there wasn' no one else here dat could do it at da time it sho' 'nuff needed to get on done. I bet you ain't ever knowed what dat meant 'til ya went on ahead an' done it, my sweet child a da light. Me an' your momma ain't never knowed it none either while we was watchin' you get all growed up. 'Sides, we all done knows Virgil was aimin' to get hisself shot or far worse if you ain't tried to cool his heels some. Maybe God done da best He could wid a stubborn ol' mule da likes a Virgil O'Keefe."

Little miss hugged her mammy back and began to cry again. "I never fully understood the reason behind my marrying Virgil until the light was gone out of me. Then I saw that Virgil had met his end the moment he got tangled up with the likes of me, Mammy. There were some good reasons behind what happened, like our babies and keeping Virgil away from those vile men. All the same, I will always feel shame for the fact that I learned what I might one day do to that devil from that beautiful yet awful moment spent with Virgil."

Miss Leslie was quick to reply to such a troubling manifestation. "Dat be a hard one right there, my child but da lines of Mr. Virgil O'Keefe ain't hurtin' none 'round dese here parts. 'Sides, boy da likes a dat always gonna jump first afore he's been swimmin' some. Dis here darkness we comin' outta now, it gonna take some folks lots a time afore da light can safely shine down on dem lies dat dey done took for da truth for all dem years now. Otherwise, it gonna be just da same for dem as it be wid Virgil when he done tried takin' dat light all in 'bout fast as da boy could muster wid you."

Miss Leslie had spoken her piece on that topic and she was about to bring up Amos's father and little Miss's boy, Davey but Margaret Anne beat her to the punch with another troubling thought that had oft times raced through her mind while she was in the asylum. Little Miss spoke with a bit of a stunted cadence to begin due to the gravity and the nature of her worries and her uncertainty over how an honest woman like her mammy might respond. "I see that now too where it concerns what I did to Virgil, Mammy. But the things I did with those evil men…do they get to keep…do they get to keep something of me with them now like the pastor once said back in church, Mammy? That thought has been breaking my heart for nearly nine long years now. I then wonder why couldn't Virgil at least have had what Mr. Bromley had of me before he had to go?"

Miss Leslie squeezed her girl tight and spoke firmly in reply while her own tears began to stream down her softly wrinkling face. "Now you listen to me good, little Miss. I wish your momma was here to tell ya true how it be wid dat, but I reckon I'm da only one who done lived it over an' over back on Butler Island. Ain't no man get to keep nothin' offered from you if'n your heart wasn' trued up at da time. Even if your heart done been right, if he ain't da man he said he was, he don' get to keep nothin' off a ya neither. Those evil men gone now an' dey can't hurt no one let alone you. You been reborn as a woman of da flesh an' bone an' God gonna see to it dat no one ain't gots nothin' a your'n dat you ain't wanted to give 'cus a what you done for us all."

"What do you mean by saying because of what you did for us all, Mammy?" asked the promised child with that same quizzical look she oft times possessed when she was naught but a little girl. Miss Leslie shook her head in disbelief in reply and then answered little Miss thusly, "Child, you definitely bein' a da mind of a proper Southern white woman now. What I'm gon' do wid you? For all a dem years ya cain't see nothin' but daisies and sunlight. Now, you be a comin' home to me an' I needs to be knockin' dat sunlight back into ya wid a mallet. If'n it wasn' dark as da insides a da horse out here I'd jus' be tellin' ya to be lookin' around some. Anyhows, you'd be seein' dat we doin' just fine out here all 'cus a da likes a you, child. And now things is set to just keep right on gettin' better too."

The promised child regained a bit of her zeal upon seeing her mammy so worked up and egged her on a bit further while smirking playfully. She did so partially because she loved getting a rise out of the beautiful old woman and partially because upon that hour and with so much despair still infecting her mind she needed to hear the truth about her life. "What is it that I have done for you all, Mammy?"

Miss Leslie shook her head again and then smiled warmly into the passing draft a warm breeze. She spoke while she thoughtfully revisited the days and years following the promised child's arrival into her arms. "First off, while my mind concernin' your daddy still be a bit mixed, you sho nuff got him an' den all a us out from under da broom a Miss Meara. You done fixed up a broken ol' mule da likes a Mr. Laing and now Little pea be off in da Terminus fixin' to be graduatin' from dat college for da colored folk dey gots there. I never would a been imaginin' da likes a dat while I was watchin' da last a my boys die while I was bein' nothin' to my masta but a used up ol' slave mistress. I done saw da power a what it was you bein' set to do in your eyes right when I took ya from da arms a Miss Sarah. Amos seen it too when we was makin' our way back to Savannah to get you through da wash. Look how good he done come out. Amos be da fanciest colored lawyer man in all dese here Carolinas."

Margaret Anne nodded solemnly and asked, "Do you think that is enough in return for what I did to Virgil?" Miss Leslie looked the woman over carefully amidst the heavy darkness of the hour and said, "You done gave birth to Virgil's baby boy an' gots him back home safely an' ya fixed your'n sister up right nice too after dat demon took to her so she gonna be right to be carin' for Virgil's first boy. Even Miss Sarah been set right by your hand. She an' Adelaide gots dem their own seamstresses shop over in Columbia now. An' child, there ain't no tellin' what would a become of me, even if I had made dem mountains a da Blue Ridge wid Jim. I was so broken up afore da light a your'n eyes was lightin' up my heart dat I wouldn' a made it but a season afore I went mad. Is dat 'nuff for ya or do ya be needin' a bit more coddlin', my baby? 'Cus I'd just like to be stoppin' there by sayin' we all done knows what been a comin' down upon us all if dat demon had lived. I don' want to mention him none now, so I just be leavin' it at dat."

Margaret Anne smiled musingly in accordance with the sudden turn of her mood, although the gesture was hardly visible to her mammy. She played coy for just a bit longer with a woman she knew didn't take any to self-pity only because she loved the tone of her mammy's voice when it was so filled with emotion. "What of poor, Doctor Bailey then, Mammy? Surely he and his girls would have been far happier had they remained up in Virginia or New York and away from this struggle of ours to keep the darkness at bay for but a time."

Miss Leslie laughed snidely in reply and then laughed jovially before she delivered her very candid answer. "You ain't doin' nothin' but testin' me now, child. Don' you forget I been da one fightin' wid ya to wear clothes an' eat dem darned peas for years." Mammy then chortled in a bit in a self-satisfied manner and firmly gave her solicited opinion on the matter of Doctor Bailey, though she was teasing the promised child to a degree. "Let me be answerin' ya by askin' you dis, dear child. What ya think dat Doc Bailey would a been up to now if he kept on sneakin' round through dem woods to bring on da babes a dem secret mistresses?"

Before Margaret Anne could even shrug her shoulders in the manner of one feigning innocence in reply, Miss Leslie answered her own question in regard to the good doctor. "Well, I'll be answerin' da question for ya too den. Dat man a been shot dead afore he gots to his third delivery is where he'd be. Shucks, he be a bit more den lucky to be getting' out a dem woods where you was born da way Miss Jeanne an' Miss Elizabeth Ann done told of it."

The two ladies laughed in unison for a short while and then Margaret Anne smiled back at her mammy and said, "Thank you for that, Mammy. I don't know why but it helped me to hear the words spoken in the familiar tone of your sweet voice. Will you swing some with me before we head on back?" Miss Leslie smiled and replied warmly, "Of course it do after all dat ya done been through, an' of course I will be swingin' some wid ya, my baby girl. I been a waitin' to do jus' dat since you done left on da train all dem years ago now."

The two women squeezed onto the swing together and swayed gently with their arms around one another until they had cried out every last tear for all that had once been sacred to them yet had been taken by sinful, wicked and needy men. The ropes Virgil had once swung over the branch of the stalwart old oak to refashion the swing in the months following the end of the war were long since gone. The new ropes pined and yawned from the strain of their weight just the same while the original wood of the seat Clarke Osment had crafted for his baby girls nearly forty years ago creaked lightly with the stresses of its burden into the blackness of the surrounding nightfall once the crickets had gone silent. The night air was alive with the ghosts and the spirited memories of their past still haunting that old field. The rich but gentle tingling of those dusty phantasms of the mist made it seem as if all the days gone by during their shared moments together out on the farm had converged upon that solitary point in time when they both stood up from the rope swing. The two women playfully teased those old remembrances and apparitions of their loved ones while they walked slowly and in a roundabout way back across the harvested rows of cotton by way of only rote and the light of the stars twinkling above.

At times, they stepped to the beat of the rhythmic yet recurrent and in many ways soothing sounds of the chirping of the crickets and the synchronistic groans of the bullfrogs in want while being blanketed warmly in the knowing that they had reached that final leg of their unforgettable journey together. That long-awaited season of their renewal as mother and daughter had at last begun. Both women cast the last remnants of their earthly baggage somewhere out along the darkened expanse of that gently sloping field, which had provided for their earthly needs for quite some time now, with each step that they took closer to home. They had made their peace with nearly all that lurked in the very darkest corners of their past and within the scarred recesses of their once again hopeful souls.

When Margaret Anne had made out the subtle silhouette of the Laing's cabin up ahead she spoke with a slight outward twinge of regret, "There is one thing I shall not forgive myself for, Mammy." "What is dat, my child?" the physically tired and emotionally charged older woman asked in reply as they readied to begin the final approach toward home.

"Having intimately known the feel of the infinite and miserable void that governed that devil's essence, I could not love his child once I was relegated solely to the ephemeral qualities of the flesh. The boy was of him and in me and I never gave the poor creature a chance to know my heart. He was not evil upon inception as his father surely was but the world I handed him over to without so much as a tender look into his black eyes will surely see to the manifestation of such an unholy contrivance. No child deserves to be without the love of their mother, Mammy. Within the throes of my despair, I allowed the evil beast to hasten that which he will surely attempt to revive slowly as the years go by and then suddenly when the watchful eyes of our kin no longer recall or believe in the verity of what has come to pass in our time."

Miss Leslie took hold of the young woman's hands to halt her progress and then kissed her gently on the forehead. "You isn' but a woman of 'bout thirty years, my child. You just might come to know somethin' a da boy after you done had some time to find yusself as you is now situated. Da story a dat life you done now been given is only just beginnin'. Have faith an' follow dat heart a your'n when dat time done come. There wasn' a thing more you could do while bein' in such a way, my child."

Miss Margaret Anne smiled lovingly at her mammy and replied in the expectant manner of the truly thankful. "You are a wonder and a true gift of God above, Mammy. I cannot tell you how good it feels to at last be home or how much it soothes my oft times breaking heart to be with you. But do know this where it concerns that boy, Mammy; one who has survived looking into the empty, ravenous eyes of the devil is never going back to a place where that beast might once again linger in wait."

To which Miss Leslie replied, "Amen to dat, my child, Amen! Da plan for dat poor boy gots to be in God's hands alone. Da Good Lord done knowed dat da devil can't be wiped away from dis place for good 'til da day Sweet Jesus be a comin' back for us all. But you keep a spot in dat precious heart a your'n for dat boy too. Ain't never no tellin' what love might be comin' to." Margaret Anne nodded thoughtfully in reply and then turned away from Miss Leslie in fronting her stride back toward home.

When they arrived back home they were greeted warmly by both Susannah Jane and old Shug Laing upon that beautiful and eternal moment of their shared deliverance. There was singing in the heavens above and both women who had endured the trials of Job in their own differing ways and had so resplendently said yes to the Almighty throughout the coursings of their lives, offered up their now light and liberated hearts to God. From that moment on they both forever knew where to find the precious feeling of His enduring peace. There was no greater treasure to be had upon this earth.

"It is good to be home," spoke the promised child as she stepped back onto the creaking porch boards and into the arms of Mr. Laing by the light of the old post lantern. The two stood as shimmering silhouettes beneath that rekindled porch lamp when little Miss furthered her initial thought by saying, "My baby girl would have remembered such a day as this forever."

Mr. Laing replied dutifully and in kind, "Welcome home, little Miss. In time, I reckon she will intricately know each memory you keep safe for her until you see her again. Come to think of it, you were such a half pint when you set me right in all the ways an old villain like me could a been set right that it suddenly dawned on me to ask: did I ever properly thank you for the gesture?"

Margaret Anne looked up at Mr. Laing and smiled into the shifting light of the lantern with her blackened teeth and all and replied affectionately, "Every single day you woke up and took care of my mammy and my brother Amos, Mr. Laing, and of course, upon the moment you gave that angel mammy of mine a little daughter of her own. Did you know that you were the only one who could ever get me to eat those dreadful sweet peas? Don't tell Mammy though. She'll get to thinking that I always liked you better, or worse, she'll get to thinking that I'll be looking for a helping or two in the days to come." The two laughed warmly with a deep longing for the days gone by set upon their glinting eyes while continuing to exchange those precious, warming smiles that linger timelessly and are only offered over to the beloved for but a few fleeting moments in this lifetime.

Chapter Eleven

CHAOS

❧

UPON THE FIRST eve of the winter season in the year 1874, some ten years to the day that Edward Calhoun had called to order the initial gathering of the rather disparate, colorful and potently opinionated members of the fellowship of the promised child out at the Leonard Brown Plantation, Miss Jeanne Jolie Basseterre was found dead by her oldest daughter at the age of forty-eight. Her body was discovered out by the side of the lightly traveled dirt road that passed beyond the periphery of the Claibrooke farm. She was lying in the hardened loam of late-December with her eyes wide open and her mouth set frightfully agape. Those once gentle and discerning eyes remained terminally transfixed with a look of dread that no spoken word of the ages could have possibly conveyed with an equivalently evocative effect.

Those now horribly resolute and eternally enchanting orbs of legend, which had unwittingly bound the heart of many an unsuspecting man by way of little more than a passing glance, were facing up to the stars twinkling below the heavens. However, it was certain those now firmly resolute irises of haunting amber beheld nothing of that tranquil nightscape glimmering above. What they continued to behold were the grim constituencies of the moment of death in whatever guise that tricky gatekeeper to the spirit realms had assumed to quarry the elegant mistress so impulsively. While there remained many ambiguities to be resolved where it concerned the untimely demise of the beautiful siren of Uriah and former peeress of the sugar plantations of the Haitian highlands, the look forever set upon the haunting counte-nance of the departed exposed but one truth regarding that desolate evening seemingly absent of hope, she had not expected to meet her end upon the instant death had come for her.

Her partially rimy and absolutely lifeless body was resting a fair ways out from the hobbled mules pulling her flat cart down the frozen carriage way on that dark and wintry night, plagued by a soulless and sheering wind of such hibernal disposition. She had ventured to make the short journey up the road from the Osment farmstead to the Claibrooke pastures upon the arrival of the evening hour to procure some provisions overlooked amid the hustle and bustle of the rapidly approaching regalia of Christmas and in preparation for Shy and her family's arrival to Uriah from over in Augusta. She had left a note behind on the kitchen table for Maime in the event she was held up out at the Claibrooke's place but otherwise stirred up little ado con-cerning the perfectly routine affair.

Be that as it may, Miss Basseterre never returned home amidst the piercing cold of that longest and perhaps blackest night of the annum from a journey she had concluded without incident on a countless number of occasions in times past. In fact, she had normally ven-tured forth to make that particular passage without so much as an afterthought once given over to the slight ordeal of the customarily pleasant walk prior to leaving home. The somewhat distracted mis-tress of the age in those parts of the world likewise smiled warmly to her impromptu stable boy against the grain of that cold and ran-corous evening air brought about by a cutting and whistling cross-current coming in from the northwest as she took hold of the reins. Furthermore, Miss Jeanne had tipped that same groom called by the name of Thaddeus Davis well for his quick work in gearing up the disinterested beasts of burden for the abruptly contrived trip. She had gifted the always hungry young man an abundance of recently and exquisitely concocted holiday fudge just as she was pleasantly yet firmly refusing her then gracious and amiable neighbor's gentlemanly offered company down that darkened road ahead.

The occasion to celebrate upon the noontide of the morrow would be Miss Shy Jolie Basseterre-Brown's one-day belated 26th birthday. Miss Jeanne had been publicly beside her wits, almost as if for show, hours earlier upon forgetting to set aside the eggs needed to confect her daughter's cake and the other remaining appetizing sundry goods she had planned to offer her babies and Mr. Brown upon the very instant of their arrival into Uriah from over in Georgia. Given that a bewitching cold snap had settled in throughout the whole of the county and perhaps the precincts well beyond, Miss Jeanne had elected to forego the mile and half a click walk some hours after her outwardly presented lamentations in favor of her trusty team of mules as the creatures and their accompanying apparatus had not yet been properly retired for the evening.

Upon returning from her scheduled affairs at the church back in town to the cozy confines of the Osment farmhouse by way of her silver horse, Amethyst, Maime Alouette went out searching for her mother with Thaddeus's habitual partner in crime, Henry Davis. Having read the note her mother dutifully left behind, the unlikely pair embarked upon their mission to find Miss Jeanne at around 9:00 PM on that evening of 21st December; an hour that afforded Maime's mother more than enough of a spell to socialize with the notoriously loquacious Miss Penny Claibrooke and return to her planned work in the kitchen back home.

Maime found the already chilled remains of her mother cloaked in her brown winter coat of Shetland wool shortly after the search party of two had located the stalled cart and the lame mules a little ways further up the road. Henry tended to the sorrowful coddling of and then putting down of the mules while Maime wept quietly yet inconsolably over her mother's lifeless body. The echoing of the gunshots piercing the eerie and somber solitude of the gelid night air of the backcountry upon that late evening hour did little to improve the poor, grieving woman's already desolate mind. Yet, Henry knew well that Miss Maime understood the need for expediency when it came to a horribly suffering creature of God's natural order. Henry Davis was near to no better off than the distraught young lady when Miss Lulu and old Gregory fell to the earth. The creatures were true to the anticipated form of the crossbreed in their stubbornness but loyal, diligent and loving creatures all the same.

Some twenty minutes or so back in time, the initial scene upon the concerned search party of two's arrival to the dark, open gap in the road a bit less than a mile out from the end of the drive shared by both the Osment and Davis families was not one the still single woman well into her 27th year would soon, if ever, come to forget. Upon immediately sensing that something was horribly wrong, a harshly beset Henry Davis could do nothing to console the poor woman who, though she was nearly approaching spinster status according to the habitual marriage practices of the time and place, had become just about the most sought after bride in Barnwell County once her sister had given her hand over to Mr. George Ridley Brown of Augusta. At first glance, the scene loosely fit the description of a woman who had been thrown from her cart after her less than agreeable, yet stalwart all the same, chargers of a grinding and plebian sort had taken a simultaneous misstep upon overlooking a deep and disastrous chuckhole. The uncommon fissure in the road may have been uncharacteristically carved into the earth by a passing wagon of considerable magnitude due to the interminable freezing of the top soil following an inundation of winter rain not but a week back.

Shrewd Henry Davis never believed as much about the fatal blemish in the road. That is he never supposed that the hole had been opened up in due course at all. He knew the condition of that carriageway upon just about every hour of the day on that 21st of December, and given that Miss Jeanne had departed the Claibrooke farm reasonably soon after arriving, sometime near 7 PM, such a disastrous gap opening up in the earth couldn't have occurred more than an hour or two after his last trip down the lightly used thoroughfare. No heavy pack wagons would have been out there at that hour under those conditions at that time of the year. Beyond that, if such a calamity were even remotely possible, Henry reasoned further that his exceedingly wise brother Thaddeus never would have allowed Miss Jeanne to make the journey unaccompanied. Such was Gospel good and true, at least according to Henry's fairly astute reckoning where it concerned the workings of the world out in those parts.

Henry continued to view such an occurrence as near to impossible right up until the evening he died in his sleep of old age at his farm outside of Branchville. As for Miss Maime, the look set upon her mother's eyes as she lie there lifeless and near to frozen upon the hard dirt of the winter road, that is until Doc Bailey was brought out to rectify the unease garnered by that particular horror conveyed by the eternal stare of the stilled and wide-eyed visage of the dead and furthermore, properly examined and covered her remains for the short return trip home; that haunting look set upon her mother's comely visage for all eternity told Miss Maime all she needed to know in regard to what had undone the uncrowned queen of the Caribbean realms, the legendary mistress of both Sumter and then Uriah, and the guardian of her timid heart.

The real fireworks surrounding Miss Jeanne's untimely demise didn't begin to occur until the final hour of that final day in the year 1874. Such was the moment Miss Shy Jolie laid her hands upon the more than two-hundred-year-old and never before spoken of journal of the descendants of Katherine Evelyn Elaine de Jacmel, which had been updated in recent years to include the essential excerpts of the life of Miss Jeanne Jolie Basseterre. The journal was neatly tucked away beneath some floorboards in her mother's bed chamber and nearly remained undiscovered for another time and another place of God's choosing altogether. Perhaps a more settled time somewhere off in the distance and a time when the remaining secrets of the enchanting woman's extraordinary life would be less incendiary to those among the living and therefore were set to be revealed by her as of yet unborn kin of the ensuing generations that settled in behind her beloved daughters out at the Osment farmstead. Though little of the contents written by the recently deceased within the ancient, leather bound scroll of the Basseterre clan were openly revealed by Miss Shy or any others for that matter, one could safely reckon that the town of Uriah was never quite the same beyond the moment Miss Shy noticed that slight and otherwise inconsequential gap in the perfectly trimmed, pine floor boards of her mother's room.

Of the few yet pertinent and highly notable secrets not to be revealed upon that hour, or perhaps ever, by her protective daughter and properly endowed guardian of the golden cross, the most shocking find was without a doubt Miss Jeanne's candid portrayal of what took place during the retiring hours of 22nd May, 1858. When Miss Shy read over the scandalous and distressing avowal that detailed the events surrounding the coming to be of the ascendant yet peculiar and perhaps eccentric young woman of fifteen years now occupying her childhood room, she dropped to the floor and passed out momentarily upon receiving the dull yet potent blow of such a sordid shock. The only person with whom Mrs. Brown initially shared those particular contents of the journal was the good man of such refined judgement and sacred ties to her half-sister, Doctor Emmet Bailey. She would not disclose the particulars of the dour and scandalous tale left behind by her late mother to the far more puritan mind of Maime Alouette or the young woman whose life would be forever altered upon receiving such true yet rag-worthy news until she wrote two separate letters from her somewhat new yet always troubled homeland of Haiti nearly a decade later in 1884.

Within the journal was revealed the fullness of the awful shadings, miscreant sounds and vile scents forever etched into the then shattered mind of the distraught woman regarding the appalling events surrounding the otherwise unattended visit to the Osment farmstead of Union Army Captain, Lucian Reed Morgenthau. Upon those timeworn leaves of hearty vellum, her mother described in horrific detail, albeit by way of rather abstract and emotionally charged though almost incoherently detached prose, the Yankee officer's defilement and unholy abomination of the sanctity of her pious and heavenly given person. Captain Morgenthau had threatened to kill the first, or perhaps even both if such became necessary to conceal his identity, of her daughters to return home to the farm from their daily afternoon lessons back in town. He would do the deed slowly and easily before her very eyes if he was not granted what he personally had longed for of her corporeal conformation and that which his dark and always wanting masters commanded him to have from the beautiful mistress of Uriah; a stalwart, alluring and powerful child of the line of the golden cross pledged to the most sinister orders of the accursed realms.

Following her slow and sorrowful rendition of her mother's words that so abstractly brought to life the nearly indescribable horrors of that afternoon that Miss Jeanne had remained pledged to only her inviolable promise of keep her daughters safe from harm, such was clear to Miss Shy that her mother knew precisely what that horrible beast had so callously yet purposefully and thoroughly done to her. Those were the eternal hours of her mother's suffering and wait; the hours upon which the poor woman abided by the sickly wants of some unknown demon of the northlands. The sickly wants of an outwardly charismatic though soulfully demented creature, which through some strange yet primeval provincial connections held some form of deadly sway over the proximate affairs of the Carolina countryside long before the Yankees had marched on through these parts.

From Miss Jeanne's written words, Miss Shy was able to suitably discern that her mother knew well and knew as much upon the instant that the sour fruit of that man's awful deeds of that May afternoon would carry on well into the years to come. He had chosen the proper time as if he scented the rutting of his mates like some rabid beast of the wild striving to compel the proliferation of its line. What the abused did not know when she penned her words as something of a curative and appropriately damning exercise was that those of the divine realms capable of guiding her spirit and her soul, by way of her unwavering faith and the ancient talisman of the golden cross, would endeavor to deliver a delicate creature in lieu of that woefully intended demon spawn. They would deliver unto the land and the proper line of the golden cross a delicate creature which in accordance with the laws of nature possessed a potency equivalent to that which the shadowy beast had seeded deep within her.

Those of the angelic realms were not capable of undoing his malicious sway under the bounds of the age. Nevertheless, they could by way of a divine miracle reorder the source which possessed command over that raw vigor by sending forth a promised child of the light not meant to fully reconcile with her mortality until the source of her flagrant capacity was no more. Furthermore, those of the heavenly realms would do so for the sole purpose of ending that unholy and accursed abomination to the lands of the west by once again splintering those dark powers the devil had consolidated within over the coursings of the centuries.

The possibility of such far more agreeable premonitions and inklings regarding the craven seed of her womb made little sense to the reader's mother in the hours of her tears of desolate sorrow that followed the consummation of the act. However, such was true only because of the hellish nature and maddened cravings of the source of such a gift. In short order, Miss Shy's mother did indeed come to discern, purely in accordance with the hallowed premonitions given over to her with such force by the golden cross immediately subsequent to the terrors of that day, a time when she was confined to her bed with a raging and near fatal fever for three days, that the tender kernel of a child of great light had been delivered into the world as the result of her indescribable suffering. His seed was in her but somehow the source of that demon's vile and unbound will was transformed into a prodigious light of the age; a light capable of confounding even the most miserable depths of the darkness.

Be that as it may, she continued to despise the very pith of the premise behind the child for a short while longer due to the nature of its brutal father. However, while wandering through the depths of what appeared to be little more than delusion to those carefully watching over her while her fever raged on through its final day, the woman said yes to those appointed to tend to the promised child from on high. She said yes at least as it concerned the concealment, preservation and future provision of the unborn child upon her birth and in the years to follow. Furthermore, the then healing, but still troubled woman knew of but one way to achieve such a seemingly impossible demand.

Doctor Whittingham of Uriah had notified Edward via currier of Miss Jeanne's perhaps terminal condition in the late spring of 1858. Edward arrived out to the Osment farm seven days after the onset of her unspeakable and entirely undisclosed torments in response to the news of her known illness. In spite of the fact that by the time of his arrival out to the farm the rather stoic looking ward of the old and affable doctor to the local townsfolk was feeling and behaving much more akin to her normal gracious and wholesome self, the gallant aristocrat of the thriving antebellum planter class accompanied the lady and her young yet splendidly blossoming daughters back to Sumter. His intended purpose in returning Miss Basseterre to Sumter was to allow her to spend time in her old quarters out on the plantation under the supervision of one of the best physicians in the state of

South Carolina. Be that as it may, to say that the man was feeling a bit feverish over the prospects of the gallant woman's temporary return to her former quarters on the grounds of the estate would have been a gross misrepresentation of the man's true feelings upon the hour of their departure from the pleasant climes of the Uriah countryside. The man forever hoped where it regarded his Haitian princess.

In the ensuing days after their arrival to Butterworth Hall, Maime and Shy thrived running about the place with the Calhoun daughters and even Aubrey while Miss Jeanne prepared for the inevitable. The girls were quite familiar with the grounds of the estate and the Calhoun children. They had come often to visit with their mother while she continued to do what she could to keep Edward's Caribbean merchant trading operations in line while raising her family out at the farm. Seeing all of the children so happy together made Miss Basseterre's looming task at least somewhat easier to bear as the moment of her given opportunity swiftly approached.

Though she was certainly never directed or in any way inspired to approach her given task regarding the sanctity of the promised child under the cover of deceit, she fell victim to the sin of doubt. Therefore she envisioned no realistic occasion by which Edward would consent to such a dreadful stain upon his name under the usually auspicious, yet in this case much maligned, circumstances of the truth. Her lack of faith in both God above and the man who loved her dearly would have been proven imprudent, but her conjecture of such a nature was always destined to be relegated to the bounds of supposition just a short, sweet, memorable while into the offing. The perceived way forward of things back then for the woefully abused woman was simply the nature of the chaos spawned by evil left to be tamed by way of the enduring pureness of the heart only after such delicate lessons have been learned. As such, the only question that remained to be properly understood regarding her chosen course of effecting Edward's dutiful aegis unto the graces of her unborn child would be the severity of the wound inflicted as the result of her treachery.

Although Edward Christopher Calhoun had mistakenly written some years later on in his life that the intended seduction of Miss Basseterre had occurred on 25th May 1858, the actual time and date of the event, which would serve as something near to the man's metaphorical anchor for many of his memories tied to the beautiful things offered in this life, was the afternoon of Monday, May 31st, 1858. Miss Basseterre's quarters were empty and would be for some several hours until her girls returned to her from a trip into town with Susannah Jane and Elizabeth Ann. She lured the lord of the manor down to the gorgeous and perfectly manicured premises of her abode with a brief note and a pink spring tulip delivered by Miss Marney. Miss Marney was a stout and delightful older woman with a lively and enchanting African accent that was accentuated by captivating Dutch inflections and who worked several odd jobs around the main manor of the estate.

Miss Jeanne knew that Edward always spent Mondays up in his classically decorated office adjoining the master chamber of the manor. He was generally filled with a certain brand of some strange form of wanderlust on those days he spent focused upon the more mundane tasks of managing his prospering and well-endowed enterprises. Upon Miss Marney's arrival to his quarters, Mr. Calhoun smiled and graciously took the note from the glowing maidservant while the charming woman smiled that wily smile of the knowing. He read the words so beautifully written upon the parchment in an elegant hand while standing before the suddenly and rather impulsively beaming elder woman as she awaited his response.

He did not reveal anything of the letter's contents verbally to the kind and always expectant woman standing before him in wait. However, the man seemed to so naturally borrow something of the apportionments of the beaming glow of the maidservant in such a brightly or perhaps brazenly displayed manner that Miss Marney near to blushed on the gentleman's behalf. Needless to say, Mr. Calhoun did not delay in jotting something down by way of responding to the note. He then thanked Miss Marney for her perfected service and proceeded to make his way down the hall and off to the mistress's residence to see what Miss Basseterre's slightly peculiar and curiously provocative correspondence regarded. For the first time since the exquisitely elegant siren of the soft and exotic easterly breezes of Hispaniola's marriage to Mr. Osment all those years ago now, he hoped where it regarded the woman of his dreams. He hoped as he bounded down the main stairs of the manor toward her quarters. Miss Marney giggled in knowing that the clearly bemused man would arrive well in advance of his hastily scribbled reply intended to be delivered by none but her still serviceable yet old and tired legs.

The rest of the interlude that caused Edward to believe he was indeed the father of Miss Margaret Anne has been spoken of elsewhere, heretofore and in more intimate detail. Still and all, it would be prudent to mention that the moment of his beautiful relief from the very deepest of his most intense and enduring aches was not in any way something less than what he had always imagined it would be. In fact, when the Haitian mistress delivered the news of her dishonorably inadvertent pregnancy to him early in July of that same year, the man held no doubt whatsoever as to the verity of her claims. He wholeheartedly believed her due to the pureness and piety of her nature and the tenderness displayed by Miss Basseterre during the enduring hours of their affection, which were retraced nearly continually and without relent amidst the heavy warmth of that enclosed room on an otherwise pristine afternoon of late spring.

Now, as to why Miss Jeanne actually found her person alone out on that cold, dark road of frozen dirt for a time on the night of 21st December 1874, there existed far more to her primary and rather innocent claim of procuring some desperately needed eggs from Miss Penny Claibrooke that evening. She had consorted with Miss Shy back during the Thanksgiving holiday of that same year regarding the diminutive probability of mischance where it concerned the event of her untimely demise. She spoke candidly to her daughter in an effort to glean Miss Shy's thoughts on a matter that was infinitely troubling to her heart as her daughter was the proper bearer of the golden cross she had come to rely on for so long in that present moment. Miss Jeanne spoke of her promise to Edward to secure the vow of Miss Margaret Anne to the unknown consort of Mr. Morgenthau hailing from Vermont.

Of course, Miss Shy had balked at the horrible pretense behind little Miss's arranged marriage altogether. Yet, she did so only of the accord of her habitually hot-blooded demeanor and not some premonition given off by the ancient cross forged of gold centuries ago, perhaps somewhere up along the Pyrenees if not during those years the relic's artisan spent living beneath the Temple in Jerusalem. While Mrs. Brown was indeed the perfect custodian of the golden cross for the times to come, the sassy and opinionated young woman still perceived the relic as little more than a family heirloom and the key to some ancient and unproven treasure she sought to one day return to Haiti to protect. Thusly, while the cross was speaking to both women in its own indirectly offered manner, given both the prodding the cross delivered to Miss Jeanne concerning the timing of the gift and the lingering detachment to the cross's spiritual proclivities exhibited by its wildly temperamental bearer of the present hour, Miss Jeanne was left wanting for the benefit of those forceful premonitions regarding defining matters she had received in times past.

Miss Shy's return to her mother's homeland and the land of her maternal forebears would in time be effected on her behalf. However, her deportation would not be fashioned in a willing manner. Her relocation to the island with her children would be the direct result of what she had come to learn from her mother over that Thanksgiving holiday and then from her mother's journal over the fortnight following her death. Mr. Reed saw to the blazing young beauty's permanently, and without the pretense of choice, offered accommodations in the land of her maternal ancestors from his station always lurking somewhere behind the scenes of all which transpired back in Uriah.

In conjunction with the lack of proper restraint set upon her tongue when the fiery young woman perceived even the slightest hint of a miscarriage of justice stirring anywhere within her sphere of influence, that highly toxic to many and heretofore wholly clandestine information regarding both the lineage of and the conjugal intentions forced upon the promised child were indeed the absolute and non-negotiable reasons behind Miss Shy's involuntary move to the island and furthermore, something of the young woman's ultimate undoing. Still and all, once Miss Shy was forcibly domiciled in Haiti against her will, and although she was deported only once her mother no longer lived to stand for her, most who had the pleasure of knowing the Carolina firebrand during her tumultuous island years would have agreed that her sassy and politically divergent tongue served as the bearer of her ultimate and final ruination. The country of Haiti continued to exist amidst a perpetual state of social upheaval and lingering colonial persecution from the very instant it had declared its independence from the French back in 1804. That irascible human discord, which appeared near to irrevocable by the date of Miss Shy's arrival to the island, was set against a backdrop of the pristine yet luxuriantly wild natural beauty of the one-time Pearl of Antilles.

As it concerns Miss Jeanne's travails on the night of 21st December, 1874, specifically, the following excerpt from Edward Christopher Calhoun's private journal was shared with Maime Alouette some years following the day Edward passed in the summer of 1901, near to the eve of his 80th birthday. The only surviving rendering of what occurred on that fateful night was delivered to Mrs. Maime Alouette Osment Duval, the proper legal name the oldest daughter of Miss Jeanne carried following her marriage to the travelling preacher man and father of her children, by the late Mr. Calhoun's forty-two year old caretaker, Miss Annie Grace Oriana. Miss Oriana hand delivered a copied transcription of the page in person to both of Edward's intended recipients when she returned with her long-time companion and their two sons to the Southern realms of the sandy clay she knew so well and the fields of cotton of her birth.

The unedited entry was copied in precise accordance with Edward's wishes and set to be delivered as an individually separate article transliterated from the pages of the required remittance of the entirety of his official biographical memoirs to Mr. Sommers's record keeping replacement, Miss Sally Kingston, back at the Calhoun family archives in Sumter. The genuine and heartfelt representation of what transpired that evening of 21ˢᵗ December 1874 was scheduled to be provided to Miss Jeanne's oldest daughter and Miss Elizabeth Ann Calhoun. Such was also certain, given that she served as Edward's posthumous scribe and standard bearer in the years that the full truth of the intent behind Mr. Calhoun's questionable deeds was set to be unveiled to those aforementioned select few, that the constructs behind Mr. Calhoun's carefully chosen words were no secret to the majestic Haitian mistress of lore's youngest daughter all the same.

New York, New York – 7 March 1891

Description of the evening events of 21 December 1874 as recalled some years later by a man known amongst the living to be someone of ill repute

By the looks of her steadily shivering frame, she had been waiting in the darkness and the cold for some twenty minutes when our carriage arrived at the spot along the frozen dirt road where she had stopped. The temperature on that night was well below freezing and the winter wind was not without the occasional sharpness to its razing, late-December teeth as we approached the otherwise open stretch of the lane, the place beside the three long-standing magnolias. The spot where she had instructed Mr. Morgenthau to meet her thirty minutes prior to the eight o'clock hour. She kept no lantern on her cart. Therefore, we only knew that we were approaching close to where she was awaiting us due to the sudden unwillingness to proceed of our impeccable twin steeds boarded out of Sumter.

As devilish and deviant as he was beneath his repugnantly attractive human exterior, Mr. Morgenthau picked up on the scent of the stalwart animals' fear upon the instant. He whistled sharply to call the horses bearing us hence to a halt. Though they had no familiarity with the man outside of the hour we had spent together on this leg of my journey over from Sumter, the blowing and sharply agitated beasts obliged.

We were perhaps twenty yards shy of reaching her flat cart but I presumed from the moment of our rather abrupt halt that the demon of the night preferred things that way. I began to step down from the coachmen's seat that I shared with my business associate of a frightfully eternal bent but he spoke harshly in reply to my swiftly adopted intentions. "Remain here with the animals. I shan't be long and I have no wish for the woman to know you are present unless I need to remind her of the consequences to her reneging upon her promise to consent on behalf of the young lady."

Though I distrusted the man and despised leaving her alone in his presence along that darkened stretch of only intermittently traveled country road, I surmised that it was my neck on the line in accordance with our contract signed in Charleston back in 1871. As such, I nodded and remained silent until he walked away, at which point I drew my single-shot pistol and kept my ears pricked to the ready. The sound of his slowly departing boots crushing the frozen clumps of dirt along the road beneath his cloven feet was rather ominous and unnerving with the high pitched whistle of the wind occasionally grating my ears.

Unfortunately, I could not hear all of which they spoke at a distance of twenty measured paces with the wind then screaming its way through the low trees and the high winter grass of the orchards out beyond as it was from time to time. What I did hear her exclaim clearly before I was called to approach was, "I shall never consent to a marriage that is not of the child's own accord. I love Edward dearly. Yet neither of us possesses that right where it concerns the child's future. I am sorry that I lead you both to believe otherwise."

At that moment a pack of coyotes howled somewhere off in the distance. They did so inauspiciously and in unison, as if they were present to support the whims of the demon man. When the dogs were silent once again, Mr. Morgenthau called me over to bear witness to the presentation of his answer to the then rather obstinate and obdurate woman shivering before him in the road. She stood with a blanket loosely wrapped around the brown winter coat I had bought for her over in Scotland a time ago.

The demon man addressed me coldly. "Mr. Calhoun, please step forward and join us if you don't mind. There seems to be a flaw found by the lovely lady within the terms of our initial arrangement. There is a new price to be levied in exchange for her change of heart."

I was scared beyond my wits for not only my own sanctity, as the man owned my soul to a degree while he lived and breathed in his human form, but for the safety of my eternally beloved Miss Jeanne as well. I tried to cock my pistol clandestinely when the wind picked up but the rising sheer betrayed my intentions when it died down to an eerie calm, as if the demon man furthermore controlled something of the very intentions of the natural order at that hour.

He cackled wickedly in his usual frame when he heard the hammer lock into place and remanded me to join them with or without my weapon then placed at the ready. I, of course, elected to bring the weapon in the knowing that I would not abide to stand by idly if the woman of my every loving intention fell under his hand. I walked slowly and evenly until I reached the place where they stood like two shadows amidst a differing realm, with only the shinning whites of their eyes marking them as both present and living beings alike.

When I was standing directly next to the man and facing Miss Jeanne, he walked up to her and clasped her head in his dreadful, long-nailed hands. I was but six feet away from the man and I raised my pistol to his head while imploring him thusly, "Unhand her, you demon of the night! You have no bargain with the concerned mother of the intended bride to be!"

Mr. Reed laughed in response to my command. Furthermore, he laughed in such a way that I felt as if I stood there before that demon of the night as little more than an impotent child, though I possessed a weapon of grave and cataclysmic consequence to him at our current distance from one another. Such was true irrespective of the uncertain pretenses caused by that menacing and abounding cover of darkness. While his unnerving laugh settled down into the quiet yet rushing flow of the cold, winter wind, Miss Jeanne sensed that something had gone horribly wrong and called out to me, "Honor your agreements, Edward. That is the only way. Otherwise you will know far worse than the earthly end to either of us here and now."

Mr. Morgenthau sensed that my beloved was trying to relay something to me well beyond the apparent and direct meaning of her words and that the element of his tantalizing moment of surprise was slipping away into the very wind blowing evenly at his back. He squeezed her face something dreadful and she screamed. I fired the pistol into the square of his back upon hearing the outcry of her torment. I did not want to risk missing him by trying for his head when I could see so very little before my gelid and wind-watered eyes. Expecting him to fall as the result of the ball striking his back from such close range, I threw the pistol down into the frozen dirt of the road and prepared to tend to Miss Jeanne.

To my abject horror, the vile man only laughed again and furthermore gave me a moment to sharpen my senses for what was to come. I rushed towards him and then heard the cracking of her neck and spine as he twisted his limbs swiftly upon inhuman coursings more rapid and violent than the hastily hissing outer wall of a low moving tornado. She sighed a final whimpering and exasperated breath and then fell to the road onto her back. I stepped forward smartly to tend to her but the man took hold of my neck with his right hand. I pulled helplessly at his gripping claw but he simply squeezed the tender place violently until I saw nothing but blackness and then the ceiling of the carriage as we made towards Sumter under cover of that devastating obscurity some hours later.

I did nothing but weep for her while he lamented my useless insolence and his having to dig the chuckholes into the frozen earth of the road for the sake of appearances. He mentioned rather enjoying the breaking of the lead legs of the mules but such was to be expected of that eternal menace set to defile anything given over to the earth in God's intended way. I wept inconsolably like a child as he spoke but I remembered the last of his words. "The consent of the child's legal father by enjoined though hidden decree in the absence of her mother's earthbound will shall suffice under the proper terms of our agreement and the eternal laws by which I must abide. Give me your consent, Edward and I will deliver you unharmed to your home and bother you naught until the day I return to deliver the young woman unto her husband up in Vermont in accordance with said promise."

I stood my ground for a time out of outright hatred for the man and to sell the remnants of her plan, though we had made such a catastrophic error in underestimating both the physical capacity of the demon man and my ability to stand in for the child's mother in the event any harm befell her. However, those are details for another twist to our saga to be known at another and still to be appointed time. For the record, I will end my tale of that evening by saying that I consented to the man on behalf of the child. For the sake of my honor, I offer only that such consent was not made for the benefit of my own neck or the future provisions of my wealth.

Though many would come to suspect that I was responsible for the death of my beloved due to their knowledge of her insistence on withdrawing her consent for Margaret Anne's betrothal, Mr. Morgenthau did clear my pistol from the road. I shall never know what became of the errant ball, yet none could ever prove or posit that I stood upon that darkened road with her that night at the hour of her death. In the shadow of her great sacrifice to see the vile demon of the age on to his end, I took my lonely and *silent solace for a time in the fact that all things would one day be revealed in accordance with God's plan for us all.*

In the end, the woman was honorable to the blessedness of her daughter and protected me until she was no longer able. I will never know if she expected the outcome that came for her that night out on that cold and lonely country road, but I do know that she was at peace with whatever came to pass whilst she remained true to those she loved and true to her dear child saddled with such an unimaginable burden that was beyond even her own. She was a complex and elegant woman, whose heart was often shrouded in mystery, but she was loyal and loving to both her children and to me in the ways upon which my own shortcomings and the meddlesome workings of the world allowed. There can be no regret, only the provisioning for of the promise that remains and that which is destined to come.

I love her dearly and I always will. That truth shall remain no matter what those given over to write the history of these turbulent, viciously defiled and politically charged days will chose to believe and therefore convey to posterity. There was always a reason beyond the means for my unwavering commitment to the revival of the Calhoun name and the once again thriving estate. I was simply the one to draw him one step closer and without warning to that which he had always truly coveted. The eternal contract from which her promised child's grace and light absolved me and countless others at such a cost to the innocent still bears the mark of my blood. Yet, due in large measure to the bravery of my beloved, there are none but I that remain party to the agreement upon the hour of this declaration. May God have mercy upon my soul.

The funeral service for Miss Jeanne Jolie Basseterre was held in town at the Episcopal Church at eight o'clock in the morning on the second day following Christmas. The properly given date was Sunday, December 27, 1874. The extended families of many were gathered in and around the town of Uriah for the Christmastide. As such, nearly all of the men present for the service excepting the oldest and the infirmed among them were forced to stand in the back and along the outer walls of the standard looking house of worship of the day, which was painted white and constructed of a durable pine.

There were, or course, many rumors swirling about Uriah pertaining to the untimely demise of the youthful looking woman who none present would have guessed was near to approaching her fiftieth year when she was presumed to have fallen so harshly from her cart. The beautiful family was well known to everyone in town and many had an opinion regarding Miss Jeanne's enduring relationship with the gallant Mr. Calhoun. Moreover, Miss Jeanne, her two proper daughters, her rather angelic and oft times Anglo appearing adopted daughter, and her fondly remembered late husband, Clarke, had remained distinguished and unwavering staples in town in some form or another since back in forty-four. That was the year that handsome devil of a man, Mr. Clarke Joseph Osment, first arrived in Uriah to sharecrop the lower forty of the current configuration of the Osment farmstead under contract with Edward Calhoun.

Miss Jeanne Basseterre had followed Clarke out to the property from the Calhoun's old Congaree estate where Edward and his children spent much of their time to escape the constant oppression of Miss Meara not but a year and a few seasons later and upon the Saturday following their wedding day of Friday, 17th October, 1845. Though the property was not officially recorded in her name until the summer of 1858, when Miss Jeanne had come to town she wasted no time in laying claim to that once idle tract of Calhoun land Clarke was working and which had last been tended to by an eccentric and intemperate distant cousin of Mortimer Calhoun by the name Aloysius Hamilton. Mr. Hamilton had wandered out to the property in November of 1822 and by all accounts was never heard from again following the summer of 1826. Many in Uriah back in those days suspected that Mr. Hamilton was involved in the nasty business of the hangings, persecutions and near deadly floggings of more than a hundred folk down in Charleston, which were the dreadful derivates of the resolving of the Denmark Vesey affair.

Constable Samuel Johnston, one of the town's two keepers of the peace and a tall, sturdy gentleman of a rather rough and impersonal demeanor, kept a watchful eye upon the assembled mourners from his standing position just below the raised podium of the lectern. The overzealous law man was prepared to quickly diffuse any emergent signs of trouble that might arise due to the brightly burning passions of the culturally divergent members of the congregation upon the hour, though such an outbreak of any violence whatsoever was quite unlikely to occur in a house of worship down home in Uriah. The constable was also diligently scanning the audience for any suspicious activity or perhaps any inkling at all that might guide him towards a clearer understanding of the plausible yet strange circumstances surrounding Miss Basseterre's untimely and somewhat brutal death. He shivered a bit from head to toe when thinking of the mules blindly stepping into that deep and narrow chuckhole, causing the poor woman to be thrown from her cart so harshly that she broke her neck clean through just above the spine on that frozen dirt of the wintry road.

Although he was the subject of a few of the rumors swirling about in regard to Miss Jeanne's passing, largely due to the cryptic rumblings of Miss Shy, Edward Calhoun and his three daughters still residing in South Carolina were all present for the eulogy so graciously given over to them all with the patent fervor of Father Morrison. The Calhoun women also stood present for and walked in the procession that followed the service out to the site of Miss Jeanne's internment. Mr. Reed lingered nearby, skulking somewhere out beyond the property line of the church in an effort to remain out of sight while keeping an informal eye upon things. He dared not set his foot upon any corner of that hallowed and duly consecrated ground. The vile man fretted over very little while enmeshed within the wares of the current state of his human condition. However, seeing all those present whose lives he had inflicted such havoc upon gathered in the same place while under the spell of the charged emotions that follow such loss left him quite uneasy while he paced to and fro from beneath the cover of the woods beyond.

Though her presence was a surprise to nearly all in attendance, Elizabeth Ann was indeed present for the ceremony of the gallant woman she loved so dearly. She had made few public appearances since the winter months of 1872 and with good reason. The young woman was devastated by the loss of her nanny of a few years and her surrogate mother for many, yet she appeared strangely contented or perhaps at peace throughout the entirety of the morning while she endured the constant unease of Virgil O'Keefe and the visible derision of many in town. A preponderance of the God-fearing folk in Uriah considered Miss Calhoun to be something of harlot while basing their opinions solely upon what they knew or had heard rumored of the woman's prior reputation. Still and all, the mother of a blooming two-year old boy was not the same person that had been tainted by the man now pacing the woods beyond. Little Miss had cured her of that once deeply rooted and malicious seed.

Among those with such a shaded view of the once again lovely young lady and secretive mother of one, were Lloyd Brooks and Ephraim Moncton. The two miscreant louts of her yesteryear were both now otherwise idle or merely skirt chasing men known to be heavy into the drink and who possessed knowledge of a religious nature concerning the woman they openly mocked, yet continued to secretly pine for, as the sick and sadistic seductress by the name of Miss Calhoun. Mary Grice and Blair Raimi had made an effort to straighten Mr. Brooks and Mr. Moncton out some prior to entering the church but the two bawdy young men understood little of the ladies' uppity, carriage-class language and had been further embold-ened by a healthy ration of the bust head prior to scampering off for the church. Other than the aforementioned, for their part on that sad and solemn winter morning of 1874, the sisters of Elizabeth Ann, Mary Grice and her once again privileged daughters and Blair Raimi did little more than endure the crowds and the quaint setting of the emotionally burdensome countryside affair.

Following the moment of Miss Jeanne's internment, which was a difficult ordeal for the groundskeeper of the Episcopal Church, Mr. Lester Bowen, amidst the continuing nightly freezes of that particular week, Miss Shy, Maime, Elizabeth Ann, Blair Raimi, Virgil O'Keefe and Miss Margaret Anne walked together back to the post at the front of the church to which Edward's team and carriage were tied. Mr. and Mrs. Laing, Little pea, Amos, Doctor Bailey and the Satterfield clan followed behind them and Edward, Mr. Sommers and Mary Grice and her family remained at the rear of the informal procession that represented the melding of most who constituted Miss Jeanne's makeshift and immediate families.

Sometime later, after Edward and his family and the Satterfield's, including the still mute and broken Miss Sarah, had begun their return journey to Sumter, the remaining mourners for and daughters of the deceased sat sorrowfully and solemnly gathered within the passable confines for such a pack, the adjoining kitchen and pantry of the Osment farmstead. Of course, Miss Shy began the discussion with a kinder, gentler prodding of the facts and circumstances surrounding her mother's fall from her cart than was her usual manner of addressing the tenets of her oft times turbulent agendas. Miss Leslie, Little pea and Mr. Laing had returned to their cabin with Miss Shy's two very young children, Andre Francis Basseterre Brown and Bailey Leeward Basseterre Brown. Therefore, the remaining contingent left to mull over Miss Shy's soon to be quite vocal concerns stood as Doctor Bailey, Amos, Maime, Miss Margaret Anne and Virgil. George Ridley Brown had little interest in any of it and for good measure had retired to the sofa out in the living room for a sorely needed nap some time ago.

"Now, I didn't want to bring up such a thing, mind y'all now, but doesn't anyone else find what happened to momma rather strange?" began Miss Shy in a tone that was quite suggestive and only beginning to approach abrasive.

Doctor Bailey had examined the deceased woman's neck with his own hands more than few times. He did not believe that a fall had caused such a clean separation of the woman's neck and spinal cord. Nevertheless, the only alternative methods by which the good doctor could conceive of such a casualty occurring were all far less plausible than the currently accepted provisions offered up for the benefit of the masses to explain Miss Jeanne's death. Therefore, the good doctor answered Miss Shy's opening salvo flatly with a twinge of consternation given for effect and to convey his distaste for the young lady choosing to travel down such a road at all. "I did find the injury strange and not likely to be correlated with a fall the likes of the one your mother was presumed to have endured that night. However, Miss Shy, are you to have us believe that a bear or some other beast of the wild contorted your mother's neck so viciously only to leave her lying there in the road as is? Certainly no man of this earth destroyed the soundness of her cervical vertebrae in such a manner."

Maime grew uneasy and stood up from the kitchen table to pace the room as the discussion continued. Virgil thought back to the strange man lurking in the southern woods that had fired his rifle in the direction of him and Elizabeth Ann on that fateful day he first kissed Miss Calhoun while he offered up his own undeveloped yet not wholly preposterous theory for consideration. "Y'all, perhaps there is somethin' dat haunts these here grounds dat ain't no man or common beast a dem there woods at all. Y'all seen all dat little Miss can do. Gots to be a reason for dem there inexplicable graces too."

Doctor Bailey shook his head and spoke firmly in reply, "If it were something set against little Miss here, the strange and inhuman beast would have made its presence known the night she was born. If it weren't for the grace of God and a blind shot taken in the night by Elizabeth Ann when Miss Calhoun was but a child, our promised child wouldn't be here with us at all. That near fatality was the result of only Miss Meara's dirty man. Why would some demon of the night miss a chance to have her while she remained so vulnerable?"

Virgil grew a bit agitated upon hearing Doc's reply. He was hoping something would give credence to his still unbelieved story from back in sixty-eight. He shook his head at Doctor Bailey and joined Maime in rising from the table while saying, "I don' know what makes dem evil dogs tick like 'dat, Doc. But I do know where you find somethin' that ain't common there is sure enough gonna be its natural nemesis somewheres nearby. Dat's just bein' the law of the jungle and all."

Doctor Bailey nodded wide-eyed and bit dubiously in acquiescence to Virgil's unassailable common sense if little else. He then turned back to the young woman who had instigated the discussion and asked, "What are your thoughts, Miss Shy? What do you think happened out on that cold, dark, lonely road that night? All I know right now is whatever it was that overtook your poor mother or caused her to hit the ground so harshly; it sure as heck wasn't what we presently believe it to be. That old dog simply won't hunt."

Miss Shy closed her eyes and took in a deep breath to steady her thoughts and apply a proper governor to her tone. When she was once again settled, she spoke temperately and evenly so as not to cause her more delicate older sister to fret beyond the limits of her capacity to endure. "Momma told me somethin' about little Miss when I was in to visit over Thanksgiving. I swore I wouldn't tell a soul but that was before she went and got herself killed."

Doctor Bailey raised his chin in surprise and interjected a few words of caution before Miss Shy continued. "Be quite careful about what you are about to say, my dear girl. I have no notion as to what it concerns as of yet, but I do know any secrets of your mother are by rule kept that way for only very measured reasons."

Miss Shy nodded firmly in the direction of Doctor Bailey and took in another slowly and purposefully drawn breath while she continued to think. When she was confident she was doing the right thing by candidly revealing the truth, once again of her own accord and not the prodding of the ancient cross of gold dutifully resting upon her breast-plate, she spoke solemnly to all present. "Momma told me that Mr. Edward had gotten hisself into some trouble with the wrong kinds of folks when he was out doin' business down in Charleston. As a result and to save Mr. Edward's neck, momma done promised the hand of our little Miss to a man livin' somewheres way up in the Yankee North."

Following that rather scandalous expose of a sort, everyone in the room began to say something differing yet all at once. Miss Shy hit the table firmly but not aggressively with the palm of her hand in response to the convergent chatter and called out, "Now, listen y'all! Momma also told me she was set to undo that awful promise of hers and that Mr. Edward was just goin' to have to live with the consequences of his actions. She'd be sayin' little Miss done deserve far better and wasn't to be held to account for their mistakes and all."

Virgil stopped pacing, turned and slammed his open palm down on the kitchen table before exclaiming, "Now, dat be just flat out crazy talk! I for one don' aim to stand for such a disgrace as a filthy Yankee ring bein' set upon dat purdy little hand of my little Miss! I'd done march straight on up there and blow the fella's head clean off a his shoulders afore I'd ever go on and allow an accursed thing the likes a dat to ever happen to a proper Southern lady!"

Miss Margaret Anne remained visibly contemplative in her typi-cally silent and lighthearted manner, no matter the seriousness of the situational circumstances gripping the emotions of those near to her. Doctor Bailey attempted to interject but Miss Shy clearly wished to further provoke and thereby bait the combustible young man for the benefit of her little sister, who potentially remained pledged to that abhorrent initial decree of her mother. "What exactly is you gonna do about it Virgil? Master Edward and Miss Elizabeth Ann walked all over you like you was below the dust of the earth once afore and you just be sittin' here pickin' at that cotton out in the field year after year! Who is to believe that you gonna stand in the way of Master Edward when he got the shady backroom men huntin' after him!"

Virgil stepped forward and leaned across the table so that he might have a good and proper look into Miss Shy's beautiful but hastily raging brown eyes. When her fiery irises were assertively locked upon his glowering stare, he spoke directly to her with a sense of purpose and with passion. "You watch what you be sayin' now, Miss Shiloh Brown! Who do you think done kept dis place goin' all these years now once you run off to Augusta to find yusself a sugar daddy who plays dat fiddle a his all over town?"

Shy cocked her ample hand back suddenly and then just as swiftly and violently slapped Virgil O'Keefe across his smug and salty mug while he continued to lean across the table and stare her down. She slapped him cleanly across the cheek and the resultant sound of wet, smacking flesh firmly striking enamel made those present in the room flinch accordingly. No one spoke a word as they watched the young man carefully to study what he might do in response to such a blatant show of both disdain and disrespect.

Virgil grabbed hold of Shy's dark, slender wrist as if it were the neck of a cottonmouth coiled upon a rock in the grass and ready to strike. When she stopped resisting the potency of his hold he spoke back to her in an equivalently venomous manner. "I'll tell you exactly what I aim to do, sister Shiloh. I aim to marry your sister and there ain't a thing dat murderous Yankee scoundrel stands to do about it!"

Miss Shy pulled her hand back toward her body and Virgil let her wrist slide free before saying further, "You must be knowin' dat I will always love the Cap'm no matter what he done to me and his daughter. He opened up dat room of his only departed boy to me when I ain't had nothin' and nowheres else to go. He'd a had his reasons for what he done to us even if I ain't knowed 'em yet. Dat bein' said, I ain't one built by God to stand by and watch dat man undo my precious angel of the light. Are you hearing me right good and clear now, sister Shiloh?"

Miss Shy nodded purposefully in a blatant show of her understanding. Virgil O'Keefe then stood up straight and tall and announced before everyone present and God above, "If the Cap'm be needin' to learn the hard way 'bout the kinda men he be dealin' with, so be it. He ain't got no right to offer up even one precious hair on this sweet woman's purdy 'lil head. I don't care me a lick if he bein' her daddy and all or not."

Miss Shy stood up from the table and replied coldly, "That's quite good of you, Virgil. But I wouldn't let no moss get gatherin' up on that flat backside a your'n. I'm guessin' that momma told some man somewhere that the Yankee man can't have her. Still and all, I'm also supposin' for all present to hear me that your beloved Cap'm disagreed. She ain't got but a few months 'til she be sixteen and momma said somethin' 'bout dat too!"

After delivering those words, Miss Shy stepped away from the table and quietly out of the room. As she passed by the living room she huffed in anger at the state of her still sleeping husband, who had stayed up all night getting drunk with some of the Davis boys for no particular reason at all. The hot-blooded young woman then marched up the stairs with a slight twinge of piss and vinegar still audible in her hasty yet heavy footsteps before she retired peaceably to her room. With Miss Shy gone and Virgil still stewing in his own simmering juices over being slapped and publically demeaned in addition to the troubles facing his angelic charge, Doctor Bailey stepped forward to interject some form of reason and organization into the chaos left behind by the fiery young woman's brazen assault upon them all. Regardless of the fact that the majority of her cutting provocations were directed solely at Virgil, they all felt duly challenged and somewhat belittled by Miss Shy's highly combustible invective. "What are your thoughts on the matter, little Miss? Perhaps none of the options set before you are indeed ideal. All the same, it would appear that you do have a choice to make."

Little Miss smiled wistfully at Doctor Bailey and stood up from the table without saying a word. She pranced on over to Virgil as if she were some sort of pixie dancing in the wind and then kissed the young man smartly upon the cheek. When Virgil blushed horribly while turning to look at the beautiful young nymph who had instantly and simultaneously snuffed out his anger and fired up the long-dormant warmth of his heart, little Miss responded in a near offhand manner to the inquiring doctor, "The honor of marrying Mr. O'Keefe would be all mine, Doctor Bailey."

She then winked at Virgil, turned back toward the kitchen table, and furthered her startling thought with, "That is once he figures out how a gentleman goes about accomplishing such a thing. I am no poor date." Virgil turned bright red from the overwhelming qualities of both his excitement and the superseding buzz of a bluntly confounding confusion. Hers was a loaded and altogether unexpected response and the young man had much to consider before he spoke in reply. Miss Maime drifted slowly out of the room without saying a word and diffidently joined her sister upstairs.

Later that evening, after the dust of a long and trying day had settled some and Amos had actually come in to the kitchen from the living room to loquaciously offer up his own drawn out and legally couched rebuke of the idea of Virgil marrying little Miss before abruptly departing the house with a bit of anger still furrowing his brow, Doctor Bailey and Miss Margaret Anne remained talking alone at the kitchen table. They sat there by the low, flickering light of a single lantern some hours following dinner and the abrupt explosion that was the delivery of Miss Shy's now plainly revealed agenda. Virgil had returned home with the hopelessly hungover Mr. Brown and that man's two children, who had been playing down at Miss Leslie's cabin with Little pea, primarily to keep old George Ridley away from the Davis clan and off of the buckskin which he favored while traveling with the family. Miss Shy spoke of making the arrangements for the night on behalf of her family so that she might spend some time with her sisters. However, much of that talk was simply poppycock offered up as cover for the man that had become such a hard drinker as opposed to the formerly casual and gregarious partaker of the spirits he once was back when they started having children. In any event, Miss Shy and Miss Maime were both worn out from the emotions of the day upon which they buried their beloved mother and were fast asleep upstairs.

With none remaining to intervene upon their shared moment together, Doctor Bailey took a sip of his fine, triple-malt scotch and stated rather as a matter of fact, "I have to say, little Miss, I was quite surprised by your agreeing to the plan to marry Virgil away from your mother's current or former promise."

Miss Margaret Anne smiled and spoke softly and near longingly in reply. "Every man deserves something good in his life, does he not, my lifelong tutelary and eternal guardian of the February Cabin of my birth?"

Doctor Bailey smiled warmly at the comforting beauty of the young woman and replied in kind, "That we do, my dear lady. Still and all, surely that was not the entirety of your reasoning behind consenting to the rather haphazard arrangement. Was it now?"

Miss Margaret Anne giggled at coming head on with the analytical mind of such a bright but inherently temporal creature by way of his musings. She then answered him thusly, "Why yes, indeed it was, my dear man. I do not perceive the world as you do. I have no lists that speak to the reasons to accept a given tenet set against the reasons to oppose. I simply follow the warmth rising up in my heart or heed the absence thereof when a given thought is made manifest."

Doctor Bailey nodded and smiled in the manner of one quickly blindsided by a suddenly apparent and undeniable truth. He laughed a bit, took another sip of his scotch and then rejoined her. "Are you not worried about the ramifications to those you care for as the result of such an undertaking?"

Margaret Anne got up from the table, walked around its short side and took up the empty seat next to the warmly glowing doctor. She took hold of his free hand while he sipped a bit more on his drink and asked of him, "Do you feel that, Doctor?" Doctor Bailey could in fact feel the strange tingle emanating from her hand and he answered her candidly. "I do indeed feel that pulsing energy coiled up within you. Although I feel warmer and far more luminous, which is in and of itself quite remarkable, I possess not the slightest inkling of any further wisdom on the matter proposed before us."

"So many words you speak, man of my deliverance into this strange and ephemeral place," was the gracious young woman's reply. "Fine then, let me try things your way," she then supposed for the benefit his further deliberation. "I must always consider that in my current state, which is set to deliver something wicked back from whence it came, that I am unfit to be a bride of human flesh and warming blood. Virgil is perhaps the only one among you all, outside of my dear mother and Miss Leslie, who has always understood that about me. His love for me goes beyond nearly all that you might consider looking for in a suitable bride, my dear man. I am not one capable of denying such a beautiful light burning within the young man's heart. To one such as I am, there is no sin more horrible. Does my answer now seem more sensible to your rational mind, doctor?"

Doctor Bailey smiled warmly and then asked the question that still gnawed at his own soul upon that midnight hour. "What of your father then, my dear? Do you not worry for the harsh care certain to be given over to him upon your flight from his promise offered within the guise of your dearly departed mother's pledge?"

Miss Margaret Anne stared off into the darkness beyond the small burning lantern of the kitchen and answered, "I would not feel Virgil's love in the way that I do if that love came at such a price. You can draw your own conclusions from such a statement, my dearest, but such is how I clearly see through to the truth."

Doctor Bailey nodded in reply while the reminiscent twinkle in his eye from the flash of the flickering flame of the lantern spoke of his thoughts that relived the moment of the miracle of her birth and her arrival out to Sumter under the cover of a new identity not but a week later. He then raised his eyes to the ceiling and replied, "What I do believe is that you understand the proper deliverance of your inner light, my precious little angel of the west wind. With that being accepted as fact, do you have any notion that Edward came here to harm your mother in an effort to save his own life?"

Miss Margaret Anne stood up from the table, kissed Doctor Bailey on the forehead and made her way into the darkened hall leading to the stairs. When she was about to take a step upward, she saw a vision of her mother wrapped in the white halo of some form of purified, ethereal light which radiated forth from a younger rendering of her earthly frame. Her mother was shaking her head at the promised child, just as she used to do when Margaret Anne tried to avoid the difficult questions of her sisters when she was but a child. At that moment, the promised child knew to answer the inquisitive doctor before making her way up the stairs and into bed. She spoke fragrantly and with an appropriate intonation of poise over her left shoulder in reply to the tender hearted man.

"In some ways, my dearest doctor, I do believe that Edward was present to save his own skin as you might term the expression. I will tell you further that I am not speaking through premonition alone when I say to you that while his reasons for doing so are precisely what you believe, the true intentions of his heart dwell far beyond those perceived motives for empire and his blood contract alike. Those intentions of Mr. Calhoun are far nobler than you would have ever presumed the man capable of espousing. My trials and Edward's own are tied to one end and the same. However, my sister has changed the course of our affairs here tonight. Though her intentions were also pure, her appeals to spur my aegis into conducting his deeds in accordance with her will were not. I must protect Virgil from further harm and in the afterglow of such haste there is but one way for me to accomplish such a thing. Does my response make things any clearer for you, my dear man?"

Doctor Bailey smiled warmly and nodded in agreement, though the promised child could not see him. He then called out to her, "Abundantly clearer, my dear child. Thank you! Is there anything I may do to assist you with the reconciliation of the current predicament?"

Miss Margaret Anne replied warmly yet still cogently enough to allow her voice to carry out into the kitchen. "Your work here in this place once so foreign to you is nearly done, my dear, sweet man. Watch the way the world unfolds before your eyes in the years ahead, and in so doing bask in the Love and the Light of the One set to answer all that you ask regarding what is taking place around you in His due and perfected time."

Miss Margaret Anne then began to slowly ascend the aging wooden stairs of the quaint and perfectly country Osment farmhouse. As she knew he would, Doctor Bailey called up to her, "Thank you again for that, my dear. I will be here for you regardless of what you may require of me in the days ahead. Goodnight and sweet dreams, my darling angel of the west wind."

The promised child slowed her steps until she had stopped three rungs shy of the hallway at the top of the stairs. She turned to face the direction from whence she had come, gently kissed the two lead fingers of her right hand and lovingly blew the gesture down the stairs in the direction of the kind and gentle man to whom she owed such an enduring debt of gratitude.

"Sleep well, my dear," she whispered, "for none see the future as they do the present day and we all walk with our hand in God's lest we lose ourselves in the bramble laid out beside the road by evil and jealous men beset by death. The passing of the good woman marks the beginning of the days set to try my soul. Pulling such a deeply rooted and evil weed from an imperfect and snugly sown garden is never clean and never permanent. There is much harm delivered to the beautiful flowers nearby. Yet the deed must always be done before the weed grows beyond all measure of control, as this one nearly has. Lest our time shared together shall never have happened at all."

Chapter Twelve

DISAVOWAL

⚜

P ER THE TURNINGS of tradition and the antiquated ways of usual custom in those parts, the midsummer picnic of July of 1890 was held in Sumter out at the home of the unofficial mistress of the county and fifty-year old widow of the cause, Mary Grice Decker. By the time that final decade of the 19ᵗʰ century had arrived, the average denizen of the provincial fiefdoms of Sumter and Uriah would have been able to genuinely say that those of the postbellum generation were near to fully taking hold of the reins of governance from their forebears who had carried the torch of their people through the heart rending years of the great conflict and that strange and corrupted period of the Reconstruction which followed. Duly in accordance with the aforementioned, Mary Grice's two daughters, Mrs. Constance Emmaline Samuels and Mrs. Tamsey Libby Worthington, who were both married at the time, mothers with little children of their own, and proximate enough to the marker of thirty years of age for the likes of government work, had seen to the majority of the planning and provisioning for the much anticipated and always festive event.

Miss Margaret Anne had returned to Uriah the preceding fall under the cover of both darkness and a new identity. She lived discreetly during those months of her purgatory out at the farm and certainly her present semblance to that of her former self did little to give her diffident presence away to those that remained unawares of her properly veiled homecoming. Her legend and the legend of

Mr. Virgil O'Keefe had become living, breathing entities in their own right, though, of course, entities deficient of corporeal form, in the quaint provinces of the Carolina midlands while she was away for fifteen years. The contrast between the notoriously remembered woman that forever belonged to the lore of the age and the worn down mistress who was purportedly kin to Miss Leslie and currently occupying Virgil's old cottage out at the farm were stark and evocatively ironic.

Doctor Emmett Bailey and his dutiful wife Eustace had returned to their beloved Virginia a dozen years prior. Furthermore, the good doctor had been turned away hat in hand from the gates of the Brattleboro asylum a half-dozen times while visiting the native haunts of his youth up in Saratoga County, New York. Both the veracity and significance of what had transpired up in Vermont in the summer of 1880 would be made known to but a scant few. The good doctor would in due time become one amongst that elite cadre of living souls that possessed the capacity to bear indirect witness to the demise of the only circumstantially provable four-hundred-year old demon of the Western age.

Miss Susannah Jane Calhoun had continued to research Mr. Lucian Reed Morgenthau in the years that followed her permanent return to South Carolina. She had journeyed back to her long-time home up in Boston only once, and the occasion was to bury her estranged husband, the late Union Army Colonel, Mr. Stanford Meeks Devening III. Subsequent to a score of archives research and first-hand interviews with various gatekeepers of legend, the former academic socialite of Boston town and once again Southern lady of leisure was rightly stunned by the number of texts in which one fitting Mr. Reed's description appeared in the written histories of the first settlers of Virginia and within the posthumously transcribed legends of the lost colony of Roanoke. Furthermore, Mrs. Devening came to learn that the lore of the indigenous peoples of Virginia and the Carolinas also told the tale of a demon hailing from beyond the great ocean of the Occident, a fiend who possessed reddened eyes and a tireless want to consume the flesh or souls of his fellow man by all means available to the outwardly mortal yet inwardly hellborn creature. One such legend referred to said man as the red-eyed devil that had arrived to the Americas aboard the good ship Lion.

In regard to that darkest secret of all, the truth of little Miss's blood father, such a woeful tale was never openly revealed to any. The discovered secret was only indirectly revealed to Miss Shy and subsequently, those who had received the letter from the late Miss Jeanne's middle daughter before the exiled firebrand of an untarnished legend amongst those of true Carolina stock passed through the accursed gates of a Haitian prison for a second time in May of that same year of 1890. Miss Shiloh Jolie Basseterre would live out the remainder of her days within the confines of that foul asylum. And so it went that the secrets of the past of the promised child continued to lie somewhat dormant while resting upon a powder keg of devastating capacity for destruction as things back in Sumter clicked into place in accordance with the natural human progressions of converging upon the prosaic tendencies of a new era.

Francis Virgil Calhoun was about as bright and industrious a man as Edward had ever been back in his prime. The young man was near to assuming total legal responsibility for the various and thriving industrial and agrarian interests of the Calhoun Empire that was reborn from the ashes of the war at just seventeen-years of age. He was indeed something of a prodigy but an obstinate young man with an overall deportment not so dissimilar to that of how his father may have behaved had Virgil O'Keefe been educated in accordance with the teachings intended for the sons and daughters of the aristocrats. As such, Mr. Francis Calhoun levied a grudge for far too long against even those who had only lightly harmed or disrespected him or one of his own.

Now of course, Edward still retained final approval on the major business decisions of the day while he still lived and remained of sound mind. That fact was primarily due to the demands of the elder Mr. Calhoun's not entirely disinterested business partner, a stout and competent yet aging man who hailed from the woods of Maine by the name of Erasmus Sinclair. Mr. Sinclair operated as fiduciary for Margaret Anne's second son, a boy whom his mother had laid her angelic eyes upon but once and went by the name Robert Chandler Morgenthau at the behest of that same Mr. Sinclair. Robert was presently a boy of only near to ten-years old, and therefore far too young, in addition to being far too demented for the consumption of the public eye, to monitor his inheritance in any appreciable way.

In a surprising move to nearly all who knew him closely at the time, Francis Calhoun invited Miss Margaret Anne, under the guise of her then current identity, to the mid-summer picnic of that July of 1890. Since extending an invitation to someone who was publicly little more than a distant and reclusive cousin to Miss Leslie would have appeared quite suspicious otherwise, Francis also cordially summoned the others connected to the Calhoun family in some unspoken way or another still residing over in Uriah. He did as much even though the town was close to being incorporated as the Negro establishment of Blackville, in large part due to the tireless work of Mr. Amos Martingale Laing, Esquire. Although Elizabeth Ann doubted her son's sincerity in extending the unexpected invitation, she saw no harm that could possibly come to her sister in accepting the offer. Therefore, Mistress Calhoun vocally encouraged the woman still recovering from the aftereffects of nine long and maddened years spent in an asylum to attend the celebration and see some of the old Sumter folks she hadn't laid her eyes upon since the unfortunate incident with Virgil back in seventy-five.

The whereabouts of Virgil's other secret son, Mr. David Emmet Bromley, now aged fourteen years and called by the name Basseterre in accordance with his mother's wishes, were another matter altogether. Few knew that Miss Margaret Anne had in fact seen the growing child upon first returning to the Carolina of her birth and only Miss Leslie knew where the boy was secretly being raised. The spot was a remote and unspoiled place up in the Blue Ridge Mountains. To be a bit more precise, a rise looking down upon a beautiful valley inhabited by those who remained among the living of that hunted band of Miss Leslie's daring compatriots making their escape from Butler Island; those brave souls who were hung out on the crossroads to surely hang, or get whipped until they wished that they were stretching, back on that February morning of 1859. That was before little Miss Hastings arrived upon the scene wrapped in the devoted yet horribly frightened arms of Miss Sarah. Though Black Jim Martingale had been taken into captivity some years after their escape from the Island by Miss Meara's man near to where those refugees from the Weeping Time had settled, Mr. Jim was both noble enough and clever enough to keep the permanent whereabouts of the remainder of his accomplices from being discovered.

Over time, the lot of those brave former runaways and their children had thrived up in those mountains and now formed quite the abounding community while David remained under their care. David's deliverance from his exile in the mountains and his becoming established as business man of fine repute down in Charleston remained some years off at that juncture, yet his predestined prosperity was always looming out on the horizon. The young man thrived up in those ancient and hallowed mountains while Jim and his extended family continued to care for him and raise him up to be a fine and upstanding young man. David Basseterre was a known and always welcomed quantity at nearly each backwater outpost of their people strung out along an upland rise of some little known corner of the primordial and wildly beautiful Falling Creek Gap.

Also worthy of annotation when reflecting upon that stifling summer of 1890 was the fact that Little pea had completed her undergraduate studies in Atlanta back in May and graduated cum laude as Miss Louisa Sanders Laing from the university. Her momma couldn't believe her eyes at the sight of such of thing when she thought back to the end she was sure to face when she took that white looking baby wrapped in a Cherokee throw up into her arms from the pleading Miss Sarah. Miss Leslie Butler Laing had endured and lost much over the course of her life as both a slave and a freed woman set to express the embodiment of her God-given rights, but the sight of her last baby graduating from college was an occurrence that remained beyond the scope of her wildest dreams when the formality and traditional pageantry of the moment had finally arrived.

Little pea was to remain home for only the summer months before she would begin her graduate studies back in Atlanta in September. As a woman of temporary leisure about that quaint and endearing countryside in the summer of 1890, she had elected to join her parents and Miss Margaret Anne on the journey over to Mary Grice's once again illustrious summer celebration. Thaddeus Davis had agreed to coach them all on over to Sumter in Mr. Laing's homemade contraption that served as something of both a flat cart and a buggy.

The low angling morning light was quite raw upon the eyes as they made their way eastward and into the glare of the rising sun upon the six o'clock hour but that time of day was likely to be the only hour of daylight that remained bearable for a spell. The thick and heavy vapors of summer being simmered by the emergent aurora would soon enough be settling in low and oppressive over the fields and prairies of the land now glistening with the refreshing chill of the morning dew. All was continuing to progress along quite nicely with the Laing's journey out to Sumter as the five freshly rested travelers passed beyond the barns and fences that marked the eastern outskirts of Uriah.

Thaddeus Davis, who was then a fine and hardworking man of God yet still without the gifts of a proper bride, kept them all laughing with his pleasantly mischievous country boy charm. He did so primarily in an effort to impress the recently minted college graduate from over in the big city known as the Terminus of the South, though Miss Margaret Anne was also unwed and far closer to Mr. Davis in age. Thaddeus's behavior might have revealed something about little Miss's lacking physical state in those years following her committal to the asylum, the lingering effects of her almost mythical yet somewhat infamous reputation out in the Carolina countryside, or simply the young man's lack of appropriate decision making skills regarding a proper Southern lady, which had rendered him single into his thirties.

In any event where it concerned the partiality of Thaddeus Davis's whims upon the moment, the presence of Constable Jemison waiting in his pocket-sized, single-horse wagon out by the origin of the overland road that would carry them on over to Sumter did not produce a warm and welcoming feeling for any riding in the carriage with Miss Margaret Anne present. No mention of her arrest for the crimes of her past had been made by any upon her return home. Few close to her overtly worried about such assuredly dated nonsense primarily stirred up by the Yankee carpetbaggers back in the day, as it was now some fifteen years after the fact. Most of the proximate and lingering Yankee influence that was a throwback to the Reconstruction Era had seemed to slowly fade off into the sunset with the passing of Mr. Reed and perhaps even Mr. Bromley, though the latter gentleman was verily only seen in these parts by a scant few during the closing stanzas of the war. Be that as it may, most back in town never knew that the promised child had returned at all. Therefore, any presumptions concerning the men of influence that may have still been harboring a desire to exact retribution upon the savagely beset young woman of just thirty-one years were likely to have been formed in accordance with shoddy provision.

There were still plenty around that believed the old stories of what the promised child had done to their beloved Virgil, but none vocal enough that one might presume those of the sort concealed plans to deliver some sort of vigilante justice or worse, to betray one of their own. The folks of these quaint and country provinces were loyal Confederates. The thought alone of the handing over of a native child to any of those remaining carpetbaggers that had kicked up such a dust storm where it concerned the pretty young lady before she had even had her proper day in court was a sin far beyond blasphemy and in accordance with the most vile crime of all, treachery. Francis Calhoun was among the most vocal of those still keeping the old legends of Virgil O'Keefe alive on behalf of the memory of his father. As such, the extension to little Miss of his direct invitation to the mid-summer jamboree back in Sumter was received as the all clear sign for Miss Margaret Anne by nearly all that knew her well and called Uriah or Sumter their home.

Constable Jemison however, was perhaps something of an unresolved problem for the fugitive from the law in several states and the one man both capable of and potentially willing to initiate the process of justice on behalf of the state against the already dourly persecuted woman. Furthermore, Constable Jemison's ties to the vulgar sorts and tainted elite throughout the state made him the most likely to detain the poor, long-suffering woman at the behest of any of her enemies up in the North. As such, Thaddeus Davis clicked his tongue aggressively and gave his lead pony a fanning of the whip to speed things up as they approached the constable's wagon. The law man took due note of the increasing speed of the approaching contraption, which was decidedly of Mr. Laing's handiwork, and stepped down from his perch atop his light and agile wagon and out into the road. Constable Jemison then raised his hand to Mr. Davis with the streaming light of the orange sun rising at his back. He flashed that open palm in the manner of one gesturing that he sure enough would appreciate it if

Thaddeus kindly stopped before he had to flash something far more disastrous than his empty appendage.

Thaddeus looked back in an inquiring manner at the full complement of his passengers upon the sight of Constable Jemison's raised and open hand. Miss Leslie turned her palms upward while simultaneously shrugging her shoulders in a show of her own nescience as to the Constable's desire to hold them up for a pause. Thaddeus nodded in reply to Miss Leslie and spoke only to try and impress the ladies or at least make them giggle a whit given the rising tensions of the moment. "Well, it's prolly best we be stoppin' for ol' Bradley now. Maisy and Delilah ain't likin' it none but they'd be lucky to outrun Methuselah at this stretch a time in their service."

Little did pea laugh some due to the fact she was almost too young to remember all that was going on with Miss Margaret Anne back in the day and because no one told her much about what was happening with her sister before she left them to live up in the North anyhow. Mr. and Mrs. Laing exchanged uncertain glances with one another while little Miss curiously studied the look set upon the face of the constable as they slowed and approached his wagon. She was still quite unaccustomed to not knowing at least the immediate turns of her own fate.

Thaddeus stopped their buggy promptly next to the law man and tipped his cap promptly after spitting some tobacco juice into the warm, settling dust of the road. Mr. Laing promptly took the reins on addressing the constable. "Mornin' Bradley, fine day we's havin' but I reckon it'll be hot enough to scald a lizard in short order."

Bradley Jemison tipped his cap in the direction of Mr. Laing and walked up next to their buggy to inspect each of the passengers. While making his initial inspection of those on board, the calm and appropriately mannered constable replied to old Shug as if he were preoccupied by what he might find at hand, "Sure enough on that, Mr. Laing. Mornin' to ya, now. And to the lovely ladies you be bringin' along so nicely today too. You mind if I ask where you all is headed?"

Mr. Laing tipped his cap rather thinly in reply to Mr. Jemison and replied, "We's headed on over to Sumter for the Calhoun's annual mid-summer gala. Why you fussin' about over us all the way out here past town and all?"

Mr. Jemison looked over to Little pea and congratulated her on the receipt of her degree. Mr. Jemison was of the once privileged class but his family remained on the outside looking in following the war, at least for the time being. Thus, he had been stranded out here in Uriah working the same job keeping the peace for going on nineteen years now. He wasn't much of a bigoted man by his nature but he lamented getting caught out in the sticks while many he once consorted with found their way back to at least some semblance of their former prosperity. When he was done exchanging niceties with Little pea, Constable Jemison turned back to Mr. Laing and answered his question. "Well now, Shug, I hate to be the bearer of bad news but the young lady accompanying Mr. Davis up front has a warrant out for her. I really do hate to do it with y'all having such a big day planned for tomorrow and all, but the law is the law out here. Y'all knows that."

Shug Laing stepped out of the back of the buggy and then placed his feet and still lumbering frame directly in front of Mr. Jemison's line of sight onto little Miss. He tipped his cap at the law man again, though soberly this time, and replied, "That there is the Missus's cousin from way back in her Georgia days. She ain't got no trouble followin' her into or out of town; if ya properly understand my meanin' here, Bradley."

Mr. Laing had grown old and he moved a lot slower than he did in his bounty hunting days. Nevertheless, Bradley Jemison wanted no part of the affable until provoked gorilla of Uriah. He stepped back very cautiously and pulled a drawing from the seat of his wagon that held some resemblance to the promised child back when she first went to prison. He walked back over to Mr. Laing and handed him the drawing while saying, "That's the pretty lady I'm looking for, Shug and she's right on up in your fit out over there."

Shug took a quick look at the reasonable likeness of how little Miss appeared in the winter and at the apex of her womanly and spirted shine. He handed the parchment back to the constable as if he were disinterested and laughed coldly at Mr. Jemison's clearly erroneous presumption. "Bradley, I known you to be a lot a things over these twenty or so years now but blind to both the particulars of beauty and color ain't never been a one a them. Miss Solomon here clearly ain't a white woman and she sho 'nuff don't gots no pearly white teeth such as that there picture presumes."

Bradley looked down at the ground and cautiously contemplated his next chosen words. Bringing the lady in was worth some shiny gold dollars to him but not a red cent if he wound up dead. Shug Laing was a pastor of sorts now and a man of God but he wasn't likely to stand by and see any further harm come to that woman he helped raise up after all that she had been through. Irrespective of even that rather sound logic however, there was a price to be paid equivalent to or worse than Mr. Laing's fury if he let them pass. After thinking for a bit longer on the matter, Constable Jemison responded by attempting to reason with Mr. Laing from the position of that of a common man beset by a more sinister order. "Come on now, Shug. This ain't a big place and we all knows who the lady ridin' up there with Thaddeus is. I don't make the rules, I just bring in the ones they be tellin' me to."

"You's still at the sniffin' a dem Yankee hindquarters after all these years! Ain't ya now, boy?" was Mr. Laing's rather harsh reply.

Bradley Jemison sensed the last of the moment available to him to get the drop on the old ogre coming to pass and rather deftly jumped back and drew his pistol on the man. Such was a dangerous proposition and would have ended Constable Jemison right there and right then if Miss Margaret Anne hadn't approached from the front of the buggy with her wrists kindly offered up as a sacrificial gift to the trembling law man while speaking sweetly to soothe her father, "You all go on out to Sumter, papa. I'll get everything squared away with Mr. Jemison here while you are gone. I'll see you back at home in a few days' time." She then smiled warmly at her father and added, "I'm certain this is all nothing more than a terrible misunderstanding."

Bradley let out some heretofore halted and slightly exasperated winds of relief. He then quickly nodded in a show of appreciation to the poorly kept but in some ways still pretty young lady who had just saved his hide. He stepped forward, lightly bound her wrists and escorted her up on to his wagon like a proper gentleman. While Mr. Jemison was so kindly and gently arresting her daughter, Mrs. Laing stepped down onto the road and soothed her maddened husband to keep anything bad from happening. Mr. Laing begrudgingly obliged Mr. Jemison's taking of little Miss into custody but he had Thaddeus Davis follow the constable's wagon right on into the heart of town until they reached the square out in front of the jail at near to the same instant.

Shug Laing stepped down into the trodden dirt of the main square when they arrived and spoke sternly to his wife and daughter, "I'll stay here and see what this is all about. You all run along and bring Amos back as soon as you be findin' him."

Miss Leslie leaned forward, kissed her husband lovingly and pliantly agreed to his plan. In accordance with such, she let the distraught goliath know that she would see him again soon. Mr. Laing nodded determinedly to all three of them that remained up on the buggy and then turned away hastily and plodded his way across the town square. He barely slowed his gait for long enough to cool his hot and dusty heels before storming his way into the front door of the Uriah jail. Back out in the nearly vacant town square of those early morning hours, the sun rose over the quaint collection of buildings clustered into the center of Uriah from somewhere off to the east as the Laing's fit out slowly rolled its way westward and on toward home. Miss Leslie began to cry as Little pea hugged her at the shoulders and wondered what was to become of her visibly tormented older sister.

When old Shug arrived inside the station, Miss Margaret Anne was being escorted into a cell in the back. "You hold on sweet girl," he called out to his daughter as she passed back to the rear of the building and beyond his line of sight with her wrists still only ceremonially bound. "Don't you worry about me, papa," she called back. "It is now long since time that I paid for what I done to poor Virgil. Such is not Mr. Jemison's fault. The burden of the guilt is my own."

Shug replied to her gravely in order to put a halt to her confession, whether such a declaration was indeed intended as such or otherwise. "Don't you be talkin' like that in front a no one, little Miss! You hear me? I'll be right here waiting for you. You ain't gotta do this turn alone like you done up North!"

"I'll be quite fine, papa," was the currently serene woman's calmly stated reply. "There is nothing to worry about. Everything is always and everywhere precisely as God intends for it to be. Go get yourself something to eat for breakfast over at Jody's place. Her biscuits always seem to tickle your belly just right."

Mr. Laing groaned a bit inwardly in reply and then called out to none but the empty space between the brick walls of the front room of the building, "Your brother will be brought in soon to settle this matter. I can promise you that, my sweet child!"

About an hour later, Amos ran into the front door of the county jail like a kid just set free from the schoolyard. Shug had nodded off to sleep but heard the commotion of his boy's raucous and disorderly entry. "Amos!" the large, aging man belted out across the front room of the building as he lifted the warm, salty brim his stale smelling old hat from his eyes and attempted to rise from his seat fast enough to catch hold of the always rather spry young man. Amos had clearly approached the building with an agenda to proceed straight back to the confines of the holding area without delay. Moreover, Amos was far too swift and his motion so pure and directionally true that Mr. Laing never had a chance to grab hold of him or slow him up any.

"Wait here, Papa. I'll be back soon with some news. Everything is going to be fine," cautioned Amos as he stepped through the door to the holding area and out of sight. Shug grunted once again, this time in reply to his son's brazen lack of respect. Nevertheless, the big fellow was at least somewhat comforted by Amos's presence upon the premises. He began to pace the length and width of the musty smelling front room all by his lonesome in the moments that followed his boy's disappearance into the back of the building.

Amos joined Mr. Jemison, an unidentified marshal from over in Georgia, a state's attorney from up in Columbia and Miss Margaret Anne in the roomy and heretofore unoccupied main holding cell. Any man or woman in possession of a more scrutinizing bent related to their opinions of the legal system in the state of South Carolina, or Georgia for that matter, might have been brazen enough to openly presume that the men knew the prisoner would be arriving sometime during that very July morning. Amos, the state's attorney and the law man from Georgia held a brief side bar at the far side of the barred room where Miss Margaret Anne was stationed that neither the prisoner nor her custodial attendant, Mr. Jemison could quite decipher. When the three men were finished speaking to one another, Amos took a seat at the small writing table next to his long, lost sister while the two gentlemen from out of the area promptly departed the holding area and then the building by way of the little used back door.

When the two gentlemen were heard exiting by way of the back door, Amos stood up and invited his sister to do the same by waving his arms and open palms upward. When she impishly obliged quite true to her past form, that is to say in doing so not at all and then all at once, Amos hugged Margaret Anne before addressing her as such, "Sister little Miss, it is so very good to see you after all of these years!"

Margaret Anne smiled warmly at the dashing and familiar, though much older, face of her brother and replied lovingly to him, "It is so good to see you as well, brother Amos. Apparently your extremely important work back in Columbia has kept you held up right up until this very moment."

Miss Margaret Anne then lifted her eyes to the ceiling to think for a moment and colored her prior thought with, "Perhaps you had not been made aware of my arrival to town. Few were told of my return and I was even given a new name, though none here that I have spoken with believed such childish nonsense. Just the same, good Mr. Jemison seemed to remain a bit uncertain as to the true nature of my identity until I testified to the truth of my proper name." Miss Margaret Anne then giggled a bit at the silliness of such a thing as attempting to maintain an alias in a small town like Uriah before saying, "You appear as if you are doing quite well for yourself after all these years that I have been away. How are Layla and your children? I have heard so much about them from Mammy and Papa since my return home. I simply cannot wait to meet them all!"

Amos smiled in return but a bit uncomfortably at this turn and managed to give a reply in a caring and hopeful but lightly distanced tone, "They are all doing wonderfully, though I do continue to spend far too much time away from home of late. We are so very close to incorporating Uriah as the Negro Hamlet of Blackville. The things we will show to the world then, little Miss! There will remain not even the slightest semblance of a doubt as to the unbridled capacity of our freed people once we are fully liberated to build, work and prosper of our own accord!"

Miss Margaret Anne returned to her seat and frowned a bit upon hearing the news delivered from the mouth of her brother. "Perhaps I shall only return to visit in the summer months then, brother Amos," she gently chided him or perchance merely sulked openly and audibly for her brother's benefit. "Why do you feel the need to drive the people of Uriah apart after all of the years we have previously endured of that same separation, oppression, and even hatred? Certainly, those behind your maddened push to create some semblance of a Negro Utopia cannot be men of high moral character. Do any of the honest and hard-working folk here even notice the color of one's skin any longer?"

Amos Laing shook his head in a frustrated manner and pleaded with his sister to see his point of view. "Do not frown upon our endeavors here, little Miss. The Jim Crow laws are taking hold every-where and continue to severely disadvantage, and in many ways, sub-jugate our people in the cities and towns where they exist and are so brutally enforced. I for one will not stand idly by and continue to live in a place that abides by legal principles established solely by way of the old doctrines of wanton prejudice. The only way to show them all that we are a people of equivalent and industrious capacity is to create a self-sustaining place of our own where we are truly liberated and treated equitably under the law. We are so near to achieving just that dream, Margaret Anne!"

Miss Margaret Anne lowered her eyes from her impassioned brother and asked, "Is that what this is all about, Amos? Is the reali-zation of this faulty dream of yours how they honeyed your lips with their melliferous assurances and in turn drew forth your tongue to deliver me forth? What then, may I ask do you have planned for me next, dear brother? Perhaps you shall offer me a smaller and far less transitory version of this delightful habitat across the river in Georgia?"

Amos quickly turned his back to the now woeful looking creature that he recalled once possessed such a brilliant and untouchable inner light and outer shine. He had figured that the young woman he last eyed some years ago yet remembered so well could pass through here in a month's time without incident and that all would then be well for her when she came out clean on the other side of a trial certain to con-clude in her favor. She could get on with living her life without those Yankee devils always dangling such a menacing threat over her head.

While those initial thoughts of the ambitious attorney were all well and good absent the taint of his own desire, this rendition of the promised child that Mr. Laing falsely believed had once overshadowed even the finest of his earthly accomplishments and who was now returned to him was fragile to the point that he wondered if she would last even the night behind these bars of cold iron and walls of sodden brick after the horrible ordeal she must have endured up North.

Amos answered his sister in the terms she understood well. "There were powerful men that wanted to see you pay in full for what happened to Virgil. Not only for what happened to Virgil, but for other reasons they did not make manifest to me. They appear to despise you as they despise no other. Therefore, I took it upon myself to free you from the clutches of the consequences of those awful and unintended proceedings of the past. I believe that I have cleared the path forward for you. However, you must stand trial in front of a jury of your peers here in Uriah. Only then will they expunge the records, rescind the warrants and furthermore, forever put an end to the leverage those vile men hold over the sanctity of your liberty."

Upon hearing her brother admit the truth of his obfuscation brought about by his desire to see his dream for Blackville on through to fruition and accordingly, the truth of his unintended betrayal of her, Miss Margaret Anne began to cry. She did not cry because she feared a trial in her hometown or telling the story of what happened on that night of her accursed honeymoon to those she had known for her entire life. No, she began to cry because she was now wholly a creature of the flesh and because her precious brother's heart had been corrupted by his yearning to show up the white men; those harsh and taunting men who had run his true father off into the mountains and then scorned him and belittled him for so long, and continued to do so even now after all that he had achieved in accordance with the rules of their own game and in the face of near to insurmountable odds. From the moment they were both sold over to Mr. Calhoun back in

Savannah, Amos had always possessed a compulsion to show them all that he was better than that of human chattel or some chained beast of the field. He had always needed to show his oppressors that they were all better than that and always had been.

For her part in that enduring struggle of the American age, Margaret Anne had simply always wondered what one might reveal to such demons to press for even little more than the return of their God-given human suffrage. As far as she was concerned, Amos had always been driven to impress the wrong sorts in his quest for a return to the natural order of human equality. The men Amos sought to impress would twist the necks of their own earthborn mothers for the sake of the proliferation of a prosperous lie or to further confound their human prey. Just as little Miss once remained so confounded by the human acknowledgment of sorrow or the pangs of loss because she was filled with the ethereal light of the eternal realms; the men Amos sought to influence were equivalently and hopelessly bereft of the capacity to feel the warmth of love or the sweet joy of true fellowship. They were usurpers and Amos would forever remain just a silly little black boy to those men no matter the dizzying heights of his earthly achievement for the simple reasons that he was not heartless as they were and that in seeking their approval he granted them the authority over his person they craved above all else.

What poor Amos never understood was that the color of a person's skin was not the root cause of the misery and scorn or even the subhuman treatment which their people had endured. Their trials, from the earliest days of slavery onward were always, and for as long as the practice of their abuse thrived, would forever be predicated on the constant battle raging between the darkness and the light in the temporal realms. The tribulations of the slaves were the result of those eternally shrouded in said obscurity forever seeking to gain an advantage over the many, and doing so by dividing them and oppressing them severally in rendering hopeless and helpless the still faithful denizens of humanity. The point of such soulless madness was always to sanction their brutal will and thereby defile the intent of God's creation. The economies of physical slavery in the Americas were a stark example of just how cogently the minds of men might be proselytized into losing their hold upon even the most self-evident truths of the Divine Creator. In the eyes of the promised child, the color of their skin was in truth no different than the blues and the greys of the uniforms of those that had blindly marched off to war, and it was in the stigmatizing of those uniforms or their creed upon which hatred spawned from misery, want and the confusion of deeply seeded deceit.

No intended fix that legitimized the same intolerance those freed souls still endured and were set to continue to endure through the legality of segregation manifest in the separate but equal doctrine of the courts was set to change any of that for the better. Though she now saw the world through entirely human eyes, Margaret Anne continued to understand that hate begot hate and that only love, like the love the good people of Uriah now openly displayed for one another, would bring about an end to their continuing persecution. Either love, the very public hanging of the truly wicked, or some combination thereof was set to deliver equitable relief to their people for the centuries of their suffering. Margaret Anne preferred that love might reign. Be that as it may, having glimpsed into the dark heart of the very worst of those demons living among men, she understood that those of pure wickedness were indeed the ones that existed as a breed apart and were incapable of comprehending the warmer graces of the human condition. As such, the worst of them could be restrained only by permanent measures of debilitating force or unyielding confinement.

If her brother could only know and furthermore, believe that she had driven away the very worst of those earthly demons responsible for the subjugation of them all, white and black folk alike, to the eternal sins of slavery, both visible and otherwise of the mind, maybe Amos Laing, Esquire would have felt differently about what he was so certain he needed to set apart for the sake of his people. However, such a turn of events would not occur on this day and at the very hour the veil placed before her brother's eyes at such a young age in the form of his lingering anger and his consuming desire to have his retribution served upon his tormentors by way of his proven success had been lifted. In much the same way that Virgil's heart and mind were not prepared to so rapidly bear the truth of the spectral innocence of the light, Amos's heart was in no way capable of accepting those suddenly revealed axioms of his humanity. He would not long endure the painful revelation that his own driven anger had been slowly and imperceptibly converted into the idolatry of his useful vanity over time; a thought perhaps properly best colored as the very thing which was now made flawlessly manifest to Mr. Laing by the sorrowful look set upon his sister's dulled, amber eyes.

In truth, that sorrowful look spoke directly to his heart and revealed to him that so many of his sacredly held beliefs were patently false. All the same, Amos would never submit to the sudden assault upon those now nearly instinctive credos at the very instant he realized he had sold over the beaten down and broken body of his own sister by rite to the very men he despised for the legal charter to the town of Blackville. The slowly enacted plans of those wicked men and the demons of the world were always the same. Deceive the overzealous hearts of men and then leave them to wallow crippled in the foul braise of that deceit in accordance with their ensuing shame when their eyes are then opened to the truth. The result would be no different for her poor, sweet brother from the days of the very first of her tellurian memories. He had been overwhelmed by his righteous yet misguided ambition. That was the true reason why the promised child wept so sorrowfully and for him.

Amos Laing, Esquire was beginning to feel the sudden pangs of his guilt and therefore asked of her, "Why are you crying, my sister of those open fields set out upon the crossroads?" Margaret Anne lifted her eyes and replied, "I am sad because those same men you seek to influence have already corrupted your heart and are only now allowing you to see the truth of it. Their bargain is always the same. I fear that you will not remain sound enough to survive the ordeal to come. I am but an ordinary woman now, brother Amos. There is little that I can do to rescue you from the depths of your troubles when they effect their reprisal upon what little remains of me."

Amos lowered his puzzled eyes and otherwise wounded mien and replied, "It is you who remains lost in the darkness of your ordeal and is therefore seeing things all wrong, gentle Maggie. You are confused and broken because of what they have already done to you. All will be well for you in time and you will soon see the vibrancy of that truth just as clearly as I do now. I must go to meet with the judge in secret on the outskirts of town to begin the process of expediting your trial. I aim to free you from this awful place before the summer is at an end. When you leave here, you will be forever washed over in the waters of your freedom from those vile men. I will return first thing in the morning and we will begin plotting out your defense to the charge of the murder of your lawful husband, Mr. Virgil Denton O'Keefe."

Miss Margaret Anne halted her tears and shifted the intentions of her still viable words to soothe her brother while she remained able to afford him such a grace. She spoke to calm the lost looking man standing before her upon that instant despite her continuing sorrow because she abruptly understood that she would not see him again. She believed in her breaking heart that the tender notions she might still offer Amos presently were all which she possessed of this world to freely give him that might in some way insulate her brother from the desolation of his remorse following whatever was to become of her.

"Fret not, my sweet brother Amos," she pined in a tone so endearing that it nearly lured him free of the invisible chains of his mind that now bound him. "All will indeed be well in this world or in the next. I too must faithfully continue to believe as much for the sake of Virgil and for the sake of my baby girl whose precious lives were the collateral cost of my given errand. You hold no blame for anything that has ever or may yet take place where it concerns me. Remember only that I love you and that I always will. Remember those words even in your darkest hour by returning to the way we once were before the will of the world consumed so much of us. When your eyes are properly opened to the plain truth of the men you sought to bargain with for my sake, keep fighting for the sanctity of your soul. Keep fighting with the same love you poured into this misguided, though pure by way of your intentions, establishment of Blackville."

Amos shook his head a bit haphazardly as he became overwhelmed by his sudden confusion upon listening to the angelic cadence of her pleading voice. He then began to deny the once subtle but now forceful prodding of the truth made readily apparent to his once blinded eyes; like the trickle of water emanating from just a small, harmless crack in a dam so suddenly turning into the diluvial flood that follows the fury of the foundering. "I will see you in the morning, my beloved," Amos replied vacantly as his eyes drew wide and expressionless. "Try not to worry. Everything has been precisely aligned to set you and all of our good people here in Blackville free from the grasp of the white man's tainted law. By sometime in September, both endearing gifts will make it seem as if the long-cherished and secretly shared fancies of our childhood have returned to warm our chilling hearts. These things to come were once little more than the whimsical wishes that lingered about the shifting mists of our minds as the impossible dreams of starry-eyed children. But right soon, those dreams stand to be turned into reality."

When Amos had finished speaking, he turned his hollow-framed and wandering eyes quickly back to her own still pleading orbs of soft and alluring amber and then rather precipitously put his head down and began to take his leave from the confines of her cell. Miss Margaret Anne cried a bit more but then quickly suppressed that openly displayed manifestation of her grief and called out to the then swiftly departing gentleman, "Amos, I'm sorry that I fixed up Mr. Laing and kept your daddy from coming around more when we were little. I'm sorry Mammy never told you about him until you were off being a lawyer. Given what they had done to those two men out on those crossroads, she didn't want anyone coming after you to get to him. You should know that he saved me and my boy up in those haunted mountains up North. You should know that he was always watching over you too!"

Amos continued walking slowly down the hall but halted for a moment and spoke to her firmly while facing off in the other direction, "Mr. Laing is the only father I have but he's white and we can't dine together back here in town. At least not before we get the new charter settled. That other man by the name of Martingale has a family of his own somewhere up those mountains. He never came down when I was little because Miss Meara took him to get at you. They were all always trying to get at you, but you showed Virgil and those other gentlemen what you had to give. Now get some rest and keep quiet while I work on getting you out of this fix since you presently seem to be a danger to none but yourself. I will see you in the morning."

She sobbed a bit more and called out to her brother as he began again to walk away, "I love you, Amos. Hold on to that eternal pledge of mine no matter what happens in the days ahead. Such is the only way you will keep them from breaking your will and then your beautiful spirit."

Amos did not turn back to look at her when he entered the hall outside the cell while Mr. Jemison ceremoniously closed the barred door behind him, locking his sister inside. When he had passed by her in the prior moment, she reached for his hand but the only black barrister in Barnwell County pretended to be preoccupied by his sudden rush to make his next appointment on time and denied her the feel of his skin upon her own. He regretted as much for the remainder of his days.

Constable Jemison understood little of what was transpiring below the surface when those men were all gathered together in that cell, but he knew enough concerning the way things worked around these parts to correctly surmise that the resultant outcome was not likely to go well for the seemingly manic, at least where it concerned the pursuit of his cause, and foolishly trusting Negro attorney. As such, Bradley Jemison also knew that things were not likely slated to go well for the broken woman once again weeping in her cell. The broken woman with the rotten teeth and slouching bones that were the result of too much time spent in some ruthless and insipid insane asylum up in the North. Such was a real shame Mr. Jemison figured, because she was once such a beautiful specimen of the possibilities existing upon the delicate blending of the two breeds kept starkly separate and worlds apart by decree and to serve a far darker purpose down here in Carolina. Though Bradley Jemison did believe that the woman blew the top of that winsome O'Keefe boy's head clean off over in Augusta, he felt for any woman that had clearly endured so many of the worst of the trials of this life before being sold up the river by her own kin.

As such, Mr. Jemison thought to check on his ward before departing the holding area for the quaint quarters of his office up front. "Is there anything that I might be gettin' for you, Ma'am? Some water maybe or perhaps even a spot of tea for some lips parched by the summer dirt of the overland roads? It might be some time yet afore folks is let in to see you again."

Miss Margaret Anne peered back through the bars with her large, moistened eyes and woefully blackened teeth and replied, "No, thank you for offering though, Constable Jemison. Perhaps later, after I have had some time to consider the unexpected events of the morning, if such a continuing burden would remain agreeable to your wishes."

Bradley Jemison nodded and replied somewhat hopefully, "Well now, Ma'am, I'll be sure to have a nice supper brought in for you. Do you like them biscuits from over at Miss Jody's place?"

Miss Margaret Anne smiled warmly at the suddenly tender hearted man and then answered him back as she returned to her chair and set her head gently to rest upon the wooden table in the holding cell. "Thank you, Mr. Jemison. I do love Miss Jody's biscuits so. They taste just like home. They taste just like Mammy's."

After a brief pause to take in a fleeting memory of her mammy serving up her warm, country biscuits on a Sunday morning back in the days of her childhood, the presently exhausted woman added, "I think both ladies whip and butter them up about the same but I wouldn't say a thing like that outside of these walls."

Bradley chuckled as he opened the doorway leading up to the front of the building and then replied in kind, "That there is a wise policy to adhere to, Ma'am; very wise indeed. I'll bring some still warm biscuits and some supper back for you after you rest for a while."

She believed that she awoke with a start in the middle of night on August 8th, 1901. Her Harlem apartment was as hot as the gallows were down in Augusta on that day back in 1890. Though she thought she was attuned to the strange contrivances of that present world of hers amongst the living, the black sack cloth remained pulled down over her head and fastened tightly at her collar by the rope that was meant to break her neck in much the same fashion that her mother's upper spine had been severed by Mr. Morgenthau some years prior. Her knees were trembling in her bed and she called out for Mr. Abraham White, who she presumed was somewhere at her side. When dutiful Abraham did not answer her frightened appeals offered up to the confines of the night, she pulled frantically at the blinding and suffocating sack cloth wrapped snugly around her head.

She could see nothing yet knew she was waiting only for the instant of her violent end, the occurrence of which rested far beyond the diminutive bounds of her control. Her preordained fate had been delivered into the hands of the hooded and soulless execution man and would come as certain as the sun would rise again upon the morrow. She listened carefully for any given sign that the contraption had been sprung but the hastening of her trapped breath and the drumming of her heart were all that were afforded her to mark the solitary trice in time of her demise. The boards beneath her feet creaked eerily and thereupon began to give way. She dropped rapidly and screamed with all of the terrors of the damned for but the flashing of an instant upon the timeless heavens out beyond the firmament. Then she awoke.

When her eyes could sense only the near blinding haze of the warm, soft morning sunlight of August in the Carolina Lowcountry, she timidly opened them to the scenery of a place that she could not possibly remember so intimately, yet seemed as natural and comforting to her finely attuned womanly senses as that of any place she had ever visited upon this earth. When the last of the fog lifted from her tender, parting eyes, she saw the man that was for a time her father sitting across from her and smiling in a loving manner. She was confused and out of her expected time and place altogether. Mr. Calhoun stepped across the inside of one of Mr. Satterfield's fine carriages, sat next to the still mildly disordered woman and gently wrapped her in his arms.

"Where are we, Edward?" she asked while looking out the windows in an effort to try and gauge their location. Edward followed her haunting eyes as they examined the scenery of the same wooded lowlands she had journeyed through with Miss Leslie, Amos and Mr. Laing back into the teeth of the darkened evil assembled along the auction oval of the Weeping Time. "I am sorry if you are still quite groggy, my dear child. There were those that would have remained unsatisfied if they had not witnessed your remains following the spectacle of your very public yet slightly shrouded hanging. The aftereffects of the elixir should wear off entirely by the time we cross over into Georgia and thereby reach Savannah."

Miss Margaret Anne was starting to catch on and offered up a wry and devilish smile to her escort while she interrogated him. "Mr. Edward Christopher Calhoun, did you return Captain Pierce's carriage that left Miss Sarah and I stalled out upon the crossroads into service just for this trip?" Edward laughed heartily and replied, "Frankly speaking, that was not the question I expected you to ask, my dearest."

Miss Margaret Anne reached forward and hugged the man lovingly. She then drew her eyes back a bit and interjected excitedly while she continued to rapidly return to the fullness of her senses. She locked onto his aging, blue eyes that were not but six inches from her own sparkling, kaleidoscopic orbs of the moment while she spoke. "Well then, do tell! Did they go on with it and hang me, you cunning man? The last thing I remember is the creaking of the unsteady boards beneath my boots!"

Edward smiled in his own boyish and slightly cunning manner. He then spoke with that excitable and winning charm that his voice had always possessed, and continued to exude even now while the man was near to approaching seventy-years of age. "Well, my dear, we had to put on a good show for those Yankee boys watching on in silence. The hangman knew to pull the boards before you fell. You had begun to wobble some from the medicine, yet it sounds as if the masked man's timing was rather exquisite. One would never have guessed that Thaddeus Davis would come up to be such a proficient chap." Edward then shrugged in reply to the astonished guise of little Miss as if to say, what else was to be done with the mess we were handed.

Miss Margaret Anne laughed like a school girl in such a way that her inner shine made even those rotten teeth of hers glisten in the morning sun coming in so plentifully through the steadily progressing carriage's ample windows. She straightened up excitedly and forced her hands flat against the perfectly polished black wood of their seat as she pressed the catty yet joy-filled man for more. "You hung your own daughter then, you devil! I thought I had endured it all as it regarded your antics when I returned to Uriah from that awful asylum."

Edward laughed joyfully and replied in a rather nonchalant manner, "I wouldn't complain too much, my dear, the rope was just a hair too long and we had a man expecting you beneath the stage. If there is one present entitled to the airing of a grievance I daresay that would be yours truly. That devil of a friend of the late Jackson Satterfield drove a bullet clean through my best cap."

Miss Margaret Anne looked away from the charming and delightful man basking in the moment of the long awaited deliverance of his child by decree from the evils set upon the world that had stalked them both without relent from the moments of their respective births. While she looked away from the brilliant flash of Edward's blue eyes, the still young woman of just thirty-one years took in the pleasant spectacle of a flock of lowland marsh birds taking flight in unison after being startled by the horses and the wheels of the carriage turning in unison over the cumbersome tread of the road. She suddenly felt just as free and easy as those birds startled into making their way back toward the ocean slightly ahead of the schedule issued by their prior whims. When she had pieced most of what had taken place together, Miss Margaret Anne turned back to her accompanying gentleman in wait and asked of him as if she were shocked by the mere thought of such an idea alone, "You don't mean that…certainly it can't be that we are…"

Edward smiled wide and then jumped to cut her off before she perhaps revealed the most astonishing of his secrets, "Yes, my dear. We are as dead as dead can be and as such, just as free as those birds making their way back to the sea."

Miss Margaret Anne gasped and replied in some form of mock horror to continue humoring the man who was clearly quite excited by the brilliance of his escapade. "What if the rope had been sized correctly for its intended purpose, Mr. Calhoun?"

Edward beamed quite smugly in reply to the joyfully received existence of her wonderfully displayed astonishment, which was tinted with the perfect dose of consternation. "Such an unfortunate miscalculation was *always quite impossible, my dear. They have tried to hang Mr. Lemarque several times now and he is a man of very precise and cunning deliberation,"* replied Edward only partially in jest.

"Oh, Edward! I nearly died from fright when they stood us up upon that stage while not knowing the particulars of your plan! I would rebuff you properly for such an oversight this very instant if my arms did not remain so deadened from that vile potion by which you poisoned me."

Miss Margaret Anne then thought for a moment and spoke rather pensively as if she were now helping to plot out that which had already transpired. *"Perhaps it is best that you didn't tell me. Mr. Lemarque has been known to get distracted quite easily and such thoughts concerning the potential for his negligence may have been worse to endure than the certainty of death before they dropped the floor from beneath my trembling feet. Lucky for you both I was prepared to meet my maker and behold my baby girl with open arms. Still and all, I must say that knowing the approaching moment of one's demise, no matter how prepared one may be for such an eventuality, is a rather fretful circumstance for the fragile wares of the human nous."*

Edward smiled a bit vacantly, continued to process what the young lady had said to him and then rejoined her reverently in saying, *"I am truly sorry for the existence of such a circumstance, my dearest child. Amos's hasty abjuration of both you and our ability to care for our own in these quaint provinces of the former Confederacy was both a blessing and a curse."* Margaret Anne nodded solemnly and silently in reply as she was not yet prepared to address the unfortunate turn of the moment of her brother's disavowal.

Shortly thereafter, the two now freed from the torments of their given trials upon this earth openly discussed many things from the blessed confines of their shared past. They laughed and smiled like children set free of the yolk of their prior burdens and their sins before the interminable will of God. As the stagecoach approached the wharfs lining the Savannah River, Edward and little Miss discussed their trip to Haiti to visit Miss Shy in prison and provision for her two children where beneficial. Edward had business of a sort to conduct with the boy, Andre Francis. However, he did not elaborate much on the circumstances tied to those intentions but to say that Miss Shy had once asked him to watch over her babies if anything ever happened to both her and her mother. Both Edward and Mr. Sommers had been made aware that Andre Francis Basseterre was the current legal custodian of the golden cross by Miss Shy in accordance with the provisions of *The Articles of 1858*.

While Margaret Anne stared up at the glorious colossus that was the steamship that would deliver them forth to the islands of the Caribbean and then on to New York, Edward pulled something from the deepest precincts of his black, leather travel bag. The item was his old auction purse and the ancient buckskin pouch was stuffed to the drawstring, just as it was when Mr. Sommers had dutifully carried it down to Mr. Lemarque's auction stand. Miss Margaret Anne eyed the purse but said nothing as Edward held it loosely in his hand before his chest. She allowed Edward to carry on with the pomp and flair of his deliberately planned ritual by remaining silent.

"There is one drawback to being dead, my dear," Edward gallantly announced while he weighed the brown satchel by way of bouncing the purse delicately while it rested in his open palm. She indulged him perfectly in reply, with that of a coy and innocent query that feigned her ignorance concerning her consort's intentions. "What may such a drawback be, dearest Edward? Such would appear to me that we are now free to roam the world without consequence to our actions."

Edward smiled willingly and placed his unoccupied left hand upon her shoulder. He then spoke purposefully in reply. "Well now, that little dilemma which we currently face, my dear, is that dead men possess no assets of this world. All was signed over to the children, grandchildren, your proper descendants and Francis Virgil Calhoun by Mr. Sommers following my vengeful demise at the scene of your hanging. Of course, such was precisely in accordance with the directives of my last will and testament."

Miss Margaret Anne frowned quite emotionally and attempted to comfort the once affluent man of commerce and agrarian affairs. "I am so sorry, Edward. You shouldn't have relinquished all of your wealth and your vast business holdings on my account. I will never be able to repay you for such kindness." Edward smiled again in reply. This time wryly and he answered her by saying, "You owe me nothing at all, my dear. It is I and all who will live out their days in this beautiful land of my Carolina that remain forever indebted to you."

The once beautiful in the flawless manner of human apportionment and now physically worn down yet wildly ragged promised child took hold of Mr. Calhoun's hands and squeezed them softly. His skin was soft and cool to the touch. She then spoke longingly in reply to what her mind accorded as such undue commendation. "Thank you for that, Edward. When I do see my boy and my baby girl again, one in this life and the other in the next, I hope that they will come to understand the given purpose to which I was bound by the heavens above. I no longer recall the acceptance of the heavenly ordained provisions of my task, yet I know well the capacity for desolation that lurked within my mark. If I was once one amongst the angels, surely, I had somehow forgotten the pangs of the trials and tribulations of the human heart when I foolishly agreed to splinter the crux of that old demon of the age."

"Those you have loved will all come to understand the grace of your sacrifice, my dear. I do not know what my children or my grandchildren will ever come to understand of this dreadful yet necessary ordeal or the truth of my legacy in its aftermath. Nevertheless, I do know that God will make such things known upon the proper time. The truth will always shine brightly, my dear child. In fact, and in accordance with that very belief, I shall begin to write my memoirs while we are abroad."

Edward paused for a moment to properly couch his guise in the manner of one set to reveal another, though perhaps not the last of his kept secrets and spoke in addendum to his prior statement. "I plan to finish those memoirs once we are domiciled up in New York. Perchance one day it will be safe for you to pass certain servings of those haphazard scribblings of mine on to some of our kin as circumstances permit."

Miss Margaret Anne raised her eyebrows quizzically and asked, "New York, Edward?" "Why yes, my dear; there is no better place in the world to get lost in plain sight. I have provisioned ahead for a residence for the both of us up in Harlem and for a few other of life's necessities before I died," replied Mr. Calhoun while he winked smartly at his once again seemingly puzzled traveling companion.

Edward Calhoun then raised his hand, which held the strings of the heavy purse and added, "And there is this, my dear. Something owed to you to set you free on this wonderful journey that awaits us." Miss Margaret Anne hesitantly took hold of the purse upon it being offered to her. She was surprised by its uncommon heft and in sensing what may be contained within she assertively queried the giver of such a substantial gift, "And just what is the meaning of this, Mr. Calhoun?"

Edward smiled a bit abashedly and shifted his eyes down to his knees. He answered her in a tone that was a bit severe for the purposes of imparting upon her the symbolic importance behind the conveyance. "Within the purse rests $3,500 in gold coin in exchange for the redeeming of the soul of Mr. Edward Christopher Calhoun, my lady. I found the price to be rather exorbitant for the deliverance of one as meager as I am, yet I shall never argue for the sake of little more than spiting divine providence or negotiating against that of my own advantage. I shall simply remain thankful that any amount offered was acceptable at all, due only to your courage and devoted care for that of your fellow man."

Miss Margaret Anne covered her widening mouth with her still long and delicate hand in knowing that so much money rested within the purse. "I could never, Edward! Due to the fact that I never believed you owned any human soul in the eyes of God, you have tendered the money for the sake of gaining nothing in return once already. Twice would be far too much to ask."

Edward placed the purse carefully into her hands and wrapped his own hands around hers to hold the old purse within her uncertain grasp.

"If I possessed a hundred of the same it would not be enough to ever repay you for releasing me from my obligation to that vile devil and so much more that the child who blew in with the coldest of the western winds has meant to us all."

She awoke again during the small hours of the same evening of 8th August, 1901. On the first actual occurrence of the previously imagined event, she could see Mr. White lying next to her. She could also see the light blue walls of the room that surrounded her in the afterglow of the streetlamps just below, which were set upon the four corners of the nearly vacant intersection of 101st Street and 1st Avenue. The church bells that rang out from the steeple located directly across the street announcing thee o'clock hour had just tranquilly chimed. She had not heard those high pitched bells toll before she awoke. All was quiet but for the ticking of the grandfather clock out in the main room of the sizeable apartment.

After gathering her bearings for a moment, she hastily surmised the reason behind her call to rise from the depths of her rushing dreams. Something was happening with Edward. She warily stood up from her bed and stepped into the short hallway of the second story apartment without covering her narrow and dainty feet. She looked around cautiously as if she believed something were moving beside her in the shrouded light whilst she approached the room of the presumably sleeping and freshly inducted octogenarian. The door to Mr. Calhoun's room was always kept open some so that she could hear him if he needed her assistance during the night. He was not stirring and clearly not suffering during these final hours of his traditional span of rest, yet there was a look set upon the elder man's shaded mien that beckoned her to enter his room and check on him.

She approached slowly and silently so as not startle Edward if he was in fact partially awake. After less than a dozen quiet steps taken along the old and worn out yet firmly settled hardwood floors of his room, she found herself standing over and watching the old man sleep by way of the low, simmering light of those same street lamps that kept her room aglow during the evening hours. Edward began to breathe a bit uneasily for a brief span but not to the point of alerting her. Subsequent to that slight irregularity, and for no apparent reason that the woman could fathom, the old man's breathing stopped altogether. She squeezed his hand firmly and could immediately sense that he was departing this world. She watched him intently but did nothing to disrupt his passage. Edward was not well and had been confined to his bed since early on in the summer. The tears began to well up in her eyes as she considered that this poor man, disavowed by nearly all of those that he loved so dearly, was set to die alone in his sleep but for the sentinel of her loving presence watching over him.

She let go of his hand to wipe away the first of the tears that began streaming down her cheeks. Before she had swept away the last remnants of those tears, she was promptly startled when the man's blue and seemingly childlike eyes frightfully shot open wide amidst the dim and milky light of the room. His chest then expanded hastily outward as if he had suddenly received an unwelcome jolt of electricity that was passing through the entirety of his body. She quickly regained her composure from the terrible fright the old man had delivered unto her wits and once again clasped his hand in her own. He inhaled savagely in a ghastly expression of his quite sudden and rather unexpected need for oxygen, coughed violently for a spell and then peacefully settled his spine back down upon the bed. When Mr. Calhoun was calm and breathing somewhat normally, he looked into the whites of her eyes, which were all that remained visible to his aging and fully dilated pupils in the dim and borrowed light of the room. She reached for his reading lantern resting beside his bed as if she might set about the task of lighting it but the old man pleaded with her not to continue on with that task. "Please, no, my dear. This will progress far better without the ill-shadings of my inconsistent lantern."

She returned the lantern flatly to the gentleman's nightstand and asked, "What may I do for you, father?" Edward tried to laugh in that pleasant and soothing way of the Southern gentleman of a bygone era, in the manner he always did, but a hacking cough promptly overtook his wind. When he was stable again, he whispered audibly, "Nothing at all, my dear. The already dead are remanded to die a second time alone and without provision. Perhaps you could deny that trend by sitting with me for a while. My time is not far off now."

"Of course, father," was her persuasive and diligently loyal reply. "But please, do stop talking of such things. We have much to finish discussing regarding your memoirs tomorrow."

Edward smiled without making a sound in reply and gently scratched at his head that was adorned by such an elegant cropping of cottony, white hair. After a brief pause, he replied to her in a fuller but not disruptive voice, "Yes, my dear. Of course, that must be the reason I returned. Thank you for reminding me."

She knew that the old man was serious about the finality of his condition now because he had put off discussing the distribution of certain portions of his memoirs for years now. "What of your memoirs then, father? What is it that you need me to do?" she asked of him.

He thought for another brief moment and then replied a bit distractedly. "Of course, the entirety of the journal is to be remanded to the sanctioned archives back in Sumter as we discussed. Beyond that, there are two pages I would like you to copy and deliver into the care of Elizabeth Ann when you do return to Uriah one day. Pardon my oversight on the matter, my dear; the place would be termed Blackville now in accordance with Mr. Jim's divine rescuing of his son and your suicidal brother upon the moment of your death. Such an occasion certainly would have made for poor theater after all of our efforts to deliver you hence from the gallows over in Augusta. I do hope that Amos fares well up in Chicago. In time, he too will understand the way of things as he should. He is a bright man with a good heart that found his wits blinded by the ways of vindictive men at the wrong moment in time, just as we all have for a spell or more."

Miss Margaret Anne smiled at the old man who would remain sarcastic up until the instant of his last breath. She rubbed his forehead after pulling up a chair next to the bed and considered how much she was going to miss this gentleman and gentle man of the harshly fostered Confederate era. She spoke soothingly in response to the dying man. "Yes, father, I do believe Amos will return to the warmer auspices his innate inner light in time. He is a good man and he will once again understand that to be true." She paused for a brief moment to consider Edward's initial request and then queried him as she settled back into the firm straits of the old wooden reading chair. "What entries do you request I deliver to Elizabeth Ann on your behalf before your memoirs are properly sealed for submission and initial review?"

"Actually, before we get to that, my dear, please do remember not to return home until the ages also have old Mr. Sinclair and he has joined me in the afterlife. I do pray nightly that our quarters will be in differing parts of town, if you properly surmise my meaning. I dare not fathom that the demise of the Yankee gentleman shall be meaningfully subsequent to that of my own. Your boys by Mr. White are growing up fast and this is no place for Southern gentlemen to learn the ways of the world. This exorbitant city is meant for the dead such as us, those who live without consequence."

Margaret Anne laughed affectionately at the dying man's continuing wit and retorted, "I have grown to love it here so, father, but I do promise you that my boys will not remain strangers to those of the Carolina countryside when that day arrives."

"Good, such is very good to hear, my dear. While our friends back home have certainly made a mess of reconciling with those to whom we owe such a debt of gratitude, certainly your boys will be welcomed into Amos's conclave with open arms. In any event, let us get on to business now, my lovely child. My wind grows short. There are two pages set within my memoirs that should clear the air as it were on a few items of considerable import to those that do still love me. The first of the aforementioned is my testimonial regarding the events that transpired on the night your mother died. As the scrivener of the transcription you are left with little choice in the matter, nevertheless such is good that you should read my written words concerning the woeful affair. I thought it best to wait until you had made a go at living like the rest of us for a while before I made the details of that foulest of evenings known to you. Make certain you sister Maime is also made aware of what happened to my dearest."

"Yes, I will most certainly see to it that my sisters both know what happened to our mother," Margaret Anne responded in earnest before asking, "Was it the father of my maligned child who so harshly undid her?" Mr. Calhoun nodded remorsefully but spoke not a word in reply to keep the memories of that night from entering the confines of his already myriad and tumultuously swirling thoughts before he passed on.

"What else remains that you would have me do for you, father? What does the other page you would have me transcribe and deliver concern?" Margaret Anne asked in the name of a preference for expediency and in deference to the uncertain condition of the dying man. She was also attempting to pry her own considerations away from the various images her suddenly distraught mind was cogently conjuring up concerning what had befallen her mother on the night she crossed over.

Edward faltered for a moment. His eyes closed abruptly and his chin dropped down and over toward his left shoulder rather suddenly. Little Miss squeezed his hand firmly to draw him back to her. When she received no response, she summoned him with but a searching whisper that seemed to wane near to the instant that her hushed call met with the warm, heavy stillness of the vapors of the room. The sound of her voice then faded into oblivion in accordance with the oscillations of the dusky immersion of the light then only

intermittently rising up from the spent gaslamps flickering on the woefully haunted yet otherwise unattended street corners below, "Father,
father, are you still with me?" she called into the enchanting hollows
of the tremoring nightshade.

Edward did not move a muscle and never opened his eyes in this
world again. He whispered back to her with as much potency as he
could muster. His words were spoken in much the same way that a
child drifting off to sleep might reply to a loving guardian watching
over then, "Nearly time to go now, my darling angel of the west wind.
You were always mine from the moment I bought you away from his
kind. You should know that I knew the truth hiding deep within your
mother's eyes long before you and your sister spoke of as much down
in Haiti. She meant to tell me once upon a time, as she could never
conceal at least the most effusive confidences of her heart from my
discerning eyes for long, yet Miss Meara held something over her back
in those uncertain days when the war raged on and took my boy. No
matter, my child, what I need you to understand presently is that I
loved you dearly anyway, no matter what may be presumed of my
intentions to conceal you in the past...and I will always love you just
the same. Keep that sentiment close to your heart as a favor to a dying
gentleman of those days of ours now gone by."

Margaret Anne attempted to seal his thoughts away from such
self-approbation at the very moment of his dying spell of clarity but
she was rendered silent when he did squeeze her hand in return. He
did as much to still her anxious tongue and save what remained of his
wind for the last of what needed to be said. "Remember that sentiment well...and remember that you have my love always...my dearest
child. Be that as it may, from this moment on you will be forced to
produce your own quips by which to take that once tainted love into
your boundless heart."

Margaret Anne smiled longingly at his last grasping breaths of
fresh wit and she smiled longingly for the days shared with him that

had in that moment all come to pass when taken within the guise of a mortal reckoning. When the tender old man had spoken those endearing words of his dying breaths, she lovingly squeezed his hand in return. She then bent forward to whisper into his ear and gently kissed him there while she softly laughed out some diminutive parcel of the oncoming potency of her need to cry. "You have my love always too, father. You keep that close to your heart while we are apart, you beautiful gentleman of such memorable Southern charm of a bygone era. These years spent with you, Abraham and the boys in these realms of loosely controlled chaos will always remain dear to me. I shall never believe that we were truly dead instead of, at last, brilliantly alive. Otherwise, my heart would not be breaking so."

Edward's chin drifted closer to his shoulder while he continued to fade. He had taken one breath softly into his lungs that he knew was set to be his last. He gathered up some loose semblance of an earthly thought while he journeyed into the outskirts of the spirit realms. He breathed out as slowly as his expiring lungs would allow and whispered, "Do you remember what we discussed before dear Shiloh was wed?"

Margaret Anne nodded into the rising glow of one of the unevenly burning gaslamps out beyond the windowpane and replied, "Yes, father," while her tears began to stream down her angelic countenance. Edward whispered, "Tell that tale in your own words instead of mine to your sister Elizabeth Ann when it is safe for you to do so, my love. Likewise, tell them all I love them dearly…and that I will always love them dearly."

The old, white-haired man went silent for a moment while little Miss squeezed his hand in the hopes that she might feel anything of the motions of his gentle caress but one time more. Edward then seized up violently and exclaimed suddenly, "Joy unto you, my promised angel! He no longer lingers in wait before the pressing of the light! There is such wonder!" With those words spoken in earnest, Edward

Christopher Calhoun passed on from this earth upon reaching the age of eighty.

Miss Margaret Anne crawled into bed beside her father and held onto his hand until it began to grow firm and cold. Afterward, she covered him up to the top of his head in his favorite patchwork quilt and returned to her room to recall the discussion they had back in the summer of 1871. It was late-July or perhaps early-August, a short time before Shy was set to be married and but few weeks after she had first dreamt of the death of the man from the picture made upon the event of her eighth birthday back in the winter of 1867. The man who was father to her heart had by that time known much of what Mr. Reed was and had already presumed that one day she would be his undoing. Sometime thereafter and following the dour abuse of his beloved Elizabeth Ann, Edward had taken the decisive risk of signing his name upon that man's eternal contract in blood based upon his faith in her alone. Likewise, such was also true that Edward never slept soundly while Mr. Reed still lived once he had made his mark upon that agreement, and he continued on in such a dismal way until Margaret Anne was delivered forth from her captivity and what remained of the child of the light was returned to the majestic woodlands and cotton fields of her birth.

On the day that Edward and little Miss had discussed Mr. Reed, her father by jointly signed decree had committed every resource at his disposal over to the promised child to learn what she might about such an entity whose cold and soulless bearing seemed to reconcile with only that of legend. Though she was just twelve at the time, she found that her understanding of the devil lurking within the manifest corporal embodiment of Mr. Reed had transcended even the moment of her birth. Furthermore, looking back on the moment of that frightful discussion now, following what the Edward had just said to her about buying her from out beneath that man's wicked and eternal bondage and knowing back then that she was the child of another, she believed that Edward had somehow come to intuitively understand at least something of what was to be written down upon Miss Shy's letter of 1884 long before they had visited with the woefully emaciated frame of her former sister in that distressingly derelict Haitian prison. Sadly, if Edward had addressed the reasons behind his pledge to remit the promised child into the hands of the very man that had violated their mother by way of an arranged marriage with Miss Shy back in 1890, the poorly treated woman had never accepted a word of it as truth.

Margaret Anne continued to deliberate upon the subject of Mr. Lucian Reed Morgenthau while lingering in the afterglow of Edward's peaceful passing and the gentle light of the breaking of the new day. She realized that the subject of Mr. Reed was one that she and Edward had continued to let lie very still in the passing decade they had spent living together amidst the hustle and bustle of Manhattan. She began to wonder if Edward Calhoun had known that the devil had come searching for its own upon the moment Elizabeth Ann had been despoiled and grossly infested with the man's vile flavor for despair. Perhaps Edward had seen something malignant lurking deep within those pleasantly unexpected bedroom eyes of her mother, or maybe Edward simply was that adept at reading the mind of another even if it were the devil incarnate. As far as the promised child was concerned, none of those presumptions amounted to a hill of beans upon the passing of the moment.

The truth was that Edward Calhoun did love her and always had, no matter what those seasoning Articles of 1858 were set to timelessly imply. Furthermore, the fine yet misunderstood man had sacrificed much and risked far more than one could possibly imagine in allowing her to complete her anointed deed of fracturing the essence of the one that would have continued to prey upon them all like a starving lion. The shame of it all was the thankless nature of his sacrifice, which would appear as exactly otherwise to many of those that knew only something or perhaps nothing at all of the true nature of her former inner light and the primordial curses set upon the Calhoun family; many of which had died, though others remained, only with the passing on of the sorceress of Sumter and her near to immortal consort of the highest order.

Margaret Anne then recalled the now timely, yet strange upon the given moment of his vocalized thoughts, words of some half-concocted wisdom Edward had offered up for her consideration when they spoke after dinner last night. "The world in its present state was never meant to understand the true gift of your light. Your radiance of the other side was granted to you only because he was here. Yet, you, your mother and Elizabeth Ann have suffered through the worst of his persecutions and in some ways, so have I, your sister Shy and dear Virgil. The shaded minds of those who cannot see off into the heavens or feel God gently prodding them so lovingly along their heartstrings will never comprehend the meaning behind the pureness of your gift."

After the two had traded thoughts on that topic for a short while, Edward added a further thought for the sanctity of the record, "This earth in its present condition is set to test the faith of men and the love they have been eternally granted and carry forth from the moment of their birth. Here, in these temporal climes, the light cannot exist without the natural contrast of the darkness. Yet, with our hearts and our eyes always watching for God above and holding on tightly to His hand, there is nothing that can hide its true intent from our faithfully searching eyes when brought before the Light of the world. Those that follow us are condemned to face the same trials and tribulations of our day, the only difference being that the suffering of their time will be dressed up in a different society gown. The vast preponderance of men in the days to come will not recognize those things we leave behind for them as the resolutions set to alleviate the banes of their own time."

After a brief moment of contemplative thought, Edward had then concluded his thoughts on the matter of the promised child's true gift to the world. "Yet, because the very worst of that darkness set to roam the earth was so confounded by the essence your light, those that bear our name and the bloodlines of our ancestors to follow in our often uncertain footsteps will remain free to choose the path they walk. Perhaps none but you, your mother or Elizabeth Ann will ever understand the depths of the concentrated evil lurking within the unknown margins of that ravenous entity. Nevertheless, when the time comes to speak of such things, none will have believed what we spoke of to be true until the balance of power shifts back to one such as Mr. Morgenthau or those that have taken hold over the country in the aftermath of the debilitating war to absolve our enduring sin. The hour remains dim, but the light of God's hope still shines because you have been sent in accordance with His promise to the faithful."

Edward had then lowered his eyes back to his journal and spoke of a premonition recently given over to him in the manner of a dream. "The continuing legacy of the age of the Calhoun family, of which you and yours are now an integral part, my dearest, will at last be settled at a time of God's choosing when one of the bloodline of Virgil O'Keefe overcomes the other that chooses to walk the path of the fickle. The gold presently held safe in both keeps is likely to be near the same once Francis Calhoun properly settles the rift caused by Miss Meara and marries the Calhoun line back into the auspices of the Pinckney Trust. Perhaps the enduring badges of honor for our own day lie in the continuing potency of our final disavowal; our closing act so to speak and our enduring exile, which serves to allow the struggle to march on toward its appointed destiny."

Mr. Erasmus Sinclair did not pass on for more than a decade following the death of Edward Calhoun. He died on April 15, 1912 while journeying to the bottom of the North Atlantic Ocean with the bisected hull and sundry remains of the RMS Titanic. He was told not to make the journey for some odd reason or another, but perchance the wicked man of such potent premonition saw no better way to meet his end for several and varying reasons alike. In any event, Margaret Anne Basseterre's young boys born out of wedlock and aged fourteen and fifteen years, respectively, Abraham Marion White, Jr. and Calvin Eoin White joined their mother and their father on a one way journey down to the mysterious lands of the Deep South and the sedentary town of Blackville, South Carolina that ensuing May. No one stirred up any trouble when the then fifty-three year old woman of a bygone era returned to town along with her gregarious family.

Margaret Anne was recognized by none but her sister and a perhaps a Davis boy or two upon her return to the beloved cotton fields she once roamed in the days of her youth. Such was precisely as she had expected things to be when she arrived. Some twenty-two years had passed since the legendary death of Miss Margaret Anne Basseterre by way of a public hanging in 1890 for the murder of Mr. Virgil Denton O'Keefe near to a lifetime ago back in 1875.

By the morning of her nearly unnoticed return home to raise her boys and settle her jazz musician of a husband out of his fast-paced Harlem lifestyle by way of some righteous, down home country living, Little pea was married with grown children of her own and well-settled in her long-time home of Atlanta, Georgia. Mr. and Mrs. Laing had passed near to just a year apart back in 1907 and Thaddeus Davis, who ran things at that time over at the Davis place, never dared mention the curious yet lighter skinned likeness of his new neighbor to the woman he inadvertently helped serve up to the hangman over in Georgia.

Of course, Thaddeus Davis and the hangman had become one in the same for a day back in 1890 after Thaddeus had paid a visit to Georgia and gotten his longtime friend, ol' Wick Thomas, far too drunk, or at least far too drunk to awaken and pull the lever over at the gallows situated in his hometown of Augusta the following morning. Therefore, Mr. Davis was one of the few who knew that little Miss had never found the end of that lengthening rope. Later on, and sometime during the last of his years, the old man would swear up and down that the woman who along with her family had taken over Virgil's old cottage and then the main farmhouse out at the Osment place for a time was the promised child; the promised child whose legend had by then grown beyond that of even the fabled lore of the wicked Miss Meara Calhoun. Unlike back in 1868, no one listened to a thing that hard drinking old fool of the Depression Era said when he had finally decided to get on with the spilling of the last of his earthly secrets.

The Claibrooke family had been encouraged to move to the outskirts of Columbia by Amos. That was back when Blackville was officially incorporated in 1891. However, Amos's heart remained far from engaged by the once fiery cause once his sister had been hanged; due in no small part to his own negligence when stated in the legal parlance to which he was more accustomed by that time, but flat out pigheadedness and stupidity when uttered by most around those more informal climes. In truth, only Miss Maime and her family remained of those once sacred to the child secretly reared out at the February Cabin. Yet, the indelible folktale that was the partially embellished in some ways and undersold in others story her life would always remain. For it was her enduring tale that had perfectly embodied so many of the struggles of the times proximate to and following the war. By way of lore, she was forever to remain the child who blew in one night with a gale force west wind of a steadfast resolve akin to none but the arctic hinterlands of the northern Canadas, a mulatto girl of uncertain yet diversely presumed stock; a half-breed of the spirit realms, and a phantasm of the mythical order of those in possession of the light with a fickle will to rain down vengeance upon those who attempted to possess her in any way.

Some five years after Margaret Anne's return to Uriah, Miss Maime and her family were set to move down to Haiti to escape the resurgent racial antipathy of the South and moreover, at the request of Miss

Shy's son, Andre Francis. Andre had been experiencing a brief spell of success down on the island, but unfortunately, that success would turn out to be rather fleeting. Maime probably would have stayed on out at the farmstead to live out the last of her days in spite of the deteriorating social climate in the South and upon receiving Andre Francis's repeated requests for both Maime and her family to return to their "homeland" if not for the youngest son of Mary Grice's oldest daughter, Mr. Bramlage Samuels-Calhoun. Bramlage was a self-professed evangelical, yet in actuality an insane man of some deep and burning racial hatred of an unknown source. As such, the man had taken it upon his honor to chase out the last of Miss Jeanne's remaining line from the Carolinas. Whatever the truth behind his motives was, Mr. Calhoun's reasons for such an unnecessary and useless witch hunt regarding the sweetest, old and God-fearing woman to ever grace the Carolina countryside were certainly not honorable.

In any event, the two women and sisters found themselves standing together yet otherwise alone on the front porch of the Osment farmstead as the sun was preparing to set on the anniversary of what would have been their mother's 91st birthday; May 5th, 1917. Maime's grown boys and her husband, Jefferson, who by that time had farmed the Osment acreage in some fashion or another for more than thirty years, had left a week prior for Charleston with the things they planned to take down to Haiti. Mr. Duval wished to make certain that all of their furniture and sundry items were properly handled during the move. At that moment, Miss Margaret Anne, under the guise her fictitious yet locally accepted name, told her sister the truth about who their mother believed her father was and what that man had done to their mother. Needless to say, Maime was shocked and also saddened by the truth of her sister's lineage and her own further disconnection from the already quite distant Calhoun clan of the Sumter she remembered from the earliest days of her childhood. The antics of a madman like Bramlage Calhoun were to be expected. However, to Maime's still rather puritan mind, the lack of support for her family from any back in Sumter marked the end of that long and storied relationship that had existed between various factions of the two families.

The two women sat out on that porch for hours and talked through it all. Such was the most Miss Maime Alouette had spoken to anyone since her father died when she was just eight-years old back in 1855. When dusk had settled in over the land and the budding stalks of cotton set out in the field in their perfected rows were no longer visible, the two aging women walked hand in hand down to the old rope swing that the youngest of the Davis grandchildren or great-grandchildren kept in perfect working order. They swung together side by side in the seat of the swing in much the same way Edward and Miss Jeanne used to do from time to time during the years of Captain Calhoun's wonderful exile from Sumter.

When the darkness had quietly blanketed that now pristine patch of downward sloping farmland, the two remained sitting together upon the swing Maime's father had crafted all those decades ago now. They discussed further all of the shared comings and goings of their eventful childhood. There was still something of a shroud of darkness that forever hung over those turbulent years both before and after the war but also a beautiful, binding ray of light that would forever enjoin the oldest and youngest of Miss Jeanne Basseterre's three daughters.

Be that as it may, the perfected hindsight applied to those joyfully shared memories of those vivid and forever sacred days would not be traded by either of them for anything of this earth. Those days so fondly remembered were their days, and the words now so affectionately shared between them were their words that marked the time. Taken together as a whole, those hours spent together were the heavenly ordained moment of the full and solitary telling of their story to none but the apparitions of the past still haunting that old field and God above; it was the time of the telling of the eternal tale of the great joys shared by them all and the story of the continuing struggle of the age that would abide well into the years that they too were naught but the lingering ghosts of the field when visiting this little corner of the world just beyond the crossroads out to nowhere.

As such, the two remaining sisters and living daughters of Miss Jeanne Jolie Basseterre sat swaying gently beneath the stars for the benefit of those they loved; for the tender knowing of the memories of the ones who had for a time passed through these sacred fields of cotton and the homesteads just beyond. For in truth, when the two wistful women offered up to the Almighty those softly spoken reflections of their shared past, whereby for but an instant they relived those fondly remembered days now shining in their minds like untarnished aurum glinting in the twilight of their own lives, those words so softly spoken into the lingering stillness of the soothing night air were the true account of the beautiful tale of their own deliverance unto Him.

Some years later, perhaps the late-Spring of 1920 being the best any mere mortal might presume concerning the actual timing of the event, as there were no records of the forbidden rendezvous ever taking place, Miss Annie Grace Oriana paid a visit to the presiding matriarch of the Calhoun Dynasty. The once fledgling enterprises of Edward Calhoun that were founded in the aftermath of the war had by then once again become a thriving empire comprised of varied businesses which had been reunited with the Calhoun's for a time alienated Pinckney blood. Miss Oriana had been up the coast and back in town to visit with Mr. David Emmett Basseterre, an ascendant businessman of his own right hailing from Charleston, earlier in the week. As the direct result of those prior days spent with Mr. Basseterre, the aging woman was beaming in the way any proud mother would upon once again witnessing the gallant and gracious nature of their prospering child.

In the case of the mother and her first-born son, such a glorious and heartfelt reunion was upon the occasion of being momentarily reunited after remaining predominantly separated for the entirety of the coursings of their rather eccentric lives. There were certainly those few and intermittent visits paid during the rare intervals when the circumstances of the day afforded them such a luxury. Still and all, the two had been estranged for so long that several differing lives had been lived by them both since the very last of the days they so innocently shared in the tender joys of near to every waking moment spent together; spent together as a young mother and her baby boy in a far-off land up in the furthest reaches of the Yankee North, a memorable place which possessed a tamed yet ancient natural beauty.

Miss Elizabeth Ann Calhoun was in fine shape for a woman in her early seventies and effortlessly completed the not insignificant journey from the parlor of her Beaufort estate home to the front foyer. Miss Calhoun had been summoned by her lovely maidservant, Alana, who had dutifully and in a pleasant manner alerted the lady of the manor to the arrival her entirely expected midday guest. "Thank you, Miss Alana, I shall arrive to greet our guest in but a flash," Miss Calhoun called out in reply to the buxom, middle-aged Carolina woman as the lady of the manor approached the elegantly adorned archway leading into the spacious, white-marble floored foyer. Miss Alana notified their waiting guest of Miss Calhoun's impending arrival and then graciously and gracefully stepped away to prepare the tea for the ladies' rather casual gathering.

Elizabeth Ann appeared about as elegant and radiant as a woman of her age would ever dare whilst she purposefully approached with her hand offered to her slightly slouched and timidly postured guest, a woman of perhaps sixty who was clearly domiciled somewhere out in the country. Miss Oriana smiled brightly with her kaleidoscopic eyes and the passable dentures of her mouth shining brightly in the abundant sunlight of the grandiose and graciously illuminated front hall of the estate while her gallant hostess approached. The still reclusive but by then widely renowned matriarch to such a once again enduring fortune seemed as dashing to Miss Oriana as she did on the night she accompanied Mr. Virgil O'Keefe to the New Year's Eve celebration back in Uriah some fifty years ago. Miss Calhoun hailed her guest as she stepped to within the proper distance of offering up a cordial greeting, "Miss Oriana, it is such a pleasure to meet you! Thank you for coming all this way to visit. I am so excited to hear of what you have learned as it regards my father. I find such a verity almost hard to fathom that dearest Edward passed on from us near to thirty years ago now."

Edward's legacy for the public consumption was quite fine or perhaps suitably intact in the year 1920. He was indeed known as the man who had reengineered the Calhoun legacy in the years following the war. Much of the family's troubles existing back in those days and, of course, Edward's secret ties to the murderous woman of Uriah with an unknown lineage had been properly cordoned off and then scrubbed from the communal record over time. In fact, the entirety of the life of Miss Margaret Anne Basseterre had reached the status of a well-guarded secret pretty much everywhere in South Carolina outside of Uriah. The efficacy of that truth was now such that Miss Oriana's presence at the estate home of Elizabeth Ann Calhoun was not a riskless proposition given that so much water had passed under the bridge since her garish hanging for the murder of the man who was the one true adoration of the woman standing before her. Furthermore, the woman so exquisitely presented before Miss Oriana was clearly and presently given over to the contingent propositions of a society woman.

"The pleasure of being here in your beautiful home on this fine day belongs to me, Madam. I will not keep you long. There are just a few items of your father's hand that were found out at the farmstead in Uriah when Miss Maime was preparing to move. My sis..." Miss Oriana rushed to cover her mouth in a fright while Elizabeth Ann interjected potently yet with a notable twinge of puzzlement glossing over her tone, "I'm sorry, my dear. I didn't quite take that all in for the benefit of my discernment. Would you mind repeating what it was that you just said?"

Miss Oriana abashedly removed her hand from her mouth and quickly set about waxing over her near to fatal mistake. "I am truly sorry, Ma'am. I thought I felt a nervous hiccup approaching to make its way to the fore. I do not receive the gentle graces of standing before one so elegant in such a beautiful home often. What I had intended to say was that Miss Maime felt those belated and latently discovered transcriptions would be suitably handled only by way of being delivered personally into your care. That was back when she was directly engaged with and therefore fully immersed in the throes of preparing for her trying move to Haiti. It has taken me quite a while to gather up the nerve to stand before someone of your distinction and prominence with these old notes of your father's hand that are quite likely to stir up those now hardened sentiments of our past."

Miss Elizabeth Ann waved her hand playfully at the poor, near-to-trembling woman and laughed a bit to comfort her while she spoke in reply. "Nonsense now, my dear, there is nothing of Edward's past that is news to me. Of course, none of us speak openly or perchance even otherwise of those things that may prove harmful to the family's reputation any longer. Such compulsory discernment comes with the rarified air of wealth and the broadly presumed refinement of our caste I suppose. Personally speaking, I'd rather be in your shoes and enjoying those beautiful sunsets out at the farm back in Uriah." Miss Oriana beamed brightly in response to such human talk emanating from her sister but did not speak in reply while she did little but intently study the mistress of the manor's current form.

That was the moment Miss Elizabeth Ann had a novel yet peculiar thought cross her mind. She impulsively shook off the bulk of such a ridiculous urging but not the concept in its entirety. "I'm sorry, my dear, would you remind me again how it is that you came to inherit the place out in Uriah from Miss Maime?"

Miss Oriana continued smiling warmly and answered, "Why of course, Madam. I am the cousin of Miss Leslie and I have three eager men that do mind me from time to time and are quite willing to work the place. With both of her sisters passed on, I reckon Miss Maime figured that I was about as close to family as she was going to get where it concerned the legacy of the beautiful old farmstead."

Miss Elizabeth Ann nodded pensively and then responded to Miss Oriana a bit hastily. Something about this woman who possessed the remnants of an old skeleton or two from her father's closet was suddenly making her a bit nervous, though she had no earthly idea as to why. "Yes, yes, of course, my dear, I do remember you saying as much now that you ever so gently remind me. Is there anything else that you had planned to discuss before you turn my father's posthumously discovered writings over to me?"

Miss Oriana could sense that something was crossing up her sister's refined and after all of these years deeply ingrained ability to wipe away every last trace of the sorrow and abuse of her past. Beyond that, the slightly bent and meekly displayed woman of the Carolina countryside eruditely surmised that the very thing triggering Miss Calhoun's sudden unease was that woman's familiarity with something of her own appearance or innate nature while she remained lingering in the presence of the dashing socialite; a true lady of the modern gentry that might have passed for far younger than she herself was while her senior by more than a decade. Such a distinct prodding from a remembered trait possessed by one once bound to the beholder's heart was a powerful portent that Miss Oriana could do little, if anything at all, to conceal. Due to that certainty, Miss Calhoun's sister of a prior time now only vaguely remembered where it concerned the formal registries of the agendas of the present day answered back in the manner of one expediting an affair onward to its desired conclusion.

Miss Oriana made an effort to speak with even more of slow, country drawl and to reflect her given mannerisms as yet more timid than in the prior moments in an effort to further disguise her identity, "No, Ma'am, not at all. If such suits your current fancy, Ma'am, I was hoping to do little more than deliver this here parcel directly into your lovely hands and be on my way back home to the quaint pastures of the upland."

Miss Elizabeth Ann nodded hastily yet agreeably enough for the bounds of proper etiquette. She then reached out her hand to receive the fine envelope of a diminutive yet sturdy make while looking directly into the eyes of the woman who for some reason confounded her thoughts so upon the moment. When she had clasped the parcel safely in her hand, Miss Elizabeth Ann asked of her counterpart, "Will you at least sit for a while and take some tea with me while I read through the old scrivening of my father?"

Miss Oriana shook her head in a nervous and hurried manner by way of refusing the once again settled and now all the more enchanting woman. "I am so very sorry, Ma'am, yet I cannot oblige you no matter the depths to which I have wanted for little more than that very thing for so many years now." With those words being kindly spoken, Miss Oriana turned starkly, showed herself out of the fine coastal estate home, and made her way quickly down the stairs of the veranda and out to the buggy that had been awaiting her return from the manor. She accomplished as much without even a proper look see given in the direction from whence she came.

Upon the moment of Miss Oriana's sudden departure, Miss Elizabeth Ann pulled the three written letters from the envelope as she strolled reticently back toward the parlor. Her lovely visage remained fully aglow in the all but blinding sunlight of the noon hour, which permeated her home that was situated just beyond the reflective waters and sandy beaches of the coast. Because she knew that none were scheduled to be present in the house during the hour of her scheduled taking of tea with Miss Oriana beyond Miss Alana, who was back in the kitchen preparing the selected blend of said leaf upon the instant, Miss Calhoun spoke in whispers to the indulgent presumptions of her thoughts. She did so as she began to unfold the first of the curious letters while she slowly wandered back to the plush comforts of her lavish reading chair.

"What a strange creature that Miss Oriana is," Miss Calhoun offered up to the vacant and brilliantly illuminated confines of her handsome parlor. "Certainly she must have been lovely beyond compare in the days before the world exacted its pound of flesh from her. Be that as it may, there was something so familiar about the way her eyes lit up when she smiled and that slightly carefree nature of hers hiding behind her abounding reverence for the pageantry of the showing off of the wares of our society. If only she knew the true cost of being surrounded by such exquisite yet temporal and fickle beauty."

When Miss Elizabeth Ann was seated in her chair, she saw the date set atop the first of the letters she unfolded. Before reading a word beyond the heading, she quickly set the letter and the accompanying envelope down on her round, wooden side table of an antique fabrication and paced rapidly back toward the front door. She pulled the door open, though she had grown quite unaccustomed to the labor of such a thing, and called out, "Miss Oriana, Miss Oriana, surely there is some mistake! The first of your parcels from Edward is marked as having been written in New York...and quite impossibly in the year 1891! The man died the same day my sister was executed back in 1890!"

Miss Oriana heard her sister very clearly as her buggy made its way down the road that ran alongside the beautiful marshlands of the island back channels. She offered not a word in reply, yet did urge her son to increase the tempo of the drawing steeds. The gallant count of Charleston town smiled in return while kindly obliging his lovely and loving mother. Miss Elizabeth Ann never got a clear look at the lineaments of the driver of the carriage. However, for some odd reason she would have sworn that she recognized the queer hat of Miss Oriana's coachman as the unmistakable stetson of a Confederate mountain ranger. The hat was a rare item to be brandishing in these heady and modern times, and a style which she had last seen flamboyantly worn by little Miss's boy, David, at a society function up in Charleston. David was known by her alone among the living to be half-brother to her son, Francis Virgil. Having been quickly worked into a richly textured froth by the strange events of the present moment, Miss Calhoun shook her head in nearly exasperated disbelief whilst she grew ever more certain she had spent the last quarter-hour in the presence of an apparition.

She returned to the house and got straight to the reading of the letters or journal entries of the late Edward Christopher Calhoun. Nevertheless, she remained a hard woman to impress upon, no matter how passionately she wished to believe in the verity of those now sacred missives of her long-belated father. The time for her to confirm or reject her suspicions regarding the letters would not arrive until she returned to Sumter in July for the 1920 rendition of the Calhoun's mid-summer gala. While spending some time in the town of her birth, she paid a visit to the Calhoun family archives unannounced. By then, the documents contained within the underground vault were seen by none without the measure of a formal appointment requested through the supervisory trustees and the diligent oversight of Miss Kingston, a woman who knew everything contained within each document piling up along the walls and within the bureaus of Miss Meara's old lair deep beneath the town square.

Miss Kingston smiled into the shaded light of her reading lantern when Elizabeth Ann arrived at the bottom of the stairs to the crypt and announced, "I thought you might never arrive. Francis had hoped that you would never come. He will undoubtedly relieve me of my duties if he finds out I have accommodated your wishes this afternoon, my lady. He worries so over the family's reputation ever since he married Miss Delilah Pinckney."

Elizabeth Ann smiled in return and replied warmly to Miss Kingston while flashing the folded parchments held within her left hand. "Such is certain that I never would have come but for the arrival of these letters to my door. They were delivered by an angel and portend to be transcribed by the very hand of my father. I am here to confirm the authenticity of those letters. As far as my son is concerned, you needn't worry about that meddlesome boy in the slightest, my dear. Mothers know incriminating things about their sons that not a person otherwise would ever believe to be true."

Miss Kingston giggled smartly at Miss Calhoun's quip and then quickly read through each of the letters in just minutes. She was something of a savant when it came to committing the written word to memory. When she had finished reading the pages, she looked up at Miss Calhoun and smiled with a beaming grin that just about beat the Dutch. The archivist then nodded exuberantly and announced excitedly, "Yes, those are the precise words of your father, Ma'am!" Miss Kingston then walked across the dimly lit subterranean room and pulled the actual completed memoirs of Edward Calhoun from the top drawer of one of the bureaus lining the wall. "Here, mistress, you may look and see of your own accord. Edward Calhoun's memoirs are all written here. They were delivered and properly archived in the summer of 1912 by his attendant up in New York City, a Miss Oriana I believe."

Elizabeth Ann shook her head in disbelief once again and snapped back, "Pardon me, my dear but did you say Miss Oriana delivered my father's memoirs to this place and that they were written up in New York City?"

Miss Kingston giggled a bit and answered her matriarch in reply as professionally as she was able under the circumstances. She had waited for the passing of nearly a decade for someone beyond Francis and the few attorneys to the trustees of the estate who had reviewed the memoirs under the strictest terms of confidentiality to discover the truth regarding the life and times and Edward Calhoun. "Yes, indeed they were, Ma'am. Most of them anyway, some of Edward's earliest writings were composed while he was down in Haiti or out at sea. You are familiar with Miss Oriana then?"

"Why yes, I am familiar with Miss Oriana, my dear," replied Elizabeth Ann somewhat vacantly while shading much of her outwardly directed focus inward to the parsing through of the vivid recollections of Miss Oriana's visit to her home in back May. Miss Calhoun concluded her brief answer by saying, "She is one and the same as the woman who delivered these pages to me but a few months prior to the present hour."

A short while later, as the elegant empress of the formidable Calhoun Dynasty built for the industrial age poured through the memoirs of her father by the light of two lanterns Miss Kingston had so graciously set out for her upon the reading table in the middle of the crypt, she asked of the warm yet methodically particular archivist, "Do you believe the dates and the descriptions of the latest of my father's memoirs to be accurate or simply the ramblings of a lonely woman who knew him well and had suffered the trials of the damned up in that Dickensian Yankee metropolis?"

Miss Kingston looked down at the industrious woman poring over the writings of her father by the simmering light of the reading lanterns and answered her rather stoically. "What I believe is of little consequence, Madam. What is of consequence is what you come to believe in your heart. After reading through all of the records Edward has provided throughout the years while he lived and even long after he was officially laid to rest, what I can say with certainty is that your father wished to keep you safe and adequately provided for above all else. Furthermore, I would add that he clearly wished for you personally to accept God's peace into your once troubled heart."

Miss Elizabeth Ann looked up from Edward's journal. After a brief moment taken to gather her thoughts, she spoke into the depths of the silence and the ominous shadows shifting against the primordial brick walls of that old dungeon that stood beyond the simmering light of the reading lanterns, "I see, my dear. I must say that you sound quite confident I will indeed come to such a resolution, though such a wished for blessing has avoided my anxious thoughts for all of these years now. That is to say, with the exception of the years that followed the moment the promised child cleansed my heart of an indecent stain and rendered me fit for the raising of a child."

Miss Kingston sat down next to Miss Calhoun at the table, placed her hand gently upon her back and replied in an empathizing manner. "I should not have allowed you in here. However, after reading all of what Edward clearly left for you to find within these walls, I came to believe that neither the Calhoun nor the Pinckney trustees nor Francis Calhoun had any right to keep a daughter from the loving thoughts of her father. Those words of Edward's always belonged to you, though they had remained hidden from your tender eyes out of some quite real and then perhaps perceived necessity for so long now. That feeling of knowing that your father's words were down here waiting for you probed the very depths of my soul, Ma'am. Therefore, and to answer your question more succinctly, that answer is simply, yes. I do believe you will find such a lasting and perhaps eternal peace lying within these cold and musty walls. I will even show you Edward's copy of the blood contract he signed with Mr. Reed if you like, though I find the act of even touching my skin to the parchment of some ancient and foreign origin to be rather unsettling."

Miss Elizabeth Ann shivered fitfully upon little more than the thought of that vile demon of her haunted past. When she had settled some from the terrors of such a dreadful rumination she replied coldly and without emotion to her guide. "That will not be necessary, my dear. I am perfectly and perhaps in some ways, eternally attuned to what that man has to offer. Solely by virtue of my sister, born of the sheering west winds and a bloodstained flogging cabin, that foul creature is no more."

Miss Kington nodded into the low light preceding the deforming shadows lurking upon the macabre walls of the crypt and replied, "I understand such an aversion perfectly, Madam. I presume the truth of the matter to be that you know more of the nature of that forbidden deed and the true capacity of a man capable of offering such temptations than I will ever know."

Miss Elizabeth Ann nodded grievously and replied solemnly to Miss Kingston, "Pray! Pray in earnest, my dear! Pray to God above that you never will!"

Some hours later, after pouring through the myriad offerings of Edward's works written throughout the years, Miss Elizabeth Ann Calhoun hugged Miss Kingston and wished her well. She then ascended from the murky darkness of Miss Meara's dank crypt, which scented of cool brick, settling parchment and lamp oil, and stepped smartly into the resplendent sunlight and sweet smelling vapors of a mid-July day up upon the street level in Sumter. Miss Calhoun had returned two of the letters that were included within the parcel delivered to her by Miss Oriana to the confines of her walking purse. She continued to hold one folded page prominently in her right hand. She intended to read the short offering one final time when her carriage had reached the field out by Dingle's Mill. The partially developed tract of land to the south of town was by the year 1920 nearly unrecognizable to those who had skirmished there more than a half-century ago, yet the former battlefield did remain suitably designated by the placement of a few monuments erected in honor of the fallen on that final day of the war.

When Elizabeth Ann arrived at a pleasant cluster of habitation adorning the stream Virgil had often described as the spot where he had met her father while attempting to run down some separate and hopelessly cornered Yankees, she read her father's words and allowed the beautiful thoughts written within to cascade over her settling soul. She had learned much in regard to her father from both the letters offered over to her by Miss Oriana and her time spent reading through her father's secretive and formally posthumous memoirs. She then raised her contented guise to the sunlight shining through an open patch of the thick and cottony clouds carelessly drifting by overhead. She did as much for the purpose of allowing the precious sentiment of her own forgiveness of those who had for a time broken her spirit to radiate with permanence into the glorious light of the summer skies, and after all of these years gone by now, to at last permit the constant stain of her guilt to be disavowed and thusly empty forth from her soul and onto the confines of that hallowed ground of her own renewal; the hallowed ground where the two men who had shaped her once again still pure and delicate love over the coursings of her life had come together as one.

Elizabeth Ann Calhoun saw Miss Oriana only one time more. The lady of Sumter wished to keep that precious angel of the light from any of the lurking troubles of the day still waiting to consume what remained of her poorly born yet perfectly faithful sister. However, when Miss Elizabeth Ann Calhoun died peacefully in her sleep with almost a century of living under her belt and shortly before America entered the various theaters of the Great War, she dreamt of the beautiful promise of the child of the west wind she knew so well from her younger days spent grooming the cotton of the field out in Uriah and the years before those blissful days. The page she carried in her hand on that fine summer day of 1920 read as follows:

> *"Our lasting moments of peace while we walk this earth and our eternal joys both, those precious gifts cherished above all others, they come simply from intimately knowing our Almighty Creator and coming to adore His presence within the ones we love and esteem so dearly. Those gifts abide not in any way from the temporal possessions that are gained or lost in this life. Such things*

that do come and go are naught but fleeting upon the passing of the moment and offered as little more than the shared treasures of our sentiment to be given again and by which we might commence with the understanding of His infinite and abounding glory and enduring love for us. The promised child born of that peculiar cabin of those haunted woodlands, which held onto the buried memories of the unspoken sins of our past, she and her dear sister, who herself endured that coldest of February nights to stand for the one I had relegated to an old and derisively dreaded flogging chapel; they both taught me that beautiful and unassailable truth. Edward Christopher Calhoun —c. 1900

Sometime during the summer of 1924, Miss Annie Grace Oriana stood upon the rotting floorboards of a decrepit and unfurnished room somewhere in the upland pine preserves of South Carolina dedicated as such by the Calhoun estate. She was staring up at the same notched beams that ran beneath the hollow steeple of the roof of the February Cabin just as her mother did on the night she was born. While the same thoughts were running through the mind of the curiously disposed sixty-five year old woman as her mother before her, Miss Kingston asked of Mrs. Adelaide Satterfield Martin, "Mrs. Martin, according to the written testimony given to you by your mother and attested to by Judge Milton Franklin and Mr. Douglass Aiken, both of Sumter proper, is the woman now standing before you the person born as Miss Margaret Anne Hastings upon this very place in the first of the morning hours of February 24, 1859?"

Adelaide knew her sister well for a brief time but kept to the script while she watched Miss Oriana stare up into the moldering rafters of the February Cabin. "Yes, Ma'am she most certainly is one and the same. My momma told me she promised Miss Jeanne she would bear witness to the child before she passed on, and that's exactly what she did back in 1920. She died in my arms not but thirty minutes after the fact. She was a woman of her word, my momma. She kept all my sister's secrets right on up to the moment she wrote and signed that declaration that be sittin' in your hands too, Ma'am."

Miss Kingston nodded firmly in agreement to the then sixty-two year old woman and turned to face Mr. Albemarle Newton, the Calhoun's top trust attorney of the day, and asked of Miss Oriana, "And Miss Oriana, those are your boys present with you; Mr. Abraham Marion White, Jr. and Mr. Calvin Eoin White?"

Miss Oriana never took her eyes off of the ceiling when answering back in a somewhat distrait tone, "Yes, Miss Kingston. Those are my beautiful boys. Although, I suspect they may be rethinking the bargain presently knowing where their momma was hatched all these years ago now. The world was a far different place back then but this old haunting hasn't changed a bit but for the rot and the peeling of the paint."

Miss Elizabeth Ann Calhoun carefully inspected the few remaining planks still somehow hinged to the doorframe and then probed the opening in one of those planks as the spot where her bullet had surely passed. Upon remembering the miracle of that frozen hunting rifle bobbing in her trembling hands, she called over to her sister, "You are most certainly right about that, my dearest Margaret Anne. It's as if I can still feel that horrid wind freezing my fingers stiff before I squeezed the trigger for no other reason than that of a ghostly tap upon my shoulder."

"Well now, Madam, you are the last among the living that stayed the night with us out here in the woods on the night of my birth. Though your father convinced me to believe Doc Bailey had always suspected what Edward and I were up to back in seventy-five, I'll never know if my gracious guardian of this place was more impressed by your blind shot through that door or the angels making it possible for him to go on and rip me backwards outta my poor momma's womb."

Elizabeth Ann laughed and replied, "Well, the good doctor should know. The only person he ever hit with a bullet of any sort was me." Both women laughed and seemed to speak out in unison, "I do miss that man so!"

At the end of the affair and against the proper protocol of her duties Miss Kingston asked of Miss Oriana, "Not that your answer makes a bit of difference, Ma'am, as everything was legally sealed when Edward passed on, yet in your opinion, who do you believe your father truly was?"

Miss Oriana turned away from the empty window pane she was then studying for no particular reason but the feel of the years gone by and answered, "That will remain the question of the age, my dear Miss Kingston. I believe that Edward and the man I shall not speak of were near to mirror images of one another. Mind you now, no woman of the present time is silly enough to believe that she could possibly be of the life-giving seed of two gentlemen, but there were times before the light was sent out of me that I could read Edward's thoughts and feelings as if they were my own. Even the memories of his childhood were not foreign to me."

"However, when my fourth child was born in the way that he was, I came to believe that at least something of my momma's intuition was correct and that my flesh was certainly of the demon man but that my spirit was kin to my daddy and that it always will be. No man I have known was braver in the face of the ultimate and eternal sacrifice had I failed in my task. As far as the demon man goes, you can only serve to splinter his essence into the wind and force him to slowly draw that darkness back unto its pith. But such is the difference between the heavens and the earth, the darkness and the light and the varying thoughts of us all of still trying to find our way back home."

The room remained silent for a time until Miss Kingston asked, "Are you set to go, Ma'am? We have all that we need to properly administer over the Articles of Edward and Miss Jeanne going forward. Miss Oriana looked deeply into the eyes of her sister from across the room. Elizabeth Ann remained her aegis and her shield and the one who had also endured the horrors of this February Cabin of her birth and the sickening taint of that devilish beast. While taking solace from the taciturn resolve emanating from the current matriarch of the Calhoun family, Margaret Anne replied to the archivist willingly, "Yes, Ma'am. I do believe that I am ready to leave this place. Perhaps it is only fitting that my sister of that same west wind shall be the one to show me the way home from here."

Miss Elizabeth Ann began to tear up as she walked across the room to take her sister by the hand. When they crossed the threshold of that once haunted cabin for the final time she said, "Thank you, my baby sis and my promised child of the light. I believe your work in this place is done. My heart has been renewed in all the ways that such a thing may come to pass. Let us return to the front porch that will forever belong to the days of Edward and Jeanne and remember all of the beautiful things in this life that have come to pass between us with the love of God set upon our hearts."

Miss Margaret Anne Basseterre smiled warmly into the light and a soothing west wind blew at their backs until they came out from beneath the wooded canopy and into the near blinding aurum of late-August hand in hand and forever as one. For the mothers of the two men of one father, men who were already well on their way to shaping the final acts of the enduring legend of that ancient and peculiar cross of gold that had once rested so beautifully upon the chest of the woman they both had loved as a mother of differing forms and which now sat lying very still on that legendary island of that elegant woman's fanciful lore, there was much of which to speak fondly.

When night had settled over that beautiful verdant field of blooming cotton resting below the swirling apparitions of the days gone by, Miss Margaret Anne spoke to her sister in the last before retiring for the evening. Amidst the staid calm of the cool, blanketing shade of the eventide, Margaret Anne had no way of knowing that the haunted mistress of their years spent in exile following the war had already drifted off to sleep and joined those memories lingering thick out in the night that had been calling her hence. She spoke somewhat wistfully to honor the past but also with a spirited joy that had overcome so much and would forever continue to overcome. "I am eternally heartened by the light I once held, but more so presently, I am heartened by the hope in God I came to know when I was near to overwhelmed by the years of my enduring futility. I wished for so long that we could have done more with the gifts and the time we were given. Yet, I know there will come a day when the one set to finish what we have started here will arrive. All shall be done in God's perfect time, my dear sister." And the night held those words safe until the gifting of the splendor of morning light.